LUTHER'S HOUSE OF LEARNING

Gerald Strauss

LUTHER'S HOUSE OF LEARNING

Indoctrination of the Young in the German Reformation

The Johns Hopkins University Press

BALTIMORE AND LONDON

Publication of this book has been aided by a grant from the
National Endowment for the Humanities.

Manufactured in the United States of America

The Johns Hopkins University Press, Baltimore, Maryland 21218
The Johns Hopkins Press Ltd., London

Library of Congress Catalog Card Number 77–18705
ISBN 0–8018–2051–0

Library of Congress Cataloging in Publication data will be found on the last
printed page of this book.

For Alice

Come to me, you who need instruction,
and lodge in my house of learning.
Why do you admit to a lack of these things,
yet leave your great thirst unslaked?
I have made my proclamation:
"Buy for yourselves without money,
bend your neck to the yoke,
be ready to accept discipline;
you need not go far to find it."
See for yourselves how little were my labours
compared with the great peace I have found.

Ecclesiasticus 51: 23–27.

CONTENTS

ACKNOWLEDGMENTS

I have received much help and kindness in the various stages of my work on this book. To mention financial assistance first: A faculty summer grant from Indiana University in 1971 gave me leisure to organize my research and orient myself in the secondary literature. In 1972, a fellowship in the Shelby Cullom Davis Center for Historical Studies at Princeton University enabled me to continue reading and provided me with a group of lively listeners and critics headed by Lawrence Stone. In 1972, also, I was awarded a fellowship by the John Simon Guggenheim Memorial Foundation, whose generous support made possible a lengthy period of research in Germany. Most of the book was written in 1975–76, in the incomparable setting of the Institute for Advanced Study at Princeton, of which I was a member during that academic year, supported in part by grant FC 10503 of the National Endowment for the Humanities. No mere expression of acknowledgment can make adequate return for the intellectual and spiritual lift given a scholar by the opportunity to work in the ideal conditions created, in large part, by the Institute's director at that time, Carl Kaysen, and by Felix Gilbert and John Elliott of its School of Historical Studies. My university came to my aid once more in 1977 with an offer to absorb the cost of typing the finished script. I am deeply grateful to all these organizations.

For assistance of another, no less tangible, sort I am indebted to the many experts who made things easy for me during my visits, in 1973 and in the summers of 1974 and 1975, to more than twenty-five archives and libraries in the Federal Republic of Germany, the German Democratic Republic, and the city of Strasbourg. I never failed, while rereading my notes as I worked on my manuscript, to experience a vivid sense of place as the pleasant circumstances of my sojourns in these splendid institutions came back to mind. I know of no greater satisfaction than the reflection that the past has been well spent. The six years I have devoted to the preparation of this volume have left me with many happy memories of people and places. I hope my book is worthy of them.

Chapter 3 appeared in somewhat altered form as "The State of Pedagogical Theory c. 1530: What Protestant Reformers Knew about Education," in *Schooling and Society: Studies in the History of Education*, edited by Lawrence Stone and published by The Johns Hopkins University Press in 1976. Parts of chapter 13 appeared as "Success and Failure in the German Reformation," in *Past and Present*, no. 67 (May 1975), pp. 30–63. I am grateful for permission to use these materials again.

With a few exceptions, which are noted, all translations in this book are my own. Quotations from the Bible are taken from the Revised Standard Version, except for the Apocrypha, which come from the New English Bible.

LUTHER'S HOUSE OF LEARNING

CHAPTER 1

INTRODUCTION:
REFORMATION AND EDUCATION

In the history of education, the reformations of the sixteenth century hold an important place. This familiar fact is not only supported by a modern scholarly literature of formidable weight and volume,[1] but contemporary sources attest to it as well. Schools grew in number and quality as a consequence of both the Protestant and the Catholic Reformations. They profited—some more, some less—from the energetic scholarship of two generations of European humanists whose enthusiasm for teaching touched every level. Instruction became more professional. Orderly bureaucratic processes brought about a desirable measure of coordination among schools and universities. In outline at least—since no generalization about the sixteenth century can stand unqualified—the shape of an educational system appears on the historical horizon. A vigorous sense of purpose imparted fresh impetus. Religious goals and civic objectives combined to gather the ways of teaching and learning in that web of ecclesiastical and secular administrative procedures that is the true image of the established Reformation.

These matters, though well known, are not without their unanswered questions. How innovative were the reformers as educators? What substantial gains, if any, did Protestant schools and universities add to the centuries-old curriculum of the better institutions of primary, secondary, and higher learning?[2] How important was the reformers' role in the extension of popular education?[3] What was their effect on literacy?[4] Was schooling still repressive, despite Luther's outbursts against pedants who kept their pupils "locked up in a kind of dungeon"?[5] Did the evangelical revival broaden public respect for learning, and, if so, did this change in the climate of education touch the system where it really counted: the attitude of the pupil? In their approach to these and similar questions, historians of education have usually concerned themselves with the mechanics of their subject, the formal institutions and activities of instruction: schools founded or reformed, teachers appointed, curricula and textbooks, fees and salaries, school attendance, and so on. All these tell us much about what was taught and learned, and why, but by no means do they say everything.

There is another side to educational thought and practice in the sixteenth century that has not had its share of attention. The Reformation would have been less than the great experiment in renewal and restoration it was had it failed to set its educational goals far beyond merely teaching good Latin, sound learning, and the principles of the evangelical faith to small groups of favored young men. It did try to do more—and here the Lutheran Reformation in Germany is of particular significance because it tried to do it first. It embarked on a conscious and, for its time, remarkably systematic endeavor to develop in the young new and better impulses, to implant inclinations in consonance with the reformers' religious and civic ideals, to fashion dispositions in which Christian ideas of right thought and action could take root, and to shape personalities capable of turning the young into new men—into the human elements of a Christian society that would live by evangelical principles. In pursuing this objective, the German reformers did not confine their efforts to the small circle of young men traditionally held to be educable. Not content with the limited goals of formal instruction, they broadened their aims to include the population at large: city dwellers, small-town folk, villagers. To reach these ordinary people, they devised instruments of indoctrination (in no pejorative sense of that word) and developed techniques of conditioning (as they must now be called), acting in what they conceived to be obedience to the divine command to propagate God's revealed truth and to show their fellowmen how they could live by it. Education, they believed, was the best of pious works, and in this light they saw their own actions.

This enterprise is the subject of my book. With its highly problematic outcome it makes an absorbing story, and it reveals some of the still-unexplored terrain of the German Reformation. Involving the highest ambitions, fondest hopes, and most energetic efforts of the reformers, the story carries considerable emotional power as we pursue it to its disheartening denouement. Most of the leaders of the Lutheran Reformation came to fear that their labors had failed.[6] Their disappointment and their sense of despair can be most effectively explained by setting them against the vaulting expectations of the movement's pristine years.

To many of its students the Reformation—at least that part of it now called the "magisterial" Reformation, the part that established and institutionalized itself in close alliance with the state—appears abstract. Its great figures are cast in bronze. Its burning religious issues, once capable of rousing men to violent polemic and at times to mutual slaughter, are academic now, or at least they seem so to the historian. The subject of this book, by contrast, presents the Reformation at its most human and, as it happens, its most topical. Both in what they attempted to do and in what, in the end, they failed to accomplish, the reformers and their pedagogues meet us as fellow contenders in a profoundly human struggle. We are all enlisted in it, often frustratingly, as uneasy observers of our social scene, as teachers, parents, engaged citizens. We struggle to replicate and perhaps to improve ourselves intellectually and morally in our children. We attempt to assure the survival of our values by impressing them on our offspring. We all try to shape the future by molding the young. Lutheran reformers were no less eager to mold and to shape than men have been in other times. Their great experiment in pedagogy (the word I shall use here to describe their attempt to remake the human personality) is a small patch of ground on which we still meet them face to face.

2

The pedagogical procedures of the German Reformation were evolved over a long stretch of years and rarely progressed in uniform motion or in a straight line. Such a pace was of course characteristic of the time; in this respect pedagogy resembles most undertakings of the Lutheran movement. Policies were occasioned by unpredictable events and conjunctions of events and personalities, most often in response to a sudden crisis. This generative process is the subject of the next chapter, in which the guiding principles of Lutheran pedagogy will be related to their intellectual roots and to the historical circumstances that had decisive influence on their formulation. Before considering this course of events, however, some sense must be conveyed of the particular administrative frame within which the Lutheran pedagogical program was developed. As is well known, reformers collaborated eagerly with their respective governments in creating systems of schools and universities. Wherever the Reformation was formally established (by government legislation always, no matter what the sources of its original impulse), it solidified itself in institutions and procedures that grew ever more rigid in the course of the sixteenth century. Schools and schooling were at once symptom and beneficiary of this process of institutionalization; Luther, Melanchthon, and their associates and successors acknowledged this from the 1520s on as a fact of religious and political life. Education was to take place in a setting of fixed institutions governed by bureaucracies whose competence pervaded entire domains, from capital to hamlets.

The acceptance of this constraint by Luther and other early reformers represents a major concession to intractable reality. Luther's first thoughts on the subject of Christian education were considerably at variance with the compromise he eventually came to accept. His many remarks on teaching and learning show him arriving most reluctantly at the conclusion that voluntary effort, parental direction, and community enterprise were weak reeds from which to construct a vigorous educational program. It caused him a good deal of pain to admit the failure of his early conviction that a change of heart must precede the imposition of doctrines and rules.[7] He never completely abandoned his hope for an inward transformation of the individual through the gospel. But as the events of the mid-1520s and 1530s overtook him and his young movement, the fulfillment of this hope became ever more distant.

Luther's early ideas reflect his personal distaste for system and uniformity in matters of religion. In the light of later developments this is not without a touch of irony. But in the early 1520s Luther believed that a true evangelical renewal in individual and society could come only from within the individual person and the singular Christian community. He therefore recommended as a model (*ein gemeyn exempel*) for Christian congregations the constitution of the town of Leisnig in Saxony (drawn up with his assistance and published in 1523 with a vigorous preface by him), in which it is stated that "every householder and his wife shall be duty-bound to cause the wholesome, consoling word of God to be preached to them, their children, and their domestic servants, so that the gospel may be impressed [*eingebildet*] on them for their betterment."[8] Although Christian education was primarily the responsibility of preachers, their sermons could not always reach those who stood in greatest need of instruction: children and simple people. Householders therefore had to do their part. Where the preacher stopped they were to take over. They were "bishops in their own homes."[9] To guide them in this office Luther had written a number of useful manuals for "the simple layman": sermons on the Ten Commandments (1518), an explanation of the Lord's Prayer (1519), a "Little Prayer Book" subtitled "How to Pray: Instructions for Children" (1522). Others were to follow. The Greater and Shorter Catechisms of 1529 are the culmination of these early efforts to assist those who provided Christian education in the home and in the world outside. By 1529, however, Luther had other purposes in mind too, as will become clear.

Luther's emphasis on domestic instruction was shared by other reformers. Johann Bugenhagen, whose influence on the Reformation in northern Germany was second only to Luther's, argued that "if we are ever to produce able preachers for our country, parents must make a beginning by teaching good discipline in their homes, as God commands them to do."[10] "Good discipline," meaning Christian instruction, demanded more than memorizing prayers. Luther always insisted on the need for understanding, for "meaning it." Don't speak the words "coldly, without reflection," he said. Don't reel them off in singsong. Think about each word as you pray, and what it means; for instance, the "our" in "our Father," signifying "that we should recognize each other as true brothers and sisters in the Lord"; in other words, it was a prayer "for brotherly love and harmony."[11] Such "opening up" of the words required, Luther thought, the closeness of the family gathered at the hearth. The hidebound ways and repressive air of the medieval schoolroom as he remembered it were ill suited to inducing heartfelt religious understanding, although teaching did require the stern voice of authority and, at times, the use of the rod. But in this respect too the family was well suited to indoctrinate its members. Presided over by its head, the paterfamilias, the household formed a political society in miniature[12] and was governed accordingly. A touch of uneasiness creeps into Luther's early assertions of these views. What, he asks, if children fail to respond? What if householders lack the necessary skill, or are ignorant or indifferent? Still, he seems as long as possible to have held to his conviction that home was the best place for training the young in their Christian obligations and in the tasks they were to perform in life.[13]

Academic subjects were learned in schools, of course, and Luther had well-formed opinions on how to turn the "donkey stalls and devil's dens" of his own childhood into places of Christian instruction.[14] He favored local initiative, as exemplified by the citizens of Leisnig, who appropriated funds from their community treasury to employ a schoolmaster for boys and an "honest woman of advanced years and spotless reputation" to teach reading, writing, and the elements of "right Christian conduct" to girls under twelve.[15] In his famous address *To the Christian Nobility of the German Nation* of 1520, Luther had rashly called for adopting Scripture as the basic text from which to teach and learn.[16] He soon amended this recommendation to include all the subjects of the time-honored liberal arts curriculum.[17] The church needed pastors and theologians; governments required lawyers, bureaucrats, geographers, and medical doctors. The traditional subjects of the trivium and quadrivium were retained for their conventional purpose, to prepare the able-minded for higher learning toward advanced degrees. In the early 1520s the reformers imagined that popular support and governmental goodwill would suffice to promote a voluntary and locally supported program of Christian and academic instruction.

Events soon proved them wrong. Whatever zeal for the support of education may have been aroused by the excitement attending the first years of the Reformation, it rapidly evaporated as burghers, and the town councils representing them, discovered the cost. With sources of money drying up, teachers departed and pupils played truant as their families began to doubt the value of formal schooling.[18] In 1524 Luther and his colleagues saw schools approaching a state of desolation.[19] It was also becoming manifest that parents were neglecting their duty of supervising Christian upbringing in their homes. Some lacked the piety for it, others did not seem to concern themselves about their off-spring's welfare, were too busy, or did not know how to do it.[20] Luther began to doubt the practical applicability of his principle that the parental hearth was the best place for Christian nurture.[21] Even more destructive to his early ideas about education were the religious and social disturbances of 1521–25: the troubles in Wittenberg, the knights' re-volt, the peasant uprisings. Clearly, people were not yet prepared to receive the saving message of the gospel. They could not be trusted with the new freedom Luther had offered them, meticulously defined, or so he thought, in his treatise on Christian liberty of 1520. Where so many mental aberrations led to such widespread tumult, only firm con-trol could restore and preserve order. A change of emphasis suddenly becomes apparent in the reformers' thoughts on education, and a stri-dent tone betrays their deep anxiety over the drift of events.

This transformation is most evident in Philip Melanchthon, whose mental balance was grievously upset by the experiences of the 1520s.[22] A paternalistic strain is unmistakable in his response to events. Schools are needed more than ever now, he said in 1525, "so that young people may be raised to be peaceful and decent."[23] As preservers of the peace and order of the community, schools come under the power of govern-ments. Magistrates exercise rights equal to those of parents in deter-mining what shall be taught.[24] Fearing that the decline of schools would cause a return to barbarism, Melanchthon now devoted himself to the revival of academic disciplines. By the mid-1520s he had come to the conclusion that the legal and moral authority of government offered the best hope for preventing total intellectual and religious col-lapse. Only under "worldly justice" was there some prospect of making an impression on the great body of nonbelievers, the young, the simple, the *dumme Volk, tolle pöfel, hoc vulgus nostrum, Herr Omnes, das tolle Volk*, the "wild crowd" making up the overwhelming mass of fallen humanity.[25] He cites Rom. 13:4 to prove that rulers are appointed over men for their own good. He reminds people of their place as subjects and their necessary condition of acquiescence. His thoughts on educa-tion now reflect his conviction that people must be inoculated against the host of dangerous ideas swarming in the febrile atmosphere of the 1520s. This, he thought, could be accomplished only by a carefully trained cadre of pastors and teachers operating under the aegis of benevolent, but strong-willed, governments.[26]

Luther gave his support to this shift of educational authority from private to public jurisdiction, from voluntary to compulsory participation, and from associative to institutional organization. "What if parents don't do it [i.e., teach their children the elements of faith]? Who is going to do it then? Will it remain undone and children left abandoned? If so, what excuse will governments offer for themselves?"[27] Like Melanchthon, Luther blamed the decline of schools on the spread of a know-nothing ideology among the people. It was a vicious circle that could be broken only from above, or so he now thought. Hence the appeal, first to municipal councillors (whom he flattered by portraying their territorial lords as too far gone in drink and hunting to be able to act),[28] then to the rulers themselves. In 1526 he assured his prince, the Elector Johann of Saxony, that "as the supreme guardian of our young people" (oberster furmund der iugent), he had not only the right, but also the high duty to step in where a town or village failed to give adequate support to school and pulpit. "If they themselves will not do it in the interest of their own salvation . . . Your Grace has ample power to compel them."[29] Surely a government that can make its subjects bear arms in war "can use even greater force to compel them to send their children to school."[30] Luther reminded fathers and mothers that children belong first to God and only in the second instance to their parents. A delinquent father, he warned, forfeits to God his right over his offspring, and God delegates this prerogative to political authorities.[31] The raising of children was no longer regarded as a private matter. Luther writes: "No, my dear fellow. If you have a child fit to be trained, don't imagine that you are free to raise him as you please, nor to set him on any path of life that happens to suit you. Your task is to help God in his benevolent effort to advance his [spiritual and secular] realms."[32] But how many among us, he asks, now actually perform this God-ordained office? "Nobody trains children nowadays to do anything other than earn a good living. They think they can deal with them according to their whims, as if there were no God who had commanded them to do otherwise, or as if they themselves were gods and sovereigns over their children! If we had strict and honest governments in the world . . . they would soon punish this wicked lot in their persons and their properties, or better still drive them from our midst as a poisonous and pernicious breed on earth."[33] Unless we change our course, Luther warns, men will become "wild beasts and pigs, good for nothing except to stuff their bellies with food and drink."[34]

These vehement, almost hysterical cadences—quite out of tune with their occasion (a brief preface written in 1529 to introduce Justus Menius's Oeconomia Christiana), betray Luther's despair over the slack response to the many opportunities he had opened to serve God and the evangelical Reformation. Given the phenomenally rapid spread of his movement throughout Germany, he could make no sense of this. In a tract written a year later, in 1530, entitled "A Sermon Arguing That Children Should Go to School," his anger erupts in apocalyptic warnings of the ravages to come down on men should they persist in their neglect of learning: divine wrath, inflation, the plague and syphilis, bloodthirsty tyrants, wars and revolutions, the whole country laid to waste by Turks and Tatars, even the pope restored to power.[35] There was still time for people to come to their senses, he wrote. But even as he pleaded for a hearing the only practical solution seemed intervention by the ruling powers. He therefore urged princes and magistrates to compel their subjects to enroll all children in schools.[36] This was, at least at present, the only realistic hope, and Christian rulers could do no less. Reiterated by his followers, Luther's argument soon became a commonplace. "In this case [i.e., when parents slight the education of their young] children cease to belong to their parents and fall to the care of God and community."[37] "The public weal has a higher claim than that of parents to wield authority over children."[38] It is unlikely that these claims had the approbation of the population at large. But there is no doubt that they had a galvanizing effect where it really counted—upon rulers and magistrates in Lutheran territories and cities.

The actions of early Protestant school organizers show the practical consequences of these arguments. Working in close alliance, reformers and governments drafted school ordinances (*Schulordnungen*) to set down policies and regulations for teaching and learning. Being in most cases integral parts of comprehensive ecclesiastical constitutions (*Kirchenordnungen*) that established and defined the Reformation in a city or territory as a fundamental law of the state, educational ordinances charged schools with a vital role in molding the religious and civic life of the community. Education was now joined to that grand design of a spiritual renewal of state, society, and individual which endowed early Lutheranism with its strongest source of appeal.[39] Thus Bugenhagen, the author of ecclesiastical constitutions for the cities of Braunschweig (1528), Hamburg (1529), and Lübeck (1531), acknowledged the failure of domestic Christian instruction (while holding to the essential soundness of the principle),[40] and placed responsibility for schools in the hands of municipal councillors. They were to exercise it, he writes, "to the honor of God almighty, for the sake of our youth, and according to the will of the whole city."[41] This reference, in the Braunschweig constitution, to an expression of communal will was no empty phrase. Before it was adopted as a basic law, the draft constitution had been circulated for examination and comment among the city's guilds and corporations; it had even been sent to outlying villages. In Hamburg the school board (*Scholarchat*) included, in addition to senior councillors and pastors, a number of elders chosen from the city's four parishes. But in this respect, too, the fervor of the early decades did not endure. In the course of the years, supervision and decision-making slipped from citizens into the hands of a proliferating secular and ecclesiastical bureaucracy,[42] and it was not long before friction developed between these rival groups over what was to be taught, by whom, and how.

More important in the present context is the fact that schools were given pride of place in each of Bugenhagen's influential constitutions,[43] a sign of the vital, not to say determining, role assigned to education in the planned restoration of religious and moral life. Luther, too, spoke in his treatise of 1530 of "schools where children are trained in the liberal arts, in Christian discipline, and in the performance of faithful service to God, and where . . . [they] are raised to become responsible men and women who can govern churches, countries, people, households, children, and servants."[44] The final point was the one that counted. Schools must train competent administrators for church and community and thereby assure posterity of a steady stream of replacements for its present generation of leaders. Bugenhagen described the institutions he founded in these very terms. They are places, he writes, where "our poor ignorant youths are taught the Ten Commandments, the Apostles' Creed, the Lord's Prayer, and the sacraments with as much explanation as they need to know; where they learn to sing Latin psalms and read Scripture in Latin. . . . And they study these subjects not for themselves alone, but to the end that some among them may grow up to be preachers, jurists, physicians, or God-fearing, hard-working, honest, obedient, content, cheerful, learned, peaceful burghers who, in their turn, will bring their children up to be God-fearing Christians. And so it will continue from generation to generation."[45]

Indoctrinating society at large was not yet the main goal. A competent professional pastoral and instructional cadre first had to be trained. Only then could one begin to undertake what was at once the major objective and the essential precondition of giving a semblance of reality to Luther's hopes for the "priesthood" of all believers and the sanctity of all worldly callings: the diffusion throughout society of a Christian ethic based on intimate knowledge of Scripture. Luther's catechisms of 1529 were to serve this broader pedagogical purpose, and he had high hopes for their success. "To those who have accepted it," he wrote, referring to the doctrine set out in his catechisms, "my reformation has brought not a little benefit, peace, and virtue."[46]

Events were to prove Luther's confidence somewhat premature. The results of a visitation in Electoral Saxony in 1528 were disappointing. Elsewhere, too, signs of popular indifference were becoming painfully clear. As for the "peace and virtue" resulting from the acceptance of his reformation, the evidence was, to say the least, ambiguous. In any case, what did it mean to claim that someone had "accepted" (*angenommen*) Luther's reformation? Had he received it into his heart or had it been imposed on him by political fiat? This was the dilemma, first faced by Luther in the late 1520s, that was to keep his successors enthralled for more than a century, now lifting their hopes, now throwing them into despair. Reacting to the events of these early years, Luther too, veered from excited optimism[47] to deepest gloom.[48] But whether encouraged or despondent, he made it evident now, as did his colleagues, that they no longer counted on individual effort and personal zeal. Only dimly aware of the fateful consequences of their decision, they welcomed the good offices of political authority and embraced them as the most promising agent for accomplishing their pedagogical objectives.

3

By the late 1520s, then, the ground had been prepared for establishing political control over education.[49] In view of all that had happened, it is not surprising that the schools of the Reformation turned out to be "instruments of magisterial education," as they have aptly been called.[50] It was a role admirably attuned to the purposes of the early modern state. The very idea of a Christian polity presupposed an intimate association of political and ecclesiastical governing functions. Schools played a central role in such a scheme. In conjunction with other instruments for disseminating approved ideas, they were expected to imbue people with opinions and values not only wholesome in themselves, but conducive also to the preservation of the body politic and its social and moral cohesion.

The political mentality characteristic of sixteenth-century rulers found little to admire, and less to trust, in the teeming world of instincts and actions they tried to control. All human creatures were selfish. Left to themselves, to their natural impulses, they went their several ways driven by self-love and swayed by passion, unstable, heedless of the future, doing injury to themselves and their kind. Holding them in check and keeping society from falling to pieces called for throttling their natural inclinations. This was the function of laws. Laws served to point out to men their appetite for malice and their tendency to hypocrisy and self-deception. Laws also served to restrain men by enmeshing them in a vast net of dos and don'ts to catch every misdemeanor. Laws touched highborn and low, rich and poor. They entered every corner of life, ignoring distinctions between private and public domains. Backed by surveillance and enforcement, laws were intended to regulate every action, to let no evasion go undetected and no transgression unpunished.

Needless to say, governments were not nearly the successful guardians of peace and order that their ambitions dictated. Governing was a frustrating and thankless task, and one gets the impression that those who were charged with it gained little satisfaction from their duties. This dyspeptic attitude goes some way toward explaining why Protestant reformers received a ready hearing in so many council halls and audience chambers. Their theological image of man as a self-seeking, intemperate, rebellious creature, and their emphasis on law as an unbending standard against which to measure his inability to fulfill his obligations, seem to have evoked a sympathetic response from rulers and their counselors, who had come to recognize that their conventional models of man were inadequate to the task of governing him in his unregenerate ways.[51]

In any case, princes and magistrates listened attentively as reformers conveyed to them their hope that a system of improved schools would bring about a significant amelioration in individual and society. No one saw a conflict in this fusion of religious and secular objectives. Protestant reformers regarded it as a part of Christian education to train people in the habits of patient and obedient citizenship. Rulers, for their part, never doubted that the conscience of their subjects was the legitimate business of the Christian state. Reformers tried to imbue magistrates with a sense of their obligation to supervise religious life and teaching. Preachers in Nuremberg, for example, urged the city's council to consider the use of coercion—"as it used to be done under the papacy"—to compel citizens to memorize the new catechism.[52] Elsewhere it was said that, like a natural father attending to the raising of his children, "government as a common father"[53] should establish and maintain schools in the great household of a territory or city. This, wrote Urban Rhegius in a catechism for the education of princes, is why magistrates are called *patres patriae*. It follows that rulers owe their subjects effective instruction in Christian principles. "I consider it a gross error," Urban writes, using the vivid words of his time, "to think that a ruler is like a cowherd who cares only about the skin and bellies of his beasts. Rulers are called to a much higher duty, namely the enforcement of God's commandments; . . . and of all the matters that concern them they must show the greatest regard for the instruction of their subjects in the Christian religion according to the word of God. They must establish schools and see to it that these remain in good working order and provide sound instruction in Christian virtue and all other good things."[54]

Governments were not slow to act on such appeals. The manifestos of general purpose, in which the ecclesiastical constitutions of reformed states were framed, identify the grounds on which political intervention in religious matters was now being sanctioned. They also reveal a new agreement of religious and political purposes in the governance of society. A passage from the 1538 ecclesiastical constitution of the city of Gengenbach may serve as a case in point. Now that the pure word of God is heard everywhere in the city, it begins, and the old errors have been discredited, a new and happier time is at hand. "But as it is not given to everyone to possess the faith and grace to hear the divine word (these being free gifts of God and not the rewards of human effort), we sadly note the great obstinacy and treachery still being manifested in our midst by those among our fellow citizens who do not have the precious gift of grace. This situation is exceedingly troubling to citizens of pious minds but weak consciences . . . and is one which, mindful of our divinely appointed office, we are no longer willing to tolerate, and therefore we now mean to correct it."[55] What better way to commence reform than by providing for the indoctrination of the young? This, said the Gengenbach councillors, is the most immediate and far-reaching measure that could be taken by "a Christian government and father over all young people."[56]

The benign but firm paternalism resonating in this pronouncement (which is typical of its kind) suggests that Protestant theological doctrines had struck a responsive chord in the minds of magisterial authorities, whose eyes had been opened to the deep source of that human obstinacy so frustrating to them in their fussy solicitude for their subjects' behavior. Despite some inevitable discords, the working relationship of church and state in Protestant lands was not to be broken. Pastors and theologians felt secure in the knowledge that they could call on the state's power when pulpit admonitions failed to obtain good results. Rulers and magistrates for their part rejoiced in finding secular purposes sanctioned by theological premises and scriptural authority. This new symbiosis is reflected in the literature of religious instruction:

> Our Lord instituted two kinds of government in his Ten Commandments. One is external; the other is spiritual. Seeing that the whole world is corrupt and unwilling to allow itself to be healed by good words and deeds, God has appointed political rulers to enforce discipline, honesty, and good administration among men, so that through the external ordering of things there may be peace, prosperity, and justice in the world. And for this reason God has given the law into the hands of rulers.

> But God's commandments ask something more of us than external obedience. They demand spiritual, divine, and heavenly piety, and this must come from the ground of our hearts. For the sake of this piety God has made his law into a mirror in which we see reflected our true condition, namely our misery and blindness, our sinful and corrupt nature, our faults

and debilities. Seeing ourselves as we really are, we can never presume to hope that our own powers and efforts will suffice to reach the state of divine piety.[57]

Men unable to raise their fallen natures; men prone to obstinacy if bereft of grace; men capable of a socially useful life only if led by instruction and restrained by law. And yet much could be done to improve them, if not in their basic character, at least in their actions, thoughts, motives, and impulses. This much the reformers thought they could do. Governments were prepared to join them in the effort.

The concrete result of this conjunction of purposes, in the 1520s and early 1530s, was a host of school ordinances issuing from governments in cities and territories all over Germany.[58] The earliest of these were framed for cities and towns, mostly with the help, sometimes under the authorship, of the major reformers: Luther himself (Wittenberg and Leisnig, 1523), Agricola (Eisleben, 1525), Melanchthon (Nuremberg, 1526), Johann Brenz (Schwäbisch Hall, 1526), Johann Aepinus (Stralsund, 1525, and Hamburg, 1529), Bugenhagen (Braunschweig, 1528, Hamburg, 1529, and Lübeck, 1531), Bucer (Ulm, 1531), and many others. Urban ordinances in turn proved seminal for the reorganization of schools in the larger territories: Hesse (1526, 1537, and 1566), Electoral Saxony (1528 and 1533), Pomerania (1535), Brandenburg (1540), Braunschweig (1543), Württemberg (1559), to mention only the most influential of the more than one hundred *Schulordnungen* laid down before 1600.[59] As organic parts of voluminous ecclesiastical constitutions, school ordinances tended to be wordy documents exhibiting to a fault the preoccupation with minutiae, and the paternalistic inclination to direct every activity, that are so typical of their age. As early codes were modified in response to changing circumstances, they grew ever longer and more unyielding. In many cases their fastidious pettiness all but destroyed the religious and pedagogical principles on which they had been based. One senses the old nagging distrust at work, the fear of leaving anything unregulated, no matter how trivial.[60] Hence the attempt to set patterns, fix lines of authority, ensure identical curricula and methods ("as is the custom in Wittenberg," "as done by the professors in Marburg"), to spell out for everyone exactly what to do and what not to do, every hour of the day. Success in achieving these objectives varied from place to place and from time to time. But there is no doubt that, even where the outcome was not wholly favorable, school legislation produced a major change in the ways of teaching and learning.

One must not distort these procedures by seeing them through the lens of modern bureaucratic operations. Governments did try to obtain an administrative handle on education, but they were content to work within existing facilities, attempting without great haste or excessive pressure to bend them to their purposes. It is true that governments began to insist that schools serve the secular as well as the spiritual welfare of their subjects, and that they enhance the authority of the state and increase respect for its rulers. But such objectives were not revolutionary in the sixteenth century. The instruments developed to attain them were modest and their employment tentative. It is all a matter of perspective. From the vantage point of the Prussian General Territorial Law of 1794, the school ordinances of the sixteenth century seem all patchwork and vacillation.[61] But from the other end of the continuum the transformation appears impressive. Governments were now counted upon to make education available to their young subjects, and they were eager to comply with this expectation, goaded by theologians and churchmen. Citizens were enjoined to cooperate by paying most of the cost and by offering their children as pupils. They responded with something less than alacrity, a reluctance that never failed to puzzle and dismay school officials. Along with the proliferating sectarianism of the late sixteenth century, this lagging public response to the new educational opportunities was the main impulse to extending and tightening school regulations.

For a closer look at this process, let us make an example of one document, the *Schulordnung* of the duchy of Württemberg of 1559. Württemberg had turned Protestant in the mid-1530s, but its first ecclesiastical constitution of 1536 had been set aside after the Protestant defeat in the Schmalkaldic war and Württemberg's acceptance of the Interim. In 1550 Duke Christoph, a staunch Lutheran and intelligent politician, recommenced the interrupted reformation of his land, aided by an able staff of theologians and administrators. The culmination of their labors was the great ecclesiastical constitution of 1559, of which the school ordinance is a major part.[62]

A preamble announces the chief objective of formal education. Learned men are needed for preaching, for secular administration, and to function satisfactorily as heads of households. Such men can be produced only in particular (i.e., Latin) schools. All towns, large and small, in the duchy should have such schools. Recent surveys (the territorial visitation of 1557 is meant) have revealed a proliferation of teaching practices. This confusion must be brought to an end. From now on all school curricula must follow to the letter the model given in this ordinance, whose articles all teachers in the duchy shall be sworn to obey. The sequence of grades and schools prescribed in the ordinance, and the curricula and methods it mandates, will ensure that no able scholar will in the future escape detection and none will go to university unprepared.

In keeping with these aims, the major sections of the ordinance are devoted to the reform of particular schools (for boys only) and to the establishment of training institutions for pastors. The former are to be graded—identically throughout the duchy—into five forms, each class receiving its uniform teaching program and list of books. Fully developed five-form schools could of course exist only in the larger towns. But even the smallest village ought to offer two grades, or at the very least one, in which children should remain until they have learned to read and write. The brightest of them could then go on to higher forms in other schools (if they could get stipends) or to the *Paedagogium* in Stuttgart, a five-form boarding school with low fees, established for deserving poor students. In the larger schools boys of comparable ability should be gathered in the same class "so that the schoolmaster can evaluate their talents by comparing them." In the lower grades good students were encouraged to proceed at their own pace. The curriculum rises from simple and traditional fare—Donatus, "Cato" (an early medieval compilation of moral precepts)—to Vergil and Isocrates in the fifth form. Much is made of the need for identical books and teaching methods, not only to serve the principle of uniformity, but also to enable common examinations to be held in all schools in the duchy. The study of Latin is not made out to be an easy task. On this point the ordinance takes cognizance of long-standing humanist criticisms of traditional ways of language teaching. Grammar in particular is acknowledged to be a difficult subject, frightening to many children. Teachers must suit their methods to the ages and comprehension of pupils. They are to say and to do nothing to discourage them. "Tell the children that Latin is not as hard as it seems at first. Show them how all Latin words can be divided into eight portions, called 'parts of speech.' Say that once you have memorized one or two words from each portion, you will learn the rest very easily." Just as one counts money by putting pennies in one stack, shillings in another and so on, "you count speech by separating words into *partes orationis*, which you might think of as eight columns of words into which you stack all the words in the language." There is much more of this sort of advice, intended to introduce adults to the child's conceptual world. Kindness and sympathy are demanded from teachers. Do not press the boys beyond their comprehension, the ordinance advises. Crude threats, browbeating, and indiscriminate punishment are expressly forbidden,[63] though it is unlikely that the statute was completely effective in banishing all forms of classroom cruelty.[64]

The hoped-for product of these efforts is enough learning to serve the ablest pupils as a foundation for further studies. By itself this was not sufficient. Without "good discipline [*Zucht*] and the fear of God," *eruditio* is an empty shell. Equal weight was therefore given to means of "implanting" the fear of God in boys and to ways of imbuing them with the approved configuration of attitudes: obedience, reverence toward elders and betters, modesty in speech, dress, and behavior in and out of school. While teachers try to make the appropriate impression on pupils, pastors must strive to gain the attention of their parents. You cannot educate your children at home, they were instructed to say from the pulpit; you are too busy and you lack the talent and training for it. You must send them to school. Pastors warned also against excessive permissiveness and enjoined parents to be severe with their children whenever they strayed from the discipline learned in the classroom. But professionals alone formed their minds and characters. Rigorous selection was to ensure that teachers possessed the appropriate qualifications. Every candidate for a teaching post was investigated as to his origins, education, religious opinions, conduct, and manner of life. He had to present references from previous employers or former teachers and give one or two sample lectures before a group of Tübingen professors and one or two members of the ecclesiastical council—the *Kirchenrat.* Then came the obligatory examination in catechism and the Augsburg Confession, and next a reading of the full text of the school ordinance in the presence of the clerical and secular officials of the town where he was to be appointed. Finally, he received a ceremonial admonition to accept his calling as "a high, precious, and God-ordained office and instrument for preserving the ministry and worldly government by instructing children in Christian doctrine and teaching them the fear of God."[65]

To assure that all these requirements were met, the ordinance arranged for supervision by a team of school inspectors, including the pastor and three other "learned men" from each town or village. Monthly visits and quarterly examinations of all pupils were to keep this group well informed. All infractions had to be reported to the superintendent and the *Kirchenrat.*

The overriding purpose of Württemberg's school program becomes clear only in the chapters—which form the longest section of the ordinance—on "monastery schools," former monastic houses turned by the Reformation into Lutheran theological seminaries. It was the "entire and sole purpose of these schools to train young men to be teachers and preachers in the church." Fees were minimal, but parents were obliged to sign a formal statement of consent to allow their sons to serve the church.[66] Successful completion of three or four years in a monastery school led to advanced theological studies at the Stipendium founded in Tübingen in 1536. Candidates for places there had to be native Württembergers educated in the duchy (for doctrinal reliability); they must present a first-class academic record and excellent references; and they were obliged to pledge under oath to follow no other career than that of pastor or teacher. Stipends were not distributed with a free hand. Pupils competed in periodic countrywide examinations. The duke and his ecclesiastical council kept all candidates for the ministry under tight control; painstakingly precise rules defined their studies and conduct while at school. Those who stayed the course must have been as reliable in character, belief, and walk of life as human nature made it possible to be.[67]

Only at the very end of the long ordinance do we find a chapter entitled "Concerning German Schools" and devoted to the education of the general public. Its inclusion in the document is itself not without significance. Vernacular schools for the "unlearned," as they were termed, tended to be denounced as injurious to serious studies and to the institutions where these were carried on. As recently as 1536 a Württemberg visitation instruction had deplored their deleterious effect on Latin schools in draining from them "many boys who would be able to learn Latin and serve the honor of God and the advancement of the common good." In towns and large villages where Latin and German schools clashed with each other, the latter were ordered closed.[68] The instruction of 1536 reflected the suspicion of many reformers, including Luther himself, that the utilitarian interests prompting parents to send children to popular schools to learn the three Rs were in large part responsible for declining enrollments in academic institutions.

But in the context of the ecclesiastical reform of 1559, a supervised system of vernacular schools seemed not only unobjectionable, but advisable. Duke Christoph and his councillors now recognized that "there are many hard-working people in our larger villages who cannot find the time to instruct their own children." To enable these youngsters to learn to read and write "for their own sake and for that of the common welfare" and to assure their instruction in basic religion, the ordinance provides for the establishment of German schools staffed by "persons examined before appointment" who were to teach reading (with "distinct and pleasing pronunciation"), writing (with emphasis on legibility), and "above all other things" the fear of God through the study of the catechism, the words of which were to be "impressed on the child's mind" until he knew them by heart. Girls as well as boys were to be taught in this way,[69] but in buildings apart, or at least in separate rooms. As in the Latin schools, discipline was to be strict but not cruel. Wherever possible, Latin school inspectors should keep their eyes on the German schools; where this was not feasible, the local pastor had to look in. Although little more than literacy was expected of German teachers, and though their engagement was the prerogative of the community, they were in fact never appointed without "prior examination [by the *Kirchenrat*] for honest birth, life, and conduct," also for orthodoxy of belief, legible handwriting, and a thorough understanding of the catechism. Teaching the catechism was the small-town and village teacher's chief duty; learning it was the pupil's main obligation.

The school ordinance does not say so, but we know from other sources that the responsibility for financing these vernacular schools remained in local hands. This explains the checkered pattern of schooling in Württemberg (as in other territories) in the sixteenth and seventeenth centuries. On the other hand, it comes as a surprise to conventional assumptions about preponderant illiteracy to discover from the Württemberg visitation records that schools were common in villages and small towns across the duchy.[70] Visitation documents note for each parish the presence or (in rare cases) absence of a school, along with a brief comment on the teacher's competence. Not all schools carried on year-round operations. Many were only *Winterschulen* because pupils could not be spared from farmwork during spring and summer. Schools often disappeared for a time as money dried up or the population fell; this regularly happened in plague years. But nearly always they started up again, and, if the visitation records can be trusted,[71] most performed tolerably well, even under adverse conditions. Ecclesiastical authorities were now in agreement with the duke that basic instruction should be made available to the largest possible number of youths, "not only for the sake of their salvation, but also for our common welfare."[72]

The documents also reveal the extent to which the system had been centralized. Again one must guard against judging this shift by modern criteria. But by the standards of an earlier epoch the duke and his councillors had, after 1559, considerable leverage in directing educational policy and compelling compliance. Huge bundles of correspondence reposing in the archives bear witness to the fastidious care given by chancellery and *Kirchenrat* (after 1590 called the consistory) to all questions, large and small, affecting education.

Most problems, and most of the writing back and forth between Stuttgart and towns and villages, touched only routine affairs: the condition of school buildings, the number of children enrolled, their ages, candidates for teaching positions and their competence, above all money. The enormous volume of correspondence about finance indicates that though the Württemberg dukes were eager to see Latin and vernacular schools widely and well established in their territory, they were also prepared to haggle interminably about the price.[73] Controversies about trifling sums tended to drag on for years. At the same time the *Kirchenrat* and the ducal chancellery received long fitness reports on all candidates, including not only the required handwriting specimens, but also sample compositions on set topics.[74] Once a man had been proved acceptable, the haggling commenced on whether and how to divide his pay and the cost of his perquisites with the community he was to serve.[75] The least one can conclude from all this activity is that the government was kept exceedingly well informed about the state of education in the duchy. Where necessary it intervened forcefully; most often this happened in cases of obvious incompetence or suspicion of heresy.[76] Books thought to be dangerous, especially those betraying a "Zwinglian" influence, were removed from schoolrooms and private shelves.[77] But there were limits to a sixteenth-century government's ability to enforce its laws. Although the school ordinance of 1559 enjoined year-round school attendance, reports from visitations in small-town and village parishes showed the impracticality of this goal. Nor could people be forced to attend catechism classes where this obligation collided with resistance or apathy.

But in the historical perspective, it makes more sense to judge reformed educational structures by what was achieved than by what remained undone. Seen from this vantage point, the accomplishment is impressive. Those who brought it about recognized the intricacy of social, political, and human factors whose concurrence alone would make the system work. Pastor Lucas Martini, for example, who drafted a memorandum on the preconditions for an effective *Gymnasium* in Nordhausen, can hardly be charged with taking a simple view of the problems of education. All who are associated with a school, he wrote, must be Lutherans. They must pray daily for its success. Pastors must constantly remind parents of their duties and parents must respond. School administrators must be magnanimous and open-handed in their policies, especially toward teachers. They must be always on their guard and, once a flaw is detected, act resolutely without respect of persons. In school itself, lectures must be kept brief and "useful." Discipline must be strict but punishment moderate. Frequent examinations should be held in the presence of school supervisors. But these procedures will bear fruit, Martini concludes, only if parents really wish their children to learn. Preachers and officials therefore have a job of persuasion to do. Mandates and surveillance alone will not work.[78]

Let us try to gain a synoptic view, bearing in mind the fragility of generalizations based on impressions from so diverse a political stage as sixteenth-century Germany. By means of ecclesiastical constitutions and school ordinances, Protestant cities and territories (and Catholic ones as well) organized coherent school systems to take the place of the uncontrollable educational conditions of earlier times. Instead of a bewildering number of types of schools—cathedral, parish, monastic, municipal, private, and many others—operating without proper supervision and according to no common standards, there came into existence[79] a more or less rational network of educational institutions serving a common purpose. Particular schools[80] led the able pupil to an advanced secondary school, usually called *Gymnasium*, a favored humanist term, or *Paedagogium*,[81] where he perfected his Latin, learned Greek and Hebrew, and was prepared for studying theology at the university, thus putting a stop to the most frequently criticized failure of medieval schools: the matriculation at the university of boys ill-trained and often much too young for serious study. "Monastery schools" or "prince's schools" (*Fürstenschulen*) were supported by territorial rulers for training their future ecclesiastical and secular bureaucrats.[82] Universities stood, as before, at the apex of the structure.

"German schools" (*deutsche Schulen*) are the most troublesome to classify and confusing to evaluate, but they are central to this book. Older Lutheran historians have argued strenuously that it was the evangelical thrust of the Reformation that led to the establishment of popular schools in towns, markets, and villages all over Protestant Germany.[83] They acknowledge the reformers' partiality to Latin schools serving a learned elite, but they see the Lutheran movement quickly gathering enthusiasm for the religious, moral, and civic education of every Christian person as a member of the church. More recent interpreters have found the drive behind the founding of vernacular schools to be the mid- and late-sixteenth-century Protestant state's fear of heterodoxy and the attempt to check its spread, and ensure religious conformity, by means of controlled indoctrination.[84] Without trying at this point to answer the questions posed by this debate, it may be said that while most of the members of Luther's own circle of reformers were ambivalent on the advisability, indeed the value, of fostering literacy and book learning at the village level, their successors, with responsibilities as ecclesiastical administrators and spokesmen for politically sponsored theological orthodoxies, became convinced of the wisdom of this move. Other impulses were at work, notably the wish for literacy shown by small-town and village folk themselves. The case for this will be made in a later chapter. The evidence for it varies enormously from place to place, but there is enough of it to suggest that the impetus for extending schools into the countryside came from below as well as from above.

The case of Hesse serves to demonstrate the role of the state in making schools available to the population at large. In his great "Reformation," sanctioned by the synod of Homberg in 1526, Count Philip ordered that "there shall be schools in all cities, towns, and villages where boys can be taught the rudiments of learning and writing to prepare those who are able for going to the university in Marburg. Wherever, especially in villages, these rudiments cannot be taught [for lack of schools or teachers], let the pastors or their assistants teach reading and writing to the boys." Girls were to be given some proficiency in reading, writing, and needlework. Religious instruction was to consist of psalms and selected scriptural passages.[85] None of the provisions of this reformation was implemented, however, for Luther advised the count against issuing such a "pile of laws" without prior spiritual preparation by pastors working in the parish.[86] Visitations as late as the middle of the century revealed that only an occasional sexton carried on some catechism teaching, and only the larger towns boasted Latin schools.[87] This situation changed after the division of Hesse following the death of Count Philip in 1567. In Hesse-Darmstadt the energetic superintendent Johannes Angelus utilized obligatory confirmation, instituted there in 1574, to encourage religious preparation in schools established for this purpose. When neighboring Hesse-Kassel turned Calvinist in the early years of the seventeenth century, the threat of heterodoxy introduced a new element of urgency, translated into vigorous promotion of schooling in the towns and countryside of the Lutheran part of Hesse.[88] Early seventeenth-century visitation records show that a large number of schools did in fact exist, though by no means everyone in the land was eager to send his children to them. But where persuasion from the pulpit and mandates from the chancellery had their intended effect, school attendance became common rather than rare.[89]

Events in other territories exhibit similar trends. It would be tedious to amass examples, but a few additional instances may prove instructive. The school ordinance issued in 1544 for Schleswig and Holstein by Christian III of Denmark deplored the general ignorance revealed by recent visitations and provided for a sexton in every village to teach reading and catechism to the young.[90] In the free city of Hamburg no arrangements for German schools had been made in the ordinance written in 1529 by Bugenhagen, who was not much interested in popular instruction beyond "something evangelical and a few Christian hymns."[91] But the proliferation of unlicensed private schools, and the confessional controversies of mid-century, changed this attitude. Pastors clamored for the introduction of German schools to compete with the ubiquitous *Klippschulen* to which, they argued, people would be sending their children as long as Latin schools were the only alternative.[92] In 1556, accordingly, Superintendent Johannes Aepinus issued a new ecclesiastical constitution that included provisions for sextons in all urban and rural parishes of the city's domain to teach not only the catechism, but also reading, writing, and reckoning.

In Saxony rural education in the middle of the century was still confined to twice-weekly catechism exercises. But the school ordinance promulgated in 1580 as part of the "General Instructions" for the great visitation of that year demanded, under the title "Concerning German Schools in Villages and Townlets," that every church in the land employ a sexton capable of reading and writing, and of teaching these skills, along with the catechism, to the young. This ordinance, which copies the Württemberg *Schulordnung* of 1559 almost verbatim, refers to the urgent need to reach culturally isolated subjects in villages too small and poor to afford a Latin school, whose children "should not be neglected, but ought to be instructed not only in the catechism, but also in writing and reading."[93] A visitation in 1617 revealed a far larger number of these *Küsterschulen* in existence than in the 1570s.[94] At about the same time Duke Johann Casimir, taking over the Coburg part of Saxony as an independent principality, urged the establishment of German schools upon his new realm, because, he wrote, "our untamed young people ought to be brought up and instructed in the fear of God, right doctrine, the catechism, and good discipline."[95] The Saxon visitation protocols, which are exceedingly rich for the 1580s and 1590s, show that village schools taught by sextons or schoolmasters were the rule rather than the exception. Popular response to them varied considerably. In many places it was very slack. But where people wished, or could be persuaded, to send their children to school, boys, and often girls too, acquired at least a smattering of simple writing and reading along with their required drill in the catechism.[96]

In the eyes of government and church officials, the growth of literacy in the population served some highly desirable objectives, as long as it remained tied to the system of indoctrination and control established in ecclesiastical constitutions. What were these objectives? First, to reach the greatest number of subjects in towns and rural parishes, so as to shape their religious and civic behavior. Second, to achieve the greatest possible measure of uniformity of belief and practice. In defining this latter goal, two impulses seem to have operated. One was a preoccupation with administrative order and simplicity, a drive that could be illustrated ad infinitum from the documents: "the same in all schools,"[97] "the uniformity of all ceremonies is hereby ordered,"[98] "no one to deviate from the orderly observance of these rules,"[99] and so on. The operative term is always "orderly" (*ordentlich*, in accordance with the prescribed *Ordnung*, which means both ordinance and order, the latter with its associated meanings of stability, constancy, logical arrangement, and normative authority). Governments evinced a horror of diversity and complexity, both of which they equated with chaos[100] and attempted to eliminate, or at least reduce, through explicit regulations. They took it as axiomatic that uniform rules "contribute to peace and unity among burghers and to the greater tranquility and stability of all things."[101]

A second impulse to uniformity arose from the pedagogical persuasion that sound learning at every level of intelligence was the product of constant reiteration of immutable formulas. "Uniformity is to be maintained throughout so that the young and simple shall become accustomed to hearing the same words spoken again and again";[102] "everything must be reduced to one simple form which can be impressed on children";[103] "so that lack of uniformity and frequent changes in the texts may not prevent children from learning and make them fall into errors."[104] "Avoid multiplicity in all possible ways," warned Melanchthon in his advice to the pastors of Saxony.[105] On this point, too, examples could be multiplied almost infinitely. Sixteenth-century officials seem never to have lost their implicit faith in precise prescriptions to govern every activity and every single case. This trust led them, among other efforts, into a determined (though rarely successful) struggle against private schools operating outside the official school system. All ecclesiastical constitutions outlawed these independent schools, but except where governments entered into agreements with educational entrepreneurs, as in Augsburg, Ulm, and Nuremberg, the attempts to suppress them came to nothing.[106] The archives hold scores of complaints about privateers who lured boys away from public schools, "first two or three, then four, . . . and soon the greater number of my pupils."[107]

Another source of contention was compulsory school attendance. In principle, children able to walk to school, or church, or to a sexton's dwelling, were expected to present themselves for instruction. But parental prerogatives over children were too firmly entrenched to enable reformers and pedagogues to do more than plead. Reminders of God's prior claims remained vague threats in the face of stubborn parental resistance. Various inducements were tried. The Württemberg ordinance imposed fines on parents whose children were seen on the street during school or catechism hours. This device was employed elsewhere too.[108] In 1619 the *Schulordnung* of Weimar ordered pastors and schoolmasters to keep "careful attendance rosters so that we can reprimand parents whose children are not in school, and, where necessary, use the secular power over them."[109] In Ulm written excuses from parents or guardians were demanded from a truant child.[110] In Stralsund the beadle was sent after absent children.[111] In Hamburg school authorities paid heating costs during winter when it was discovered that parents were reluctant to let their children sit in frigid schoolrooms.[112] But none of these expedients worked to satisfaction.

Comparing actual performance with the regulations saves us from judging the success of sixteenth-century bureaucrats only by the forceful language of their decrees. This is a useful corrective exercise. But the long view obliges us to give due weight also to what they attempted to accomplish and what they did to implement it. On balance, their achievements appear by no means negligible. Deeply rooted customs and attitudes do not change overnight, or in a hundred years. A century after the Reformation was introduced into German cities and principalities, educational organization still exhibited many of its medieval traits. Private and local initiative was by no means eclipsed by intervention from above. It remained an essential factor in the working of the system. Students and teachers were still itinerant, though much less so than in earlier times. Poor pupils continued to go begging from door to door.[113] Rural teachers were still moonlighting in other jobs, and many a village schoolmaster conformed to Vives's description of him as one "who smells worse than a goat and instructs his three-penny classes in his school which abounds in dirt and filth."[114] Particular schools continued to prepare students for the clergy; the medieval proverb "*Schülerlein jung Priesterlein*" (schoolboy today, priest tomorrow) holds for the Reformation as well. For the masses education still meant mainly religious teaching, though it came to be more effectively organized.[115] Actuality still fell far short of expectations. On the other hand, a great deal had already changed and more was changing. The trend toward system, uniformity, and centralization is unmistakable, as is the political drive behind all instruction, religious and literary. Teaching and learning became institutionalized activities. A common sense of purpose emerges, and a determination to close the gap between what was desired and what was being done. Educational aims joined the other objectives of church and state in extending the bureaucratic reach beyond what had traditionally been thought feasible and tolerable. This trend did not in itself guarantee success. But it went a long way toward creating circumstances more favorable than ever before to achieving the objectives of Lutheran pedagogy.

4

Nowhere is this interpenetration of the old and the new more symptomatic and the direction of change more evident than in the disposition of financial problems created by school reform in the Reformation. There is good reason for seeing in the intricate political manipulations required to raise the needed sums of money the best effort of the Protestant educational enterprise.

Whatever success one is prepared to grant to educational reformers, they clearly could not have achieved it without the help of the state. Political mandates and legislation made the support of education a matter of public policy. Government enlisted the pulpit to exhort and employed its officials to obtain compliance. Its bureaucratic apparatus gathered accurate data on the condition of schools and schooling. It brought isolated local efforts into coherence and marshaled scattered resources. Above all, it persisted in urging, nagging, prodding a reluctant citizenry, thus preserving by political means the impetus generated charismatically in the early phase of the Reformation.

The reformers themselves urged governments to give all possible support to schools. Luther has already been quoted on this point. His followers kept up the pressure. One of them, writing in the late 1520s to the elector of Saxony, put the case succinctly: "Two kinds of people attend [Latin] schools: great lords and the sons of the rich on the one hand, and commoners on the other, that is to say, children of burghers and peasants. The former study to attain honor and fame, the latter to make a living. The former never become pastors, preachers, or school-masters, for there is no honor to be got nowadays from these professions, only trouble and hard work. We must therefore count on the common people for supplying us with our clergy and teachers."[116] But how can the poor and those of the "common middle sort" (*gemeine mittelmässige bürger*) afford to keep their sons in distant schools? The writer urged his prince to persuade the wealthy to give substantial help to the poor so that their children could study. Private benefaction did in fact become one of the means of funding learned education.[117] Theologians and preachers acclaimed the support of learning as a most meritorious work in the practice of Christian love, "commanded by God, and also bearing his promise of rich reward."[118] But this kind of munificence helped only professional studies, in the large cities. For the mass of particular, German, and catechism schools in towns and countryside the money had to be raised in other ways. These involved government actively and directly.

In principle, governments continued to regard education as a charge upon localities. If funds could be provided on the scene, rulers refused to consider external financing and restricted their role to collecting precise information on how much was, or might be, made available and how much was being disbursed. They badgered town councils and village elders to raise and spend larger amounts for educational facilities and salaries. Ecclesiastical constitutions tied school financing to municipal common chests and to the secularized church revenues that fed them.[119] Understandably, local worthies attempted to shift part of the burden to territorial governments. Taking at face value their princes' acclaim of the godliness and social merit of education, they made persuasive cases for their respective towns and villages as suitable recipients of public subsidies. Huge correspondences ensued; this has already been noted in the case of the duchy of Württemberg. They exist in equal bulk for nearly all territories. In principle, again, rulers were willing to grant augmentations of locally raised funds. But their means were limited, and they had to be selective. In 1544 the town council of Schilda in Saxony pleaded with the elector for an annual grant of forty gulden to hire a second teacher. We have sixty boys in school this year, the council wrote, and only one master, who is also our town scribe and the sexton of our church. These labors take so much of his time that he has to neglect his teaching. Will the elector, whose interest in improving schools is well known, grant an augmentation? Not until

1545 did the elector reply. We get too many such requests, he wrote, and must in this case say no. He could do no more than suggest palliatives to relieve the unsatisfactory situation.[120]

In other instances, however, the elector responded affirmatively. It was a matter of negotiation in each case.[121] If a ruler decided to help, a sum was usually available from a sequestrated monastery or other income-yielding property. Most rulers demanded a detailed inventory of local resources before entertaining requests for augmentations.[122] Letters went back and forth for years: pleas for help, calls for more information, refusals, renewed pleas, final rejection or, after a change of heart in high places, a grant from the central treasury or an award of property.[123] Periodic general and special visitations produced meticulously detailed charts showing the provenance of revenue in every parish. Visitors investigated each stoppage or delay in the flow of income and tabulated the figures for the use of chancelleries and consistories. Where individuals or groups failed to give what they owed—and it was a rare parish whose pastor and schoolmaster did not have complaints on this point—the government intervened, though it did not normally go beyond the usual dunning sequence of reminders, admonitions, repeated proddings, and threats. Where a source of revenue had disappeared, it attempted to make a replacement.[124] Meanwhile it also gathered information on salaries and living and working conditions of schoolmasters (and, of course, clergy) and made determined efforts to remedy serious inequities. Territorial visitors had standing instructions "wherever possible to raise incomes,"[125] that is to say to persuade local authorities to furnish increments. Many localities were too poor, however, to do anything of the sort. This fact, too, emerges starkly from visitation documents. "Children are kept at home because their parents cannot afford school fees." "The people hereabouts are too poor to pay school fees and [the village school] has only five pupils in the winter and none at all in the summer." "The wretched inhabitants of this village would gladly send their children to school [wrote a visitor from Coburg], but they cannot afford the stick of wood each child has to bring to school during the winter. If we could provide a few cords of firewood for these people their school would surely flourish."[126] In such instances small sums were often made available from outside sources.[127] Generally speaking, where visitation reports showed town or village people able and willing to spare their children from work, and interested in having them learn, and where sufficient resources were available for maintaining a building and a modest salary for a teacher, governments were willing to help out, as also in cases where abject poverty precluded these prerequisites altogether. There is no doubt, moreover, that the incessant investigating, and some shrewd intimations of possible help if local contributions were raised, had the desired effect. They produced a significant quickening of local effort, which in turn was rewarded with a more generous allotment of public funds.

The resulting pattern of financial support was, for the most part, a patchwork of bewildering complexity, whose extreme precariousness explains the waxing and waning fortunes of schools in the later sixteenth century. In the small town of Dommitzsch in Electoral Saxony, for example, the schoolmaster's income in 1575 was listed as follows:

> From the common chest and the *Comthurhof*, 30 gulden, given quarterly, 7½ each time. Also 3 pennies' worth of bread from each burgher given on John the Baptist's day, which comes to about 1½ gulden per year. Also 4 groschen from each schoolboy, coming to 1½ gulden per year, but this sum is to be shared with the cantor. Also 3 gulden for scribal work in connection with the common chest; also 4 gulden at Christmas. *Summa:* 36 gulden, 4 groschen. Also 36 *Scheffel* grain, paid out of the common chest. Also one loaf of bread from each house. Also the use of a field one-half *Hufe* in size, for which he is to pay 14 groschen, 2 pennies in interest to the administrative district of Torgau and 8 *Scheffel* in grain to the church. Also free lodging in the schoolhouse. Also 6 *Klafter* of firewood annually to be supplied by the council. Also accidentals: for each funeral 1 groschen if he goes with the whole school, and from each wedding he may take food back to school for the boys who do the singing.[128]

In Dresden the schoolmaster had a small salary from the elector, a loaf of bread annually "from each burgher and peasant who owns a large house," some grain in sheaves from outlying villages and more grain in the sack from a wealthy teamster, ten groschen twice a year for washing the altar cloth and greasing the clock, fifteen groschen from the town council, and in addition small accidental sums for leading his choir at funerals, marriages, and baptisms. He also had a field, a kitchen garden, and school fees of two or three pennies per week from each pupil depending on whether the boy was learning only to read, or also to write.[129] Most incomes were composed of such tiny bits: petty sums from land, brooks, house and school pennies, also grain, bread, eggs, peas, sausages. Victuals were still picked up in the teacher's *Umgang*, his perambulation to houses from which payments in kind were due, but were often grudgingly given ("baked in a small loaf and from spoiled flour")[130] or not at all. The archives contain thousands of petitions addressed to their governments by small-town and village schoolmasters unable to make ends meet and facing a destitute old age.[131] Wherever possible, rulers and their agents procured increments from local sources. But even when they declined to lend a hand, their responses betray touches of human sympathy for forlorn widows and veteran teachers who had been able to save nothing for their declining years.[132]

Urban schoolmasters were much better off than their colleagues in the country. Latin masters always earned more than German teachers.[133] At the bottom of the heap was the sexton who drilled village children in the catechism. One cannot help wondering how much skill and dedication these wretches brought to their teaching duties. Looked at from a different angle, on the other hand, the situation astonishes us in a positive way. The bulk of documentation illustrating these intricate financial arrangements makes it clear that a host of schools had come into being in the German territories, Catholic as well as Protestant.[134] The best of these gave solid training in traditional learning and evangelical religion. The worst of them provided at least a smattering in catechism and the ABCs. Seen in historical perspective this was no mean achievement.[135]

The principles of Lutheran pedagogy were formulated by men who helped in the building of this educational structure. Despite frequent disappointments, they kept their faith in the assumptions on which it rested. They believed that the minds and habits of their fellowmen could be shaped by indoctrinating the young. The network of schools created in the course of the sixteenth century provided a framework within which the basic postulates of this endeavor could be put to the test.

PART 1

ASSUMPTIONS
AND EXPECTATIONS

CHAPTER 2

PEDAGOGICAL PRINCIPLES

Readers familiar with the religious literature of the sixteenth century may have discovered an implicit paradox in the explanation just given of the genesis of the Lutheran educational program. In its structure and operations this program suggests permanence and trust in the future. On the other hand, few among the reformers believed that human institutions could long endure or that much time remained before their demise. Judgment Day was near; most men accepted this as a certainty in their lives. To many its imminence was assured. As for the persistence of human effort on earth, a long backward glance over the history of empires and kingdoms told them that all man's works were fleeting. Why, then, so much planning, organizing, and building? The laws and institutions of the Reformation were made to last. Why build so well if time was running out?

This paradox was not resolved; indeed, it was not even faced, at least not on the conscious level of analysis and explanation. But its symptoms are everywhere apparent, most notably in the strangely ambivalent tone suffusing much of what was said and done in the early and middle years of the Reformation. Expressions of hope in the future were not lacking. But anticipations of doomsday sounded a persistent counterpoint: "In this year of our Lord 1532, about five thousand, four hundred and seventy-four years have passed since the beginning of the world. We may therefore hope that its end is now near at hand." Thus wrote Johann Carion, whose universal chronicle, edited by Melanchthon, became a kind of official outline of world history as seen from Wittenberg,[1] demonstrating above all other things the inconstancy of life and the insubstantiality of human labors.[2] Melanchthon himself was deeply pessimistic about the time left to Christians to put their house in order. In 1559, the year before his death, he added this dejected note to an earlier edition of his *loci communes:* "The prophecy of the prophet

Elijah: The world will last 6,000 years, then it will be consumed by fire. Two thousand years of desolation, two thousand years under the law of Moses, two thousand years in the time of the Messiah. But because of our sins, which are many and grave, the fullness of years remaining to complete the last two thousand will not be granted to us. Written in the year of our Lord 1559 and in the year 5521 counting from the beginning of the world. This reckoning shows that the day of the last judgment of our Lord Jesus Christ is now not far away."[3]

As early as the 1530s Melanchthon had begun to regard the sectarian divisions shaking the Lutheran movement as sure confirmation of the rapid running down of time.[4] His close attention to astrologers, who produced doomsday datings as their stock in trade, and the evidence he himself had gathered on the apparent senility of nature[5] added force to his prognostications, which darkened as the century passed its halfway mark. Even when the signs were not in themselves unfavorable, they tended to be read in the context of these covering schemes, surely a symptom of the compelling psychological power wielded by the theme of decline as an explanatory paradigm. Thus Johann Aurifaber, who edited Luther's Table Talk in 1566, laments in a bitterly disillusioned preface to this widely read anthology: "It seems to me that God has decided to bring the world to an end with this last preaching of the word [i.e., Luther's doctrines as taught in Saxony] and to smash it into a pile of rubble. As a candle or fire, when it is about to die, flickers for a final instant into a brilliant flame and gives off a great flash of brightness and then at once succumbs, the gospel has been burning as a bright last flame and sermon, casting a splendid light. But soon it will go out."[6] If Luther was the prophet Elijah returned, as many of his supporters claimed after his death, "then it is certain that the end of the world is on our doorstep, for Luther has preceded the second coming of Christ as John went before the first."[7] Preachers and pamphleteers drove the point home: "We clutch a tiny last corner of the world," they warned, "but soon it will slip from our grasp,"[8] for we live in a "cold, sad time when the world is sinking into death,"[9] "when the world has fallen into decrepitude."[10] On the ground of this reasoning many Lutherans opposed calendar reform in the 1580s, for if the cosmos was racing to dissolution, what was the use of making computations about the coming centuries?[11]

In earlier centuries, Christians had faced this dilemma more uncompromisingly. The primitive church had drawn the lessons of its eschatology and given only the most casual attention to building permanent institutions and preparing a new generation of leaders.[12] Not so the reformers of the sixteenth century. They too meant what they said about the nearness of Judgment Day and the apparent acceleration of the pace of disintegration. But such assertions did not persuade them to remain passive while all about them the signs of decline clamored for action.[13] They were not of a temperament to wait patiently while events took their natural course. The nearer Judgment Day, the more urgent the need to make ready for it by commencing the systematic religious and moral training of their fellow creatures. It may be that this simple line of reasoning allowed them to reconcile the conflicting claims of eschatology and reform. But the balancing of these two largely incompatible orientations was a difficult act that took a heavy toll. It left them with an inner tension that often sapped their confidence and was quick, when things went badly, to throw them into despair.

2

Reformers were no less ambivalent on other matters, and a chapter devoted to fundamental pedagogical ideas must take stock of these. Most profound in its influence on the development of educational principles was Luther's own wavering position on the scope and limits of instruction. His pronouncements on this subject were remarkably unsystematic, if not self-contradictory.[14] While affirming the feasibility of traditional teaching in the proved ways of the arts curriculum, and while holding the child's parents accountable for basic instruction in religious knowledge, Luther seemed also to deny the possibility of effecting by means of human effort any lasting change in the inclinations of men. Human ingenuity cannot make Christians of non-Christians. This transformation is the work of God, who fashions each Christian anew, even as he once created the cosmos out of nothing.[15] God's work alone can educate (*erziehen*): "Let God draw [*ziehen*] you by means of his word," Luther said.[16] Parents and pedagogues can do no more than lead the young to it. For this they may use compulsion if need be,[17] but even this power is incapable of altering a man's nature or redirecting his impulses. Christian education is impossible through human effort.

Luther's pedagogical thought rests like his anthropology on the bedrock of his image of man as a fallen sinner. "For the imagination of man's heart is evil from his youth." This line from Genesis (8:21) defined for him the innermost corruption of all human instincts and the impossibility of changing these by rational argument or humane appeal. It also identified the psychological source of that irreversible egotism that he saw as the all-pervading symptom of human perversion.[18] Not merely "inclined to evil" (*in malum prona*), but evil in substance, evil through and through. In principle, Luther was therefore forced to deny conventional educational wisdom along with the traditional anthropology of the schoolmen.[19] Their insistence that the human sinner could be improved by appeals to his mind and senses was unacceptable to him as a facile meliorism that ignored the root cause of the human condition. When he faced it in the person and writings of Erasmus he rejected it out of hand. Only God could educate, if education meant learning to rise above the limits imposed upon human understanding and behavior by the depravity of human nature. "Unless the Lord builds the house, those who build it labor in vain": Psalm 127 spoke the literal truth. Human ingenuity and human strength were inadequate to the tasks of directing human affairs.[20] Men may respond to God's call, but only God can summon them and remake them in a new act of divine creation.[21]

So much was said to satisfy the claims of theology. But when it came to actual practice, Luther allowed much greater scope to education, particularly to the education of young children, whose condition—innocence or guilt—confronted him with a difficult problem of reconciling Scripture with sense evidence. His reading of the Bible obligated him to impute to even the very young the depravity so evident in their elders ("the imagination of man's heart is evil from his youth [ab adolescentia sua]").[22] "We have hardly passed our fifth year," he comments on Gen. 8:21, "when we look for idleness, play, wantonness, and pleasures, but shun discipline, shake off obedience, and hate all virtues, but especially the higher ones of truth and justice." Before long "lust and the hideous passions of the flesh, . . . quarreling, fighting, and murder" join the catalog of vices.[23] On the other hand, Luther's experience with the young, and his feelings as a man and a father, told him that children were in fact tractable, open to suggestion and receptive to mollifying influence. He agreed with his contemporaries that the storms and tensions of early adolescence clouded the serenity of childhood at the very time that experience of the world brought inevitable contamination. These changes set in at about the age of six, when the human person begins to make use of his reason (qua homo incipit ratione uti).[24] From then on his conduct proves the truth of the proverb that "by the time he grows up, the little angel has turned into a devil [Junge Engel, alte Teufel]." In his early years the child is still untainted. Indeed, childish innocence is a wonderful thing to observe, as Luther insisted repeatedly.[25] He never tired of watching his own and other children as they amused themselves in their guileless ways. Their artless games put him in mind of the pristine condition of man in the Garden of Eden.[26] They still retain the right faith, he said.[27] Their innocent minds should be an example to us all.[28] "Observe," he said, "the wondrously pure thoughts of children as they face heaven and death without a doubt in their hearts."[29] All this suggested to him that the young, at least the very young, were still pliant and receptive,[30] open not only to the imposition of external discipline but also to the implantation of religious and moral impulses. Thus human reason and the dictates of parental love and political responsibility did suffice to effect by means of instruction a beneficial change in the thoughts and behavior of men.

This does not mean that evil inclinations could ever be expunged from the human heart. But they might, by means of discipline, be "to some extent" (aliquomodo) corrected and restrained.[31] Unfortunately Luther is elusive on the concrete details of this process. At what age exactly does innocence cease and the inheritance of sin assert itself? Up to what point can conduct be altered by discipline? How do constraints relate to impulses, and outward behavior to motivation? In what sense are children "tractable" ("weil sie sich noch ziehen, biegen und leiten lassen"), and how should the pedagogue utilize this capacity? Nor is Luther's position without internal contradiction. Still, one may find in his assertions enough encouragement to support the conclusion that educational efforts are by no means wasted or without object and direction. At least as an aspect of natural law and external discipline ("ein heidnisch eusserlich ding"), education is not only possible but indispensable.[32] Luther himself made no attempt to remove the confusions arising from the coexistence of these two distinct strains in his thought. He emphasized now one, now the other, as his argument or the exigencies of the moment demanded.[33] The resulting ambiguity was to plague the conduct of Lutheran pedagogy for decades.

In any case, a number of reasonably firm conclusions could legitimately be drawn from Luther's pronouncements and given the cachet of his vast authority in the movement. First, if education were to succeed at all, it must begin with the very young. That the older generations were too far gone in stubbornness was a matter of universal agreement. "Let them go to the devil," said Luther.[34] "These people are deaf and dumb to all appeals and warnings." said Johann Agricola; "there's nothing we can do with them because their minds are shut and their senses hardened."[35] If the Christian Church is ever to rise again, Luther wrote, "we must make a new beginning with children"[36] who, not yet spoiled by the ways of the world, respond with an innocent heart and an open mind. Throughout the sixteenth century Luther's followers reiterated these contentions, for which a formidable weight of traditional authority could also be cited. "Men who are to serve their country must be raised to it from childhood," wrote Justus Menius; "in no other way can an impression be made on them."[37] "Let us with God's help try it again with children," urged Agricola in 1528. "It's our only hope for restoring corrupt Christendom."[38] Fifty years later they were still trying. "That saintly man Martin Luther admonished us to be mindful of our duty to train children. He said Christendom is now in so sorry a state because we have been neglecting the young.

And things will not get better until we have made a new beginning with our children. As you want people to be when they are grown up, so must you raise them in their youth."[39] Other writers could be quoted to the same effect.[40] Their words were charged with alarm and urgency. A start must be made at once, or another generation would be lost. The proverb "soon ripe, soon rotten"[41] conveys something of the sense of pressure felt by all those who based their hope for a restored Christendom on the reform of its youngest members.

Second, it was concluded that indoctrinating the young was essentially a matter of religious and moral, as opposed to academic, education. Young people, said Luther, must be taught above all other things to "learn to know God and understand his word."[42] This is the heart of Lutheran pedagogy.[43] School subjects are important, of course, but languages and the liberal arts do not touch the core of the pedagogical problem as it was perceived and being defined by the reformers. The arts curriculum offered some helpful tools for acquiring a knowledge of God and the human condition. But superior and simpler means were at hand for gaining this central objective, for Luther and his associates had developed useful instruments for the religious indoctrination of lay people, especially of children. This indoctrination is best accomplished in public schools—this is the third conclusion—not at the hands of parents but under the care of professionals and the aegis of the Christian state. Luther's acceptance (after 1525) of the superiority of school over home as the place of nurture and education meant a sharp break with his early preference for parental supervision of Christian education. But he knew now that even with the best will—rare enough in those times—most parents, being too ignorant and too deeply mired in mundane affairs to give sound instruction in an age of dangerous theological drift, lacked the gifts for instilling religious knowledge and moral precepts in their offspring. Though he never acknowledged the full dilemma posed by his shifting position, Luther came to reject the amateur in education. "Discipline taught in the home, without the help of schools," he noted shrewdly, "tries to teach by utilizing our own experience [erfarung]. But before this can bring results, we are a hundred times dead and have acted foolishly all our lives, for experience needs a long time before it can tell us something."[44] In other ways, too, experience proved a poor guide to the Christian life, by charting an uncertain course toward undefined goals. In the context of the 1520s and 1530s, the school of experience could bring only the profligate diversity of heterodox beliefs, with moral and social chaos as the inescapable consequences. Hence the insistence, near-universal among reformers, on authoritative teaching by proved experts under controlled conditions.

Fourth, Luther outlined—though again not without ambiguity—the pedagogical approach to be taken to reach the young: no rigid, formal schoolmastering, but a humane fellowship between the child and an adult personality secure in its grasp of sound principles. Luther's own writings furnished a treasury of examples of the simple language and picturesque imagery suited to this approach.[45] He urged adults to enter the child's world, to inhabit his realm of play and imitation. "Let no one think himself too clever for such childishness," he warned. "Christ himself could not draw men to him until he had become a man. If we want to teach children we must first become children. Would God such childish games were now in use everywhere! We would soon have great plenty of Christians among us, and souls rich in the knowledge of Scripture and God."[46] This posture represents his innermost conviction as preacher, father, and pedagogue. "Let a father raise his child so that it will never have cause to lose trust in him. Let him avoid all cruelty lest he shake the child's faith in him."[47] God's way with men set the pedagogical model: "A father should deal with his children as God deals with us,"[48] he said. This was Luther speaking as feeling man and loving parent. As a theologian he could talk very differently, as will be seen later in another connection.[49] In this instance, as in many others, Luther employed contradictory precepts as the occasion demanded, without confronting their incompatibility, much less reconciling it.

Finally, Luther gave support to the conviction that religious knowledge and understanding were attainable goals with the aid of a well-functioning system of schools. Although in important respects at variance with his theology, Luther's trust in the restorative power of education struck resounding echoes among his contemporaries. They overlooked its implicit inconsistencies (which in any case were muted in the process of popularization) and adopted the optimistic outlook as the most congenial posture for the reforming temper of their age. To be sure, Luther's ambivalence rose to the surface whenever calamity called for a pessimistic response:

> Everything lies in God's power, especially whether a person prospers or goes to ruin; and this includes children. Human nature being evil, we despise laws and experience, and profit nothing from instruction we receive. God therefore reserves to himself alone the right to determine who shall fare well and who will be destroyed. We have proof of this in the families of the biblical patriarchs, some of whose sons were made wicked by God, to serve us as examples that it is not education and discipline [*Zucht*] that make children good or bad, but God's will alone. Abel was pious, Cain a scoundrel. Sem and Japheth were good, Cham was a rogue— and yet each of these pairs was born of one father![50]

Pessimism did not often have the last word, however. More typical are expressions of "hope that, if we teach Christian discipline and doctrine to our foolish young people in their tender years, we will in a short time, and with God's help, see a heartening evangelical change taking place among us, and a much improved Christian society established."[51] Many Lutheran preachers seem to have believed that lasting benefits were the assured result of such a program of religious instruction. Veit Dietrich, for example, the theologian and pastor in Nuremberg, convinced the city fathers of Ravensburg that their fellow citizens were bound to be uplifted by the city's newly inaugurated classes in catechism and religion:

> You will now see daily improvement and steadily increasing well-being in body and soul in your whole community and within each household. For it is impossible [unmüglich] that God should refuse to honor and reward those who keep his word ever before their eyes. . . . Nor is it possible that people who go to church and listen attentively to the preaching of the Old and New Testaments should fail to be much improved in their understanding, in their faith, and in their lives.[52]

Such implicit trust in the efficacy of education—and many more illustrations of it could be given[53]—was strengthened by growing evidence that schools and schooling enjoyed wide support in both high and low places in society. Luther's praise of public schools, given in his open letter of 1524 to city councilmen, evoked a deep and lasting resonance.[54] Most of the early school ordinances were drafted in response to its appeal. But from the grass roots, too, there came signs of approval, townspeople and villagers exhibiting a hitherto unsuspected interest in literacy and learning. The evidence for this is spotty, of course. But clearly there was enough of it[55] to convince proponents of mass education that their voices were not crying in the wilderness.

The main objective of general education—all reformers were agreed on this—was to prepare people to give willing service to God, each in accordance with his native gifts.[56] Predisposed by their respective talents to fill two major roles in society, they were trained to be either teachers or learners—preachers and teachers of Scripture or listeners and attendants. To these roles people must be prepared from childhood. "For it is surely God's will"—the passage comes from the ecclesiastical constitution of Zweibrücken—"that some should be taught to read, study, and afterward instruct their fellowmen in the writings of the prophets and the Apostles, . . . also in reading, writing, languages, and the arts; and that there should be others whose special function it is to attend to these teachers [etliche besondere zuhörer] and to learn and thereby help preserve books, languages, and Christian doctrine."[57] To be sure, learning also helps win material rewards, both for individuals and for society.[58] But this is not the main objective. Paul's advice to Timothy was often quoted in support of the religious purpose of education: "Paul counsels his friend Timothy, who had learned to read in his youth, to keep it up all his life."[59] "From childhood," Paul says, "you have been acquainted with the sacred writings which are able to instruct you for salvation through faith in Christ Jesus" (2 Tim. 3:15). The passage was immensely useful in helping to bridge the theological gap between human effort and divine intervention. At least on the rhetorical level—for purposes of preaching and exhortation—it suggested an exalted role for instruction in Scripture. Only in formal theology was a sharp and final distinction made between human effort and divine grace. In practice, especially the practice of pedagogy, doubt was not allowed to weaken the proposition that right-thinking and right-living men and women would emerge from a systematic program of religious and ethical indoctrination.

For an informed voice on this crucial issue one may listen to the Nuremberg preacher and former Wittenberg professor Wenceslaus Linck. In 1524, the year before his city went over to the Reformation, Linck published a tract entitled *On Christian Nobility; or, the Freedom of the Children of God*,[60] addressed to the vital problem of the formation of the Christian person. A blank slate (*ein blosse tafel*) at birth, the human mind and character can be shaped (*formirt*), he affirms, by utilizing three native tendencies. First, some among our natural inclinations dispose us to seek the good. "God's image dwells within every person as a natural spark, and this directs him to seek good things even as his depraved nature erupts violently on the surface." This innate ability to recognize and want the good can be reinforced by nurturing. Through the development of this trait men may be conformed to honesty and a rational life. Second, human beings respond to the influence of custom and habituation. "Practice and habit have their effect on the lives of individuals as long as they are accustomed from childhood to good burgherly discipline and taught to acquire other traits indispensable to our social existence. In this way our natures are formed." Habit, an important pedagogical concept in the sixteenth century, conforms men to good morals and manners.

Third, we respond to the force of law "which by compelling people to adopt standards of piety and justice, directs them away from self-seeking and leads them to the love of neighbors and God." Law therefore conforms us "to spirituality and holiness." These three natural tendencies do not purchase salvation for us. Salvation is God's work, a new creation in the course of which "men are reborn, formed and taught by God as they receive God's word into their hearts through faith, becoming regenerate creatures, true children of God." Decent instincts, good habits, and law cannot turn a sinner into a true Christian, although in a way that remains unexplained they help engender Christian thoughts and Christian conduct; and these traits, in turn, do in effect make Christians of those who exhibit them in their lives. The distinction is less than perfectly clear. In practice it was further blurred by a tendency to imply that the right-thinking, right-acting Christian, as one especially pleasing in God's sight, was certain to be favored by the deity. In practical theology and the care of souls the distinction was all but obliterated. Thus Melanchthon warned Saxon pastors in 1528 against confusing the faithful with abstruse explications. "It is not necessary," he told the clergy, "to deliver subtle disputations on merit and whether or not God gives it in exchange for our efforts and works. Simply tell people that God approves of good works and compensates us for doing them, though you must tell them also that he bestows rewards freely, without counting any merit of ours."[61] A tidy division of human effort and divine determination was possible only in the realm of metaphysical abstraction. In real life and among real people, it was always undercut by the need to provide inducements for the learner and encouragement for pedagogue and preacher.

Bugenhagen's school ordinance of 1528 for Braunschweig provides a good example of how this theological predicament impinged on practical school administration. Its prefatory declaration of religious principles[62] states that baptized children are innocent but, like the rest of us, prone by nature to acts of wickedness. All too soon this inclination asserts itself, and with it comes the serpent reason, goading children to attempt all manner of vice, and prompting them to blaspheme against the gospel and reject the bond with Christ created in the sacrament of baptism. "This is the moment to seize them," Bugenhagen advises. But who is there at home to instruct them? There is no one, for all members of the household are locked in the service of Mammon. Thus godless parents raise godless children. As they themselves have been brought up, so do they bring up their own. Bad eggs, bad chicks. And thus the power of Satan grows over humankind.

For these reasons, the preface continues, it is of the utmost necessity to establish good schools "where our poor ignorant young people can be trained in discipline and taught the Ten Commandments, the Apostles' Creed, the Lord's Prayer, and the sacraments . . . not only that the knowledge of the doctrine may be increased, but also that some among them will become schoolmasters, preachers, jurists, and doctors . . . to be of use to themselves and to society, for the salvation of their souls [*zur seligkeit der seelen*] and the preservation of government on earth." We will not succeed with everyone, the preface concludes. But why cut down the tree because a few of its fruits are wormeaten? The great majority of the young will profit from our discipline.

One wonders, in reading this text today, whether the good people of Braunschweig followed Bugenhagen's subtle differentiation between the uses of education for salvation and for procuring social benefits.

Most likely not. But the very softening or blurring of this distinction is sure to have enhanced the appeal of education among ordinary folk, and this effect could not have been unintended. Reformers and pedagogues, for their part, must have found in such vague formulations much-needed encouragement in their efforts to use the power of indoctrination to fashion good Christians for a better society.

Bugenhagen did not extend his recommendation to the establishment of vernacular schools, although the preface to his school ordinance seems to point him in that direction. Like the other early reformers, he tended to draw back when it came to a firm commitment to popular education. Their low opinion of the mass of men persuaded them that easy access to German schools would further deplete indispensable academic institutions.[63] But, as has been seen, subsequent developments convinced governments and their theologians that general literacy and education were desirable goals. This position too had been prepared by the reformers, giving still another instance of their ambivalence. "Learning to read," said Bucer in 1525, "makes the common people more polite, peaceful, and disposed to a civic life."[64] As ecclesiastical and secular authorities struggled to retain control over the turbulent events of the 1530s and 1540s, they reinterpreted the principles of Lutheran pedagogy. Adapting them to their own purposes, they discovered in them the means of exerting influence and a measure of control over the thoughts and behavior of their subjects. As a result of this shift, religious orthodoxy and compliant citizenship became the heart and core of general education.

It has been seen that the experience of the early and mid-1520s persuaded most Lutheran reformers to welcome law and authority as necessary restraints upon men's natural tendencies to sectarian fragmentation and social turbulence. This acceptance had fateful consequences for education. The sequence of events beginning with Karlstadt's actions in the castle church at Wittenberg in December 1521 and culminating in the revolutionary mayhem of the peasant uprising of 1525 built up into a religious and social crisis of momentous consequences for the completion of the evangelical reformation. In the light of this crisis the reformers now saw the gravest threat to the divine order of things in the misguided individual's self-arrogation of the right to change long-standing traditions on the basis of whims, visions, narrow self-interest, and willful suppositions. Owing to the concurrent and—from Luther's point of view—highly destructive antinomian challenge to his position on law and gospel (which itself received definitive formulation only in reaction to the crisis of the 1520s), the Lutheran response to these events acquired a heavy, not to say heavy-handed, emphasis on the role of law in Christian society. The discussion of this issue swung widely between two levels of meaning and two frames of reference. Against those who rejected the force of Old Testament law over Christian believers in the gospel, it was argued that education through law must precede the preaching of the gospel if the latter were to prove effective. In this sense the making of a Christian individual recapitulates the development of the human race in its passage from the old dispensation to the new. But below this theological plane of argument one detects the suspicions of worried observers of unpredictable social events, frightened by the breaking of traditional bonds, uneasy over the effects of innovation, fearful above all of what might happen "when common people take matters into their own hands."[65] True Christians need no law; this was certain. Nor do they need the gospel. They live wholly in their faith. But as only God knows for certain who these true Christians are, contends Luther, "both law and gospel must continue to be preached and people forced by the law to be outwardly pious. For this purpose God has placed men under the worldly sword, as confirmed by Romans 13 [3–7], so that those who are not pious enough in their hearts may be prevented from behaving wickedly. . . . In short, it is even more necessary to preach and practice God's [Old Testament] law than the gospel, because so many people are evil, and only through the constraints of the law can they be kept out of harm's way."[66]

Law also fulfills its role as disciplinarian by awakening the believer to the full consciousness of his sin. Until this happens inward piety cannot take root: this explains the obligatory first place given to the Decalogue in all Lutheran catechisms. Theologically speaking, law offers men instruction toward justification—*paedagogia ad iustitiam*.[67] But the argument is not limited to theology. From the 1520s on the Lutheran camp also exhibited a great practical interest in law and legislation. "God has ordained civic laws, indeed all laws, to restrain transgressions. Therefore every law was given to hinder sins," Luther said in 1531 in his course of lectures on Galatians, the most systematic statement of his doctrine of law.[68] In a disproportionately wordy section of his *Instruction of the Visitors to the Pastors in Electoral Saxony* of 1528,[69] Melanchthon enjoined ministers to preach often and vigorously on the legitimacy of civil law and the folly of every attempt to tamper with it. "Let the old laws stand undisturbed for the sake of peace, oppressive though they may be. Our forefathers who made these laws knew that our crude, untamed people have need of the threat of punishment." There are many now, Melanchthon continues, who preach revolution "and these were in part responsible for the tumults of two years ago [i.e., 1525]." It is for us to respect and obey existing laws and the authorities who stand behind them. Pastors and teachers must train their parishioners and pupils in this respectful obedience.[70] The law being a "pedagogue [*Zuchtmeister, paedagogus*] toward Christ," schoolmasters must drill it into the heads of the common people, and especially the young. Only the discipline of the law, and the power of those charged with enforcing it, can keep the Lutheran movement from coming to grief in a violent and complacent world.[71]

One detects behind these utterances the corrosive distrust of human nature, the suspicion of men's motives, and the tendency to expect nothing but the worst of them that reformers shared with so many thinkers and with most of the lawmakers of their time. The events of the 1520s did nothing to soften these misgivings. "The foolish mob" (pöbel), "the crazed mob," "the crude mass" are tags used increasingly and ever more indiscriminately in Reformation writings to designate the common man. "It's the way it goes when the disorderly rabble gets into the act," said Luther. "Nothing troubles me more now than this great mob of people . . . among whom there is no one who can tell good from bad." He concludes: "the mob must be ruled by force as a donkey needs blows."[72] Melanchthon, writing in the aftermath of the peasant rebellion, included all commoners in Germany in his holy wrath: "Such a wild, disobedient people as the Germans ought to be given even less freedom than they enjoy now," he wrote, and "German people are so ill brought up, reckless, and bloodthirsty that they must be ruled harshly from now on, as King Solomon advises us in Proverbs 26 [3]: 'a whip for the horse, a bridle for the ass, and a rod for the back of fools.' "[73] Luther now began to express himself cautiously in public for, he said, the mob is bound to misunderstand it all,[74] turning a good cause into a bad one. The more wicked a cause the greater the number of followers it attracts.[75] Everything said on the subject of the common people (and a great deal was said) supported the conclusion that firm hands and strong wills at the top were the only guarantors of peace and order in a volatile society forever on the brink of turmoil.

The upshot of the Lutheran response to the disturbances of the 1520s, then, was a great augmentation of the role of government in the management of affairs, not as a matter of principle—Luther still distrusted political autocracy, especially at the hands of princely rulers, most of whom he regarded as callow worldlings—but as a matter of expediency in managing men and situations in a condition of crisis. Reformers still hoped for a general change of heart in response to preaching and Scripture reading. But governmental intervention seemed to offer the only realistic expectation of swift correctives. "Where young people stay neglected and undisciplined," wrote Luther to his duke in 1526, "it is the fault of the government."[76] Sins and abuses among the people continue to wax daily, wrote Justus Menius in 1548 after discussing the state of affairs with his fellow superintendents in Saxony and Thuringia, "because government has not yet brought them under control." Preachers, he continues, can accomplish nothing with people who turn a deaf ear to the word of God. "The harder we try, the more we are despised, not only among the common mob, but even by the governing class."[77] Political acts alone will help now, he concludes.

The city of Strassburg provides an interesting case in point of how the observations and reflections discussed in this chapter were turned into suggestions for government policies. Two fundamental points of educational policy guided Strassburg's magistrates and preachers, led by the reformer Martin Bucer. First: the purpose of schooling was to secure the survival of humanistic studies on the one hand and the diffusion of religious knowledge in the population on the other ("for it is our desire and purpose that everyone gain a modicum of understanding, and that whoever is called to higher things be advanced to these").[78] No one was to be excluded from advancement on the grounds of his station or income, "for," the preachers wrote, "in a free city every man has a right to better himself." Second: the supervision of schools must rest in the hands of the municipal council, delegated by it to a college of school supervisors.[79] This group of laymen, the *Scholarchen*, controlled all aspects of education from basic policy to routine administration.[80] The protocols of their sessions, which have survived, convey an insider's viewpoint on school politics and administration in that important city where Zwinglian and Lutheran ideas contended for dominance over religious, social, and diplomatic policies. In Strassburg, as elsewhere, public morality and religion left much to be desired in the 1520s and 1530s. Church attendance lagged, catechism classes were sparsely visited; blaspheming, drunkenness, and disorderly conduct abounded.[81] The Latin schools were suffering a continuing drop in enrollment[82] while students gambled, picked bloody fights with citizens, and perpetrated other acts of hooliganism.[83] Public response to Reformation and gospel was clearly less than wholehearted. Moral persuasion proved to no avail; the documents show plainly that preachers had given up on this for the present. If people's behavior were to be conformed at least outwardly to Christian standards of conduct, government intervention seemed the only answer.[84]

This is the background of a long memorandum addressed in 1547 by Bucer, Zell, Vogius, and Marbach to the Strassburg council. The document gives much insight into Protestant thinking on matters of education. After furnishing a long and painfully explicit grievance list of the many ills of their society, the preachers addressed themselves to steps to be taken to correct them. Let us begin with children, they said. The instruction of the young in doctrine and discipline is our only hope now for a basic improvement in public morals and religion. "First and foremost," then, "it should be understood that everyone who wishes to reside in this city shall be obliged to send his children to catechism instruction." But since appeals of this kind have not worked in the past, stronger action is needed now, "for children belong more to God and the community—we mean both the religious and the political community —than to their parents, and for this reason the authorities and governors of both communities must make certain that all baptized Christians fulfill what they have pledged to do and what they are by law obliged to do." No well-ordered state, the preachers argue, can permit a man to bring up his children in disobedience to his government. "How much less, then, shall Christian magistrates allow parents to raise their off-spring in hostility to God and his congregation? . . . And how much more are Christian authorities obliged to ascertain that all who are baptized shall be raised, educated, and required to behave in a manner pleasing to God and conforming to his divine law?" If people refuse to comply, they must be coerced: "Parents who will not act voluntarily in this spirit should be made to feel the full severity of the law. No one can be left free to dedicate his children to the service of Satan." The obligation of government to eliminate gluttons and drunkards (a reference both to Deut. 21:20 and to the unceasing complaints about these most characteristic of German vices) shall be a warning to every person that "a Christian reformation requires above all other things a government willing to hold parents to their duty to raise children to serve the common purpose of the community [*zu nutz der gemein*]."[85]

The Strassburg city council was not yet prepared to assume the Draconian role suggested to it in 1547 by its ministers.[86] It preferred instead to continue for the time being its familiar, tried, and unproductive expedients. The sweeping Mosaic ruthlessness implied, if not explicitly recommended, in the preachers' memorandum, though part of the arsenal of every sixteenth-century government, was still used with reluctance by most magistrates and rulers. But given the prevailing public indifference toward religion, there seemed to be little choice between rigorous repression and ineffectual persuasion. Other governments were no more resourceful than Strassburg in matching performance to intentions. Though they acknowledged their responsibility, as it was being put to them by theologians and preachers,[87] they were at a loss to know how to force citizens into compliance. In the end they always fell back on the usual entreaties, as in Württemberg in 1559:

> At least twice a year, once in spring and again on the approach of winter, each pastor shall make in his sermons serious admonition to his parishioners that they must be diligent in sending their children to school. And let him stress the great benefit bound to come from this, schools being necessary not only for learning the liberal arts, but also the fear of God, virtue, and discipline. Where the young are neglected and kept out of school, permanent harm, both eternal and temporal, must result, as children grow up without fear and knowledge of God, without discipline,

like the dumb beasts of the field, learning nothing about what is needed for their salvation, nor what is useful to them and their neighbors in worldly life. And the pastor shall inform them, furthermore, that school-mastering is a troublesome office and laborious, thankless work for which teachers should be honored and respected, and their hard-earned pay given to them willingly and without grudge.[88]

If pleas failed, as they usually did, only threats remained. Thus the Thuringian church administrator Caspar Aquila, in commenting in 1538 on the fifth commandment, gave first place in the company of homicides to neglectful parents:

> Who violates the fifth commandment? . . . All those are murderers in the sight of God who feel envy, hatred, anger in their hearts. . . . And he also is a slayer of men who covets his neighbor's goods, which God has been pleased to grant him. Also whoever curses, blasphemes, tells tales—these are all murderers before God. . . . And no less is he a murderer who fails to raise his children in the fear of God and in good discipline. Indeed, such a one is a worse murderer than a man who has struck another dead in anger.[89]

Such words—reiterated in countless variations into the sixteen hundreds[90]—express the impotent frustration of the reformer whose most heartfelt counsel was sown into the wind. A deep pessimism saturated Lutheran literature in the second half of the Reformation century. And yet the old hopes were not dead. Even as he warned people against placing excessive confidence in their children—"Christian fathers had better abandon all natural joy, ambition, and trust in their godless children"—Caspar Huberinus, a prolific writer of popular religious books, insisted that only in a new generation, raised in humility and brought up in the fear of God, was there any hope for suffering Christianity.[91] The evidence was overwhelming that "nothing is [being] accomplished with our preaching, calling, appealing, and writing."[92] "Everyone, young and old, lives in a state of arrogant security [*sicherheit*] and indifference."[93] "Many a person has been learning the catechism for twenty, thirty years, and still understands less of it than a papist who has never even heard of it."[94] These charges were raised again and again, and on good evidence. But few believed, or admitted, that the principles of their pedagogy had failed them, and preachers continued to implore citizens and governments to redouble their efforts to bring to life in a new generation the conditions of a godly Christian society.

Psychologically, at least, Lutheran theologians and preachers could countenance the defeat of their best efforts even as they refused to relax their labors. Their equivocal posture toward humankind in general, its educability in particular, and the waning time in which they lived out their years, enabled them to keep up the good work while acknowledging its lack of success. To be sure, frustration and despair did break through on occasion. "Our headstrong Germans will not come to their senses," wrote Andreas Musculus; "they will mind neither God nor the devil until, like the rich man in hell, they have lost everything, the door of grace has been slammed shut, and no one is left to show them pity or give them help or counsel."[95] Too much was at stake, however, to abandon the struggle. Knowing themselves even in a losing war to be fighting on God's side, the reformers persisted in their endeavors. In the late decades of the sixteenth century the bloom of great expectations had faded from their enterprise, but the momentum gathered in its first, heroic years continued to impel them.

CHAPTER 3

THE PEDAGOGICAL TRADITION

It will be useful at this point to ask: What did sixteenth-century theologians know about education? What sources supplied their information about children and the young? Did they express new ideas or merely restate the conventional wisdom compiled during centuries of reflection on the question of pedagogy?

No one familiar with their epoch will be surprised to learn that what these men knew was what they had read in books. Not that they lacked interest in real-life youngsters. Luther himself can be quoted for a number of acute, and often very touching, observations on his own and other people's children.[1] Nor would it be difficult to cull from autobiographies and other writings enough evidence to show that adults regarded children with concern and affection.[2] A growing corpus of pediatric treatises also suggests that the young were being studied with something like the care we now feel they deserve.[3] But the empirical attention devoted to children was never systematized. It remained fragmentary, occasional, and—except for medical writings—subjective. The literary tradition, on the other hand, furnished reformers with an internally coherent set of propositions on the nature of the young. It also offered reliable predictors of their behavior at each phase of their physical development. Given the receptivity of sixteenth-century intellectuals to traditional opinion, it is not surprising to see them turning to this pedagogical literature for their ideas about the young, for clues to the scope and limits of education, and for practical suggestions and methodological hints. A rich and prolific body of writings on education reaching back to Plato carried a cumulative authority that was hard to resist, even at points where it conflicted with observed or sensed reality. In any case, in the context of their culture it was a natural move for reformers to consult the past for solutions to conceptual and methodological problems concerning the education of the young.

To answer our question, What did sixteenth-century reformers and theologians know about education? let us assume that they were familiar with the entire body of pedagogical literature from Plato to their own contemporaries Vives and Erasmus. This supposition is not as farfetched as it might appear on first glance. The sixteenth-century intellectual was a voracious reader. He took pleasure in compendiousness. He knew that the problems of education had occupied the great minds of pagan and Christian antiquity and of the philosophical schools of the Middle Ages. He also knew—and here we move closer to the realm of the practicable—that earlier authors had, for their part, drawn on older books, much as he himself was inclined to do. When he read Vincent of Beauvais he also came to know Hugh of Saint Victor, Jerome, and Quintilian. In Jacob Wimpheling's *Adolescentia* he found a large mosaic of pedagogical bits and pieces gathered from more than a score of earlier writers.[4] Otto Brunfels's *Catechesis puerorum* of 1529, written for the school supervisors of Strassburg, provided an easy introduction to Quintilian, Cicero, Plutarch, and Jerome, as well as a good sampling of fifteenth-century Italian educators.[5] Readers could also fall back on an assortment of anthologies of educational classics that would have given them a speaking acquaintance with the pedagogical tradition all but indistinguishable from a firsthand knowledge of the sources.

The publication of such anthologies is itself an interesting piece of evidence of the sixteenth century's serious concern with education. Though editions of ancient sources had become more readily available, they were not, of course, within the reach of everyone who might wish to consult them. A market therefore existed, for digests and compendiums of educational classics. A good example is Antonio Mancinelli's *On the Education of Children by Their Parents,* which contains entire chapters on Plutarch, Quintilian, Plato, Aristotle, the *Cyropaedia* of Xenophon, Cicero, Quintus Curtius, Diogenes Laertius, Seneca, Jerome, Augustine, Basil, and—from Scripture—Proverbs, Ecclesiasticus, Matthew, and Paul.[6] Otto Brunfels has already been mentioned; in addition to his *Catechesis puerorum* he compiled a florilegium of educational thoughts and observations taken entirely from classical antiquity.[7] Several abridgments were published of the works of major pedagogical writers, including notable contemporaries,[8] as well as numerous reductions of pedagogical classics to aphorisms and didactic precepts.[9] No one in the sixteenth century needed to be ignorant of what the great thinkers had said on the subject of education. There was plenty to read for those who liked to browse in digests, and convenient editions, and innumerable references to them, awaited the scholar who preferred to go to the sources.

This body of literature supplied its readers with a wealth of useful information. More important, it put a solid foundation under their implicit trust in the power of instruction. As has been seen, such a trust could only with difficulty be derived from Luther's theology; no more plausibly could it call on observed reality for confirmation, for reformers were inveterate pessimists when it came to judging the lives of their fellowmen. Confidence in the ability of some to teach and others to learn must therefore in large part have come from the many authors who in the previous millennium and a half had written on the very questions now preoccupying the reformers. These lessons from the past were by no means unequivocal. The pedagogical tradition did not speak with one voice. It was not a dogma to be adopted but a critical discussion to be confronted. But on two points, at least, there was substantial agreement among all authors: that men could and should be taught, and that one must begin with the young. These tenets became Archimedean points from which Reformation pedagogues proposed to change the course of events. The pedagogical tradition furnished the arguments with which they made their case; it also convinced them that they spoke for a powerful historical consensus.

It follows that reformers lacked neither incentive nor opportunity to steep themselves in the literature of the pedagogical tradition. Let us examine this literature to see what principles they extracted from it and what actions it suggested.

2

At the root of all that was said on the subject of education lay two contradictory convictions about the child's essential nature. The approbation of natural instincts, and their adoption as beneficial impulses to learning, was most attractively summarized by Quintilian, whose observations on children and their upbringing (in the first book of his *Education of the Orator*) cast a lasting but not unequivocal charm over sixteenth-century pedagogues. Quintilian's "Nature brought us into the world that we might attain to all excellence of mind"[10] can stand as the motto of the sanguine school, which accepted the fundamental soundness of human nature at least to the point of denying its inescapable corruption. Most children are intelligent by endowment and eager to learn by instinct.[11] The function of education is to deepen and extend this promise.

An equally eloquent opposing view rejected nature as a basis of trust and severely limited the expectations and scope of education. Corrupt from birth, or corrupted within a few years of it, human impulses exist only to be restrained, not to be allowed to unfold. This pessimistic view, firmly anchored in the Old Testament (Gen. 8:21, as has been seen), was given momentum by the compelling assertions of Augustine on the subject of infants and children and by a large company of pedagogical writers from Gerson to Wimpheling and Vives who had come under Augustine's spell. Their position is epitomized by Augustine's gloomy introspections on the motives underlying the childish pranks and petty deceptions of his own childhood. "Is this childish innocence?" he asks, after giving a revealing account of them, "It is not, Lord, it is not. . . . These are the same things, the very same, which as our years go on . . . are done with regard to kings and governors, business and profit."[12] Among the Protestant reformers this pessimistic strain produced a lasting echo. In a large body of the Lutheran literature of pedagogy it is the prevailing theme.

Pedagogical ideas and assertions exist in astonishing profusion in Augustine's works, although they lie scattered, some in his early writings, many in his late works. His sixteenth-century readers could not have drawn a coherent system of educational thought from Augustine, but they were bound to have been struck by the acuteness and psychological force of his observations. Augustine's position is far from simple. Quite apart from the polemical purpose of much of his writing (of which his sixteenth-century readers need not have been aware), and from the serious internal inconsistencies that have often been pointed out, the bishop of Hippo harbored shifting attitudes toward the early stages of life and their influence on adult behavior. For the purposes of this inquiry, however, it is not as important to discover what he really meant—this question has been meticulously examined[13] —as to know how he was read in the sixteenth century: as the apostle of extreme pessimism. From his *On the Merits and Forgiveness of Sins and on the Baptism of Infants*, later readers could, if they so wished, extract passages to prove the wickedness of the babe in his cradle.

> Seeing now that the soul of an infant fresh from its mother's womb is still the soul of a human being, . . . not only untaught, but even incapable of instruction, I ask why, or when, or whence it was plunged into that thick darkness of ignorance in which it lies? If it is man's nature thus to begin, and that nature is not already corrupt, then why was not Adam created thus? Why was he capable of receiving a commandment? . . . Whereas [the infant], although he is ignorant where he is, what he is, by whom created . . . is already guilty of offense. . . . Where, when, how have [infants] by the perpetration of some great iniquity become suddenly implicated in such darkness?[14]

Augustine is here at pains to prove against the Pelagians that original sin is inherited, that baptism makes no sense without assuming this, and that sin does not have to be committed to exist; it is our human heritage.[15] In the *Confessions* the same point is sharpened by the author's portrait of himself as a natural sinner. "It is the physical weakness of a baby that makes it seem 'innocent,' not the quality of its inner life. I myself have seen a baby jealous: it was too young to speak but it was livid with anger as it watched another baby at the breast."[16] Augustine shows that the young child, the infant even, displays all the signs of human depravity: greed, envy, lust, the prodding will, and the *amor sui* that is the heart of sin. Without grace the infant remains in the "thick darkness of ignorance," incapable by his own powers of surmounting his animallike condition. He is all instinct, and his behavior reveals the direction of his infantile drives.[17]

But Augustine does not have to be read quite so dismally. Jean Gerson, whose influence on the religious strain in early modern educational thought almost equaled the bishop of Hippo's,[18] while also rejecting the innocence of infants as a Pelagian heresy and pointing to overt signs of *concupiscentia* as proof, insisted on a basic natural goodness in the child that, he says, renders him capable of positive responses to influence and instruction. Gerson denied that every human instinct was depraved, preferring to speak instead of an inclination or susceptibility to concupiscence, a tendency that could be counteracted.[19] As an educator, which he was with a passion, Gerson built on the existence of germs of goodness and reason in the child that, with careful cultivation and guarded by a "wall of discipline," could be nursed into virtues.[20] Gerson believed in restraint, particularly in matters relating to the senses, and he worked out comprehensive rules for making beneficent impressions on children.[21] His writings show that the Augustinian position on inherited sin need not necessarily lead to unmitigated pessimism, and they persuaded many who found Augustine himself too hard to accept. Jacob Wimpheling, who was much influenced by his older French colleague, worked up Gerson's suggestions into a comprehensive (though incoherent) theory of pedagogy which he advanced in his *Adolescentia*.[22] Although he found the young full of undesirable inclinations, he identified four means for reaching the residue of virtue persisting in each child. These make training possible. They are the efficacy of divine grace, the influence of intelligent parents, good examples, and direct appeals to his mind and character. Small children, being least corrupted by life, offer the best prospects for training by educators charged with creating a favorable educational milieu in which every influence tends toward the desired end.[23] Wimpheling suggests that only within this all-enclosing pedagogical environment can the slender shoots of virtue prevail over the proliferating weeds of natural and worldly vices.

In Reformation pedagogy the straight Augustinian position was usually advanced as an argument for the unflinching use of severe restriction and coercive conditioning in the education of the young. One naturally wonders whether this was a case of theology leading to educational ideas or, conversely, an empirical sense that the young ought to be subdued seeking and finding a postulate on which to rest educational practice. However this may be, the question of the innocence or depravity of young children had a profound influence on the form and content of religious and secular instruction in the sixteenth century. Authoritative opinion was available to argue that even the slightest extension of freedom to the young would be misused by them to indulge the self-destructive urges in which concupiscence manifests itself in all human beings. The only correctives were restraint and control.

Equally impressive opinions existed, however, to furnish a different set of guiding principles. Relatively little was made of theological arguments for the natural innocence of infants and young children,[24] or of the affecting appreciation of the child implied in Jesus' injunction (Matt. 18:3) to "become like children." Childlike qualities acclaimed in this and many other gospel passages[25] tended to be invoked as correctives to adult trespasses, constantly in sermons, frequently in pedagogical writings. But they offered nothing in the way of concrete suggestions for educating the young.

Much more promising as a starting point was the idea of "crude matter" that pictured the infant at birth as a neutral entity and placed on the educator the burden of turning the raw substance into something good and useful. Taken from Quintilian into the sixteenth century, and acquiring in the passage a faintly Augustinian overtone, the *rudis massa* concept is prominent in the educational thought of Erasmus, especially in his *De pueris instituendis,* his pedagogical best-seller first published in 1529 and of great influence on Reformation pedagogy. Quintilian, in denying the naturalist claim that native talent requires no instruction and need only be allowed to unfold without hindrance, had argued that crude nature must, by mental discipline, be broadened and developed.[26] All men, without exception, are teachable, but education must proceed systematically if it is to be effective, "That there are any who gain nothing from education I absolutely deny,"[27] he concluded. To Erasmus, who followed Quintilian on this point, as on many others, "nature" was simply the ability to be taught, not the source of wickedness in children. Men accuse "nature," he says, when they should blame themselves "for ruining the minds of children by allowing faults to be acquired before directing them to the good."[28] This position explains Erasmus's emphatic insistence on early childhood training that is the chief purpose of his treatise and that became, as we have seen, a pedagogical axiom in the sixteenth century. Quintilian had given the classic empirical proof of this position: "The mind is all the easier to teach before it is set. This may be clearly proved by the fact that within two years after a child has begun to form words correctly, he can speak practically all without any pressure from outside.

On the other hand, how many years it takes for newly imported slaves to become familiar with the Latin language. Try to teach an adult to read and you will soon appreciate the force of the saying . . .: 'be started young!'"[29] Education begun in infancy molds the unformed mass into the shape of a man (*in hominis speciem*). Left to itself, Erasmus asserts, the substance will turn "naturally" into the image of a beast.[30] Erasmus is not free of latent pessimism, but he believes in the power of instruction. As dogs are born for hunting and birds for flying, man has been created to recognize truth and virtue. Every creature is capable of learning the skill for the practice of which it is born. The human child, when properly taught, is quick to acquire good discipline. But without such teaching he is speedily corrupted, for human beings are always ready to choose the lesser over the greater.

It is easy to see that Erasmus failed to resolve the contradiction posed by his conflation of classical and Christian sources. He rejected, often indignantly, rigorous Augustinianism. He agreed with Quintilian that education was efficacious and beneficial. But he was enough of a Christian to tinge with an Augustinian stain Quintilian's insistence that education should do more than simply assist in the development of natural abilities. Unremitting vigilance is essential in dealing with the young, Erasmus believed, for they are driven by desires, not by judgment. "The good is more quickly forgotten than the bad, which we remember much longer," he wrote.[31] This tendency of children to succumb instantly to a bad influence had been unquestioningly accepted since antiquity. It was a matter of common knowledge that, if unreformed by discipline, the young were a rebellious and fickle lot. There was no disagreement with Plato on this point: "Of all wild creatures, the child is the most unruly, since the fountain of reason in him is not yet regulated," or with his proposed corrective: "When he leaves the care of nurse and mother, he must be under the management of tutors."[32] This conclusion could be buttressed with passages from Augustine to the effect that the young were naturally lazy and irresponsible, capable of effort only when placed under constraint.[33]

Such assertions about the basic traits of children tended to be made indiscriminately across the age span from infancy to adolescence. But this does not mean that authors failed to distinguish among the obvious stages of biological development. Classifications of childhood and youth into the three periods of *infantia, pueritia,* and *adolescentia* were ancient. Pagan as well as Judeo-Christian sources supported this tripartite division, along with finer discriminations based on observed behavior within each phase.[34] Thus Augustine distinguishes between the nursing and the learning-to-speak phases of infancy, and between the *puer loquens,* who has just emerged from childish imbecility, and a later condition of *pueritia,* just preceding puberty, when reason begins to be active.[35] Far from being mere periods of physical growth, the stages of youth leave profound and lasting impressions on the psyche. With the development of memory in infancy comes the retention of experiences. Augustine maintains that all early impressions are stored and constitute the formative ingredients of the adult. When the power of will first asserts itself, also in infancy, the child begins to notice the outside world, encountering it as an object of resistance to his instinctive wishes. Taking his own will as a command, he responds violently if denied. Thus the will is established early in life as the driving agent it will remain throughout adulthood.[36] Augustine's psychological perspicacity is unusual among the sources of the pedagogical tradition. But Varro, Isidore of Seville, and many other writers shared Augustine's recognition that human life was lived in stages, the onset of each of which signaled an important physical and mental transformation.[37]

There was no doubt about the significance of one such stage, adolescence, held to begin at age fourteen.[38] It would be difficult to improve upon the portrayal of the inner storms and passions of puberty, the restless longing and seeking for something not clearly perceived, that is conveyed by Augustine in his *Confessions*.[39] A similar, though very much cruder impression, emerges from Vincent of Beauvais's and Aegidius Romanus's books on the education of young princes, in which the adolescent's rampant pride, arrogance, and rebelliousness are evoked.[40] All authors clearly identify the source of these tensions and excesses as sexual: "the fires of youthful manhood."[41] Unrestrained by experience of consequences and with no care about the future,[42] adolescents, in the first flush of their physical powers, are driven to "natural" vices: lying, blaspheming, violence and cruelty, theft, disobedience to parents and disrespect toward their elders, idleness, gambling, recklessness and lack of shame, and "voluptuous desires that consume the body and mind." Catalogs of this sort are frequent in the pedagogical literature. The one just given is from Wimpheling's *Adolescentia*[43] and is taken mainly from Gerson, who was fixated on the apparently irrepressible sexual drives of adolescent boys, the gravest peril to their souls, as he saw it.[44] Sensuality had to be suppressed to the extent that it was possible to do so by influencing youthful minds. Gerson never ceased to plead with secular and religious authorities for help in guarding the young from corruption. At the very least, he thought, these safeguards would delay sexual maturity until the boy had acquired some self-discipline.[45] All authors agreed that a more or less rigorous system of control was needed to keep boys of fourteen and fifteen from destroying themselves for life. Even those who, like Erasmus in his *Colloquies*, make no attempt to conceal the unabashed sexuality that seems to have been overt among the young deplore its effects on the mind and character. Few writers, needless to say, addressed themselves more than cursorily to the problems of female adolescence; although when Vives, writing of the education of girls, quotes Jerome's "neither the burning of Etna, nor the country of Vulcan . . . boils with such heat as the bodies of the young,"[46] there is no doubt of what he means.

Everything written on adolescence, then, pointed to the conclusion that in this, as well as in the earlier even more impressionable phases of young life, nothing beneficial to the individual and to society could result from keeping the young on a slack rein. All authors advocated kindness and understanding. But the idea that the young might be allowed to develop with a minimum, rather than a maximum, of restrictive authority was—if discussed at all—declared to be abhorrent. Quintilian had wished the young to show spontaneity and initiative ("the young should be more daring and inventive and should rejoice in their inventions, even though correctness and severity are still to be acquired").[47] But his sixteenth-century followers rejected this aspect of his pedagogy. They were not persuaded by his warning that "exuberance is easily remedied, but barrenness is incurable"[48]—a proposition they were prepared to turn inside out. Instead they paid attention to writers who looked on childhood and adolescence as stages to be transcended, as a segment of life the sooner surmounted the better. The early years were obviously important to educators, but they were regarded as a period of privation, a state leading—if correct means were employed—to something higher. Child into man was a passage from imperfection to, if not perfection,[49] at least something less imperfect. Adulthood signified success in having learned to overcome the traits of childishness rooted in the instinctive, untaught, unrefined nature of man. To be a child, wrote a Scholastic author in a widely quoted passage, means saying whatever comes into your head, thinking only of the frivolous cares of the moment, enjoying uncleanliness, being unreliable and fickle, reacting to the world with superstition and fear, desiring everything you see and wanting it all at once, showing lack of consideration for others, and being thoughtless and self-centered.[50] Similar descriptions of childish traits were common in the literature. No one idealized the young.[51]

3

Everything said so far relates to the nature of the young—that is to say, to the instinctual, emotional, and biological drives supplying their natural impulses. Against nature, understood in this way, was set mind, intellect, *ingenium*, the seat of intelligence and the ability to learn. If nature was force, mind was restraint, holding the reins and, if properly trained, able to guide impulses and control drives. The training of the mind is the first specialized task of the educator, for (to quote Augustine writing in a less pessimistic vein) in the child "reason and intelligence somehow slumber, as if non-existent, but ready to be roused and developed with the increase of age, so as to become capable of knowledge and learning. . . . Thanks to these faculties it may imbibe wisdom and be endowed with the virtues so as to struggle . . . against errors and the other inborn vices and conquer them."[52]

How do we learn? The answer to this question—a critical one for Reformation pedagogues—will be the subject of the next chapter. Here it may be said in summary that the pedagogical tradition presented to its sixteenth-century readers a consensus assuring them that learning was an orderly, methodical, and essentially simple process. Provided one knew how it worked and used appropriate techniques, nearly everyone could be made to learn. Intellectual differences among students were recognized, of course;[53] the gifted were quickly identified and advanced to special schools, as has been seen. But there was also the conviction that skillful instruction can level the talents unequally bestowed by nature. To clinch this point, nearly every educational writer retold Plutarch's story of Lycurgus and his experiment with two dogs. One animal was highly bred but ill trained, the other a mongrel but carefully drilled. In the test the latter performed better, proving the superiority of nurture over nature. "Nature can do much," comments Erasmus on his own version of the story. "But instruction is better because it can do more."[54] Education was mainly training, and every child had the capacity to be trained. The modest expectations harbored by Reformation pedagogues for all but the brightest of their pupils could be met by all minds in normal working order.

This conviction was supported by another set of assumptions about the pupil's responses to learning situations. According to these, every human being exhibits certain basic psychological impulses affecting his interaction with his fellowmen. If presented in the form of appeals to these impulses, learning was not only a possible, but a highly likely result.

The most rudimentary level of the personality was affected by the pleasure-pain principle. Plato had held this principle responsible for the initial impetus to all actions,[55] and educators made use of it in many ways. Erasmus argued that learning should be a pleasant pastime for the young child—make it a game, he said—but he was only repeating a commonplace, first uttered by Quintilian.[56] It was, after all, simple good sense, supported by experience, to acknowledge that children seek delight and avoid pain.[57] Hence the many injunctions to "make play a road for learning" and to offer frequent rewards "so that [the child] may love what [he] is forced to do, and it be not work but pleasure, not a matter of necessity but one of free will."[58]

Sterner pedagogues could draw from the same principle a more rigorously physiological interpretation and employ positive and negative reinforcement techniques to produce desired responses. Plutarch's popular treatise on the education of children suggested how this might be done. Counseling against the use of corporal punishment as inappropriate and pedagogically unsound, Plutarch recommended instead the use of methodical praise and rebuke. "It is well [he wrote] to choose some time when children are full of confidence to put them to shame by rebuke, and then in turn to cheer them up by praises, and to imitate the nurses who, when they have made babies cry, in turn offer them the breast for comfort." "These two things," he concludes, "hope of reward and fear of punishment, are, as it were, the elements of virtue."[59] There were other ways, too, some less gentle than Plutarch's. In view of the common notion of early theories of education as a set of variations on the theme "spare the rod, spoil the child," it should be said at this point that traditional authority stood emphatically against this principle. We have already seen that the framers of sixteenth-century school ordinances attempted to outlaw cruel punishment. On the other hand, there seems to have existed in many minds an irrepressible suspicion that natural wickedness required unnatural punishment. The Old Testament supplied a wealth of vivid passages to prove that parental and institutional punishment was a good and godly thing. Indeed, it has been pointed out that the very word for education in Hebrew came from the term for chastisement.[60] These passages exerted a certain influence on sixteenth-century teachers. However, there is hardly an educational writer of the classical, medieval, and early modern periods who fails to insist that severe and frequent punishment is counterproductive. Quintilian thought beating disgraceful and, in any case, bound to fail, for the type of child who will not follow instructions is quickly inured to blows.[61] Plutarch held corporal punishment fit only for slaves.[62] Benedict's rule limited beating of pupils to extreme cases.[63] Augustine suspected that the threat of punishment made people worse rather than better.[64] Guarino da Verona agreed with the ancients that blows were unsuitable chastisement for a free person.[65] Maffeo Vegio wondered how one could hope to teach the child moderation while subjecting him to humiliating examples of adult rage.[66] Wimpheling advocated as little physical punishment as possible,[67] while Erasmus thought that even a good-tempered child would turn surly if accustomed to a diet of blows and other humiliations.[68] Opinions were, of course, also available on the other side. No writer was prepared to banish corporal punishment altogether. But even those who thought it a useful tool argued for restraint. Vives, for example, who disagreed with the more militant opponents of corporal punishment, regarded corrective blows as most effective if held in abeyance as a threat. The utilization of this inborn wish to avoid pain must have suggested itself by way of common sense and observation. If authorities were consulted on this point, however, the arguments against harsh punishment as an inducement to learning not only were more numerous and eloquent, but also were more sensible than those in favor of this practice.

Beyond simple reactions to pleasure and pain—but of course not independent of them—operated the innate urge to compete for success. Appeals to this impulse were highly recommended in the literature, but for Reformation pedagogues the principle of competition was a two-edged weapon, as easily turned against their best efforts as likely to advance them. Their model of the evangelical person was of a creature freed from the ultimately self-destructive drive of ambition. Nevertheless, they recognized the competitive urge as a biological fact of life and made use of it for what they hoped would be good purposes.

The principle of competition was said to depend on the instinctive operation of two urges, the ambition to excel, to win fame and honor, and the equally pronounced wish to avert disgrace and avoid shame. The possibility of appeals to these desires had, of course, long been recognized, and the literature furnished abundant proofs of their effectiveness and many illustrations of their application to practical teaching. Writers who, as Christians, deplored the persistence of the deadly sins among men, nevertheless endorsed the sense of pride as a beneficial impetus to achievement in the classroom. Jerome was often quoted: "Let her [the pupil Paula about whom he was writing] have companions in her lessons, so that she may seek to rival them and be stimulated by any praise they win. . . . Let her be glad when she is first and sorry when she falls behind."[69]

It goes without saying that authors of the Italian Renaissance supplied most of the arguments for the urge to excel as the psychological ground of successful instruction. Battista Guarino denied the very possibility of teaching where the desire to excel was absent. This, he says, was recognized by his famous father Guarino da Verona and made the starting point of his practice.[70] Maffeo Vegio suggests a number of techniques for awakening feelings of honor and ambition in young boys. No human being is so low, he argued, that he fails to respond to the appeal of praise that, bestowed on some and withheld from others, produced a "noble contest" among students. Never hesitate, he said, to give preferential treatment to those who excel; this will be sure to spur the rest to greater efforts, which is a good thing not only for performance, but also for character.[71] Vergerio thought that love of achievement and pleasure in fame must be developed in earliest infancy.[72] Few writers took the trouble to explain the inconsistency arising from their juxtaposition of the principle of competition and their evangelical morality. Some, indeed, made the incongruity obvious. Thus Wimpheling argues that an avid desire for praise, honor, and fame is the best sign of a suitable disposition in the young.[73] This he takes from Piero Paolo Vergerio's *De ingenuis moribus,* where it is asserted that a sound nature is stimulated by praise. Upon this stimulus rests emulation, Vergerio writes, "which may be defined as rivalry without malice."[74] On the other hand, Wimpheling ends his treatise with a set of cautionary precepts taken mostly from Petrarch (alphabetized for easy reference), prominent among which is the reminder that fame is an empty bubble: "Fama ventus est, fumus est, umbra est, nihil est."[75] Wimpheling may never have reflected on the contradiction between the two attitudes demanded by these contrasting pieces of advice. He was not much of a thinker. But his books were useful compendiums of wisdom gathered from others, and the received wisdom approved of ambition and proposed to make good use of it. Only Vives among early modern pedagogues maintained enough fidelity to his religious morality to reject it.

As effective as the wish to be praised was the fear of being put to shame. Most pedagogical authors advise relying on this as an alternative to physical punishment. Inflicting pain and humiliation is not needed where the dread of failure and the sense of shame are invoked.[76] These fears are innate in human nature; it is the teacher's job to bring them to the pupil's consciousness and establish them as impulses to action. The teacher who does this well is a good teacher.[77] A visible manifestation of the sense of shame is the tendency to blush. Boys who blush readily reveal their tractability, says Wimpheling, quoting Vergerio again.[78] *Pudor,* the "fear of deserved censure," is an effective internal control and obviates the use of the rod in all but desperate cases.[79]

By playing on the child's supposedly inborn inclinations, then, the knowing teacher could shape his pupil's mind and mold his personality, confident that indoctrination early in life would determine the direction of an individual's development. The pedagogical tradition supported him in this conviction. Plato's system of compulsory training, prescribed and supervised by a board of philosophers according to fixed norms and rules, was too distant from recognizable reality to be of practical use, but it did make available a powerful argument for systematic indoctrination in the service of an ideal. Where the ideal mandated a renovation of the human personality, as in the attempt at a Christian reformation through the education of children,[80] Plato's *Republic* was a relevant text. But the entire pedagogical tradition could be summoned to support Plato's contention that the child, at a young and tender age, could "be molded to take the impression one wishes to stamp on it."[81]

The extreme position on this point is Plutarch's lapidary "moral virtue is habit long continued."[82] Christian writers ought not, perhaps, to have adopted so readily this interpretation of the moral character as a neutral substance to be shaped by habit. But Plutarch's observation was never explicitly challenged. In its weakened form, also given by Plutarch, "youth is impressionable and plastic, and while such minds are still tender, lessons are infused deeply into them,"[83] it was certainly unexceptionable. The plasticity of young natures had always been taken as a truism. "Mold while the wax is soft and it will permanently retain its shape," said Maffeo Vegio.[84] It was the same with mind and behavior. Let children learn "not to see and hear" objects catering to base instincts, wrote Aegidius Romanus, for what they absorb early in life they will remember always.[85] Jean Gerson argued indefatigably against exposing the young to impressions that would make them lifelong slaves to passion.[86] He advanced many concrete suggestions of how to shape children into good Christians.[87] Like all writers on the subject, he too used the plastic argument: the child is like wax, you can make of him what you wish. Examples from nature furnished the analogy of young shoots and saplings. Bend the twig and the tree will incline as you want.[88]

Comparisons with animal training are even more revealing of how pedagogical writers imagined the molding process to work. Erasmus has much to say on this, and he says it very entertainingly in his book on early education. You train a puppy from birth; why not a child?[89] He cites examples from the animal kingdom, from parrots to elephants.[90] His *Declamatio* is, in fact, of all pedagogical treatises the most emphatic on beginning the conditioning process in infancy, almost from the moment of birth. To fail to do this is to waste the most receptive years and to miss the only chance of making a lasting impression. Without the shaping hand of the educator, Erasmus says, the child will grow into a wild creature, not a man. Teaching is everything. The crude mass of life must be pressed into form. There is no use in deploring the effects of sin. It is we who are at fault if a child turns out badly, for we have allowed him to develop defects before directing him to the good. It is impossible to unlearn bad habits, but easy to be trained to good ones.[91] We cannot choose our parentage, Erasmus declares elsewhere, but minds (*ingenia*) can be formed and behavior shaped,[92] as long as this is done in infancy, the only time to establish the foundation of a good life.[93] No author disputed what had, at least since Quintilian, been called "the pliability of childhood."[94] Even Vives, who, always more circumspect than others, held that human nature is essentially impervious to manipulation, maintained that it may "be amended by means of learning."[95] A more representative voice was that of Christoph Vischer, a Lutheran popularizer and author of many educational treatises, who argued that: "No beast of the forest is so wild that it cannot be tamed and made docile, as long as this is begun while it is still young. It will not entirely lose its natural traits, but one can largely break it of its habits [abgewöhnen]. Should we not, then, be able to tame a human being with the aid of God's word and Christian discipline?"[96]

It would be otiose to compile passages from the literature to show that pedagogical authors spoke with one voice on the need for early conditioning and proved their contention by citing the child's puppy-like tractability, his innocence and trusting openness, and the facility with which he absorbs and retains what he has been taught in his earliest years.[97] How does one get him started? There was agreement on this point too: utilize the child's natural love of imitation to get his physiological and psychological impulses under way. The imitandi libido exists even in infants. You may see it, says Erasmus, in the signs of joy they give when they have succeeded in imitating something. They are like monkeys. It is this eagerness to imitate that makes children "docile," teachable.[98] The competent educator will use this capacity methodically, moving from imitation of simple acts and words to emulation of complex ones. As Quintilian said: "repeated imitation passes into habit" ("frequens imitatio transit in mores").[99] Quintilian is at pains to point out that no more than a learning technique is suggested here. The purpose of education is not imitation but to lead the student to inventiveness and independent judgment.[100] Nonetheless, "it is expedient to imitate whatever has been invented with success."[101] For the first years of life this is the cardinal rule. Directed imitation passes by frequent repetition into habit, and—to quote Plutarch again—"moral virtue is habit long continued."[102]

"If one were to call the virtues of character the virtues of habit," Plutarch continues, "he would not seem to go far astray."[103] This proposition—ascribed to Plutarch, who said it epigrammatically, but resting on the authority of Aristotle who developed it at length in his Nicomachean Ethics—fortified educators in their labors. "Moral virtue," Aristotle explained, "comes about as a result of habit, whence also its name [ēthikē] is one that is formed by a slight variation from the word ethos [habit or custom]."[104] Moral virtues, far from being innate in us, are acquired by practice:

> We get the virtues by first exercising them, as happens in the case of the arts as well. For the things we have to learn before we can do them, we learn by doing them, e.g. men become builders by building and lyre players by playing the lyre; so too we become just by doing just acts,

temperate by doing temperate acts, brave by doing brave acts. . . . Thus, in one word, states of character arise out of like activities. . . . It makes no small difference, then, whether men form habits of one kind or of another in their very youth; it makes a very great difference, or rather it makes all the difference.[105]

It was this explication of virtue that aroused the ire of Martin Luther, who saw it as the very antithesis of his own deeply pondered conclusions about the relationship of human nature to human actions. He proposed in 1517 "that man, who has become an evil tree, can produce and will nothing but evil."[106] This is Aristotle stood on his head. Far from acting well or wickedly according to whether we are innately good or bad, as Luther would have it, we are, in Aristotle's analysis of moral action, made virtuous only as a result of the habitual performance of virtuous deeds. When we begin to take enjoyment in practicing a virtue, he added, we have in fact become virtuous, habit having turned into second nature: "For the man who abstains from bodily pleasures and delights in this very fact *is* temperate. . . . Hence we should be brought up in a particular way from our very youth, as Plato says,[107] so as both to delight in and be pained by the things that we ought, for this is the right education.[108]

Aristotle's position was adopted as the basis of Scholastic ethics; Thomas Aquinas's commentary on the *Nicomachean Ethics* does not modify Aristotle in any important respects. "Moral virtue is derived from customary action," Thomas wrote; we have a natural aptitude for acquiring the virtues, but they are the product of repeated use. "Like actions produce like habits," and habits long continued become virtues. It is therefore essential "that one become accustomed to perform . . . good . . . actions from earliest youth, for we retain longer the things impressed on us as children."[109] Thomas's pupil Aegidius Romanus, in his book on the education of princes, applied the Aristotelian position directly to religious teaching. Since the Christian faith cannot be proved by reason and is best accepted in the spirit of naive credulity, he writes, it is most efficaciously instilled in earliest youth. Children do not question what they learn. They believe it in all simplicity. They can be made Christians by implanting in them the simple substance of the faith and habituating them to the practice of it.[110] This argument, which was stated in similar terms by many other writers, could not have been lost on Reformation pedagogues despite its evident irreconcilability with Lutheran doctrines on sin and works. If virtues resulted from habits, the task of pedagogues was made both feasible and indispensable. Over habits they had some measure of control. If, in his actions and reactions, the finished person was indeed the sum of the habits instilled in him, they had grounds for hope of success in their endeavors. Plutarch's dictum and Aristotle's analysis did not need to be taken literally for educators to devote the most careful attention to that part of their activity that dealt with the formation of habits.

Man, according to Aristotle, shares with all animals the propensity for modifying his nature by means of acquired habit.[111] Understood as a way of acting and thinking with sufficient frequency and regularity to become unconscious, habit turns into a kind of second nature. "Consuetudo est quasi altera natura" was a commonplace among medieval and early modern educational writers.[112] If bad habits learned early in life are inextinguishable,[113] good habits may be as firmly implanted by means of practice and endless repetition. This argument evidently appealed to Christian writers confronting a rigorous Augustinian pessimism. Man's mind is capable of moving in several directions, said Vives, and can be turned by practice and counsel.[114] His nature, though inclining to evil, may "by learning be amended (*disciplina emendatur*)."[115] "Habit is a wonderful thing," he wrote in 1531 in his book on the art of teaching; "the opinions inculcated in us at an early age we retain for the rest of our lives."[116] Stoic philosophy could be taken to reinforce the point. Seneca, whose moral essays were widely read, taught that men acquire virtue by practice.[117] He was referring to adults, who knew what they were doing, but the principle applied a fortiori to children, who were unresisting subjects to conditioning.

Extravagant claims were sometimes made for the power of habit. Vives encouraged women to think that a mother's intimate control over young children empowered her "to form [their] dispositions. For she may make them what she will—good or bad."[118] Such an assertion was not mere rhetoric, for supporting evidence could be found in the literature on pediatrics from Galen[119] to the medical popularizers of the sixteenth century, who declared that good habits, inculcated early, were capable of changing a child's entire "complexion."[120] Few words turn up with greater frequency in the school ordinances and policy statements of the Reformation than "habituation" (*Gewöhnung, consuetudo, usus*). No other pedagogical idea is more confidently accepted as a good thing and more insistently applied as the only method. It was hoped that comprehension would come in due course, and with it the internalization of rules and doctrines first imposed by rote drill. But at the beginning came inculcation of sound habits. "For the young cannot grasp our teachings," it was said, "unless they are first habituated to them by means of verbatim repetition."[121] Where the hoped-for understanding failed to materialize, where the required repetition of habit-forming acts did not mature into internalized norms of conduct, it was comforting to know that the habits themselves would stick and education had not been entirely wasted.

4

Nature, impulses, responses, habits: the pedagogical literature had much to say on these. It had accumulated a large body of pedagogical declarations and reflections that—profound or not, empirically verifiable or not—generated confidence by showing that writers of unassailable authority had agreed on a wide range of important problems.

To what general educational purpose were pedagogical ideas related? What were the goals of education implicitly accepted and explicitly recommended in the literature? One might begin by grasping some underlying assumptions concerning educational activity itself. It was generally agreed that education must proceed from a guiding purpose. Defining this objective was not, of course, the function of educators themselves, but unless they embraced it they labored without aim. Second, education could not limit itself to one side of the human personality or one compartment of life; it must instruct the young in religion, in the arts, and in civility, and it must instruct them in these simultaneously. Finally, educational activity must be not only high-minded, but also technically competent. The pedagogical literature set high standards for the professional teacher. It also made some practical suggestions on pedagogical methods, although these were rudimentary and often naive.

Specific educational goals were diverse, but they were not often clearly defined in the pedagogical literature, at least not clearly enough to permit tidy classification. There seem to have been three principal objectives. The first described the purpose of education as an aspect of civic well-being, society being the general object of education, the citizen's place in society its particular goal. At its most grandiose this objective aimed at creating the ideal state, or radically reforming an existing one, by reeducating its citizens. More modestly considered, education undertook to inculcate in the individual a code of civic ethics likely to make him a useful member of his commonwealth.

Plato's state—the ideal state of the *Republic* and the model state of the *Laws*—furnished a compelling instance of the harmony of education and politics.[122] In the sixteenth-century context Plato's propositions had no practical application; but Lutheran theologians and pedagogues would have been well advised to heed Plato's demonstration of how a guiding ethos might be transmitted by methodical education to the new generations who were to uphold and practice it in the future. There is no doubt that many of the leading proponents of the Reformation harbored the hope that this was a feat to be accomplished in their time. One wonders if they noted the passage in book 7 of the *Republic* in which Plato explains how the philosopher-kings propose to transform their society into a new kind of commonwealth:

> They will begin by sending out into the country all the inhabitants of the city who are more than ten years old, and will take possession of their children, who will be unaffected by the habits of their parents. These they will then train in their own habits and laws. . . . And in this way the state and constitution of which we were speaking will soonest and most easily succeed.[123]

Such extreme measures were of course hardly to be contemplated. But at the very least reformers must have come to recognize the symbiosis of religious and civic virtues, and to advocate early indoctrination in both. It was a truism to say—and nearly every writer in the pedagogical tradition had said it—that the commonwealth could flourish only while its citizens accepted its principles as their own, or at least acted as if they did. The culture of the community determines the education of the individual. Education was therefore a public concern. Nearly every writer from Plato, Aristotle, and Quintilian to the Renaissance affirmed this.[124] Few Lutheran pedagogues evinced much interest in the republican virtues on which Italian Renaissance educators placed such emphasis.[125] But they knew that peace and prosperity in the community depended on the good behavior of its members, and they quoted the "Christian" humanists on the important place to be given in pedagogy to civic education.[126]

The second objective was predominantly religious. At the maximum it sought to create in the individual those dispositions that were the preconditions of salvation. The moral and religious restoration of Christendom was to be the aggregate result of this effort in individual reform. Augustine defined the problems and indicated the possibilities of this endeavor. The origin of sin lies in man's natural pride (*superbia*). Pride is expressed in thoughts and acts of egotism (*amor sui*). Only grace can deliver man from this condition, but hope of grace is open only to those who have faced up to their predicament and entered the state of humility in which they recognize themselves as sinners.[127] This image of man and his condition defines the role of education: destroy the old man, the "old Adam," and raise up the new man. Augustine considers the aims of Christian education most concretely in *De vera religione* (which argues that Christianity grasps fully what Platonism had seen but dimly). He passes before us the ages of man: infancy and the purely nutritive existence; childhood, when memories begin to be stored; adolescence and the onset of sexual power; manhood with its responsibilities; and last the calm after the storms of life, old age. "This," he concludes, "is the life of man so far as he lives in the body. . . . This is the 'old man,' the 'exterior or earthly man.' " Some among these "old men" are reborn: "With their spiritual strength and increase of wisdom they overcome the 'old man' and put him to death and bring him into subjection to the celestial laws. The result is 'the new man,' 'the inward and heavenly man.'"[128] All education, then, augments and reinforces the qualities necessary to the inward creation of "the new man." With Christ as his paradigm, the educator selects specific goals and procedures conducive to the restructuring of the sinner's personality, insofar as it is amenable to human manipulation. Augustine did not raise much hope on that score. But he did reject passivity and resignation, encouraging men instead to be energetic in their attempt to supplant the self-seeking impulses of the old man with the humility of the new man.

It goes without saying that Augustine's design is too schematic to be a prescription for teaching anyone or anything. His ideal types are as abstract as the concepts of Plato. They are about Man, not men. Still, the religious and moral force pulsating in Augustine's sentences exerted a strong hold upon sixteenth-century theologians and pedagogues, who succeeded in bringing Augustine down to earth by translating the abstract qualities that defined his "old" and "new" men into concrete vices and virtues, recognizable to every observer of the human scene, and largely congruous with the traits enumerated by secular-minded pedagogues as the attributes of good citizenship. The great majority of Christian writers on pedagogy described their hoped-for result, the end result of right education, as a young person exhibiting habits of obedience, humility, modesty, submissiveness, a bland passivity of behavior, and lifelong docility.[129] Vives thought that human faculties could stand much blunting. Not that he wanted boys made dull or stupid; but the end result of their education should be a simpler, more honest, less cunning, above all less self-seeking personality than that of the "natural" creatures they had been before their training began.[130] This end product of Christian education was a long way from the exuberance and precocious self-confidence of Quintilian's ideal youngster, who "runs riot in the luxuriance of his growth."[131] Christian ethics are not the only explanation of the distance between the two types. It was also that writers in the early modern period saw the violence and tensions of their age as consequences of the permissiveness with which parents and society as a whole had been allowing the young to mature. In the days of antiquity, Erasmus notes perspicaciously, pedagogues had been able to count on the homogeneity of their culture to do much of their educating for them. Alas, such conditions exist no longer.[132] The young must be taken in hand. They must be taught. There is no other way to individual improvement, nor to the reformation of society.

A third school of educational writers concerned itself less with social objectives than with the individual's drive to self-fulfillment. It will be obvious that this group had least to say to sixteenth-century reformers, who lacked sympathy with the implicit postulates of Renaissance humanism. On the other hand, its liberal and often very eloquent pleas on behalf of the mentally and emotionally, as well as physically, maturing young person could be taken as a corrective to the suppressive tendencies embedded in Lutheran educational ideas. To enlarge the mind,[133] to direct the growing person toward *virtus et gloria* as the only worthwhile pursuits,[134] to create in him resources for becoming the *vir probus atque perfectus* or the *uomo virtuoso*,[135] to build a foundation for self-respect by encouraging methodical self-examination[136]—these were noble objectives. They were beyond the reach of all but the select few to whom pedagogical writers in the classical tradition had always addressed themselves.[137] They related to a social and political setting increasingly alien to the conditions for which Reformation theologians were legislating. Above all, they offered no concrete suggestions for solving the most vexing of the problems facing reformers in the 1530s. But as reminders of a humane tradition they never lost their force, and in Erasmus's eloquent and reasonable fusion of these ideals with the cause of religious reform, Lutheran pedagogues could find justification for tempering their theoretical and empirical pessimism with the benign gentility of classical humanism.[138] Erasmus's ideal of a *sapiens et eloquens pietas* was an attainable goal for that part of Reformation pedagogy that concentrated on training a professional elite. But Lutheran pedagogues wished to cast a wider net. And to their purposes of mass indoctrination in basic religion and citizenship, the humanist model could make no practical contribution.

5

The pedagogical literature not only spoke of fundamental questions relating to guiding purposes and methods, it also offered suggestions on a host of corollary issues on which the counsel of tradition was sought by sixteenth-century reformers ill prepared by experience to take action. Is education best accomplished in public institutions or in the home? This question answered itself in the 1520s and 1530s, as has been seen, but it was comforting to know that the pedagogical tradition spoke overwhelmingly with the reformers in urging the creation of public schools. "Since the state as a whole has a single end, it is plain that the education of all must be public and not private, as it is in the present system, under which everyone looks after his own children privately." Mutatis mutandis, Aristotle's words[139] could have come from the lips of a Lutheran reformer after 1525. Quintilian, who weighed the pros and cons carefully, also pleaded emphatically for public over private education;[140] his clinching argument, that parents' vices are inevitably transmitted to their offspring unless the children experience countervailing influences away from home,[141] was often reiterated in the following centuries. Maffeo Vegio thought that common instruction in schools would not only counteract the corrupting experiences of the home but also accelerate the learning process.[142] Wimpheling deplored the home as a place of instruction,[143] and Erasmus, despite the sardonic attitude toward schools and schoolteachers he had gained in his own life, thought that only in the most unusual cases—he cites that of Thomas More[144]—should the training of a young person be left to his parents, although he exempts from this rule the child's earliest years, before formal schooling begins.[145] Vives, like Quintilian, discusses opinions on both side of the question. He found little good to say about the schools of his day; nonetheless he thought public education best.[146]

In pressing these views, no author intended to reduce the family's role in the young person's education. Like the sixteenth-century reformers, the writers of the pedagogical tradition affirmed the indispensability of household support, in every sense of that word. The more literate the home, said Quintilian, the easier the work of educators.[147] Augustine's mother, Monica, as her son portrayed her in his autobiography, became everyone's model for the intelligent, caring, devoted parent.[148] Collaboration between parents and teachers was thought to be essential to final success.[149] But on the question of control over the policies of education, tradition was nearly unanimous in insisting that authority must be lodged in public, not private hands. Erasmus's uncompromising phrase "opportet scholam aut nullam esse aut publicam"[150] epitomizes the discussion reaching back to Quintilian, and brings it up to date with an excoriation of the stupefying, often harmful teaching of monks and incompetent privateers. Erasmus's idea—and he shared it with most authors—was that school be open to all and regulated by public authority. Where every head of a household determines by his own lights the training of his children, one finds, as Aristotle said, a primitive society "like that of Cyclops in the ancient days."[151] Only publicly regulated uniform education could assure conformity with overarching purposes. "The education of children," wrote Vergerio, "is a matter of more than private interest. It concerns society, which indeed regards the right training of the young as, in certain aspects, within its proper sphere. I would wish to see this responsibility extended."[152] Opinions could be quoted on the other side as well.[153] But to Lutheran reformers they held little merit in the face of the religious and social crisis of the 1520s and in the light of a tradition that clearly favored public and centrally controlled education.

Should learning and teaching be rigidly structured or left informal? Arguments existed on each side of this old debate, but writers whose concerns coincided most closely with those of the reformers recommended formal curricula and instruction.[154] The literature was also informative on the question of the education of women—whether or not, how much, to what end. It supplied quotable views to press either alternative, but, again, the most persuasive authors favored rudimentary intellectual training and religious instruction for girls, at least in their early years.[155] The literature also abounded in detailed suggestions on practical teaching and instructional devices. The adoption of these in the sixteenth century meant that curricula and methods remained entirely conventional. Only the introduction of the catechism as an instrument of mass education offered opportunities for new departures. But these were rarely grasped; even the innovative possibilities of printing remained largely unrealized. Experimental teaching, in the sense of trying methods not advocated in the classical and medieval literature, was unknown. The tradition was persuasive, finally, in pressing for high standards of professional skill in teachers; indeed, teacher-training—to the extent that this could be carried out in the sixteenth century—owes much to the idea, ubiquitous in the literature, that formal education should be so systematic that, as Quintilian wrote, if anyone fails to learn, "the fault will lie not with the method but with the individual."[156]

In general it may be said that the pedagogical literature gave powerful support to ideas and assumptions already firmly lodged in the reformers' thoughts. Few pedagogues could have approached the problems of education with an open mind. They came to them with their guiding concepts firmly settled. The literature supplied them with a battery of arguments for presenting their case. It also gave them the confidence of knowing that behind their own efforts stood an ancient and intellectually unimpugnable tradition. Above all, it sustained them in their sense of being engaged in a profoundly important enterprise on whose success or failure rested the future of their reformation.

CHAPTER 4

LEARNING

Confidence in the soundness of their cause came to the reformers from other sources as well as from the classical tradition. They needed to be convinced that what they were doing was both right and practicable. What was the likelihood of succeeding with their task? Reassurance was needed above all in their approaches to the young as learners. Hoping to instill in them the precepts of the new evangelical religion, they had to assume the teachability of Christian doctrines, not merely to a favored few, but to all who could be reached by instruction. As will be seen in a later chapter, the catechism became their principal pedagogical tool. In form and method, catechization was a technique uniquely suited to what was presumed to be the mental condition of the multitude. But how did Reformation pedagogues imagine the learning process itself? How was information conveyed to the mind, stored in the memory, turned into action? What distinguished able intellects from plain? What mental operations linked knowing to doing? How should one present information to the learner to enable him to absorb it easily, retain it firmly, and act on it resolutely?

The answers to these questions constitute an important chapter in the story of Reformation pedagogy. All hopes of success rested on the reformers' adoption of a model of the mind capable of persuading them that learning was a natural activity and, as long as appropriate instructional techniques were used, not much of a burden to a normally endowed human being. Seen as a simple mechanical process that could without great difficulty be set and kept in motion, learning was not a serious obstacle to pedagogues facing large numbers of pupils of diverse natures and talents. This lesson, drawn from the small stock of psychological treatises available to them, did much to shore up their confidence and direct their efforts. It will be useful, therefore, to give some attention to the prevailing assumptions about the mind and the psychology of learning.[1]

Sixteenth-century intellectuals were as inquisitive about the workings of the mind as their colleagues in earlier epochs. Philip Melanchthon's book on the soul, *De anima*, that is to say, on the life-giving faculties of the organism, was printed in more than a dozen editions during the sixteenth century.[2] Although intended as a text for university students,[3] it became required reading for all Lutheran theologians, especially after 1542, when, in a notorious academic controversy, it was the object of an assault by a fellow professor at Wittenberg, Veit Amerbach. For both scholars the bone of contention was Aristotle himself, specifically the true meaning of his explanation of the soul, its properties, and its functions. In fact, Aristotle remained throughout the century the starting point for every discussion of psychology. Even those who looked for a way beyond the received wisdom —Juan Luis Vives, for example, whose *De anima et vita* was published in 1538—were locked to Aristotle's terminology and problematics. Melanchthon's orthodox Aristotelian treatment was probably the most influential psychology book of the century. Stephen Batman's encyclopedia of 1582 reproduced without modification or additions its thirteenth-century Aristotelian source on the soul.[4] Disagreement with the master called for justification. Juan Huarte's *Examination of Men's Wits,* published in 1575 and an instant best-seller with a score of editions in the original Spanish and translations into seven other European languages, presented itself as a polemic against Aristotle and his restrictive intellectualism, which, Huarte charges, had too long withheld useful information about the mind from ordinary people who might have gained great practical benefits from understanding it. From Melanchthon in 1540 to Giacomo Zabarella[5] and Robert Burton's *Anatomy of Melancholy*[6] in the early seventeenth century, Aristotle dominated all discussions and controversies on the vital principle.

Aristotle's preeminent place rests on his apparently precise and objective description of the operations of the soul. His coherent and comprehensive account, which furnished a satisfying explanation of the whole principle of life, continued to hold as long as his scheme of inquiry remained in force. In Melanchthon's day, as in Aristotle's, the questions about the soul were: What is it? What are its parts and how do they relate to each other? How does it interact with the body and its environs? Above all: What does it do and how does it work? Since the essential nature of the soul escaped detection, the scholar's main task was to enumerate and describe its functions. Aristotle's definition (advanced after a review of all theories before his own)[7]— soul is the form, or idea, of animate matter—was not very helpful to nonphilosophical readers in later centuries. But even where a scholar found it irrelevant it was not explicitly rejected,[8] and as the starting point of a systematic investigation it served its purpose in an age that valued dictionary definitions as the opening move in an orderly train of thought.[9] In any case, Aristotle gains firmer footing with the assertion that the soul is what it does[10] and should therefore be defined by its four faculties of nutrition, sensation, thought, and movement—the powers necessary to life—whose functions he proceeds to examine with his customary care. Aristotle's terms—"faculties," "powers," "functions," "parts"—were interchanged rather confusingly in his own and subsequent discussions, but this did not seem to have detracted from their utility.[11] His description of the soul as the ground of the four vital powers made good sense (never, of course, being subjected to empirical verification) and remained an indispensable source. It was of special relevance to scholars occupying themselves with problems touching on intellectual capacities, for Aristotle's account of sense perception, discrimination and judgment, imagination, memory, reflection, and reason seemed outstanding in its physiological concreteness and apparent agreement with observed reality. Unlike Plato, whose discursive and ambiguous views of the soul offered little to readers looking for practical guidance, Aristotle's *De anima*—transmitted to modern times in the Latin terminology and with the utilitarian bent of Cicero[12] —served as a point of departure for all writers wishing to modify, extend, or surpass ancient authority on the soul.[13]

In the middle of the sixteenth century the best key to Aristotelian psychology was Philip Melanchthon's *On the Soul*, written in 1540,[14] a handy summary of received ideas and, coming from the leading academic theologian of Wittenberg, a work accepted nearly everywhere in Lutheran circles as an authoritative statement of classical psychology for the modern reader. Melanchthon's book is our best clue to what his contemporaries knew about the mind and its operation.

Questions of definition need not detain us. Melanchthon adopts Aristotle's own—"of the accuracy of which," he says, "there is no doubt"[15]—advancing objections to it and defeating them in a Scholastic game designed to make a clean sweep of all competing definitions, while placing them before the reader. More to the point is his ensuing account of the body's physiology according to Aristotle's proved method of giving as exact a description of each organ as contemporary medical knowledge permitted. In this respect, Melanchthon improved on his source, having provided himself with up-to-date information about the anatomy, function, and pathology of the parts of the human body.[16] This enumeration, in turn, serves as the organic basis for the discussion of nutrition and sensation that follows. Aristotle had represented the soul (an organ with no definite location in the body, being diffused throughout its parts)[17] as possessing two species of powers: nonrational ones, promoting nutrition, growth, generation, and appetites and desires; and rational powers, practical wisdom and, ultimately, knowledge of truth.[18] Melanchthon uses the same scheme and a related system of classification as he demonstrates how the body is nourished, how it grows, how it regenerates itself, and so on, before proceeding to a topic more germane to his major concerns: sensation, or the ability to perceive, feel, and learn. Although withdrawing somewhat from Aristotle's philosophical empiricism, Melanchthon follows him in assuming that all knowledge of the world comes to us through the five senses, each of which he describes according to the traditional method of asking, What is it? What is its organ? Its object? Its medium? He explains: perception occurs when an external object (color in vision) transmits its perceptible properties through the appropriate medium (light) to the organ (the eye). Stimulus of object on organ occurs as motion, an outer motion that takes place in the medium between object and organ, and an inner motion transmitted through a similar medium within the organ, to consciousness. Melanchthon depicts these processes in concrete terms. External sense organs reflect a mirrorlike image (*imago*) of the object. This act of reflection occasions vibrations in the interior sense, the *spiritus vibrati*. These vibrations in turn create a copy (*similitudo*) of the object and conduct it to the brain where, by means of other vibrations peculiar to that organ, the copy is kept alive in a sequence of constantly renewed impressions (*simulacra*) that constitute the material of memory. The common sense (*sensus communis*, a Latin expression for the term Aristotle coined to denote the mind's ability to synthesize and discriminate among the data presented simultaneously by the five senses) distinguishes, combines, and classifies the impressions conveyed in this way. It is situated, Melanchthon says, in the forward part of the brain. Judgment—the product of the common sense—resides in the middle brain, memory in the rear.[19] Although Aristotle had given little emphasis to the brain as a center of vital activity in the living being, sixteenth-century authors knew enough anatomy to assign to that organ a major share in organizing the body's cognitive functions. Other vital motions originated in the heart and the liver. But the brain was the thinking organ par excellence.

As understood by Melanchthon and his contemporaries, then, the chain of knowledge moves from simple sense impressions to the discriminating activities of the common sense to memory, thence to judgment, ultimately to cognition.[20] The first two links in this sequence are natural, inborn, involuntary; every normal human being possesses them. It is otherwise with memory, judgment, and their end product, knowledge. These faculties are determined only in part by natural endowment. To a large extent they are the product of training and thus are susceptible to manipulation. Equally subject to conditioning is the faculty of conscience (*conscientia*), to which Melanchthon, unlike Aristotle, gave an important place in his system,[21] following on this point both the Stoic postulate of an inner source of sound conviction and the Scholastic idea of an intuitive grasp of moral imperatives conceded to men even after their lapse from grace. Melanchthon explains conscience as a function of the soul's appetitive power—the tendency to strive for a desired object and the attempt to obtain it—particularly of the so-called voluntary appetite which, as it causes us to reflect on the moral choices we must make, generates conflicting emotions. Appetite goads us to crave objects or to escape from them. The feelings it engenders affect us with sensations of pleasure or pain—pleasure at having obeyed the moral laws in pursuing our desires, pain at falling victim to our base instincts. The "soreness of the heart" we suffer upon every transgression of the ethical code is one effect of conscience—an important one, because in this manner it brings our sins uncomfortably to the consciousness. But conscience is more than a voice. It also acts as judge, approving or condemning every moral action and discriminating between good and bad. Combining the faculties of knowing (good and bad), judging (a good from a bad act), and feeling (joy at having done well, pain at having done ill), conscience represents a fusion of faculties singularly susceptible to the influence of methodical conditioning.

The prominent place given to conscience in Melanchthon's scheme owed much to Luther's identification of *conscientia*, or *Gewissen*, as the place in the soul where faith and arrogance contend for dominance within the individual.[22] For Luther this was a struggle between submission to God's law and the complacent trust in one's own powers. But from the pedagogue's point of view, the faculty of conscience served another, more operational purpose: of internalizing imposed rules and autonomizing directed motives. As the inner voice of normative authority, its message was loud and clear. Men are weak, blind, forever falling into sin (these phrases are from the sermon of a Wittenberg theologian, preaching in the mid-sixteenth century) but their hearts know the full gravity of their crimes, throwing them into constant anxiety and dread of God's anger.

> This is why small children say to each other 'If you're bad and do wrong, you'll go to hell, for God will surely punish you.' Children do not need to be taught this. They know it naturally. As soon as we commit a sin we feel it at once in our heart, which accuses us by thumping and pounding inside our breast like an executioner setting out the tools of his trade. For conscience is the living voice of the hangman saying 'You have just done a wicked thing. There is a judge whose wrath will come down upon you for your sin, and who will punish you, don't you doubt it.'[23]

If despite such internal warnings obstinacy persisted, preachers stood ready to elaborate on the direct link between transgression and punishment until the lesson was learned and conscience replaced the outer disciplinarian.

Conscience, as the faculty enabling the individual to develop "that dependence on himself which makes him, in turn, dependable,"[24] needs the intellect to inform and guide it. But what is intellect? Melanchthon answers: the power to apprehend, judge, and reason about particular things and universals.[25] All animals respond to single sense impressions, but only man abstracts universal ideas from these, grasps them, and uses them to organize his experience. Intellect is one of the two faculties of the *potentia rationalis*, the reasoning capacity, mind. The other faculty is will, which is the tendency to strive for an object identified as desirable by the intellect, or to evade one viewed as abhorrent. Intellect is superior to the senses because it reflects on the vast number of pieces of information communicated to it by our sense organs and transmutes them into universal statements. It excels also because it possesses innate ideas. Melanchthon insists on the real presence of innate ideas in the mind. No one denied them categorically in his time, but by his emphatic affirmation he chose sides on an ancient subject of contention. Prominent among innate ideas, along with numbers, logical concepts, and so on, is the concept of a moral law, a law— Melanchthon says, quoting Paul—written in the heart of every man. Innate ideas are our *criteria*, our *norma certitudinis*, standards of certain knowledge of whose validity and truth there can be no doubt.[26] Without them we would be able neither to judge nor to decide.

Nearly all pedagogical writers rejected the radical sensationalist position according to which the mind is a blank slate until sense experience records impressions on it. Nonetheless this view surfaced at times (difficult as it was to reconcile it with a Christian theory of knowledge reaching back by way of Augustine to the transcendentalism of Plato) when an author wished to present the molding of young minds and the shaping of pliant personalities as an easy task whose success was virtually assured by skillful utilization of the mechanics of sensation. For such an argument the *tabula rasa* concept—always credited to Aristotle but usually taken out of the context in which it occurs in his *De anima*[27]—was prodigiously useful. Melanchthon himself does not advance it, but others did. Bartolomäus Metlinger, for example, a physician specializing in the care and nurture of children, had claimed that "Aristotle says 'the soul of a child is an unwritten tablet upon which nothing is written. One may, however, write on it what one wishes!'"[28] Similarly, the Nuremberg preacher Wenceslaus Linck, speaking of the roles of teaching and habit-forming in the education of Christians, asserts that "man's mind is at birth a blank slate [*ein blosse Tafel*] with nothing written upon it and without any form," on which, he continues, we write his life's program by means of discipline, instruction and habituation.[29] At least as a handy metaphor[30] the *tabula rasa* idea was of great help in demystifying mental processes, making learning appear to be an uncomplicated, not to say automatic, activity of the mind. None of the authors quoted as asserting the blank slate actually accepted it as an analogue of the learning mind; not Aristotle ("nothing is in the intellect that was not beforehand in the senses");[31] not Thomas Aquinas ("since all the knowledge of our intellect is derived from sense experience, what is made known to us by our senses is known prior to what is known by the intellect");[32] not Vives ("the senses are our first teachers, in whose home the mind is enclosed").[33] Statements such as these relate to information conducted to the mind from outside, not to the means available for judging and interpreting this information. But in reducing otherwise abstruse mental operations to a simple and graphic emblem, the image of a *tabula rasa* was an ingenious device and an immensely reassuring one to Reformation pedagogues as they contemplated the task of indoctrination that lay before them.[34]

2

Ideas may be guided, then, by regulating the data conducted to the intellect by the sense organs. Similarly controllable is the power of acting on ideas—a capacity residing, as already shown, in the will.[35] Thought, arousing an inclination for or against something, stimulates the appetite and causes the will to become active. "The soul moves the living being," Aristotle had written, somewhat vaguely, "not by mechanical force, as Democritus taught, but by the thinking processes issuing in the response of the organism."[36] This response expresses itself as an action of the will. Melanchthon here adopts the so-called intellectualist position, which held that the will depends on the intellect to define the ends of its action rather than being itself the aggressive initiating force (as claimed by the voluntarist school) in choosing the most desirable from among the ideas presented to the soul. In principle, the will's object is to attain the good and escape from the bad. Robert Burton describes this aim in a vivid phrase: "[the will's] object being good or evill, the one hee embraceth, the other hee rejecteth, according to that Aphorisme, *Omnia appetunt bonum*, All things seek their owne good, or at least seeming good."[37] The will can "will and not will,"[38] or it can delay action. It is therefore free. But because of man's original lapse into sinfulness these primary powers have been deformed by the debasement of human instincts. The will can still aim for the good: Melanchthon is emphatic on this point, rejecting all theological claims of total depravity. To argue for this, he says, is tantamount to asserting that ethical norms no longer apply to human life. It is also to deny any distinction between choosing freely and acting on compulsion.[39] But the will has been seriously flawed, and it requires constant support from Scripture, by action of the Holy Ghost.

Men, too, play a determining role in guiding one another's wills. The psychological ground on which such human intervention takes place is habit. Habit, says Melanchthon,[40] governs actions. It does so in two ways. The first is by working in the memory as instant recollection of perceptions deeply and frequently impressed upon the mind at an earlier time. Aristotle had made much of the importance of habit in training the character, which, he wrote, "is as its name indicates something that grows by habit [ēthos from ethos, cf. chap. 3 above], and that which is under guidance other than innate is trained to a habit by frequent motion of a particular kind."[41] Some of these motions occur in the mind, notably in the memory, which instantaneously and accurately (if it is a good memory) reproduces impressions previously conducted to the sense organs. The more vivid the impressions when first made, the more frequently they are repeated; and the more orderly their arrangement, the greater the likelihood that full recall will occur the moment the series of recollections is triggered by an impulse from within or a signal from without. "What we often rehearse in our mind, we easily recollect," Aristotle had written, "custom becoming as it were second nature."[42] This mental aptitude—the intellect's susceptibility to a predictable routine of thought based on automatic recollection—was an attractive starting point for systematic pedagogy.

But habit operates not only in the intellect. It works with equal effectiveness on the will (now following Melanchthon again, near the close of his treatise). Frequently repeated similar actions condition the will to strive more constantly and resist more steadfastly. "These acquired habits," Melanchthon writes in summary,[43] "we call virtues and vices." His allusion here is not merely to individual habits, but to habitus, which he takes to be a moral disposition, or inclination, or character (again, the terms are interchangeable) resulting from the possession of desirable habits—in other words it is the condition of being well habituated. For corroboration of this important concept we may turn to Vives, who explains the origin and function of habitus in greater detail.[44] Vives, too, affirms the indispensability of incessant repetition in habit formation. Habitus, the desired state, is not an assured product of consuetudo, habituation, unless the latter continues to operate without interruption. Habitus tends to weaken with lack of practice. Relax the pace, particularly after the middle years of life (for aging also depletes habitus of its acquired characteristics), and all will be lost. Since a person's character and disposition are the result partly of his nature and partly of his acquired habits,[45] the inculcation of habits, not only early in life but throughout life offers the only hope of exerting a lasting influence on thought and behavior. The suggestion was strong in the entire psychological literature that this process was an automatic one. "Like actions produce like habits," Thomas Aquinas had written in his commentary on Aristotle's *De anima*.[46] "Moral virtue comes from customary activity."[47] "When we act repeatedly according to reason, a modification is impressed in the appetite by the power of reason. This impression is nothing else but moral virtue."[48] It could be concluded, then, that if one habituated people in their earliest youth—"for we retain longer the things impressed on us as children"[49]—there was every reason to expect that moral virtues acquired in this fashion would, with continued practice, be retained throughout life. Needless to say, the reverse is also true. Harmless infantile sins turn in later life into destructive habits, as frequent sinning focuses the mind on corrupt inclinations until the "custom of sinning takes away the sense of it."[50] In either case habit determined behavior by means of the will as much as it formed impulses through the intellect. Melanchthon accepted this Aristotelian-Scholastic proposition. It was an integral part of his intellectual training; but it also brought incidental benefits in postulating an image of the mind singularly encouraging to all who wished to shape the thoughts and direct the actions of their fellowmen.

A less conventional explanation than Melanchthon's is given in Vives's monograph on the soul, a treatise that reinforces the central argument of this chapter: that pedagogical reformers imagined learning to be a simple, essentially mechanical activity. Since all descriptions of the soul were of the nature of a priori speculations, there was no logical reason for choosing one over any other, except on the ground of functionality. By this criterion Melanchthon, being simpler and more schematic, must have scored higher than Vives. Vives, however, furnishes a more interesting analysis, and it is useful to compare the two books and note agreements and differences.

A minor distinction is Vives's substitution of three powers, or faculties, of the mind—intelligence, will, and memory[51]—for Melanchthon's two (intellect and will), and his division of the process of cognition into four functions: the imaginative, receiving and absorbing impressions made on the senses by objects; memory, retaining received impressions for later recall; fantasy (*phantasia*), combining and discriminating impressions (like Aristotle's *sensus communis*); and finally the so-called *facultas aestimatrix*, which appreciates and assesses impressions and forms judgments concerning advantages and disadvantages.[52] A variety of activities, or motions, within these faculties—

their precise nature and relationship are not made clear—starts the process of learning. *Consideratio* sifts what has been received by the senses and stored in the memory. Having found what it is looking for, it turns into *recordatio*, recollection. *Collatio* then compares and contrasts impressions, accomplishing this important task by means of *discursus*, a scanning operation in which the mind sweeps back and forth across the spectrum of impressions, searching for the required data. This in turn engages judgment, *iudicium*, from which emerges *voluntas*, the will, one of the soul's three constituent powers, whose function it is to move the organism to action, seeking the good and avoiding the bad. When sense impressions cease, as the sense object is removed, fantasy takes over. Its special task is to recapitulate the lost image from memory or, if no image has been recorded there, to construct one from related material filed under cognate headings in the memory. In this way, says Vives,[53] we form mental images of places we have never seen, as also our ideas of God, angels, and so on.

Vives appears somewhat uneasy about *phantasia*. It is a fragile faculty, he says, easily thrown off balance and misdirected in its efforts. Many human errors originate in a disturbed fantasy;[54] more often, however, they arise from the intrusion of passions on the thinking process.[55] More than any other writer on psychology, Vives does justice to the role of emotions in men's lives.[56] He studies their arousal and dissipation, their mutual relationships, and above all their place in learning and cognition. This concern with the affective part of the soul lends his work a lifelike quality unusual in the literature, a verisimilitude helped also by his considerable emphasis on the importance of individual distinctions in memory capacity[57] and *ingenium*, mental aptitude or talent.[58] Unlike Melanchthon, who said little of interest on memory, Vives devotes a long and suggestive chapter to it.[59] Memory is a *picta tabula*, an inscribed tablet from which the inner eye reads the signs impressed there. A simple process of recollection (*recordatio*) recalls them for use; a more complex one, "reminiscence," searches the memory systematically, proceeding by means of association of ideas from the known to the unknown[60] until the required piece of information, though apparently forgotten, has been recovered. Whereas recollection is a capacity shared by all animals, reminiscence is a distinctively human trait. Men have it unequally according to, first, their humoral balance[61] (Vives, a follower of Galen in this respect, stresses the physical basis of all mental processes); second, their intellectual abilities (*ingenium*, intellectual aptitude arising from *natura*, natural endowment); and, third, the amount of training they have received.[62] The young have the liveliest memories,[63] being of a serene, unperturbed state of mind most conducive to learning. The quality of a young person's memory is the best sign of his intellectual ability, although *ingenium*, like memory, varies among individuals according to the combination of their bodies' basic qualities and humors.[64]

Individuals are therefore variously endowed with mental gifts and aptitudes, and Vives enjoins teachers to make careful discriminations among the young so that no sluggish mind is overtaxed, which would lead only to frustration and rebellion, and no able intellect remains unchallenged, a sad waste of human resources. His advice was well heeded. School ordinances enjoined schoolmasters "to inform themselves with the utmost care of each pupil's particular complexion and nature."[65] But native endowment does not render an individual impervious to the force of habit. Of all human faculties, only those controlling sense perception work unaided in the soul. All others require practice, *exercitatio*, lifelong training leading to *assuefactio, consuetudo*, habits "which," Vives said, "consist not only of a facility for doing things, but also of the inclination [*pronitas*] always to do them."[66] Habit thus tends to level the natural differences among *ingenia*, bringing some conformity to the otherwise profligate diversity of human constitutions and endowments.

It seems clear, then, that sixteenth-century views on education were rooted in classical theories about the soul. The reception of this ancient psychological model was a critical factor in the development of Reformation pedagogy, identifying its objectives and determining its techniques. A summary of the reformers' educational ideas will demonstrate the crucial importance of this adoption to the conduct, as well as the outcome, of their pedagogical enterprise. What enables the mind to know? The question may be narrowed at once. Pedagogues had mundane concerns. They worked toward inculcating practical disciplines, the possession of which defined the useful member of the religious and civic community. Metaphysical knowledge did not enter their province, for they accepted Augustine's distinction between two levels of knowing: grasping essential truth, which is a matter of illumination and available only to a few, and ordinary knowing—acquiring necessary and useful information—which could be done by all. This distinction does not affect the work of practical teaching, in which the subjects are communicated by means of language and other "signs."[67] Sixteenth-century pedagogues were for obvious reasons unable to adopt the ideal tutoring situation proposed by Augustine in his book on the teacher, a relationship—in their own context a Utopian idyll—where mentors guided and suggested while pupils "consider within themselves whether what has been said is true . . . by gazing attentively at that interior truth, so far as they are able."[68] Its impracticality aside, this procedure would have seemed in the 1520s and 1530s a highly hazardous undertaking. In any case, pedagogues faced very different problems in the age of the Reformation. They must, however, have shared Erasmus's conviction that "there is no branch of learning for which the human mind is not receptive." Erasmus added a proviso: "as long as we do not fail to supply instruction and practice."[69] This, indeed, was the province of pedagogues. Knowing and willing depended on the inculcation of disciplined habits by means of instruction and practice. *Ingenium* came from nature, but instruction and practice "depend entirely on our industry."[70] Here solid work could be done.

Nearly all authors agreed that three elements were necessary to effective learning: natural endowment, instruction (*disciplina*), and practice (*exercitium* or *exercitatio*). If learning was the development of potentiality into actuality, as suggested by the useful Scholastic model,[71] practice and discipline were the means by which this transition was effected, the teacher himself being the efficient cause of the knowledge engendered in the pupil. Thomas Aquinas had shown how the mind works on its own, by the method of "discovery" (*inventio*). Good instruction imitates this method: "Natural reason by itself reaches knowledge of unknown things, this way is called 'discovery.' In the other way [i.e., in education] someone else aids the learner's natural reason, and this is called 'learning by instruction' [*disciplina*]. . . . For the teacher leads the pupil to knowledge of things he does not know in the same way that one directs himself: through the process of discovering something he does not know."[72] Natural, unaided learning proceeds by moving from concepts at first only indistinctly grasped to concrete and particular knowledge. In the same way instruction moves from the general to the particular, aiming above all at orderly arrangement.

What was learned was stored up in the memory through an activity sometimes called "gathering" (*colligere*). This was a simple process accomplished by "reducing to a brief and compendious outline things that have been written and discussed at some length."[73] The faculty of memory had since antiquity been regarded at the best indicator of a mind's ability to learn easily and well. Quintilian had said so, and what he said was restated by nearly every educational writer who followed him.[74] "The salient signs of an able mind," wrote a sixteenth-century pedagogue, "are memory and imitation [*imitatio*]. A good memory has two powers: to perceive easily and retain faithfully; imitation is the mind's eagerness to learn from others and fix in the memory precise copies of what we have learned."[75] The capacity of the human mind that had so excited Quintilian—"so swift and nimble and versatile that it cannot be restricted to doing one thing only"[76]—depended in the first instance on memory. In Augustine's persuasive presentation, memory is pictured as the scene where thought takes place; understanding (*intelligentia*) works with the materials found there and subjects them to imagination and reasoning; the will acts as catalyst, setting the thought process in motion by giving it direction and purpose.[77] Memory, understanding, and will, although affected by inborn endowment (*natura*), are subject to conditioning. The many mnemotechnic devices employed by professional pedagogues attest to their conviction that a good memory, though to some extent a matter of native talent, was in large part the result of training.[78] Even authors with a less mechanical view of memory—Vives, for example,[79]—emphasized the indispensability of constant practice. No other faculty, says Vives, benefits so much from *exercitatio*. With the memory in top form and the subject matter well arranged, learning was not much of a problem. Occasions had only to be provided, and able instructors, and some form of compulsion to overcome inertia. Behavior was similarly manageable, for when the will had been trained by systematic habituation, action ceased to be erratic or capricious. Thus the entire chain of psychological responses from perceiving to learning to judging to knowing to acting was seen to be an orderly, controllable, and—to a considerable extent—predictable process.

Some authors went very far in their eagerness to portray learning as a reliable and simple procedure. Rudolf Agricola, for example, a well-known German humanist and pedagogical writer (whose *De formando studio*, written in 1484, was first printed in 1518 and often reprinted thereafter) posed the question revealingly. What distinguishes the scholar's mind, he asked, from his commonplace book, in which he enters under appropriate headings the hoarded riches of his lifetime's reading? There is little difference, he answered, except that the mind is more efficient and, if possessed of a good memory, quicker in its operations than even the best-organized reference volume. Able minds, he says, have swift recall. More important, the mind can use stored material for novel purposes not foreseen when information was first registered in the memory. Exactly like the commonplace book, however, the mind works with governing concepts ("virtue," "honor") to which facts are related as we learn them. We store information in the memory under these general headings; then, as occasion arises, we call it back. In its essential operations, therefore, the mind closely resembles a book of reference. Agricola recommends rigorous training exercises for conditioning it to this purpose.[80]

This kind of reductionism, which pictured the mind as an efficient engine with discrete parts and a tidy division of mechanical operations, made matters considerably easier for pedagogues. Simplification was further aided by the concrete imagery in which popular writers on psychological subjects tended to express themselves. The English physician Timothy Bright suggested clockwork as the best analogue of the mind and its operations. "Observe," he wrote, "how one right and straight motion, through the aptnesse of the first wheele, not only causeth circular motion in the same, but in diverse others also." Windmills and waterworks illustrate the same process. "Note how so many actions diverse in kinde rise from one simple first motion, by reason of variety of ioynts in one engine."[81] Other writers saw the motions of the soul sustained by the harmonic equilibrium of that organ's structural and humoral members. As long as this balance remains sound, argues Juan Huarte, quick learning is a natural activity of the well-tempered mind, the senses supplying required information, the intellect "instantaneously capable" of grasping ideas.[82] Like Bright's mechanical metaphors, Huarte's physiological determinism[83] stripped the workings of the mind of their inscrutability.[84]

Reformation pedagogues were ready to put this knowledge to the service of their project. Given their jaundiced views of human nature and the corruption of native impulses, habituation seemed an ideal tool. Intellectual habituation utilized the force of acquired habits over the recall of sense-impressed data in the memory. Voluntary habituation employed the conditioning power of frequently repeated actions on the will. Knowing and acting were subject to habit formation. Intellect and will both needed the steadying control of custom. A person's nature might tend to move him in a certain direction, but only habit could make this tendency continuous and predictable. Inculcation of habit was therefore the only available means of turning impulses and motives from—as Aristotle had put it—potentialities into fixed states.[85] Left undirected, the soul will always follow its perverted inclinations. But this need not be allowed. Raw nature may be habituated to approved conduct, most easily during the early years, for, as the German proverb says, "bent in youth, inclined for life."[86] An English medical writer makes the same point: "By nature (if we may call custom another nature, as Hippocrates does)[87] we love those things . . . that we are brought up with and accustomed thereunto."[88]

To sixteenth-century pedagogues, therefore, the constraining and directing power of habit over life was much more than a fond hope, a rhetorical commonplace, or a rule of thumb taken from experience. They accepted it as a scientific doctrine, one that explained the operation of the mind and the process of learning, offered them an instrument of indoctrination for remaking their fellowmen into decent Christians, and even promised to bring within their reach the truly formative kind of education of which Plato had written that it "leads you always to hate what you ought to hate and love what you ought to love from the beginning of life to the end."[89]

CHAPTER 5

PERCEPTIONS OF CHILDHOOD AND YOUTH

In a world made by adults, what happens to the young is governed by adult attitudes. This is true regardless of how much or how little is known about children, how right or wrong-headed their elders' perceptions of them, whether they are glimpsed stereotypically from above or observed closely and sympathetically from up close. Ideas about childhood are tied to adult anticipations of the future: whatever else children mean to their parents and their society, they are pawns with which the future is held in pledge. Fears, hopes, fantasies about the future determine the expectations set for the young. The clearer the shape of things to come, and the broader the agreement about it among dominant groups in society, the more categorical are the prevailing doctrines about children and their nurture, about young people and their incorporation in the social order.

In the sixteenth century, as before and for a long time thereafter, perceptions of childhood and youth were adult perceptions, reflecting the ideas of men (and never of women) preeminently occupied not with the young themselves, but with their own concerns and their own world. Their attitudes toward youth were shaped by a received wisdom that had little to do with the lives of actual children. They did not seem to remember what it was like to be young; nor did they wonder whether young people's personal and social needs were being met and, if not, with what consequences for their development. From our modern perspective, this apparent lack of interest is inexplicable. It is much deplored in the rapidly growing body of literature on the history of childhood. Men who lived in centuries altogether innocent of our post-Freudian fascination with the early and earliest stages of human development are made to bear a heavy burden of blame for their indifference to the problematic aspects of childhood and youth.[1] But this is a misconceived judgment. If certain questions were not chosen for discussion, this does not mean that they failed to trouble men's minds. Nor does the prevailing tendency in the sixteenth century to treat the child as a potential adult force us to conclude that men were innately insensitive to the appeals of childhood. Their reluctance to give rapt attention to each and every phase of growing up, and their disinterest in childhood and youth as subjects of psychological and sociological investigation, do not necessarily denote coldness toward the young, or a lack of concern and solicitude, or even ignorance of the profound implications of the obvious fact "that the human being starts life as an infant, that to be human begins with being a child, that each person is always, somehow, archetypically the child he once was"[2]—in other words, that the child is father to the man.

One could, perhaps argue that the pains and dangers facing all children in late medieval and early modern Europe made childhood such a traumatic experience that there was a strong incentive to blot out memories of it. This hypothesis would explain the disinclination to think seriously about the significance of childhood as a stage of development. There is indeed enough evidence to show that death, illness, and discomfort touched nearly everyone growing to maturity, and nothing to suggest (as some modern scholars do) that daily exposure to these ravages created an apathetic acceptance of suffering as a fact of life. The few childhood recollections that do exist from the sixteenth century do not make pleasant reading. The most evocative among them, at least for Germany—the autobiography of the Cologne burgher Hermann von Weinsberg—conveys little nostalgia for a golden age of childhood. Although raised in a well-to-do and mutually sustaining family living comfortably in a large house in a prosperous city, Hermann and his siblings escaped none of the horrors visited universally upon the young. At the age of two he had the measles, which made him so sick, he says, "that my father had to get up during the night and whistle my favorite tunes to stop my crying."[3] Before he was nine he had had several kinds of fevers, including the sweating disease of which several of his acquaintances died within twenty-four hours, also mysterious temporary paralyses, boils, sores and scabs on his scalp, "foul flesh in the mouth" that a barber cut out with a pair of shears, worms giving him vertigo, diarrhea and violent vomiting, constant toothache followed by extraction of most of his teeth by hand, hernia, and the plague. He comments: "O, how numerous are the ailments all of us must suffer, old people, young people, and children. Being subject to so many diseases, is it any wonder that scores of people die every day?"[4] Though he himself lived to describe these agonies, he observed death at closest hand. When he was five, in 1522, he and his two sisters fell sick with smallpox. He writes: "The three of us were laid out together, bedded down in the great hall at Weinsberg. And even though we had the best of care, counsel, and protection, it was God's will that first my sister Merg should die, and shortly thereafter my sister Drutgin. . . . And so I was alone again, left without sisters or brother."[5] It was a common experience.[6] Albrecht Dürer lost all but two of his seventeen brothers and sisters, "many of them," he said, "in their youth."[7] Mortality statistics expressed in percentages or plotted on graphs tend to conceal the psychic toll of such experiences on survivors. One wonders, for instance, as one reads the dry minutes of the meetings of the Strassburg school board for the year 1541, what the emotional impact of that plague year must have been on the surviving schoolboys there. "Magister Sebastian lost 36 children and has only 28 left now. Magister Hartman: about 40 of his children have died; he has 43 left but because of the dying has closed his school." And so on.[8] Everyone working in archives discovers such depressing tabulations. One can only guess, and by an act of the imagination try to recover, the lasting effect on the young psyche of the pervasive presence and apparent inescapability of pain, terror, and death.[9] It seems plausible, however, to suppose that few people carried into their maturity remembrances of a childhood appealing enough to persuade them to try to reconstruct it for themselves and to write about it for their own offspring.[10]

In any case, whatever the scenes of childhood lingering in the memories of adults, they were superseded by concern with the crisis of their time and perplexed speculations about the future. The model youngsters they recommended for emulation[11] had little in common with real children; their praiseworthy lives and deeds could not have rung true to the men who invented them. This was not, of course, their purpose. They were not taken from life. They were stereotypes, meant to point to the growing incompatibility between the desired ideal and perceived reality, a trend pedagogy was expected to reverse. There was good reason to dislike what was being observed in the world, and better reason still to mistrust the drift of things. The outward manifestations of this drift were believed to be discernible with special clarity in the young. Schemes for their socialization[12] were therefore the product of well-pondered thoughts about the present and the anticipated needs of the immediate and distant future. As expressions of an ideal intended to transcend human instincts, these schemes could not have borne much resemblance to real life. There was every reason, indeed, why they should neither resemble nor reflect the experiences of real youngsters.

2

These considerations should not be taken to suggest that sixteenth-century educators were unfeeling men. Enough has been said in an earlier chapter to indicate that pedagogues recognized the differences between their abstractions and the living young people crowding their classrooms. It should be added that there is much evidence to show that children were valued, loved, and cherished by their elders. In its most rudimentary form, this interest in the young from infancy to adolescence reveals itself in an increasingly intelligent concern for their health. Traditional children's medicine, as written in antiquity by Hippocrates, Galen, and Soranus of Ephesus, and by Rhazes and Avicenna in the Middle Ages,[13] was scarcely improved upon in the centuries following these venerable theoreticians, as medical textbooks continued to lag behind the clinical observations of practitioners.[14] But a surge of interest in pediatrics marked the sixteenth century when, as one of the students of early medicine has pointed out, scholarship and printing brought to this branch of medicine a kind of international collaboration. More important, and from our point of view more interesting, the growing respectability of vernacular languages freed practicing doctors from their profession's subservience to its classical and Arabic predecessors.[15] This, as will shortly be seen, was all to the good.

A sign of this escape from the weight of an ineffectual orthodoxy was the emergence, in sixteenth-century pediatric treatises, of the young person as a human individual with a claim to serious attention. His survival was obviously of the greatest importance to parents and physician alike. Children's diseases engaged the interest of medical men, but what is more to the point is that the latter now began to give some careful and perhaps not altogether useless thought to the effect of their ministrations on the infant's development into child, youth, and grown person. Why, they now asked, does the baby scream after parturition? Theologians say it is because he is at once made conscious of his heritage of sin. This is nonsense. As the infant is thrust suddenly from warmth to cold, from well-being to discomfort, "he is shocked and frightened, for babies are the most delicate of creatures."[16] To lessen the trauma of this abrupt plunge into the "cold and rude world"[17] and to increase the chance of survival, all authors advise the use of trained midwives. Only a small segment of society could afford them (this segment can be easily identified from the dedications preceding the many manuals on infant care and midwifery),[18] but Protestant reformers were trying to broaden access to them. Bugenhagen included a chapter on birth help in the ecclesiastical constitution he wrote for Braunschweig in 1528. It is a disgrace, he wrote, that the poor cannot afford the services of professional midwives. We must do what we can to reduce suffering and death at birth, and the first step to take is to make midwives available to all. If God decides to take the lives of mother and infant we cannot grumble. But there is no excuse for allowing our own negligence to cause death or deformation.[19] Most reform constitutions followed this line of reasoning; indeed many cities had long had statutes for the employment of public midwives to assist the poor.

Midwives did not, of course, guarantee the prevention of early death or debilitating disease. How much danger there is in childbirth, laments Felix Würtz, a barber-surgeon and (one surmises from the circulation of his books in several languages) a widely trusted medical adviser. So many deaths; so many crippling injuries! Only a midwife who has herself known pain will, he thinks, do reliable work. He has seen enough hurt inflicted on children, he writes, "to make me want to weep with the little worms, so great is the pity I feel for them in their needless suffering."[20] Like most of his colleagues Würtz opposes casting the newborn into the alien arms of a rustic wet nurse. Not only is mother's milk more healthful, being of the same constitution as the nourishment received in the womb, but it is also "much more pleasant for the infant to suck at the breast of his mother."[21] The Italian and French upperclass custom of farming out babies to the homes of wet nurses (*mamma* was the word for wet nurse in many parts of Italy)[22] was rejected in Germany, on psychological as well as physiological grounds.[23] An impressive battery of scientific argument going back to Galen defended a preference for the nursing mother, whose milk alone was said to transmit to her child the harmony of temperaments keeping her own body in tune (no one, of course, considered the use of cow's milk). A famous passage from Tacitus's *Germania* (a work arousing great excitement in Germany at the time) made a moral issue of the mother's feeding her children at her own breast.[24] But pediatricians were clearly concerned also with the baby's senses and feelings: "Imagine what goes on in him [*wie im sey*] as he feels the touch of rough hands on his tender skin and is chafed by coarse woolen cloth or scratchy swaddling bands. What do you think it feels like to lie on a hard board covered with prickly straw, sharp-edged planing chips, or crumbled birch leaves?"[25] Felix Würtz, the writer of these lines, betrays an astonishing sympathy for the sensations of little creatures lying in the crib, and he is by no means the only physician to do so.[26] He deplores the head holes cut in crib boards (to help produce a nicely shaped head) because these make it difficult for the infant to shift his position, which induces "a sense of fear and anxiety." He opposes swaddling for the same reason.[27] Those who did advocate it (not many) recommended loose binding to allow maximum mobility. States of insecurity induced by discomfort, injury, or excessive restraint recur in nightmares, Würtz thinks. If they persist they will leave the child with a permanently melancholy disposition.[28]

All writers advised close attention to the infant and prompt response to every sign of discomfort. Change him as often as needed. Rocking, singing, and soft words will console him nicely.[29] Keep him clean by daily bathing[30] and spotless clothes.[31] Make teething as painless as possible by easing out the milk teeth when they are ready to go, and by rubbing a mild narcotic on sore gums.[32] Wean him slowly to lessen the shock to stomach and habits. Let him suck for a while on a nipple-shaped plug of bread steeped in sugar water.[33] The actual utility of such advice need not be exaggerated in order to establish its importance. While most of the vernacular writers held to their bookish reliance on the ancient tradition of their profession, it is also evident that they made friends of their young patients. An implicit agreement seems to have operated between parents and medical men that children ought to be closely observed, raised in hygienic and comfortable surroundings under close parental and medical supervision, and that their development should be carefully studied. "Parents should be kind to their children and give them their attention at all times."[34] Words of gold, from Otto Brunfels, though surely not always heeded, even among the social classes for which these books were primarily written. But even the best medical counsel could not prevent or alleviate the numberless ailments wasting children and traumatizing childhood. Each of the books mentioned here (and many others not mentioned)[35] supplies a frightening catalog of childhood diseases, followed by a pitifully small repertory of remedies and palliatives. These may not have made things worse; but they are not likely to have helped very much. Childhood and youth were times of peril, confinement, pain, and death. But this was not for lack of attention to the young, nor for a deficiency of care for them.

On a more personal, familial level, this concern can be exemplified by expressions of affection that would not sound out of place on our lips today. Any suggestion that people in former ages took less pleasure in their children than we do in ours, or felt less pity for their pains and grief at their death,[36] ignores the testimony of the sources. The selfless and, if necessary, self-sacrificing love of parents for their offspring was taken for granted as a natural instinct in the hearts of all creatures: "God has made this love a part of nature—not only human but also animal—so that parents would rather themselves come to harm and sorrow than let their children suffer."[37] This has nothing to do with expectation of rewards, immediate or future.[38] It is pure intuitive love. "The weaker and more helpless the babe, the greater his parents' fondness for him. They will attend the sick more gladly than the strong. Loving all their children equally well, their hearts still go out more tenderly to the sick child than to the healthy one."[39] "That parents love their children more than they love themselves,"[40] that "a father's heart beats with a natural [angenaturte] affection for his children . . . is [to most authors] as clear as is the light of day."[41]

The claim is sometimes made that fathers in earlier times felt less attachment to their daughters than to their sons. As far as we can tell from the (admittedly scant) evidence, this is not true. The story of Jephthah's grief for his only daughter was as often told and moralized as was old Laertes' love for Odysseus, but a much more immediate example is at hand in Martin Luther's reaction to the illness and death of his fourteen-year-old daughter Magdalena in 1542. His words, in which he struggled to reconcile the depth of his human sorrow with his implicit faith in God, were recorded verbatim by his friends.[42] As his wife sobbed inconsolably by the child's bed, Luther tried to comfort her. "He said 'I love her very much, but if it is your will, O God, to take her, I shall be content to know that she will soon be with you.' " To the girl he said, " 'Magdalena, my child, would you be glad to stay here with me, your father, but will you also go happily across to your other father?' The dying girl answered, 'Yes, father dear, as God wishes it.' Her father replied, 'My dear, dear little girl. The spirit is strong but the flesh is weak.' And he turned his face away, saying, 'I love her so very much.' And as the child Magdalena lay in death's throes he fell on his knees at her bedside and wept bitterly."[43] Only the death of a beloved spouse, he said, exceeds in bitterness the pain felt by a parent who has lost a child, adding "I have myself experienced and suffered this."[44]

Luther's open and warmhearted interest in children has been noted several times in these pages.[45] Unlike many of his fellow reformers he seems to have treated the young without condescension. He could enter their world. When he spoke to them, or of them, he sounded no false note. Describing paradise to his son Hans, then aged four (the year was 1530 and Luther wrote from the fortress at Coburg, while anxiously watching developments at the Diet of Augsburg), he said:

> I know where there is a lovely pretty garden. Many many children go to play there. They wear golden doublets and gather sweet apples from beneath the trees, also pears, cherries, and yellow and red plums. They sing, run about, and couldn't be happier. They play with pretty little horses that have golden bridles and silver saddles. When I first saw this garden I asked the man who owns it, "whose children are these that play here?" He answered, "They are pious children who like to pray and learn." Then I said, "Good sir, I too have a little child. His name is Hans Luther. May he also come to play in your beautiful garden? I know he would enjoy the taste of your delicious apples and pears and he would like to ride the little horses and play with the other children." And the man said, "If he prays gladly and learns well, and is pious, he can come and play in my garden. When he and his brothers arrive, they will have

music of pipes, drums, and lutes. They can dance, or, if they prefer, they can practice target shooting with the crossbow." And he showed me a splendid meadow in the middle of the garden where some children were dancing. And on a nearby table I saw golden pipes laid out, and drums and several fine little crossbows made all of silver.[46]

There is no evidence to suggest that the delicacy of emotion revealed in these words was unusual in Luther's time. On the contrary, pedagogical literature abounds with injunctions to parents not to let their natural fondness make them indulgent, softhearted, and foolish toward their offspring. These warnings are given so often and so repetitiously that one is tempted to conclude that the child pampered by permissive parents was the rule, and the unloved, unattended, and battered waif of which one hears so much nowadays[47] the exception. It goes without saying that this conclusion, like the evidence on which it rests, relates to burghers, artisans—people leading an orderly and comfortable family life. Unlike the mass of rural villagers (the crudeness of whose lives is fully documented in visitation protocols, as will be seen), urban citizens seem rather to have coddled their children than abused them. If few fathers matched the caricature of the doting daddy ("What piece of meat would you like for breakfast, my little darling? Ah, wait, I know what you will enjoy. Take this capon wing here. It's the most delectable morsel!"),[48] most seem to have felt and displayed toward their children the love and concern we ourselves regard as natural and normal.[49]

Other evidence serves to reinforce this point: the dreadful anguish felt by parents whose infants died unbaptized—a terror that preachers did their best to assuage;[50] heartrending laments for the souls of dead children and exultant thanksgiving for the lucky ones who recovered;[51] legal sanctions against parents guilty of what was clearly regarded as unnatural neglect of their young, even of the handicapped or otherwise abnormal.[52] But our strongest confirmation comes from paintings, sculpture, and book illustration: "tales from the childhood of Christ" (*infantia Christi*) in which the scenes are portrayed lovingly with obvious feeling for the bonds of affection uniting children and adults;[53] epitaphs for dead children showing them being blessed by Christ, as in Matt. 19:13–15; Cranach's figure of Christ as he cradles an infant in his arms while extending an expression of deep sympathy to a circle of mothers and children gathered close to him;[54] Dürer's sympathetic studies of young children;[55] the many family portraits painted for the well-to-do and suggesting a by no means casual attachment of parents to children.[56] One could lengthen the list, particularly from religious art in which both the joys and the sorrows of familial affection received their most intense expression.[57]

There is, of course, no dearth of recorded instances of harsh treatment and cruel punishment. This catalog is always led by Luther's recollections of the bloody beating he received from his mother for having stolen a nut.[58] In commenting on what parents should and should not do to discipline their young, religious writers often addressed themselves to the vexing matter of corporal punishment. Their text was always Paul's warning to the paterfamilias (Eph. 6:4) "do not provoke your children to anger." This does not mean, they hasten to add, that one must never punish them: "But it does forbid, and on God's own authority, their chastisement without good cause. Children are not to be beaten out of envy, anger, or hatred. Each of us knows some strange types [wunderliche Köpffe]—found most often among stepfathers and stepmothers—who vent their bad tempers on helpless children or take out on them their vicious resentment of the care they are obliged to give them. They scold and nag them without letup until the children turn numb and listless. Or else they pay them no heed at all, never speaking a word of reproach, even when punishment is deserved."[59] A good father, the authors advise, "brings up his children with kindly words and tempts them with promises of pleasant rewards to do the right thing." Unfortunately there is another sort, "who beats them about the head, punches and pummels them until he has made them into deaf-and-dumb fools and broken cripples."[60] Such a brute seeking license for his savagery could find it in a notorious passage from Ecclesiasticus, a book of counsel much quoted (under the title "The Wisdom of Jesus, Son of Sirach") in the sixteenth century:

> A man who loves his son will whip him often
> so that when he grows up he may be a joy to him.
>
> . . . .
>
> An unbroken horse turns out stubborn,
> And an unchecked son turns out headstrong.
> Pamper a boy and he will shock you,
> Play with him and he will grieve you.
>
> . . . .
>
> Break him in while he is young,
> Beat him soundly while he is still a child,
> Or he may grow stubborn and disobey you
> And cause you vexation.[61]

The evidence suggests, however, that this prescription was not often acted upon.

3

But this is far from the last word to be said on the subject. Attitudes reflect more than emotional responses. Perceptions of childhood and youth were compounded in the sixteenth century of a rich mixture of ideas and notions, some of which collided with, and deflected, the adult's fondness for children and prevented the individual's instinctive affection for his own offspring from becoming a general disposition of indulgence toward the young. "Natural" human impulses were regarded with suspicion. Presumption, ambition, and self-serving were rejected as disturbers, if not destroyers, of social tranquility. They were held responsible, not only on religious grounds, for most of the restlessness afflicting society in the age of the Reformation.

The extent to which children and adolescents possessed these distressing qualities was the subject of an anxious debate. How much do the young partake of the egotism, instability, and rebelliousness characterizing the "natural man," the Old Adam? What are the effects of the corruption passed by every parent to his child? What consequences follow for his nurture and training? The timeliness of these questions is shown by the attempt to bring them down from the stratosphere of academic theology, where they were most vigorously debated,[62] to the arena of action where people did or did not respond to calls for prompt infant baptism, where parents pampered their children or disciplined them, and where society accepted or ignored the pedagogical duties urged upon them by the reformers. To counteract comforting but, in their view, perilous assumptions based on familial feelings, Lutheran ecclesiastics thought it vital to demonstrate that children, infants even, were not the innocents they seemed to be. Doctrinal formulations of sin and guilt were not easily put across to ordinary folk, but theological popularizers—and the German Reformation produced many notable ones—tried their best. It will be useful to listen to one of them, the Nuremberg pastor and ecclesiastical administrator Andreas Althamer, expounding his point of view in a vernacular pamphlet on original sin.[63]

Some say, Althamer begins,[64] that children live in a state of innocence because they have not yet learned the law of God. To support their contention, partisans of this doctrine point to Rom. 4:15: "where there is no law there is no transgression." Small children, they say, lack all experience, and must necessarily be ignorant of the law; they cannot therefore be said to transgress it. Not so, counters Althamer. To argue that young children are in a state of innocence because they do not know the law is to advance a false proposition. Adam's sin is everyone's sin. "The young sinned in Adam as much as the old." We are all "by nature children of wrath" (Eph. 2:3). "Now, if the young are children of wrath, they cannot be innocent. Like the rest of us they are sinners." Psalm 58 affirms that "The wicked go astray from the womb, they err from their birth, speaking lies" (Ps. 58:3). From this assertion Althamer concludes that "law is law and sin is sin, know it or ignore it, it makes no difference, it's all the same. Adam's sin damns us whether we know the law or not." Empirical proof of infant guilt is all around us, Althamer continues, most incontrovertibly in the dreadful evidence of infant mortality: "Would they die if they had not sinned? No one dies unless he has sinned; 'for the wages of sin is death.' It follows that, if infants die, they must have sinned, and they do die, as we all know. Why this is so, why they must suffer death without having lived long enough to have learned the law, is a question we dare not ask. It is God's judgment. He reaps where he has not sown [Matt. 25:24]. . . . It is not for us to make out the deeper meanings of any of this. We must leave it to God." "Their very birth damns them," Althamer concludes, "and woe to them that die unbaptized." "And should one of you now ask, How is it that little babes are damned if they die without baptism, seeing that they have done nothing either good or wicked in their short lives? Is it their fault that Adam committed a big sin? I answer: Let us hold our tongue. Let us not meddle in God's judgment. God is just. He owes us nothing. How dare we argue with him and interfere in his affairs?"[65]

Althamer's vehemence is in part the product of his polemical objective. Like many other Lutheran controversialists of the time (his treatise was published in 1528), he was making a case against "the Swiss," which is to say, against the Zwinglian denial of the causal link between original sin and personal guilt. Zwingli was prepared to admit guilt only where an individual had willfully chosen to act on his inherited "natural infirmity." This "disease" is not sin, implying guilt, but only a contaminated condition. We are "by birth contaminated by inclination to sin," said Zwingli, "but the contamination harms not, for its poison has been taken from it through Christ." [66] This position obviously let off infants and small children. To Lutherans, on the other hand, being born helplessly into sin in no way diminishes guilt. Children share the human condition of culpability. No matter how leniently one chose to apply this doctrine to real life, its theological weight was unshakable. It was soon to be anchored in the Augsburg Confession, the Schmalkaldic Articles, and the Formula of Concord:

> Because of Adam's fall, all men, born in the natural way, are conceived and born in sin; that is to say, from the womb they are all filled with evil desires and inclinations and can by nature have no true fear of God and no true faith in God. And this congenital plague [*Seuche*] and inherited sin with which we are born is a true sin, and it damns under God's eternal wrath all those who are not reborn through baptism and the Holy Spirit.[67]

It was a small step to combine this doctrine with "experience" and "reflection" and to arrive at propositions about the young that deviated considerably from friendly inclinations dictated by natural affection: "Is original sin then inherent in all human beings? Yes, in all, Christ alone excepted. For all of us who have observed them know that children, when left to themselves, will always turn gleefully and eagerly to every sort of wickedness, while detesting the good and refusing to do it except under duress and against their inclination."[68] Even the babe in the cradle is guilty, and his behavior shows it. So argued the prominent theologian Andreas Osiander in his *Nuremberg Catechism or Sermons for Children* of 1533. He admitted that feelings and reason argue against this. "But," he concluded, "it is not for us to judge by reason, but by the word of God."[69]

Had this contention made its intended mark, the loving parent's softhearted affection would have been powerfully counteracted and socially neutralized. In any case, there now emerged in the writings of theologians and pedagogues a stereotyped image of the young person, not as an individual boy or girl who may or may not have been lovable to his kin and neighbors, but as the abstract incarnation of traits ascribed to children as their defining attributes by a wary, suspicious, and, by the late 1520s, thoroughly alarmed company of adults. More than a sweeping generalization, this was a blanket judgment on the nature of the young. It stamped them in the eyes of those who directed their maturation and tried to determine their lives. It sanctioned the repressive (in a sense to be explained in a later chapter) methods of indoctrination to which, by general agreement, all children must be subjected if they were to be kept from doing irreparable harm to themselves and their society.

"Wild," "unbroken," "crude" were the adjectives most often applied to youths in their "natural" condition, their undisciplined state. "A child brought up at home is like an unbroken bull," asserted a contemporary proverb;[70] given his own way by permissive parents, a youngster will remain "stubborn, obstinate, incapable of ruling himself, and bound to come to a bad end."[71] Man, "who in his childhood is no more than a brute beast and has no other powers than those of anger and concupiscence,"[72] needs to be tamed, and the earlier this is done the better. "A child is like a wild tree standing alone in a field," wrote the Lutheran superintendent Christoph Vischer in a treatise on education.

> Unless you graft a good nature onto its rude and wild stock it will bear you sour fruit all its life. To gather sweet fruit from a tree, you must first trim off all the wild branches and then insert into the cuttings buds of a sweeter kind. Treat the young in the same way. Their nature is wild, they are children of wrath, conceived and born in sin; their instincts and drives are unfailingly wicked. Into this rude stock you must implant a better nature. Suppress their rebellious impulses. Use the knife of God's

word to cut off the branches of their contumacious will. Raise them in the fear of God. And when their wild nature comes up again—as weeds always will—and the Old Adam stirs in them again, kill it and bury it deep in the ground, lest the newly grown good nature once more revert to its wild state.[73]

Only drastic means could modify nature and avert the fateful implications of Christ's metaphor of the tree and its fruits (Matt. 7:16–20). Unless altered in their native character, youths were bound to remain *natura mali*, as Luther said in a sermon.[74]

The general anxiety about the young, and the fear of the havoc they might do, are revealed in the vast exaggerations and the piling up of pejorative adjectives to which some authors resorted whenever they mentioned "the raging, cocksure, brash, reckless, ignorant but know-it-all young:"[75]

> Let us hear Jesus, son of Sirach on this point,[76] namely how much filth and viciousness there is in all children, unless this is eradicated in them in their first years and they are turned away from it by means of discipline. But how easily they slide back and turn again into wild, willful, and destructive brutes. Pamper them the least little bit, and at once they will rule their parents and cause them grief, heartache, and terrible sadness. Parents who spoil their children are the greatest of fools. They fondle them, give them their way in all things . . . and before they know it their folly has made them objects of scorn and disgrace.[77]

The rasping tone and bilious vituperation—characteristic of clerical authors who may well have been kindly men in private life—emphasize the schematic abstractness of this pedagogical image of youth. As a type, it was a figment of the imagination, although religious dogma and empirical evidence, selectively gathered, lent it a certain weight and appearance of verisimilitude. But as a piece of special pleading for indoctrination and discipline, it had obvious utility. It quickly made its way into school ordinances and educational mandates that proclaimed that "these foolish young people of ours,"[78] "ever inclined to frivolity and wickedness,"[79] "should not be left free to make decisions for themselves, seeing that they will always reject what is good for them and take up instead whatever arouses their foolish fancy."[80] Without the fear of God instilled in them in earliest childhood they would remain as they had been born, "stubborn animals, creatures of their whims, and sure to destroy themselves, *ut quotidie experimur*."[81]

Lutheran pedagogues had of course not invented the stereotype of the headstrong youth, self-destructive unless tamed by discipline. The social havoc likely to be caused by the wild boy whose unruly energies remained unharnessed had been for centuries the rhetorical stock-in-trade of religious and civic reformers.[82] Aristotle is the ultimate

source of this image of the young boy as an engine of crude and rampant psychic and physical energies. Aristotle's description (in his
Rhetoric)[83] persisted into the sixteenth century as a pattern stamped
indiscriminately on the young. Modified at the obvious points to agree
with doctrine and "experience," and employed where required, Aristotle's portrait of the young was accepted as consensus orthodoxy:

> The young, as to character, are ready to desire and to carry out what
> they desire. Of bodily desires they chiefly obey those of sensual pleasure
> and these they are unable to control. Changeable in their desires and soon
> tiring of them, they desire with extreme ardor, but soon cool. . . . They are
> passionate, hot-tempered, and carried away by impulse, and unable to
> control their passion; for owing to their ambition they cannot endure to be
> slighted, and become indignant when they think they are being wronged.
> They are ambitious of honor, but more so of victory, for youth desires
> superiority. . . . They are not ill-natured but simple-natured, because they
> have as yet not been often deceived. . . . They are high-minded, for they
> have not yet been humbled by life nor have they experienced the force of
> necessity. . . .
>   In their actions they prefer the noble to the useful; their life is guided
> by their character rather than by calculation. . . . All their errors are due
> to excess and vehemence and their neglect of the maxim of Chilon ["Never
> go to extremes"], for they do everything to excess, love, hate, and every-
> thing else. And they think they know everything, and confidently affirm
> it, and this is the cause of their excess in everything. If they do wrong it is
> due to insolence, not to wickedness.[84]

"High-minded," (*megalopsuchoi*) and "noble" (*to kalon*) do not quite
fit the Augustinian mold preferred by most Lutheran pedagogues, and
one finds no mention of such traits in their writings. But every other
youthful attribute identified by Aristotle agreed with their suppositions
and mightily shored up their preconceptions. Restless, mutable, tending to extremes, passionately impulsive while lacking self-control,
ambitious and domineering, smugly self-confident despite a naive
gullibility exposing them to influences of every sort, the young were
humankind in the raw, Old Adam unbound, natural man at his coarsest,
destructive and vulnerable, objects of both pity and fear.

Now it is obvious that Aristotle's description is of the adolescent,
not the young child. Christian authors, on the other hand, when they
speak of the innocence, or apparent innocence, or the trusting openness and tractability of children, do not always identify the stage of
life to which these characteristics apply. "Children [*Kinder*] are the
purest and best part of the whole human race," wrote David Chytraeus,
a prolific religious and pedagogical writer and church administrator.[85]
This declaration served to introduce his catechism and must have been
meant to designate youngsters of school age. Indeed, the assertion was

a commonplace, turning up whenever and wherever an argument was being made for supporting Christian education. The "purity" it extolled seems difficult to reconcile with the sinful intentions and uncontrollable behavior seen by many Lutheran theologians as deeply rooted traits in young children. But if an ambiguity was perceived, it was not resolved. "Children are the purest and finest part of the human race, the loveliest blossoms of the Christian church, and the most beautiful flowers of paradise": this from the writer of a visitation protocol in the Palatinate principality of Neuburg, in 1584, who goes on to plead in very practical terms for the endowment of a Latin school for talented boys of seven or more years of age.[86] In this case, *Kinder* obviously does not refer only to children of preschool age. Innocence could therefore extend into the teens. This claim was asserted, and believed, whenever occasion demanded. The prayers of boys and girls gathered in school and church were regarded as effective means of warding off danger or gaining relief from calamity.[87] Their natural guilelessness also had its judicial and political uses, as when lots had to be drawn in a trial or a candidate chosen for civic office.[88] Jörg Wickram, a novelist and writer of didactic plays, relates a grisly story about a group of youngsters who, carried away while playing a game called "butcher, cook, and pig," slit the throat of one of their playmates and made a blood pudding. Baffled by this bizarre incident, the judges invited the "butcher" to choose between an apple and a gold florin. The boy happily took the apple, which, in the eyes of the judges, established the blamelessness of his appalling deed.[89] We are reminded here of Luther's words in exaltation of childish innocence. "Children live in innocence [*leben in Unschuld; summam innocentiam esse in pueris*]," he is reported to have said. "They know no sin, they live without greed, . . . they will take an apple as cheerfully as a coin."[90] Coming from Luther himself (in 1535), the remark speaks volumes about the unsettling ambivalence created in people's minds by the conflicting claims of theological natural affection.

Luther makes an elusive witness for one seeking clarity among the reformers' pronouncements on the nature of the young. He evidently cherished and treasured them, or at least some of them, but he also joined in the chorus deploring their typical faults and vices. Even the most sympathetic and best informed student of his educational thought, Ivar Asheim, whose book brings together all Luther's declarations on children and youths, does not find them consistent.[91] We have seen how spontaneously Luther responded to the affective appeal of the seemingly innocent ways of children. But he also knew that appearances were deceiving. Original sin is as deep-seated in the infant as it is in the adult. In the child it lies dormant, not yet ready to reveal itself in overt actions. But this situation changes between the ages of five and seven.[92] The ego now begins to assert itself. The child becomes psychologically and mentally active, moving rapidly into his inheritance of sin, the acting out of which will turn him into a fullfledged human individual. Luther distinguishes in emphatic black and white the child's apparent innocence from his manifest guilt: "Children under seven years of age have not developed real [rechte] thoughts. We know this because they do not feel the urge to kill and commit adultery. Still, sin has begun to stir in them, as is evident in their tendency to steal, snatch sweets, and so on."[93] Seven-year stages were for many authors, classical and modern, the fateful segments of human development.[94] Every seventh year a crisis stirs the individual's life, brought on by his need to come to terms with unsettling new situations for which the experiences gathered during the previous phases had not prepared him. Each crisis constitutes a new test for the growing, maturing person.[95] The most disorienting of these turning points comes with the awakening sex drive at age fourteen. Luther had much to say about this, as will be seen in a moment. But at earlier stages, too, physical and psychic developments mean trouble. Soon after the fifth year, the hitherto latent power of sin "awakens." Immediately it finds work to do as the child is taken captive by an overpowering desire to have his will in all matters, to gratify his own pleasures, and to escape from all responsibility and authority. At fourteen, aggressiveness and sensuousness are added. At twenty-one, with full manhood, come greed, pride, ambition, and arrogance, as the individual, having learned to hide his low impulses behind a pious mask, sets out to use these traits in the exercise of his concupiscence.[96]

Luther's genial comments on the innocence of childhood therefore seem to touch only on the first five or six years of a child's life, although, compared with the twenty-one-year-old adult, the growing youth is still relatively innocent (if there can be such a thing) at every preceding stage.[97] It is a matter of perspective. The younger the child, the purer his instincts. Jesus' warning that "Unless you turn and become like children, you will never enter the kingdom of heaven" (Matt. 18:3) makes of the initial years a model [muster] for all subsequent ages.[98] Man at his best is man at his youngest, a time of his life when his thought and behavior show unquestioning trust in God and innocence without guile or cunning. No wonder Luther found himself reminded of paradise when he observed young children at play. "God's little fools," he often called them affectionately.[99] But he knew that their blessed time was short. "Oh, how wicked the world," he exclaimed, "and how soon in life things start to go wrong!"[100] This too was a commonplace. Johann Agricola, in explaining a proverb on the ages of man, states it as a familiar fact that "a child wants only to play, flies quickly into rage, is fickle, and soon loses interest in what he does. An adolescent [*Jüngling*] likes to hunt, ride, and roam about. He can't stand being contradicted and, like a monkey, imitates whatever he sees others do, good or bad. He wastes much time, he is arrogant, he craves attention, and he soon tires of everything."[101]

Luther's remarks on children and childhood can be disentangled and classified, but this is not equally true for his contemporaries and followers, who are much more difficult to pin down. They tend to use *Kind* and *puer* indiscriminately to refer to all ages from infancy to late adolescence. *Jüngling, adolescens, iuvenis* were terms generally avoided by pedagogical writers, who preferred in their books and ordinances to speak of *Kinder* and, generically, of *Jugend*.[102] The reason for this imprecision is not hard to find. *Kinder*—children—were tractable. In contemporary usage the word suggested receptivity to instruction, docility. Often its use was accompanied by expressions of an avuncular solicitude: "our poor, simple-minded, inexperienced children whose heads are so easily turned,"[103] "who are quickly thrown into confusion."[104] "Our poor children who bend this way or that, like twigs in the wind, unless they are strengthened by discipline."[105] As long as they were *Kinder*, they remained elastic enough to bend to the preceptor's shaping hand. Once they had become adolescents it was too late. The longer the "childhood" stage, therefore, the better the chance of succeeding with the program of mental and moral conditioning that constituted the chief objective of Reformation pedagogues.[106]

The urgent need to prolong childhood explains why the more systematic of pedagogical thinkers attempted to create for their pupils an environment that could postpone the onset of puberty. Their object was to delay the psychological acceptance of sexual maturity[107] (as opposed to biological sexuality, over the timing of which educators had of course no control), that is to say, to retard as long as possible the young person's acknowledgment of his sexuality and his readiness to employ it. This, it was thought, would give educators time to form his mind and shape his habits.

A moratorium on sexuality, and the consequent extension of childhood, could be achieved only in the near-total control of the boarding school: the *Klosterschulen*, princes' schools, and seminaries of the Reformation. Such institutions illustrate the connection between schooling and the modern concept of a "long childhood" to which Philippe Ariès points in his celebrated book on family life and childhood in the early modern period.[108] But schools of this kind enrolled only a few, and Reformation pedagogues aimed at the population at large. They recognized the difficulty of their struggle to counteract natural tendencies in a natural environment. It seems to be the consensus of most recent investigators that sexual maturity came early in the fifteenth, sixteenth, and seventeenth centuries in Europe.[109] Childhood tended to be short, a brief span of time quickly transcended by adult life, which in many respects—games and pastimes,[110] clothing,[111] behavior in public,[112] early apprenticeship and university admission—coincided with puberty at age fourteen or so.[113] With adolescence and incorporation in the "world"—a loaded word when used by reformers, meant to warn of "the terrible disorder and perverse manner of the world which in all things stands opposed to the word and ordinances of God"[114]—the young were lost to good influence, impervious to appeals and threats. The "ripeness of youth" placed the young person permanently across the threshold dividing innocence from guile. Observe the adolescent, wrote Thomas Elyot, translating from Plutarch, "and you will see riottous lyvynge consumynge substance and inheritance, inordinate and chargeable gaminge, ingurgitacions and surfettes, defloracion of maydes, corruptynge good women."[115] One must take hold of him early and keep him a "child" as long as possible by delaying the dreaded symptoms of adolescence, whose onset extinguished all hope of molding him to the accepted pattern.[116] Philippe Ariès could not be more wrong than when he asserts that "due to the indifference with which strictly biological phenomena were regarded at the time . . . nobody would have thought of seeing the end of childhood in puberty."[117] In fact, puberty made all the difference, signaling the end of pliancy and docility.

In launching their futile attempts to contain the sexual impulses of their pupils, or at least to keep their overt manifestations at bay, Lutheran pedagogues seem to have forgotten what the reformer himself had written concerning the irresistible force of the sexual drive in normal men and women. Luther's extraordinary description of the sexual urge, and of the psychological harm done by its suppression, was published in two polemical tracts in 1522 and 1523,[118] which should have taught his colleagues something about the hopeless task they were setting themselves.

Sexual desire, says Luther, "is not a choice we make or a decision at which we arrive. It is a necessary and natural thing. Every man needs a woman, every woman must have a man."[119] This need is not only natural; it is God-ordained. The divine command to "be fruitful and multiply" is "not up to us to resist or ignore." Satisfying our sexual wants is "more urgent than eating, drinking, . . . sleeping and waking. It is rooted in us as part of our nature and species."[120] The treatise from which these passages are taken, *On Wedded Life*, was an attack on monasticism and a justification of the married estate. But Luther was not only polemicizing. He clearly argued as one who knew. He restates his case with heightened effect in his commentary on 1 Corinthians 7, always the proof text for debates on the relative merits of marriage and celibacy.[121] Writing in his most graphic German, Luther gives a cut-ting edge to Paul's advice to those who cannot control their passions. "For the sake of the spirit," Luther says, a Christian needs no wife. But a Christian's flesh, "corrupted by Adam and Eve and filled with evil lusts," differs in no respect from a Turk's or a heathen's. "His flesh rages and burns and must spill its seed."[122] "Nature never lets up." Without normal release "we are all driven to the secret sin. To say it crudely but honestly, if it doesn't go into a woman, it goes into your shirt [*fleusset es nicht ynn das fleisch, sso fleusset es ynns hembt*]."[123] "Nature will out. It wants to spurt its seed. . . . The fire in the flesh never stops raging, giving us no peace with our daily need for a woman or a man."[124] Luther heaps scorn on monkish claims that this fire can be extinguished. He voices outrage at parents who consign their youthful sons and daughters to the cloister, expecting them to deny or control their sexual urges. "It's like being told to hold your urine and dung. . . . Most of them can't stand it; they do what they must to satisfy themselves." He adds: "I don't want to write about this now." But he clearly understood the deep psychological anguish inflicted by irrepressible conflicts between physical needs and religious vows. "When they do relieve themselves, outside marriage, at once conscience jumps up and starts clamoring. And then they suffer the most unbearable self-recriminations and become the most wretched people on earth."[125] Luther did recognize a vocation for chastity in both men and women. But this is a special grace, rarely given.[126] It is an exception to the rule. Most men have no choice. We crave sex "and it is impossible to stay away from it."[127] Should your wife refuse you, Luther advises, tell her "if you don't want to, there are plenty of others who do. And if the wife says no, call the hired girl."[128] This passage has caused modern Lutheran commentators some discomfort.[129] But it does, in a crude way, sum up Luther's acknowledgment of the irresistible power of the sexual drive and the futility, as well as the trauma, in any attempt to hold it back.

It was not, of course, the adult's carnal desires that Reformation pedagogues tried to inhibit, but the young boy's and girl's first sexual explorations. And it was not sensuality alone, but everything for which the all-powerful sex drive stood as symbol: aggressiveness, ruthlessness, egotism. Their aim was not to eradicate sexual needs, but to postpone and, if possible, moderate them. Delayed sexual maturity would prolong the innocence of childhood. Pedagogues can be presumed to have been thoroughly familiar with the signs of adolescent sexuality. Aristotle had described these in his matter-of-fact way,[130] and sixteenth-century medical writers were also giving attention to the subject. They agreed among themselves that privation and repression normally led to physical and mental distress.[131] They cautioned against sexual activity "at inappropriate ages, that is to say in childhood or, worse, in old age,"[132] and, like the reformers, they affirmed conjugal love as its only approved form.[133] But they left no doubt of the imperious power of the sexual urge and the natural tendency to satisfy it by masturbation if no other outlet was available.[134] From the physician's point of view this was neither illicit nor immoral. Pedagogues disagreed, of course; they were the true heirs, in this respect, of Jean Gerson and the educational reformers of the preceding century.

But how could they impose a moratorium on sexual maturation? Only by removing all stimulants to the prurient fantasy. Parents must keep their small fry from running about naked before going to bed in the evening, "a disgraceful and objectionable practice, unfortunately very common nowadays, through which children are at an early age accustomed to impure thoughts and lack of inhibitions."[135] Public baths offended for the same reason. In schools, boys and girls should be segregated, in different buildings if possible, or at least seated separately.[136] If parents protested on grounds of inconvenience, "tell them that it is being done for the sake of decent conduct among children."[137] Only men should teach boys, only women girls.[138] Never allow youngsters to gather in small groups in obscure places. Keep your eye on a boy who goes off by himself.[139] "You can't watch them too carefully at that slippery, furtive age," cautioned Martin Bucer.[140] Boarding school dormitories should be spacious (no dark corners), and "in each large sleeping room let a candle burn all night long."[141] Suggestive clothing should be outlawed,[142] dancing, stage plays, and other sensual excitements placed off limits.[143] Admonitions and censure were to ring constantly in young ears. Catechism writers never tired of describing the dreadful consequences of disobeying the sixth commandment ("you shall not commit adultery"); some, indeed, were so explicit in naming the sins against it that their descriptions of sexual transgressions must have put some thoughts into children's heads:

> *Father:* What are the sins against the sixth commandment? *Child:* All carnal, impure, and unchaste thoughts and wicked desires such as seeking illicit stimulation and excitements, making lewd gestures and provocative talk, singing indecent songs, telling ribald jokes, reading salacious stories or gazing at voluptuous pictures for the purpose of exciting oneself to corrupt lusts and thence to unchastity. *Father:* And what are the good works done in observance of the sixth commandment? *Child:* Pure and spiritual thoughts, a chaste heart, seemly speech, virtuous conduct. In other words, avoiding everything that may incite to indecency, luxury, voluptuousness, and arousal of the senses.[144]

It would be strange if these suggestive allusions had failed to arouse sexual thoughts in children. When they read in a "Response to the Devil's Book of Lies" [*Lügenbüchlein*] that Satan was ready to lure them with "all sorts of filthy, gross obscenities, indecent words and talk, and fornication" in order "to distract our poor, simple young folk from their Christian conduct,"[145] they must have been tempted to fantasize concretely about these enticements. To the question, "What are the sins [against the sixth commandment]?" catechisms replied: "whoring, unchastity, and all the other impure actions you can imagine."[146] But life among ordinary folk in towns and villages could not have left very much to a child's imagination. Sexuality was open and, one gathers, uninhibited.[147] Popular stage comedies, especially at carnival time, when children were usually among the spectators, abounded in comic sexual situations and suggestive wordplay. Sermons often referred no less explicitly to sexual matters. Catechisms included schoolboy prayers for relief from syphilis.[148] Chastity and celibacy were still acclaimed as the most godly walk of life, but this assurance was given only halfheartedly. Some few men and women have God's singular gift of continence, it was said. "These have a special commission to do God's work,"[149] and whoever has this gift, "let him thank God for it and pass up the married state without regrets."[150] But these special cases have no bearing on the lives of ordinary men and women who must seek sexual partners, not only to reproduce the race, but also to assuage their passions.

Sixteenth-century pedagogues may well have realized that they were fighting a losing battle for the containment of something that had no bounds. The short reins on which they proposed to hold the young could not restrain them in a condition regarded as unnatural by the world around them. As their advancing years hardened the child's natural pliancy, as their burgeoning adolescent appetites stripped them of their docile temper, how were the young to be kept out of harm's way? Only one answer suggested itself: by means of hard work. The prescription to keep them always busy was intended to consume their energies and demonstrate to them the seriousness of life:

> All youths [jungheit] need discipline because they must be kept from vices and taught the fear of God. Young people are inexperienced. They are subject to great temptations; most of all those who go to school. Working youngsters are less exposed to corrupting influences because hard work breaks their impudent nature. But pupils are always being tempted to vice, having much time on their hands to think about it. It's the Old Adam stirring in them. Let them be free, indulge them, and they will always give themselves to vice and frivolity. The more freedom, the more corruption.[151]

Steady toil and constant occupation, even if it was only busy work, were the best correctives for youthful high spirits, or so it was believed. Idleness bred mischief. Young minds and bodies with time to kill were easy prey for the devil. Working at their assigned tasks, memorizing and reciting the catechism, sitting still in church while listening to the preacher would, it was hoped, teach them the fear of the Lord and respect for authority. No other means existed for holding them in check.

4

Whatever private feelings Lutheran pedagogues may have brought to their work, their perceptions of childhood and youth were determined by their religion's Augustinian anthropology and their culture's general suspicion of human motives. These attitudes set the style of their pedagogy, compellingly reinforcing their postulates and substantiating their guiding precepts. Childhood offered opportunities for molding, since receptivity of mind and malleability of character were then at their highest. At seven, the age of "reason," the senses were in working order, memory alert, understanding intact, habits still unset. This was the time to begin. But even at that tender age the seeds of obstinacy and malice were ready to burst into full-grown weeds to choke the delicate fruits of good instruction. At fourteen, the age of pubescence, opportunity had passed unless sound ideas, good habits, and correct responses had already been firmly implanted. But even if this had been accomplished, the reconstructed personality might prove no match for the powerful destructive forces unleashed as the individual came into his sexual maturity.

Perhaps this uncertain outcome was the best to be expected. Pessimism was implicit in the cultural and religious misanthropy that pedagogues shared with most of their contemporaries. Nevertheless, they were determined to stay the course. Seven or eight years might be time enough to remake the young. Methods could be improved, techniques refined. Better books, more effective preaching and instruction should eventually leave their mark. Informed and disciplined Christians, the products of their pedagogy, would sooner or later begin to transform a society still perceived largely in terms of adolescence: volatile, rebellious, filled with tensions and violence, incapable of self-regulation, requiring control.

Such doctrinaire assumptions did not necessarily leave Reformation pedagogues insensitive to the young people they tried to press into their mold. But in setting their policies they did allow bloodless stereotypes to dominate their sense of life. It was not the human individual that mattered to them, but the faith they preached and the religious and moral disposition of the society that lived, or did not live, by this faith. They may have been responsive to the charms of childhood and the excitement of youth. But in their pedagogy the young counted only as the recipients of their ideas. Pedagogues thought in abstractions. The "natural child" was one such abstraction; a second was the finished indoctrinated product conceived on the model of a biblical Tobias, an Isaac, or a Joseph. The good society peopled by such types was a third. They had few illusions about the gap separating this ideal from reality, but they remained confident that the means at their disposal sufficed to close it.

CHAPTER 6

PEDAGOGY AND THE FAMILY

Between pedagogue and pupil stood the family. What was its part in the child's religious and civic education? Did this role match the family's social authority as established in custom and law? Preliminary answers to these questions have been suggested in earlier chapters. Events in the 1520s compelled reformers to modify their original hopes for a voluntary program based on family and community participation in Christian instruction. As education came under bureaucratic control, its aims and operations underwent drastic changes. But this altera- tion was not intended to eliminate the household as a focus of child- rearing and socialization. The family remained an indispensable ally in the reformers' pedagogical undertaking. Didactic writings addressed to the heads of households defined the terms of this partnership and enumerated its responsibilities. We may draw on this literature for some concrete clues to the shifting relations among church, state, and family in Reformation pedagogy.

It is a commonplace in Reformation historiography that Luther was instrumental in raising the married state and the family to a new level of theological and social respectability. The contention is true as far as it goes. To make it a significant observation upon events, however, it must be placed in its context. Beyond doubt, marriage and the Christian household were crucially important to reformers. The sheer volume of their words on this subject establishes this. What is not quite so clear is the originality of their contribution. Very little of what they declared on marriage, parenthood, and household man- agement had not been said before. Critical distinctions must therefore be sought not in the novelty of their assertions, but in peculiarities of emphasis and nuance.

Protestant doctrines on matrimony and its many attendant prob- lems—sexual gratification, withdrawal to a private realm of self-interest, interaction with the larger social, political, and religious community, use and abuse of paternal authority, child nurture and first instruction—rested on the same biblical prescriptions as Catholic teachings developed during the three centuries before the Reformation. But agreement on the sources to be cited did not constitute unanimity of interpretation. Few scriptural injunctions were clear enough to be applied without considerable explication. The New Testament offers highly ambiguous guidance on the Christian's duties to home and faith. Depending on where he places the accent, the believer faces or avoids conflict in meeting his obligations. Matt. 10:34–37 seems to call for an uncompromising rejection of all conventional ties: "He who loves father and mother more than me is not worthy of me; and he who loves son or daughter more than me is not worthy of me."[1] The passage's meaning had to be explained, not only in the interest of preserving the stays of traditional society, but also in the light of seemingly competing demands made elsewhere in the gospel. Obedience to the fourth commandment, Honor your father and your mother, is the most imperious of these;[2] no less binding are the rules for the conduct of a Christian household scattered through the Old and New Testaments. Without exception these precepts emphasize the cohesion and closeness of the family as a unit of cohabitation, work, mutual support, loyalty, and love.[3] These maxims—among them the so-called *Haustafeln*, rules for the household about which much more will be said in later pages—evidently presupposed the endurance of family and domestic bonds. Their explicit analogies between domestic obedience and submission to God, between the affections uniting family members and Christ's love for the church,[4] powerfully reinforce the affirmation of family and home as the nucleus of social organization.[5] The household may be an earthly copy of the heavenly home whose head is Christ, but its temporal frame is no less solid for that. The Old Testament offered a wealth of supportive passages[6] on the need to shore up this framework. How then should the Christian divide his allegiance and his duty? How much belongs to Christ ("the head of the body, the church; he is the beginning, the first-born from the dead, that in everything he might be pre-eminent")[7] how much to kin and hearth? If Scripture presented a paradigm for the organization of Christian life, it was one that called for much interpretation.

Few systematic theologians of the later Middle Ages evaded this responsibility. All affirmed that wedlock is a godly estate, serving to propagate the race, to neutralize (through the sacrament of marriage) the concupiscence inseparable from the human need for sexual gratification, and to make visible in concrete associations the indissoluble union of Christ with humanity. This last signification, the symbolic meaning of marriage, was most powerfully expressed in Eph. 5:31–32:

"For this reason a man shall leave his father and mother and be joined to his wife, and the two shall become one. This is a great mystery, and I take it to mean Christ and the church." The passage made an effective rejoinder to denunciations of marital life as a contemptible surrender to the demands of the flesh. Since most medieval discussants of these questions were themselves in holy orders, they could be expected to treat with a certain sympathy the conventional claims to the superiority of celibacy over matrimony. But as commentators on Christian ethics they dared not ignore the pragmatic needs of their society and of the men and women in it. A kind of consensus therefore conceded as a matter of principle the rarer purity and sanctity of the celibate life, while confirming that wedlock was for the great majority of men and women a sensible, proper, and divinely ordained condition, one that allowed them to live at peace with themselves and with God, and to serve nature as well as their faith.[8] Luther accepted this Scholastic solution to the ambivalence of the New Testament, agreeing with the theologians of the church that marriage was sanctified by its nature as a sacrament, as a covenant of fidelity, and as a union issuing in progeny.[9]

Throughout the later Middle Ages one could, of course, hear the voices of ascetic revilers of every concession to carnal needs, and of ferocious misogynists who denounced any and all contact with women.[10] But these fulminations are no more typical of medieval thought on marriage than the erotic fantasies of courtly poets at the opposite end of the continuum. "If bodily nature has been designed by a God who is good," wrote Thomas Aquinas, "it is impossible to assert that a thing which has to do with conserving bodily nature, and which nature prompts one toward, is thoroughly evil."[11] One might regret so grudging an acknowledgment of natural instincts. But it was not a viewpoint confined to "medieval" or Catholic theologians. Luther's views on sex and marriage arose from the same speculations and differed in no important respect from those of Thomas Aquinas. Scholastic authors approved of marriage as a social good and, for ordinary men and women, a haven from lust. Marriage manuals transmitted these views to common folk.[12]

Protestant approaches to the problem of marriage were from the beginning less equivocal than those of their Catholic predecessors. This distinction came not so much from Lutheran theologians' personal preference for marriage, or its propagation as a general good, as from the polemical thrust of Luther's initial pronouncements on wedlock and family life. His early writings on the subject served his stratagem of setting marriage in clear opposition to clerical celibacy, especially to the monastic ethos based on a rigorous interpretation of the vow of chastity.[13] His primary target was the monkish affectation of superior spirituality and holier virtue. Luther's emphatic rejection of these pretensions led him inevitably to a sweeping exaltation of the matrimonial state.

"What a truly noble, important, and blessed condition the state of matrimony is, if properly conducted," he said in a sermon in 1519.[14] Wedlock is a spiritual estate. Those who call it secular have been deluded, especially monks and nuns who—far from being spiritual—are revealed by their lives to be more worldly than lay people.[15] Sanctioned by God's command to men and women to be fruitful and multiply (Gen. 1:28), matrimony is a spiritual association sealed by the unselfish love of husband and wife for each other. The sacrament confirming their union makes of it a sign of something sacred.[16] Every action taken in married life expresses the spirituality of the estate. To earn a living, to keep a roof over the family's head and bread on its table, is to learn a daily lesson in the need for total trust in God, from whose hands all blessings flow. Monks are shut off from this source of faith. But matrimony, with its daily cares and worries, "drives all who live in it to put their faith in God."[17] The ceaseless work required of both partners renders their shared life godly—again in contrast to the useless existence of monks.[18] But the highest spiritual advantages of marriage are brought by the children born of the union of man and wife.[19] To raise one's offspring in the fear of God, to bring them up as Christian servants of their fellowmen—this is the godliest of labors, justifying even the satisfaction of sexual appetites that, were it not for the begetting of children, would be mere fornication, "the destroyer of body and soul."[20] Paul declares (Heb. 13:4), "Let marriage be held in honor among all, and let the marriage bed be undefiled; for God will judge the immoral and adulterous." Luther comments: So much for the "spiritual" celibates of the church. We all know how they keep their chastity. "God will judge them, harlots and fornicators, but he will not condemn faithful husbands and wives."[21] Normal men and women (that is to say, those who are not "eunuchs" in the sense of Matt. 19:12) cannot exempt themselves from God's command to be fruitful; nor does the profession of chastity give them the right, even if they had the power, to suppress "what God has created within them."[22] God has intended us for marriage, the better to serve his purpose in the world. "To a Christian," Luther says, "the whole world is holy, pure, useful, and pious."[23] Considering the deep stain of defilement usually ascribed to "the world" in Lutheran circles, this was a powerful endorsement.

It is evident that a positive strain of thought competes in these sentences with Luther's attack on celibacy and monasticism. In the early 1520s he still thought that the reform of Christian society could best be accomplished through family and congregation. The Christian household was a much more fundamental concern to him than his polemical tilts against the Roman priesthood. He saw it as the source of evangelical impulses in society. He and his followers therefore set out to raise the moral tone of wedded life and household governance. Scripture offered many signposts to this objective, but its suggestions needed to be amplified and applied to domestic use. A whole literature was created to accomplish this task, as will be seen in a moment. The families of Lutheran pastors were to serve as wholesome examples of wedded life, and it is clear that Luther regarded his own household as a model of conjugal and paternal conduct in both its private and its public aspects.

In view of the important role Luther assigned to the reforming mission of matrimony, it is astonishing how little his tracts on marriage say about this objective. The reason is not hard to find. In the 1520s, Luther's comments on marriage and the family moved on conventional paths long ago laid down for the discussion of this topic. The straightest and shortest of these roads led to the conclusion that marriage offers the only acceptable alternative to fornication. Its proof text was Paul's contention that "it is better to marry than to be aflame with passion" (1 Cor. 7:9). Luther comments, "Here Saint Paul shows us the chief reason for marriage, and I can think of no stronger or better one myself: the sexual need. That's what it is, a need [*Not heysst es*]. Nature will out."[24] Praying and fasting are of no help in allaying such a powerful urge. This contention, too, we have on the authority of Paul (1 Cor. 7:5), and we can see its truth in the cases of wretched monks and nuns who "burn" (*brennen*) with lust and are made miserable by it.[25] The answer, then, is with Paul: "Because of the temptation to immorality [Luther renders it "because of whoring"] each man should have a wife and each woman a husband."[26] Luther's final word on this aspect of the problem is entirely traditional.

No less so is his lengthy analysis of the nature of true chastity—again a subject to which his attention was impelled by New Testament proof passages and the Scholastic authors who had commented on them. As was seen in the preceding chapter, Matt. 19:12 gives the only legitimate exemptions from God's command to "be fruitful and multiply." If one is naturally impotent, or has been made so by castration, one clearly cannot marry. There exist also some rare individuals who, as the gospel puts it, "have made themselves eunuchs for the sake of the kingdom of heaven." Luther calls them "spiritually rich and exalted persons, bridled by the grace of God, who are equipped for marriage by nature and physical capacity and nevertheless voluntarily remain celibate."[27] Continence of this high order is a divine gift. Those who possess it need not take wife or husband. "But whoever has not been granted the grace to remain joyfully and devotedly chaste, let him enter marriage."[28] Luther admits—his source and the momentum of traditional interpretation compelled him to do so—that "in any comparison of chastity and marriage, chastity appears as a nobler gift than marriage. But," he promptly adds, "marriage is as great a sign of God's favor as chastity. A man," he continues by way of proof, "is, as everyone knows, a nobler creature than a woman; but this does not mean that woman is a lesser example of God's handiwork than man."[29] It is the same with marriage. He concedes, following Paul and indifferent to contradictions within his own argument, that the celibate "tends to be keener in the service of God"[30] than the married person. But one should not conclude from this contention that the apostle denigrates marriage. "It is true," says Luther, "that the state of celibacy is more serene and offers us greater liberty, but the married state is also good, that is to say it is without sin and is pleasing to God; and therefore everyone is free to choose it." "To sum up this whole chapter, then: No one should marry unless he feels the need to do so. But this need exists wherever God has not by his grace bestowed on a person the noble gift of chastity. No man was ever made by nature to be chaste. On the contrary, we were all made to beget children and to bear the burdens of married life."[31]

These burdens of wedded life formed another conventional topos to which Luther had to pay his respects. "Only a fool takes a wife," said the proverb. "Thus speaks the world," adds Luther, "and our wise men agree."[32] His allusion was to the contemptuous remarks about wives, wedlock, and children that fell from the lips of distinguished scholars in his time. Luther himself disagreed. Misogynists among his colleagues were, he said, merely aping the prejudices of pagan writers "who went out of their way to malign women and hold marriage up to ridicule. 'Short bliss, long disgust'—that's what the world says about it."[33] Luther was at pains to dispel this fabrication. "This is what happens when natural reason, clever harlot that she is, looks at married life. She raises an eyebrow, curls her lip, looks down her nose, and asks, 'Am I going to rock the cradle, wash diapers, make the baby's bed, smell its stench, get up nights to stop its crying . . . ? Will I nurse my wife, slave all my days to feed and clothe her, do this, do that, suffer this and put up with that, not to mention all the other troubles and miseries brought on by wedlock? No, I shan't be caught on this hook. I'll stay single, thank you."[34] To these objections the Christian has but one reply: God made marriage; I am his servant; I comply with his wishes.[35] To the reflective man Luther offers another thought. Let skeptical bachelors and embittered husbands learn to see marriage for what it really is: a godly work, a spiritual service, a condition of Christian life, an image and likeness of heavenly peace and love. If they could but grasp this form, their grumbling would cease.[36] To be sure, painful moments are in store for all who wed. These, Luther

From *Ein kurtzer ausszug auss der christlichen Oeconomia
Justi Menii . . .* (Regensburg, 1554).

insisted, were a wholesome corrective to the pleasures of the marriage
bed. But neither domestic bickering nor sexual desire could subvert the
spiritual nature of the marital bond. To open the eyes of his contemporaries to the true quality of this union was the paramount objective of
everything Luther said and wrote on marriage and family life.

Luther's followers continued this discussion in its established
vein. They wrote advice to young people about to enter wedlock,
"marriage mirrors" (*Ehespiegel*), commentaries on the domestic
maxims in Ephesians 5–6 and Ecclesiasticus, precepts for the Christian
home (*Haustafeln*), bridal sermons, instructions on childrearing, and
so on. For the most part these are bulky volumes, anthologies of prodi-

gious numbers of didactic and moralizing counsels for people who were giving thought (perhaps in response to the Lutheran effort to make them do so) to their obligations as Christian husbands, wives, and parents. Most books of this kind were intended to be studied in the home, to be read aloud to the assembled household. Woodcut illustrations show how reformers imagined the scene: paterfamilias at head of table, wife and daughters to one side, sons to the other, servants at the lower end, the whole company respectfully attentive to the patriarchal voice reading aloud from a huge tome resting before him.[37]

What did the household learn from these books? The first lesson was that God's world is governed by three estates or offices, of which matrimony is the first, the other two being the preaching and the secular power.[38] Foolish "philosophers and other worldly-wise [Weltkluge]" men have misrepresented the matrimonial office as the least of these estates. On the contrary, matrimony is "the mother of all the other orders": "For this reason, if you were to make a picture of matrimony, you would draw it in the likeness of a splendid and beautiful woman of kindly aspect, and under her cloak or seated on her lap you would show a priest with his book, a king holding his sword, a peasant with his hoe, and so on: every trade and station with its special sign and device."[39] More ancient in the order of creation than spiritual and secular government, "matrimony is the source in which all other estates have their origin."[40] Its priority as the first institution given by God to men sanctifies it. A Christian marriage is God's own work. He selects the spouse, "and no human desire or interest can change his choice by a hair's breadth."[41] Instituted to advance God's purposes in the world, "marriage is a conjunction or association in God's word of a man and a woman who, each having agreed to enter their union, promise to stay together until death, avoiding sin and bringing forth good fruit."[42] All writers proclaim the serenity and happiness in store for those who submit to this divine plan: "Christian husbands and wives can say joyfully to God: 'See our dear, loving Lord, how happy we are in the certainty that what we do finds pleasure in your sight.' No priest, monk, nun, or other hellish vermin living in celibacy can say this."[43] In no respect is wedlock inferior to celibacy: Luther's equivocation on this point was abandoned by later authors.[44] Although Christ himself never took a wife, he clearly favored matrimony: "The fact that our dear Lord Jesus Christ was bidden to the wedding [at Cana] and showed himself so willingly and gladly among the guests at the feast is surely a sign of the special honor in which he held the married state."[45] Christ denounced the Pharisees who scorned marriage. He loved children, and must therefore have favored the union that produces them.[46] His spirit lives in the ties joining husband to wife:

If each partner to a marriage is convinced that his spouse is the
fairest and best person on earth, neither will ever become stale in the eyes
of the other. The sun itself shall not smile on him so sweetly as his life's
companion and bed partner whom Christ has given him for wife.[47]

No writer pretended that everyday married life conformed to this
idyll. In fact, a point was made of balancing praise of matrimony with
sober warnings of the many troubles to be expected. "This much is
certain," wrote one author, "God makes the married man bear many
a cross and much sorrow. Unchristian people, wishing to avoid such
troubles, refuse marriage. But the God-fearing Christian consoles himself with the knowledge that God has ordained this union for men's
benefit and will always provide for those who enter it, even changing
water into wine if necessary."[48] The defensive tone pervading such
passages makes one suspect that marriage was held in low esteem
among the public at large: "maligned and rejected, held in contempt
as a nuisance and a bother," as one writer complained.[49] There is some
evidence for the conclusion that traditional male prejudices continued
to be at work in many quarters against the obvious targets: scolding
wives, the cost of raising children, the drudgeries of running a house,
and so on. Lutheran marriage books gave useful advice on how to cope
with these hardships. As for the remaining woes, the remedy was
forbearance. "No Christian can be without his cross."[50] "He who
enters matrimony in obedience to God's command suffers its inescapable trials in good cheer, for he finds his happiness in the fulfillment
of God's word."[51] Perhaps such "consolations to husbands and wives
in times of trouble"[52] gave a measure of help where help was needed.
Their tone is never excessively commiserating. Far from it. By citing
Scripture, precepts, and examples, Lutheran authors gave reassurance
of the godliness and joyfulness of marriage. Wedlock was the right
and proper condition of life, "ordained for a remedy and to increase
the world and for the man to help the woman and the woman the man,
with all love and kindness." The words are William Tyndale's, but the
spirit is that of Wittenberg.[53]

2

If obeying the command to "be fruitful and multiply" was a Christian's first duty to God, his second obligation was to devote himself to
the instruction of his children. All reformers saw this task as the cor-
nerstone of the evangelical society they hoped to build. Merely begetting offspring is not enough, said Luther in 1519. Pagans do this no less
well than Christians. "But to raise children to the honor and glory of
God, and to seek no other goal than this," is a Christian thing to do.[54]

In 1581, long after the major responsibility for religious instruction had been effectively removed from the home, another Protestant pastor thanked God for having "preserved the catechism in our homes and among our parents so that they can, in the morning and again in the evening, explain to their children the commandments, the Apostles' Creed, and the Lord's Prayer."[55] This still seemed the best way, and as a basic principle of evangelical reform it was never renounced. "To bring [children] up as Christians and God-fearing people, to instruct them in the knowledge of God, to teach them to depend on God more than on the world: these are the finest gifts [parents] can make to their children and the richest bequest they can leave behind.[56]

Taking a step or two back from the evidence at this point will allow us to see these expressions of piety in their social context. It does not disparage their spiritual intent to establish the relevance of this context as a vital element in the compound of assumptions, inferences, and responses constituting the Lutheran position on the family. Nor does it lessen the religious force of their pronouncements on the Christian household to demonstrate how closely the reformers were attuned to the family's place in custom, law, and economic life, and how mightily they reinforced its stability while at the same time responding to subtle but unmistakable social shifts affecting its inner cohesion and its position at the foundation of society.

By insisting on the generative priority of the estate of matrimony, Lutheran theologians had themselves introduced the social nexus as a problem for analysis and comment. In the family of their day they recognized, with no less clarity than does the modern social historian, "the final unit of society and . . . the citadel of its values."[57] *Oikos*, the family household, and *oikonomia*, the rules by which this tiny community governed itself,[58] concerned them not only as the focus of private behavior, but also as the matrix of the public community and its moral condition. Reformers made an explicit connection between these two crucial functions of the household. Thus Justus Menius's *Oeconomia christiana*, for which Luther wrote a brisk preface in 1529, prescribed "how each household should be managed in a Christian manner and what the duties of each of its members are toward one another, so that everything in the house will answer to God's commands and ordinances. For," Menius adds, "there can be no doubt of this: from the management of the house flows and derives, as from a fountainhead, the governance of the entire country." *Oeconomia* and *politia* both rest, he says, on the bedrock of the fourth commandment, and this order of things will last as long as the world endures.[59] "Power passes from parents to governments, from householders—who rule privately over their wives, children, and servants—to magistrates and princes who exercise their might publicly over the mass of men."[60]

For this reason magistrates are called *patres patriae*.[61] The semantic power of "father" in civic and religious discourse was greater than the Latin tag suggested (more will be said about this later). But politically, at least, the master of the house was the node linking the private home with the larger community and the commonwealth. Lawyers and theologians agreed on this point. "All orders of human society derive from the first estate, matrimony, which was instituted by God himself [wrote Justin Göbler, a writer of vernacular law books for laymen]. On this origin and foundation stand all the other estates, communities and associations of men. . . . From the management of the household, which we call *oeconomia*, comes the administration of a government, a state being nothing more than a proliferation of households."[62]

The constant reiteration of these venerable commonplaces points to a phenomenon long recognized in the social history of early modern Europe. As in many of their other efforts, reformers were in this instance engaged in a rear-guard action for the stabilization of something that was in fact undergoing a slow but unmistakable transformation. The very vehemence of their insistence on the family's place as the bastion of society's moral and religious health demonstrates their anxiety over its real condition in their day. Frightened witnesses to what they feared was the slow disintegration of the family, they described the overt symptoms of its breakdown, crudely but—by their lights—accurately: shrewish wives, defiant children, impudent servants, irresponsible fathers remiss in performing their duties. Viewing these signs *sub specie societatis*, they observed the drift of things and tried to alter it. But the very remedies they applied were bound to accelerate the current they were attempting to reverse. Setting aside the family's traditional role in education in favor of administrative action directed by the state inevitably speeded the erosion of the household as the source of moral values in society. In pursuing this pragmatically justifiable course of action, reformers were in step with large-scale, long-term impersonal trends toward the restructuring of European society. Forms of organization and social relations were moving toward the bureaucratization of hitherto private functions. Forces largely beyond their control impelled reformers to join this tendency. But their emotional allegiance, and their rhetoric, remained with the ancient ideals. The core of their reforming zeal was and continued to be a conservative, or restitutional, impulse to return to origins. Expediency and necessity dictated a different course. Plainly, the two directions were at odds, although this conflict was perceived but darkly at the time.

Two trends, complementary but mutually contradictory, have been identified by recent historians of the family in its early modern phase of development. One is the prominence in the social fabric of European society of the simple family household,[63] the basic conjugal or "nuclear" family, "not as a unit of cohabitation, which it had always been, but as a focus for psychological loyalty and devotion."[64] Man, wife, dependent children (sometimes with a servant or two) formed the *oikos*, the household, as a dwelling place and, more importantly, an association striving to attain self-sufficiency in the mutual allegiance and support of its members and in the acquisition and conservation of property. This reduction of the family to its essential members seems to have been assisted by the fading of a larger circle of relatives whose kinship ties had once played a significant role in governing family affairs. If this diminution of the "extended family" did in fact occur— historians debate the issue[65]—it happened over a long stretch of time, at a glacial tempo, and with unequal pacing in the various strata of society. All attempts to fix the historical landmarks of this transformation have been frustrated by scarcity of data. It also seems that the family had never been, and did not become in the sixteenth century, the exclusive repository of individual loyalties. A proliferation of formal and informal associations claimed the time and attachment of household members according to their respective ages, sexes, and stations.[66] Nonetheless, despite the vagueness left in our minds by the sketchy and often contradictory evidence, it is a demonstrable fact that during the period under examination here the conjugal, nuclear family household received from many influential quarters the sort of riveted attention that proves its place of importance, even if it does not fully explain how it got there.

But as loyalty shifted from the extended family to the *oikos* at its center, it encountered a second trend straining in the opposite direction. Real authority and concrete power were slipping from the conjugal family into the hands of political rulers in city, territory, and state, and of ecclesiastical bodies acting as their agents. Characteristic functions anciently performed by the family and honored as part of its inviolate preserve of rights and traditions disappeared into the realm of public affairs.[67] State and church, even as they seemed to be mobilizing all available resources of law and exhortation to strengthen the power of husband over wife, father over children, master over servants, were engaged in draining the household association of essential responsibilities. Sermons and proclamations, religious tracts and law books extolled the authority of the paterfamilias. But the real object of these rhetorical acclaims of the fourth commandment was to inculcate in the population habits of submission and obedience leading beyond parents to the higher authorities governing state and church. The two contradictory trends coincided in the sovereignty accruing, or appearing to accrue, to the master of the house. The political community insisted on the subordination of subjects to constituted authority. The religious establishment preached the virtues of acquiescence and complaisance. Within the walls of its home firmly governed by the paterfamilias, the conjugal family was expected to exemplify these traits, the practice of which now constituted its essential social function.

This larger social and political setting explains the reformers' exaltation of the patriarchal family, and of the paternal sovereignty that held it together. Not that this magnification was a new theme. Since ancient times paternal power had been solidly rooted in political custom, law, and theology.[68] Protestants reiterated these familiar formulations, but they did so with an urgency betraying their alarm over the disintegration of society (as they perceived it) and their conviction that a return to social cohesion demanded as a precondition the restoration of familial authority at the center of the social universe.

"Each house under one head, and that head absolute, but not a tyrant." This formula served as the motto for Lutheran homes. "In the good household all things must stand in their proper order. But such an order can exist and endure only where the house is governed by a single head, the husband and father, the master of the house. Should his wife also attempt to be master, the house would have two heads, which is a monstrous thing and repugnant to God's will. Such a house would be divided against itself and it would surely fall."[69] This passage, chosen more or less at random from a large number of similar pronouncements, upholds and justifies, but does not explain, paternal power in the house. Once again one may turn to Luther for explication. *Hausvater*, literally father of the house, is Luther's translation into German of *oikodespotes* in the Greek and *paterfamilias* (with its Roman law associations) in the Vulgate rendition of Matt. 20:1.[70] The word conveys the husband's and father's right to rule the domestic enclave, imperiously but not arbitrarily. Paternal mastership of the house is a considerate, modulated power. While insisting on the close parallels between paternal control and political sovereignty—if the former is shaken, all authority is undermined—Luther is also at pains to discriminate between the two according to the immediacy of each to the natural order of things:

> There is a difference between the power [*Gewalt*] given to parents and the power bestowed on governments. Parents feel a more anxious concern for their children, and their solicitude for them is much greater than is the interest of a government in its subjects. . . . This difference is due to the father's and mother's power being a natural and voluntary [*freiwillige*] power, a dominion over their children rooted in the natural order of things. Governmental power, on the other hand, is an unnatural [*gezwungen*] power contrived by human artifice and ingenuity.

Political authority can therefore be little more than "a watchman over the fourth commandment," as Luther puts it, "like the cat over the mouse." "And this is why parents stand in greater dignity than governments, and more veneration is due them. For they are the fount and origin of the fourth commandment."[71]

Luther's repeated appeal to parents to act as bishops within their four walls[72] defines the nature of their authority. Of their right to total filial obedience Luther permitted no doubt and brooked no qualification. He himself could never forget his father's taunt about his infringement of this absolute right when he entered the monastery in defiance of his father's express wish.[73] But if parents demanded complete obedience, the quality of their rule was to be "fatherly," meaning severe, rigorous, vigilant, but also kindly. This qualification gains great force from the constant parallels drawn between the *Hausvater* ruling his little flock and God the father as sovereign over all his living creatures. God's defining attributes were grace, not vindictiveness, forgiveness, not retribution. The housefather, too, was distinguished from the petty domestic tyrant by his kindness and solicitude. Catechisms often made this comparison explicit. They suggested it also by means of verbal analogues, bound to make an impression on pupils. The Old Testament was particularly persuasive on this point. Sternly but lovingly chastised ("for the Lord reproves him whom he loves, as a father the son in whom he delights"),[74] certain to find help and comfort when needed ("with weeping they shall come, and with consolations I will lead them back"),[75] but never for a moment forgetful of the obedience owing to his begetter ("He said to me, 'You are my son, today I have begotten you' "),[76] the child was to learn at his father's knee that attitude of unquestioning submissiveness combined with trusting dependence which, in the management of the household as in the government of the world, constituted the appropriate response to the divinely established order.

The God-father analogy was the heart and sinews of a stable domestic, political, and religious universe. It lay at the core of every book of religious instruction:

> *Father:* Prove to me that our Lord God wishes to be your father and not your judge and executioner.
> *Child:* I answer with Deut. 32:6, "Is not he your father who created you, who made you and established you?"[77]

"Father is a comforting word," wrote Johann Spangenberg, "for if God is our father, we are his beloved children, and I know that my heavenly father will use me as graciously as a housefather treats his beloved child."[78] God, government, parents were one in possessing the quality of patriarchal dominion with its characteristic amalgam of severity, justice, watchful anxiety, and infinitely caring solicitude. Parenthood deserved to be revered for the troublesome, time-consuming, costly, and self-denying service required of all those who exercised it: "Our parents give us life, true; but they also do much more for us. They nourish us, clothe and instruct us, show us wholehearted devotion and generosity, acting from feelings of deep love and shirking no toil, pain, bother, trouble, or expense. They will gladly suffer poverty and privation for our sake. Day and night they worry about us, even risking their lives and limbs to give us the best of care. They eat their own bread in sorrow and distress so that we, their children, may be happy."[79] God, too, had suffered sorrow for the sake of his wayward creatures. Every child should recognize the countenance of God in his father's careworn features. A verse from a primer conveys this merging of images:

In my dear par-ents will I see
Your hon-ored like-ness, Lord,
As they, with ten-der love for me
Pro-vide my whole sup-port[80]

Similarly, political rulers were to be honored not only for the majesty inherent in their office, but also for their willing assumption of the thankless burden of government. *Hausvater, Landesvater, Gottvater* represented, respectively, the concentric domains and intersecting orders of home, state, and universe. They were united in the exercise of a paternal power combining the sway of unimpeachable authority with the benevolence of loving care. In the coincidence of these qualities one detects the principles of a future political paternalism, whose first outlines were sketched in Lutheran manuals for the master of the house.

Paternal authority and the cohesion of the patriarchal family were moored to solid legal supports whose chief object was the preservation of family property. A variety of props shored up this status quo. Legal majority (and therefore the right to dispose of inherited goods) was fixed at an advanced age, usually twenty-five. Elaborate provisions regulated the wardship of orphans and young people "of frivolous disposition," even if they had attained majority age. A parent's right to disinherit children was sharply limited; on the other hand, filial obedience and "gratitude" were made a condition of coming into bequests. A child's right to choose his own spouse was drastically curtailed.[81] In each of these and similar instances reformers upheld tradition. A later chapter will examine at some length the part played by Lutheran pedagogy in protecting the stays of established society.[82] To be sure, there had been a good deal of slippage in the ground on which these supports rested, and Protestant observers deplored this. They could not escape a measure of blame for it. Luther was well aware of the Pandora's box he had opened with his rejection of monasticism —an action whose purpose had nothing to do with, but which was bound to affect in a most serious way, the property management of families accustomed to conserving their resources by dispatching daughters to nunneries.[83]

At the same time, Luther's extravagant praise of matrimony, and the apparently libertarian bent of his religious message, must have swelled the number of young people prepared to ignore their parents' wishes in choosing marriage partners. Reformers responded vigorously to this mutilation—as they saw it—of the family's authority. Sermon after sermon deplored this abominable form of disobedience, and every catechism made acquiescence in an arranged marriage a proof of loyalty to parents, the social order, and God.[84] Similarly, the generous words about wives and mothers in the Lutheran marriage literature are likely to have raised both the expectations of women and the misgivings of reformers incorrigibly disposed to suspect the female of scheming to exceed her place.[85] In all these respects things seemed to be going awry. The bonds of society were coming loose. Reformers believed that the repairing of these ties must be accomplished where they had had their origin: in the family.

3

As on so many other issues, then, reformers found themselves ambivalent on the role to be played by the family in the moral and religious training of children. They demanded that Christian education be given in the home, and they praised domestic instruction as the most suitable of pedagogical settings. On the other hand, they also exhibited a deep distrust of the individual parent's judgment and, in the end, turned away from private instruction. They never relinquished their conviction that the family represented the ideal milieu in which to learn one's first lessons in telling right from wrong, good from bad, and what one owes to God from what may be given to the world. The tragedy was that so few parents lived up to the ideal. Forced to recognize this fact of life, reformers had to find an alternative. Let us now take a closer look at this process.

We have seen that Luther's original plans for the reform of religious and civic life called for spontaneous actions by individual congregations. As late as the mid-1520s he imagined the Christian congregation as an association of men and women engaged in mutual teaching and learning. Householders would study the Bible "at home, each in his own house, mornings and evenings with his wife, children, and servants so as to make Christians of them, not memorizing and reciting only, but asking what each article means and how they understand it."[86] Trained pastors expounding the doctrine from the pulpit would—Luther thought—guarantee its orthodoxy, while *Hausväter* passing it on to their dependents would disseminate it among the population. Luther's catechism first appeared in a form appropriate to this purpose, printed on a single sheet to be mounted in a prominent place in the home.[87] This was no new departure. Handwritten or printed tablets showing the Lord's Prayer, Apostles' Creed, and Decalogue had since the late Middle Ages been displayed in churches and, occasionally, in private houses.[88] But Luther's catechism caught on as no preceding publication of its kind had ever done. Bugenhagen issued it in book form "for the use of every Christian master of his house,"[89] making available to him "a brief synopsis and compendium of all of Holy Scripture,"[90] as Luther said. Formal catechizing did not, of course, exhaust the parent's teaching responsibilities. By daily example and counsel he was to guide his children's steps on their Christian journey. "This duty makes parenthood immensely rich in good works," Luther said, "for God has given this estate the care of souls upon whom parents may lavish a great plenty of Christian works. Fathers and mothers are apostles, bishops, and pastors to their children as they raise them in the knowledge of the holy gospels. No greater and nobler power exists on earth than that of parents over children, for it is a power both secular and spiritual."[91] Thus parents cooperate with God in his work of redeeming souls.[92] As for themselves: if they perform their office willingly and well, they will find it "the straightest road leading to heaven."[93]

The family's fellowship in Christian instruction was the heart of Luther's evangelical program in his early years as a reformer. If matrimony was validated in the offspring it produced, parenthood justified itself by making Christians of children. Luther's successors reiterated his exhortations to act on these responsibilities. Caspar Huberinus argued in his *German Postil* of 1545 that

> Children are God's gift to husbands and wives. Parents should truly love and cherish such divine treasures, raising and keeping them to the best of their ability in constant remembrance of God's benevolence. When you realize that your children represent God's special blessing and bounty, you will feel for them not only the natural and carnal love that one can observe even in animals, but also a godly and Christian love. In this spiritual love you should raise, guide, and instruct your children to be good Christians and God-fearing people. For it is the richest bequest and the most generous dowry you can make your children that you bring them up to rely on God more than on the world.[94]

Luther's friend Nikolaus von Amsdorf contended that public preaching was not by itself capable of bringing the gospel to people's hearts. What child, he asked, attends so closely to the sermon that he can remember what he has heard? Only the *Hausvater*, repeating it word for word, will cause the lesson to sink in. Amsdorf amplified his argument in a pamphlet entitled *God Has Commanded Parents to Repeat and Explain the Sermon to Their Children and Domestic Servants in Their Home*,[95] a work representative of many books written by earnest Protestant clerics for "the use of the simple, well-meaning Christian householder."[96] Intending to turn the latter into a "home theologian [*Haustheologe*]" to his family,[97] they tried to train him to instruct "each person in his house on how he is to conduct himself, first and foremost toward God and his holy word, and next toward his neighbors, that is to say the authorities [*Oberkeit*], father, mother, wife, children, servants, friends, enemies, and everyone else."[98] All such volumes reflect the clergy's serious concern with the progress of the Reformation, and the conviction that without the continued impetus of domestic instruction its pace and direction would not be maintained. By mid-century many parishes were still without trained pastors. Public response to the new creed was falling well short of expectations.[99] Most disturbingly, deviant doctrines and sects were disfiguring the evangelical movement and sapping its strength. If these defects were to be counteracted, immunization must begin in earliest childhood, in the intimate environment of the home where lessons are learned most willingly and lastingly.[100] But the spread of Lutheran orthodoxy through society was not the only objective of domestic instruction. Believing and living were too closely enmeshed to allow reformers to miss the opportunity of extending their influence to right conduct in public and private life, to the management of home, estate, and business, to the duties of citizenship. These matters received due attention from authors whose chief qualification for offering such guidance was an unquestioning acceptance of the evangelical precepts on which rested all principles of life in society.[101]

It would be idle to attempt to convey a sense of the quantity and bulk of these books. Caspar Huberinus (or Huber), the most prolific writer in this genre, compiled as the capstone of his career a tome of more than six hundred folio pages giving comments ethical and practical on every aphorism in the book of Ecclesiasticus. Entitled *Mirror of Domestic Discipline* (1553), it repeated and amplified much of what Huberinus had already said in earlier books: a *German Postil* in two volumes (1545), several catechisms for home teaching, and a book of sermons (1550).[102] Other writers rearranged Ecclesiasticus topically in the manner of a commonplace book,[103] gathered digests from Scripture under appropriate headings,[104] composed short sermons "to be read aloud by the Christian master of the house,"[105] or turned the catechism into a form suitable for questions and answers at the family table.[106] Most authors tried to bring system and, above all, habit-forming regularity to religious instruction: prayers, catechism questions and answers, Bible passages to be recited "when [children] rise in the morning, go to table, prepare for bed, go out and come in again."[107] The advice to "give them nothing to eat or drink until they have said it correctly," proposed a simple technique of reinforcement.[108] All writers believed that orderly habits were a precondition of effective learning, and that there was no better time to acquire them than infancy and no better place than the home. A somber earnestness speaks from their assurance to fathers and mothers that in their hands rested their children's future lives. Those who evaded this highest duty of their estate, or who performed it badly, faced terrible threats uttered in tones of Old Testament wrath:

> Truly, such parents must pay to the living God a heavy price for having so wickedly despoiled and destroyed their own flesh and blood. Indeed, what they have done is more hideous than the ghastly action of those Jews in the Old Testament who cast their children into the flames as a sacrifice to Moloch. For the pain of the Jewish children lasted only a moment. But the agony to which neglectful parents commit their unfortunate children lasts forever.[109]

This was written in 1573, by Christoph Vischer, a prominent Lutheran ecclesiastic. More than half a century earlier Luther had himself cautioned men and women entering wedlock: "Truly, a noble, great, blessed estate, the estate of matrimony when well conducted," he wrote, "truly a terrifying, dangerous estate when it is abused!"[110] As the decades passed, the dangers appeared more imminent and more grave. It should be noted that in trying to meet these perils, reformers did not limit themselves to exhortations. Nearly every Protestant state included in its civil code laws requiring parents "to raise their children in the fear of God and good discipline, and to give them sound instruction."[111] Ecclesiastical constitutions also made this duty a matter of legal obligation.[112] But enforcing the laws was difficult and frustrating work, as a later chapter will demonstrate to repletion.

In any case, threats and warnings are uncharacteristic of books of domestic instruction, which were intended instead to inspire and encourage, and above all to inform. Much practical advice was given the householder on when, how, and what to say to his family: "When you come home from work in the evening, let this be your foremost task: summon your children and servants to your table, ask them what they have learned that day and what they remember of it. . . . Then read to them a passage or two from the Bible and bid them memorize it well."[113] The evening meal provided the most convenient occasion for instruction: "A pious master of the house will make it a custom for his children to give a devout recitation of the whole catechism each evening before the meal is served."[114] Such mealtime devotions are fondly evoked in a scene from a contemporary play, where a widow recalls peaceful hours around the family table:

> We lived in fear of God, we four.
> Seated at table we broke bread
> While from the word of God he read,
> And nourished us more from the good book
> Than from the food and drink we took.[115]

Servants, too, were considered to be under the householder's spiritual charge. Before taking on hired hands he must, he was told, ask not only "whether they can cook, sew, scrub, but also how well they know the main articles of Christian doctrine and if they can sing the words and melodies of our common Christian hymns." He must include servants in all family devotions and see that they go punctually to their catechism classes.[116]

An important question has for some time been lurking in the background of this discussion, and it must now be brought to the fore: the problem of literacy. Reformers and their governments seem to have taken it for granted that nearly every head of household could read, not painfully or haltingly, but with fluency and expression. Could this have been true? How common was literacy in mid-sixteenth-century Germany? Did reading competence reach the level of what would appear to have been the reformers' expectations?

An extended analysis of this puzzling problem must be postponed until a later chapter.[117] Here I wish only to suggest that the ability to read with fair facility was evidently much more widespread in sixteenth-century German society than is ordinarily recognized. General illiteracy would have made nonsense of the Lutheran endeavor to promote domestic instruction. It could therefore be reasonably argued that the reformers' ceaseless efforts to involve the family—at least among the urban and rural well-to-do—in Christian instruction constitutes in itself a kind of proof of extensive literacy. But there is better evidence. Mandates and visitation directives in Protestant lands plainly assume literacy as the norm, illiteracy as the exception, and not only in populous cities. Pastors in Saxony, for instance, were told in 1555 to make annual visits to every large village (*Flecken*) in their parishes and "summon the members of each household to appear before you and give a catechism examination to all those who cannot read."[118] This seems to suggest that a good proportion even of rural parishioners were presumed literate enough to study the catechism. In towns and cities expectations were even higher. In his *Mirror of Domestic Conduct for Simple Housefathers and Their Servants* of 1552, Caspar Huberinus urges householders to enroll their sons in Latin schools, particularly if they themselves are ignorant of the learned tongue, so that, he said "someone in the house will be able occasionally to recite a passage in Latin." He does not appear to have doubted the housefather's ability to read in the vernacular.[119]

Particularly interesting corroboration comes from Bavaria, where possession of Lutheran texts was automatically equated with opposition to the Catholic regime. Bavarian visitation officials had instructions to ferret out suspicious books, and the result of their probes (in the 1560s) is exceedingly suggestive. "The common man [*der gemain man*] here keeps in his home Lutheran catechisms, postils, and other poisoned writings"—this from the bishopric of Eichstätt.[120] "The priest here" (a parish in the city of Wasserburg) "thinks that outlawed books are hidden in every house in the city."[121] He would scarcely have had reason to worry about this had he not assumed the presence of a reading householder in each home. Nor was this phenomenon limited to the cities. "Many peasants [*paueren*] hereabouts own misleading and corrupting books"—from a village in the bishopric of Freising.[122] In many places the authorities found "that the reading of wicked, sectarian, heretical Bibles, Gospels, postils, prayer books, hymnals, polemical tracts, and books of slander, has done grievous harm in people's minds."[123] The mandates issued by the Bavarian government under Duke Albrecht in the 1560s strongly suggest that literacy in the countryside was more pervasive than anyone had suspected. The total picture is of course much more differentiated than that, and this will be noted in due course. But it is clear that a large enough proportion of the ordinary people in Bavaria could read to make literacy appear to be a source of danger to the stability of the state.

Among Protestants reading was—or at any rate it was hoped that it might be—one of the chief means of implanting the evangelical faith in the individual. It will be seen later how reading was encouraged, taught, and promoted. The story is complicated and requires a more balanced presentation than seems appropriate in this chapter. But it is clear that the writers of books of domestic instruction felt certain of access to a sizable readership. Common sense and simple arithmetic will tell us that this circle of readers must have been limited by the high cost of buying books. But, given interest and reading ability, books could be, and probably were, borrowed and shared,[124] and authors knew of this practice. They appealed to their readers to employ their reading skill in the service of the reforming enterprise, above all to use it in doing their duty to children and other dependents in their homes. If this were done, and done well, immeasurable gains would result: a harmonious, mutually supporting household, confident, cheerful labor among all, paternal authority reinforced, children able to face both life and their maker as Christians, and above all a pious deed precious in the sight of God and sure to be rewarded by him. Biblical and historical examples gave proof of the blessings conveyed on everyone who performed this most demanding and essential of good works.[125]

Was it in fact done? The sources give some hints that occasionally, at least, it was. Felix Platter, the Swiss physician, recalled late in life how deeply he had been impressed by family Bible reading when he was very young, in the early 1540s. "My father used to read to us, before we went to church, and preach from holy Scripture. This affected me mightily, and I can remember thinking, 'how is it that there are godless people? Are they not afraid of hell?'" He adds, "I have often since reflected that I was more pious in my childhood than later in life, when I got involved with the world."[126] This slackening of religious commitment was a common phenomenon. The question for reformers was not only: How well is instruction given in youth? But also, does it last throughout life? The evidence on this point was discouraging. It is interesting, however, that the ideal situation portrayed in books of domestic instruction seems to have been most closely approximated where Lutherans were a harassed minority. Some illuminating facts about this come, once again, from Bavaria, where Duke Albrecht V moved in the late 1550s to extinguish all forms of Protestantism. Visitations in 1558 and 1560 brought to light telling information on how Lutherans, separated from the mainstream of their group, managed privately to keep their spirits up and their religion alive: "In Matrigkofen the count reads to his whole household every Sunday from the gospel and from Luther's postils. If someone misses these readings he gets nothing to eat that day."[127] Precisely the procedure suggested by Lutheran authors! In another parish all members were listed as good Catholics save one who, according to the local priest, "reads to his children from Luther's postils."[128] In 1565 it was said of a suspect in Ingolstadt that "his five children have in their possession little booklets containing the gospels and epistles for Sundays and the other holidays. He says that he reads these books with them to instruct them in the word of God and in what their duties are."[129] These Bavarian samples seem to show that in this respect, as in so many others, strength of conviction grew from adversity.

But where people had settled into the routines of officially established orthodoxy, they seemed to lapse into indifference. Lutheran ecclesiastics themselves verified this. From the middle of the century, visitation after visitation discovered that "few parents pray with their children before the meal; they do not even say the evening blessing."[130]

Most books of domestic instruction take note of these disappointing signs. "Many parents are neither pious nor well-meaning enough to be entrusted with the education of their children."[131] Too busy, incompetent, or merely indifferent,[132] "they think they have done enough if they feed and clothe them and put aside a little money for a dowry or an inheritance."[133] These typical comments acknowledge the facts of the situation, but they do not admit failure. Householders continued to be reminded that they must do better. But the notion, once set forth in all seriousness, that reform could proceed from within the home and the congregation was now being abandoned as a matter of practical procedure.

A dual policy thus evolved. In principle, parents were responsible for the Christian instruction of their offspring. Even where circumstances clearly made it impossible for them to possess or deploy enough knowledge to train their children to minimum standards of Christian citizenship, they were nonetheless expected to do so.[134] On the other hand, as a matter of preeminent public policy, all states and state churches possessed, or adopted in the course of the sixteenth century, instruments for usurping parental responsibilities for the instruction of children. In a time of divisive sectarianism and heterodoxy, this was in any case the safest course.[135] Nearly everywhere school attendance was demanded (made obligatory is too strong a word, though this was the intention) and assiduously promoted. "Although no decree ought to be necessary to compel parents to do their duty to their own children," stated the school ordinance of the city of Nordhausen in 1583, "we are aware of a great failing on their part, because so many of them do not know what it means to instruct children. Parents and guardians shall therefore send their children to school so that in their early childhood they may learn to pray, know God, and acquire discipline, decency, and sound skills."[136] Primary parental responsibility was never abrogated. But when not acted upon, which was usually the case, it was resolutely superseded.

Ideally, the two authorities worked in partnership. The family was too vital an element in the structure of society for a reduction of its role to be countenanced, particularly in an activity with such far-reaching political, social, and religious repercussions as early education. Parental authority was so important a cohesive factor in society that its weakening could not be permitted. In his total dependence on his parents the young child first experienced the terrors and joys of the individual's relationship to God. From the respect and obedience owing to them he first learned to acknowledge his place in the system of superordination and subordination defining all associations, human and divine. It was in the small world of the household that he learned his first lessons as God-fearing Christian and faithful citizen.[137]

Family and household were sacred institutions. Both state and church sought to invigorate the bonds among the members of this little community. Far from allowing public instruction to divide children from parents, church and government sought to utilize it to bring them into closer union. Nearly everywhere regulations required children to share with their parents the fruits of their learning. "Let the boys read to their parents every day an article from the catechism and also sing them a psalm or two."[138] "On Saturday evening children should read the Sunday gospel to their parents and the whole household.[139] Wherever possible parents ought to oversee instruction, encourage, spur, and—if required—punish their children. Christoph Vischer, so often quoted in this chapter, saw in this collaboration the chief service of parenthood.

> In addition [to public instruction and examinations] all parents are obliged on danger of losing their souls to teach the catechism to their children and domestic servants. Every day, let your children recite the main articles of the catechism, taking care that they speak clearly and pronounce distinctly. Ask them also what they remember from last Sunday's sermon, and, if they remember nothing, admonish them to pay closer attention. And if kind words don't help, take the stick to them or give them nothing to eat and drink for supper until they have repeated something from the sermon.

For, he concludes, "parents are truly bishops in their own homes. What the pastor is to his congregation, the master of the house must be to his family."[140] Lutheran reformers never gave up hope that this wish might one day be turned into reality.

PART 2
DOCTRINES AND INDOCTRINATION

CHAPTER 7

MODELS AND IDEAL TYPES

A set of linked assumptions and expectations impelled the German reformers to proceed with the indoctrination of the young and dictated their choice of a method. Religious and moral instruction was a necessary stage in the sanctification of the Christian individual and a precondition of reform in society. The religious and social agitation of the 1520s made it a matter of urgency to begin such a program of instruction as soon as possible. Their analysis of the human mind had convinced them that mass instruction in the rudiments of religious and civic morality was practicable. Received opinions concerning character formation and the shaping of conduct encouraged them to suppose that a beneficial alteration of the human personality was a feasible undertaking. The only proviso was that systematic instruction commence in early childhood and that rigorous methods of habit forming be employed. Governments stood ready to supply initiative and drive. Pious households gave support where it was needed at the grass roots.

These were compelling presuppositions, but Lutheran reformers were not so naive as to count on easy work and swift success. Expecting little from the generation already grown to adulthood, they attached their hopes to those still young enough to be molded to their exacting standards of right thought and conduct. What were these standards? Before examining, in the next two chapters, the techniques of indoctrination available to Lutheran pedagogy, let us consider the models set for both pupils and pedagogues as the paradigms of religious and moral attitudes and behavior.

1

All Lutheran pedagogues agreed on the qualities of mind and

135

heart to be fostered in the young. Compared with the liberal educational goals of a later day, these traits strike us as restrictive, not to say repressive. Far from setting out to prepare the child to exercise independent judgment, encouraging in him flexible attitudes, training his mind to assimilate the greatest possible number of experiences while convincing him that his personality is complex, the reformers attempted by means of rigid discipline to subdue those traits that promoted in the adult person contumacy, self-absorption, assertiveness, curiosity, and the restless search for new satisfactions. They saw the greatest danger to man's soul in his tendency to relate all experience to himself and to take his own senses as the measure of all things. Their model Christian was an essentially passive being prepared to acquiesce rather than struggle, distrustful of his own inclinations and reluctant to act on them, diffident, ready to yield where his personal wishes collided with approved norms, unsure of his private judgment, hesitant to proceed where no one guided him, certain only of his weakness as a creature and of the mortal peril of his condition as a sinner.

This type emerges forcefully, and with special relevance to the subject of education, from a striking passage in Luther's response of 1525 to Erasmus's treatise on the freedom of the will. In the course of his passionate refutation of Erasmus's insistence on the necessity of free moral choice, Luther seized upon an analogy used by Erasmus to illustrate the relationship between God's role and man's in the process of salvation. A father, Erasmus wrote, will always support a small child taking its first steps. He will point to an apple placed a short distance away, suggest with encouraging words and signs that the child can reach it, then steady its faltering steps to the object, "so that led by its father it obtains the apple which the father willingly puts in its hand as a reward for running." Not so, counters Luther. Fathers act quite differently in such a situation, and with the opposite end in mind: "How often do parents have a game with their children by telling them to come to them, or to do this or that, simply for the sake of showing them how unable they are, and compelling them to call for the help of the parents' hand!" This, Luther contends, is God's way with men. It is his manner of showing us our incapacity. "God is putting us to the test so as to lead us . . . to a knowledge of our impotence." He plays with us like an austere father who, by asking his child to do the impossible, demonstrates its total dependence on him, thus impressing on it a sense of its utter helplessness whenever it lacks support from above.[1]

Obviously, as man and father, Luther did not act with the calculating coldness of the paternal doctrinarian in his example. But as a theologian Luther saw things differently. The sturdy arms of the law with which God appears to prop up fallen man serve only to cast him down again. Constantly exhibiting man's inability to fulfill divine expectations, the law is the voice of God's wrath and the sign of his stern justice. The little nursery vignette from Luther's *De servo arbitrio*, while concrete and vivid *in conspectu Dei*, thus hovers above the human scene as an ephemeral abstraction. Far from reflecting reality, or intending to do so, it represents the normative values of a theology grown distant from life and the realm of human motivations. No one could have recognized or accepted it as a practical guide to childrearing. But its agreement with fundamental points of doctrine made it a highly suggestive paradigm of the human condition, and its schematic father and child figures became the symbols held up by generations of Lutheran educators as models of good Christian qualities.[2]

Personifications of these qualities filled the pages of educational books. The most representative and most often cited of them was the youth Tobias who, lifted from the rambling narrative in the book of Tobit,[3] stood in the didactic literature of the Reformation as the exemplar of a devoted son and dutiful Christian. Mindful of his father's counsel on how to bear himself in life (Tob. 4:3–19), observant of the divine law, especially of its fourth commandment, Tobias was everyone's favorite son. "Who is the child who never caused his parents any grief?" asked Michael Saxo in his *Christian Pastimes and Spiritual Riddles*. "Answer: Young Tobias, who refused to pay court to a woman while he was away on a journey, explaining that he did not wish to cause his parents grief by acting without their consent. Nor did he tarry long in that distant place, fearful of giving them concern over his long absence."[4] Jörg Wickram's verse drama about Tobias, a play "profitably to be read by all Christians, young and old,"[5] reveals Tobias's exemplary qualities in every life situation. He trusts God, he displays devotion and obedience to his parents, he receives his father's instructions with a willing mind and an open heart. His speech and manner are modest. He shows respect to personages in high places, kindness to fellow Christians in all stations, and generosity to the unfortunate. Every line he speaks points a salutary lesson.

> My father, your command always
> I shall obey, as is my place
> By right and by divine decree,
> Which children must learn willingly.[6]

Eager to spare his parents needless distress, he politely but firmly declines his host's invitation to extend his stay:

> No no, my father would be grieved.
> My mother, too, weeps many a tear,
> Her heart oppressed by pain and fear;

> They count the hours night and day
> And find no peace while I'm away.[7]

His every action exemplifies the principles imparted to him by his father on the eve of his journey.

> Throughout your life, my son, keep God
> Before you as you walk abroad;
> No step you take, no word you say
> Shall cause your deeds and thoughts to stray
> From virtue and from God's commands,
> And from his holy ordinance.
> Give to the poor a daily share
> Of your receipts, it's right and fair
> To help where charity is due;
> God will reward you for it, too.
> Do unto others as you would
> Have them use you: be true and good.
> Give to the hungry drink and bread,
> Offer the homeless roof and bed;
> Keep clear of sinners, never go
> With sons who cause their parents woe.
> Always ask counsel of the wise.
> Above all, raise to God your eyes,
> Beg him to guide your steps, and pray
> That you may follow in Christ's way.
> Each day take stock of what you've done,
> And keep these precepts, my dear son.[8]

Forever held up as a model to the young, Tobias stood in the posture of obedient and respectful compliance appropriate to all Christians, young and old. Having tested these qualities in life, moreover, he proved that they did not go unrewarded. Tobias died, the book of Tobit notes, "greatly respected at the age of one hundred and seventeen" (Tob. 14:14). Revered by men and loved by God, he was an example of a Christian life well spent.

Pietas—dutiful conduct motivated by reverence willingly given to God, parents, and others in positions of sovereignty—*pietas* was the salient attribute of the evangelical youth. Its essence was unquestioning and unqualified submissiveness. "Who were the most obedient of all children?" asks Michael Saxo in another of his Christian riddles. "Answer: the first was Isaac, son of Abraham, who in silent compliance with his father's instructions gathered the wood to build the altar on which he was to be sacrificed, and then held still under his father's hands while he was bound and made ready to be slain with the sword. The second was Jesus Christ who, in full obedience to his father, bore the cross on his shoulders, carried it to the place of execution, and there gladly and patiently suffered a most humiliating and painful death."[9]

History furnished many other salutary models. Telemachus in the Odyssey illustrates the lengths to which a loving son goes in the service of his father. His story was to be read "as an example of a child's most pious duty, the obedience and reverence he owes to his father."[10] "Galen, the excellent physician, whose like was not seen again after the death of Hippocrates, loved and honored his father above all measure, for he never failed in his medical writings to make affectionate mention of him, recording many admirable things, and at such length and with such evident delight that whoever reads his books will agree that it was Galen's greatest joy to honor his father's memory, a sentiment which we may take as evidence of the sincere filial love he bore in his heart." This story, from Zacharias Rivander's *Example Book*,[11] is supported by scores of similar cases in point. "Pomponius Atticus, a Roman knight and scion of a noble family and lineage, had such heartfelt filial piety for his mother that he used to swear by the heavenly powers that in his entire life he had never once angered or in the least degree offended her. Indeed a lasting peace and unity reigned between them until the day she closed her eyes and died. A wholesome example for us all."[12] Charlemagne loved his mother so fervently that "to the end of her days his behavior toward her gave evidence of a willing obedience and submissiveness. Let this exalted sovereign serve as a distinguished example of a son's love and devotion to his parents."[13] Even the animal kingdom honors the obligations of the fourth commandment. "In the lion" (still quoting from Rivander), "God has given us one of the best examples of a child's love and piety for his parent. When the king of the beasts grows too old to seek his food by hunting and prefers to lie safely in his den, his young sons invite him to go with them some distance on their predatory prowls; when they have killed a prey, they make a loud roaring to summon their father and faithfully divide their booty with him."[14]

Such nature stories proved that disrespect for parents was not only a violation of the divine command, but also an unnatural and perverse act. A stirring example of this rule (from Rivander again) occurred in the life of the German emperor Henry V, who, goaded by pope and bishops and "acting contrary to all divine and natural precepts, hounded his father to death. But even in so spoiled a child there flickered a spark of that natural love that all children feel for their father, providing us with another example to show that God has so fashioned his creatures that children must needs love and honor their parents." The Church having refused hallowed ground to receive his father's body, "Henry's heart spoke within him" and prompted him to give the old emperor Christian burial. Rivander comments: "From this case wicked children should learn that whenever they offend or distress their parents, they at once feel the gnawing of their bad conscience. Let every child heed this warning and guard with all his might against offering any slight or insult to his parents. Let him honor and obey them at all times and perform willingly and in good faith whatever deeds may contribute to their pleasure and comfort."[15] Admonitory examples abounded of disobedient, disrespectful, or even mutinous sons. "Let these wretches be judged and condemned by the fourth commandment," says Rivander.[16] The bad end awaiting such an ingrate—"miserably dragging out his life in gaol, . . . excluded from the Christian church and handed over to the devil"—was persuasive testimony to "that ancient truth first pronounced by the wise pagan, Orpheus":

> Who holds his parents in contempt
> Will suffer painful punishment.[17]

An important extension of the obligations arising from the fourth commandment was the insistence that honor and obedience owing to parents are not diminished by unbecoming conduct on their part. Parents and, of course, others in authority command respect not only when they appear dignified and admirable, but also, or especially, when they are seen in circumstances that tend to humiliate them or when, being merely human, they have blundered. Defined as "an attitude that condones, forgives, and overlooks the transgressions of our parents and superiors,"[18] this duty received a graphic emblem in the so-called drunkenness of Noah. The episode, lapidarily described in Gen. 9:20–23, was expatiated at great length in Reformation didactics. The book of Genesis relates the incident as follows.

> 20. . . . [Noah] planted a vineyard; 21. and he drank of the wine, and became drunk, and lay uncovered in his tent.
> 22. And Ham, the father of Canaan, saw the nakedness of his father, and told his two brothers outside.
> 23. Then Shem and Japheth took a garment, laid it upon both their shoulders and walked backward and covered the nakedness of their father; their faces were turned away, and they did not see their father's nakedness.

Sixteenth-century woodcuts and engravings depicted this scene vividly: Noah slumped unconscious on the ground, his bloated Silenus face besotted with drink, his genitals exposed by the disarrangement of his cloak as he had fallen in his stupor. Shem and Japheth hurry to his side with a covering garment, respectfully averting their eyes. Only Ham looks on, staring fixedly at his father's private parts and, lest the direction of his gaze be missed, pointing with forefinger extended.[19] "Shem and Japheth covered their exposed father, and were blessed for it," one catechist commented. "But Ham, who mocked his father's

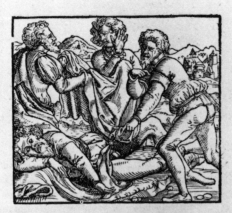

Honora patrem tuum & matrem
tuam.

Quæ eſt ſententia ?

Parentibus & ſuperioribus tuis pro-
pter Deum obedias, & præſtes officia de-
bita cum uera reuerentia cordis, agno-
ſcens à DEO ſic ordinatum eſſe ut obedias.

Quid præcipit ?

Sancit ſocietatem in genere humano
& ordinem politicum,conſtituit Regimen
inter homines, & præcipit obedientiam
                                    erga

From Valentin Trotzendorf, *Catechesis scholae
Goltpergensis* . . . (Wittenberg, 1558), E 7r.

nakedness, was cursed." Noah's "nakedness" being explicitly obvious
in all illustrations of the scene,[20] the sexual ingredient added a sinister
resonance to the main thrust of the message, which was, of course, the
political imperative contained in the fourth commandment. "Moses,
therefore, holds up Ham as a horrible example that should be carefully
impressed in church," Luther wrote in commenting on the Genesis
passage, "so that young people may learn to respect their elders,
magistrates, and their parents." Ham, Luther adds, pushing his argument as far as it will go, "felt a satanic and bitter hatred against his
father." His despicable act, and Noah's shame, he goes on, "are
recorded for the sake of their descendants and of every one of us to
take warning." From Shem and Japheth, on the other hand, we should
learn what we owe to all seniority and authority, and the spirit in which
we should perform our obligations.[21] "Let Noah's good sons be an

example to us," wrote the well-known Latin teacher Valentin Trotzendorf in his catechism. "They averted their faces from their father's disgrace and covered his nakedness. Let us learn from this to overlook, rather than point out, the frailties of our governments, which are in any case due less to the errors of those who rule over us than to the troublesome times in which we live."[22] "You must avert your eyes," warned another catechist, "from the weaknesses of your parents and of all those whom the fourth commandment places in your parents' stead."[23]

Pietas, then, calls for an attitude of reticence and forbearance toward one's superiors. This lesson was incessantly driven home. "Humility is a child's highest virtue," declared Caspar Huberinus in his *Mirror of Domestic Conduct*, commenting on Eccles. 3:17.[24] "It is the nurse and mother of all moral excellence in children," added Christoph Vischer, who goes on to define it as comprising "tenderness [*Sanftmut*] and leniency [*Glimpflichkeit*],"[25] attributes for which Christ himself is the exemplar, a patient sufferer content to make God's will his own. Training to this attitudinal disposition was begun in early childhood. Among the short monosyllabic sentences in a primer printed in Nuremberg in 1534, one finds the following: "It is not my will"; "No good thing is in us"; "You will be saved without your own work."[26] Used as points of indoctrination for the very young, these affirmations of naive trust reveal the religious and psychological source of the child's humility: his simple and total reliance on divine predisposition. Scripture, history, and literature supplied the evidence that this trust was not misplaced. Thus the heroine of Paul Rebhun's biblical drama *Susanna* points to the happy ending of her trials as vindication of her unswerving reliance on God. She says to her children:

> My dearest boy, and daughter, too,
> Let this be an example to you.
> Place love and trust in our Lord God,
> Honor him well in deed and thought,
> For you have witnessed here how he
> Has wonderfully rescued me,
> Has saved my life and reputation,
> Brought to an end my tribulation.

The boy, Benjamin, agrees:

> Yes, mother dear, we do avow
> To be more pious than ever now.

And the girl, Jahel, chimes in:

> And I'll try harder to obey!

Mother adds:

> Yes, girl, and don't forget to pray.[27]

Stage plays, incidentally, were considered of great utility in influencing the minds and consciences of the young and simple. Jesuit pedagogy is well known for the integral place given to the theater in its system of education,[28] but Protestants had learned this lesson much earlier. "In our present situation," wrote Wenceslaus Linck, the Nuremberg reform preacher, in 1539, "we must use rhymes, songs, proverbs, comedies, and tragedies to dress up God's word and doctrine. The mad world, and especially the ignorant and indifferent young people in our midst, will not sit still long enough to listen to a sermon or a word of friendly counsel. But by means of these entertainments we may win them over to the lessons we want to teach them."[29] Linck presented this argument in an endorsement of Leonhard Culman's *A Christian German Drama, Showing How a Sinner Is Converted into a Contrite Man,* an entertaining masque that made use of bizarre incidents and comic divertissements to convey a serious underlying message laid down with a heavy didactic hand. Unswerving trust in divine grace, so went the lesson, is the Christian's only path to salvation. Ambition, friendship, and worldly success may gratify him briefly; and the play depicts these joys entertainingly with a wealth of theatrical detail.[30] But the emotional impact lies in the contrast between men's frantic exertions for worldly honors and the confidence and calm displayed by the true Christian. The moral is never less than blatantly explicit. It is acted out in the plot, announced in programmatic declarations by leading characters, reiterated by the narrator, and summarized by an epilogue as a word of parting advice to spectators and readers. In Culman's *A Pleasant and Spiritual German Play about the Widow* (i.e., the woman in 2 Kings 4 whose sons were rescued from enslavement by Elisha) the concluding moral is put in the mouth of the boy, Aser, who speaks it in the authentic voice of the Lutheran catechism:

> Dear God, our Lord in heaven high
> Your name be praised eternally!
> You've paid our debts, with grace to spare
> To count before your judgment chair.
> You promise aid when we're in need,
> As in your holy writ we read.
> On this pledge rests our entire trust.[31]

The pedagogical effectiveness of biblical dramas may be gauged from the eagerness of both Protestant and Catholic authorities to instigate and support theatrical performances in conjunction with catechism classes.[32] But theater was only one of the many means for reaching the young and simple. "Example books" gave vivid instances of approved behavior suitable for emulation, and they had much to say on the virtue of humility. "A fine example of humility" was pointed out by Zacharias Rivander in his anthology of wholesome cases in point. He tells the story of Frederick, first margrave of Brandenburg, who was unwilling to pass his crown to his heir Johann, deciding instead to elevate a younger son. Johann's speech in response to the news was, according to Rivander, a model of Christian humility and filial submissiveness. "To this discovery Johann replied as follows: 'For some time now, dearly beloved father, I have suspected that you hold my brother in greater affection and esteem, for you have shown him more openness of spirit than you have been able to show me. But I see now how kindly disposed you are toward my person, and I accept with deep gratitude your decision to assure my peace of mind by keeping from me the heavy duties of government with which, in your new will, you have burdened my brother.'" "This," Rivander concludes, "is a most praiseworthy example of a son's humble and trusting acquiescence in his father's wishes."[33] He did not need to underline the parallel to God's way with men. Erasmus Alberus's *Ten Dialogues for Children Who Are Learning to Talk,* originally written for the author's own three-year-old daughter and her playmates, recounts, in the preface "To the Children of Hamburg," the tale of the girl Cecilia who died in an edifying manner, exhibiting her perfect love and trust in God. "And when it was time for God to call the beautiful little Cecilia to come to him, and she lay on her bed ready to die, she once more affirmed her belief that it was for our sake that Jesus was nailed to the cross to die. And having said this, she stretched out her arms like Christ on the cross, and thus gave up the ghost."[34]

In the short conversation pieces of which his book consists, Alberus prepared the intellectual and psychological ground for such an act of peaceful surrender. Counting her blessings—Jesus is her brother, she herself is at once his sister, his daughter, and his bride—the little girl in the dialogues expresses her joy in the "unspeakable splendor" of her condition. Her father asks: "How is it, dear child, that such distinction comes to one of our humble station in life?" She answers, "it comes from God's mercy alone, father dear." "Shall we then thank God in all eternity?" "Yes, father, I shall always be grateful to God." "Who has given you mouth and tongue to thank God with?" "Our dear Lord Jesus." "Who has given you eyes to see him with?" "Our dear Lord Jesus." "Who has given you ears to hear . . . feet to walk?" "Our dear Lord Jesus." "Did our Lord Jesus give you all these?" "Yes, all these, father; our Lord Jesus has given me everything." "Why, child, he must be a gracious good lord indeed, who shows us so much kindness!" "That he is, father." "And can this gracious lord also be angry with us?" "Yes, he can be angry, too, although he does not like to show his wrath, except to wicked people who hate him. But whoever humbles himself before him, confesses his sins and craves his forgiveness, will receive from him all that his heart desires."[35]

Submissiveness and trust were the dispositions most insistently pressed upon the young. Their antithesis was epitomized in the word *sicher*—meaning self-assured, cocky, safe—the epithet invariably employed to designate, first, a false sense of security leading sinners to consider themselves shielded from God's wrath; second, that pervasive human inclination to assertive self-confidence coupled with indifference to consequences, which most reformers blamed for the rampantly asocial and self-destructive drift of things in their time. *Sicherheit*, ignorantly insolent self-assurance, is the mark of the unreconstructed sinner whose impenetrable shell of smugness insulates him from the spirit of the gospel and the exhortations of its ministers. "Never have people been more cocksure of themselves [*sicherer*] than in our own time," wrote Andreas Musculus,[36] recalling the days of the early martyrs, "when the world was not yet so deeply set in its great wickedness and complacence [*Sicherheit*]."[37] Luther's Table Talk records that "in the year 1539 the conversation turned to the great *Sicherheit* of people in this last age. Doctor Martin said, 'would that people were not deluding themselves with this false sense of security. They don't realize how many powerful adversaries and enemies are against us— I mean the devils, of whom there are so many that one cannot count them.'"[38] Another time he said, "'when people have become overconfident [*sicher*] . . . it's a sure sign that God is about to deprive them of his word and pure doctrine and is ready to abandon them to the arrogance of their false hearts.'"[39] To Melanchthon, a "false sense of self-sufficiency in life [*Sicherheit des Lebens*]" was the characteristic trait of the unregenerate.[40] The more calamitous the time in which men lived, the more brazen their reckless self-assurance. Apocalyptic writers did not fail to interpret the increase of *Sicherheit* as a sign of doomsday approaching.[41]

Sicherheit was the attitude diametrically opposed to that unconditional acceptance of human sinfulness which admitted that (to quote from a catechism) "man's natural powers—reason, understanding, heart, sentiment, sense, and will—are set against God; man is God's enemy, and there is nothing good in us."[42] It was the delusive presumption of *Sicherheit* that made the world into "a foul sty inhabited by evil, disgraceful people, enemies and blasphemers of God."[43] With *Sicherheit* a man succeeded in the world, growing fat on the misery of his fellows, "robbing, stealing, deceiving and defrauding because he is ashamed of Christian poverty."[44] "By imbuing us with a false sense of our security, the world's riches and honors lure us from the straight path to salvation."[45] "The topsy-turvy way of the world"[46] was the path of foolish aims and misconceived goals. "He prays rightly," wrote Andreas Musculus in his *Directions for Prayer*, "who sees in himself the cause of all that is ugly and contrary in his life. He also prays rightly who claims no credit for the good he does."[47] *Sicherheit* was irreconcilable with man's recognition of himself as a sinner. It was the function of pedagogy to instill in the child the full measure of this self-awareness, thereby inuring him to the blandishments of a false sense of security promoted by a fraudulent world.

2

We shall see in the following chapters how pedagogues endeavored to convey this self-image to their pupils. Here it should be noted that the catechisms serving them as their main teaching tool supplied, in their docile child respondents, the most consistently developed examples of approved attitudes and sanctioned behavior in the young. Heard from only when spoken to, tractable to a fault, gratefully receptive of good advice, betraying no trace of boldness, erudite on holy subjects and conversing on them like a book, the responding children of Lutheran catechisms are the very models of Christian youth mindful and observant of its duty. A world of religious and intellectual presuppositions separates these types from the pert youngsters of Erasmus's schoolboy dialogues, who give every indication of having formed their own ideas of what they should think and do.[48] Not so the children of the catechism. They ask questions by the book and answer by the book. Their curiosity is fully satisfied by what is said to them. They believe with all their heart. Doubt and suspicion are as foreign to their nature as disbelief.

One example will convey the sense of this ideal type. I take it from Caspar Huberinus's *Shorter Catechism for the Instruction of Young People*, published in 1544. The questioning father asks: Can we, with the aid of our own powers, avoid grave sins and perform good works? No, we cannot, replies the child. Human nature, he continues, has as a result of Adam's fall been so corrupted and become a thing so feeble, fragile, and defective that, blinded from birth, we can neither know nor learn what is right and wrong, not to mention act on it. How, then, continues the father, can we be saved? Child: God can do it for us. All things are possible to God. If this is so, the father insists, why has God laid heavy commandments upon us, seeing that we cannot keep them even if we try? The question touches the heart of the problem of religious and moral indoctrination. The reply to it is a critical place in every catechism. There are two reasons, the child responds.

In his Ten Commandments the Lord God has laid down two kinds of authority for us, one external, the other spiritual. Seeing that the whole world is wicked and will not let itself be reformed or pacified with good words, God has appointed magistrates, and empowered them to exercise outward authority through effective governments, to the end that order, peace, and equity may be maintained in the world. This is why rulers and magistrates have been made custodians of the law.

The other reason is this. God requires something greater of us than external piety. He also demands a spiritual, godly, and heavenly piety which, flowing from the very ground of our hearts, must be practiced with the utmost fullness of joy and love. But in our contemplation of this heavenly piety, we see as in a mirror held up to us by God, a reflection of our misery and blindness, our sinful and corrupted nature, our derelictions and utter helplessness, so that, fully aware of what is expected of us, we will never presume to attempt with our own feeble powers to attain this heavenly piety.[49]

Here we have the official portrait of the Christian as impotent sinner, incapable of self-help, wholly dependent on powers outside himself not only for his salvation, but for the order and stability of his earthly existence as well. To keep this picture ever before the eyes of the young person, and to convince him that it was his own true likeness, was the paramount task of Lutheran pedagogy. "Every Christian must know three things," one reads in a children's catechism of 1554, "and the first of these is to recognize himself as a sinner, being under the curse of the law and deserving the rewards of sin, which are death, the wrath of God, and the everlasting pains and tortures of hell."[50] Everything else followed from this self-perception, which was the deep source of the traits and attributes constituting the evangelical personality and a necessary impulse to their internalization. Upon the acceptance of the scriptural authority and divine truth of this self-image depended the assimilation of attitudinal norms and rules of behavior to which the young were expected to conform.[51]

The problems posed by this assimilation will be the subject of a later chapter. Here our concern is with the norms and rules themselves. A sampler of them is easily assembled from books written for the young. "A child's virtues are endurance, silence, and patience."[52] "Don't speak except when asked."[53] "Four special virtues form the golden chaplet gracing the head of a Christian youth: fear of God, obedience to parents, true humility, and the zeal to learn and work."[54] "Honor your parents with patient forbearance, especially when they are old, ill, poor, tired, irritable, or distressed."[55] Be content with your lot in life; to wish to rise above your place is presumption. "What the world counts as eminence is despicable before God."[56] "The vice of presumption," it was argued, "can be eradicated only if we teach children neither to judge nor to despise their playmates. If we fail in this, they will all grow up to be scoffers and scorners."[57] Don't attempt too much in your adult life, especially in the world of business, because "in the end you will gain only worry, misadventure, taxes, fines, inflation, pillage, and destruction of property."[58] Resist the lure of novelty. Beware of the newfangled and untried: "Always prefer old and traditional things, for they are more true than what has been newly invented. Stay away from innovations; they are likely to be false and dangerous."[59]

One could run on indefinitely quoting from catechisms, sermons, and books of civility. But the point does not gain by cumulation. Advice of this kind clearly presupposed the model of a quiescent, pliant, conscientious (but never enterprising or venturesome), essentially passive individual, amenable to direction and respectfully attentive to authority, a loyal follower, a diligent believer. Much too good to be true, he came to life only in the improving novels, stories, and plays that seem to have enjoyed the favor of many readers of the time—a time, be it noted, that also relished the scoundrels, rogues, and scalawags of picaresque and satirical tales. Didactic fiction abounds in good-as-gold youngsters, products of sound Christian nurture and discipline. Some of them have already made their appearance in this chapter. Two more will round our our sampling. First, young Benjamin, son of Susanna, the falsely accused woman in the apocryphal book, as dramatized by Paul Rebhun in 1535. Exhibiting the model qualities acquired in his upbringing, the boy approaches his mother in a scene in no way connected with the play's plot. He exclaims:

> O mother dear, I overheard
> Just now a dreadful, ugly word,
> While chancing, I don't know what for
> To pass the open kitchen door.
> Within the hired girl made free
> With a most horrid blasphemy.
> Does she not hold our Lord in dread?
> You tell us every night in bed
> "To God give fear and honor both,
> And never, never say an oath!"
> Will God permit this girl to offend?

Susanna concludes:

> No, child, he'll punish her in the end.[60]

From such a scene, insisted its author, "we must draw wholesome lessons tending to strengthen our faith, brace us to bear our cross, teach us patience, and show every man, woman, child, and servant what they ought to do and what not to do."[61] How effectively the drama (including its easily available printed text) impressed this point on its audiences must be left to the imagination. At least it offered moments of diversion and put on the boards a few recognizable characters who, even while mouthing truths better suited to a morality play, showed themselves in homespun attitudes and colloquial dialogue that may well have touched the audience.

Not so the novels. Their stilted and preachy tone and their cloying sentimentality rob them of all verisimilitude. Jörg Wickram, the century's most successful purveyor of edifying tales and novels, illustrates this feature. In his *Good and Bad Neighbors* of 1556, he attempted to bring several kinds of improving influence to bear upon his readers. He wished to show how pious families can live together in peace and friendship. He tried to demonstrate that hard work in one's appointed calling leads to public esteem and inner contentment. He sought to portray a well-governed Christian household as a happy community. Finally, he gave advice on the proper raising of children. The novel's numerous chapters on education show how the professional literature on children—medical, pedagogic, theological—had seeped to that middle layer of culture and status where a man like Wickram, the illegitimate offspring of a patrician clan in Colmar, a municipal secretary by trade and a mastersinger and storyteller by vocation, could assimilate and transmit it to his public as a consensus view. Wickram's pedagogical principles, as they are expounded by the characters in his novels, hold no surprises for us: "It is often said, in fact it is now a common proverb, that 'what you first put into a new vessel leaves a permanent taste in it.' It's exactly the same with the delicate and soft minds of our youths. Train and educate young people to good things, and you will find that they will accept them willingly and grow up with these good principles firmly rooted in their natures."[62] Wickram's case in point is young Lazarus, son of old Lazarus, the latter a dutiful Christian householder who had learned by heart the lessons taught in all the books of domestic comportment.

> Old Lazarus had no other thought than to raise and keep his son in the fear of the Lord, knowing that by his nature the boy was from birth somewhat inclined to this virtue. Eagerly and happily young Lazarus went to school, paying the closest attention to his master's words of instruction and not resting until he had completed his assigned work to the teacher's complete satisfaction. As a result of these efforts he soon became his master's favorite, learning his lessons without ever hearing a harsh word spoken in censure and never feeling the sting of the rod on his back. Within a short time he had exceeded all his classmates in learning, a fact of which the master not infrequently reminded his other pupils.

The boy also had other habits worthy of imitation.

> Never did he leave his parents' house without having first wished his father and mother a good and blessed day; nor did he fail to extend this wish to the kitchen maid and the stable groom. Following these greetings, he cleaned and combed his hair and washed his hands. If there was a soup or porridge for breakfast, he tasted not a drop of it until he had praised God and thanked him for the many blessings he had bestowed upon his family. Then he took up his copy books and writing utensils and went off to school, where he applied himself most industriously to his lessons. [63]

The remainder of young Lazarus's exemplary qualities may be inferred from these samples. Their power of provoking emulation may be open to doubt. But no contemporary scorned the norms of Christian behavior as portrayed by Lazarus and his fellow paragons, and magistrates and prelates all over Germany codified these norms into regulations for the young. In the county of Schwarzenburg in Thuringia the following comportment was prescribed for mandatory Wednesday afternoon catechism lessons. After bell ringing, hymns, and opening prayers, "two boys, and in alternate weeks, two girls, step before the group. With hands folded and faces composed in simple and gentle piety, the first child bids the other recite an article of the catechism, taking a different article each week, and the second child giving the answer in all devotion and with becoming modesty." [64]

The assumption, or at least the hope, underlying these rules was that this fitting modesty was the outward expression of an inner state of trust, calm, and docility, the posture of a young person who had learned to know his place with respect to God in heaven and his betters on earth. The actualization of this ideal type required nothing less than an alteration of the human personality. Let us now consider the pedagogical tools available for attempting this fundamental transformation.

CHAPTER 8

TECHNIQUES OF INDOCTRINATION: CATECHISMS

"In a boy all virtues grow out of fear and the feeling of shame." So wrote Jörg Wickram in the preface to his *Mirror of Young Boys,* spreading the conventional wisdom. "Where these two lights are snuffed out," he added, "little good remains in young people and old."[1] Readers of the preceding chapters will take the meaning of Wickram's words. Fear was of God and of the punitive power given to temporal authorities: parents and magistrates. Shame (*pudor*) was the mortification resulting from the child's perception of himself as sinner and the humiliation attending failure of his unaided efforts. Fear of God's anger was the indispensable psychological precondition of faith and trust. Shame worked as the most effective impulse to the internalization of imposed rules and their transformation into dictates of conscience. But neither fear nor shame were innate in the young; they had to be learned. Fear and shame were therefore concerns of pedagogy. Implanting them as the roots of all virtue was the principal task of indoctrination.

This is how reformers defined the objective of mass education. The chosen few endowed with the intellect and perseverance to pursue higher studies had access to superior schools, where they were prepared for special responsibilities in church and society. But the rank and file needed to know only what was necessary to them as Christians and citizens. "We have issued this ordinance," stated the authors of the Württemberg school constitution of 1559 (a model of its kind, it will be remembered) "to ensure that all children in our German schools will learn the fear of God, right doctrine, and decent conduct [*Zucht*]." These essential goals required, in turn, some competence in reading and writing, and the self-restraint induced by disciplined habits: modest speech and demeanor, punctuality, conscientious performance of assigned duties, and avoidance of idleness, loose chatter, and similar kinds of "impious behavior."[2]

151

Only public education could introduce these traits uniformly and equitably;[3] the fate of the entire commonwealth was therefore thought to hinge on effective public teaching of doctrine and discipline. Since truth and morality must be learned, contended a Lutheran pedagogue, Johann Michael Dilherr, a government's foremost task is the teaching of virtue, "without which laws are useless and warnings are given in vain."[4] Melanchthon persuaded the governing councillors of Nuremberg that schooling offered the only hope of implanting virtue in their subjects.[5] The preachers of Strassburg urged their magistrates to launch a comprehensive program of civic and religious education and suggested that all baptized children be entered in a register to allow officials to control their progress through catechism instruction and school,[6] adding the assurance that "schooling will benefit not only our Christian religion, but also the general good [*gemainer Nutz*]."[7] The blend of acquired skills and imbued virtue that was the hoped-for result of the kind of pragmatic training contemplated in these memoranda[8] was the vital prerequisite of the Christian society envisioned by the reformers. As such it was, or ought to be, the sovereign concern of public authorities.

Laws and regulations set the criteria for social and private behavior, and energetic magistrates endeavored to conform their societies to these standards. But they saw no hope of a lasting improvement in religion and morality until people's guiding aims had been transformed. How could religious and moral precepts be imprinted so lastingly on men's hearts, minds, and characters as to redirect their impulses? Protestant theology and pedagogical practice clashed on the answer to this question. This struggle of principles has been examined.[9] The conflict was not irreconcilable. All agreed that only God could turn the individual's heart; man could not do it by himself, nor could it be done for him by a teacher, a method, a book. Nonetheless, Protestant educators proposed to bring about just such a fundamental change in men's natures. Luther himself pointed the way toward this transformation. The word of God, he suggested, can be impressed (*eingebildet*) upon the hearts of men to allow the divine spirit to do its work there. Devout attention to the words of Scripture can draw God's spirit into their souls. This is the purpose of study, of preaching, and above all of catechism practice:

> God wants us to ponder his word diligently in our hearts, and so impress it on ourselves that at length it will become a natural thing to us [*das wir sein wort fleissig in unserem hertzen bewiegeten und so einbildeten, das schier natur daraus würde*]. Solomon says in the Song of Songs [8:6]: "Set me as a seal upon your heart." God's word must be in us like such a seal or brand mark, burned in, not touching the heart lightly, as foam on water or spittle on the tongue which we want to spit out, but

pressed into the heart to remain there as a distinguishing sign [*mal-zeichen*] which no one can remove from us, as if it had grown there naturally with strong roots never to be torn up again.[10]

Luther was here referring to the divine spirit contained in the words of Scripture and to the impact of these charged words on men's souls, hearts, and minds. Although later Protestant pedagogy shifted the emphasis from the spirit to the words themselves, and from God's living presence in Scripture to the Bible as a code of doctrine, *einbilden* (to impress, imprint, incise deeply and lastingly) became a critical methodological concept and an indispensable pedagogical technique in Protestant education.[11] Since truth and error were perceived as opposites, and the well-being of society was understood to demand the annihilation of false opinions, indoctrinating the young required that they be so deeply imbued with right ideas as to determine their thoughts and actions for the rest of their lives. Since the canon of knowable things was limited and arranged in a fixed hierarchical order, teaching proceeded from authority; spontaneity, initiative, and subjective judgments were considered destructive, and their exercise was interdicted. From childhood the individual must be shaped to desire only what agreed with sanctioned precepts.

Classical models reinforced this principle. A particularly compelling case in point was Xenophon's *Cyropaedia,* a text familiar to pedagogues from the 1470s on. It contained a passage that showed that, if from childhood a person were molded to wish only what is good for him, little external direction was needed to control him later in life:

> [Cyrus] was educated in conformity with the laws of the Persians; and these laws appear in their care for the common weal not to start from the same point as they do in most states. For most states permit every one to train his own children just as he will . . . and then they command them not to steal and not to rob, not to break into anybody's house, not to strike a person whom they have no right to strike, not to commit adultery, not to disobey an officer, and so forth; and if a man transgresses any of these laws, they punish him. The Persian laws, however, begin at the beginning and take care that from the first their citizens shall not be of such a character as ever to desire anything improper or immoral.[12]

Ancient and modern educational writers agreed that mental and behavioral habits securely implanted in childhood molded the human being for life. This was the position epitomized in Plutarch's dictum: "character is habit long continued."[13]

Lutheran educators thus embraced habituation as the only method promising to effect the personality change on which the evangelical reform of individual and society depended. They had great faith in its instrumental power. "What you get used to doing while you are young you will still do when you are old [*jung gewonet, alt getan*]"

—no one disputed this piece of folk wisdom.[14] "Let the young be habituated [*angewonet*] from childhood to silence and attentiveness, for once a tree is fully grown it cannot be bent."[15] "Habituate [*gewehnen*] children to regular church attendance, for trees must be bent while young."[16] "What you are not habituated to do while young, you will never learn later in life."[17] The Württemberg school ordinance justified its regulations with the recurring phrase "so that [the pupils] may be habituated to it [*damit sie gewont werden*]."[18] After urging parents to read stories of God's wrath to their children, Spangenberg insisted that "these tales . . . be repeated every day without ceasing or letting up, for when children are habituated in this way to fear God's anger and praise his benevolence, they will bear it in mind as long as they live."[19]

Emotions and mental states, no less than behavior, were considered subject to habituation. Christoph Vischer argued that tenderness and leniency (*Sanftmut und Glimpflichkeit*), "the noblest of virtues, can be learned only by becoming habituated to them while young."[20] Bugenhagen assured the city fathers of Hamburg in 1526 that the Christian society of the future could be prepared "by educating and habituating a new generation of pious and Christian young people."[21] Protestant pedagogues endlessly repeated Luther's advice that the young should be accustomed to open their minds to the word of God and let it impress itself upon their hearts. Huberinus, for instance, declared that "early in life, in tenderest youth, children can be habituated to a willing, even an eager reading and hearing of God's word, to ponder it diligently and impress it within themselves."[22] And the ecclesiastical constitution of Jever stipulated that "our young people . . . be accustomed as early as possible in their lives to the chief articles of the Christian religion, so that these articles will become firmly impressed [*ynbilden*] and rooted [*geplanted*] in them."[23]

Repetition and memorization were the only means to this end: "the more frequently and diligently a thing is repeated, the better children will grasp it."[24] Memory being a trainable faculty, subject to habituation by exercise,[25] pedagogues made considerable demands on mnemonic powers, not only of the gifted,[26] but of ordinary children as well. Every child was presumed capable of committing to memory the catechism, some prayers and hymns, and the penitential psalms. To facilitate retention and recall, these texts were presented to them as simple and incontrovertible truths, Luther having insisted that ambiguity inevitably leads to doubt, and doubt sows confusion and irresolution.[27] "The delicate and untouched minds [of children]," he argued, "must be shaped by simple, necessary, and undoubted doctrines which they can accept as certain truths. Before a beginner can learn anything," he added, "he must believe."[28] Started in the first year of school, and maintained unremittingly throughout the impressionable years, habituation was a form of conditioning[29] intended to mold pliable souls by impressing on them a set of characteristics never to be expunged and a disposition never again to be altered.

Most primers, Latin grammars, and ABC books included among their phrases simple sentences designed to get the indoctrination process under way at the very start of formal schooling. The effectiveness of these formulas must remain open to doubt, but one imagines that a steady diet of such phrases as

> "take pity on us Lord, we are lost sheep, forlorn sinners, damned souls."[30]
> "God gives grace to those who fear him,"[31]
> "come to me soon, says the Lord,"[32]
> "se-que-re De-um."[33]
> "Much wickedness a child must see/and evil is learned easily./Protect, dear Lord, this little lad/so that he will learn nothing bad"[34]

left its mark on the young psyche. But it was the catechism that offered to sixteenth-century pedagogues a most powerful conditioning instrument for shaping habits of thought. "Young people cannot grasp the doctrine unless they are habituated to it by means of verbatim repetition," declared the eccesiastical authorities of Saxony[35] in ordering obligatory catechism recitation in their territory. When the Nuremberg council adopted Luther's Shorter Catechism as the basic textbook for its German schools, it confidently expected that "when children become habituated [to it] they will grow up in the right Christian religion."[36] Every German government committed itself in similar terms to catechization as the surest, safest, most feasible, and most effective instrument of religious and civic instruction.

2

In the 1520s, 1530s and 1540s, confidence in catechism instruction was still unclouded by the disappointments that overtook Protestant leaders in the second half of the sixteenth century. In 1528 Luther, in a mood almost manic when compared to his dejection soon afterward, exulted, "I declare, I have made a reformation that will make the popes' ears ring and hearts burst."[37] For more than a century now, he said, men have been talking about reform, but now he, Luther, has accomplished it.

> By the grace of God I have brought about such a change that nowadays a girl or boy of fifteen knows more about Christian doctrine than all the theologians of the great universities used to know in the old days. For among us the catechism has come back into use: I mean the Lord's Prayer, the Apostles' Creed, the Ten Commandments, and all that one should

know about penance, baptism, prayer, the cross, how to live and how to die, the sacrament of the altar, also about marriage, civil obedience, the duties of father and mother, wife and children, father and son, master and servant. In short, I have established the right order for all estates in society and have brought them all to a good conscience so that each will know how to live and serve God in his appointed role. And to those who have accepted it, my reformation has brought not a little benefit, peace, and virtue.[38]

Luther's own catechisms, to which he makes reference here, had been in preparation since 1523 and were about to appear in print.[39] In 1530 he again took stock of accomplishments. To his territorial ruler, Elector Johann of Saxony, he boasted that

there is no other land in the world to compare with Your Electoral Grace's territories for excellent pastors and preachers. Nowhere else do they teach so piously and purely and help maintain such serene peace among men. Our tender young people, girls as well as boys, are now so well taught in catechism and Scripture that my heart grows warm as I observe children praying more devoutly, believing more firmly, and discoursing more eloquently on God and Christ than, in the old days, all the learned monks and doctors.[40]

The accuracy of this description is open to question (Luther was trying to encourage the elector at a difficult moment), but it was generally acknowledged in Lutheran circles that 1530 marked the zenith of the movement in Germany.[41] When Luther rejoiced in "the good which the gospel has accomplished not only in the individual conscience, but also in the conduct of public affairs and in family and household life,"[42] he was inclined to attribute this happy result to the effect of catechization, notably to the success of his own Shorter Catechism—"the most exalted book on earth," as his contemporaries called it, "because it teaches the whole of Scripture in a brief sum or compendium."[43] By 1530, Lutheran leaders had come to regard systematic catechization of the laity, particularly of the young, as a distinguishing feature of their movement and a decisive break with the past. This is what Melanchthon had in mind when he claimed in his *Defense of the Augsburg Confession* of 1530 that "among our adversaries children receive no catechism instruction whatsoever."[44] Like Luther, he counted it a major achievement to have brought back the catechism, the adoption of which[45] set reformers on a wave of optimism that was to carry them over the setbacks of the second half of the century.

Catechisms play so important a role in Reformation pedagogy that time must be taken here to consider them as a genre.[46] Reformation theologians showed a keen interest in the origins of their catechisms; indeed, it was their search for precedents that convinced them of the originality of what they were trying to accomplish.[47] They knew, of course, that the early church had given instruction in "the words of the faith and of the good doctrine" (1 Tim. 4:6) to people being prepared for baptism; hence *catechizare*, to teach by word of mouth, as in Augustine's *De catechizandis rudibus*, where *rudes* refers to those still untutored in the Christian doctrine.[48] Since instruction was for the most part oral, the method of repeating every word aloud established itself early in the Christian era, while the question and answer form characteristic of later catechism instruction evolved out of confessional manuals and devotional dialogues.[49] The major incentive to catechization in the early church seems to have disappeared, however, with adoption of infant baptism. Lutherans therefore believed that they had revived an evangelical tradition dead for nearly a thousand years. This was an exhilarating thought to them, and one source of the enormous energy they brought to their efforts.

Actually the medieval picture was not as bleak as Protestants imagined it. To be sure, nothing undertaken in earlier centuries matched the Protestant and Catholic Reformations' systematic programs of catechization. It is also true that not until Luther's time did the catechism become a self-contained book encompassing the main points of Christian doctrine in a rudimentary form suitable for instructing the laity. But the medieval church had not failed to prepare people for confession and communion, and for the responsibilities of parents and godparents.[50] The fourteenth and fifteenth centuries, especially, saw the appearance of explanations of the Apostles' Creed, the Lord's Prayer, the sacraments, sins and virtues, and the works of charity,[51] and the early printing press brought out a host of confession manuals that gave some basic religious instruction to their readers, for the purpose of inducing in them a sense of sinfulness and a craving for penance.[52] From the Protestant point of view, these tracts were sadly lacking in order, clarity, and singleness of purpose. They could not be regarded as fitting successors to the catechetical instruction of the patristic age. On the other hand, the popularity of these manuals[53] must have helped persuade the reformers that an eager public stood ready to respond to their own more rigorous efforts.

Medieval catechisms differed from their Lutheran counterparts in another important respect. Confining their appeal to religious responses, they ignored the social articulation of piety that was a major Protestant concern from the very beginning.[54] One need only remember the setting in which the Lutheran pedagogical program was undertaken to grasp the point of this broadening of scope. In the mid- and late 1520s, as the first Lutheran catechisms were being prepared,[55] the religious and secular problems clamoring for attention were so entangled that reformers could not fail to use religious instruction in their attempt to reverse dangerous trends in society, politics, and culture. Serious concern with secular ethics was, in any case, a natural product of the new theology. The attempt to elevate the tone of temporal life, implicit in the principle of the priesthood of all believers, demanded that catechization address itself no less vigorously to secular grievances than to the religious conscience. Lutherans would have been false to their movement had they failed in their catechisms to respond to the call for reforms in secular life.

As has been seen, Luther did not quickly or easily bring himself to acknowledge that formal procedures and administrative constraints were required to spread religious knowledge in the population. He had at first imagined a very different setting, one in which individuals would seek instruction and then come forward to be tested in their knowledge. Attention to preaching, independent study, voluntary examinations: these were the public responses Luther had anticipated. The events of the 1520s smothered these expectations. In 1529 he recommended that no one be admitted to the Lord's table who had not first given proof of his understanding of the faith.[56] The visitation of 1528–29 in Saxony had revealed appalling ignorance.[57] Most people were uninformed about their religion and had little or no access to sources of instruction, small-town and village clergy being for the most part as benighted as their parishioners. Something would have to be done if the evangelical religion were to escape a drastic change of character from a broadly based reform movement to a cult for the few who had the brains and interest to grasp it.

Two things were done, one a decision made under the duress of the visitation reports, the other a step long contemplated and slowly brought to maturity in the minds of Luther and his associates. The former was the extension of catechization to the population at large, with special emphasis on the young, making it a legal obligation for all subjects. Relying for enforcement on the procedures of the territorial visitation—still to be fully formulated—Luther implicitly held all Christians responsible for knowing the main articles of their faith and for submitting to periodic examination of this knowledge. Commenting on the tone of Luther's correspondence during the 1528 visitation, Zezschwitz, the historian of catechetics, remarks that "on an objective reading of these letters one can scarcely escape the impression that Luther suddenly began to see himself as a visitation official acting on the authority of his prince."[58] That, at any rate, is what his successors became. Alarmed by the ignorance, and therefore the vulnerability, of the population, Lutherans abandoned their voluntaristic and participatory ideals in favor of an obligatory system of instruction and examination. "Interrogate and instruct [*verhöret und unterrichtet*]"[59] was the maxim now.

The second consequence of the crisis of the 1520s was the preparation of Luther's two catechisms. Few of his works received more of his care than these unpretentious compendiums of basic religious knowledge, and none was closer to his heart. No man can ever learn the catechism well enough, he said in the preface to the Larger Catechism, "for while you read, recite, and reflect [on the catechism] the Holy Spirit is always present, steadily deepening your insight and piety, so that you will love and understand it better and better, as Christ has told us, saying 'where two or three are gathered in my name, there I am in the midst of them' [Matt. 18:20]." The study of these holy texts will never grow stale, he promised. "The more time you spend with them . . . the more you will wish to learn."[60] This gave the lie, he said, to "cocksure" and "presumptuous" people who disdain the catechism as a childish thing, fit only for the very young and the very silly. "Speaking for myself," he said, "I am still a child beginning to learn my catechism. Every morning and whenever I have time during the day, I read and recite the Lord's Prayer, Decalogue, Apostles' Creed, psalms, etc., word for word, and in this way I stay forever a child and a disciple of the catechism, and I am very happy in this condition."[61] Catechism is *Kinderlehre*—doctrine for children—but in a profound sense, not literally; for becoming a Christian demands as a prerequisite a return to childhood, that is to say to the guilelessness, candor, and docility of one's early years before reason and ambition destroyed innocence.[62] True Christians are always "children and simple-minded people." All stand to profit from "an unaffected exposition of the doctrine, simple and—as they say—childlike [*kindisch*]."[63] No one, said Luther, ever surpasses the catechism in wisdom. Nor is anyone so witless as to find it beyond his modest capacities.

The religious instruction of all Christian men and women was one objective of the catechism, but there was another. Luther's Larger Catechism was published in April 1529, compounded of a series of sermons the reformer had given the year before. The Shorter Catechism appeared in May of the same year.[64] Both were intended as handbooks for pastors, telling them "what they shall teach and preach,"[65] giving authoritative formulations of the five chief articles of the faith. The larger version gave succinct commentaries in the form of short sermons in Luther's personal style. The shorter furnished concise explanations in question and answer form,[66] of great use, Luther thought, to ill-trained country parsons confused by sudden demands made upon them in the Visitation Instructions of 1528, which declared pastors answerable for their parishioners' religious knowledge. Both catechisms were therefore meant to instruct the pastors themselves, because in a time swarming with "heretics," "sectarians," "enthusiasts," and "false seducers" (read Zwinglians, Anabaptists, spiritualists, and antinomians) definitive statements of doctrine were of the utmost importance. Luther implored his fellow pastors to "help us instill the catechism in people, especially in the young. Take up this broadsheet"—he meant the placard on which the earliest version of his catechism was printed—"and impress it word for word on people's minds."[67] We cannot coerce people in matters of faith, Luther warned. We must give them the impulse to learn, and this can be done only by means of preaching and catechization. These efforts rest on the work of pastors, a calling very different now from what it was under the papacy. "For now it has become a grave and saving office."[68]

Thus Luther's catechisms paved the way for obligatory religious instruction to be given by ministers. From the time of the Saxon visitation of 1528 Luther had regarded this step as a vital necessity. The experience of those unhappy months in the fall and winter of 1528 was very much in his mind as he put the final touches to his catechisms. In the preface to the shorter version he admitted that "the deplorable need and misery to which I was recently a witness when a visitor have forced me to put the catechism into this small, plain, and simple format. So help me God, what pitiful things I saw then, how the common man knows absolutely nothing about Christian doctrine, especially in the countryside, and how a great many of our pastors are just as ignorant and utterly incapable of teaching it."[69] These facts prompted him to insist that the primary duty of a pastor is to drill his parishioners in the words of the articles. First make them memorize the words, he advised, then explain their meaning "so that they will know what they are saying."[70] He gave some examples of how this could be done in a simple way. "What does it mean to believe in God our Father? Answer: it means that my heart has complete trust in him and feels certain of his grace, goodwill, help, and consolation, in this life and in eternity. What does it mean to believe in Jesus Christ, his son? Answer: it means that the heart knows we would be lost in all eternity had Christ not died for us."[71] Those capable of some understanding might receive more elaborate explanations; but these do not really matter. What matters is the text itself and its inculcation in everyone's mind. Don't leave it up to individuals to decide whether they want to learn the catechism, Luther cautioned. "It is true that no one can be forced to believe. But we must exhort and incite [halten und treiben] the throng [haufen] to the faith, so that they may know what is correct and what is false. . . . And those who don't want to learn, tell them that they have rejected Christ and are no Christians."[72] Such people should be kept from taking the sacrament, he adds, and ought not to be allowed to act as godparents. The Christian freedom of the evangelical reformation was not for them.

By 1529 Luther was clearly beginning to suspect that most of his contemporaries fell into the latter category. He railed against the "crude, lazy, ignorantly arrogant, self-righteous, and time-serving" people everywhere to be seen now.[73] The only hope lay in starting over with the young. For this objective the Shorter Catechism was the best instrument yet devised, while the larger one suggested how an awakened faith might be deepened into understanding. To those who understood, Luther held out the promise of a sovereignty never before claimed for Christian commoners. A man who has truly learned the Ten Commandments, Luther announced, holds the key to the whole Scripture, and "such a man is entitled in all matters and cases to advise, help, console, decide, and judge things spiritual and temporal. And he may be a judge over all doctrines, estates, ideas, laws, and everything else that exists in the world."[74] The priesthood of all believers could scarcely be asserted more boldly.

Luther's two catechisms won instantaneous recognition. Most Protestant state churches recommended, and later required, them as the chief instruments of religious instruction. They also generated elaborations and adaptations, Luther himself having called for free use of these two prototypes. "Choose any form you like," he told pastors in his preface to the Larger Catechism, and interpret and comment to the extent of your parishioners' ability to understand, as long as you always hold fast to the same basic form and style.[75] In response to this invitation, a veritable explosion of catechism writing took place in Germany during the half-century or so after 1529. A recent student of the subject goes so far as to suggest that "something like every third pastor drew up a substantial catechism of his own."[76] But in the 1570s and 1580s, as theological rivalries fragmented the Lutheran movement and orthodoxy became the salient criterion of religious instruction, theologians called for a return to the source, and ecclesiastical constitutions demanded the universal adoption of Luther's authorized catechisms, "without adding anything or taking anything away."[77]

Luther determined the Protestant catechism in several important respects, beginning with its order of arrangement: Ten Commandments, Apostles' Creed, Lord's Prayer, and sacraments. Why start with the Decalogue? Luther had answered this question as early as 1520, in his treatise on the "Freedom of a Christian Person."[78] Unless the human being sees himself as the sinner he is, his heart will never feel true piety. The Decalogue confronts him with the inadequacy of his efforts. Try as he might, he cannot keep the commandments. The sense of his failure brings him to the realization of his own corruption, and thence to the fear of God's punishment. His heart thus emptied of pride and boasting, the sinner discovers in faith his only hope.

Luther's insistence on primacy of place for the Decalogue is in part explained by his opposition to antinomian tendencies that began to surface in Germany during the gestation years of his two catechisms.[79] Far from having been freed from the Mosaic law, he argued, Christians are bound to it more firmly than the Jews. This relation determines the order of the articles in the catechism. "For these three articles," he said in his treatise of 1526 on the German Mass, "Decalogue, Creed, and Lord's Prayer, contain plainly and completely everything a Christian must know. . . . First he must know what he shall do and not do; second, seeing that he cannot by his own powers do or refrain from doing anything, he must know where to seek and find this power. Third, he must know how he is to seek and obtain it."[80] From law to faith to prayer: this was not only the inherently right order, but also the only psychologically compelling progression in awakening the religious consciousness. There could be no true piety without the fear of God engendered by the individual's perception of himself as an inveterate sinner.

Most catechisms elaborated this necessary connection in unmistakably explicit terms. Daniel Kauxdorf, commenting on Luther's Shorter Catechism in 1575, illustrated it with an analogy to illness and restoration to health. First, he wrote, we must discover the nature of our ailment. We learn this from the Ten Commandments, which say to us: if you want to be with God, keep these laws; if you don't, be doomed for all eternity. We soon discover, however, that we cannot keep the divine laws. Realizing this, we are struck down by conscience, appearing to ourselves, no matter how clever of mind or proud of bearing, for what we are: sinners, lost sheep, damned souls. "The Decalogue, therefore, shows us our debility and innate wickedness. It is the true mirror of man's self." Having acknowledged our disease, we look for a physician. That such a helper exists we learn from the Apostles' Creed, where we are assured that God pities our wretched state and has sent Christ as our deliverer. Knowing his physician, the invalid now asks what medicine he has ordered for him. It is the Lord's Prayer, for prayer is the sinner's only means of making himself heard in heaven. A strengthening potion is his next step, to help him back on his feet. This he finds in the sacraments, which invigorate his heart with God's promise of eternal life. Only one thing more is needed for complete recovery: a regimen of religious and moral exercise "through which we become practiced in the faith and are improved by it."[81] This strict regimen will keep the convalescent from relapsing into illness.

Emphasis on the sinner's full and honest acceptance of his impotence was therefore balanced by the assurance of God's mercy and the promise of his grace. Stress on the dark or light side of this spectrum varied among catechists. As will be seen in another chapter, some elaborated the sense of sin and the concomitant need for supports and controls. Others touched on it only lightly. None failed to give pledges of certain mercy, vouchsafed in the Apostles' Creed, the Lord's Prayer, and the sacraments "by which we are made sure in our hearts of God's grace and fatherly benevolence, confident that by his covenant of grace and testament he has chosen us as his children and heirs to eternal life. . . . Of this we must have no doubt whatever."[82]

Luther's sense of the purpose of catechization affected its practice in another important way. From the first the reformer had put special emphasis on the indoctrination of the young. Rulers and churchmen agreed in principle with this aim. But the initial momentum of their policy was not always sustained. In the face of general public apathy, the education of the young was the most difficult and at the same time the most essential task to pursue. Remaining faithful to the reformer on this critical point of Lutheran pedagogy, Lutheran preachers kept a steady pressure on their respective governments. Throughout the Reformation era they made fresh efforts to turn Luther's catechisms into effective teaching instruments for the young, producing special catechisms for use in schools, turning them into primers,[83] dialogues,[84] hymns set to music ("so that our Christian doctrine may in many different ways, through preaching, reading, singing, etc., be impressed on young and simple people"),[85] and pictures for the illiterate.[86] Their authors' names—obscure for the most part—make a very long list.[87] The important point is that Luther's insistence on instructing the young and the very young was not lost in the decades following the reformer's death.

No less significant was the broadening of the catechism to encompass secular as well as religious concerns. Some medieval precedents existed for this extension of objective. But the substantial weight given in Lutheran catechization to civic and social behavior constituted an innovation. In this shift, too, Luther can be seen leading the way. His powerful evocation of the believing Christian's authority over things spiritual and secular fused the two realms into a single domain of evangelical action. His proud—not to say boastful—claim to having with his catechisms "established the right order for all estates in society" argues for the interpenetration, in fact, the inseparability, of religious conscience and civic morality. To make this junction explicit to all, even to the simplest and youngest, Luther appended to his Shorter Catechism a so-called *Haustafel*—a list of precepts for the Christian home—derived from Paul's epitome in the fifth and sixth chapters of Ephesians of the duties of husbands, wives, children, masters, and servants.[88] In later years Luther enlarged these lapidary remarks,[89] and his followers amplified them further.[90]

Explanations of the fourth and seventh commandments became the favorite vehicle for making social and political comments in the catechism. I shall defer analysis of these interesting reflections of the reformers' social ideas to a later chapter. But here it is worth emphasizing again that catechization was from the first regarded as a promising means for internalizing rules of moral and social conduct.

The many dos and don'ts of the law imposed external rules of behavior. But as a spiritual code, the law also touched a deeper level of motivation. Catechisms identified this internal source of lawful action:

> *Question:* How are we to understand [the fourth commandment]?
>
> *Answer:* The law, being a spiritual law, demands not merely external conformity and observance, but asks also for fulfillment in the depth of the heart [*des hertzens grund*]. This means that you owe your father not only outward respect and honor, but also a fundamentally good will [*einen grund guten willen*] of which your deeds must give proof.[91]

Obedience was not enough. The law also required solicitude, consideration, anticipation of just demands, and a willingness to sacrifice one's own interests for those of parents and other superiors. "For to be subject to your elders is to give proof of your humility, and God, who opposes the proud, gives grace to the humble."[92]

Fundamentally formative though it was, Luther's hand was not the only shaping force of the Protestant catechism. Independent catechisms came from theologians and reformers such as Johann Brenz and Philip Melanchthon, from professional schoolmasters like Valentin Trotzendorf, and from ecclesiastical administrators and preachers like Huberinus.[93] These in turn generated their own emulations, each trying to make a contribution to the common enterprise. The result, by the third quarter of the century, was a proliferation of catechisms so prodigious in number that it strains the imagination to take stock of them. Only one scholar has attempted to survey the entire lot, the German-American theologian Johann Michael Reu, in a work published early in the present century and frequently cited in the notes to these pages.[94] Huge as it is, his collection of texts and synopses is far from complete; nor would it be possible for a single scholar to catch every title. A two-volume *Bibliotheca catechetica* cataloging holdings in the Thüringische Landesbibliothek in Weimar contains well over a thousand items. In Hamburg alone more than fifty different catechisms circulated during the sixteenth century, and not until 1693 was the city's senate successful in banishing all but Luther's from its schools and churches.[95] In Nuremberg eleven or twelve were in use until the council published an official *Kinderlehrbüchlein* in 1558, but even then rival catechisms could not be entirely suppressed.[96] Saxony used thirty or forty, before the ecclesiastical constitution of 1580 declared Luther's catechism to be the only legitimate one. Printed catechisms represented only a fraction of those actually in circulation. Schoolmasters and preachers often wrote their own, but few have survived; most manuscript copies were small in format, unbound, and passed from hand to hand, dog-eared and torn to shreds, before they crumbled to pieces.[97] Printed catechisms were published in small editions for local use, to be handed by one generation of pupils to the next.[98] Surviving copies still make a formidable bulk in the archives and libraries of Protestant territories. But they are only a fraction of the vast numbers once in existence.

Several explanations for this profusion come to mind. Luther wrote his own catechisms to suit the special circumstances created by the 1528 visitation in Saxony and the continuing need for pastoral and domestic instruction. Both the Larger and the Shorter Catechisms required exegesis. To supply this need, longer versions soon made their appearance. The shift of religious education to schools and formal catechism classes created a demand for teaching catechisms suitable for successive levels of age and intelligence.[99] For a while Lutheran authorities encouraged local pastors to try their hands at supplying these, a move that accorded with Luther's original intentions, as has been seen. Church administrators in Gengenbach, for example, asked their pastors in 1538 to "draw up brief, distinct, clear, and easily understood handbooks of the main articles of the Christian doctrine, strictly in accordance with Scripture but also in an attractive manner to please children."[100] But in the 1540s this casual procedure no longer made sense. Bugenhagen rejected it in 1542, saying that "it is not a good idea for each theologian to write his own catechism, because if this practice were to continue, the poor ones would drive out the good ones. As for me," he added, "I do not plan to write one, for I know that Dr. Luther's catechisms are much better than anything I can produce."[101] Some orthodox Lutherans suspected foul play. "Many catechisms are written now for no other purpose than to drive that noblest of books, Dr. Luther's Shorter Catechism, from the church and replace it with a slippery and sectarian theology," wrote Johann Tettelbach, a pastor and superintendent in Saxony, and author of *The Golden Treasure,* a simplistic but faithful rendition of Luther's catechism.[102] The theological quarrels troubling the Lutheran movement almost from its start inevitably led to the multiplication of catechisms as each camp sought to advance and defend its version of disputed doctrines. Agricola was tainted with antinomianism, Meckhardt in Augsburg with Zwinglianism; Huberinus supported the Interim. Each of these men propagated his views in a substantial catechism. Meanwhile, many a pastor, believing himself to be an abler teacher than his colleagues, decided to publish his own text.[103] Thus the numbers grew, each new title demonstrating its author's confidence in the effectiveness of the catechetical method.

3

When fully organized, catechism instruction proceeded in three simultaneous stages. Huberinus was one of many who described how the system was intended to work. Pastors speaking from the pulpit expounded Luther's catechisms "somewhat more copiously and circumstantially," addressing themselves especially "to young people possessed of some understanding, and to other simple-minded folk not yet sufficiently grounded in the true Christian religion." Meanwhile, at school, beginning at the lowest level and continuing in all grades, schoolmasters drilled boys and girls in the Shorter Catechism or one of its variants, taking one article at a time and concentrating on the words. Finally, at home, parents—"who are our first teachers from childhood on"—instructed their children in the commandments, the Creed, and the Lord's Prayer, stretching their memories, explaining, taking recitations at meal times, and generally informing themselves on their progress in knowledge and understanding.[104] Huberinus adds that Protestants exiled in Catholic states were compelled to rely on the last of these stages alone. But without the supports of pulpit and school the evangelical doctrine was a fragile shoot, easily crushed. Accordingly, every Lutheran government issued regulations for catechism teaching, first as part of its ecclesiastical constitution, frequently repeated thereafter as articles in visitation instructions and religious edicts.

In Saxony, which we may take as a case in point, the 1528 *Instruction of the Visitors* required pastors to read the catechism to their parishioners every Sunday afternoon, and schoolmasters were to practice it with their classes throughout the year.[105] Saxon cities continued for a while to follow their own customs; Wittenberg, for instance, observed Luther's practice of giving four series of two-week catechism sermons during the year. But later on, the rift within the Lutheran camp and the unsatisfactory conditions discovered by the visitations[106] prompted church and government to press for strict compliance with their decrees. Parents who refused or neglected "to send their children to catechism" (the constant phrase) were to be identified and reported to local administrative officials for further action, by the central authorities if necessary.[107]

In 1580 a new constitution for all Saxony consolidated older catechism rules into a comprehensive order.[108] Only Luther's texts could be used in church, school, and domicile. The Shorter Catechism was to be read from every village pulpit every Sunday "in a loud voice and distinctly," and without adding comments or explanations. Afternoon catechism classes were made obligatory for all. In larger towns pastors were encouraged to give some explanations, but they were told to refrain from "making a display of their theological cunning with far-fetched digressions and excursions which will only spread confusion among poor ignorant folk." Parents were held responsible for their children's attendance of sermons and classes. Those who failed to comply risked "severe censure and punishment." One afternoon during the week was set aside for catechism examinations by the pastor, especially of children approaching first communion. The annual Lenten examinations, conducted by visitors, covered every parish in the land. In the cities and towns they proceeded from lists of inhabitants furnished by municipal councils. Every householder was required to send his children and domestic servants to be examined to "give proof of their faith by demonstrating their knowledge of the catechism." At least one parent had to be present. Churchmen were cautioned against humiliating anyone on these occasions: no harsh words, no dressing down before the congregation. Instead, they were to display a friendly, fatherly, modest manner and to be generous with praise for serious effort. Older citizens should not be placed in embarrassing positions by being subjected to public questioning, but this was a courtesy extended only to urban dwellers; adult villagers had to submit to examination along with the "young and simple." Schoolchildren memorized the Shorter Catechism, reciting the answers "with a loud and clear voice, so that they will become accustomed to saying it before the whole congregation in church." In Latin schools, too, the catechism was practiced every week throughout the school year. Parents were obliged to interrogate school-age children during the Sunday meal, and to acquaint even their youngest with the Decalogue, Apostles' Creed, and the Lord's Prayer. Illiterate householders were urged to offer a free meal to a needy student who could read the catechism to their children and servants.

Saxony was not alone in taking this systematic approach to catechism study. In Hessen a comprehensive "Ordinance for the Practice of Christian Discipline," of which Martin Bucer was one of the authors, established catechism instruction and examinations as a prerequisite for confirmation in the church.[109] In Kassel the catechism was read three times a week in every parish, for an hour every Sunday and for thirty minutes on Tuesdays and Thursdays.[110] Poor parishes found it hard to meet these obligations, but governments tried to distribute funds at least to the extent of providing weekly catechism readings by a sexton in even the most destitute of villages.[111] Regulations attempted to set minimum literacy standards for pastors' assistants.[112] School ordinances fixed sequence and frequency of catechism instruction.[113] In Coburg, Superintendent Maximilian Mörlin established a schedule in 1578 calling, in addition to thrice-weekly catechism sermons in church, for daily practice in school: Mondays the Decalogue, Tuesdays the Apostles' Creed, Wednesdays the Lord's Prayer, Thursdays baptism, Fridays confession, and Saturdays the sacrament of the altar.

The frequency and intensity of these exercises tended to increase in the last decades of the sixteenth century. Pupils in Augsburg had catechism lessons once a week early in the century; in 1581 the council augmented these with two additional weekly sessions.[114] In Ulm, in 1586, the city's teachers were held answerable for accurate catechism memorization by all children.[115] In the bishopric of Magdeburg pupils were promoted to higher grades only if they passed an examination in Luther's catechism.[116] To ensure that all pupils understood what they were memorizing, regulations called for the use of the German catechism in Latin school, "for the object is not to study Latin from it, but to learn religion."[117] Teachers experimented with graded catechisms of increasing difficulty as children advanced through school. A schoolmaster in Plauen in Saxony, for example, drilled his lower grades only in the words of the articles, but used his own "Instruction in Christian Doctrine," for intermediate pupils and a more demanding "Handbook" for the upper forms—all, of course, containing the same basic material. This was in 1525. Four years later he abandoned the "Instruction" as too difficult and substituted a rudimentary *Elementa pietatis; or, Synopsis of Christian Doctrine in Three Short Dialogues,* in Latin and German. "We have boys here," he confessed in the preface, "of short grasp and weak memory. For their sake I have written these attractive dialogues, keeping them as short and simple as possible. Pray God my pupils may learn well enough to move on to better catechisms than mine!"[118] It was a prayer echoed in many another preface.

Examinations kept everyone on his toes, for governments had no illusions about the willingness of people to learn without coercion.[119] To reinforce the tests given locally by pastors and schoolmasters, visitors held formal catechism examinations in which a certain number of parishioners were selected for testing, some young, some old, women and men, to "recite their Commandments, Creed, and Lord's Prayer to see how well they know them and how well they understand."[120] In Hamburg, visitors monitored parish and school examinations by questioning schoolchildren and parishioners during the annual Lenten visitation. Results varied widely, but they never satisfied the visitors, who rarely discovered anything to praise and nearly always found something to deplore.[121] Elsewhere the story was much the same. Examinations themselves were not always well attended. Often only the schoolchildren came, having been marched to church by their teachers, who had no choice in the matter.[122] Some visitors tried to sweeten the pill by awarding favors for correct answers.[123] They also tried to keep good records of results, taking down the names of persistent malingerers and compiling lists of children who had given good answers. Exceedingly modest in their expectations—"boys who can say the Lord's Prayer in part or in full"; "boys and girls who know all six articles of the catechism"—these catalogs tell us something about the criteria by which the religious competence of the general population was judged.[124]

In one respect, at least, the regulations were successful: they gradually convinced preachers and schoolmasters of the virtue of uniformity. Nearly every school ordinance espoused this principle, usually justifying it by quoting Luther on the bewilderment resulting from variety and mutability in religious instruction.[125] Administrative orderliness was an equally compelling consideration, diversity and change being synonyms for chaos. "Orderly procedures will never come about," wrote the preachers of Nuremberg to their council in 1531, "unless teachers have specific instructions to implement our schedule."[126] Governments obliged with meticulously detailed ordinances to assure "that uniformity is maintained in impressing the catechism on children,"[127] "that no new words throw children into confusion,"[128] and "that the same text be taught everywhere, and our young and simple people be accustomed to hearing and repeating the same words year after year."[129]

These inflexible directives make sense only if one recalls that the catechism, as the basic learning book for all children, played a political as well as a religious role. Governments promoted its use because they believed in its power as a habituating instrument for the molding of future citizens. The dutiful subject was the secular counterpart of the evangelical Christian. Many catechisms propounded a coherent social ethic as they discoursed—in accordance with the conservative (that is to say change-resisting) principles of the time—on worldly estates and their reciprocal obligations, on justice in government, business, and daily work, on malcontent and grumbling, unrest and rebellion. They sanctioned the social order as a holy and godly arrangement[130] and prepared the individual for accepting it. Indeed, one recognizes in the spectacle of public catechism recitations a kind of communal declaration of loyalty, in which the young set a salutary example for the adult congregation. When schoolchildren in Württemberg stood up in two facing ranks, antiphonally intoning questions and answers from the catechism,[131] the intended effect must have been that of a cultic affirmation and rededication of the entire community to the established order.

The direction of so many catechisms to the young and the simple of mind (*Kinder und einfeltige leute, pueri et rudiores* or *simpliciores*) illustrates the change in the nature of catechization following its adoption by ecclesiastical and political bureaucracies. Responsible adults could be allowed to depend on their pastors' sermons for their knowledge of the faith. The weight of catechism instruction was therefore shifted to the young, to mold them, to the volatile crowd of unattached and unsettled wage earners, to control them, and to country folk, to civilize them. Toward these groups of individuals, Protestant pedagogues displayed a consistently low regard. With a minimal attention span, feeble memories, slack incentives, and an incurable frivolity, they made ungrateful subjects for Christian instruction. They could be approached only like children, and with children they sat while receiving instruction and stood while being examined. This was a far cry from Luther's spiritual interpretation of *Kinderlehre*. "There follows the examination in the church," one reads in visitation records, "and let the hired men and boys stand in one place and the hired women and little girls in another."[132] In the end these humiliating arrangements proved self-defeating. But Lutheran churchmen had never expected much of a response from their adult subjects. Their hopes were set on the young.

While these hopes, at their highest, aspired to the development of an evangelical personality in the unformed child, pedagogues, thinking realistically, were prepared to accept much less. But even their minimum expectations would—if actualized—have brought about a considerable elevation of popular religion and morality. Mere memorization of the catechism was beneficial. "Like the soldier in wartime, who is cast out from his troop and killed like a foe if he does not know the password, the Christian person who has not learned his catechism is no Christian at all, but an enemy of God."[133] Learning the catechism therefore required no more than repeating the words, which was the best to be hoped for in prevailing circumstances: "Here [the small town of Weinbach in Hessen, in 1592, the pastor reporting] we have no schoolmaster. But during the winter I [the pastor] take on a few boys and teach them to help with the singing in the service and on Sundays to recite the articles of the catechism to the other children."[134] As the Holy Spirit was present in every authorized catechism, word-for-word repetition was in itself an efficacious act: "The words in Luther's Shorter Catechism are not the words of a man, but of the Holy Spirit. Catechism doctrine is the true word of God."[135] Merely saying them aloud released their intrinsic power. Pedagogues developed compelling analogies and metaphors to carry this message to the populace. "That best and most experienced of alchemists, the Holy Spirit has distilled from God's sacred word a quintessence containing the marrow, vital force, sap, and kernel of the whole of Scripture, . . . an *aqua vitae* to strengthen the heart and give it power to work wonders."[136] As "the layman's Bible,"[137] the catechism was as divine as Scripture itself, designated by God for common folk lacking skill and time for immersing themselves in the Old and New Testaments. It was God's gift to the plain man, proving his gracious disposition toward the human race:

> You recognize a kind, well-meaning father when you see how a man lifts from a child's back a great weight and burden, which is too heavy for him to bear, and takes it on his own shoulders, giving the child a smaller burden to carry. . . . In the same way we recognize God's superfatherly or supermotherly [*überveterliches oder übermütterliches*] heart going out

to his forlorn creatures and feeble little earthworms when he draws the sap, vital power, and taste of the whole Bible, which is a book much too long for poor lay people to grasp and remember, into the extract of a slender and easy catechism.[138]

If such appeals fell on deaf ears, it was not because Lutheran churchmen had failed to try hard enough or lacked talent or conviction. In any case, their faith in the catechism as a teaching instrument remained undiminished.

It was a highly useful instrument also for guarding orthodoxy, an objective second in importance only to that of propagating the doctrine. Protestant states and cities always introduced catechism instruction as one of their first acts of reformation. From the beginning they incorporated anti-Catholic propaganda.[139] Antisectarian apologetics were included a little later, and around the middle of the century, when the contention among religious factions preoccupied Lutheran theologians, catechisms tended to become overtly polemical. Caspar Huberinus, the most prolific of catechism writers, urged his colleagues to use the catechism for this purpose. "You should," he pleaded, "do more than merely explain the words and meaning [of the catechism] to the young. You should indicate also that from earliest days heretics have attacked and opposed each of its articles, and how these articles can be defended against unbelievers, so that young people stand warned against false prophets and develop a loathing for all past and present heresy."[140] The roster of latter-day heretics lengthened with each passing year. "*Question:* Who are now the false prophets who spread errors and confusion in the Church of God? *Answer:* The following: Jews, Turks, papists, sacramentarians, Anabaptists, Schwenckfeldians, interimists, adiaphorists, Majorists, synergists, antinomians, Osiandrists, and many more."[141] An age of ceaseless religious bickering needed a firm criterion for testing the soundness or falseness of rival doctrines. Catechisms facilitated this judgment. "If [an unfamiliar belief] agrees with our beloved catechism you may accept it," it was said; "if it conflicts with it, avoid it like the plague."[142]

Our most impressive testimonials to the propaganda power of catechisms come from Catholic regions, where officials looked upon the Lutheran catechism with both alarm and undisguised respect. Catholic visitation documents report the rapid spread of Protestant catechisms into Bavaria, the bishopric of Bamberg, and many other territories still loyal to Rome in the middle of the century. To constant Protestants living in fear of prosecution, the catechism must have been a mainstay of their faith and the chief means of passing it on to their offspring. Catholic officials who had the job of rooting it out[143] soon paid it the compliment of emulation. Wherever they governed they instituted catechism instruction in church and school, on the

Protestant model.[144] These measures were as vital to the Catholic Reformation as to Protestants. Both sides regarded the catechism as the best medium for propagating the right religion, the only feasible method of mass indoctrination, the most reliable shield of orthodoxy, and the most efficient agent of uniformity.[145]

Methodologically, the catechism was perfectly suited to the pedagogical model transmitted from the past and adopted by the reformers as an answer to their special needs. Although the Reformation coincided with the first flowering of the culture of printing and is generally thought to have been one of its chief beneficiaries,[146] it was the catechism's suitability to oral instruction that made it seem a panacea for all problems of mass indoctrination. Many authors emphasized this advantage. Huberinus rejoiced in the direct communication between catechist and catechumen, which is, he said, of the greatest profit to the young. "The catechism is our cabala," he wrote, alluding to "the secret doctrine of the Jews, kept alive only by word of mouth." Of course one cannot, in the middle of the sixteenth century, do without writing or printing, he said. But the instruction of the young proceeds much more efficiently by oral means than by reading, for "the word of mouth stays with them longer, being more powerfully impressed and more deeply rooted."[147] Contemporary attempts to conceptualize the principle of catechization reflect this faith in the spoken word. In 1531 the magistrates of Nuremberg invited their preachers to comment on the merits of catechism teaching, the citywide establishment of which was then under consideration. The ministers wrote: "Catechism is Christian instruction for children [*Kinderlehr*], although it is not only for children, but for all Christians to learn and say from childhood on. Its name comes from the word 'echo,' meaning reverberation, and for the following reason. In the days of the early church the catechism was read aloud to a new Christian and he repeated it word for word, like the voice coming back when one shouts something in a great hall or a forest or a mountain range. And this speaking aloud and answering must be kept up until the children can repeat the whole catechism correctly."[148]

Apodictic speaking and rote repetition agreed also with prevailing notions of the unstable character of the young, and with the general disinclination to consider initiative and spontaneity as acceptable incentives to learning. Theology, psychology, the received wisdom, and practical experience were in perfect accord on this point. To hand down the word from above and to receive and repeat it faithfully from below was a holy, methodical, safe, and sensible pedagogical practice. It was ideally realized in the three ways of learning the catechism, "by questions, by interrogation, and by preaching [*fragweis, verhörweis und predigweis*]."[149] It conditioned the mind and formed desirable habits. "What is the advantage of our way of doing the catechism?" asked Johann Tettelbach in his *Golden Treasure*. He replied "it accustoms children from their earliest years to pay attention, to grasp a thing quickly, repeat it accurately, and speak up distinctly and without fear."[150] A practice "agreeable and congenial to human nature," the erotematic method offered the most direct and artless approach to learning and teaching.[151] It facilitated the reduction of complex subjects to manageable units. From the very outset it prepared the learner for the examination that tested its results at the end of the learning process. With unchangeably familiar questions and predictable answers it was the very paradigm of the safe and static condition in which the reformers hoped to come to rest after the headlong mutability and confusion of their own time of troubles. In the most developed form of catechism practice, where children stood up in pairs to ask each other the prescribed questions and give the required answers,[152] the procedure approached the ideal of a fully internalized and self-perpetuating system of indoctrination.

Not everyone accepted these results as the best to be obtained. Visitors could scarcely avoid noticing that nearly everywhere children tended to drone in vacant and mindless automation. Throughout the later sixteenth and the seventeenth centuries, reformers within the reform movement tried to convey to people an understanding of their faith, or at least make them wish to understand it. Their success was minimal, as will be seen, although this result did not keep them from persisting. The chief trouble was that the catechetical method had suffered a change of character in its transplantation from the days of the early church to the age of the Reformation. Having read Augustine's description of his own work as a catechist, sixteenth-century reformers ought surely to have been alerted to the inevitability of this alteration. Augustine had addressed himself to mature individuals and devoted close attention to their responses and the growth of their understanding. We cannot look into a catechumen's mind, he wrote, to discover whether his reception of the doctrine is obstructed by religious fear, or by a skeptical disposition, or a weak intellect, or natural shyness. We must try every approach likely to involve him actively in the learning process: "We must by questioning him find out whether he understands; and must give him confidence so that if he thinks there is an objection to make he may freely lay it before us."[153] This personal, empathic, and intellectual approach obviously became impossible when catechization turned for its objects to the young and simple, applied itself to the multitude, and sought to implant, imbue, and impress rather than persuade. Settling into a rigidly formal, not to say hidebound, routine, it tended to evoke perfunctory responses from its involuntary subjects. It could coerce people to memorize words and reproduce them mechanically when called on to do so. But it was not a technique likely to arouse curiosity and promote comprehension.

On the other hand, words were better than nothing, and reformers refused to give up hope that sooner or later the holy catechism would take root in the hearts of the young and begin to promote religious understanding. They continued to work toward this goal, imploring their audiences to apply themselves more willingly, warning them of the wages of indifference and neglect: "Let no one think himself so clever and wise as to imagine that he has finished with his catechism and can put it out of his mind. There will come a time when the Son of God will give the examination and ask each of us what he has learned. And we will have sore need of it then, if we have learned it!"[154] Trying their best to make catechism study as painless as possible, they avoided overtaxing young and simple minds, forever abbreviating, condensing, digesting.[155] "Don't burden the young with long explanations and subtle discourses"[156] was the watchword. "Never keep them longer than an hour."[157] "It would be best if the entire procedure, from bell-ringing and hymn to sermon and the children's examinations, were completed in less than an hour, for we should not intrude on people's enjoyment of their Christian leisure time after a hard week's work."[158] When addressing young audiences, pastors should "preach only fifteen minutes or, at most, half an hour."[159] In many places children could earn favors by performing well: a penny or two in Nuremberg and Saxony, a loaf of bread in Halberstadt, dancing in the market square in Zweibrücken.[160] But even where such inducements were used, the catechism did not often stick in the mind, as pastors were discovering in the confessional.[161] Pedagogical theories notwithstanding, rote memorization did not seem to suffice. Johann Tettelbach, who as pastor and superintendent in Saxony had many years' experience studying the catechism with all kinds of people, young and old, identified the root of the problem. "I have been noticing," he wrote in 1568, "that schoolboys and other children merely memorize this precious book. This is a praiseworthy thing to do, to be sure. But they remember it without having thought or reflected on what it means, and they parrot the words with so little feeling that when one asks them a question about it, they can't explain even the simplest thing."[162] Like every author before and after him, however, Tettelbach believed he had in hand a superior method to enable him to succeed where others had failed. It did not occur to him to admit defeat.

As for adults, they appear to have remained cool to assurances that with respect to the holy catechism they would remain forever children. Visitors in the duchy of Braunschweig-Grubenhagen reported in 1579 that "people over eighteen years of age are ashamed to be seen at catechism practice, and none of them will go to it."[163] It was even suggested that the embarrassing name "Children's Doctrine" (*Kinderlehr*) be dropped in favor of *Christenlehr*, "because that word *Kinderlehr* makes grown men and women feel disgraced to be seen in a catechism class."[164] Here too we find religious writers and ecclesiastical officials prepared to convince themselves that no more than an adjustment was required to reverse the unfavorable drift of things.

Detailed demonstration of their failure to effect this reversal will be the subject of a later chapter. In the present one I have tried to do justice to the endeavor itself. Successful or not, the Lutheran experiment in mass indoctrination brings one of the central objectives of the Reformation into focus and suggests a criterion for judging its achievement. A conscious, systematic, and vigorous effort was made to change the human personality through pedagogical conditioning. The chief instrument of this process was the catechism. This was an unprecedented venture whose failure, never fully acknowledged at the time and not adequately described since then, brought to an end the sixteenth century's most radical effort to put the ideal of reform into action.

CHAPTER 9

TECHNIQUES OF INDOCTRINATION: SCHOOLING

In planning and implementing their program of indoctrination, Protestant educators did not differentiate between the objectives of religious teaching and the aims of formal schooling. Both rested upon identical pedagogical assumptions and were directed toward the same goals. Educational reformers felt pressed for time. Alarmed by the symptoms of academic decline in the 1520s and 1530s, they wished to expedite learning. Their psychological and pedagogical postulates convinced them that success in this endeavor lay within their grasp. Indeed they often boasted of the dispatch with which the pieces of knowledge could be assimilated with the aid of their techniques. We have encountered these claims in the preceding survey of catechization. Similar assertions were made for teaching languages, literature, history, and geography. Given a modest aptitude on the part of the pupil, learning was a matter of applying the correct procedure under favorable conditions. This procedure consisted of dismembering subjects into small segments and committing these to the pupil's memory, bits at a time and by means of ceaseless repetition. Once a subject was broken down and tied by associational links to cognate topics, each leading to and from the other, instruction became an orderly, mechanical "method."

These ideas will be recognized as a reduction of the educational theories of Peter Ramus.[1] But the simplifying and "methodizing" technique later known as Ramism was advocated by Protestant pedagogues long before the books of Ramus and his followers began to circulate in Germany.[2] Its adoption was a natural consequence of the generally accepted model of the mind. The persuasiveness of this model was bound to lend a certain crudeness to pedagogues' claims that they held the key to effective learning. Michael Neander's *Memorandum on*

Guiding and Instructing a Boy from Six to Eighteen of 1580 is a case in point. Its author, a prominent Lutheran preceptor at a famous Latin school in Ilfeld in Saxony, tried to condense a lifetime of experience into a pedagogical system that he hoped would prove useful to his colleagues. Successful teaching, according to Neander, removes the intellectual discomfort normally associated with learning. "Without exertion or distaste, hardly aware that he is learning anything, the boy will gain knowledge and keep it firmly in his memory as long as he lives."[3] The secret was to reduce the daily intake to tiny portions, four lines of grammar a day, no more, "and whatever you do, don't rush him, make him repeat these lines daily, precisely and without missing a word, a syllable, or a letter, and do this every single day, adding something new each time, but very little, and every day make him recite from the first to the last word everything he has learned." In this way, without quite knowing how, a boy masters grammar in as little as half a year. In ten years he will have assimilated a curriculum that used to take twenty, "and he will not only have learned it completely and accurately, but he will also know how to profit from it."[4]

Pedagogical method thus involved nothing more than disjoining a subject into its smallest teachable parts and having the pupil ingest them in an unvarying diet of repetition. "Never give children too much to learn at one time," it was recommended, "but repeat often what you give them, and always in the same manner and words."[5] Some pedagogues thought children in primary grades should study only two hours a day; others recommended four. Part of their time should be spent at games; hard work will come soon enough in their lives, one pedagogue said, "and once it has started it will last until they are dead and buried in the ground."[6] "Don't overwhelm them with books and homework, don't make them get up too early in the morning, don't press them too hard"—this from a Saxon school ordinance.[7] The principle of this policy[8] was a commitment to method rather than a humane regard for the young, although it would be wrong to conclude from this preoccupation that pedagogues were unfeeling toward their pupils. "Take pity on [their] innocence," teachers were told. "Don't frighten them. Never humiliate them."[9] Don't be too quick to tell a boy that he lacks ability. "In this case, too," the school ordinance of Württemberg noted, "it is possible that the last will be the first." Always take a boy's age and background into consideration."[10] Sometimes talents lie dormant under a cover of shyness and inexperience.[11] In any case, the world of learning is so diverse that everyone, no matter how modestly endowed, can find in it something of value. "It is as if you led your pupils into a lovely flower garden," said Huberinus. "One child will pick this blossom, another that; one gathers an armful, another only a few. This is how it is in the garden of the mind."[12]

The age for entering school continued to be the traditional six or seven, most educational theorists favoring six as the most suitable year in which to begin formal study.[13] At this age a boy's intellectual faculties were fully developed, while his character was still pliable and his disposition flexible enough to respond to the pedagogue's shaping hand. For at least three years, more often for five or six, he remained in Latin or "particular" school; then, if he was to continue his studies, he went up to the gymnasium before enrolling at the university. But the correlation between age and school form remained as haphazard in the Reformation era as in earlier periods, and it was not unusual for a boy of twelve to share a bench with youths four or five years older.[14] School administrators were combatting this untidy arrangement, which they regarded as a troublesome holdover from the past. On the other hand, they seem also to have known, both from experience and from theory,[15] that children do not all develop at the same pace.

Young as they were, pupils found themselves subjected to two kinds of pressure: for the majority it was to conform and comply, for the able, to excel. These constraints were thought to be complementary; their objective was of course a social one and had little to do with individual boys. Conforming the young to the approved type was, as has been seen, the chief aim of mass education. But the selection of an intellectual elite was a goal no less energetically pursued. The apparent decline in the number and quality of Latin students in the 1520s had persuaded Luther and his associates that they must warn against the proliferation of vernacular schools.[16] Suspecting that the lure of a cheaper and utilitarian educational alternative would rob higher education, and eventually church and government, of a host of good minds,[17] they prepared to counteract this temptation, especially after the second half of the century, when the establishment of German schools became an object of government policy. Officials roamed the land looking for "good minds" in town and village schools. From Neustadt in the principality of Coburg, visitors reported that "we found some able young minds here, but they are children of wretchedly poor parents." In Eisfeld they discovered "two boys with promising minds, but both from poor homes." Their names were forwarded to the capital.[18] Where school systems were centralized, as in Württemberg and Saxony, this procedure often produced positive results. Bulky dossiers on deserving pupils attest to the time, care, and—occasionally —money invested in the advancement of promising young scholars.[19] Visitors routinely reported the names of students who excelled in catechism examination,[20] and governments often followed through with scholarship aid, or at least with encouragement.[21] But often their efforts were frustrated by parental resistance. And always there was the struggle against time. "Where we find a boy of some promise," a

Coburg visitor observed, "his parents are likely to take him out of school and set him to minding the shop or keeping pigs. And once he is grown up he will be ashamed to go back to school."[22] Unless rescued early, such a boy was forever lost to the common benefit.[23] Some territories staged an annual *delectus,* a screening operation designed to discover "which among our pupils have suitable natures, sound heads, and good intellects."[24] The criteria for making this choice were not in dispute. Everyone held talent to consist of a quick intellect, a tenacious memory, a strong desire to learn, the ability to persevere in hard work, good health, and a tranquil spirit.[25] A boy who possessed these qualities had the makings of a theologian, lawyer, or scholar and should not be left to waste his gifts in a workshop or in the field.

In order to nurture these talents, school administrators "streamed" classes wherever enrollment was large enough, and teachers were available, to justify this action. "Unequal minds [*ingenia*] sitting together impede effective learning," it was said.[26] Or, as the Electoral Saxon visitors stated in their *Instruction* of 1534: "pupils must be divided into groups so that no one will be held back in his studies."[27] Ideally, classes should be homogeneous and large enough to allow pupils of roughly equal gifts to test their wits against one another.[28] Competition for academic distinction was regarded as an effective impetus to attaining excellence,[29] and ambition was encouraged. As long as they were directed to intellectual and spiritual pursuits, achievement-oriented impulses were not considered incompatible with the reticence dictated by the evangelical model. No Protestant educator went as far as Jesuit pedagogues, who spoke of a *sancta aemulatio*.[30] But the zeal (*Eifer*) to excel and surpass, and to relish personal success,[31] was as assiduously fostered in the budding captains of the Protestant church, state, and academy as it was suppressed in the mass of their future subjects.

Mention of suppression raises the subject of corporal punishment and the question posed by the ineradicable impression that rod and paddle were throughout the early history of education the essential instruments of instruction. Needless to say, pupils were whipped at times, and the threat of physical pain played a part in their education. But the relationship between schooling and punishment is much more subtle than the connection implied by the proposition that "lickin' and l'arnin' goes together."[32]

It has been argued that a sin-oriented religion possessed an inherent psychological justification for the use of physical pain as a principle of correction,[33] and it is true that a search among Christian pedagogical authors yields many telling passages to support this contention. The fifteenth-century Dominican Giovanni Dominici, for example,

asserted it as a simple fact that "frequent chastisement is of great benefit to the young because it improves them." He explained: "Being
especially prone to wickedness and naturally disinclined to do the
right thing, children need to be controlled, and this is best done by
means of frequent punishment." Dominici advised that children be
trained to beg to be punished, and to express gratitude for blows received. "This mode of education," he commented, "should not stop in
the fourth or fifth year but must be kept up as long as needed, even to
the twenty-fifth year."[34] Dominici's ideas lingered long in the pedagogical literature. If necessary, they could be reinforced with ferocious
injunctions from the Old Testament (for example, Ecclus. 30:12) to
prove that bodily punishment was wholesome and good. "Of what use
is the rod to the young?" asked the author of *A Book of Christian
Counsel for Children*, published in Wittenberg in 1536. He answered:
"it rescues their souls from hell. Prov. 23 [13–14]."[35] Folk wisdom
chimed in: "the bigger the rod, the better the child." Tenderhearted
objections could be neutralized with the comforting reflection that
"God has created the human buttocks with a generous amount of flesh
so that no irreparable damage will be done when a child is whipped."[36]
If anyone pointed out that the pain inflicted might be psychological, as
well as physical, he could be pacified with the warning, taken from
Prov. 13:24, that "he who spares the rod hates his son." We hear of
children intoning, under the watchful eye of their master, a hymn to
the birch rod:

> O, my dear rod
> Teach me to fear God;
> Make me good, I beg,
> Or the hangman will have my neck,[37]

to which the proverb added: "better the teacher's wooden stick than
the executioner's iron bludgeon."[38]

This brief anthology could be expanded to show that corporal
punishment had a place in sixteenth-century pedagogy.[39] The question is, How prominent a place? Modern critics who are out to prove
that physical discipline in the fifteenth, sixteenth, and seventeenth
centuries was not only severe but brutal and degrading—that it reveals,
as Philippe Ariès would have it, society's "insistence on humiliating
childhood"[40]—have looked at only part of the evidence. It has been
noted in an earlier chapter that the consensus of traditional pedagogical
authority, from Quintilian to Erasmus and Vives, was emphatically
against the indiscriminate use of pain and terror. The educational laws
of the Reformation (Catholic as well as Protestant) reflect this abhor-
rence of inhumane correction. It is possible, of course, to read official
prohibitions of brutal beatings as proof that barbaric practices were in

fact widespread in the early sixteenth century. There is some auto-biographical evidence to support this contention. Luther's recollec-tions are a familiar case in point, and others, too, tend to show that child-beating was not uncommon in homes and schools.[41] Indeed, it would be surprising if schoolmasters—most of whom lived in anything but comfortable circumstances—had not on occasion resorted to the stick to vent their frustrations.

Contrary to the model suggested by Ariès, however, the conscious intention of governments seems to have been to mitigate this practice. No one argued against the need for an occasional scolding or cuffing. The saintliest educator and fondest of parents conceded that beating was sometimes necessary and helpful.[42] But moderation was of the essence. "Confine your punishment to words and a few strokes of the birch," the governments of Strassburg and Ulm instructed their teachers. "Let your words give no personal offense or insult, and limit your blows to those parts of the body least likely to be injured. Don't beat them about the head, never use your fist or bare hand on them, and don't pull them by the hair."[43] Minor misdeeds should be overlooked.[44] "Everything in good measure," advised a Saxon visitation order, "for excessive punishment will turn young people against their studies."[45] Luther had made the very same point. "How many good minds," he complained, "have been ruined for learning by the violence and brutal-ity of some of our schoolmasters."[46] The ordinances themselves some-times convey a glimpse of such a brute at work. The Nordhausen *Schulordnung* of 1583, for instance, warned against "acting tyrannically, striking boys until they are bloody, kicking them, lifting them by their hair or ears, beating them about the face with a stick or a book."[47] All governments tried to put an end to this abuse. The archives of most territories and cities contain dossiers on individual cases of brutality brought to official attention.[48] Once an incident had been reported, usually after a visitation or upon a local complaint, it was investigated and the offending teacher charged with having by his lack of restraint violated the idea of "fatherly castigation" to which he had been sworn. If the charge stuck, he was fined or even discharged.[49]

Where the state failed to act, parents tended to take matters into their own hands. They had the legal right to revoke the transfer of disciplinary authority from household to teacher;[50] but whether they knew of this right or not, they often rushed to the defense of their young. These incidents illustrate both sides of the argument over the limits of corporal punishment. Teachers constantly protested that even a modest reproof, not to mention a flogging, brought an irate father or a furious mother storming into the schoolhouse. "Even a cross glance at a boy is enough to make his parents remove him from school," said one.[51] On the other hand, parents often charged school personnel with being "unduly severe," showing "a sour and mean disposition," or practicing "relentless and cruel discipline, particularly in using the rod."[52] Such accusations may be proof of the prevalence of brutality in the classroom. Or they may substantiate what many religious and pedagogical writers said at the time: that scandalously permissive parents were raising a generation of loafers and troublemakers.[53] It is impossible to decide this question from our distant perspective. What seems clear, however, is that sensible people were striving for a balance of kindness and severity in raising the young. Luther's advice to "punish children in such a manner that they always see the apple while they feel the rod"[54] was exemplary. "Punishment will work if it is not too severe; tenderness and moderation are good if kept within bounds," wrote the physician Otto Brunfels.[55] Reflecting on the experiences of his childhood in which a quick-tempered father had often been restrained by an indulgent mother, the Stralsund patrician Bartholomäus Sastrow expressed the hope that "my own children will find the right way to discipline their offspring, neither injuring or intimidating them with excessive punishments, nor pampering them with foolish doting."[56] Government regulations turned these prudent sentiments into laws.[57] Although they are not likely to have restrained every village teacher, the modern historian who finds irascible martinets and cane-swinging bullies in every classroom before the eighteenth century has seen less than half the picture.

2

Another matter for state intervention was the material condition of schools and teachers. Visitation documents give a vivid, and mostly dismal, picture of the circumstances in which mass education took place in the sixteenth century; but in reading these sources it is worth remembering that the information conveying this impression was brought to light by officials eager to make improvements. Nearly every defect ultimately turned on the problem of money. No one denied that a modicum of space, light, and ventilation, adequate heating in winter, and a few sticks of furniture (benches with backrests for pupils, a podium and table or lectern for the teacher, a blackboard, a candlestick or two, a cupboard) were necessary if any benefit were to be had from schooling. An educational reform program that could not provide these was not likely to have much of an impact. The question was: Who had the responsibility of paying for such amenities or, rather, how should the bill be divided? We owe most of our knowledge of sixteenth-century school conditions to the documents generated by the everlasting bickering among central and local governments over who was to pay for what.

For example: in 1562 the city fathers of Coburg agreed to appropriate a sum for rebuilding their Latin school, "provided," they insisted, "our Gracious Prince and Lord be willing to grant us a subsidy . . . in this time of galloping inflation."[58] The present edifice, the magistrates went on, "is ramshackle, stuffy, damp, and so gloomy that the boys who sit in it suffer from weak and inflamed eyes." This is a typical picture.[59] Many a schoolhouse was a derelict building, usually a private home donated for the purpose or purchased at a bargain price. Too small even to give adequate shelter to the teacher and his family, it often held, as well, a number of student boarders in a garret under the thatch, and on the ground floor a classroom or two. In the poorer villages conditions were appalling. A single room where the teacher or sexton and his wife and children lived, slept, and cooked, accommodated village children of all ages and both sexes for what reading and catechism they could absorb under such conditions.[60] Often there was neither a cellar for storing wood and vegetables nor an attic. For heat in winter, each pupil brought a piece of wood.[61] "A tumbledown structure," "worm-eaten," "a low ceiling," "smoky," "much too small for four classes"—these are characteristic descriptions.[62]

Failure to improve things in the course of the century was not due to want of trying. All governments agreed that schooling ought to take place amid suitable surroundings. This principle underlay their investigations of actual conditions. "Still no schoolhouse in this market village [*noch immer keine schule erbaut*]," we read in a report on Annaburg in Saxony, a place of 340 communicants, in 1583.[63] This formula suggests that the existence of a proper school building in such a place was regarded as normal. But the standard was not always met. Major cities boasted splendid edifices: the Saint Nicholas school in Leipzig, the refurbished Franciscan monastery serving Ulm as its Latin school, the Saint Anna Gymnasium in Augsburg. But elsewhere schoolmastering continued in physical surroundings whose disheartening features go a long way toward explaining its unsatisfactory results.

Equally dismal—but again with notable exceptions—was the plight of those who worked in these depressing structures. Given the enormous economic disparity among and within German territories, the pay and keep of school personnel differed according to no single criterion except the time-honored usage that it was more remunerative to teach in Latin than in German, at a gymnasium than at a particular school, in a city than in a small town, and in a town than in a village. But this rule covered a huge spread, from a comfortable living to utter penury, with the latter predominating. Not many teachers existed in a state suited to the exalted role written for them by the reformers.

In fact, some of the blame for their penury should go to educational theorists who helped perpetuate the myth of the dedicated teacher whose sense of vocation inured him to material privations. If, as Murmellius had said, a good teacher should be *pecuniae contemptor*,[64] why overpay him? Vives's recommendation that "teachers [should] receive a salary . . . such as a good man will desire but a wicked man disdain,"[65] when translated into fiscal politics, served to justify the payment of a pittance. While a handful of distinguished scholars at renowned schools enjoyed fortune as well as fame, their lesser colleagues lived in a servile state, figures of ridicule and contempt in folklore and anecdotes,[66] hampered by humiliating restrictions on their private lives,[67] condemned to spend their careers in demeaning poverty. One must read through the enormous documentation on matters of school policy to take the full measure of these abject conditions. Thousands of pleading petitions to the Duke of Württemberg, for instance, coming from teachers in all corners of his territory, describe their deteriorating situation owing to inflation and implore his assistance, however small.[68] To give substance to their pleas, teachers itemized their incomes down to the number of eggs and candles due them at Eastertime. They complained of tight-fisted parents cheating on the quarterly pupils' fee, withholding it altogether, or taking their children out of school just before it fell due (a common custom). They described their beggarly one-room shacks with roofs like sieves and the pigs sharing the family's quarters for lack of a sty. And they depict their wants:

> All week long I take nothing but water to drink at my hard work so that on Sunday I can treat myself to half a measure of wine with my meal. Is there a stable groom in Your Grace's duchy who doesn't have his daily cup of wine? But we schoolmasters, to whom you entrust your children, are forced by our poverty to chafe our lips on the water jug all year long![69]

The point at issue here is the incongruity between the actual condition of teachers and the high and godly task they were expected to perform. Governments were not insensitive to this paradox. They tried to ascertain the facts of the situation[70] and when these cried out for redress, as they usually did, attempted to remedy them. But their best efforts were defeated by the steady rise in prices and the foot-dragging of local authorities and individual householders. In addition, there appears to have been an oversupply of candidates for teaching posts, which further eroded teachers' economic position. Nearly every archive holds bundles of applications from job seekers—young men just out of school and veterans looking for a change.[71] A kind of grapevine must have operated among them, for the inquiries began to arrive as soon as a place was vacated by death or removal. But not many vacancies occurred after the period of educational expansion in the middle of the sixteenth century. Most teachers remained in their jobs until they dropped dead. Few instances of voluntary retirement are known, but there are many of a tenure in the same post lasting twenty-five, forty, even fifty years.[72] Governments were very much alive to the peril of allowing aging schoolmen to continue in office. They watched for danger signals. Visitors observed "old and embittered," "feeble-bodied," "dull-witted," "half-blind," and "failing" teachers still at work.[73] Just why such individuals were not replaced from the pool of younger candidates is difficult to say. The documents suggest that visitors turned a humane face to the plight of aged pedants staring at total destitution in their last years. They allowed them to remain in office even when their incompetence had been demonstrated.[74] Negotiations for a new appointment were always time-consuming, with government agents and local elders pulling in opposite directions. Vacancies therefore occurred only at death or upon proof of criminal turpitude, or heresy, or doctrinal unreliability, the last of these being the most common cause for dismissal.

Remuneration differed so widely from place to place that there is no sense in trying to convey more than an impression of it. The crucial point to make here is that the very individuals upon whose skill and dedication depended the success of the Reformation's pedagogical program were consistently the worst paid, most wretchedly housed, and least-esteemed members of their profession. Whereas the rector of the Hamburg Latin school earned 200 marks in 1530, Camerarius and Eobanus Hesse 150 gulden per annum in Nuremberg in 1526, Thomas Platter 100 gulden in Basel, and the preceptors of the upper gymnasium forms in Ulm and Augsburg at the beginning of the seventeenth century from 240 to 300 gulden in addition to free housing (a figure they regarded as inadequate), the Kolmar schoolmaster had only 40 gulden in 1545 (plus minimal fees from all but his poorest pupils), as did his colleague in Altdorf near Nuremberg in 1560, compared with 30 gulden for a Wittenberg schoolmaster in 1555, 26 gulden in 1588 for the teacher in Pattensen (a district capital in the duchy of Braunschweig-Kalenberg), and 15 gulden for the third assistant in Saint John's school in Halberstadt in 1589. Visitations in Albertine Saxony in 1542 brought to light a salary spread from 120 gulden in Dresden to 50 in Lammatsch, down to 15 gulden for an assistant master.[75]

Discrepancies between Latin and vernacular teachers were enormous, a state of affairs often deplored by visitors but left unchanged throughout the century. Visitors in Coburg in the 1570s, for example, noted that "German teachers have a small income here, no more than about 10 gulden per year each," whereas a Latin school rector, they reported in 1578, had 61 gulden with free housing, the cantor 49 gulden and his firewood, and the "third" 38 gulden.[76] As for the average village teacher, he had to make ends meet with the minuscule pupils' fees to which governments tried, wherever possible, to shift the major burden of financing public instruction,[77] plus various emoluments obtained by him in his *Rundgang* from door to door at Christmas and Easter.[78] In some small towns and villages he even went about for his daily dinner. Most teachers pursued other trades as well. Authorities did not like this but, in view of the miserable pay, closed their official eye.[79] Usually German teachers were also full-time sextons or town scribes or copyists, helped out in church, carried on a trade in books, or did all of these. For instance:

> Concerning Sebastian Hopf, charged with being lazy in performing his duties as schoolmaster, we [the Nuremberg territorial visitors, in 1560] have found that in addition to his teaching service, he works as municipal secretary in Greifenberg, court scribe and tax recorder in Hildpolstein, and he also greases and sets the clock in the town hall at Grevenberg. From all these jobs he has only 38 gulden per annum and cannot afford to pay an assistant to give him more time for his duties in the school and church. He also complains that his schoolhouse is too crowded for his wife, children, and pupils, especially when his wife is confined to her childbed.[80]

With such distractions occupying Sebastian Hopf's mind, one wonders how much teaching and learning were going on in his schoolroom.

One also wonders at the gaping disproportion between such a scene and the reformers' great expectations of what pedagogy might accomplish. Their working assumptions suggested that dedicated teaching would draw positive responses from pupils and support from their parents. Conversely, if the public reaction was slack, teachers must be at fault for having failed to make their mark.[81] Raising the standard of instruction was declared to be a matter of high priority, and involved not only the teacher's professional competence, but also his humane approach to pupils. "A school," rhapsodized the rector of the Latin school in Eisfeld in Saxony, in 1568, "is like a young orchard where, under the care of a devoted gardener, tender saplings grow and mature into strong and fruitful trees."[82] Governments attempted to prepare teachers for this delicate task. By the second half of the sixteenth century, firm criteria for the appointment and supervision of teachers were in use in nearly all German states. Candidates had to show testimonials from former preceptors or employers. An unemployed teacher without a letter of reference was automatically suspect. Intellectual and doctrinal fitness were subject to examinations, often before the consistory or *Kirchenrat*, the highest ecclesiastical authority. If a man's competence was in doubt he was shunted "to a small school where he does only the catechism," provided, of course, he could meet the religious test and was certified to possess "a good understanding of the divine word."[83] Files were gathered of handwriting specimens and lists of "books read during the past year."[84] Authorities tried to ensure "that [the candidate] can show children how to form letters and syllables, read and do sums, and that he himself writes a legible hand."[85] They investigated his origins and travel in foreign parts. They probed for signs of a "disputatious nature"—a sure mark, it was thought, of Calvinist influence.[86] They demanded an upright walk of life, for teachers were expected to set an example to the young.[87]

Clearly, then, there was an intent—although largely confined to schools in populous and well-to-do places—to turn teachers into a professional corps.[88] But the outcome of this endeavor depended directly on the supply of money and the willingness to spend it. Most governments supported serious academic learning in Latin schools, gymnasiums, seminaries, and universities; these represented a political investment well worth making. But they tended to be far less open-handed with the instruction of the general public, evidently having convinced themselves that in the catechism they had a cheap instrument of mass indoctrination that required neither expensive teaching talent nor costly facilities. This, it turned out, was a fatal miscalculation.

To a considerable extent this error arose from the preoccupation with fast learning techniques to which attention has already been called. In a conscious break with the older "medieval" predilection for long, arduous study and bulky erudition, Reformation pedagogues pursued the shortcut to learning. Their first experiments drastically curtailed the time needed to gain essential knowledge. Luther in 1524, and Bugenhagen in 1528, claimed that no more than one or two hours a day were required to train youngsters in rudimentary skills and basic religion.[89] But in the realm of formal schooling, as also in vernacular teaching, these optimistic estimates were soon abandoned, and pedagogues returned to the time-honored schedules of the medieval academic program.

Latin school pupils started their day at six or seven o'clock in the morning (in winter usually at eight), went home for the midday meal, returned at one and remained until four. In principle, classes continued through the calendar year, but in practice vacations at Christmas and Easter broke the routine. Wednesday afternoons were usually free, and, of course, Sunday all day, to let children attend church and catechism practice. Vacations were rare.[90] But it was customary to cancel afternoon classes during the hottest weeks of summer and to take a holiday at the time of the annual fair. There were free hours for sports and games, as long as these could be enjoyed "in a decent and honest manner."[91]

Country schools recessed for the harvest and operated by a haphazard calendar determined by situation, climate, the state of the economy, the educational interest of parents, and the schoolmaster's dedication. In some places school was held only in the winter, farm work keeping children occupied during the rest of the year. In others it was closed from November to March since most children could not or would not make their way across difficult terrain in freezing weather or were too poor to bring the required piece of wood for heating the classroom. Vernacular and catechism schools in rural parishes set their hours to accommodate the children's domestic and agricultural chores. Five to nine A.M. school days were not uncommon in the summer; seven to eleven in winter.[92] School attendance was obligatory in theory, but incessant pleas by the authorities indicate that this duty was not taken seriously by many.

Although the organization of mass instruction in Lutheran Germany was innovative in many respects, formal learning remained entirely traditional, both in concept and in execution.[93] Apart from the religious component, only its administrative rigor and uniformity were new. Every detail was stipulated in supervisory regulations that bound teachers and pupils to an immutable order. "Unless a school organization [Schulwesen] operates according to definite laws and ordinances, it cannot work efficiently, nor will it, in the long run, escape destruction"—this from the preamble to the school ordinance of the gymnasium at Regensburg.[94] Obedient to this general principle of educational policy, rectors and schoolmasters in nearly every German city and territory submitted to the ecclesiastical or political authorities their Schulordnungen, lesson plans, timetables, and reading lists. The archives hold a stupendous mass of these documents.[95] Owing to the drive for uniformity, they are very much alike, which makes it easy to summarize the contents of Latin education in the sixteenth century.

In the first grade, beginners struggling with ABC books or primers sat beside more advanced boys already doing their Donatus (who, according to Luther, was still "the best of grammarians").[96] By the end of the year all were expected to read simple texts and write legibly. By then they had also done Leonhard Culman's sententiae pueriles and a few of the distichs of "Cato," the proverbs of Solomon, some psalms, gospel readings with brief explanations, and the catechism in Latin and German. They had memorized hymn tunes and were singing these at Sunday service. In second grade the elements of formal grammar were added to the curriculum. Pupils continued with their "Cato" and went on to Aesop (in Joachim Camerarius's Latin translation), to the scholastic dialogues of Mathurin Cordier after their publication in 1564, or the simpler colloquies of Erasmus, some Terence, as well as a conduct book such as Erasmus's *De civilitate morum puerilium* or Camerarius's *Praecepta morum.* In some schools the study of Greek began during the second year. Catechism study continued in this and all subsequent grades.

The third-year curriculum added Melanchthon's textbooks in Latin grammar and syntax, also the epistles of Cicero, more Terence, Ovid, and, in Greek, Isocrates and the Greek gospel. Music theory and practice was continued, as was gospel reading (in three languages now) and the catechism. There was also some Latin dictation. Fourth grade extended Greek to Plutarch and Theognis, Latin to the study of prosody with Horace's *Odes* and Vergil's *Eclogues;* more Cicero, some Livy, and synonyms from Erasmus's *Copia verborum.* Finally, if there was a fifth grade (not all Latin schools had one) it took up the *Aeneid,* Melanchthon's *Dialectics* and Greek grammar, Hesiod, the *Iliad,* and practice in translating from one classical language to another; also, at long last, arithmetic.[97]

Except for a few of the required authors and the thread of catechism practice running from one end of the curriculum to the other, nothing in this program would have given pause to a medieval theorist of the liberal arts, such as Isidore of Seville in the seventh century or, for that matter, Martianus Capella in the fourth. As in the old days, all learning rested on the bedrock of the Latin language, the intensive study of which formed the core of erudite education. Latin was still learned by the so-called natural method. Children listened to a sentence spoken by the teacher and repeated it aloud while looking at the written syllables in their ABC book or tracing the letters on a wax tablet or scrap of paper. The rote memorization encouraged by this procedure seems to have left many youngsters less than fluently literate, and later in the century the "natural" method was challenged by a "modern" way that separated learning to read and learning the Latin language into two distinct operations. But the old way allowed teachers to quickly distinguish able from ordinary students, which was one of the chief objectives of the Latin school, at least in its lower forms.

There was, however, one new element in this course of studies: its religious content and the explicitly indoctrinational slant of some of the reading material. This too was perhaps more a matter of emphasis than of innovation, for primers had traditionally been used to exert a moralizing influence on the pupil. But by insisting on a direct link between piety and the written word—"without the written word [*litterae*] no one can be sanctified," wrote Melanchthon in the preface to his *Elementa puerilia*[98]—the reformers departed from the ways of the past. Melanchthon's primer, as a case in point, first gave the alphabet in capital and small letters, then the vowels and diphthongs; then— leaving it up to the preceptor to make the transition—went directly to the Lord's Prayer, Ave Maria, Apostles' Creed, the sixty-sixth psalm, chapters from Matthew and John, a collection of sayings attributed to the Seven Sages with comments by Erasmus, and a few prayers. Primers like Melanchthon's (most others much easier than his *Elementa,* which, despite its title, was considered a difficult book)[99] were used in every school. Many laced their practice texts with rules of conduct, ranging from tags like *obsequor parenti* to conversations on salutary subjects like the following, taken from Sebald Heyden's *Formulae puerilium:*

> Where were you yesterday? I was at home, having a bath. How long did you bathe? A whole hour. Who bathed you? My parents. What did you do after your bath? I dried my hair. Why did you not return to school? My father forbade it. Why did he do this? Because my hair was still wet. You are a delicate boy![100]

Heyden's *Nomenclatura,* adopted at the Nuremberg school where he taught, started pupils on a religious vocabulary: Adam, tree, serpent, death. Other "name books" gave grace, temptation, Wittenberg, and so on,[101] each word providing an occasion for explanation and comment by the preceptor.

A little more demanding, and offering better opportunities for inculcating ideas and values, were the "sentence books," which had been a staple of Latin teaching since the Middle Ages. "Cato's" *Disticha de moribus ad filium* dominated this field. The author was not Cato the Censor or Cato Uticensis (although the book was in fact attributed to one or the other of these until the day of Scaliger) but a fourth-century compiler of simple-minded wisdom, in hexameters and in the form of Polonius-style advice from father to son, with Stoic and Christian tinges eminently suitable for pedagogical purposes:[102] "Avoid excess," "Keep your word," "Don't start what you can't finish," "Read good books and remember what you read," "Silence is golden," "Be content with little," "He who fears death loses that which is the aim of life." Such conventional precepts appealed to educators everywhere. The themes are moderation, contentment with little, the inevitability of death, respect for one's elders, the insubstantiality of earthly life. Easily memorized and incessantly repeated, these versified home truths may have helped mold character while at the same time giving useful practice in Latin. Cato's only serious competitor was Leonhard Culman's *Sententiae puerilis,* a compilation of material taken from older authors and offering wholesome advice, in handy alphabetical arrangement, such as *Libenter disce* (learn willingly); *Magistratum metue* (fear your magistrates); *Ab Adamo peccatum in nos derivatum est; Absque deo nihil possumus;* and so on.[103]

For the great majority of schoolboys these sayings contained the sum of the education they received. To the extent that they were remembered, perhaps believed, possibly internalized and acted upon, they offered a socially beneficial training. But they conferred little of practical worth or spiritual profit upon those who copied and recited them. Only the few pupils whose aptitude, tenacity, and ambition qualified them for professional careers, and to whom the particular school was only a stepping-stone to higher learning, obtained from their primary training something of lasting value. It initiated them into the exclusive company of men whose mastery of Latin and intimate knowledge of a received canon of texts entitled them to make the rules in the interlocking realms of religion, law, high politics, and erudition. It stripped them of the telltale signs of their origin and permitted men from obscure backgrounds to mingle with the guardians of the established culture. The suggestion has been made that Latin study in early modern Europe functioned as a kind of extended puberty rite, in the course of which a boy advanced from ignorance to approved wisdom and from the vulgar circumstances of family, home, and native place to the select company of international cultural mandarins.[104] While the analogy does not fit precisely, a kind of passage no doubt took place, and the Latin tongue served as the vehicle of transition.

If language enabled the novice to enter this inner circle, grammar conferred on him its intellectual regime. As "the beginning, the source of all the other arts," the *"alma mater* of all learning,"[105] grammar was the core of the liberal curriculum. Like the catechism, with which it was always paired as a foundation discipline, grammar was practiced from the first year of formal schooling to the last. It could never be learned well enough. "First etymology, then syntax, then prosody," advised Melanchthon in his *Instruction of the Visitors* to Saxon pastors and schoolmasters of 1528, "and as soon as this sequence has been completed, start again from the beginning and in this way impress grammar upon the minds of your pupils. For if this is not done, all learning will be in vain and for nothing." No greater harm, he said, can be inflicted on arts and letters than to allow grammar to fall into desuetude.[106]

But the state of the arts was not the chief concern of pedagogues as they appealed for greater rigor in the study of grammar. They clearly recognized in it a mental discipline by means of which they could foster desirable traits in their pupils. "There is no better way of preparing young people for right discipline [*Zucht*] and sound learning than to teach them the catechism and turn them into firm [*gewisse*] grammarians."[107] What can this proposition mean but that with its rigid and binding rules, its subordination of individual expression to fixed paradigms, its distaste for innovation, and its methodical drills and rote repetition of memorized patterns, grammar was, along with the catechism, the primary training discipline for conditioning the young to approved habits of thought and behavior? In an age that judged excellence by its conformance to a fixed standard, grammar offered pedagogues a practicable regimen for bringing intellects and characters into line with sanctioned models.[108]

In view of the importance of this and other subjects, the right to adopt textbooks could not be left to individual teachers, but was placed in the hands of ecclesiastical or school authorities.[109] In the case of grammar, the choice, for Protestants, was an easy one: Melanchthon's *Grammatica latina*, first printed in 1532 and frequently thereafter. But Catholic teachers also liked this text, as Bavarian investigators discovered in their periodic attempts to rid the duchy of heretical literature. In fact, the furor aroused by the *Grammatica Philippi*'s penetration of the Catholic lands[110] confirms our earlier observation about the intimate association made in the minds of contemporaries between schoolbooks and their ideological message. It also supports the Protestant claim to have "methodized" and speeded learning. "These people," declared the Bavarian school administrators in 1569, referring to Melanchthon and his fellow grammarians Erasmus Sarcerius and Johann Rivius, "have adopted a style and method [*methodus*] that seem to make learning easier and less painful than it has been according to the custom of the older schools." But, they cautioned, "our youth ought to be protected from such writings, in which we have found heretical examples freely mixed with rules and paradigms."[111] Bavarian visitors had standing instructions to send to Munich lists of textbooks used in local schools, from which the works of suspected authors were then ordered removed. This, it was explained, was a necessary step because "even the most unassuming ABC booklet can be mixed with a large dose of poison."[112]

There was substance to this suspicion. In an age of confessional rivalry, no book was entirely neutral. Some, indeed, might be judged propaganda in disguise. An example is the *Book of Precepts for a Christian Life*, published in Frankfurt in 1536, by Erasmus Alberus, an indefatigable schoolmaster, philologist, preacher, churchman, and controversialist. His *Precepts*, culled from the Bible and classical authors and arranged under the headings of the Ten Commandments, are innocuous enough—*gravissimum est imperium consuetudinis*—until one turns to the catchy German rhymes in which the vernacular paraphrase of the Latin tag is given:

> You can't with all your main and might
> Turn off a habit overnight.
> You'll never make the papists see
> Their thousand-year-long villainy;
> For truth won't penetrate the mind
> Of one who has so long been blind.[113]

Similar barbs directed at Catholic (and also rival Protestant) opponents lie buried in editions of Melanchthon's *Elementa puerilia,* Camerarius's *Praecepta morum,* Lutheran versions of such old standbys as Murmellius's *Pappa puerorum,* and scores of catechisms. "Who is Antichrist?" "Antichrist is the entire papacy, spawned by the devil." "Who is the god of the papists?" "They have a god they call Stuff-My-Guts."[114]

Anthologies of passages from literature were meant to prepare the pupil for life, as well as give him exercise in Latin. Students were trained early on to make their own collections of noteworthy sentences from the literature by recording and indexing them in their commonplace books. Pupils in Augsburg began to do this as early as the second grade[115] and kept it up to the end of their schooling. Equally common in the curriculum were dialogues and colloquies with the aid of which pupils were coached in spoken Latin, from morning salutations to conversations on ethics, politics, and religion. Such books, said the school administrators of Ulm in reference to Erasmus's colloquies, "are more suitable to our time than Cicero."[116] They were read with roles divided or acted out in class. They taught boys how to make small talk, ask for a loan or a room at an inn, send out invitations, what to say at a *convivium* or a funeral.[117] From some exceedingly frank talk about love and lovers they could even pick up some sex education.[118] The *gravitas* of the classical curriculum was therefore not without its occasional touch of *levitas,* and young candidates for erudition were not necessarily cut off by their learned tongue and sententious speech from the tastes and habits of the popular crowd.

To speak of a "widened gap between literate and oral cultures," therefore, as recent students of the social impact of printing have done,[119] is to exaggerate. If there were two cultures, they interpenetrated so deeply and at so many points that neither could have flourished independently. This is not to deny that graduates of institutions of learning differentiated themselves from their "nonlearned" countrymen. Indeed, I will argue later that this separation, insofar as it set clerics and churchmen apart from their flocks, is a factor in the Reformation's failure to make good its pedagogical promise. But the distinction between the learned and the laity was a function more of the offices to which formal education gave admittance than of education itself. It was certainly not a product of literacy, which in any case was by all appearances much more widespread among the broad population than has usually been recognized.

3

Literacy touches the subject of Reformation pedagogy at many critical points and raises questions of great interest to historians of early modern Europe. The relationship between the Protestant Reformation and the extension of reading has intrigued scholars for a long time. It was also of concern to the reformers themselves, who saw it as a difficult and problematic issue. Clearly, they encouraged reading among their followers, favoring—in principle at least—the spread of literacy to the whole population.[120] But in the aftermath of the events of the 1520s and 1530s reformers experienced some misgivings about the wisdom of a massive application of this principle. Expansion of vernacular education appeared to be starving serious learning of its recruits, while independent Bible reading was coming under suspicion for nourishing the seeds of an uncontrollable sectarianism. These doubts were never completely laid to rest. Throughout the century they surfaced at moments of stress and anxiety.[121] With the adoption of the catechism as a corrective to religious instability, however, and with revitalized gymnasiums and seminaries promising a reliable supply of trained pastors, literacy became a safe policy to pursue. Magistrates and rulers had their own reasons for encouraging this trend,[122] and in response to the shift in their attitude elementary schools proliferated in the second half of the sixteenth century, as has been seen.

The educational laws of the Lutheran Reformation give concrete expression to official intentions of propagating literacy. In Saxony, for example, the school ordinance of 1580 stipulated that even in the smallest and poorest villages, where the people were too hard-pressed to instruct their own children, too poor to hire a teacher, and too thin on the ground to support a Latin school, a sexton ought to be available to teach reading and writing "because children of working people [*arbeitender leute Kinder*] should, for the sake of their own and our common welfare, receive in their early youth instruction in prayers, catechism, and writing and reading."[123] In the duchy of Lauenburg, also in 1580, visitors admonished country people to "keep their children in school so that they will learn to read and write."[124] Householders—as has been shown in an earlier chapter—were expected to preside over Bible readings, and although it was acknowledged that not every *Hausvater* and *Hausmutter* could perform this duty, the assumption was always that they ought to be able to do it.[125] Indeed, literacy seems to have been regarded as a normative, certainly as a desirable, skill. Those who lacked it could turn to teach-yourself books, whose titles explain both their purpose and the nature of their appeal: Jakob Griessbeutel's *A Most Useful Book of Sounds, Illustrated with Figures Giving the True Sound of Each Letter and Syllable, from Which Young Men, Husbands and Wives and Other Adults, Also Children, Women as Well as Men, Can Easily Learn to Read in as Little as 24*

Hours; Valentin Ickelsamer's *A Correct and Quick Way to Learn Reading* and *A German Grammar from Which Every Man Can Teach Himself to Read* . . .; or Peter Jordan's *The Layman's School: An Easy and Quick Method for Learning to Write and Read. With a Technique for Instructing the Hard-of-Learning and Dull-Witted without the Use of Letters, but through Figures and Characters Attractive to Look at and Easy to Remember.*[126] "Such books," writes Jordan, "are used everywhere. Each year a new title appears on the market."[127] With some initial help from a practiced reader (even a child would do) an interested layman could now achieve functional literacy by himself. Ickelsamer, the favorite among these popular "grammarians,"[128] advocated the phonetic method as the best approach to teaching adults. Teach the alphabet from the sound of the word, he said, not vice versa. "Take the name Hans," he explained; "You have four sound changes in this word, which are represented by four letters. First, you hear a strong exhaling noise, as when someone heaves a deep sigh. This is the H, which you breathe into the vowel A. Following this there is a sound through the nose and finally you hear a sibilant like the hissing of a snake." For the next step, Ickelsamer continues, imagine a picture to associate each of these sounds with a written letter. Let us say that you want to read the word *Mertz (März,* March). First note the four sound changes, then think of an animal or object vividly representing each of these sounds. Draw a cow over the moo-sound M, over the goat sound E put a goat, a dog over the growl R, and finally a bird over the sparrow cry Tz. Nothing could be easier or more entertaining.[129]

There is much evidence that a strong interest at the grass roots supported the attempt to raise literacy. Whenever a government moved to curtail or abolish a vernacular school, either for the sake of economy or in order to protect the Latin curriculum, it met stubborn opposition from the affected community.[130] The municipality of Heidenheim in the duchy of Württemberg is a case in point. Its town fathers engaged their prince in a heated correspondence in the mid-1560s over the closing of the German school in their borough. "Our young people," they wrote to Duke Christoph, "most of whom have no aptitude for Latin and are growing up to be artisans, are better served by a German teacher than a Latin master, for they need to learn writing and reading, which is of great help to them in their work and livelihood." They did not like the alternative of a new Latin school, where all boys would learn to read, and a few would stay on to become scholars. Their interests were practical, and reading and writing was their foremost concern, "for these skills," they maintained, "do honor to God and promote trade and an honorable walk of life."[131] When the Bavarian government proposed the closing of German schools in the duchy's villages, the territorial estates objected, saying that "not all peasant children want to be like their parents, . . . and whoever can't read or write his mother tongue is little more than a dead person."[132]

Literacy was coming to be recognized as an indispensable skill for every occupation tied to commerce and exchange. "Our burghers here," reported the pastor of a town in Württemberg, where the German school had closed down, "deem it their greatest complaint that their sons have been deprived of the opportunity to learn writing, reading, and reckoning before they are apprenticed to the trades."[133] When asked how a smallish city like Coburg could support three vernacular schools in the 1560s, a local official explained, "because we have so many artisans, journeymen, and vine dressers here."[134] Apart from the utility of literacy, there was, of course, the pleasure to be derived from reading. Printed books made quick converts. "My father," wrote Hermann von Weinsberg, the advocate and politician of Cologne, "although a layman, went to school to the age of twelve and, having learned to write, read, and reckon, he developed such a taste for . . . books that he spent all his time studying them, telling the rest of us at table every day of the things he had learned. And he never ceased to marvel at the riches contained in books. . . . Indeed, he often praised book reading as a source of useful and helpful knowledge to men."[135] This is not an isolated story.[136] If most men made slower progress than the elder Weinsberg, who advanced from ABC and primer to Livy and Herodotus (in German translation, of course), few lacked the opportunity to acquire a serviceable command of the written language.[137]

A religious motive was rarely given for the wish to become literate, but Protestant churchmen declared reading to be a normative obligation on all Christians. "Attend to reading, preaching, and teaching," the authors of the school ordinance of Mecklenburg quoted from 1 Tim. 4:13 (somewhat out of context), adding, lest the point be missed, "in saying this, Paul has intentionally put reading in first place."[138] Authors of books of self-instruction also believed that by teaching people to read they were helping to prepare them for the word of God.[139] "Now that the Bible has been printed in German," wrote Johann Kolross in introducing his *Manual of German Orthography* in 1530, "all the artisans and housemaids, though working all day in the sweat of their brows, want to spend their evenings pondering the word of God."[140] The observation may not be entirely accurate, but its motive was genuine. "Only a few rare spirits achieve enlightenment without reading," said Ortholph Fuchssperger in his *Art of Reading* in 1542. "Most of us depend on books for what we need to learn about our duties toward God and our fellowmen."[141] "I was moved [to write this book]" Valentin Ickelsamer explained in the preface to his *German Grammar* of 1534, "not only because I know that reading brings much pleasure to those who have mastered it, but also because this skill is a splendid divine gift, which we should use to honor God by reading, singing, and writing. Never before has the art of reading been so beneficial," he added, "as in our day, when each man by himself can know and judge the word of God." (Ickelsamer, it is pertinent to interject, had been a partisan of Karlstadt's in the early 1520s.) He suspected that a corrupt world would ultimately prove unworthy of this divine gift. But to the few true Christians among the host of sinners it would, he thought, bring great spiritual profit.[142] Ickelsamer did not fail to list some mundane advantages as well. "Everybody nowadays wants to be adept at a skill with which one discovers, understands, and remembers everything in the world and can communicate it to others, no matter how far away they are." His book, he contends, can prepare anyone to be ready within a few days to read and write. He himself had taught people to read in as little as a week; in fact, he says, it can even be done overnight.[143] A promotional interest is certainly not absent from these claims. On the other hand, it is true that, given the incentive to learn, some leisure time, and a bit of help at the start, no one needed to remain illiterate.

But adults were not the main concern of the Reformation pedagogues who had attached their hopes to future generations. Turning the young into qualified readers was clearly a problem of schooling. As has been shown, vernacular schools sprang up nearly everywhere in the course of the sixteenth century. Strassburg had nine elementary schools for boys and six for girls in 1535.[144] In Hamburg each parish had not only a school for boys, but also one where girls learned "reading, writing, sewing, and the fear of God, good manners and honorable conduct."[145] In other German cities—Catholic as well as Protestant—the situation was similar. A visitation in Munich in 1560 showed that every parish had an elementary school.[146]

For small towns, villages, and hamlets,[147] the evidence is spottier, but the conclusion seems warranted that most rural people had access to elementary schooling (though they did not necessarily avail themselves of it). The school situation in Württemberg was described in an earlier chapter; abundant visitation documents in the Stuttgart archives suggest that every town and every large village (*Flecken*), as well as a preponderance of the smaller villages, had, from the 1550s onward, a vernacular school where, no matter how unsatisfactory its physical condition, reading, writing, and catechism were taught to as many children as parents saw fit to send.[148] The same can be said of the principality of Coburg,[149] as shown by notations in the Coburg visitation documents in the 1570s: "small school here, children learning to read and pray, hard-working schoolmaster"; "pious sexton, does his best in reading and writing with the children"; "tiny school, reading only, difficult to get a teacher to stay here"; "teacher not very competent, only catechism and German hymns"; "schoolmaster here is an artisan, hard-working, has 4–5 pupils in wintertime, teaches reading and praying."[150] When the Upper Palatinate was visited in 1579 and 1580, the inspectors found that more than three-quarters of the territory's *Flecken* and villages had some kind of school (many of them poorly attended, however).[151] In the Electorate of Saxony, village schools were common by the 1570s, as the protocols in the archives of Dresden and Weimar demonstrate. But the same sources show also that numerous communities were still without teachers in 1590, and that many schools survived precariously, attended only occasionally by half a dozen peasant children and taught by an overworked and underpaid sexton ("a poor old man," "a hard-working but unlearned man") or a rural artisan ("a poor day laborer," "a poor bookbinder" or linen weaver, cooper, printer, or carpenter).[152]

On close inspection of the documents it appears that the fate of a village school, and the number of pupils it attracted, were functions less of the support of territorial rulers or magistrates than of the concern with education, or lack of it, of the local elite: village elders, jurors, church deacons. Where these worthies valued book learning, where they could persuade or browbeat their neighbors to pay for it, and where their own children acted as examples to the rest, a school usually survived.[153] Governments played their part, of course: prodding, dangling the promise of financial help before an eager or a reluctant commune, occasionally granting a subsidy. But local interest was of the essence, and the visitation protocols tell us where it existed and where not.

Needless to say, economic and social conditions had much to do with the response villagers made to schools. "People here are unwilling to send their barefoot children to the school in Grossenbuch during the winter months," states a Saxon protocol; "the cold, snow, and storms are so severe that no one would chase a dog over the raging brooks and narrow planks."[154] If a little money could be squeezed from the public treasury, such an isolated community might set up its own subsidiary school (*Nebenschule*) to spare children the long trip to the parish village, where the *Hauptschule* was situated. Many of these tiny ABC and catechism schools had a mere handful of pupils: "Sachsenburg: few inhabitants, school has only three or four boys, but they are all learning their prayers and the ABC."[155] Sextons did the teaching where no schoolmaster could be hired.[156]

Governments set the procedures used in teaching reading and writing in German-speaking schools. These rules had not changed since antiquity and were not much influenced by the theories of advocates of "method" in education. Moving from the simple to the complex, from parts to the whole, ABC learning started the pupil on letters (learned by name and sound), advanced him to syllables, then to words, eventually to sentences, from there straight to the German catechism. Compared with this "synthetic" system, the phonetic, or analytic, method[157] advocated by Ickelsamer seemed natural and fast-moving, but it did not make its way into the schools, where tradition reigned with its reliance on slow, repetitious, cumulative, habit-forming drill. Under this system it took a six-year-old child one to two years to learn to read, provided, said Neander, he was not rushed but was allowed to progress slowly and methodically at his own pace.[158]

Although unattractive on psychological grounds, the synthetic system probably worked as well as any. Its proponents, at any rate, were enthusiastic about it, and even its detractors could criticize only its demands on the child's memory and attention span.[159] The following example shows how one teacher, Hans Fabritius, author of a manual on his craft, conducted his elementary reading lesson:

> *Master:* My dear pupil, say after me: a.e.i.o.u.
> *Pupil:* I can do this already. M. Tell me, then, which is the a among these vowels? P. Is that what they are called, vowels? M. Yes, they are called vowels. You cannot write a word without the use of one. That's why we must learn them especially well. P. Write them out for me, please. M. Here they are: i.u.a.e.o. Now say them. P. I.u.a.e.o. M. And now in reverse order. P. O.e.a.u.i. M. Do you think you will remember and recognize them from now on? P. Yes, surely I shall.

And so on to consonants.[160] In Augsburg (according to a *ratio docendi* submitted by one schoolmaster to the magistrates) the scene looked as follows: "Prayers finished, the youngest boys stand before a board on which the letters of the alphabet are written. One letter after another is read out to them and its shape explained. For example: O is like a ring, a short stroke with a little dot on top is an i, and so forth. This is kept up until all children have learned the letters,"[161] after which they attempted simple words, written out in spaced syllables, before going on to Luther's Shorter Catechism. Critics occasionally scoffed at so mechanical a routine and pointed to the distorted sense children were apt to gain from intoning "Him–Him–el–el: Himmel, Christ–Christ–us–us: Christus."[162] But the old procedure remained inviolate. "If the word is a long one, let the boys say the first syllable twice; otherwise they will forget it before reaching the end of the word."[163] In Saxony, in 1580, according to the school ordinance,

> When young boys first come to school, give them a copy of the ABC booklet specially printed with Dr. Luther's catechism. Don't press them too hard at first, but be sure that they repeat all the letters from the beginning every time they learn a new one. To discover how well they remember

them, have them occasionally name a letter outside the regular order, from the middle or near the end of the alphabet. When you are certain they have mastered the alphabet, teach them the syllables, using the Lord's prayer as your text. All this time pay close attention to their pronunciation, and do not allow the boys to slur or drawl their vowels and consonants in the manner of their natural speech, but make them separate and distinguish the sounds clearly from one another, as it is done in Latin diction.[164]

The rest was drill: "What is the first letter in *pater*? It's a p. Show me the p in the alphabet. What comes after the p? An a. Show me the a."[165] And so on.

What do these facts suggest about the literacy of the general population? And what is the evidence for my contention that reading and writing were more widespread among the common folk of early modern Germany than has been thought? Let it be admitted at once that the evidence is circumstantial. Students of the incidence of literacy in traditional societies have usually resorted to counting signatures given in circumstances that allow them to relate signers to their social origins, and then quantify the results.[166] Such data exist for Germany too. The so-called Fraternal Book (*Bruderschaftsbuch*) of the city of Frankfurt am Main, for example, holds for the years 1417 to 1524 hundreds of signatures of artisans from all parts of Germany.[167] Another quantifiable, albeit secondhand, indicator is the large number of entries in Frankfurt's citizen registers (*Bürgerbücher*), where the names of applicants for lower municipal offices in the fifteenth and sixteenth centuries bear in nearly every instance the note "can read and write."[168] Most of my exhibits, however, are of the kind usually disparaged as "impressionistic" or "literary"—in other words they are indirect. None will by itself, nor will they all together, constitute a demonstration. I offer them here for what they are worth.[169]

The strongest argument is the distinct sense one gains from the sources that by the middle of the sixteenth century literacy was taken for granted in the elevated ranks of society, regarded as normal among artisans, and noted without astonishment in the peasantry. One can take the heroes and heroines of Jörg Wickram's courtly novels (written in the 1530s, 1540s and 1550s) as an initial example. They are prolific letter writers, all of them, and Wickram evidently thought it unnecessary to explain or justify their writing skill. This is no less true of the burgher novels, where nearly everyone reads and writes.[170] Wickram's popularity, and that of the half-dozen or so writers who equaled his contemporary fame as a storyteller, is itself a comment on reading ability in urban circles.[171] But books and pamphlets were found in the homes of the lowly as well. The learned peasant encountered by Wickram's pilgrim errant[172] could not, despite obvious exaggeration, have struck his readers as an absurdly implausible character without stripping the poem of its chief didactic point. That there was reading in rural cottages is known also from more immediate sources. Investigations in Bavaria during the reigns of Albrecht V and Wilhelm V brought to light a large number of materials lumped together as "wicked sectarian and seditious Bibles, postils, prayer books, scurrilous pamphlets, and tracts, translated into German and put into print."[173] along with the discovery that a considerable portion of the population "in towns and larger villages [*Städte und Märkte*]"[174] could read these books. The Bavarian authorities say explicitly that this group included "common burghers" (*gemeine bürger*), artisans, "ordinary men" (*der gemein man*), as well as peasants.[175] When the government instructed officials in the Munich district to "visit [i.e., inspect and report on] the homes of all those peasants who can write and read and possess written or printed books,"[176] it must have known that the search would not be for a needle in a haystack.

While evidence of this kind has no statistical force, it does help provide a context in which to interpret more ambiguous pieces of information. For instance, pastors in Albertine Saxony were instructed in 1555 to make an annual house inspection in the sparsely populated outlying villages of their respective parishes "and subject those inhabitants who cannot read [*so nit lesen können*] and who are unknown to him to a catechism examination."[177] I take this as an indication that literacy was, to say the least, not uncommon among the Saxon peasantry. There is, of course, evidence on the other side as well. The preface to Ambrosius Moibanus's catechism of 1534 refers to the continued need for preachers "in this age of printing, when books can be read at home, but not by those who do not know how to read at all, and these are always the greater part. Books benefit the minority," Moibanus continues, "and we need preachers and teachers to serve the majority who cannot read."[178] Another example of counterevidence comes from a prosperous region in Württemberg, where visitors reported at the end of the sixteenth century that although the district had "many substantial villages and farms, few people in them can write and read."[179] At about the same time the *Geistliche Rat*, the highest ecclesiastical authority in Bavaria, reported to the duke that catechism instruction in the diocese of Freising was proceeding very slowly because "our subjects there can neither read nor write."[180] If these statements are true as they stand, they seem to represent atypical situations. Of course the larger the town and the better off its citizens, the greater the inducements to literacy. *Winkelschulen*—unlicensed private schools where only utilitarian skills were taught and the time-consuming burdens of catechism drill and hymn-singing were held to a minimum—flourished in many of the larger towns despite determined attempts to suppress them. The stubborn support burghers gave to these schools is strong evidence for the interest of townspeople in gaining and preserving the skill of letters.[181]

The direct connection between literacy and elementary schooling is, at any rate, no longer a matter for debate.[182] Sixteenth-century governments were convinced of this link. Since the proliferation of vernacular elementary schools is a documented fact, it can, I think, be taken that literacy increased commensurately. Of course there are reasons to hedge this assertion with caveats. School attendance was a serious problem, particularly in the countryside. Nonetheless, one who has spent much time with the sources cannot suppress the conclusion that reading was a common rather than an uncommon pursuit for a large number of people in nearly all walks of German society in the sixteenth century. The pedagogical endeavor of the Reformation presupposed a society whose members were, or were being trained to be, readers. The evidence suggests that they were not wrong in this supposition.

CHAPTER 10

THE USES OF SIN

Latin pupils in Augsburg near the end of the sixteenth century practiced the verbs of the first conjugation with the following examples: "*amo*—I love; *beo*—I save, gladden; *clamo*—I cry out; *damno*—I damn; *dono*—I grant; *erro*—I err; *fugo*—I put to flight; . . . *ligo*—I bind, confirm; . . . *pecco*—I sin."[1] Even without explication, these words confronted the schoolboy at the very beginning of his academic preparation with the central problem of the Christian faith. *Fugo, damno* sealed the divine act of rejection following man's rebellion against God. *Erro, pecco* held him captive in the consequences of his fallen condition. *Clamo* sounded his wretchedness and gave voice to his appeal for help. *Amo, dono, ligo, beo* spoke of God's unmerited regard for his sinful creatures and pledged the healing action of his fatherly affection.

These themes, reiterated in sermons and catechism, were meant to turn the schoolboy's mind to holy things. According to the theory of habituation, their repetition in daily grammatical drill could not fail to internalize the religious message. Most textbooks chose vocabulary and paradigms to support the main thrust of Protestant religious indoctrination. Leonhard Culman's *Sententiae pueriles* went through the alphabet with *Ab Adamo peccatum in nos derivatum est* (from Adam sin has come down to us), *Calamitas omnis peccatorum poena est* (misfortune is the punishment of sins), *Deus solus et gratis remittit peccata* (God alone and freely forgives sins), *Homo ad calamitatem nascitur* (man is born to misery), *Hominis cor ex natura sua malum* (man's heart is naturally evil), *homo sibi ipsi calamitatem auctor* (man is the author of his own misery), and so on.[2] Selbald Heyden's *Nomenclatura,* a Latin primer, began with *Deus*—God, *pater*—father, *filius*—son, *salvator*—savior.[3] Konrad Mercklin, a schoolmaster in Rothenburg on the Tauber, included in his *Important Sayings in Latin and German Culled from the Old and New Testaments, for Beginners* such sentences as *Non est homo qui non peccet*—There is no man who does not sin.[4] Nearly every ABC book thus did service as an instrument of religious training, augmenting the catechism in preparing the child to accept the evangelical faith.

It is tempting to interpret this preparation as an act of repression done for ulterior purposes. Much of what has been said in earlier chapters concerning the reformers' endeavors to imbue children with a sense of their innate depravity could be represented as a scheme for internalizing effective disciplinary constraints by using sin as an instrument of control. Badgering boys and girls of an impressionable age with the grim consequences of their perversion, sapping their self-confidence, terrifying them with the signs of their inherited corruption —these might indeed be part of a Machiavellian pedagogy designed to keep them subdued and pacified. There is some evidence to support such a judgment on the motives of Lutheran pedagogy, as will be shown later in this chapter. But it is not the whole story, which is, as always, more complex than a selective reading of Protestant homiletics might suggest. There is no doubt, however, that sin had a prominent place in religious education in the sixteenth century, and its use in Lutheran pedagogy is well worth a closer look.

How was sin explained to the young? Let us listen to Sebastian Fröschel, a Wittenberg pastor and religious teacher, who in 1559 printed a collection of catechism sermons for children. He had been urged to publish by Bugenhagen, who praised his preaching for its sympathetic approach to young audiences.[5] "What is sin in general?" Fröschel begins.[6] He answers: "Sin is everything done outwardly or inwardly to violate God's commandments." This definition is followed by a list of transgressions of each of the commandments, from idolatry and blasphemy to surrendering to doubt and despair. Such evil acts, Fröschel explains, follow necessarily from the sin passed to us by our first ancestor, which has left us blind to God's love, and subject to his reprobation: "Man born of man's seed cannot know God and obey his will, nor can he keep his commandments, for he is driven by the wish to oppose God's law, unless he is reborn through Jesus Christ." This, then, is original, inherited sin. Men make their fallen condition manifest by committing actual sins ("they are called 'actual' because we act them out from the beginning to the end of our life"), deeds performed outwardly and inwardly against God's commandments. Mortal sins are committed against conscience, that is to say, they are done knowingly; venial sins originate in the "evil inclinations, lusts, desires and turbulent emotions of man's mind and heart; these, however, can be resisted, and the sanctified do resist them, for which reason their sins are not imputed to them." Men must understand and acknowledge their sins "so that they will become terror-struck in the face of God's anger and gain a heartfelt love of the holy gospel in which they find the promise of forgiveness in God's grace, eternal justice and eternal life, and all this without any merit of our own."

Fröschel's formulations are concise, simple, and entirely conventional. They uphold the Protestant position as defined in the second article of the Augsburg Confession: original sin is man's failure to fear and trust God. But the reader's attention (and, one assumes, the listener's when Fröschel's catechism was preached from the pulpit) is almost at once deflected from the motivational substance of sin to the actual perpetration of sinful deeds. The catalog of actual sins, a time-honored instrument of pastoral care intended to encourage contrition and confession, furnished penitents with a checklist of sins of commission and omission against which to match their daily conduct. Habitual sinfulness was acknowledged, but actual sins were counted, classified, and registered. "Let us acknowledge," said Fröschel, "that many sins remain in us [after baptism] in this mortal life, to wit: evil inclinations, ignorance, doubts, injustices, cockiness, profane passions, inadequate fear of God, a weak faith and indifferent love for God and our fellowmen. Such sins we must admit and bewail in the depths of our hearts."[7] In the same manner, Johann Meckhart's catechism for Augsburg prompted children to acknowledge that "I am, alas, a poor sinner, for my whole life is composed of sin and nothing but sin, excepting only what God himself accomplishes in me." It continues: "In particular I confess that I have been disobedient to my parents and schoolmasters, often angering them and causing them to curse me." A list of petty delinquencies follows,[8] each contributing to the somber background of man's sinfulness, against which God's redeeming love stands out more brilliantly. All catechisms took this direction from sin to pardon. The more depressing the list of transgressions, the brighter the promise of man's deliverance. The object was not to wallow in actual or imagined sins, but to accept the mercy of God. The message was of hope, not despair.

On this point Lutherans were at great pains to differentiate themselves from Calvinists, whom they accused of teaching "that God has created the larger part of men for damnation."[9] This, they charged, would make an evildoer of God, one who not only looks on passively while wicked things are done in his name, but indeed takes a hand in them by hardening men's hearts, making them blind, perverting and tempting them, leading them to error and prompting them to revilement."[10] Lutherans were emphatic in their rejection of these "perverted teachings": "God has created no one for damnation. He wants to lead all men out of their ignorance and to the knowledge of truth. His only demand is that we listen to his son Jesus Christ whose voice in the gospel speaks to us with the power and virtue of the Holy Ghost to bring about the conversion and salvation of all men." It is not God's fault that many go to perdition. Refusing to turn to the gospel for help, they have only themselves to blame.[11] "If I believe firmly," said Fröschel in his sermons, "that Jesus Christ, the son of God, has redeemed us all with his body and blood and has become our true savior, then I am certain of my own salvation."[12] Some Lutheran preachers showed great ingenuity in presenting a plausible redemption scenario to their audiences:

> Christ steps into the courtroom, motions to the sinner to approach him, bends down, lifts him upon his shoulders, and carries him pickaback to his father. First he turns to the sinner. *"Confide fili!"* he says; "be of good cheer! I shall plead with our father on your behalf as earnestly and devotedly as if your cause were my own." Next, he speaks to God. "Father," he says, "here is a poor sinner who has turned to me prayerfully, seeking counsel and succor. He has reminded me of the love I have shown the world by dying and rising again in obedience to your command. I beg you now to continue to help him, as you have assisted him in the past and, when the time comes, to perfect him with your righteousness." And to this God the Father replies: "My dearest son, I am well pleased with you. You have paid for this sinner with your own obedience, having fully satisfied all my demands. I can refuse you nothing. Go, take him with you."[13]

It will help to know that this brief dialogue was written by the orthodox Lutheran theologian Andreas Musculus as a contribution to one of the heated doctrinal controversies that shook Lutheranism in the middle of the sixteenth century, the so-called Osiandrian quarrel over the interpretation of justification. The vivid courtroom scene was in fact a dramatization of Melanchthon's view of justification as a "forensic act" in which God declares the faithful to be justified on the account of Christ, whose total obedience to God achieved the forgiveness of all sins.[14] It reminds us that very little in the dogmatics of the Reformation was beyond dispute. Even at the rudimentary level of indoctrination these underlying conflicts often rose to the surface.

I have suggested that on the subject of sin Lutheran catechization did not depart very far from Catholic teachings. In order to call the catechumen to repentance and the wish for self-improvement, his attention was directed to his actual sins. Even the ritualistic formulas of Peter Canisius's Catholic catechisms[15] had their Lutheran equivalents. For instance: "Sins against the fourth commandment: I confess myself guilty of not giving enough honor to my parents, master and mistress, magistrates, schoolmaster, and pastor. I have not prayed for them and I have been many times disobedient to them. Against the fifth: Although I have not laid my hands on anyone with the intention of killing him, I have been angry and impatient with many people; I have shown a spirit of vengeance toward them, and in all my thoughts I have fallen short of the love, patience and sympathy I owe to my fellow Christians."[16] To be sure, Protestants took issue with Catholic trivialization—as they saw it—of man's inheritance of sin. Original sin not only left the individual deprived of his prelapsarian innocence; more fatefully, it induced in him a willful inclination to resist and reject, "a truly malevolent quality of sinfulness," as Konrad Dietrich explained in a training manual for catechists. Sin is "an inclination to evil," he wrote, "a perverted lust and desire to do whatever goes against God's law, a stubborn ignorance and conscious misinterpretation of divine things, a constant doubting and rejection of God in the heart, and an active resistance to God in all our bodily limbs and members."[17] This proclivity is inseparable from the human condition, "a natural corruption hateful in God's eyes and meriting our eternal damnation."[18]

In other respects, however, Lutheran and Roman treatments of sin did not differ very much. From the working catechist's point of view, the issue was not theological but mundane. How was he to lead his auditors to Christian conduct? To Sebastian Fröschel the answer to this question was the basic lesson in Christian instruction:

> The first thing to be learned from the Ten Commandments is outward discipline [eusserliche zucht], which God requires of all men. . . . By this we mean the obligation to control one's external members—eyes, ears, tongue, hands, feet, and so on—by right reason and by God's law. For we are not entitled to use our external members as suggested by our deluded mind, our evil desires, and foolish whims, but rather as God's will, written in his Ten Commandments and inscribed in the heart of every human being, commands us to do. All men are therefore duty-bound to live in external discipline according to God's Ten Commandments. . . . Second, we must know why this outward discipline is necessary. There are four reasons. The first is that it is God's order to all rational creatures, angels as well as men, to be obedient. The second is to avoid punishment in this life and the next, for it is a most certain rule that God chastises with bodily punishment in this present temporal life all overt and visible sins against his laws, such as idolatry, blasphemy, epicurean talk, false oaths, rebellion, murder and violence, adultery, robbery, deception, and so on and so forth. . . . The third reason why God requires men to live an honorable and orderly life is to allow other people to live in peace . . . , for none of us has been created to live for his own selfish pleasure and gain, but instead to serve God and his fellow creatures. . . . For this reason God has appointed governments to maintain outward discipline among men, and where rulers do not perform this duty, God himself punishes everyone with war, disease, inflation, and so on. . . . The fourth reason is the one given by Saint Paul in Galatians 3 [24], where the apostle says: "the law is a school for the young and simple [Kinderzucht] toward

Christ."[19] That is to say: external discipline is necessary because people cannot be taught the gospel while they live a wild, debased, disorderly, epicurean life, nor can the Holy Ghost do his work among mad, raging people who remain stuck in their sinful ways.[20]

We must remember, says Fröschel, "that outward obedience cannot gain forgiveness of sin and the blessing of eternal life." Christ alone has earned these for us.[21] But, he adds, we shall never have God's pleasure if we fail to subject ourselves to his holy discipline.

Responsive to society's need for stability, deeply worried about the tensions appearing to tear it apart, the catechist concentrated his religious message emphatically on the right ordering of personal and social life as a responsibility arising from the individual's understanding of the gospel. Less a theologian than a molder of men to the peaceful and useful life on earth, he shifted the evangelical thrust to the realm of works, exertion, restraints, and self-control.

In pursuing this pragamtic objective, preachers and catechists had to steer cautiously through the perilous theological narrows separating man's fallen condition from the promise of his ultimate deliverance through no merit of his own. The extreme polarity of these doctrines created problems of moral guidance. Excessive emphasis placed on either of the poles might discourage or even obviate the serious effort toward their own sanctification that Lutheran divines urged upon their followers. Too heavy a burden of guilt might cripple them in their struggle to raise themselves from their fallen state. An unconditional pledge of emancipation, on the other hand, could lead to complacence. Most catechists seem to have recognized this dilemma and faced its dangers.

One can, of course, find writers who worked the theme of human corruption for all it was worth. Caspar Aquila, pastor and superintendent in Saalfeld in Saxony in the 1530s and 1540s, tells us he made boys memorize and recite publicly in church on Sundays a series of eleven catechism sermons written by himself, which included such passages as the following:

> *Another pupil asks:* Prove to me out of Scripture what will happen to the ungrateful who hold the word of God in contempt.
> *Answer:* Jeremiah says in the eleventh chapter: "Cursed be the man who does not heed the words of the covenant," "even his prayer is an abomination," Prov. 28. God will scorn and mock such a man even as he suffers unbearable anguish, Prov. 3; he will not hear him, but punish him terribly with many diseases and calamities, Leviticus 26, to wit: fever, consumption, boils, pestilence, inflation, war, fire and arson, hailstorms, sores and inflammations. In sum, God will pour down upon him so much terror, misery, suffering, confusion, and misfortune that he will fall into utter despair.[22]

Aquila seems to have believed that sound religious instruction required self-vilification by the learner:

> *Question:* Tell me, what have you learned from the Ten Commandments? [A pupil answers:] I have learned from them that we lead a damnable sinful life and that God cannot find a single good thing in us. For the Ten Commandments are the book of our vices and the record of our disgrace, in which we see clearly, as in a polished mirror, what we are before God without his grace, namely idol worshipers, miscreants, blasphemers and violators of God's holy name, cursed robbers of his sacred temple and despisers of his eternal word. Item: rebellious abusers of our fathers, murderers of our children, envious dogs, cutthroats, whoremongers, adulterers, thieves, rogues, deceivers and dissemblers, liars, tale bearers, perjurers and false witnesses, misers and insolent braggarts. In short, we are wild, insatiable, unbridled beasts whom God must keep locked in the cage of his commandments so that our evil nature may be confined and prevented from ruining us and all around us.[23]

Common sense will tell us that such cadences went in and out of children's ears without leaving as heavy a burden of shame as they were meant to induce. One should also remember that threats and self-accusations were followed in every instance by assurances that God would not abandon his wretched creatures. "The sacraments are our sign," Aquila wrote, "that God neither will not can forsake us in our sinfulness, but will always be at our side to help and console."[24] Vivid descriptions of barely imaginable horrors[25] were meant to open hearts to an ardent desire for God's grace. Still, clerics like Aquila evidently believed that extravagant words were needed to embed the lesson of corruption deeply in young minds.

Egregious among those who took this position was Andreas Osiander, the controversial preacher, theologian, and scholar, a leading reformer in Nuremberg, and author in 1533 of *Catechism Sermons for Children* (*Kinderpredigten*), a text adopted by the council as an integral part of the new order of worship and preached publicly in all the city's churches.[26] Intended chiefly to help prepare young children for their first communion[27] (as well as to instruct the "simple of mind" assembled in the adult congregation), Osiander's sermons were meant to impart to their auditors a solid grasp of the fundamentals of Christian doctrine. To this end they were preached repeatedly and uniformly throughout the city's domain and that of the margrave of Brandenburg-Ansbach, an enthusiastic Lutheran whose lands touched Nuremberg in the west. "Once our children have begun to learn and remember," Osiander insists in the preface to his sermons, "they will easily absorb all other religious teachings and grow up to be good, pious, able, and wise Christians in their various estates and offices."[28] The social ethic ranked high among the concerns of this urban clergyman.

A child's wisdom,, Osiander begins, consists of knowing what to do and what not to do. This knowledge can come only from the fear of God, as David tells us in Psalm 111: "The fear of the Lord is the beginning of wisdom." This is why the Decalogue, which teaches both fear and wisdom, is the beginning of all knowledge. It demonstrates our inability to act in full compliance with God's laws and brings to light all the hidden lusts and desires of our hearts. Sin defines us. We are, all of us, children of sin. Our parents impregnate us with sin "as a leprous mother infects the child in her womb."[29] The consequences of this contamination are momentous. "For sin, you must know, is nothing other than rebellion against the word of God, and from this act of rebellion arises all the evil in the world. One who does not obey the divine law

> is obstinate and full of evil inclinations to disobedience, rebellion, murder, adultery, theft, lying and deceit; and these traits lead to a bad conscience, fear, sadness, terror, despair, and timidity. A person who feels these sensations cannot live long. He declines from day to day, eating his heart out as he ponders his depraved nature. He therefore feels hunger, thirst, heat, cold, exhaustion, and weakness. These bring in their train every sort of sickness and, finally, death. And because, not believing in God's word, he lacks wisdom and is blind, he is soon tempted and deluded by Satan, and from this temptation follow idolatry, sorcery, heresy and error, and all manner of false teachings. And because each of our fellowmen is as bad as the next, none better (excepting only those who believe) we are surrounded on all sides by envy, hatred, wrath, bickering, deceit, robbery, theft, insults, slander, assault, murder, lying, duplicity, fraud, warfare, and every other sort of iniquity. Such atrocious sins cannot go unpunished by God. He therefore gives license to the foul fiend to poison the air, whip up terrible storms, fan great fires, make raging floods. Some men are led to madness by the devil, others are possessed by him. He breaks their necks, drowns them, lets them burn or plunge to their deaths, and causes them to fall into despair so that they will be eternally damned. And all these evils we suffer because we have sinned.[30]

The deliberate vehemence of this passage was, of course, designed to give weight to Osiander's ensuing plea to "cry out to your heavenly father with all your faith and implore him to save and redeem you from all these evils."[31] One wonders what sort of an impression Osiander and his fellow preachers made on their teen-age auditors (whom Osiander addresses throughout, affectionately, as "my dear little children"). His catechism sermons were widely used. Urban magistrates seem to have found them to their liking. They were reprinted many times, translated into Latin by Justus Jonas,[32] and adopted in several other cities as a guide for preachers and catechists.[33] But some among his colleagues thought Osiander had gone too far.[34] The famous

Catholic apologist Johann Eck attacked him on his uncompromising application of the ninth and tenth commandments to children, infants, and even the unformed creature in the mother's womb—an attack to which Osiander responded with the ferocity of the professional polemicist.[35] In any case, he knew better. Even the babe in the cradle is guilty before God, he wrote, "as David declares, saying: 'They have all gone astray, they are all alike corrupt, there is none that does good, no, not one.' "[36]

> This is something we all sense and experience: by nature we are full of evil lusts. For we crave what is pleasing to the flesh while trying to avoid whatever causes us pain and discomfort. And this lust for pleasure can be observed even in the infant in the cradle. Let a baby lie uncomfortably, or feel hunger or thirst, or let him be too warm or too cold, and he will kick and thrash about and cry. Show him a pretty toy and then take it away, or withhold something from him when he thinks of it and wants it, and he will scream. Is this not a clear sign that the babe in the cradle, even in his mother's womb, is full of evil lusts, and therefore a sinner as much as we who are older? For we see him acting against the [ninth and tenth] commandments: thou shalt not be lustful [*du solt dich nicht lassen gelusten*].[37]

Osiander admits that reason cannot grasp this. But, he asks, "who are we to judge by reason? We must go by the word of God, which tells us that lust and desire are sin." No one, therefore, is without guilt [*unschuldig*], "for if we were truly pious, pure, and innocent we would never desire or gain satisfaction from what is pleasing to the body. We would take pleasure only in that which pleases God and is given to us to enjoy. Nor would we try to avoid the things that cause discomfort and pain to our bodies, hating instead only what God has forbidden." But this is not how we live and act. We desire without knowing or caring what God wants us to do and have; and even when we know God's will, we still lust after forbidden fruit. "This is our great sin," Osiander concludes.[38]

One cannot today read these passages without wincing. Their effect on the sixteenth-century audience is of course another matter. But it is not unreasonable to suppose that they made some sort of impression, being presented—as I have already emphasized, and as their place in the full text of the sermons makes clear—not in a voice raging with fire and brimstone, but in tones of infinite patience and loving solicitude for the spiritual well-being of the flock. Osiander was not unsympathetic to the sensibilities of his listeners; far from it. Nonetheless, other men of goodwill thought it dangerous to disorient naive young minds with so grave an accentuation of sin and guilt. Erasmus, for one, feared the effect of such a harsh doctrine on the untrained conscience. "Do not tell the multitude," he warned, writing in the same year as Osiander, "that everything man does ends in sin. In a certain sense this is true, but unlearned persons are bound to interpret it in a way that does them no good."[39] To Osiander, on the other hand, and to many another Lutheran preacher, the encounter between the impressionable young child and the ugly face of his heritage of sin was the indispensable precondition of his acceptance of the divine promise of deliverance, and the only psychological ground on which he could accept and perform his role in society.

But in harping on the consequences of the child's innate corruption, Osiander did not represent the majority view. The preponderance of Lutheran catechists preferred to play down the effects of congenital sinfulness on the individual's inner and outer life. While affirming the gravity of his inherited state, they touched with some delicacy on its effects in daily life. An interesting instance of this alternative is Thomas Lindner's catechism of 1546 for the city of Ravensburg, which is based on Osiander's sermons but omits most of the original's terrifying forewarnings. Only an appended "Manual for Communicants" brings back an echo of Osiander's voice:

> Do you believe that you are a sinner, and where do you learn to recognize your sins? Yes, I believe and know that I am a sinner; and I learn this from the Ten Commandments, which I have not kept, nor can keep perfectly because of my corrupted nature. —And do you know the penalties God has set for your sins, and what you have earned from God for your sinning? Yes, I have earned God's wrath and disgrace, also temporal punishments of many kinds, and in addition eternal damnation in hell.[40]

This kind of ritualized self-incrimination—not substantially different from medieval confessional formulas—must have diffused the impact on the young person. Indeed, such routinized declamations as "I have sinned against God, against my parents and my other fellowmen. I have earned by my conduct temporal punishments and eternal damnation. . . . I was conceived in sin and born in sin. I have been sinning all my life,"[41] or "I confess, heavenly father, that my life is filled with unclean and sinful things and that I offend constantly and in many ways against your fatherly will,"[42] could not have promoted much soul-searching in the young sinner, and sensible pedagogues may well have concluded that a succession of rote self-incriminations was as likely to dull religious sensibilities as it was to arouse serious reflection.

Most catechisms, confession manuals, "Children's Litanies," and "Christian Sentences," offered only such conventional formulas. "The beginning of the Christian life is to be frightened deep in our heart of the wrath of God and of our own sin," wrote Melanchthon in 1527 in his

Book of Proverbs in Which Is Contained the Whole of Christian Life.[43]
But most catechisms tried to induce this fear with confessional recitals
no more terrifying than the following interrogation, found in a *Kinderlehre* for the county of Hohenlohe in Württemberg:

> Are you a sinner? Yes, I am a great sinner. How do you know this?
> I know it from the Ten Commandments, which I have not kept. What is
> sin? All that goes against God's commandments. How many kinds of sin
> are there? Two kinds: original sin and actual sin. What is original sin?
> The unspeakably great impairment and corruption of human nature in
> its reason, will, and powers. For this sin we would be damned if God did
> not offer us his grace for Christ's sake. What are actual sins? All wicked
> thoughts and deeds done against God's commandments. . . . Are all men
> sinners, even small children? Yes, except for the Lord Jesus himself.[44]

The direction of the argument is obvious: fear and its acknowledgment lead to confidence in God. As Melanchthon put it: fear moves the
frightened heart "to turn to the certainty that God has forgiven our sin
for Christ's sake. And thus we are brought to the faith which alone
makes us righteous with God. When the frightened heart comes to
understand that all our merits are not enough to atone for our sins, it
turns instead to Christ and grows certain that he has lifted our sin from
us. And in this certainty our heart finds peace."[45]

In similar terms the catechism of the city of Gengenbach, in its
comments on the second article of the Apostles' Creed, obligated
children to declare that "we know we have been disobedient, damned
creatures. For this reason [*darumb*], God has sent down from heaven
Jesus Christ, true God and true man, born of the Virgin Mary, to purify
us with his holy blood, to gain for us eternal life through his own
innocent death, to justify us with his splendid resurrection, and to be
at God's side as our advocate and mediator to the end of the world."[46]
Despite the immeasurable gulf separating sin from salvation, most
Lutheran catechisms presented the way from one to the other as a
straight and short path. "Are we able to fulfill the commandments of
God? No, for we are evil by nature, being congenital sinners. Our good
works cannot therefore be perfectly good. But to help us out of our
wretched state, God the father has sent Jesus Christ, his son, who
never himself committed a sin and has fulfilled God's commandments
to the letter. If we believe in Jesus Christ, God will favor us for the
sake of Jesus Christ, his son, as if we ourselves had fulfilled his laws."[47]

Such passages imply a direct and, given the requisite of faith,
automatic transitition from sin to salvation. Even Caspar Aquila tried
to persuade his schoolboy audiences that their approach to God was
certain to be favorably received. "We do not despair in our condition,"
he told them, following his depiction of the wages of sin, "because we

know that we are forgiven and have assured access [*sichern zugang*] to God."[48] Psalm 130 was quoted as proof of this certainty: "if thou, O Lord, shouldst mark iniquities, Lord who would stand? But there is forgiveness with thee, that thou mayest be feared";[49] also Acts 10:43: "To him all the prophets bear witness that every one who believes in him receives forgiveness of sins through his name."[50] The surety of this transaction was the sacrifice of Christ. "How do you interpret the article on Christ our Lord? *Answer:* Seeing that, in Adam's fall, we have become so corrupt that no angel or man could extinguish our sins and requite our punishments, God sent his only son as our deliverer, . . . whose passion and death made good our sin and removed our punishment, and whose resurrection and ascension have restored to us our heavenly nature."[51] This assured pledge was sealed by the holy sacraments, which, wrote Huberinus, "convince us in our hearts that we may be sure and certain [*versichert und vergewissert*] of God's grace and fatherly approval, that in his covenant of grace he has adopted us as his children and in his testament has made us heirs to the eternal life. Of this we must have no doubt whatever as we persevere in our struggle against sin, death, Satan, world, and damnation."[52]

2

Most Lutheran catechisms, then, were moderate on the subject of sin and generous with promises of eternal bliss. It would have been hazardous to dishearten the young so deeply as to impair their resolve and block their efforts. A basic trust in human instincts and good sense had to be preserved, along with an incentive to venture and striving. On the other hand, promises of salvation had to be hedged with intimations of contingency to ward off complacency. This psychological dilemma between despair and presumption required pedagogues to exercise considerable tact. To preserve confidence, faith, and determination in the individual while holding off apathy and smugness, they had to strike a delicate balance.

This fragile equipoise rested on the ambiguity left in the layman's mind by the explanations given him of the doctrines of sin and salvation. Academic theology had arguments and proofs to counter every objection and put every doubt to rest; but passing this religious understanding on to the masses was another matter altogether, especially in the contentious atmosphere of the mid-sixteenth century, when a host of competing positions had to be refuted or taken into account.[53] Theology could resolve ambiguities, or explain them away. But popular homiletics neither reconciled internal contradictions nor tried to hide them. Instead it made use of them to serve the pedagogical objective.

Whose fault was sin? It was easy to refute false opinions concerning God's responsibility for evil, attributed to Calvinists, as has been seen, and to deviant brethren among Lutherans who described sin as an intrinsic quality of human nature.[54] But if God was absolved, considerable confusion was allowed to reign with respect to the role of the devil in the drama of original sin. Konrad Dietrich, the Lutheran churchman mentioned earlier in this chapter, exemplifies the difficulty residing in the problem of identifying the culprit. "Where does sin come from, and who is its originator?" he asks, replying: "The chief cause of sin is the devil, who, acting entirely on his own, was the first to turn against God and the first to sin, as we read in 1 John 3 [8]: 'the devil has sinned from the beginning.' The second cause is the perverse wicked will of man, Rom. 5:12. Deceived by the devil's devious cunning, man voluntarily acted on the evil lusts in his heart: James 2:14: 'what does it profit if a man says he has faith but has not works?' "[55]

Apart from the somewhat puzzling use of James 2:14 in this passage, how is its reader to gauge the nature and extent of human culpability in an action in which the devil played the protagonist? Who was guiltier, he or Satan? And if the latter, could the human follower be blamed for succumbing to so powerful an adversary? Catechisms were of no help in settling this conundrum. " 'Where does sin come from?' Answer: 'originally from the devil; after that it came down to us from Adam and Eve, our first parents.' 'And how did our first parents fall into sin?' Answer: 'Having been deceived by the devil, they disobeyed God and ate from the forbidden tree in Paradise.' "[56] Even more succinctly, " 'How did Adam fall, and why do we find ourselves in our distressed state?' Answer: 'Through the devil's deception and our own free will.' "[57] How these two determinants related to each other was not made clear. Trying to get to the root of the discrepancy by working through the popular religious literature leaves one more bewildered than enlightened. Nearly all preachers, following Luther in this respect, urged the faithful to be on constant guard against the devil's assaults and plots. "What are we to conclude," wrote Andreas Musculus in his pamphlet on the power of Satan, "from people's indifference and resignation to the devil's murderous attacks? We learn," he responded, "that the great mass of men live nowadays in such cocky self-assurance that they fear neither Satan nor God and let the devil do what he wants with them."[58] Musculus did not say what men might do to keep the foe away. In fact, he made a point of arguing (in the longest chapter of his book) that devils have their power "from God, who has given it to them to inflict harm on men."[59] On the other hand, he also speaks of Satan as if he were an autonomous potentate. This failure to reconcile the contradiction was typical. Neither Musculus nor his fellow preachers thought it necessary to balance the three disparate types of evil: that which was caused by man himself and for which he was fully responsible, evil perpetrated by the devil in his capacity as adversary, and the power of doing evil conferred on Satan by God as a punishment for men. With common sense helpless before these incongruities, the individual was bound to remain mystified by the nature of evil and the depth of his own involvement.

If it was inconsistent to exhort men to foil the devil while depicting him as an irresistible force, it was even more equivocal to prod them to redouble their efforts on behalf of their own sanctification while leaving them unsure about what they could do to help themselves. Ambiguity abounded in all attempts to explain in common language the nature and power of the human will. Could it be directed to good things? Was it free, and did it have the strength, to pursue the right course? Having raised these questions, nearly all catechisms left them wide open:

> Question: Has fallen man a free will?
> Answer: In external and corporeal matters touching on temporal life, man has, to some extent [*etlicher massen*] a free will which is, however, much impeded and thwarted by the work of the devil and by human frailty. But in spiritual matters touching on God and eternal life, man's free will is before his conversion utterly dead and useless.[60]

That man had no effective control over his fate in the hereafter was, of course, manifest in Lutheran theology, although even on that point theologians differed, contended, erred, recanted, anathematized each other, and vastly confused the general public.[61] When it came to the problem of making mundane choices in daily life, the issue was left entirely unresolved. How could anyone, from the passage just quoted, gauge the scope and power of his own will? Depending on what a person had been told from the pulpit and in his catechism, this capacity could vary from complete determinism to synergism and neo-Pelagianism. He was counseled to leave everything to God[62] and prompted, in equally urgent tones, to do his utmost to mend his ways and improve his standing. "Have you made a serious resolution to improve your life and conduct yourself in a Christian manner?" he was asked. "Yes," he was made to reply, "with all my heart have I made this resolution, and may Almighty God send his Holy Spirit to help me keep it. And why should you make this effort to be obedient and observe a Christian walk of life? The answer to this question I know from the catechism, and it is this: I must do good works because with good works I give proof and evidence of my faith."[63]

This answer and many similar passages clearly suggest that there was much the individual could do to help himself. At the same time his self-confidence was methodically undermined by reminders of the fragility of his strength and the uncertainty of his sense of moral direction. Reflecting on these apparently contradictory lines of advice, Charles Trinkaus has rightly noted that no proponents of a theology of grace "ever ceased to preach and evoke individual moral reform despite its seeming contradiction with their theology. Each theology," he suggests, "has its own way of reconciling these contradictions."[64] Among the abstractions of philosophic speculation this is certainly true. But on the mundane, utilitarian plane of religious instruction and moral guidance the inconsistencies remain unsolved, glaring, and enigmatic to common folk trying to fit their lives to the doctrines.

One wonders, for example, how clear an understanding, and how untroubled a conscience, could have been drawn from Nicolaus Hunnius's *Instruction in the Right Christian Faith for Young and Simple People in Home and School*, a handbook of basic religious knowledge written in a characteristically patient, kind, and direct manner. The argument—in questions, answers, and proof texts from Scripture— runs as follows.

If Christ has made atonement for all men, why is it that not all are saved? Because not all men let themselves partake of this redemption and allow themselves to be led to grace. . . . Does God call all men or only a few? He calls all, without any distinction, as Christ himself exclaims, Matt. 11 [28], "Come to me, all who labor and are heavy laden and I will give you rest." . . . Is it enough that I feel sincere repentance for my sin? No, for while true repentance always includes serious contrition, . . . it also requires complete trust in God's forgiving grace, as Christ tells the repentant sinner in Luke 7 [48]: "your sins are forgiven." How does a man come into true repentance? Not by the use of his own powers. God alone can lead him to knowledge of sin through the commandments: Rom. 3 [20]: "through the law comes knowledge of sin." . . . What is conversion? Conversion is when a man turns away from all unbelief, disobedience, sins, and hostility toward God and his fellowmen, and turns instead to faith, obedience, and love of God and his neighbor, as in Rom. 13 [12]: "Let us then cast off the works of darkness and put on the armor of light." Can a man convert himself or make progress toward his own conversion? Everyone can hear the word of God, but no man can change his own heart and nature. If we cannot turn a single hair on our head white or black, as Christ says in Matt. 5 [36] . . . , how, then, can we have the power to turn our heart to God, or help with a single good thought to bring about our conversion? If God alone converts people, why does he not convert them all? God works within us, "both to will and to work for his good pleasure," Phil. 2 [13], and he is eager to help us. But as a wounded man cannot be healed if he pushes his medicine away and refuses to put himself under the care of his physician, no one can be converted if he does not surrender himself entirely to God and continues instead in his worldly desires and concerns. . . . What, then, can a man do to assist and advance his conversion? He can hear the word of God . . . and allow his reason to become captive to the obedience of the faith, as Paul says in 2 Cor. 10 [5]: "take every thought captive to obey Christ." Seeing that all men are sinners and unrighteous, how can they become righteous before God? No man can become righteous through his own efforts or with his own works. . . . All the works commanded by God are owed to him; they cannot, therefore, earn us any merit if we do them. . . . Other works, not expressly commanded by God, avail us nothing. . . . Where, then, does righteousness come from? From Christ alone, who was created by God for righteousness' sake. . . . And how can a sinner partake of the righteousness of Christ? By believing and trusting in Christ's atonement and fulfillment of the law, accomplished for our sake, and by firmly believing that Christ has through his passion won righteousness for us as though we ourselves had made satisfaction to God.[65]

A self-canceling argument? Exercise of choice, decision, and action is strongly suggested, but its efficacy is explicitly denied. On the one hand it is declared that men must "let themselves be conducted" [führen lassen, sich theilhaft machen] to grace, a decision that seems to demand the conscious choice of a set of attitudes and a course of action leading to a turning away [Abwendung] from the flouting of God's laws, and a turning toward [Zuwendung] the love of God and one's fellowmen. They could carry out this redirection of their inclinations, or they could continue on their self-destructive "worldly" course. If it was to be the former, they must surrender themselves to God as a desperately sick patient resigns himself into the hand of his physician. This is the choice men must make. On the other hand, will it make a difference? Nothing men do or fail to do can contribute to their salvation. All that is asked is belief and trust in Christ's redemptive sacrifice, a capacity of mind not in our power either to acquire or to direct. Of what use, then, is the turning away and turning to? And how can a preacher's admonitions to do better and to exert oneself more be reconciled with the solemn assurance that nothing counts for us except resignation and trust? One is reminded here of the jingle with which Charles G. Finney lampooned the sermons of the neo-Edwardian Calvinists of his day:

You can and you can't,
You shall and you shan't,
You will and you won't,
And you'll be damned if you don't.[66]

How, indeed, could the sincere believer know for certain what he was expected to do, how much, and with what effect in the final balance? What security could he draw from the firm assurance that only faith mattered, when so much attention was also given to efforts and works? Conversely, could he wholeheartedly exert himself while being warned that all human actions were chained to sin? Protestant authorities must have realized that this paradox, as Erasmus called it,[67] caused the faithful much puzzlement. In 1539 a Saxon ecclesiastical ordinance noted that, among people who came to confession, "there are many who possess no understanding and little conscience, but are withal decent people who have never been taught by the Catholics what sin is and how one gets rid of it [*wie man ir los werden . . . sol*] and receive grace." The ordinance required pastors to "stir up their conscience until they feel their sin and accept the need for grace."[68] But they must also make it clear that efforts and exertion were required. For the sake of doctrinal purity the meritoriousness of human effort was qualified with reservations or disclaimers. But the ordinary man, learning his catechism and heeding his preachers, received a different message: "Paul shows us in 1 Cor. 15 that our future state of bliss will not be the same for all. Some will be raised higher than others, for God distributes greatness in the hereafter according to the works each of us has done, even though there is no intrinsic merit or worth in these works, which are not our works at all, but the works God himself performs in us." Works have, however, an even more fateful function; they bestow the right of admission. Andreas Musculus, the author of the lines just quoted, was at pains to clear God of all responsibility for the failure of so many of his creatures to reach heaven. God is not a tyrant, he argues, who condemns men without reason. On the contrary: "At the end of time God holds a judgment day and gives to each man what is owing to him according to his works. No one will get too much and no one too little. And no one will then have reason to cry out against God and his justice, for if he is condemned, he can cry out only against himself."[69]

One can find even more emphatic declarations that good works weigh heavily in the final balance. Johann Spangenberg, who wrote a question-and-answer version of Luther's Greater Catechism for young people, asks: "Must we all appear before our final judge?" He replies: "Paul says in 2 Cor. 5 [10]: 'we must all appear before the judgment seat of Christ, so that each one may receive good or evil, according to what he has done in the body.' I take it, then [continues the questioner], that God will judge by our works and not by our faith [*So höre ich wol, Gott will richten nach den wercken und nicht nach dem glauben*]?" The answer is curiously oblique: "Faith being an invisible thing, God prefers to judge by something one can see and touch, that is to say, by each man's works, whether they be good or bad."[70] Spangenberg explains that God, as a fair-minded judge, does not base his verdicts on secret information, hidden from men's eyes. He renders them publicly before the whole world, "saving or damning men on the strength of their works done in testimony of their belief or unbelief."[71] Elsewhere in his book he makes it clear that good works can make no contribution to the forgiveness of sins.[72] But Christians must exert themselves all the same, he says, "in unceasing practice of the fruits of their faith . . . , never lazy or slack, never sleeping, loafing, or idling, but always working and growing richer in virtues."[73] In the end they are judged worthy or wanting on the strength of these efforts, "God will say to them, 'are you a Christian? Then let me see your Christian works [so zaige an Christliche wercke].'"[74]

Spangenberg clearly fails to give an unequivocal solution to the problem of works and merit, although he goes further than most in suggesting that works count in the final reckoning. A core of ambiguity survived his and his colleagues' best endeavors to explain in popular terms the subtle interactions of sin, faith, human effort, and grace. This was not for lack of verbal skill on their part. Lutheran theologians were able popularizers. Ambiguity was not due to inept formulations; it was inherent in the conflicting objectives of their diverse roles as guardians of the doctrine, teachers of the ignorant, counselors of troubled souls, and governors of men in society. They wished to bring confidence and ease of mind but must urge men on in the lifelong contest to prove themselves. They encouraged them to raise their eyes to heaven, but directed their efforts to their earthly duties. They gave them assurance of having been cleared of inherited sin but frightened them with tales of its dreadful aftereffects. They implied certainty of deliverance but left a large residue of doubt. They asked for childlike trust in God's mercy but could not dispel a strong suspicion that men's lives lay in the hands of an unpredictable deity.

Preachers and catechists seemed to be telling their young auditors that even though God demanded nothing of them but love, trust, and faith, they would be well advised to support their claim to a place in heaven with a lifelong record of laudable deeds. A small thing to man—eating an apple, disobeying a command—Adam's deed in the Garden of Eden was a colossal crime in the sight of God, so immense a malefaction, says Andreas Musculus, "that it could be expiated in no other way, manner, or form than by the death of his only beloved son."[75] Against so huge a backdrop of sin and divine indignation, the assurance given of God's patient mercy may have echoed with a hollow sound, and the admonition to fear God may have seemed more compelling than the exhortation to turn to him in love and trust. "He who is a sinner is afraid," said Musculus, "and whenever something goes wrong with him, or when suffering comes upon him, he remembers God's anger and thinks he is being punished for his sin."[76] To be filled with fear and anxiety was itself the mark of a sinful nature; only the regenerate, Musculus said, "are happy and certain [sicher] that God is no longer angry with them."[77] But how could one gain this certainty when the object of religious and moral instruction was to crush the very roots of *Sicherheit* in the child, and to persuade him to accept himself as a creature both sinful and guilty? No catechist gave a psychologically plausible solution to this dilemma. Lutherans were not unique, of course, in burdening the young with the weight of irresolution. "People all over the world seem convinced," writes Erik Erikson in *Identity and the Life Cycle*, "that to make the right (meaning their) kind of human being, one must consistently introduce the senses of shame, doubt, guilt, and fear into a child's life. Only the patterns vary."[78] Lutheran pedagogy constitutes a paradigm of this intervention.

The child growing to maturity with the aid of the Lutheran catechism is therefore not likely to have found comfort in the pledges given him of God's love and solicitude. His birthright of sin told too heavily against him to allow him to cultivate an attitude of trust in which to face his maker with a serene and confident spirit. If religious indoctrination made any impression on him (and this is a big "if," as a later chapter will show), the sense of guilt will have remained on his conscience despite what he had learned of Christ's sacrifice and the sacramental power of baptism. Was this the object of the education he received? Pondering this question in the light of Erikson's observation, one is astonished to note how closely Lutheran pedagogical techniques correspond to practices found by psychologists in cultures where socialization depends on, or is aided by, the stirring up of guilt feelings in children. While the very young learn obedience through fear of punishment, older children, who have begun to reason and reflect, need a subtler kind of control. Fear of punishment continues to play its part, but transgressions now tend to be linked by educators to feelings of shame and remorse. Having been taught to blame himself when he strays from approved behavior, the young person experiences guilt feelings, or the anticipation of guilt feelings, whenever the thought of a transgression crosses his mind.[79] If punishment and blame are tied to the child's need for love, the threat of withholding love acts as a powerful dissuader from unacceptable behavior.[80]

A modern student of Lutheran catechisms cannot doubt that sixteenth-century Protestant indoctrinators made instinctive use of this "love-oriented technique of punishment" (so called because "it threatens the child's attainment of the goal of . . . love, yet keeps him oriented toward that goal").[81] God's love for his fallen creatures was the Christian's only hope, although he knew that nothing in him merited sympathy or affection. His catechism assured him that God wished to save all men; but he also learned that many were being condemned, God having withheld or withdrawn his compassion from them. Such reprobates had no grounds for complaint. No descendant of Adam deserved God's sympathy. Why should God love men who cannot love him? "Our entire nature is so thoroughly poisoned with self-love," wrote Ambrosius Moibanus, "that we are incapable of loving God as we love ourselves."[82] A sinner's hold on God's affection was therefore weak at best: this realization must have been the sum of a thoughtful catechism reader's reflections. It may be that this conclusion pushed him to exert himself all the more earnestly in his struggle to earn divine benevolence.

But it may also be that catechisms and other books of religious instruction provoked no such thoughts. Indeed, they may well have had very little effect of any kind. There is no evidence to allow us to claim that catechization in Lutheran Germany left an imprint on the young psyche commensurate with its pedagogical aims and its psychological potential. We cannot know what responses young people made to their lessons on sin and guilt, love and grace. Their reactions can only be inferred from the recorded evidence of their religious behavior, and this suggests that the impact of catechism teaching is likely to have been much weaker, and certainly much less durable, than pedagogues had hoped. Beyond this general observation, the historian's facts do not permit him to say whether, or how deeply, the doctrine of sin marked people's minds and affected their lives.

CHAPTER 11

THE MAKING OF A CHRISTIAN:
RELIGION AND DISCIPLINE

What, then, was the concrete lesson of religious education? If its central message remained ambiguous, as I have argued in the preceding chapter, what kind of religious understanding was passed to "young and simple" folk? Did it give laymen an intelligent perception of themselves as Christians? Did it stamp on them a sufficiently distinct religious identity as evangelical Protestants to lend some force to the contention that the Lutheran Reformation transformed the religious conscience of its time?

We have, alas, little evidence from which to draw definitive answers to these questions. Our knowledge of mentalities is too fragmentary, indirect, and superficial to permit confident judgments on the quality of the Lutheran faith as it was assimilated by the multitude. There are no windows into people's minds to let us analyze their conscious perception of formal religion and its force as an organizing principle in their lives. We do have excellent data, however, on the behavioral manifestations of popular piety, and these suggest that the general attitude toward doctrines and ecclesiastical institutions was, broadly speaking, one of detachment and indifference. In the light of more than half a century's massive sermonizing and catechizing on the individual's Christian duties, this nonchalant posture is itself a judgment on the popular religious response. Indeed, the very paucity of convincing evidence for a lasting religious commitment on the part of masses of men and women indoctrinated by the principles of Lutheran pedagogy compels one to conclude, I think, that their grasp of the formal doctrine, and of its implications, was a shallow and uncertain thing.

Three reasons seem to explain this apparent failure to transmit a clear religious message that could be consciously received and adopted.

All three are familiar to the reader of the preceding chapters and need only be summarized. The equivocacy of the communication at its crucial junctures is certainly one reason for its unproductive reception. Early enthusiasm for evangelical teachings is likely to have yielded to perplexity and indifference as a result of long exposure to confusing ambiguity. The case for this view has been presented at length. An even more important block to the internalization of the religious message, at least in the long run, was the rigid methodology into which Protestant theologians and their pedagogues were locked. Text-bound, word-oriented, wedded to a pedantic dependence on rote memorization and endless reiteration, their inflexible schoolmasterly procedures could scarcely keep from extinguishing whatever sparks of religious curiosity might have been incipient in their pupils. Their implicit faith in the power of habituation enthralled them to a mechanical learning procedure unlikely to awaken a desire to learn. Their acceptance of the very words of Scripture and catechism as holy matter, and of the reading and speaking of them as sacred acts, bound them to a regime of mindless drill and recitation. Lutheran reformers themselves are our best witnesses to the cheerless results of these labors. They were also their own most unsparing critics, but they could think of no superior method. "In no other way can you build a solid foundation for knowledge of divine things," insisted Huberinus, "than by impressing on your pupils the right Chrsitan meaning of each article of the catechism."[1] One knows exactly what this meant in practice: memorizing, drill, repetition on demand, none of it necessarily entering the thinking part of the learner's mind.

A third factor contributed to the vague impression of the religious message in the public conscience: the polemics disfiguring so much writing by Reformation theologians. Lutherans waged their assaults on Catholic and rival Protestant opponents as a relentless propaganda war. Its vehemence may have won them a measure of popular allegiance in a time of danger and agitation. But such a reaction was not likely to grow into a permanent affinity. The sense of religious identity forged in these contests was apt to be perceived negatively, in terms of what was being scorned, rather than positively as a commitment to its distinguishing virtues. To be a loyal Lutheran meant to be aware of why one was not a papist, Calvinist, sacramentarian, Anabaptist, Schwenckfeldian, interimist, adiaphorist, Philippist, or Flacian, and on what points of doctrine one differed from all and each of these repudiated antagonists. Many authors of catechisms were themselves avid apologists. Their embattled and suspicious mentality, seriously at odds with their wish to edify and enlighten,[2] must have distracted from their religious message, undermined its authority, and blurred its focus, discouraging the learner or turning him away altogether.

Protestant leaders were aware of these deficiencies, but they could think of only one way to overcome them: by increasing the already comprehensive exposure of the public to religious indoctrination. Over the quantity and frequency of religious instruction they had some control, and they preferred to err on the side of excess rather than run the risk of doing too little. "Without discipline and direction [*disziplin und zweck*] the common man will learn nothing about our doctrine," wrote a Saxon church official in 1554, referring to the need, as he saw it, of steeping the *gemeine Mann* in religious indoctrination.[3] In accordance with this principle, governments expanded catechism practice, preaching, and the time devoted to religious study in school curricula. Clearly, they took it for granted that in the absence of a pronounced public desire to learn, saturation was the strategy most likely to lead to good results.

The entire Protestant establishment seems to have joined in this campaign to immerse the population in as much religion as it could tolerate. Although the products of this collective effort give us no fresh clues to the religious thought of common folk, they do reveal what their mentors wished them to believe, feel, think, and do. They constitute a profuse and reiterative statement of the authoritative religious message delivered by the Lutheran Reformation, though not necessarily accepted by its recipients. But before turning to this latter problem—how the Lutheran doctrine was received by those for whom it was intended—it will be useful to examine the form and substance of normative religion as it was conveyed in the literature of indoctrination. This examination will support my earlier conclusion that on many points of doctrine, particularly on matters of "inner piety" (to use contemporary parlance), the message remained blurred and ambiguous. On the subject of "external piety," on the other hand—that is to say, on the life to be lived in the world and the responsibilities to be met there—the message was, as will be seen, loud and clear.

A rich religious folk literature brought Christian instruction to every house where books were read or pictures handed round.[4] Preserving a venerable medieval tradition of private devotional reading,[5] while at the same time attempting to counteract its pluralistic trend and replace it with a uniform creed based on the catechism, this literature was intended to turn every Christian home into a place of auxiliary religious instruction. The disappointing outcome of this endeavor has already been noted. In any case, the main effort of the Lutheran educational enterprise shifted from home to church and school. But the principle of domestic instruction and household devotions kept its hold on Protestant churchmen who looked for ways to improve the religious preparation of the laity. Luther's own postils provided the model for bringing religious teaching into the home, but books by Spangenberg, Brenz, Huberinus, Konrad Dietrich, Christoph Vischer —to mention only names frequently cited in these pages—were as widely used. Their chatty tone and easygoing informativeness probably explain their popularity, as does their affinity with the social position of their readers. Theologians and consistories approved of these authors because they gave plain and, for the most part, authoritative interpretations of gospel and doctrine.

Religious instruction came also from prayer books for all occasions, classes, and ages; from consolation tracts, confession manuals, books of Christian conduct, collections of psalms, anthologies of selected writings of the major reformers. Nonreaders could resort to woodblock pamphlets such as *A Brief and Correct Summary of the True Doctrine of Our Holy Christian Faith*, in which the entire catechism was condensed into nine pictures explaining, almost entirely in visual images, "The Origin of Our Inherited Sin," "Actual Sin" (vivid scenes of rape, murder, theft, fornication), "The Punishment of Sin" (death and the devil pulling a sinner into the jaw of hell), "The Law Merely Tells Us What Sin Is," "The Works of Christ Alone Earn Us Forgiveness and Salvation," "Through Faith We Partake of the Merits of Christ" (man turning his back on Reason and moving toward the cross while "Works," one foot in hell, looks on), "Faith Comes from the Preaching of the Divine Word" (a closely packed congregation sitting in rapt attention at the preacher's feet), "Good Works Are Fruits and Witnesses of Faith" (scenes of charity and kindness), and "The Christian's Tribulations on Earth and Eternal Joy in Heaven" (the righteous arranged in a semicircle below God and his angels).[6] Between the covers of this little pamphlet, at least, the message was straightforward, and one suspects that a few minutes' concentration on such unpretentious woodcuts left a layman with a clearer understanding and fewer doubts than many a compendious "Catechism with Explications."

But such popular volumes were no more than accessories to the principal thrust of religious instruction for the young, which took place in school. The proposition that "teaching piety and religion is the first and foremost duty of public instruction," enunciated by a Lutheran educational theorist, Sebald Heyden of Nuremberg,[7] became an axiom with all theologians and government officials. Heyden emphasized that religious teaching, if it were to produce the desired effect, must be linked with the two other major divisions of the curriculum, the liberal arts and the study of one's duties in life and society. "These three parts should be taught simultaneously and integrally in each school," he insisted.[8] Religion as an independent subject of

Die erſte lere iſt vom Geſaße auch der ſünden vꝛſpꝛung vnd der Buſſe.

Der erbſünden vꝛſpꝛung.

EVA   ADAM

Erſte

From *Ein kurze ordenliche summa der rechten waren lehre unseres heyligen christlichen glaubens* . . . (Regensburg, 1554).

Die würck-
lichen sünde.

Der Sünden
straff.

Das gesetz Le-
ret nur erkennen
Was sünde sey.

Volget die ander lere vom
Euangelio vnd dem glauben.

Allein die
Werck Christi haben vns
vergebung vnserer sünden vnd
die seligkeyt verdient.

From *Ein kurze ordenliche summa der rechten waren lehre unseres heyligen
christlichen glaubens . . .* (Regensburg, 1554).

Durch den glau-
ben werden Wir des ver
dienſts Chriſti tail-
hafftig.

Der glaub
kompt auß der Predig
Göttlichs Worts.

Volget Die dritte lere
von guten wercken.

Gute werck
ſind des glaubés frucht
vnd zeügen.

Der Chriſten
Zeitlich Creütz alhie/vnd
ewige freüde im Hi-
mel.

From *Ein kurze ordenliche summa der rechten waren lehre unseres heyligen christlichen glaubens* . . . (Regensburg, 1554).

instruction was a new departure in the history of education, a creation of the Reformation's endeavor to nurture and mold the maturing young person in a learning environment imbued with evangelical associations.[9] Since its position in the curriculum was always determined by official school ordinances, and owing to the voracious bureaucratic appetite for written data, we are exceedingly well informed on religious instruction in Reformation schools.[10] Visitation records contain thousands of lesson plans submitted by rectors and schoolmasters to ecclesiastical authorities who wished to exercise effective control over the scope and doctrinal reliability of the religious components of the curriculum. These plans, along with the marginal corrections and comments added by officials, constitute the best source for our knowledge of both the format and contents of religious teaching in Protestant Germany.

Tied to the academic curriculum on the one hand and the divine service—preaching, confession, catechism practice—on the other, religious instruction took up a considerable portion of the pupil's day. Quantitatively it came to a major portion, and qualitatively it constituted the heart, of the Latin and the vernacular curricula. In German schools it was, apart from reading and writing, the only subject taught consecutively in all classes. Catechism study occupied the largest block of time made available to religious instruction. In the Latin schools of Braunschweig, to take a case in point, boys began Luther's catechism in the *Sexta,* the lowest form, restudied it with explications in the *Quinta* and *Quarta,* had it memorized by the end of the *Tertia,* and only then went on to read passages from the New Testament in the *Secunda* and *Prima.* Throughout these years, they also attended catechism sermons in their respective home parishes. This arrangement, first worked out by Bugenhagen in 1528, was confirmed in subsequent school ordinances later in the century.[11] To take another example, girl pupils in Pirna, in Saxony, recited Luther's catechism on Monday, Tuesday, and Wednesday mornings and on Thursday afternoons; on Monday afternoons they read psalms, on Tuesday afternoons they answered questions on the catechism, more psalms on Thursday mornings, and on Saturday mornings the Sunday Gospel.[12] Gymnasium students in the city of Speyer memorized Luther's two catechisms first in German, then in Nicolaus Selneccer's Latin and Greek translations.[13] In Magdeburg they read Luther's German and Latin catechisms, a book of "Sacred Sentences" taken from the Old Testament, and various commentaries by Protestant theologians.[14]

This curriculum did not exhaust the religious instruction given to Reformation schoolboys. In each of their forms they were required also to pray and sing. Many detailed descriptions of these devotional exercises have come down to us, but one example, from a school in the county of Oldenburg, must suffice here. It invites quotation in extenso because, coming from the very end of the sixteenth century, it epitomizes the reformers' attempt to immerse their pupils in a milieu of Christian words and sounds.[15] But it is a very long and repetitious document, and I must limit the excerpt to a typical day's praying and singing.

Monday morning: *Veni Sancte Spiritus* in German. "Lord, When I Raise My Voice to You. . . ." Amen. Morning blessing.

Morning prayer from the school book. The five articles of the catechism: Decalogue with explication, the other four articles without it [each day a different article was taken up "with explication"]. The first penitential psalm. "O God, We Praise You Every Day. . . ." John 3: "For God so loved the world. . . ." "O, My Dearest Jesus" [and three other hymns]. Lord's Prayer, Blessing, "O Jesus, Jesus, Jesus Christ, Keep Us Safe from Devil and Hell."

Monday Afternoon: "In God I Trust," The ordinary school prayer as given in the lesson book. Lord's Prayer. Blessing. "We Thank You, O Lord." "Keep Us, O Lord, True to Your Word." "Be Praised, O Lord." Ecclesiasticus 50: "Come Then, Praise the God of the Universe." "Now Thank We All Our God." Lord's Prayer. Blessing.

Monday evening after the last lesson: "O Christ Who Is Our Day and Light." Psalm 5: "Give ear to my words, O Lord, Give heed to my groaning." Evening blessing and evening prayer from the school book. Psalm 1: "Blessed is the man." "Remain with Us, Lord Jesus Christ." Verse 25 of Psalm 73: "Whom have I in heaven but thee?" The Lord's Prayer. "Keep Me, God, from Despair and Doubt." The blessing. "O Jesus, Jesus, Jesus Christ, Keep Us Safe from Devil and Hell."

And so on through Saturday evening: catechism, psalms, Ecclesiasticus, the familiar and recurring prayers and blessings, interspersed with sacred hymns whose expressive words and melodies described the sinner's lonely way in the world and affirmed his trust in God's mercy.

The prominence of religious songs in this program—a typical one in that respect[16]—points to another feature of the religious setting in which reformers tried to situate their public. They knew, of course, that rhyme, meter, and melodies could forcefully impress minds and affect sensibilities, and they did not fail to mobilize this power. In the popular religious verse and music of the Reformation they possessed an imprinting device of uncommon potency. Christian hymns gave natural expression to human feelings and exerted a direct influence on the affections.[17] "When I read these hymns," stated Katharina Zell in the preface she wrote to accompany an edition of the songbook of the Bohemian Brethren, "I felt that this writer had the whole Bible in his heart. We have here not just a hymn book," she continued, "but a lesson book of prayer and praise."[18] A lesson book easily remembered, she could have added, for the mnemonic power of verses set to pretty tunes, long known in classical pedagogy, was recognized by the reformers. Luther himself had recommended the singing of religious verse as a means of propagating the gospel.[19] An even stronger endorsement of hymns for pedagogical purposes was given by the Rostock theologian David Chytraeus:

> Our gracious, wise and merciful God has entrusted his beautiful art of music to us so that his word, that is to say the divine doctrines, cautions, promises, and warnings of our religion, may the more eagerly and joyfully be learned, the more easily kept in the memory, and the more deeply received into Christian hearts, moving and exciting us all to fear, love, trust, and joy in God as well as to heartfelt prayer and praise. For in these hymns the articles of our Christian faith and the important acts of God, especially the justification of the human race in Jesus Christ, are set distinctly and clearly to such pretty rhymes and such beautiful melodies that, when young people sing them with hearts full of serious piety, they will be brought in a pleasant and joyful way to the true knowledge of God and the practice of virtue.[20]

These songs, said another writer, will inspire in Christians an abiding love for God's church and a due reverence toward its ministers.[21] Of the three ways of imparting the Christian message, "by preaching, by reading, and by singing," the third way was particularly likely "to impress the doctrine deeply into the minds of simple-minded young people and preserve it from generation to generation."[22]

It was hoped that verses and melodies might be passed on as part of an oral tradition of words and tunes, from mothers to children, from older members of congregations to the younger. But, as always, reformers took no chances and tried in various ways to assist the natural process of preservation. Visitors questioned pastors "whether people follow the choir in singing the German hymns and begin and finish in time with the cantor."[23] They ascertained from parishioners that "only the familiar and well known [that is to say, authorized] melodies are sung in church."[24] Schoolmasters had to give information on "what use they make of singing in their classes and what hymns they practice with their pupils, and how often they sing them."[25] Where visitors noticed poor responses—the greater part of the congregation sitting in silence, making a thin sound, end-phrases trailing off, words mumbled unintelligibly[26]—they increased the time given to singing practice in school.[27] Schoolboys were expected to set an example to the rest of the congregation in their choral singing no less than in catechism recitation. Like their medieval predecessors, Lutheran pupils played a fixed role in the musical part of the service.[28] Their function, however, was a new one: to lead the congregation in the singing of chorales. For it was in hymns and psalms set to moving melodies that the idea of a Christian community found its most evocative expression. "All spiritual singing is directed to this one end": it was stated in the Strassburg catechism of 1544, "to teach and admonish ourselves and to give thanks to God the Lord."[29] But since few people could be expected to do much more than trail along with words and tunes, boy choristers formed the nucleus of the singing congregation, and pupils were trained for this role.[30]

The many hymnals and books of spiritual songs (*geistliche Lieder, Kirchenlieder*) printed during the Reformation served the several purposes of congregational singing: to give thanks and praise to God, to express the community's common spiritual interests, to arouse the individual's religious emotions and help imprint on his mind the salient points of the doctrine.[31] From the perspective of this study, the most interesting hymnbooks were those edited to meet explicitly pedagogical needs, the *Enchiridion, or Handbook for the Constant Practice of Spiritual Songs Suitable for the Education of Young Children*, for example, published in Erfurt in 1524,[32] a collection offering the Decalogue and Apostles' Creed set to well-known melodies. Another, an anthology by Wolfgang Figulus, contained settings of the Sunday Gospels in German rhymes matched to popular tunes familiar to every child.[33] In Nuremberg the best-known verses seem to have been Sebald Heyden's twenty-three strophes on the Crucifixion, a musical passion moving from the Last Supper to the Resurrection.[34] Equally popular were the *Christian Psalms, Songs, and Church Hymns, in Which the Christian Doctrine Is Epitomized and Explained; For the Use of Preachers in Towns and Villages* by the theologian and poet Nicolaus Selneccer, comprising a selection of psalms, Luther's complete catechism turned into rhyme, and hymns for the chief holidays.[35] Perusing the lines of these verses, and humming the tunes, one is as impressed by the unpretentious honesty of their religious sentiment as by the easy rhymes and melodies in which the doctrinal message was communicated. Many such anthologies seem to have been spontaneously generated by teachers, cantors, and pastors who drew upon a huge repertoire of local songs in their regions so as to rescue, as they said, fine tunes from the salacious secular jingles to which they had been attached.[36]

There are some signs of a positive response to the musical emphasis of the Lutheran service. Once again, however, for our best evidence we must fall back on Catholic evidence, notably from Bavaria, where grass-roots sentiment in favor of congregational singing was officially resisted (and later only grudgingly accepted)[37] but where teachers reported strong pressure from townspeople to have their children taught German hymns and psalms.[38] When the Jesuits took over educational direction in Bavaria they immediately put religious verse and song to pedagogical use. A German Jesuit reporting to General Aquaviva in 1586 could not laud highly enough the power of rhyme and melody to lodge things firmly in the minds of the young. "For a whole year," he wrote, "I had been laboring with our village boys but could not make them remember even the words of the Lord's Prayer. But now that I have taught them how to sing, they learn the Apostles' Creed and the Ten Commandments in a few hours, and I doubt they will ever forget them."[39] In response to popular requests, German hymns began to appear in the *agenda*, the ceremonial books of Catholic regions,[40] thus incidentally creating another enforcement problem for Catholic authorities, who worried about the intrusion of Lutheran songs and their power to cause large-scale disaffection among churchgoers.[41] All this is spotty evidence, to be sure. We cannot be certain how enthusiastically the masses responded to these hymns. We do know that Protestant officials often complained about the feeble and unmusical singing that assailed their ears as they visited churches across the land.[42] In the end we must admit once again that we have too few clues to people's inner lives to allow us to assert that these plain but evocative and—to us—extraordinarily moving chorales stirred sixteenth-century congregations as deeply as their spiritual mentors, counting on the principles of classical psychology, hoped they would.

But it is not unreasonable to assume that in their simple and unaffected way these hymns epitomized the intended meaning and central lesson of the evangelical faith. Plainly stated, this was the emotional tension between despair and hope, fear and trust, and the gulf between man's weakness and infinite vulnerability, on the one hand, and the prodigious power and boundless compassion of God on the other. Unlike the catechisms, however, Lutheran church hymns resolve the tension and close the gulf. To be sure, they also convey a harrowing impression of fear and despair as the insupportable burden of man's inheritance of sin. Their essential message, however, is not of sadness, but unequivocally of hope and joy. No writer suggests this core of optimism more eloquently than does Luther, in his own contributions to the literature of spiritual song. We who possess the gospel sing to the Lord a new kind of song, he exulted in 1545, alluding to Psalm 96. We sing a happy tune, unlike the dejected airs of the Old Testament, because "God has gladdened our heart and conscience by sending his beloved son to redeem us from sin, death, and devil. Those among us who earnestly believe this, Luther declared, "are of good cheer and wish to sing gaily for everyone to hear and take heed." Luther does add a sharp reminder of the minatory tensions embedded deeply in the evangelical creed. "He who feels no desire to speak and sing of this joy," he warns, "must take it as a sign that he does not believe [in the redeemer]."[43] But the hymns themselves do not admit this threatening undertone. Words and melodies induce a mood of cheerful, though always serious and reflective, gratitude for the Christian's immense good fortune. This joyful spirit Luther tried to suggest in a short poem, called *The Lady Music*, which he wrote as a "Preface to All Our Good Hymn Books":

> What joy, what pleasure can compare,
> What merriment's as fine and rare
> As when we raise our voice to sing
> Or blow the flute or touch the string.
> No gloom or sorrow can abide
> Where folk sit singing side by side;
> Bad temper, envy disappear,
> Heartache and grief turn to good cheer,
> Sadness dissolves, despair gives way,
> Comfort and solace win the day.[44]

Christian hymns concentrated the believer's thoughts on the essential attitude of trust and offered him words and sounds with which to express the joy he felt in his heart. They helped disseminate the good word and disclosed its cheerful intent. This was their function in the Lutheran service as well as in Lutheran pedagogy. In their artless but poignant way they conveyed what must have been intended as the heart of the evangelical message.

One suspects that reformers relied on the sense of certainty imparted by these hymns to counteract the confusions and doubts left unresolved in people's minds by pulpit and catechism. On the level of explanation, on the other hand (always the preferred approach of preachers and catechists), the hymns' simple unequivocacy was more often than not contradicted. Nothing was asserted in the catechism that was not, in the explanation, blurred. Nothing was promised that was not somewhere taken back. Justification by faith alone—announced as a blissful release from the burden of works, a great heartease and liberator of the conscience—was at the same time presented as a most difficult and rare achievement. Reason will tell us, writes the Breslau theologian Ambrosius Moibanus in his catechism, that nothing is more easily done than believing in Christ. "Foolish reason asks 'who will fail to believe, seeing that it is much more easily accomplished than fasting?' " He comments: "Thus speaks the silly multitude, prompted by the devil. They do not know what they are saying, however, for there is no art, no labor, no effort more arduous than believing in Christ. Indeed, the true Christian faith is beyond all our natural powers and natural wisdom. The faith which only God can produce in the human heart is the most difficult work of all."[45] Encouraged to think that no more was required of him than trust and faith, the simple Christian was at the same time forever being thrown back upon his own strength and resources and cautioned that success in this most fateful of all his tasks was far from assured. Everything he did was idle; nothing he could do was enough. Protestant religious education pointed no way out of this quandary.[46]

2

If the qualities of inner piety were presented ambiguously to the young and simple, no such confusion was allowed to reign when it came to the principles governing worldly conduct. On the practice of "external piety," as it was called, Lutheran theologians, preachers, and pedagogues were clear, consistent, and all but unanimous. They accepted the institutions and conventions of the emerging bourgeois society sheltering their movement even while they deplored its defects and its inherent incompatibility with evangelical principles. Seeing in the established order the only alternative to social disintegration and moral chaos, they were determined to reinforce its structures and maintain its operations. Acting from this resolve, they set to work to persuade their followers to take their places in society and participate in its processes as a duty dictated by their Christian conscience.

Religious education provided the best means of shaping the public mind to meet this obligation, and Lutheran pedagogues turned this opportunity to excellent account. What they had to say on the duties of worldly piety was stated without the qualifications or equivocations clouding their doctrinal pronouncements. A convenient theological solution to nagging doubts about the congruity of Christian principles and the established order was provided by Ambrosius Moibanus. All human laws, and therefore all works of external piety, Moibanus wrote in his German catechism printed in Wittenberg in 1535, have their beginning in original sin. Observing Adam eat the forbidden fruit, God said to him, " 'This is the end of your piety. You will no longer be able to act piously now because you have ceased to be pious. From now on you will be a pretender.' " Moibanus was at pains to show that the need to simulate, the obligation to seem to be what one is not, is the source of all worldly piety. It is a spurious piety, of course, an act of hypocrisy before God (*heucheley fur Gott*), like its symbol, Adam's vain attempt to hide his nakedness. God is not deceived by such feints; all the same, he himself demands that men be dissemblers in the world:

> Because Adam acted against true piety, God made a hypocrite of him, a dissembler who can do no more than affect an outward show of piety. It is as if God had said to him . . . "From now on, live your external life in the semblance of honesty and sincerity. I know that in your heart

you cannot avoid sin. But at least keep from sinning with your hands and tongue. I know that you are a thief in your heart; but do not allow your fingers to steal. Your heart is full of foul desires, but refrain from committing adultery. Blaspheme and scold in your heart, but do not open your mouth to a curse. By restraining yourself in this way, you will be deemed a pious person by the world, although your counterfeit piety gains no favor in my sight."

"Out of this hypocrisy [*heucheley*]," Moibanus comments, "arise all our worldly laws, and all the rules of the outwardly honorable and disciplined life we must lead in the world. Princes and lords, kings, emperors, councillors, parents and masters originate in this hypocrisy, because their only function is to ensure that their subjects, like Adam, will always conceal and restrain the nakedness of their depraved natures under a cloak of good discipline. [Magistrates] don't ask of their subject: 'Is he a rogue under his coat? Is his heart full of evil?' They cannot change his heart or improve what is beneath his garment. They can only control what he does with his hands and feet. They can but command him to behave decently toward his neighbors and keep him from stealing and doing harm to his fellow creatures. And those who obey these commands are pious enough for this world and this life."[47]

Given the fundamentally un-Christian nature of human society, people can rest content in the performance of this surface piety. The deep-dyed sinfulness in their hearts does not prevent them from conforming their actions to the standards of external piety. Their will is not so corrupt that they cannot perform their outward duties. Though a mere cover for the low impulses teeming beneath the surface, this show of civility is not a lie in the sight of God. It cannot generate the inner piety whose possession is the sign of salvation, but as an act of obedience to God and to his surrogates on earth it is not devoid of merit. Its compensation in the final reckoning was an open question. But its immediate social utility was substantial, society's requirement of peace and order being fully met by an outward semblance of uprightness and probity.

The tinge of cynicism we are inclined to read into Moibanus's analysis should not obscure the fact that the justification he gives of good behavior as a conscious pretense, carried out in accordance with a divine command, succeeded in bridging the gap between theological principles and political needs. Not that Lutheran pedagogues accepted his explanation as the permanent condition of men in society. Far from it. The whole object of their pedagogy was to forge a motivational link between inner purposes and outward actions, to internalize the rules of Christian life as a set of guiding precepts originating in the intellect and the will. But they knew that this transformation of the nature of men would not come quickly, and until it could be brought about they acceded to the simulation of external piety as an interim solution.

How were people to be conformed to the rules of outward piety? The conventional wisdom suggested that this could be done only through "discipline"—*Zucht*—a systematic, habit-shaping regime, part upbringing, instruction, and character formation, part surveillance, control, and punishment, a procedure expected to mold and tone the personality until obedience to established rules became automatic.[48] Initiated in youngest infancy and kept up through adolescence and early adulthood, *Zucht* counteracted the youth's natural proclivities, eventually replacing them (or so it was hoped) with the traits of an evangelical personality. "We learn from the wisdom of Jesus Sirach," writes Huberinus, "how much perversion, corruption, and vice there is in children, and how easily and quickly they are spoiled, if we do not, by means of good discipline, retrieve them from their wickedness."[49] Left to their own devices, untamed and undisciplined, they bring ruin on themselves and everything around them.[50]

Such governing perceptions ensured that education in civility meant the imposition of a rigid behavioral discipline.[51] Much was made of the punitive association resounding in the word *Zucht* (*züchtigen*, to chastise). "Man has a free will to perform external works," asserted the *Saxon Instruction of the Visitors*, "as long as he is driven to them by law, discipline, and threats of punishment."[52] School ordinances brought this principle into the classroom, as for instance the Nordhausen *Schulordnung* of 1583:

> Preceptors shall maintain good discipline among their pupils in the following manner: First, they must imbue them with Christian ideas and duties pleasing to God. They must make them act according to these ideas, faithfully and conscientiously, and allow them to do nothing that has been forbidden. If one or more pupils should show the least sign of disobedience, or of sloth, boldness, discourtesy, or deceit, the preceptors shall at once give them vehement (*heftig*) warnings and a good fright by threatening them with punishments.[53]

Such documents illustrate the "oppressive sense of need for restraint"[54] with which all Reformation pedagogues approached their labors. "No child would fear God if he were not disciplined to it," declared the authors of the Württemberg *Schulordnung*,[55] and proceeded to spell out in a long list of articles what they meant by "discipline": punctilious regulations touching every moment of the young person's life, tireless surveillance, controls and constraints "to keep him from exercising his free will in any matter."[56] Luther praised monastic regulations as a model for the day-by-day organization of *Kinderzucht*. Every right and wrong action should be itemized, he said, nothing left to chance, whim, goodwill, or common sense. If and when these dos and don'ts should enter the conscience, the time might be right, Luther thought, "to stone Moses to death."[57] But this consummation had not come to pass in his day, and no indications suggested that it was around the corner. The heavy hand of discipline continued to lie on the young, conforming them to a pattern they could not have failed to find oppressive.

Civility, good manners, tidy dress, and neat personal habits were the outward signs of the disciplined youngster.[58] A modest demeanor in keeping with his age and station marked his carriage; humility and deference guided his deportment toward his fellowmen.[59] At a deeper level, his behavior exemplified his epoch's ingrained principles of sub- and coordination. He was a sturdy, responsible, but otherwise unremarkable member of his society, a docile subject, a good citizen. His foremost attachment, after his allegiance to God, was to his social and political order, his major task to uphold it. Melanchthon, who was, as has been seen, severely troubled by the social disintegration he observed in his time, gave pride of place to this obligation. In his lengthy analysis of the fourth commandment, traditionally the place for advice on the practical implications of citizenship, he noted that "we have two objects in mind as we learn to give honor to those to whom it is due under this commandment. One is that we must respect our parents, magistrates, and teachers in their persons; the other is that we must revere the political order itself [*ordnung der policey an ihr selbs*], for this order has been created by God to help us keep our burgher society [*diese bürgerliche gesellschaft*] safe, sound, and in good working condition."[60] Melanchthon invited his readers to share his pride in the social order—"what a fine and useful thing it is!" he exclaimed—and to join him in his sense of wonder at the divine wisdom shining through "this admirable association of people linked in their several groupings, namely wedlock, civic assembly, government, justice, law, and good discipline."[61] Melanchthon's was not the only catechism celebrating the delicate complexity of this social arrangement. Justus Menius, too, marveled at the harmonious intricacy of the structure. "Lords and subjects, householders and territorial rulers, housemates and tenants, parents, children, domestic servants, day laborers, hired hands, old people and young people, widows, orphans, the poor and the rich—all these estates have been placed by God in a proper disposition to each other, forming a constituted order in which we, as pious Christians, can serve him according to his word and will."[62]

But this ingenious system worked only if each member observed its rules and played his part. Catechisms gave particular emphasis to the second table of the Mosaic code, containing the laws of external piety, and especially to the first of these, the fundamental imperative of citizen and subject, the fourth commandment, with its extended application to all who governed, ruled, and taught. Willing and unstinting submission to legitimate power was the preeminent duty of citizenship.[63] In times of social turbulence—the decades following 1522–25 in the view taken by all reformers—only the quality of submissiveness seemed capable of shoring up the sagging supports of stability and propriety in human affairs.[64] Greater care was lavished on discussions of the fourth commandment than on any other article of the Decalogue. Protestants took overt pride in the emphatic support they gave to established authority. Christoph Vischer reminded rulers and magistrates that they "can never be grateful enough to our beloved gospel for having raised your estate from the mire into which the papacy and its henchmen had plunged it to the honor and dignity it now enjoys."[65] This restoration had occurred not only in laws and institutions; much more vitally, it had been accomplished in the minds of men. From childhood on citizens were now being prepared to esteem, revere, and if necessary forgive their elders and betters.[66] Christians honored *Obrigkeit* in their hearts while serving it with their heads and hands. Pleading with their sovereign to give support to a school in their town, municipal councillors in Braunschweig-Wolfenbüttel assured the duke that "obedience and willing submissiveness [*Gehorsam und wolgehaltene Unterthenigkeit*] to the state [*Obrigkeit*] will grow marvelously wherever such instruction is given."[67] Melanchthon insisted to his own pupils, and to the wider circle of the readers of his pedagogical books, that "obedience to the established powers [*Oberkeit*] is the noblest of the works of Christian love."[68] "Submit yourselves to these powers for conscience' sake, not merely because you are in fear of God's wrath," he wrote in his catechism, quoting the famous words from Rom. 13:5, which, he said, "forge the strongest chain holding the commonwealth together and giving society its cohesion,"[69] Citizenship is not merely a matter of doing the right thing in following the laws. It is the wish always to do it that counts. Motive and intention matter as much as actions. "You shall honor your father and your mother" imposes motivational obligations that cannot be satisfied by perfunctory deeds. "Take the little word 'you,' " wrote Christoph Vischer in explaining the fourth commandment, "it does not refer only to various limbs of your body, but involves your entire inner and outer person: feelings, desires, thoughts, words and works, your body and your soul, all your powers and capacities, your heart, eyes, ears, tongue and mouth, hands and feet,"[70] in other words, the whole individual, that which moves him as well as that which he moves. "How should you honor your father, mother, elders, teachers, and magistrates?" asks Johann Tettelbach in his version of Luther's catechism. "Giving them external honor is not enough," he answered. "Unless you also magnify them in your heart, unless you fear them and yield to them, you have not honored them enough. And all this must be done not so much for the benefit of their persons, as for the sake of their office and dignity, to which God has appointed them over us."[71] It is their high responsibility, and the qualities appertaining to it, not their human persons, says Konrad Dietrich, that makes magistrates worthy of being called (in the words of the eighty-second psalm) "gods" and "sons of the Most High."[72]

On the other hand, the fourth commandment could not be fulfilled with good motives alone. "More than a show of love is needed to give honor to your elders," said the catechist Johann Spangenberg, addressing an audience of children. "You also owe them external discipline [äusserliche Zucht]. Timidity and submissiveness must be exemplified in your actions."[73] Hard work and perseverance were indispensable complements to humility, for "we must not in our laziness be tempted to do less than God demands of our calling."[74] All catechisms for the young furnished lengthy lists of "good works to be done in obedience to this commandment."[75] Laudable aims did not count without exertion. The useful citizen, the loyal subject, excelled in both.

This was the secular face of religious education. Its principles and objectives were presented with a resoluteness noticeably at variance with the vacillation characterizing doctrinal instruction. Its demands and expectations were never less than perfectly clear. Indeed, "external piety" was the paramount lesson of Protestant pedagogy. To be a child in the hands of Lutheran educators was to learn to be a good subject. The child-subject analogy was made unmistakably explicit in catechetical literature. "Whom do we include under the name of 'children'?" asks Konrad Dietrich in explaining the fourth commandment. "We mean by children," he answered, "all those whom God has subjected [unterworffen] to the authority of others, to be instructed, governed, and protected: that is to say, natural and adoptive children, minors, parishioners [Pfarrkinder], pupils and apprentices, political subjects, domestic servants, and tenants."[76] Our fallen world, Dietrich continued, is apportioned between those appointed to wield power and those whose place it is to obey. Since in a Christian polity no one, regardless of rank or dignity, is without superiors, obedience is a virtue necessary to all.[77] Obedience, Dietrich declared, is the single most important lesson to be learned in childhood. In the same vein, Huberinus insisted that "God has divided mankind into parents and magistrates, who dispose and command, and children and subjects who submit."[78] It is your place to obey, a Strassburg catechist said to his young auditors. "From childhood on you must be habituated to be willing subjects [untertenig] and faithful followers [volgig]."[79]

Paul had the sagest piece of advice to give to the teeming crowd of subjects and followers, and his first Epistle to the Thessalonians was much quoted on this point: "Aspire to live quietly, mind your own affairs, and work with your hands" (1 Thess. 4:11).[80] When complied with in thought and in deed, this precept became a divine service that could not fail to be pleasing to God and therefore beneficial to men. Rejoicing in the Protestant restoration of the gospel to its place of honor, the catechist Christoph Vischer observed that "nowadays we discharge our duty to God by working as good Christians in our respective estates. We work," he continued, "in the state of matrimony as husbands and wives, as magistrates in our places of authority, and as willing subjects in our various humble stations. With hearts made pure by the evangelical faith, we can hope that our service will be pleasing to God."[81] Performed in this spirit, even the lowliest occupation was meritorious: "The artisan who toils until the sweat runs off his nose, the hired girl who spins, sews, cooks, mucks out the stable, wipes the baby's bottom, the councillor who brings malefactors to justice—each of these does a divine service more agreeable to God than all the tomfoolery of monks, priests, and nuns."[82] To accomplish faithfully what one has been called to do, to obey all rightful commands—these are the works of external piety. He who does them may justly say: "see, I am made by my efforts holier than the Carthusian who killed himself by fasting to death."[83] If, in addition to these labors, a man also "feels in his heart a sincere desire and a good will to give honest, useful service to human society [*menschlicher gesellschaft*], he has," says Melanchthon, become a truly disciplined Christian, for he has come to see "that the constitution of our secular government and the arrangement of our worldly society are God's own handiwork."[84]

Melanchthon's term—"*bürgerliche Gesellschaft*[85]—for this polity brings into focus the moral problem faced by Lutheran catechists who attempted to guide their flock in the practical world of courts of law, marketplaces, and council chambers. The Christian ethic compelled many to disapprove of the ways of the world. But none failed to uphold them and to urge their followers, for peace and order's sake, to do the same. The seventh commandment furnished the most convenient sounding board for rendering judgments, con and pro, on the burgher society and its ambiguous moral structure. Critiques were by and large conventional and jejune. Chasing wealth is a useless endeavor, for taxes, wars, misfortunes, and inflation will only take it all away again.[86] The rich, like the poor, leave the world as naked as they entered it.[87] To live for yourself, which is the way of the rich, is to lead an un-Christian life.[88] Fortunes cannot be gained without "deceit, cunning, trickery, and embezzlement."[89] Only he who is satisfied with what he has is truly rich.[90] And so on. An occasional stricture pricked with a sharper barb. Andreas Osiander used his famous Children's Sermons to pillory the merchants of Nuremberg (who were not accustomed to such interference in running their city) for taking excessive profits, weighing short, making false claims, selling high in advance of price drops, exploiting helpless pieceworkers, restraining trade through corners and monopolies. "What is this," Osiander asked, pointing his finger, "but concealed theft?"[91] In Nuremberg such denunciations struck too close to home, and Osiander found himself in difficulties over his bold words.[92] But his voice was the minority's; and even he did not take a big bite out of the hand that fed him. Most catechists and preachers supported the established economic order—not without uneasiness, but no less sturdily for all that. Sometimes their misgivings are revealed in glaring inconsistencies. Johann Böhm's *Book of Christian Counsel for Children*, published in Wittenberg in 1536, asks "Where does poverty come from?" Answer: "From laziness and sloth (Prov. 12 [24])." Very next question: "What sin is committed by him who insults a poor man?" Answer: "He despises God, who has created the pauper (Prov. 14[31])."[93] But such lapses are rare. Most catechisms praised hard work and condoned the pleasure taken in its fruits. "Can there be any doubt," asked Lucas Geierberg, "that God gave the seventh commandment to Moses as a confirmation and sanction of private property? If this had not been his intent, why would he have built a protective wall around each man's possessions by saying 'Thou shalt not steal'?"[94]

Geierberg had an easy target: Anabaptists and other "lazy fellows" who did not want to work, preferring instead, he charged, to usurp other people's hard-earned goods. Against this lot he made a convincing case, arguing on behalf of a society of fallen but enterprising men and women who, corrupted in their natures, produce and consume their goods inequitably, "one man often using up more than all the rest can create. If such a society is to survive," he concludes, commenting on the postlapsarian loss of mutual love and kindness in the world, "there cannot be community of goods among its members."[95] Luther, too, acknowledged the need to accumulate temporal goods, even to gather treasures in moderation (*messig schetze samlen*) while men struggled for a livelihood in this corrupt world. For how else, he asked, can a man find sustenance in this life?[96]

Luther's position rested on a distinction (made in the early 1530s, in his sermons on the sixth chapter of Matthew) between the true Christian, who lays up no treasures on earth, and the worldling, whose situation compels him to gain and keep worldly goods. The distinction was reiterated by many other catechists trying to gain a foothold on the slippery ground between the Christian ethic and the social logic of the seventh commandment.[97] Most writers gave the acquisitive and competitive society the same measure of interim approval as Luther:

"pious enough for this world and this life."[98] Huberinus, in his examination of the seventh commandment, asks: "Seeing that the children of God must bide their time here on earth for a while, may they in good conscience make their living by the customs of the world?" And he answers: "Indeed they may, and they can do so in good spirits and with the help of God,"[99] Making money, acquiring property, and enjoying good fortune did not violate the duties imposed by external piety. Huberinus calmed his readers' fears on that score: "May a Christian," he asks, "possess wealth and relish it? May he own a fortune and treat it as his own? Answer: all wealth is the gift of God. This being so, a Christian may in good conscience become a rich man. For both wealth and poverty are awarded by God (as we read in Proverbs 22 [2]: 'The rich and the poor meet together; the Lord is the maker of them all'). . . . From these words we may take it that money and wealth are not in themselves evil things and incompatible with godliness."[100]

To be sure, the rich man courts greater dangers than the pauper. Paul warns of this peril in 1 Tim. 6:9–10, speaking of the temptations and snares awaiting the lover of money. But, Huberinus contends, "Paul is here not referring to wealth itself, but rather to greed, which is a very different thing. It is greed the apostle has in mind when he calls the love of money the root of all evils. Wealth is indeed a wicked thing when it is joined to greed. But taken by itself, it is harmless." Is it possible, then, he goes on to ask, for a rich man to be justified? And if so, what force is there in Jesus' warning, in Matt. 19:24, that a camel will fit more easily though the eye of a needle than a rich man into the kingdom of heaven? A touchy question, this, but Huberinus is equal to it: "In saying this, Christ did not mean to repudiate the rich, or to close the gates of heaven to them. For he did not say that it is impossible for a rich man to enter the kingdom of heaven. He said only that 'it will be difficult' for him to get in. Why will it be difficult? Because the temptations and snares to which the rich are always exposed will get in their way. . . . But they should be of good cheer, for Christ says in the very same passage [26] that 'with God all things are possible.' And he said this to console the rich and give them hope."[101] True, he adds, few men of wealth are genuine Christians. On the other hand, where does one find genuine Christians in the world? "Wickedness is not confined to the rich," he argues. "We find wrongdoing in all estates nowadays, and real Christians are few and far between."[102] The wealthy are no worse in this respect than the poor or the middling sort, and no Christian should for this reason hesitate to engage in trade. He may buy and sell in the market, give and take credit, speculate, enter into partnerships. "People must feed and house themselves on this corrupt earth; let them do it, then, by the unsavory practices of the world."[103] This is not to say that the golden rule has no bearing on earthly piety. "It ought to be every merchant's scale and measure." Let him remember the pious Zacchaeus in Luke 19, who made full restoration for the wrong he committed. This, too, is a duty imposed by external piety.

One important question remains. "May a Christian," asks Huberinus, "take and give five per cent.?" His evasive answer is revealing: "This question relates entirely to public policy, which is, as you know, a matter for secular governments and courts to decide. In what ways, by what laws, under what circumstances men may carry on their business is determined by the imperial law and its courts and lawyers. Let these be the judges and decision-makers. They have their written laws to declare how a merchant or moneylender should manage his affairs."[104] The precepts of religion therefore seem to conform to prevailing circumstances. The necessary adjustments between the two called for seeing things in their proper relations. By keeping the appropriate distinctions in mind (external from internal piety; gospel from world; true Christian from secular man), a person could, while serving out his sentence on earth, discharge his duties to two implacable imperatives: the inexorable commands of God and the lesser, but more immediately pressing, needs of society.

It would be idle to point out the obvious: that the literature of domestic instruction reflected a status-conscious, not to say, class-bound, orientation whose definition of secular piety must have sat exceedingly well with the worldly-wise and upward-struggling householders for whom Huberinus, Vischer, Lauterbeck, Kauxdorf, Tettelbach, Spangenberg, and their colleagues wrote.[105] The relevance of their exhortations to small-town and village folk was another matter. Disquisitions on property rights conferred by the seventh commandment could not have struck much resonance among rural artisans, peasants, or hand-to-mouth wage earners in the poorer urban precincts. And yet it was on these people, and on their children, that Lutheran pedagogues looked as the chief beneficiaries of their program of indoctrination.

Equally evident is the contradiction between the image of the citizen described by Huberinus and the others, and the ideal type set by catechists as an example to their pupils. Clearly, the burgher ethos was at odds with the evangelical model. The former suited the movers and doers of politics, business, church, and the world of learning. The latter defined their followers, who were the subjects of Reformation pedagogy. The "true Christian," the hoped-for product of Lutheran indoctrination, lay low and kept his place. Dutiful and industrious, content with his assigned role, trusting, docile, diffident in the knowledge of his mental and moral inadequacy, hoping for a better life to come—but not on earth, where things were what they were and wrongs must be endured because fallen men deserved no better—the "true

Christian" gave no trouble and caused no alarm. No entrepreneur or initiator, he was the passive subject praised by magistrates and blessed by preachers: a quiet type becalmed by his sense of insufficiency, diligent but never self-reliant, deeply imbued with a sense of where he belonged in the patriarchal society he accepted for the peace of his mind and the salvation of his soul.

Lutheran pedagogues therefore addressed two distinct audiences. The one, well-placed and influential, could not have found the evangelical model a very useful key to contentment. The other, the vast majority, may well have perceived it as a heavy-handed attempt to thwart their rising expectations in the world. Both were entitled to wonder how the secular propositions of external piety could be made to accord with the unworldly principles of their Christian faith, and how the activist and passivist strains within the latter could be reconciled in the same life and the same religion. Here was a problem no one had faced, much less attempted to solve.

PART 3

CONSEQUENCES

CHAPTER 12

VISITATIONS
AND VISITATION RECORDS

I hope I may take the importance of the pedagogy of the Lutheran Reformation as having been demonstrated in the preceding chapters. But its place in the fortunes of that movement will become clear only when answers have been given to two questions not yet fully aired: Did the pedagogical venture accomplish its aims? If so, how lastingly? Enough hints have been dropped along the way to remove any suspense from these questions. The pedagogical experiment was not a success. So judged the reformers themselves in the 1550s, and so concluded their epigones at the end of the sixteenth century and the beginning of the next. The dimensions of their failure were, of course, a matter of discussion and soul-searching among them, and their voluminous writings enable us to participate in this debate. But an even richer source of information is available and encourages us to draw our own conclusions about the consequences of the reformers' educational labors. We can study the symptoms of their failure by examining the evidence they themselves collected as they tried, almost from the outset of their endeavor, to discover what was going wrong, and why. Attempting to explain the puzzling religious indifferences of the multitude, they gathered a vast body of data to document popular religious attitudes and behavior. This evidence, which is contained in the massive protocols of parish visitations conducted by territorial and municipal authorities throughout the sixteenth and seventeenth centuries, furnished theologians and churchmen with solid facts to guide their deliberations and policies. In our own time, these records have not begun to be put to good use. The social historian, the student of mentalities, of popular culture, rural customs, and folk beliefs will find them an almost inexhaustible mine of information. Most of what I shall have to say about the results of the Lutheran pedagogical undertaking rests on my reading of these documents.[1]

Lutherans took a justified pride in having revived the ancient apostolic custom of "visiting"—that is to say, going to see, to inspect, investigate, correct, and, if necessary, to punish (the word *visitieren* suggests all these meanings)[2]—congregations, parish folk, church and lay officials in their respective territories. Luther makes much of this restoration in his preface to the *Instruction of the Visitors to the Pastors in the Electorate of Saxony* of 1528 (a pace-setting document, as has been seen). The visitation about to be launched in the duchy, he argues, will mend a broken historical continuity. He refers to Peter and Paul, Samuel and Elijah, and to the bishops and archbishops of the early church as his predecessors in the task of roving about the land (like Christ himself, he says, "who claimed no single spot on earth as his own where he would rest his head") in order to "call on parish folk, tend to their needs, and find out from them how they live and what they are being taught."[3] Four years earlier he had not been so certain of the merit of these procedures. In 1524, when urged to lend his support to a planned visitation, he could not overcome his deep-seated distaste for bureaucratic measures imposed uniformly from above. But his fellow reformers were less hesitant than he. Quicker to see the advantages to be gained from close collaboration with political authorities, they did not shrink from partnership with a secular bureaucracy, or from reestablishing a centralized and authoritarian ecclesiastical organization. Visitations were effective ground-clearing operations toward these goals. "A noble effort," they were called by Luther's colleague Nikolaus Hausmann, the reformer of the city of Zwickau, writing to Elector Johann in 1515: "Visiting means correcting abuses and defects, admonishing people to live upstanding lives, eradicating treacherous doctrines, preaching the pure word of God, consoling faltering spirits, strengthening timid consciences, opposing local tyrants, and unmasking false prophets."[4] Hausmann went on to advise his duke that Luther himself was the best man to plan such an undertaking.[5]

Hausmann must have known that this suggestion went against the reformer's grain, but even Luther was being forced to admit that the glaring inadequacies and appalling conditions being discovered in most of the duchy's parishes admitted of no alternative.[6] Late in October 1525, he wrote to the duke in a new vein. Churches everywhere are in a state of dereliction, he declared. No one pays for their upkeep or fulfills his obligations, "and the common man shows so little respect to his preacher and pastor that, unless your Electoral Grace will agree to undertake a great housecleaning, . . . God's word and divine service will soon have vanished from the earth." To forestall this unthinkable consummation, Luther implored his prince to consider himself "God's faithful instrument" in employing the power of the state to bring the Saxon church to order. Nor must he stop there. Temporal institutions were also crying out to be reformed, Luther added, "for we hear bitter complaints everywhere about corrupt magistrates in towns and countryside." He predicted great improvements "where such visitations and correctives are undertaken."[7] He also proposed a workable scheme for accomplishing the latter. Let the electoral domains be divided into four or five districts and appoint two nobles or other secular officers to visit every parish, gather information there, and, where necessary, order immediate remedies.[8] Luther still averted his eyes from the ultimate destination toward which he was now directing his steps. He knew that Hausmann had already cautioned the elector against granting to congregations the right "in these perilous times" to choose their own pastors.[9] Indeed, he must have seen the point of this warning. But he was still opposed to peremptory laws as a means of obtaining compliance in religious matters. In his preface to the 1528 *Instruction of the Visitors* he vigorously denied any intention of imposing on unwilling parishioners the directives contained in that document. We are not issuing these instructions "as strict rules," he asserted, "because we do not want to start over again with papal decretals and such."[10] Luther was still not prepared to abandon his cherished principle of voluntarism. But events had already made an anachronism of this reluctance.

The territorywide visitation of 1528–29 (a few local ones had preceded it by two or three years) set the model for all later visitations in Germany. Its purpose was, first, to investigate deficiencies, second, to discover by examination of the population and its ecclesiastical and lay leaders how firmly the officially established doctrine was taking root.[11] Melanchthon's *Instruction* provided for those ministers still unsure of it a basic guide to the evangelical faith. We have already noted the shocked reaction of Luther and his colleagues to the conditions brought to light in the course of this visitation. Shaken by the sheer enormousness of the job of reeducation they were taking on, the reformers came to realize, still with regrets but no longer with any doubts, that they would be able to accomplish their objectives only by employing the legal authority and power of compulsion wielded by the state. They were facing a turning point in the course of events: to a significant extent the survival of the Reformation was becoming an administrative problem and a bureaucratic responsibility. This shift could not fail to deflect the movement's original purposes.[12] It was also bound to feed the governmental emphasis on record-keeping and documentation that is the major concern of this chapter.[13]

From the beginning,[14] Lutheran officials pursued two aims in planning and executing their visitations. One was to take stock of the physical and human assets of the church in their lands. The other, which ultimately became the overriding goal, was to commence, and then promote and protect, the improvement of religion and morality in the populace. These two aims were closely linked in both principle and practice. Only a revitalized church organization could preserve the doctrine and act as censor over people's lives. At the same time, only a demonstrable improvement in the moral disposition of society would justify the creation of a new ecclesiastical officialdom with its rigid procedures, shielded orthodoxy, and entrenched authority. The early modern bureaucratic state's investigatory techniques and methods of documentation served these objectives admirably.

Visitations were always formal undertakings. They began with an official promulgation, printed copies of which were dispatched to every local authority, announcing the impending visitation and stating its purpose. A lengthy *Instruction to the Visitors* (*Formula visitationis, Instructio summaria pro visitatoribus,* or *Modus visitandi ecclesias, earum res, et personas*) outlined the procedure to be followed. Not every visitation was intended as a thoroughgoing inspection. Authorities distinguished between occasional and geographically limited visitations (*simplex visitatio, perfunctoria visitatiuncula*)[15] and broadscale general visitations conducted, normally once a year, throughout the land. The latter were most carefully prepared. In Saxony in 1528, the duke's instruction requested clerical and secular officials to assemble in a *Malstatt,* a central place in each district, to be interrogated (the Latin term for the list of questions put to each person was *interrogatoria*) on a large number of points. Each official had to submit a tabulation of his parish revenues and their sources, also an inventory of furniture, vessels, sacred objects and relics, books, and so on. All preachers were tested on competence and orthodoxy. They had also to give a good account of their private lives. Other questions touched on education: Is there a school in each town? In each large village? Does the schoolmaster have an adequate income? (The evidence collected on these subjects has already been discussed.) Finally, every parishioner was to give the visitor his impression of the faults, defects, and failings (*Fel, Mengel, Gebrechen*) in his parish:

> Wherever a visitation takes place in our towns and villages, respondents shall be required under threat of severe punishment to report and enumerate to the visitors whether there are to be found among them any blasphemers, adulterers, fornicators, gamblers, drunkards, idlers or loafers, disobedient sons and daughters, and others of the same sort, leading a wicked life and exhibiting the outward signs of an evil nature. Also any people suspected of Anabaptism or of abusing the holy sacrament by practicing Zwinglianism. Also any who mutter against the govern-

ment and oppose it as though it were not a power ordained by God. All such are to be reported by name, as the Electoral Instruction prescribes.[16]

Such stock-taking remained throughout the century one of the chief objectives of territorial visitations.[17] In addition, a reasonably accurate census of the number of communicants in each parish was of the greatest importance, for a pastor's and schoolmaster's living (which it was the purpose of visitations to investigate and, if possible, improve) depended, for reasons that have been examined,[18] on contributions made more or less voluntarily by their parishioners.[19] The bewildering complexity of late medieval church organization and financing made this inventory a laborious and never-ending chore.

The modern reader of these records is at once struck by the extraordinary seriousness of all officials concerned with planning and executing visitations. Everyone agreed on the overriding goal: "to make good regulations and establish external discipline, but first and foremost to implant God's saving word," as the Württemberg Visitation Proclamation stated it in 1557.[20] "As soon as [the visitors] arrive in a place, having beforehand summoned the people to meet them in the church, they shall . . . make a formal address to the parishioners, urging them, if they know of any fault or defect in the parish, to come forward privately and make it known to the visitors." Great care was taken to create a relaxed atmosphere to encourage this exchange of information: "Let [the visitors] take particular caution lest they or their assistants say or do anything that might cause anyone distress. Those who are to be examined, be they of the spiritual or the secular order, should open their hearts and reveal their thoughts, but they will never do this if offense is given. Visitors must therefore display at all times a gentle disposition, so that every person will tell them freely, fearlessly, and fully what he believes and how he lives."[21] Not trusting a visitor's ability to establish such friendly relations on his own, the instructions usually wrote out the text of the opening address he was to make. The visitation order of 1566 for the principality of Neuburg, for example, declared that:

after the sermon, one of the visitors is to speak to the assembled populace as follows: "Our serene and gracious prince and lord Wolfgang, Count Palatine, duke of Bavaria [etc., etc.] has, in Christian love and obedience to God's word, ordered a visitation or Christian inspection to be made and has instructed us, who have come to your place of habitation, to carry it out. It is his Serene Grace's most earnest desire that we examine not only pastors and other clergy on their teachings, daily lives, and duties, but also his loyal subjects, in order to discover what they are able to recall of their pastors' sermons and whether they have become better Christians by what they have learned. Mindful of our duty to our prince, we shall fulfill his wishes in this place, as we have already done in several other places, and we will begin now by interrogating [*verhören*] first our dear young people; and then it will be the turn of their elders. And we ask you all to remain present until we have concluded the interrogation, for we shall have more to say to you then on behalf of our prince and lord."[22]

To some extent this amiable approach seems to have worked, although it is to be doubted that the visiting party's carefully cultivated air of *bonhomie* was able to break through the social and psychological barrier separating common folk from the officialdom that harassed and browbeat them in their daily lives. Still, the information gathered in this way is remarkably rich. The protocols of Protestant (and also of Catholic) visitations are among those rarest of documents in which we can hear the authentic voices of plain people. Authorities knew, of course, that they could not take all that was said to them at face value. They developed ways of cross-checking, and visitors were expected to employ these. Everyone was encouraged to tell on everybody else. In Saxony, for instance, each cleric was asked, "can you report anything suspicious about the beliefs and teachings of any of your colleagues?"[23] Visitors were always alert to possible collusion among clergy and magistrates.[24] Their deep-seated distrust of human nature persuaded them that parishioners must be pressed for observations critical of their spiritual and lay leaders. In gathering this information visitors made few attempts to distinguish fact from rumor. Whatever was said in the course of the interviews was taken down, leaving it to higher administrative echelons to discriminate between accurate observation and idle gossip.

Let us take an example from a set of questions for parishioners in the principality of Coburg, given in an official instruction of Duke Johann Casimir.[25] The questioning went as follows: Does your pastor seem orthodox in his teaching? Does he preach at excessive length? Are his sermons moderate in tone or does he sound polemical and quarrelsome? Does he appear punctually at catechism practice? Is he an effective teacher? Does he visit the sick? Does he perform the marriage ceremony with dignity and grace? Is his private life, and are the lives of his wife and children, in keeping with Christian teachings? Does he spend his evenings at home or does he sit about in taverns? Is he seen at private carousals? Has he been overheard to blaspheme? Does he keep company with persons suspected of fornication or adultery? Do he and his wife live in domestic harmony? Are his children being raised in a Christian manner? Does he earn additional income from trade or by working as scribe or "adviser" to the secular government?

Similar questions were asked concerning the schoolmaster and the bailiff. In evaluating the answers (which are often explicit enough to satisfy our liveliest curiosity about popular life in villages and small towns), officials clearly allowed their judgment to be influenced by quantity. A large amount of smoke suggested the presence of fires, and it was the function of visitors to find the sparks before they blazed into conflagrations. When the gymnasium in Hornbach, in the duchy of Zweibrücken, was visited in 1575, its distinguished rector and professors submitted to detailed questioning concerning both their academic duties and private lives. Not content with this direct evidence, the visitors turned to other school personnel, including the custodians, in order to verify the responses given by the faculty.[26] It does not seem to have disturbed governments that their open invitations to tattle were likely to undermine respect for the very dignitaries whose authority they wished to strengthen. They trusted no one, hence the prodding and pumping of everyone with something to divulge.

General reform was clearly the ultimate purpose of visitations. As an immediate step to this long-term end, visiting commissions functioned as tribunals of censors and judges over the rogue's gallery of alleged drunkards, loafers, fornicators, gamblers, shrewish wives, cantankerous husbands, insubordinate children, spendthrifts and poor providers, cunning women and makers of spells and potions named by informants. Each case was taken up on its own, with the accused person arraigned before the visitors. Interrogation, replies made, and the disposition of the case were noted in the protocol, usually under a heading such as "Names of those who live openly against the Ten Commandments."[27] No misdemeanor was too petty or private for the visitors to give it their full attention: "Veit Grauer in Hilpersdorf has been ill four weeks. His wife was cited before the visitor and asked why her husband had no grain in reserve and why he has been so imprudent a provider that she and her children are now obliged to go begging in the streets. The woman was in great despair as this question was put to her."[28]

Although admitting no distinctions between big things and little, visitors could hardly avoid making some obvious discriminations between symptoms and underlying causes. If people led unchristian lives, the fault must lie in their ignorance or inadequate knowledge of the faith. Since religious understanding was taken as the prerequisite of moral regeneration, visitations were designed to test people's comprehension of the rudiments of their creed as these had been taught them in the catechism. Governments unhesitatingly assumed responsibility for this task. They sought the aid of their consistories but placed the latter in a clearly subordinate role. Johann Georg, elector of Brandenburg, quoted a familiar proverb to justify his control over visitations in his territory. "The homesteader's eyes and footsteps enrich the soil of his land," he wrote. "For this reason," he continued, in a proclamation announcing the visitation of 1578, "faithful inspectors and supervisors must visit parishes from time to time and make inquiries there concerning the pastor's teachings and way of life, the people's understanding [of their religion] and moral improvement, public vices and nuisances, contempt for Christian doctrines and sacraments . . . and the facilities and revenues of churches, schools, and hospitals.''[29]

Testing "the people's understanding" was a relatively simple matter of asking them questions based on the catechism. Every visitation instruction gave a list of such questions as part of the printed questionnaire, or *Fragstück*, the numbered points of interrogation, in some instances seventy or eighty of them, drawn up to guide the visitors in testing each respondent. Usually visitors were told exactly whom to put to the test: local officials (pastors, sextons, schoolmasters, mayors, and councillors) and a sampling of private citizens, including men and women in several age groups, adolescents and children, male and female servants, town dwellers and country people.[30] When schools were visited, a number of children were called to the front of the room and quizzed on the catechism and related subjects.[31] It is not possible to say how representative the choice of respondents really was. We can be sure, however, that visitors, who were for the most part experienced investigators, were not likely to be hoodwinked by a pastor's putting his most attentive auditors and best pupils forward while keeping the dunces in the back row.

Armed with its questionnaire, the visiting party—often a sizable group of a dozen men or so, sometimes led by the district superintendent, nearly always including an experienced pastor, and aided by a scribe[32]—appeared at the preannounced place to which the visitation mandate had called local citizens. In the country, the site was usually the *Pfarrdorf*, the larger village where the parish church stood, and to which the inhabitants of outlying villages were summoned.[33] In a town, the visitation took place in the parish church, or in the town hall, or the market square, always depending on the size and the ecclesiastical organization of the place. After opening formalities, respondents were examined one by one, beginning with the pastor. Their replies were written on makeshift pads, formed by folding two or three folio sheets along their long sides, thus making little booklets, called *Kladden* (from *kladderen*, to scrawl, jot down), that contained the raw material later to be transcribed into protocols. Respondents' replies were numbered to correspond to the questions in the *Fragstück*. The scribe therefore needed to write only "*ad* 1," followed by the answer given, "*ad* 2," again the answer, and so on, which saved a great deal of time and—it is important to point out here—makes it possible for the modern researcher who knows what he is looking for to scan bulky records rapidly without fear of missing anything. Few of the original

Kladden survive. They seem to have been discarded after being transcribed.

Moving from place to place within its assigned precinct, the visitation team compiled a large stock of notes and documents containing the data obtained in questioning local officials and parishioners. Their tour completed, they retired to make clean copies. First they wrote a draft, taken from the *Kladden,* of the information collected in the parishes of a given district. This draft—already a bulky volume—was then revised, and a prefatory synopsis (entitled *Generalia*) added, listing the types of defects and faults (*Mengel und Gebrechen*) found in all or most of the parishes.[34] The resulting document was, or purported to be, a word-for-word record of the information gathered during the visitation of a particular district. This was then turned into a clean copy, of which the exemplar went to the secretariat of the territorial prince or municipal council. Confirmed by the seals of this office, it became the official protocol of the visitation. A copy of this document was forwarded to the consistory, or whatever the central agency of the territorial church organization was called. "Protocol" therefore refers to the complete, ostensibly verbatim, record of the visitation in a given administrative district, prefaced by a resume of general conditons. Large numbers of these protocols have come down to us. Bound in huge folio volumes, they stand rank upon rank on the shelves of state, ecclesiastical, and local archives.

But protocols were not the end products of visitations. Their inordinate length and repetitiveness made them cumbersome—invaluable sources of information, to be sure, but very slow reading for busy administrators. It became customary, therefore, to excerpt "relations" (*Relationen*) from them, abridgments faithful in substance and balance to the originals, and much more useful to hard-pressed policymakers. "So far as our visitation records are concerned," Count Philip Ludwig of Neuburg informed his cousin Friedrich of Zweibrücken, with whom he shared the administration of some of his lands, "and to avoid any discrepancy between our methods of keeping them, let us agree that protocols and relations are identical in purpose but differ in that in making the relation it shall not be considered necessary to transcribe word for word the entire protocol of the visitation."[35] Special copies of such relations were made for city and town councils,[36] for district administrators, and for lower-level bureaucrats. A great many of them remain in the archives.

Political and ecclesiastical authorities took the information thus conveyed to them with the utmost seriousness. Thanks to their meticulous secretarial practices, we can still follow in detail the manner in which visitation data were read, pondered, judged, and acted upon. Clean copies of protocols and relations redacted for consistories and government offices used only the right-hand side of each folio page. Its left side remained blank (a custom, incidentally, taken over from chancellery procedures for drafting official letters, where the left half of each page remained white for later additions and corrections) so that observations and directives made during discussion could be jotted down in the appropriate places. The documents therefore allow us to observe at close range the scrutiny given to visitation results and to follow the attempts of church and secular authorities to redress the largely unsatisfactory conditions brought to light.

In examining these volumes, one discovers again how eagerly rulers and their agents stretched their administrative arms to touch personal and public, trivial and weighty matters. Instructions to superintendents, pastors, mayors, and bailiffs[37] reached beyond incompetence of pastors and schoolmasters, beyond absenteeism from communion, sermon, and catechism, beyond malfeasance in public office, to individual instances of petty indebtedness, drinking and gambling, brawling, disobedient children, quarreling couples, Sabbath violation, blaspheming, talebearing, frivolity, and a host of other private actions considered inimical to the right order and moral health of the Christian *res publica*. Authorities paid special heed to "faults and defects" that were "universal, touching nearly all the churches [*general und fast alle kirchen betreffend*]" in their lands.[38] They also concentrated (always with a sad reflection on the thankless burden of governing so imperfect a race of people) on those failings that seemed to remain distressingly constant, being revealed in visitation after visitation. But no dereliction was too singular, its perpetrator too obscure, or its location too isolated, for the authorities to take an absorbed interest. The drive and persistence with which they pursued it, for years if necessary, seem obsessive to us until we pause to reflect that sixteenth-century administrators judged the lives of men and women by a small store of moral absolutes that infused even the most trivial act with universal significance and made it of one piece with an unfragmentable set of precepts on which depended the ordered existence of mankind in temporal society.

2

Visitations, then, served the state as effective tools for enlarging, solidifying, and perpetuating its dominion. From the administrative point of view they were a bureaucrat's dream. Control was centralized, lines of authority and jurisdiction clearly designated. A network of officials fanned out over the country, reaching every village and hamlet. Everything was put in writing and filed away—not the substantive material only, but also accounts of every penny spent on traveling, vehicle repair, lodging and boarding, candles, writing paper, and so on.[39] The interrogatory method and verbatim protocol that constitute the heart of the visitation procedure responded easily to short-term administrative needs as well as the requirements of long-range planning. Protocols were sufficiently alike from year to year to allow meaningful comparisons. They brought church and state into intimate association while emphatically reinforcing the supremacy of the latter.[40] In all these ways the visitation was a true expression of the early modern bureaucratic state.

It will be helpful to have before our eyes an example of a well-planned territorial visitation. My choice is the general (i.e., territory-wide) visitation conducted in the Brunswick principality of Kalenberg-Göttingen.[41] Its ruler, Duke Julius, a resolute Lutheran who had governed the principality of Brunswick-Wolfenbüttel since 1568 and inherited neighboring Kalenberg-Göttingen in 1585, launched in 1588 a vigorous fact-finding visitation to prepare the way for the long-overdue correction of notoriously slack religious conditions in his new land. Julius was an experienced organizer of visitations, having employed them effectively in 1568 to establish a permanent base for Protestantism in his Wolfenbüttel lands, which had been hurled by dynastic, political, and military tempests from Catholicism to Lutheranism and back again. Facing a distressing situation in his newly acquired principality in the late 1580s, he knew exactly what to do.[42]

The visitation order[43] dated over Julius's name and seal on 21 February 1588 first named as members of the deputation, commissioned to carry out the inspection, three abbots (their names were listed first, in keeping with the ancient ranking order), three members of the territorial nobility, two personal emissaries of the duke (a councillor and a secretary), two theologians, and one *protocollista*. This team was in its movements and actions strictly bound by the terms of the instruction. They were required to stay together as a group. They must interrogate the ecclesiastical and secular worthies of each administrative district at a specified time and place. Every pastor, chaplain, schoolmaster, and church deacon had to be present; illness excused him only upon special dispensation. Clergy and school personnel had to show documents validating their ordination and appointment. They must also produce for inspection the Bibles, catechisms, and other texts from which they preached and lectured. In the smaller towns all members of the council were to attend. Villages had to send their elders and five or six other residents. As for the landed nobility, a single representative could stand in for the rest of his estate, but he, like the townsmen and villagers, must remain present throughout the whole procedure.

The visitors' opening address was epitomized for them in the instruction. They were to say that legitimate governments had been commanded by God not merely to guard the social order ("according to the second table of the law") but also, in keeping with the first table, to see to it that God's saving word was being preached free of error, and uncontaminated by false teachings. In order to discover how well this obligation was being carried out, and with what results among the flock, everyone should feel free to give open and full replies to the questions about to be put to them, reporting to the visitors without fear or timidity all the shortcomings, faults, and abuses they had observed in their communities.

Thus prepared, respondents were called up one by one and put through the interrogation. Each cleric had to answer to a thirty-six-point *Fragstück* beginning with vital data—name, birth, education and ordination, appointment to present post—followed by questions on the administrative and financial conditions of his place, his performance as preacher, catechist, and minister, his colleagues in church and school, and his relations with his parishioners, their conduct in church and daily life, and to what extent this had begun to improve in response to his preaching. Visitors were empowered to order corrections of minor defects brought out in the questioning, but major actions, such as the replacement of a weak incumbent, were explicitly reserved to the prince. "Such matters are to be forthwith reported to us for our disposition," declared the duke's instruction.[44] Visitors were cautioned to preserve a critical frame of mind. "Make a habit of asking other pastors, officials, and a number of laymen whether [the pastor being questioned] is a man of pure doctrine and upstanding life and has succeeded in drawing people to his church or, whether, by his demeanor, he has turned them away."[45] Cross-checking was made obligatory. "Ask [each sexton] how the pastor, chaplain, and schoolmaster in his parish conducts himself in his office, doctrine, and private life. Are they quarrelsome? Addicted to wine? Beer guzzlers? Gamblers? Are they vain or arrogant in their behavior? Do they keep their wives and children on a tight rein? And these same questions are to be put also to village elders and district headmen."[46]

Next, each person present was examined on his religious comprehension, the clergy first, followed by the laity. Visitors were directed to keep their questions to a minimum but to choose them from each section of the catechism. All replies were written down by the *proto-collista*. Visitors then inquired about ceremonies and ordered changes to be made if these departed from the duchy's ecclesiastical constitution. This concluded the investigatory part of the visitation, leaving only the final admonition, the text of which was also given in the instruction. Look after your sheep, the clergy were told. Keep your eyes open and make a record [*nachzudenken und ufzuzeichnen*] of every individual in your community who seems lacking in respect for God's word, whose life is a public nuisance, or who fails to respond to your advice or warnings. To the laity the parting message was simple: go to church, study the catechism, obey and honor your ministers.

Everything said to this point in the instruction related to visitations in villages and small towns. Tone and emphasis change abruptly as the document turns next to the duchy's four major cities, Göttingen, Hannover, Nordheim, and Hameln. With respect to these, visitors were placed in an altogether different position. Far from approaching urban councils as plenipotentiaries wielding peremptory authority, they appeared as petitioners, "graciously beseeching" municipal leaders to designate an appropriate place and to assemble there for the purpose of a "Christian colloquy." A short address at the opening of this meeting outlined purpose and scope of the questioning, which, "if the council be willing to signify its assent," then proceeded as in district towns and country villages. But if a city government showed itself opposed to the course outlined by the visitors, the latter were first to repeat their request "briefly and in soft words"; then, should this also fail, to refrain from all further argument and make a full written report to the duke, who reserved to himself the decision on what to do next. In expecting such opposition from city fathers and urban clergy, Duke Julius could draw on ample experience. Municipal councils and pastors harbored deep suspicions of the motives of territorial visitors and were in a much better position than townlet and village elders to offer stubborn resistance to interference from above. The circumspect and reassuring approach taken toward them by Duke Julius was typical, as will be seen.

Turning the pages of the protocols from Kalenberg-Göttingen and pondering the answers given by the laity to questions on the catechism, one immediately recognizes the importance of visitations in the government's persistent efforts to implant the Lutheran religion in the minds of the populace. The most cursory questioning was sufficient to reveal the insubstantiality of people's grasp of even the main points of the evangelical doctrine. Their susceptibility to sectarian appeals must have frightened political and ecclesiastical leaders. At the same time, the latter must have seen this vulnerability as an opportunity not to be missed, for people's minds lay wide open to indoctrination, which could be supplied by effective preaching, catechism instruction, and schooling. Later visitations tested the impact of these first steps. They also compiled, year after year, a mass of concrete facts and figures from which, in their own time as well as ours, the religious attitudes and behavior of ordinary people may be gauged.

3

But how persuasive are these documents? Are they reliable indicators of the religious intelligence of ordinary folk? What conclusions do they allow us to draw about popular attitudes toward faith, clergy, church, doctrine, divine service, the gospel, and the Christian life? How solid a foundation do they make for our attempts to appraise the long-range response to Lutheranism at the grass roots and to measure the success, or the failure, of the pedagogical endeavor of the Reformation?

Having in the preceding pages acclaimed the accessibility and utility of visitation records, I must now underline the difficulties inherent in my acceptance of them as critical sources. These difficulties may, for the sake of discussion, be divided into six categories, although in practice they are compounded in every instance, always resolving themselves into the single question: How accurate a description do the documents give of actual religious and moral conditions? All problems relate to the manner in which evidence was collected and transcribed, to the real intentions of visitors and the seriousness of their commitment to the investigative purpose, and to the proportions of frankness to concealment, trust to fear, openness to withholding on the part of local folk responding to the visitors' probing, prying, nagging, and quizzing.

To begin with the question of data gathering and recording:[47] it hardly needs to be said that investigating techniques differed from place to place and from time to time. Some visitations turned up information on the basis of what we may call a "soft" questionnaire, whose interrogatory drive lacked clear focus and whose questions tended to be broad, leaving to respondents themselves the initiative for giving concrete answers. Such flexibility would naturally fail to turn up the sort of explicit data about religious knowledge and behavior extracted by probing from "hard" questionnaires whose tenacious, often ruthless mode of interrogation concentrated upon clearly defined points and obtained concrete information: names named, charges or suspicions specified, instances related. Both methods of questioning were in use, at different times, in all territories and cities. This creates problems for one who attempts to compare evidence and identify trends. But as one studies the documents in sequence, one soon recognizes that the more exhaustive and relentless the interrogation, the more disheartening the information brought to light. Pointed questions usually elicited revealing replies, and these nearly always described or represented an unsatisfactory state of affairs. The bland generalities and vague rejoinders that there is "nothing of special importance to report" (*weiss nichts besonders anzuzeigen*) of "soft" interrogations should not, therefore, be taken to cancel or dilute the largely dismal evidence collected by tougher questionnaires.

A related difficulty arises from the practice—already mentioned— of preparing from the full text of a visitation a number of extracts or digests for the special purposes of state and church offices concerned with some, but not all, the information contained in the protocols. Owing to the large number of these fragments, and to their dispersal among scattered archives, it is something of a burden to reassemble the total documentation of a given visitation.[48] For almost every visitation conducted in the sixteenth century we have separate excerpts relating to schools, preaching, the incursion of "heresies," church attendance and catechism study, and so on. While they make a confusing patchwork, they also offer compensation. A few archives, notably the Saxon state archives in Dresden and Weimar, have acquired in the course of time the greater part of the documentary record of visitations in their territories.[49] These holdings not only give us the complete texts, but also enable us to draw interesting inferences from the ways excerpts and digests vary from the full protocols. What the ruling prince was told does not always tally with what the consistory needed or wished to know. Prefatory summaries sometimes make the situation out to be less unpleasant than the protocols tell us it really was. At other times they convey the full brunt of the malignity. Occasionally they seem to make it worse. In using the records, therefore, historians must acknowledge the likelihood that officials may on occasion have altered data in accordance with what they wished their superiors to know, or with what they thought the latter might prefer to hear. An argument can be made for each of these temptations. My judgment is that attempts by visitors to aggravate or gloss over the largely disagreeable information they elicited cancel each other out and that their materials, taken as a whole, convey an accurate picture of conditions as they really were.

The actual performance of visitors is another factor calling us to caution. The documents make it clear that not every visitor obeyed his orders to adhere in every particular to the schema laid down in his instruction. Most were, in fact, punctilious in carrying out their duties. But exceptions were not uncommon. A few departed from the questionnaire, pursuing an independent line of investigation, omitting whole blocks of queries, or interpolating comments of their own. Some protocol keepers took answers down verbatim, as required; others merely summarized them, or gave brief paraphrases, and we are left to wonder whether these contain the gist of what had been said, and how accurately. These variations from the rigid norm present serious problems in interpreting the evidence of a particular visitation. But over the long run, and with respect to the situation in the empire as a whole, they are not significant. By and large (and this generalization must be understood to encompass a huge body of sources) visitors and their staffs were conscientious men. They followed their instructions, kept to the printed questionnaire, put every query to every respondent, and recorded each answer. They invented shortcuts to help them over the tedium of asking the same questions day after day: long lists of *dittos* to indicate identical answers, formulas to stand for replies that differed only insignificantly from each other, *nihils* where nothing of interest had been discovered. But despite such lapses in precision, the records contain a rich store of concrete detail.

So much for the documents themselves. There are other caveats to be observed. One would be less than prudent if one failed to speculate about the intentions visitors brought to their task. Was it not their job to find fault? And, having found it, did they not then exaggerate its gravity in order to drive their governments to prompt and decisive remedial measures? This point has been made in the scholarly literature, usually to mitigate somewhat the monotonously gloomy picture conveyed by the records.[50] One scholar has suggested that taking the protocols at face value would be like drawing a portrait of our own society entirely from the police blotter.[51] I do not find this a persuasive comparison. First of all, it is wrong to assert that visitors, and the governments and consistories that sent them, approached their task with a mind set solely on finding bad news. Of course they wished to discover what was wrong, but they were equally eager to learn that things were improving: Indeed, one can often see them trying to convince themselves that the religious and moral tone of society was rising, that the gospel was at long last taking root, and that the preaching and study of it were beginning to shape the outward lives of men and women. Both the wording and the tone of questions on the catechism suggest that people were being encouraged to do their best. Visitors generally tried to help a confused respondent over a baffling question. Often they showed themselves highly gratified by a mere recital of the Decalogue or the Apostles' Creed. Their questioning was thorough, but they were prepared, particularly in the later decades of the century, to be satisfied with very little.

Second, visitors never ceased to show dismay at popular religious indifference and to voice anger at the depressing picture of public immorality. They never seemed prepared for the worst. Each new sign of ignorance wrung from them a fresh expression of shock. Far from displaying contempt or cynicism toward their flocks, they always appeared anxious to emphasize the positive. This eagerness for pleasant things to report is implicit in the formulas they employed to record information supplied by pastors, officials, and lay people. The standard phrases go: "he has nothing to report, except that . . . [*Er wüsste nichts anzu-*

zeigen, on allein das . . .]," or: "no complaint was made here, except that the pastor complained . . . [*Es kam allhie keine Klage für, allein der Pfarrer beklagte sich . . .*], followed by the usual litany of faults, defects, and delinquencies—wordings that suggest a wish to stress the better rather than the worse. Nor must it be forgotten that protocols do record examples of good performance. Such cases always provoked touching expressions of optimism. They were few and far between. But the emphasis given them suggests that finding fault was not the guiding purpose of visitations.

The most perplexing problem posed by the visitation records concerns the attitudes of the respondents themselves. Did they answer willingly? Truthfully and accurately? Did they say all they knew, or were visitors allowed to hear only what was meant to reach their ears?[52] It should be admitted that, since the true intentions of people are never fully revealed to us, no entirely satisfactory answers can be given to these questions. But the documentation itself does provide some clues permitting indirect access to the ideas and inclinations of ordinary men and women. There are some rules of reason we can apply to this evidence. Our conclusions must remain speculative, but I think they can be offered with confidence, always remembering that the historian's world is a realm of probabilities, and he need not pose as a purveyor of certainty.

It stands to reason that townspeople and villagers in a humble condition tended to hold back. They must have felt cowed, perhaps threatened, by the pomp and circumstance of the occasion: the passage through their obscure hamlets of dignitaries representing a distant authority, the rigidity of the proceedings, the tension generated by the obligatory interrogation. No number of assurances of goodwill, and no manner of overt amiability, could have dispelled this sense of intimidation. Some among the respondents may have been resentful as well. Small-town and village communities were self-reliant political organisms, ably led in many cases by local aldermen jealous of their rights to manage their own affairs and always on guard against encroachments.[53] Surely they would not tell all to outsiders whose very presence aroused misgivings. We know little of the network of loyalties attaching ordinary men and women to their neighbors and communities (we know far more of the fears and suspicions rising to the surface whenever this web of mutual fidelity was torn apart). But we should, I think, assume that even in the face of persistent prodding most respondents maintained a certain reserve and divulged as little as possible of their religious and moral habits, of ancient folkways that in effect bound them all to a kind of underground religion and ethic. Of this the visitors from the distant capital had at most a slight inkling. They were eager to learn more, but this was not made easy for them.

What folk could not hide, on the other hand, was their lack of interest in the official religion, its doctrines, its formulations (especially the catechism), and its ministers. This fact is simple to establish. People either knew the catechism or they did not know it, and visitation examinations revealed that overwhelmingly they did not. This apparent indifference to the formal religion remained unchanged over the century. Where so many opportunities to learn had resulted in so little knowledge and even less understanding, it is safe to conclude that not much interest had been generated. The protocols, taken as a whole, allow of no doubt on this point. Evidence of widespread and enduring ignorance is too massive to be explained away.

If the laity had reason to remain on guard, the clergy had much to gain from telling all. Pastors and schoolmasters stood in a very different relationship to the investigating outsider than did their parishioners. They may have felt some allegiance to the congregations to whose needs they ministered, but they could not have considered themselves fully accepted members of the community, nor could they have felt easy in its midst.[54] Their flocks' behavior often made it plain to them that they did not belong. Much more often than their parishioners, therefore, they spoke their minds, and their depositions in the protocols are our chief testimony to the behavior of people as judged by evangelical standards. We must not, of course, accept the innumerable pastoral complaints about uncivil conduct, gross neglect of religious duties, and nearly universal contravention of the rules of godly living without remembering that their authors wished to impress upon their ecclesiastical superiors the difficulties under which they labored. Probably they were also venting some of the frustration that turned these labors into a thankless task. If they were to escape blame for their parishioners' unsatisfactory performance, they must persuade visitors to seek the fault not in the spiritual mentor's incompetence but in the pupil's obtuseness. This they endeavored to do, giving example after example based on their own observations or picked up by way of hearsay, rumor, and gossip. Visitors were aware of this bias. They endeavored to corroborate the evidence, as has been seen. They demanded names of talebearers and tried to pin respondents down on vague allegations that "it is being noised abroad . . ." or "they say that. . . ." They often discounted some of the most scabrous gossip, as we can tell by comparing relations with the original protocols. I shall observe the same restraint, preferring to err on the side of caution. But what remains of the pastors' account after subtracting probable exaggerations—and a great deal does remain—is very likely to be a trustworthy description of the authentic religious behavior of the multitude. Visitation documents are so full and so rich in detail, they cover so much ground, they are so uniform over so long a stretch of time in describing religious and moral conditions among so large a segment of the population, that we are left with no honest choice but to read them as a reliable statement of what people did and failed to do in performing their Christian duties.

One final reason for caution in interpreting our sources should be mentioned here. Our evidence is deficient in one important respect: it offers us less solid information than we would like on the larger cities. Small and middle-sized towns were well covered by visitations; our state of information on these is as good as it is on villages. It is the large metropolises, free and imperial cities and territorial capitals, that pose a problem for us. Visitations were not well received in urban parishes. Territorial visitors found clergy and parishioners there openly hostile to intrusion, often declining to cooperate. The result of this refusal was that authorities sometimes had to abandon attempts to visit cities. In Strassburg, for instance, where Johann Marbach, Bucer's successor, had persuaded the council to require annual visitations of all city parishes, so much opposition was occasioned by this decision that the visitation had to be canceled in the following year, and none was undertaken again.[55] Exemption of city parishes did not mean, of course, that rural populations under urban control escaped inspection. Visitations were as thorough in the territories of city-states as in princely domains. It is the city population itself that remains just beyond the light cast by the protocols. But the picture is not entirely dark. Many cities did in fact allow themselves to be visited, albeit not with the regularity of smaller places. And there is other evidence, as will be seen, by which to measure the response of city dwellers to gospel, doctrine, and the Christian ethic.

With these cautions in mind, we may now turn to the visitation records themselves. Needless to say, what will be offered here for demonstration is no more than a sampling of an enormous mass of materials. I must ask the reader to trust my judgment. In selecting my illustrations I have chosen instances that could easily be supported by scores of others. The force of my evidence lies not in the occasional telling point, but in the cumulative weight and consistency of the documentation.

CHAPTER 13

RELIGION AND SOCIETY

When Saxon visitors reported to the Elector Johann Friedrich in 1535 that "in many places of your Grace's realm the common people, following the example of nobles and burghers, show a flagrant contempt for the servants of God's word,"[1] their observation could not have occasioned much surprise. A mere seven years had passed since the launching of the first territorial visitation in Saxony, scarcely enough time to prepare a cadre of new pastors to minister to an untutored population.[2] Only two years earlier, in 1533, a sweeping reform mandate had defined the duties of clergy and laity. Henceforth no one was to be allowed to absent himself from divine service. All youths must attend weekly catechism classes. "Public blasphemy, cursing, profaning the name of God" were to be severely punished; also "mocking or deriding the gospel and the holy sacraments, sorcery and similar unchristian superstitions, . . . gambling, adultery, idling and loafing, drunkenness, and disobeying parents." Ducal officials and town and village elders were warned to look out for evildoers in their midst and to chastise them, "not in a spirit of vengeance, but to encourage them to become better Christians."[3] Copies of this mandate were sent to every *Amt* and town council in the realm,[4] urging all in positions of authority to do what they could to make "people desist at long last from showing such frightening ingratitude toward God."[5]

The depressing monotony with which such appeals were repeated year after year throughout the sixteenth century suggests that little was accomplished during the ensuing decades. Threats of punishments proved to be without substance as local law enforcers washed their hands of their responsibilities under the law. Indeed, as visitation reports indicate, in many places officeholders led the population in ignoring the mandates. "Since they themselves never attend service or catechism, how can they persuade others to go, or punish them if

Germany ca. 1570 (Cartographer—John M. Hollingsworth)

they don't?"[6] In his instructions for the visitation of 1554, Elector Johann Friedrich acknowledged that "little or no improvement" had taken place since 1535. "Daily experience tells us, alas," he noted, "that few of our people have taken the gospel to heart."[7] He concluded that another fresh start must be made, and therefore ordered visitors to ascertain whether parishioners could say their prayers and had learned "at least the rudiments of what a Christian needs to know."[8] But the results of this and later examinations were discouraging. People stayed away from church. In many towns and villages they did not even know the common prayers. In the district of Römhild, for instance, although nearly every village had a German school,[9] few children and fewer adults could recite the catechism. The pastor in Graim, visitors reported, had abandoned all attempts at giving catechism instruction "because [he said] people here pay so little attention to it."[10] "A crude, ignorant folk, and untaught," runs a typical comment. "Since they never go to church, most of them cannot even say their prayers."[11]

Not everywhere was the picture quite so dark, but the majority of parishes reported conditions similar to the ones just noted. What could the framers of the Saxon visitation instruction of 1569 have had in mind when they spoke of their desire "to restore the Christian religion in our lands to the splendor it enjoyed under our forefathers, the dukes Friedrich, Johann, and Johann Friedrich"?[12] Perhaps the passage of time had gilded the reality of former days. The 1560s and 1570s, in any case, showed urgent need for improvement. Visitation documents provide graphic instances of this exigency. In Notenstein the *rustici*, including church elders, could remember none of the Ten Commandments.[13] In the parish of Vierzehn Heiligen the elders could not explain how a Christian's sins are forgiven, "except for one man, named Kaiser, who after long hesitation answered 'through Christ.' "[14] Another villager, when asked to explain "who Christ is," could say only "he's up there, above us." "They know nothing of Christianity," the visitors commented.[15] Many a local pastor made a point of venting his sense of frustration to the visitors: "My first complaint, and that of my fellow ministers, is of the great ingratitude, contempt, and disdain among our flocks for the preaching of God's word and the taking of the holy sacrament; second, I complain of the laziness and ill will displayed by young people toward our beloved catechism. I constantly remind and warn them. But it's no use. They do not want to mend their ways."[16] "Most of them are gruesome epicureans," said another pastor.[17] "Great carelessness hereabouts toward the gospel. People make no secret of their scorn for the Sunday catechism and the Friday sermon."[18]

Identical complaints crowd the Thuringian visitation records of the 1580s. Nearly every pastor there "reports his auditors' negligence [*unfleiss*] in attending Sunday and weekday afternoon sermons."[19] "Not a soul comes during the week, . . . and on Sundays they usually stay away without having obtained permission. . . . They treat God's word with open derision [*verachtung*]"[20] "Children ignore the required catechism class on Sundays, and they do not turn up for the examination."[21] "As soon as the minister begins to preach, his auditors jump up and make for the door."[22] Everywhere people had recourse to sorcery, taking their problems to wizards and cunning women instead of to the priest. Forbidden practices, such as illicit meetings of young people at weekly "spinning evenings" (*Rockenstuben* or *Spinnstuben*) flourished unimpeded.[23] A few oases of piety brightened this wasteland. The townspeople of Pirna, upstream on the Elbe from Dresden in the electorate, performed very well on being examined in 1578.[24] But generally the reports were dismal. "Young people know the catechism fairly well, but hardly a single grown-up can recite a word of it. They say they can't keep it in their minds."[25] No one could reasonably contend that this ignorance was due to a lack of learning opportunities. Most regions in Saxony and Thuringia had vernacular schools, and according to the prevailing pedagogical theory a thing well learned in youth should stay in the memory for life. But this did not happen. Since the theory could not be doubted, public apathy was blamed. People were not letting themselves be taught. "It won't be long now," declared a pastor in Görnitz in 1578, "before the entire history of the passion and death of our Lord Jesus Christ will have been completely forgotten, seeing that so few (alas) of our parishioners can remember it, even though we preach it to them with all our might."[26]

Explanations were not lacking to account for the apparent flagging of religious zeal in Saxony:[27] the German civil war and the general turmoil brought in its train, bitter theological rivalries within the Lutheran church in Saxony,[28] incursions by Calvinists and sectarians, and the hard conditions of daily life to whose improvement catechism and sermon contributed little.[29] But contemporaries could not accept these as adequate reasons for the population's listless response. The report from the Wittenberg administrative circle in 1555 shocked them with its litany of glaring defects and abuses. Townspeople were as incompetent (*ungeschickt*) in catechism recitation as villagers, and just as impervious to pleas and threats.[30] As for the countryside, it was deeply sunk in vice: "Gruesome cursing, incessant drinking, tyrannical cruelty of husbands toward wives, neglect of children (whom they raise without any schooling or trade)."[31] The government's best efforts to provide good preaching and religious instruction seemed to bring almost no results, and visitors could not understand why the new opportunities they had created were having so little effect. The protocols of the 1560s and 1570s show that catechists were now at work in nearly all parish churches, even in the most thinly-populated regions.[32] In many places, for instance, "the schoolmaster studies the catechism with his pupils on Friday afternoons at three o'clock. Two boys recite one of the articles, with the explanations, and this is also done on Sunday afternoons. And afterward he examines all the boys and gives them a new article to learn."[33] But even where this was done, the general ignorance persisted.

Every expedient was tried to lure people to weekday sermons.[34] Every precaution was taken to win their confidence: "Pastors should employ soft words in addressing their poor simple-minded, hard-working auditors, so that the latter will not be frightened and prefer to stay away from the weekly [catechism] examination. Pastors ought to speak in friendly, courteous tones. At least for the time being, they should be satisfied with tolerably correct answers to their examination questions, and they must give generous praise whenever some little progress has been made in learning the catechism."[35] On the other hand, it does not seem to have occurred to church bureaucrats that catechism study was not everyone's favorite pastime. When one reads in the Saxon Ecclesiastical Constitution of 1580 that Sunday afternoon catechism classes were organized for "young people hard at work all week long and able to go to church only on Sundays,"[36] one wonders why Lutheran churchmen continued to be surprised at the poor turnout. Throughout the century pastors preached the Sunday afternoon catechism to the bare walls. But however painful their sense of failure, they did not stop looking for signs of progress. Most ministers seem to have performed their thankless duties with a conscientiousness worthy of much better success: "During the recent Lent [the pastor] gave the examination to young and old in this parish. He says he spent much effort and time on it, and has made a register of 1,091 persons, in which is shown what each person knew or did not know of the catechism. With this list he will be able in the coming year's Lenten examination to identify those who have improved their competence, and those who have not."[37] Needless to say, few incumbents were so scrupulous. And no wonder, when it was a struggle to keep their churches warm in winter and their families from starving. Throughout the century ecclesiastical officials continued to be preoccupied by the material state of the church, and its ability to carry on in the face of inadequate funding.[38] This is an important aspect of the setting against which one must judge the public's general failure to respond. How much authority could even the ablest and hardest-working minister command when, as one woman told a visitor contemptuously, "he has nothing but a watery soup to eat for his supper?"[39] Sixteenth-century ecclesiastics had to wage a two-front battle against deteriorating material circumstances and the public's increasing alienation, as it appeared to them, from the care of the church.

Whatever the reasons, the fact of public aloofness toward preachers and gospel is indisputable, being demonstrated in visitation after visitation. In 1578, "it [was] the common complaint everywhere [in Saxony] that people, young and old, do not go to catechism sermons."[40] "The pastor reports that hardly anyone comes to church to hear him preach the catechism and the weekday sermons. And if they do come, they run out again as soon as he starts preaching."[41] The superintendent of Borna reported in 1578 that "it is the chief complaint of nearly all pastors [in the city of Borna] that when they announce the catechism examination, no one will come to church. The hired hands would rather quit their places of service than let themselves be interrogated on their faith." To which the consistory added the telling marginal comment that "we will never make an impression upon these burghers [*bürgerschaft*] and their servants until the elector issues a direct order to the city council."[42] The report from Borna also showed that "people drink and gamble during the time of divine service; indeed, the councillors themselves sit in the taverns and the common townsmen follow their example. No one seems to reprimand them for missing church."[43] In the superintendency of Meissen, in 1579, "no more than six or eight householders out of a populous parish come to church [on Sundays], regardless of ceaseless reminders and admonitions from the pulpit, . . . nor can the pastor keep people from going to sleep during the sermon, or from running out before the prayer and the blessing."[44] The same conditions were reported in the superintendency of Leipzig: "absenteeism from service . . . no one punished for it . . . children and adolescents avoiding the catechism; . . . they play cards while the pastor preaches, and often they mock or mimic him cruelly to his face; . . . cursing, blaspheming, hooliganism, and fighting are common; . . . parents set their children bad examples by refusing to go to service; . . . they enter church when the service is half over, go at once to sleep, and run out again before the blessing is given; . . . nobody joins in singing the hymn; it made my heart ache to hear the pastor and the sexton singing all by themselves."[45] "No one here knows the catechism. The other day the pastor asked a sixteen-year-old boy to give him the first commandment, but he did not know it. When asked to name his maker, the boy answered that his father was Hans Lindner, recently deceased."[46]

In 1579, a territorial diet, convened at Torgau to undertake church and school reform in Saxony, acknowledged that "absenteeism from the preaching of God's word waxes daily in our land. If this trend continues, people will eventually revert to a savage, beastly life."[47] But nothing seemed capable of reversing this trend. "Everyone, young and old, has now fallen into such lax habits and such a false sense of security [*sicherheit*]," wrote the Leipzig theologian and church administrator Heinrich Salmuth in 1581, "that they think themselves too good for the catechism."[48] When questioned on their reasons for not going to church, "the people answer arrogantly that 'the Turk and the pope are not doing us any harm.' "[49] A pastor in Seifersdorf, in the superintendency of Dresden, complained that it usually took an hour's bell ringing and another hour's solitary singing to collect enough people to commence the service.[50] In Senftenberg "not one out of a hundred comes to the afternoon service."[51] Again and again one learns that the passing years brought no improvement. From Heimsdorf near Borna, in 1581: "Every defect listed in past visitations is still being observed here. . . . Threats and warnings are of no help, for people regard them as old wives' tales."[52] From Zwickau: "All the old complaints are being repeated here and we have found them justified."[53] And so on, with occasional good reports gratefully acknowledged, but no signs of steady or lasting progress.[54] Once in a while the clergy's bitter sense of frustration breaks through the bureaucratic formulas. When visitors attacked the pastor in the town of Hartha for the poor performance of his parishioners, he defended himself heatedly, saying

> that his parishioners are not angels, but sinful, frail, and in large part malicious men and women (in this parish as, indeed, in the whole world) who live and act against the Ten Commandments and the secular laws, and who will neither listen to reason nor heed warnings. The congregation, for its part, accuses the pastor of having insulted them from the pulpit by calling them 'the devil's brood'; which words the pastor, in his reply, justified by citing John 8 [44–47], saying that he had addressed some (not all) of his parishioners in these words because of their inveterate habit of missing church, because they despise the sacraments, and because they lead an abominable life and will not listen to warnings.[55]

Clearly there was another side, that of the parishioners, to the general picture the visitations conveyed of public apathy and malevolence. The documents tend to muffle this side, but occasionally a voice escapes from the cover of official disapprobation:

> The pastor [in Lastau, superintendency Colditz] complains that his auditors pay him no respect and are careless about going to church. But his parishioners say that he always preaches too long, and often about strange subjects, so that they cannot follow him. They say they would like to have a postil read to them. When we put these complaints to the pastor, he denied preaching too long (although he conceded that the hand on his clock is not working properly) and submitted that his eyes are too weak to allow him to read from the pulpit. He also asserts that he is frequently obliged to admonish his auditors for their many vices, and that they do not like to hear the truth.[56]

This deposition was taken down in 1617. After nearly a century of institutional and educational reform in Saxony conditions were still very far from satisfactory. Nor could honest churchmen see much ground for hope even in the distant future. They knew that the quality of pastoral service had improved, at least by and large.[57] The network of vernacular and catechism schools covering most of the duchy must have given them satisfaction.[58] But the public's lack of response to these benefits was unmistakable. In villages and small towns parents sent their young to school only grudgingly.[59] Too tight-fisted to pay the modest fee,[60] unwilling to release children from farm, house, or shop for catechism study (while writing and reading proceeded at a snail's pace),[61] they allowed their offspring to grow up, as one superintendent said, "like the dumb beasts of the field, without an inkling of the word of God."[62] Neglected during their formative years, the young developed obtuse minds and recalcitrant habits, passing these, in their turn, to the next generation. Authorities tried to break this vicious circle. But they could think only of instruments that had already failed them: more rigorous visitations,[63] a six-stage method of dealing with offenders from "fatherly admonitions in private" to the synodial ban against habitual deviants.[64] None of these devices helped. The visitation protocols of the mid-1600s in Saxony show no measurable departure from the familiar defects listed in earlier reports.

In the region of Saxony governed independently (from 1572) by the princes of Coburg matters stood no better. A general visitation carried out there by Duke Johann Casimir shortly after he came of age in 1586 revealed the usual apathy and disrespect among the populace. They kept their distance from church; they made for the door on hearing the first word of the sermon; they were rowdy in the yard while service was in progress; they gossiped maliciously behind the pastor's back and defied him to his face; they disregarded the laws against Sabbath work, neglected their children's religious instruction, cursed and blasphemed, enjoyed gargantuan drinking bouts attended by "swinish behavior," and engaged in sorcery, soothsaying, and magic-mongering. As usual, this dismal catalog concluded with the lament that no threats, warnings, punishments, rebukes, or appeals had made any impact on so insensible a race of people.[65] As in the rest of Saxony, the fault in Coburg could not be laid to any lack of opportunities to learn. Visitations in 1577, 1578, and 1580 showed that German schools functioned in all the principality's towns and in many of its villages.[66] Visitors asked pastors "How competent are [schoolmasters] and their assistants? . . . Are they diligent or lazy? Do they keep good discipline in school? Do they teach the catechism and Christian hymns?"[67] To make certain that ministers were actually performing their assigned task of supervision, visitors charged "some notable citizens" with the duty of watching the clergy, and reporting derelictions to the superintendent.[68] But the results in Coburg were as disappointing as elsewhere in Saxony.

Latin and German schools flourished also in the Protestant archbishopric of Magdeburg,[69] but visitations conducted there from 1570 could demonstrate no connection between schooling and religious understanding. In a few places the indications gave ground for hopes. Sixty peasants in one village could recite sections of the catechism, some of them all five parts of it. "Those who live in villages where school is held nearly always give better answers," one visitor noted in 1583.[70] But he himself suspected that this was an exception, a suspicion that rested on good evidence, for the Magdeburg visitors had spent two or three hours inspecting every village. "We have found epicureans here," they wrote in summary, "who hardly know a word of the catechism and never think about their salvation. Indeed several have let it be known that it's all the same to them whether we bury them in the churchyard or elsewhere." When the visitors asked a random sampling of villagers how they applied the Decalogue to their lives, it turned out "that a great many of them did not know how to relate their sins to the commandments, and most refused to admit that cursing, fornicating, and being dead drunk count as sins."[71] In part this situation could be attributed to ineffective preachers.[72] The root cause, however, lay elsewhere, in a human condition so fallen in its habits and so obtuse in its senses that appeals and warnings could not penetrate:

> Godlessness, open scorn for God's word and doctrine, for the gospel and the sacraments, contempt for pastors, disobedience, gross incivility and defiance have so gained the upper hand over the common people in this district [of Zinna, in the archbishopric], not to mention fornication, adultery, and every other sort of vice, especially blaspheming, fraud and deception, and swinish drinking, that it is not possible to give a sufficient description of it.[73]

Visitors were sore at heart as they watched their pastors waiting in empty churches while people took their ease "under the linden tree, in the tavern, or the gaming house," deaf to the tolling of the bell.[74] The Brandenburg consistory's verdict on such conduct as "a wild, disorderly, Cyclopic nature and behavior"[75] does not, in the light of Protestant expectations of a transformed spiritual and moral life, seem excessive.

2

Despite such expressions of disappointment and frustration there was no inclination in official Lutheran circles to abandon hope. Instead, they took every small instance of success as a sign of a possible turning point.[76] Twenty years, even thirty, they reasoned, were not long enough to eradicate the residuum of a thousand years of Roman perversion.[77] Time was of the essence. In the face of mounting evidence to the contrary, churchmen remained stubborn in their conviction that, over the long run, catechism and sermon would accomplish their transforming work in individual and society.

Events in the Brunswick duchies of Lower Saxony exemplify this perseverance. Frequent shifts of confessional alignments had sown religious chaos there, among both clergy and populace. But Lutheran theologians, and the secular rulers who stood behind them, refused to regard this state of confusion as permanent. Even as their visitations near the end of the century reported at best minimal signs of progress they persisted in this conviction.

The duchy of Braunschweig-Wolfenbüttel[78] had been made Protestant during occupation by the League of Schmalkald in 1542, recatholicized in the late 1540s after the victory of Charles V in the Schmalkaldic war, then turned Lutheran again in 1568 when Duke Julius inherited the territory from his Catholic father and reintroduced the Reformation on the model of the neighboring duchies of Kalenberg and Lüneburg. A fact-finding visitation launched in the year of Julius's accession unearthed evidence of pastoral incompetence so egregious as to be scarcely believable.[79] Of fourteen incumbents examined in the administrative district of Bockenem, none could name the parts of the gospel, not to mention the books of the Old Testament.[80] In Jerstedt a preacher scandalized the visitors by referring to Joseph as "Christ's stepfather" and declaring that Mary gave birth to five sons and several daughters after Jesus.[81] Most replied poorly (*übel, male*) to all questions; some could, or would, say nothing at all. Only a few responded *non male* and *bene*. In this light, the apathy found to prevail among the populace could cause no surprise.[82] But it did spur authorities to redouble their efforts. Visitations were rigorous enterprises in the duchy of Wolfenbüttel.[83] All pastors and schoolmasters were interrogated and pressed to reveal general and particular abuses in their respective parishes. Visitors questioned all householders and a fair number of wives, children, and servants. They recorded answers verbatim and sent bulging protocols to the consistory.[84] Two decades after 1568 these reports still reflected a state of general desolation. People could not be persuaded or browbeaten to go to service and catechism. At most, two or three householders turned up, "and there the sexton stands, all by himself, waiting in the empty church until in the end he has to abandon the catechism." Week-long drinking orgies were the rule at Easter and Whitsun, also dancing and gambling on Sundays, not to mention fornication, adultery, and horrible blaspheming to which the entire population was addicted. In 1572 the visitors reported that

> It is the greatest and most widespread complaint of all pastors here-
> abouts [the town of Barum] that people are too lazy to go to church. . . .
> Nothing helps, neither pleas nor threats. And the same obstinacy exists
> on weekdays, when the catechism is preached, and only the least part of
> the parishioners come, so that the pastor preaches to an empty church.
> . . . Is it any wonder that they respond poorly in examination and can give
> no sensible account of the articles of the catechism? Even if you find
> someone who can recite the words, . . . ask him who Christ is, or what sin
> is, and he will not know it.[85]

In a few places the outlook was not quite so hopeless. But in the district of Woldenberg, in 1586,

> after the hymn had been sung and the congregation admonished, when
> [the visitors] asked the people about the previous Sunday's gospel read-
> ing, and whether they could repeat something from it, even a word or
> two, they found not a single person among the adults or the young who
> remembered anything. . . . When asked next what each man owes to Cae-
> sar and the government, and what he must give to God, there was not a
> soul who could give an answer.[86]

There too, however, children were able to say the catechism, a fact from which visitors concluded that what they learned so easily while young, they forgot just as quickly as they were grown.[87] In 1590 the parishioners of a large and well-to-do village in the district of Salzlieben-halle "did not know who their redeemer and savior is." Their pastor vigorously denied blame for this extraordinary piece of ignorance. It is the people's fault, he said. They don't want to go to church, and where else should they learn their religion?[88] The visitors conclude: "If people will not go to church more diligently in the future, we shall be able to accomplish little with them."[89]

Even allowing for the many doctrinal shifts in Wolfenbüttel in the middle of the century, which older people could still recall in the 1590s, it is difficult to account for such behavior except as the expres-sion of an utter lack of concern with the formal religion and the obligations imposed by it. Duke Julius and his successor took pains to improve religious and academic schooling in the principality,[90] but their best efforts were defeated by the general lack of interest. In the neighboring duchy of Braunschweig-Grubenhagen, where the Refor-mation had been introduced as early as 1532 and institutionalized in 1544,[91] visitations in the 1580s tell an identical story. Indeed, so unedify-ing was the information elicited by the questioning that Superintendent Schellhammer feared "that the visitations themselves will in the end become an object of ridicule among the people here."[92] Many churches are empty on Sundays, Schellhammer reported, schools go unattended, and no one wants to learn the catechism.[93] "In nearly every parish," he wrote, "I heard the complaint that people over eighteen years of age are embarrassed by the catechism and will not attend lessons."[94] He found one man who could say the Lord's Prayer in Latin but did not know what the words meant.[95] The superintendent appended the usual list of depravities common among the people: habitual drunkenness (including brandy-drinking in church),[96] gaming, blasphemy, whoring, and magic-mongering, the latter an all-pervasive practice but difficult to trace to its perpetrators "because people are thick as thieves with each other in these villages, and no one wants to tell on his neighbor."[97] This situation had not changed by the second decade of the seventeenth century.[98] Children could sometimes say their catechism, and schools seemed to be better attended in 1617 than they had been in 1579. But the pity of it was that by the time they grew up people forgot all they had learned. As a pastor in Kalenberg told the visitor: "in cases where we are sure that a child knew his catechism years ago, we find out that by the time he had grown up he remembers nothing of it."[99] This discovery was made nearly everywhere.[100]

When Duke Julius of Wolfenbüttel inherited the duchy of Kalenberg in 1584, he prepared there an uncompromising inspection of both clergy and laity. As has been shown in the preceding chapter, this visitation was principally designed to expose and remedy clerical incompetence. Seen against the general ignorance prevailing among the people as revealed in the course of the preceding year's visitation,[101] the theological sophistication demanded of the Kalenberg pastors seems incongruous. The transcripts of the visitors' long sessions with hundreds of ministers[102] are dramatic documents. Only the totally uninformed were summarily excused. Of the rest, none was allowed to pass with evasive or confused answers. Turning the pages of the protocols today, one can still imagine these wretched pastors squirming as questions of increasing complexity and, quite often, distinctly unfriendly tone rained down upon them. The doctrine of the Trinity gave them no end of trouble. Many were at a loss to show how inherited sin was passed to all men. The problem of the will confounded them utterly. Few respondents could rebut contrary arguments. When challenged, they resorted to mere repetition, or else fell silent: "*tacet*," as the protocol keepers wrote in many cases: " 'Can man exercise his free will in spiritual things?' 'No one can do it with his own powers.' 'Prove this from God's word.' *Tacet*. . . . 'Show that we are justified by grace, and not by works.' *Tacet*. . . . 'To what end must we do good works?' 'Not for our own good.' 'This is no answer. Prove that we must do them for the honor of God.' *Tacet*."[103]

Universities and seminaries were able to raise the standard of clerical performance in the course of the following decades. But the public did not keep step. "Our pastors would be glad to do what is demanded of them," wrote a Kalenberg superintendent in 1628, "if only people would go to church."[104] He continued: "Seeing that everyone grows more wicked now from year to year, we must call on the secular authorities to support us in our holy office."[105] Collaboration between church and state was, of course, the first and lasting objective of all visitations and the decrees issuing from them. But even where ecclesiastical and secular authorities were of one mind, and where the state was well organized and in good financial shape, as in the duchy of Lauenburg (Protestant since 1531),[106] the religious condition of the people left a great deal to be desired. In the town of Segedorf, we hear, hardly anyone went to church.[107] In Gudow people talked back to their pastor and walked out on him if he undertook to reprimand them from the pulpit.[108] In Gronau "the congregation behaved disgracefully during the visitation" and would not answer a single question, "so that the examiner had to break off his interrogation."[109] Although some parishes showed better behavior, the general pattern was highly unsatisfactory in Lauenburg and remained so in subsequent visitations in 1590 and 1614. The government imposed severe punishments, but they brought no results. Anyone found sitting in a tavern after the church bell had ceased ringing was fined, as was the offending landlord.[110] Sorcery was a capital offense.[111] But all this was of no avail. Plaintive appeals went to householders to send children to school or catechism class at least "as often as possible"[112] and to discipline them when they were truant.[113] But little changed in the course of years, and the authorities' attempt to explain their failure by blaming it on Anabaptists and Calvinists in their midst carries little conviction in the face of the universal drinking, whoring, and blaspheming detailed in the protocols.[114]

Even a resolute organization could not overcome determined public resistance. If further proof of this is required, it may be found in Braunschweig-Lüneburg, across the Elbe from the duchy of Lauenburg. Although Protestant since 1527, religious instruction had not accomplished much at the time of the second territorial visitation in 1568.[115] The protocols are clear on this point. Pastors, sextons, schoolmasters, and elders from each parish were summoned for interrogation, along with as many "ordinary" people as could be persuaded to turn up. Brief summaries of conditions in each parish describe the general impressions gained by the visitors:

> People [in Molzen] will not go to hear the catechism. Only two individuals from this large parish turned up for the examination. This seems to prove that few of them have learned anything.

> The pastor appeared with only a few members of his flock. We found them

completely ignorant. He says that they drink brandy all day long on Sundays and are unmoved by warnings and punishments.

The people are sluggish and lazy about attending divine service and doing their duties. They have all turned against the catechism.

People here are completely ignorant of the catechism. Their pastor says that there is nothing he can do to make them go to catechism sermons on Sundays and Fridays.[116]

Everywhere the moral tone was set by drinking, gambling ("even during the service") foul swearing, and fornicating. A few counterindications were noted by the visitors with such expressions of delight that they stand out clearly as exceptions to the general rule.[117]

The same documents should have convinced officials that school and catechism could not automatically accomplish the hoped-for reform of private and public religion. Schooling was available nearly everywhere in the Brunswick duchies in the 1560s and 1570s. Most villages kept a sexton's school for reading, writing, and catechism; or, at the very least, "the pastor instructs several boys," that is to say, those whose parents could spare them and wished them to learn. But in fact children were being kept out of school either by poverty or by their parents' resistance to enforced education,[118] or else they were removed "as soon as they have gained a smattering of writing and reading."[119] Apart from the sons of the well-to-do, only boys (and never any girls) who received stipends remained at school long enough to enjoy the molding influence of doctrine and discipline.[120] The work of these privileged pupils was often highly satisfactory. In the salt-mining town of Zellerfeld, in Grubenhagen, for example, visitors "went to the school, where the rector first gave us a Latin oration, after which he examined the older pupils in their [Latin] catechism, Greek Gospels, . . . Terence, and other authors while his assistant examined the younger boys and presented their writing and exercise books. And they all passed admirably."[121] In major cities—Braunschweig, Hannover[122]— excellent gymnasiums and Latin schools provided sound instruction. As late as the third quarter of the sixteenth century, these elite schools were the overriding educational concern of territorial and municipal authorities,[123] as has been seen. The instruction of the general public was another matter. Opportunities to absorb the rudiments of the evangelical faith were not lacking; but there must have been large numbers of youngsters who never crossed the threshold of a school. How, for example, could one persuade boys who worked in the salt mines in Grubenhagen to go to catechism on Sunday afternoons? One scheme was to hold back part of their weekly pay until after the Sunday sermon.[124] This expedient was not adopted, but its suggestion is characteristic of devices sometimes employed to bring a minimum of knowledge to even the least-motivated members of society. For Saxony, too, as has been seen, copious evidence suggests that learning opportunities existed throughout the duchy.[125] But the point is that although elite schools produced able ministers, and many children acquired in their local schools or from their catechism teachers a smattering of religious education, very little of this transferred itself to the general adult population, on whose everyday lives and thoughts the formal religion appears to have made scarcely an impact.

Distinctions between rich and poor do not fully explain this general failure of the Lutheran program of indoctrination. In the county of Oldenburg, for example, the documents allow one to plot poor and well-to-do parishes on a small landscape divided into the Geest, with sandy soil forcing the population to a subsistence level, and the Marsch, where farms and communities were prosperous and schools flourished. But the ignorance and crudeness revealed in visitations in the county just before and after 1600 did not vary between ill- and well-favored regions. In both sections churches were largely empty, the catechism ignored, and most people led what seemed to visitors a scandalously Godless life.[126] There were exceptions in each place.[127] But indifference and ignorance prevailed nearly everywhere. Again and again visitors noted that children forgot what they had learned in school the moment they left it. This, of course, is the most ubiquitous complaint of all. "Does it not cry to high heaven," wrote the superintendent of Schleswig-Holstein from an inspection journey in 1639, "to observe how much thought they give to their domestic affairs and matters of daily life, and how keenly they keep them in mind, and then to see how they have forgotten the essential and necessary points of faith and salvation that we have so often and so distinctly inculcated [*vorgekeuet*] and impressed [*eingebildet*] in them? How can our Lord God tolerate such blindness?"[128] Over and again it was demonstrated for Protestant churchmen that as soon as the business of life claimed people's attention, they seemed to give no further thought to spiritual matters.

3

Let us move southwest, to the Nassau counties of Hesse, where several centuries of dynastic divisions had created a congeries of unstable splinter territories with confusing confessional relationships.[129] Their Reformation, that is to say the magisterial Reformation in the political meaning of that term, dates back to the 1530s. Hessen-Nassau-

Weilburg received its ecclesiastical constitution in 1533 and was first visited in 1536. Nassau-Wiesbaden became Lutheran in 1540. The victory of Charles V in the Schmalkaldic war set the Lutheran cause back in the counties, but by 1553 Protestantism was ascendant again. Not so the public response to evangelical preaching and indoctrination. In 1576, according to a memorandum of the Weilburg synod to the count, "contempt for God's word and the holy sacraments, blasphemy, fornication, whoring and adultery, . . . and unchristian conduct are common here."[130] By 1604 no improvement had taken place. On visiting the city of Weilburg in that year, the superintendent-general reported that few parents cared whether or not their children went to church, weekday and catechism sermons were poorly visited, and "blasphemous and foul-mouthed men and women, drunkards, usurers, whoring fornicators, and the like are to be seen everywhere." Weilburg had a good school and no lack of able teachers. "But it is a pity to see how few people make their children attend it."[131] Absenteeism from church on Sundays was so widespread that the synod debated whether the city gates should be barred on Sunday mornings to lock everyone inside.[132] Evidence from elsewhere suggests that this expedient would not have helped. "From day to day people grow more godless, cocksure, impudent, and reckless," a superintendent wrote to the count of Nassau. "They thumb their noses at the preacher when he admonishes them as they deserve, and they will not let themselves be governed by the spirit of God." This, he stressed, was no local aberration. "It's the misery of the whole German nation," a state of affairs that put him in mind of the wickedness of men before the Deluge.[133]

"No one wants to go to church," was the constant complaint of pastors in the Lutheran counties of Hesse-Nassau, also "great negligence in catechism." "How punctual they are, on the other hand, in going to a dance!" "The whole town turns out for revels. They come early and stay late. And what sacrilegious use of the holy name of God is to be heard there!"[134] Running out of church during communion and disturbing the sermon with loud talk were common practices as well ("long sermons are boring," people said in their own defense).[135] From Nassau-Wiesbaden, in 1594, comes the following catalog of "defects and complaints we have observed among all auditors":[136]

First, gruesome cursing and blaspheming, as for instance "by God," "by God's Holy Cross," "by God's Passion, -death, -flesh, -blood, -heart, -hand," etc., "A Thousand Sacraments," "by the Baptism," "element," "star," "thunder and hail," "earth." Also dreadful swearing by various fears, epidemics, and injuries. These oaths are very common among young and old, women as well as men. People cannot carry on a friendly chat, or even address their children, without the use of these words. And none of them considers it a sin to swear.

Everyone is lax about going to church, both young and old. Many have not been seen by their pastor in a year or more. . . . Those who come to service are usually drunk. As soon as they sit down they lean their heads on their arms and sleep through the whole sermon, except that sometimes they fall off the benches, making a great clatter, or women drop their babies on the floor. . . . At times the wailing of babies is so loud that the preacher cannot make himself heard in the church.

The moment the sermon ends, everyone runs out. No one stays for the hymn, prayer, and blessing. They behave as if they were at a dance, not a divine service. . . . On Sunday afternoons, hardly ten or fifteen of 150 householders come to catechism practice, nor do they oblige their children and servants to attend. Instead they loaf at home, or sit about gossiping. . . . In many places catechism preaching on holiday afternoons has had to be abandoned for lack of auditors.

Other complaints (and there were dozens) concerned inattentiveness to pulpit announcements; open scorn for their preacher's attempt to censure their vices; magic, superstition, witchcraft and faith healing; and the ever-present whoring, adultery, drinking orgies (particularly at Easter, Whitsun, and Christmas), gambling, and general beastliness (*viehische Art*) of behavior. Here and there, this "Cyclopic" life coexisted with a decent knowledge of the catechism, that is to say of its mere words. When the county of Nassau-Wiesbaden was revisited fifteen years after the inspection just described, the general conditions were found unimproved, but it was noted, without special gratification, that "young and old people passed the [catechism] examination tolerably well."[137] On the other hand, the visitor objected to the many dogs running about in the church, "barking and snarling so loudly that no one can hear the preacher." He was also upset to see most members of the congregation sound asleep soon after the start of the service.[138]

The report from Wiesbaden, with its reference to soothsaying, spells, and talismans, furnishes a telling illustration of the abiding conflict between formal Christianity and ancient folk practices. More will be said later of this conflict, which was an elemental condition of religious life in the age of the Reformation. Here another, much more mundane, point should be noted. Even where people felt some wish to visit church on Sundays and holidays, and had the leisure to act on this impulse, they evidently kept well to their own side of the threshold of religious saturation planned for them. Sunday afternoons were for resting, or walking in the country, or gossiping, not for attending another sermon. Weekday evenings were for talking business, or doing the washing, not for a new round of catechism drill. Even the rare model child who lived up to his pastor's expectations and was held up as an example to the rest could surely think of pleasanter companions for his free hours than the sexton or the catechist. Why were Protestant churchmen so insensitive to popular inclinations? Should they have been so shocked at their flocks' refusal to offer their bodies and minds to programmed indoctrination? These questions remain puzzling until we remind ourselves that in the pedagogical thought of Lutheran churchmen, model Christians and evangelical stereotypes had replaced the living human being. Fifty years of Lutheran pedagogy had not closed the gap between the ideal type and the authentic lives of real people, but reformers and pedagogues could not face this fact.

Descriptions of "negligent," "careless," and "casual" [*fahrlässige*] attendance of church also fill the Württemberg protocols from 1581.[139] Württemberg, it will be recalled from the first chapter, had a network of schools that, by the third quarter of the sixteenth century, reached even the smallest of villages.[140] But the duchy's visitation records prove once again that the reformers' correlation between schooling and religious understanding rested on theory and wishful thinking rather than on evidence.[141] Where pedagogues waited for people to respond to "influence" and "inculcation," they saw little good coming of their endavors. Strong-arm measures were much more likely to work, and governments willing to employ these recorded some improvement. When the need to root out Calvinism persuaded Ludwig VI of the Upper Palatinate that extraordinary means were required to instill sound— meaning Lutheran—beliefs in his subjects, he used police powers to bring children to catechism and adults to church. Bailiffs walked the streets during the Sunday service, knocked on house doors, and kept the taverns shut. If a shirker was found, he was locked up in the "dunce's hut" for the day. Two men who could not answer questions on the commandments were thrown in prison. Children playing truant from catechism were punished and their parents fined.[142]

There is no doubt that such authoritarian measures worked. In the Palatinate they even succeeded in curtailing somewhat the drunkenness and swearing that elsewhere proved irrepressible.[143] But how much religious comprehension could they induce? Count Ludwig's superintendent Martin Schalling answered this question indirectly when he assured his prince that the Calvinist threat was but a passing menace to his realm since, the official asserted, "the common man has scarcely any understanding of the difference between that doctrine and ours."[144] Questioning of ordinary people demonstrated the truth of this contention. Few could give a coherent explanation of their beliefs. A woman who identified herself as "*Zwinglisch*" was unable to say what this meant and in what respects it differed from being "Lutheran." But she eagerly promised to "learn how to be a good

Christian," provided only, she said, her pastor "stop speaking so rudely to her."[145] This unsatisfactory situation did not change for the better. Visitations held in the Upper Palatinate just before the outbreak of the Thirty Years War revealed dutiful churchgoing, but no diminution of the crudeness of life or the general ignorance of religion.[146]

There is no doubt that administrative constraints, if resolutely pursued, raised the level of religious performance, but they could scarcely have affected people's mentality or changed their natures. Going to church, keeping the catechism on the tip of one's tongue, and suppressing coarse words were far from the whole of evangelical Christianity. But they were a beginning, and by the late sixteenth century most governments would have been content to have accomplished that much.

The Palatinate principality of Neuburg furnishes an example of such a limited success. Protestant since 1542,[147] Pfalz-Neuburg was frequently and energetically inspected under Prince Ottheinrich and his successor Philip Ludwig, the latter a serious and resolute Lutheran ruler. Their visitation instructions were both rigorous and comprehensive. All *responsa* had to be written down verbatim and all *Mengel und Gebrechen* specified. Pastors were required to give proof of their ability to preach and lecture on the catechism. Secular officials faced sharp interrogation about the conduct of the local clergy, for which they were responsible: "[The visitors] shall choose from among the common people a certain number of youths and older people who shall recite to them the words of the Ten Commandments, the Apostles' Creed, the Lord's Prayer . . . ; and visitors shall also ask them the meaning of these articles and what they know of their explanation. For in no other way can visitors discover what the parishioners have learned and how well they have been instructed by their pastors."[148]

These instructions were carried out to the letter. "We have not omitted to examine a number of young and elderly persons on the Decalogue, the Creed, and Lord's Prayer," the visitors reported, "nor have we failed to ask them what baptism is and how they understand the Lord's Supper."[149] In 1558 the information thus obtained showed more *Mengel* than merits. "Public morality, order, and discipline are in a poor state in our country, as they are everywhere else."[150] Detailed reports from individual parishes list the usual defects: absenteeism from church and catechism, brandy-swilling, cursing, and so on. "And even where they attend church, they are not made better by it."[151] Eight years later the situation was the same,[152] as it was, still, in 1575. The superintendent of Neuburg, whose province included the capital city, reported in that year that children were not going to catechism, that people were slow to come to church and made their displeasure painfully clear to the pastor, while "those of the lower sort" went across to Catholic Bavaria to take communion. "It is easy to obtain the sacrament from the papists," they declared when reproached. "They don't make us learn anything before they give it to us."[153]

With such comments ringing in his ears, Count Philip Ludwig decided on intervention. His policy was centered in a *Kirchenrat*, a body with direct control over all pastors in the principality, which was expected to take a strong hand in raising the religious and moral tone of the populace.[154] A set of general articles laid down strict rules for clerics and local officers.[155] They must keep exact census figures of the number of houses in their parishes, of the adults, children, and servants residing there, and of the names of those who did, and did not, attend church and catechism. Absentees were to be admonished, "moderately at first, not in rough language, because our object is to advance the faith, not to turn the common people against it." Those who remained stubborn were to be treated severely, with fines and, if nothing else helped, imprisonment. Magistrates had to set an example for the common people. "Once our subjects observe the seriousness and zeal of their Christian government, they will be prompted to more diligent attendance of the service."[156]

This stringent policy seems to have worked. The visitation of the following year already registered substantial improvement in catechism examinations, among the "old" as well as the young.[157] Pastors reported better church attendance. "More people than before know their catechism now, in which we see the fruits of the recent visitation."[158] By 1585 even serving maids and hired hands came regularly to catechism.[159] There is not doubt that the key to success lay in the systematic use of constraints over the population of a small territory. Since the records of the Neuburg consistory have survived, [160] we can reconstruct this process of coercion. The consistory's members—four theologians and four *politici*—displayed an almost fanatic concern with the details of administration. Nothing escaped their attention. Exhaustive data reached them at regular intervals on each parish: census figures (communicants, baptisms, marriages, burials), audits of the common chest, building inspectors' reports, lists of books read by each pastor, memorandums by the local "censor," and so on. These reports were identical in form from year to year, which facilitated comparisons and the charting of trends. Punishments were executed, fines collected. This alone seemed to work wonders. "We have no complaints here this year," said a pastor in 1589, "because the visitor sees to it that penalties are carried out as ordered."[161] Absenting oneself from service and catechism on Sundays became hazardous when, as one reads in the protocol on the town of Monheim, a posse consisting of council members, the *Stadtvogt,* and a man-at-arms made rounds during church hours.[162] "Censors" sought out slackers and cautioned them or, if this failed, browbeat them into compliance. In 1587 pastors reported that since "the censor ordered [parishioners] to send their children and servants to catechism and to set them a good example by going there themselves, they have become much more diligent in complying."[163] In 1594 we hear of a parish of 580 communicants whose 90 teen-age boys could recite the entire catechism with explanation.[164]

So much for accomplishments in Pfalz-Neuburg. It is difficult to decide what they prove about the broad impact of the Reformation and the success of Lutheran pedagogy. What they do seem to demonstrate is that a resolute and able state operating in a compact territory had the means to obtain obedience to rules that, though they crossed ingrained habits and violated deeply rooted folkways, were not in themselves unreasonable, however irksome they may have seemed. But how much of this praiseworthy churchgoing and catechism reciting entered the individual's conscience? On this point we have no clues. The protocols do suggest that "natural," "epicurean," "brutish" ways were not altogether extinguished by attention to sermons and memorizing the catechism. Visitors often came upon scenes, or heard pastors speak of them, to remind them that the old vices were still active.[165] Indeed, the constraints adopted in Pfalz-Neuburg in 1576, after decades of unsuccessful trials with less authoritarian methods, are themselves an implicit admission of the impotence of indoctrination as a means of re-education. A wide gap separates the complaisant satisfaction with which Neuburg theologians contemplated their full churches from the early reformers' hopeful anticipations of a voluntary and internalized Christianity.

4

Our portrait of Lutheran Germany in the light of its visitation protocols will gain in depth if the perspective of a prominent Catholic region is added, that of the duchy of Bavaria. Fifty years of resolutely opportunistic policymaking won for the Bavarian dukes a firm grip on religious affairs in their land.[166] Wilhelm IV and Albrecht V compelled the Bavarian bishops to accept a politically controlled program of ecclesiastical reform,[167] tried to neutralize the appeal of Lutheranism in Bavaria by revitalizing the institutions and services of the Bavarian church, negotiated alliances with fellow Catholic powers,[168] and came to agreements with restive nobles and territorial estates who were using the religious turmoil as a wedge to obtain constitutional concessions. In 1558, Albrecht V began to carry out territorywide visitations. A loyalty oath was required of all teachers.[169] Censorship on the model of the Roman Index was imposed and traffic in and out of

Bavaria put under surveillance. In 1570 a College of Ecclesiastical Councillors placed the capstone on this program. As the supreme authority over the church in Bavaria, subject only to the duke, the college exercised both initiative and final authority in all ecclesiastical matters.[170] Its voluminous records reflect its government's avid interventionist policy. Every rumor was traced, every suspicious report checked. Elaborate questionnaires extracted information from suspected Lutherans and sectarians. The archives hold hundreds of library catalogs submitted by priests whose orthodoxy was under question, long lists of persons counted absent from mass, "annual inquisitions [*jährliche Inquisition*]" conducted in all parishes to identify religious deviants, and dossiers on individual citizens whose words or actions had aroused suspicion.[171]

It goes without saying that this program of surveillance and control included the duchy's schools.[172] Catholic governments faced greater clerical resistance than did Protestant states to the creation of an educational system responsive to political as well as religious needs,[173] but this struggle ended in Bavaria in 1573 when the College of Ecclesiastical Councillors was given jurisdiction over all educational policies.[174] Long before this date it had been made clear to the Bavarian prelates that "in matters scholastic our gracious lord in his capacity as territorial ruler has the power to say what shall be done."[175] Thus the Bavarian *Schulordnung* of 1569 set curricula and teaching methods for Latin and German schools, established Canisius's catechisms as the basic texts of religious instruction, laid down rules of discipline, and provided for regular visitations—a program identical (except in the choice of books, of course) with its Protestant counterparts.[176] But Bavarians, too, soon realized that it was one thing to declare policy, another to force compliance. As late as the 1620s Bavarian visitors were still trying to root out illicit catechisms and textbooks, especially in the northern parts of the duchy, where Protestantism had made the deepest inroads.[177] It took the police-state methods clamped upon Bavaria in the reign of Maximilian I to gain the upper hand on this lively traffic in Lutheran books.[178]

In the meantime, religious education in Bavaria had conformed itself to the pattern already established in Lutheran territories. The only distinction from the latter was its essentially defensive character, the overriding purpose of indoctrination being to eradicate heresy and dissidence, and to inoculate the population against heterodoxy—although in this respect, too, it resembled later Lutheran policies, with their preoccupation with divisive sectarianism. Instruction in basic Christianity was integrated with the curriculum in Bavaria; pupils intoned the daily prayers, sang German hymns, recited Bible verses; above all they memorized the catechism. Like their Protestant cousins they marched to church, where "two designated pupils, one asking questions and the other giving answers," recited the catechism to the congregation.[179] Canisius's German and Latin catechisms settled the question—an insoluble one for Lutherans, as has been seen—of how best to translate complex theological ideas into the lay idiom.[180] As among Lutherans, the Shorter Catechism was printed and bound with Latin grammars and German ABC books.[181] For Latin pupils, the Jesuit curriculum and educational methodology became standard learning fare long before the publication of the *ratio studiorum* in 1599; the work of Jesuits in the schools of Munich and other Bavarian cities was made exemplary by the Bavarian school ordinance of 1569[182] (incidentally causing much envious resentment to build up among rival educators).[183] German schoolmasters were left free to select curriculum and books (except for the catechism), the only proviso being their orthodox authorship and place of publication.[184] The principles underpinning these activities were identical with Protestant postulates. The young must be taught "in their tender years."[185] Imbuing them with "the fear of God, virtuous habits, and useful skills" would advance "good government and the public weal."[186] Latin schools sifted talents and assured the country of its future generations of ministers.[187] Regular catechism practice for adults was expected to perpetuate sound knowledge and good habits.[188]

So much for theory. When it came to gauging the success of the enterprise, Catholic Bavaria ranked no better than Lutheran countries. Only in the seventeenth century, under the aggressive rule of Duke (later Elector) Maximilian I, did Bavarian visitors begin to take a serious interest in the religious consciences of lay people; until then, outward compliance was accepted as a sufficient criterion of belief.[189] Throughout the sixteenth century visitation procedures had been as methodical in Bavaria as among the Protestants: identical questionnaires in all dioceses, cross-examination of respondents, and so on. But until the early 1600s the sole object of these exercises was "the safeguarding and preservation of our holy Christian and Catholic religion," as Albrecht V put it in his mandate of 1569.[190] To Maximilian, zealous renovator that he was, this was not enough. He therefore ordered annual school visitations, accompanied by interrogations of pupils on the catechism.[191] And he instructed his visitors to discover what people in the duchy's parishes actually knew and understood of their professed religion.

The answer was: not much. "As time goes on," complained Maximilian to the Bavarian bishops in 1607, "we note that our young people and their elders have less and less knowledge of the catechism and the articles of our Catholic faith and cannot, when questioned on these, give good answers." He blamed this decline on incompetent teaching by the clergy,[192] but the latter disagreed. It's the fault of the people, they contended, because most of them have set their minds against religious instruction. The College of Ecclesiastical Councillors, having examined the evidence gathered in visitations, came to the same conclusion. "The majority of our pastors complain that their parishioners do not attend [catechism practice] on Sundays, and therefore all their good work and effort are done in vain."[193] The bishop of Salzburg admitted that "the common man cannot even say the Lord's Prayer or the Ave Maria with the right words and does not know the Apostles' Creed, to say nothing of the Ten Commandments."[194] The bishop of Augsburg also found his "people . . . negligent in attending divine service . . . and slack about sending their children to catechism instruction."[195] "Sloth and lack of zeal" in religious matters prevailed everywhere.[196] The blame for this clearly belonged (so the clergy thought) to the laity, "who are more inclined to go to dances than to church."[197] Appeals and warnings were of no use, and ecclesiastical authorities saw themselves forced to plead for the duke's intervention against the deteriorating conditions. This service was willingly rendered by Maximilian, but in the end he was as helpless as his bishops in the face of public apathy. In fact, a good case can be made for concluding that the more unyielding the mold of religious conformity pressed upon subjects, the cooler was their loyalty to the declared creed and the deeper their alienation from its spiritual substance.[198] But no Protestant or Catholic government saw in this withdrawal the handwriting on the wall. Wedded to their commitment to uniform orthodoxy, ready always to encroach on the most private of intentions, they built a heavy-handed apparatus that, in opposition to its own objectives, worked to set aside motivation and conscience in favor of formal compliance with bureaucratic rules. To the extent that this shift extended the state's ability to manipulate the lives of its people, it discouraged their internal impulses and increased their aloofness from the institutions, creed, and ministers of the established church.

An example from a Calvinist region will reinforce this conclusion by introducing us to a variant model for controlling religious behavior. The county of Dietz, a tiny splinter territory on the Lahn River east of the Rhine, divided in 1564 between the Catholic archbishopric of Trier and the Protestant county of Nassau-Dillenburg, was toward the end of the sixteenth century forcibly brought to the Geneva confession as a consequence of Dillenburg's adoption of that creed. Its ruler, Count Johann VI (a brother of William of Orange) faced a formidable problem in having to root out the county's official Lutheranism along with the traditional beliefs of a large part of the population with easy access to Catholic churches across the border in Trier. Visitations toward this objective began in Dietz in the 1580s. They generated a mass of documents that permit the historian to observe at close range the aggressive and methodical approach to religious politics for which this ruler, and the religion he professed, are noted.[199]

Unlike his Lutheran and Catholic colleagues, but in accordance with the Genevan practice, the count concentrated his efforts on a handful of leading citizens in each community, assuming that as opinion-shapers and pace-setters these notables would exert a beneficial pressure on the rest of the congregation. Having been persuaded to adopt an exemplary Christian walk in their lives, these men, designated *seniores*, were set as censors and judges over their neighbors. "It is of the greatest importance," wrote Count Johann, "that the *seniores* appointed to assist the pastor in each place be thoroughly schooled in doctrine and ceremonies so that they may lead their communities to understanding and acceptance of the truth."[200] As "the most dedicated, outstanding, and knowledgeable members of their community,"[201] they gathered their children and servants for daily prayers and catechism practice,[202] knew the Heidelberg Catechism by heart, and gave clear explanations when interrogated in public. Their children were regular and punctual in attending religious instruction.[203] Their servants never ran "across into the papacy"—that is to say, over the frontier in the archbishopric. Aided by "clear commissions and good instructions" to "the cautious, orderly, courteous, and useful performance of their duties."[204] they were expected to raise the moral standards of all but the most obstinate of their fellow citizens.

Visitations recorded the elders' impact on their communities. Count Johann's visitation procedures, which involved the use of a model questionnaire worked out in 1583 and remaining in use well into the following century, were more rigorous, under far tighter control, and much more resolute in following through than Lutheran and Catholic visitations.[205] Each pastor presented registers of baptism and catechumens.[206] Visitors catechized every adult person and every child. In each parish they heard the pastor preach, then criticized his performance for soundness, coherence, good elocution, and a firm grip on his audience. All preaching had to be done from memory but was to be carefully prepared and delivered "in a lively and pleasing manner."[207] No detail was too small to merit the visitors' attention. They required that parents be kept occupied while their youngsters were being catechized. A well-heated room must be prepared for winter catechism.[208] To spare older people the embarrassment of public interrogation, they should be visited in their homes. Pastors should engage parishioners in private discussions, for these, it was said, made greater impression on them than sermons given in church.[209]

Having completed their inspection of Dietz, the Dillenburg visitors compiled a *Summary of Defects Found in All the Parishes of the County*. There is no doubt that these reports, from about 1590 onward, give a much more favorable picture of religious conduct than the documents from Lutheran territories. Minor flaws were noted (no midwife in a village, a school building in need of repair, some children truant from catechism class); but the general situation looked hopeful indeed. Church and catechism attendance was good, and people answered correctly when interrogated. On the other hand, do these facts signify religious understanding and, beyond that, do they prove that evangelical dispositions had been created? This is to be doubted. Replies to catechism questions were always verbatim quotations in Dietz, apparently given in a mechanical way. Even the slightest deviation from the exact wording was sternly reprimanded, and the respondent advised to go back to his book.[210] Such parroting could not have prompted much religious thinking. But discouragement of independent speculation was, of course, one of the chief objectives of catechization. As to the Christian life resulting from these exercises: Calvinists insisted even more forcefully than Lutherans that good works were a sign of right faith and that the practice of them was necessary to salvation.[211] But how can one be sure that this doctrine was in fact internalized by those to whom it was preached? Vigilant pastors and Argus-eyed elders could suppress to some extent the social vices noted in such proliferation elsewhere in Germany. But even in Dietz the documents record instances of the irrepressible habits of drunkenness, boisterousness, and blasphemy. Churchgoers had to be warned against going to sleep during the sermon,[212] and frequent references to "young people running across [the border] to the papists[213] to enjoy dances and other festivities indicate that resistance to puritanical Protestantism was bold enough even in a Calvinist state to make a brief escape worth the risk of punishment.

The moral to be pointed from this experience is that a certain amount of coercion could, nearly everywhere, assure at least some observance of the rules of external piety. Late in the sixteenth century many governments were driven to extraordinary measures in their struggle to oppose the tide of depravity they saw bearing down on them.[214] Sometimes these steps achieved the expected results. But to record reformed conduct is not to prove informed hearts. Indeed, the evidence argues strongly against making this false connection. People reeled off their catechism but could make no sense of it. They recalled its words at examination time, "but," said a visitor in Strassburg, "press them on matters of understanding, bid them prove this or that from Scripture, ask them . . . what *Evangelium* means in German, what a sacrament is, or why we call the gospel the New Testament, and you will get, even among older people, the most absurd and foolish [*absurd und ungereimte*] answers."[215] It is a typical observation.[216] "The blind lack of understanding of the catechism and the foundation of Christian doctrine" was seen as the chief, more often the single, cause of corruption in life and manners.[217] If this remained the situation more than a century after the introduction of Lutheran pedagogy, one must conclude that its program of evangelical indoctrination had not succeeded in making an autonomous moral agent of the human conscience.

3

It is left now to examine the territories of the urban states and to gather what information is available on the cities themselves. On the latter we face a problem of evidence, as was indicated in the preceding chapter. Visitation records fail us as we turn to the free cities, large and small, of the Holy Roman Empire and to the capitals and administrative towns of Protestant and Catholic territorial states. The councils of the important urban centers wielded enough power, and the clergy of major churches commanded sufficient influence, to keep unwelcome visitors from prying into their affairs. The protocols themselves note this fact. The excellent records of the principality of Neuburg say nothing about the city itself.[218] A visitation of the archbishopric of Cologne in 1569 covers thirteen of the seventeen towns of this ecclesiastical state, but exclude the imperial city.[219] In Graz, the largest town in Styria, Archduke Ferdinand's visitors met point-blank refusal from parish priests "to make their report and show us obedience."[220] Nuremberg conducted its municipal affairs without a single visitation from 1528 to 1560.[221] But other cities saw no reason, or found no ground, for resisting visitations: Dresden and Meissen in Saxony, and Leipzig after 1580,[222] for example. In Bavaria all cities, including Munich, the capital, were visited regularly;[223] also Augsburg and Rothenburg—the former owing to the confusion created by the principle of religious parity imposed there in 1555, the latter because of its special ecclesiastical relationship to the margraviate of Brandenburg-Ansbach. Lesser cities and towns[224] nearly always submitted without protest. On these our information is abundant.

For the larger municipalities there is other evidence to draw on in the absence of visitation data. The confessional was freely used to assess the general state of religious knowledge.[225] In some places householders were summoned to council chambers and consistories to be questioned on their faith.[226] Catechism examinations took place, more or less regularly, nearly everywhere.[227] Preachers and ecclesiastical administrators commented and deliberated on these procedures.

Combining these remarks with what visitation material is available, one can compose a likeness that, though it lacks the detail and color of reports from smaller towns and villages, is likely to be true to the facts.

In 1577 the council of the city of Leipzig was warned of serious "flaws and defects" among the citizens: absenteeism from church and especially from communion (the council members themselves were accused of leading their fellow members in this neglect), drinking, gambling, promenading in the market square during catechism practice, sleeping through the sermon, and so on. The same vices were observed in 1608 and again in 1615.[228] In Augsburg, pastors complained early in the seventeenth century about "the prevailing ignorance among young and old in all matters of religion."[229] The city's excellent and tightly controlled school system had not, it appears, made much of an impact on the religious disposition of burghers; even the rudimentary catechism of Johann Meckhardt, officially adopted in 1551 and further simplified in later editions, was judged too difficult for the Augsburg laity.[230] Visitors to Rothenburg, representing the margrave Frederick of Brandenburg-Ansbach, discovered in the 1560s and 1570s that hardly anyone knew his catechism.[231] In 1607 the city council observed that "churches and sermons are sparsely visited by young and old," few people attended catechism instruction, and children were not being brought up to a Christian life. To gain a firmer hold on this situation, the council ordered all burghers, and their families and servants, to be examined by their pastors in catechism and Scripture. But in 1618, as an edict repeating this instruction noted sadly, the councillors were "grieved to observe that our benevolent, zealous, and well-meaning Christian decrees have so far brought no results whatever, having been contemptuously ignored by old and young, men and women, whose godless, vexatious, disgraceful, and wicked lives and natures grow worse from day to day."[232]

The governing magistrates of Strassburg strove throughout the sixteenth century to lure people to church and catechism instruction, and to put a stop to blasphemy, drunkenness, gaming, adultery and fornication, "nightly clamor," disorderly conduct, open disrespect shown to the clergy, and the "general contempt for the word of God."[233] Ecclesiastical administrators with more than local experience recognized in these symptoms a pandemic illness. Christoph Vischer, who was superintendent in the cities of Schmalkalden and Meiningen in Thuringia, and Celle in Brunswick (and had been preacher and visitor in several other towns), deplored in 1573 the alarming decline in public catechism attendance, noting that "it has come to this now that a person feels embarrassed to be seen by his neighbors on his way to catechism class."[234] Given such attitudes, wrote Simon Musaeus in 1571, is it any wonder that even preachers are now ashamed of the catechism?

This is why "many people who have been exposed to the evangelical faith for twenty or thirty years understand as little of it as the papists who have never heard it preached at all."[235] People claim that the Christian doctrine is too difficult to keep in mind. But when it comes to "belly matters," they have excellent memories. On a visitation some years earlier, Musaeus relates, he asked a cloth merchant to repeat to him the subject of the previous Sunday's sermon, but the man recollected nothing. And the price of wool a year ago? To this the merchant gave precise answer. Why was it, Musaeus wanted to know, that he could remember wool prices for a year and forget a Christian sermon in less than a week?

> To which the man replied that these are different matters. 'Wool is my business,' he said; 'I must think about it day and night, for I can't make a living without it. As for the sermon and the catechism, I don't need them so much.'

"Is this not terrifying blindness?" Musaeus exclaims. "But this is how most of them are."[236] Veit Dietrich, writing of his experience in Nuremberg, agreed with this judgment, deploring the bad example set for the young by their elders, ("wanton prodigality in stuffing their guts and wearing extravagant clothing, also abominable cursing, lying, and deceiving"). He despaired of the preacher's ability to bring people to their senses. "You cannot make them go to church," he wrote, "no matter what you say. To worldly affairs they turn with a passion, but for church they have no time and no interest."[237]

Musaeus, Vischer, Dietrich, and their colleagues were of course not wholly objective witnesses to the religious behavior of their fellow citizens. They clearly expected more dedication than the laity could reasonably be asked to give. Moreover, each had his own theological axe to grind. On some essential points, however, they agreed among themselves and with the evidence of the visitations. Church, catechism, and doctrine held little appeal for urban people in the later sixteenth century. The evangelical message had not entered their hearts; or, if it had, it had failed to reform their walk of life. If they read the gospel, as many surely did, and if they listened while it was being preached to them, they kept their own counsel on its meaning for their mortal lives and its relevance to their hopes for the hereafter.

If this was the situation in the cities themselves, it is not surprising to find in their rural domains even less loyalty to the established creed. No more than a quick survey need be given here, for conditions were much the same in the urban countryside as in the great princely territories. A visitation of the Nuremberg Territorium in 1561, for example, turned up the usual complaints of negligent church attendance, ignorance of the catechism, unchristian behavior on the Sabbath, cursing and blaspheming, and so on.[238] Lutheran from 1535, and operating since 1533 under a joint ecclesiastical constitution with Brandenburg-Ansbach, Nuremberg and its extensive countryside ought to have been a showcase for the success of Protestant pedagogy. State and church government were firmly controlled by a small group of shrewd and energetic patricians. Most villages had German schools where prayers were taught along with reading and writing, and Luther's Shorter Catechism was the universal primer.[239] Obligatory catechism lessons had been set as early as 1531. But the impact of all this on public religion and morals remained negligible. There were mitigating circumstances to explain this unsatisfactory result. Warfare in the early 1550s made a shambles of much of the rural countryside,[240] and the lamentable conditions discovered during the visitation of 1561 might have been the consequence of this devastation.[241] But long after the war had drawn to a close, the hoped-for standard of religious and moral culture remained a goal still to be achieved. As late as 1626 we hear of people who did not know "who has given us the Ten Commandments," of a fifteen-year-old girl who thought the Trinity consisted of five gods, of peasants who could not say "on what day of the year our Lord Jesus Christ died on the cross," and so on.[242] Appalled at these and similar signs of general ignorance, the city council could recommend only old standby solutions: a simpler catechism, more drill, sterner decrees and stiffer fines, more rigorous inspection.[243]

Nowhere did such half-measures work. The city of Ulm, to take another example, held territorial visitations every two or three years from 1532 into the seventeenth century, but little or no progress was observed during this time. In 1615 Superintendent Konrad Dietrich found rural churches poorly attended, and his examination detected scant knowledge of religion among the people: this after more than three-quarters of a century of schooling and catechization in the city's townlets and villages.[244] Acknowledging this state of affairs, Julius Endriss, the historian of Ulm's ecclesiastical visitations, concludes that "if instruction in the holy catechism had in two or even three generations not brought a knowledge of the Lord's Prayer to adults and younger people, not to mention some understanding of it, one must accept the fact that no advance had been made over the conditions prevailing before the Reformation."[245] In 1605 a rural schoolmaster confessed to his inability to take his pupils to church in an orderly fashion, as prescribed in the ordinance. No matter how he begged or threatened them, he said, they would not stay in formation, making by their behavior a mockery of the occasion. "And it's their parents' fault," he added, "many of whom don't go to church themselves." He found no children who knew the meaning of the catechism phrases they reeled off on command,[246] and Ulm's visitation protocols furnish some graphic illustrations of the character of rural and small-town life at the end of the sixteenth century:

> In Geislingen they practice the following vices: dreadful blasphemy, stuffing and besotting themselves with food and drink, gambling openly in tavern and beer houses, . . . also an arrogant spirit as shown in their contempt for the sermon, catechism, and the Lord's Supper, also sacrilegious behavior on the Sabbath and holidays, to wit: they sit in front of their houses, gossiping, while the service is in progress, they allow their children to run wild about the streets without reprimanding them, they open their shops on Sunday and do their buying and selling as though we had no divine and secular laws against these sins.[247]

In Strassburg, territorial visitations turned up the same sort of evidence.[248] A partial explanation is at hand in that city's reluctance (unusual among German city-states, as has been seen) to establish schools in the countryside;[249] but even in Strassburg, catechism instruction on Sundays was obligatory everywhere.[250] Visitors discovered that this rule was not observed. "Everything is in a state of decline, especially attendance at catechism," they reported in 1586. "As for the catechism, things seem to go downhill from year to year" (1598). No wonder, then, that "disobedience, brashness, and corruption grow daily among our young people." Young boys travel abroad, or go to war, coming back brutalized, scarcely Christian, but nothing is done to counteract this trend (1600).[251] Most children in the countryside could not even say the Decalogue without making serious mistakes.[252] Similarly, visitations in the principality of Bayreuth carried out by its territorial ruler, the margrave of Brandenburg, found in 1591 "great contempt everywhere for the word of God and the sacraments, also terrible blaspheming, sorcery, adultery and whoring, excessive drinking and other vices, all practiced openly, while the common man is negligent, delinquent, and lax in attending church and learning the gospel."[253] "In nearly all parishes [in Bayreuth] pastors complain that the word of God is scorned by their parishioners, who grow daily more arrogant and cocksure in their demeanor."[254] In Hamburg visitors to the countryside also found (in 1581) "unbelievable epicurean wickedness and contempt for preaching, for the holy sacraments, the commandments, for sacred songs," along with evidence that people came habitually late to church, "laugh or make indecent gestures at members of the congregation who join in the singing," or "out of sheer mischief bring their dogs to church and let them interrupt the service with loud barking."[255] In some places children could recite their catechism. But—so went the constant complaint—adults recalled barely a word of it, and in any case their behavior gave no indication that it had had a lasting influence on their lives. Indeed, how could it be otherwise when "we cannot prevail on them to go to church on Sundays or pay us any heed when we try to preach the catechism to them?"[256]

This plaintive litany could continue almost indefinitely. But surely the cumulation of evidence has made its point. A century of Protestantism had brought about little or no change in the common religious conscience and in the ways in which ordinary men and women conducted their lives. Given people's nebulous grasp of the substance of their faith, no meaningful distinction could have existed between Protestants and Catholics—a distinction arising from articulated belief, conscious attachment, and self-perception. It seems clear, therefore, that the hopes occasioned by the pedagogical endeavor early in the century had not been fulfilled. To say this is not to deny that there were men and women of earnest, informed piety in Germany. Gymnasiums and seminaries turned out able preachers and, one assumes, conscientious laymen who took their religion seriously. One hesitates to think that the buoyant spirit in which urban circles had received and joined the Reformation in the 1520s and 1530s should have been so stifled by its subsequent routinization.[257] But it is one thing to be carried along by the surge of a young cause in its heroic phase, and quite another to champion a creaking orthodoxy. It should not be difficult for us to understand how it happened that compulsory churchgoing and obligatory catechism drill promoted resentment and opposition, boredom and apathy. By and large this seems to have been the end product of religious indoctrination. The evidence of the visitations speaks for itself in urging this conclusion.

CHAPTER 14

CONCLUSIONS

So disappointing a denouement of an enterprise so confidently launched and zealously pursued needs to be explained. Comments toward an interpretation have been offered in each of the preceding chapters. It remains to draw these fragments together and expand them into a comprehensive synopsis.

A deep-seated ambivalence toward their objective split the reformers' minds into opposing attitudes and impaired their pedagogical program from its outset with fatal inner contradictions. Torn between their trust in the molding power of education and their admission that the alteration of men's nature was a task beyond human strength, they strove for success in their endeavors while conceding the likelihood of defeat. They believed in the sanctifying virtue of voluntary actions taken by freely choosing Christians but allowed their distrust of the individual sinner to justify his subjection to administrative control and intellectual coercion. Unwavering in their efforts to conform men and women to the evangelical model, they recognized in their failure the confirmation of their worst suspicions.

This debilitating oscillation was not merely the result of their frustrating labors as pedagogues. It arose from their ambivalence toward the Reformation itself, from the painful sense conveyed to them in the 1520s and 1530s that somewhere the movement had taken a wrong turn. Luther himself blamed Thomas Müntzer for the missed direction. "Müntzer did us great damage in the beginning," he said of his great antagonist. "The work of the gospel was going so well, but along came Müntzer and spoiled it all."[1] More plausibly, Aurifaber charged in the 1560s that "politicians, lawyers, and courtiers" were taking over from preachers and theologians, "directing religious matters like worldly affairs"[2] and building an institutional shell without Christian substance. After the middle of the sixteenth century little time seemed

300

left to set things right. A mood of foreboding invades the pronouncements of Protestant churchmen, and a sense of having to make haste
"in these dangerous, wicked, and last days of the world."[3] As the signs
pointing to doomsday multiplied and the evidence mounted that men
would not listen to warnings, the reformers' innate inclination to expect the worst became a dominant strain in their reading of events.
This reaction, in turn, drained them of their energies and kept them
from responding imaginatively to the deteriorating situation.

This mental set is certain to have contributed to the reformers'
failure to organize their pedagogical program as systematically, and
to administer it as effectively, as conditions demanded. Dismissing the
proposition that men's nature might be perfected or even substantially
improved, they stopped well short of actualizing the transforming
possibilities offered by the doctrine of malleability.[4] They affirmed the
plasticity of the human mind but failed to implement a rigorous process
of conditioning it. Instead they relied on the principle of malleability merely to sanction the disciplinary measures that were always their
most immediate concern. Surveillance and restraint mattered more
urgently than amelioration, which could come to pass only in a future
perceived less in concrete social and political terms than in accordance
with eschatological expectations. But even for the limited purpose of
social control, indoctrination proceeded cautiously and halfheartedly,
far more timid in its execution than one would imagine from the tone
of tough-sounding official declarations. Psychological tools were available for leaving a lasting mark on pupils' minds and characters: the
sense of shame, for example, of which pedagogues might have made
an effective goad had they played upon it in appropriate settings such
as groups of youngsters seated in school and catechism class, or parishioners gathered in church. The public catechism examination offered
an inviting forum for promoting changes in patterns of thought and
behavior; but despite its use everywhere, this institutionalized ritual
failed to suffuse society with evangelical ideals. Recent experiences
indicate that peer pressure generated by regular gatherings of small
groups is likely to work where it is shrewdly and unflinchingly employed.[5] The age of the Reformation, too, produced some evidence
that the social matrix could be mobilized to exert a formative influence
on the individual. Calvinist regimes had some success with this technique. But Lutherans seem to have lacked the temper, or the stomach,
for such measures. They had opportunities for creating social pressure,
but they failed to turn them into a molding process. They insisted that
everyone in society should be subjected to internal and external coercion, but they shunned police-state methods (for which they lacked the
means, in any case) and treated with resigned tolerance the widespread deviation from their exalted norms.

This lack of resoluteness in the face of general defiance cannot be understood without taking into account the extraordinary tenacity of popular resistance to imposed doctrines and observances. The strength of this opposition has been consistently underestimated in traditional interpretations of the Protestant Reformation. To sixteenth-century theologians, who were well aware of it, it was a source of lasting anguish and daily dismay. Refusing to let political and church powers browbeat them into abandoning age-old folk practices and folk notions, people waged passive resistance by staying away from church and ignoring its teachings. Only in the rarest of instances were authorities successful in overcoming their subjects' tendency to withdraw. Lacking respect for the ways of popular belief, churchmen felt no compassion for the religious needs of ordinary people and gained no understanding of their disinterest in the formulas of the official creed. Insensitive to the appeal of religious experiences and expressions differing from their own orthodoxy, they treated deep-seated customs with contempt and intolerance.

One should not, of course, blame sixteenth-century ecclesiastics for having been blind to the spiritual and ethical merits of a folk piety whose worth has only recently begun to be appreciated.[6] Where we today see a rich blend of intuitions and observations affording the devotee a satisfying and, one supposes, useful integration of nature and individual life, Protestant clerics noted only obscure and clandestine superstitions. Beliefs we now recognize as the ideological cement of fraternal and kin associations in village and town they rejected as shameful symptoms of ignorance and depravity. They condemned time-honored traditions as relics of an outlived pagan and Catholic past, a body of notions to be eradicated in favor of the uplifting precepts of the new Protestant state churches. Given this lack of comprehension on the one hand, and their unquestioning self-righteousness on the other, it is no wonder that churchmen could not gauge, much less conquer, the massive opposition thwarting their policies almost from the beginning.[7] The urban academic's ingrained contempt for peasantry and rural life seems to have made Protestant churchmen obdurate to the physical constraints defining daily existence in small town and countryside. Visitation protocols cited instance after instance of the burdens and perils faced by peasants nearly everywhere: forced labor on Sundays, lack of adequate clothing against cold weather, farmhouses burglarized by vagrants while occupants attended church.[8] But to superintendents and theologians these hardships neither excused nor explained the public's indifference to church and doctrine. Nor could they appreciate the vexation of villagers and small-town dwellers over the reimposition of old tithe payments added to new fiscal responsibilities for the upkeep of churches, parsonages, and schools. The resentment caused by these exactions mounted in the course of the sixteenth century. If the events of the 1520s had kindled in people's minds hopes for a change, the collapse of the peasant rebellions and the suppression of urban uprisings had stifled these expectations: a point driven home by strong-arm intervention carried out by all governments, menacingly if ineffectually.[9] Ignorant of the social and psychological functions played in people's lives by ancient cults, time-honored associations, traditional beliefs, and received ways of coping with daily existence, the Lutheran clergy tried with a heavy hand to suppress these vestiges of a rejected past and supplant them with a mandatory and uniform set of doctrines.

Against this alien code, ordinary people maintained a vigorous religious subculture[10] that seems to have gained strength and resilience in proportion to the efforts of a combative Protestant establishment to replace the permissive climate of medieval Catholicism with an authoritarian creed.[11] The deep current of popular life nourishing this subterranean religion was beyond the theologian's grasp, the preacher's appeal, or the visitor's power to compel. Protestant visitation protocols convey a marvelously rich and detailed picture of this grass-roots piety, the operative faith of rural and urban folk. Lutheran churchmen had good reason to mistrust this autochthonous religion. They fulminated against it as an "unchristian, pagan, idolatrous, frivolous, fictitious and unfounded, lying, deceiving, seductive, ungodly, devilish" cult,[12] an overt breach of the commandments and the Apostles' Creed.[13] They also instructed visitors to probe in every parish for soothsayers, cunning women, crystal gazers, casters of spells, witches, and other practitioners of forbidden arts. Yearly interrogations turned up massive evidence of a proliferating undergrowth of magic practices flourishing amid the doctrines and ceremonies of official Christianity. Lay people rarely gave away much information about this secret level of their private lives.[14] But clerics talked freely of it, venting their frustration with the impossible job of sifting superstitious pagan and medieval ingredients from evangelical elements in the religious practice of their flock. The mixture must have been maddening to conscientious pastors. People said the Lord's Prayer while casting lead to tell fortunes.[15] They gathered occult substances on Christian holidays and invoked the names of the Father, the Son, and the Holy Ghost to protect chickens from hawks and humans from the evil eye.[16] They rang church bells against storms and hail,[17] addressed Christian prayers to the devil, used altar vessels to locate missing objects,[18] and crossed the border to Catholic regions where obliging priests blessed their herbs, roots, potions, and wands.[19] *Segensprechen*—pronouncing charms and incantations, making signs and casting spells—was carried on with the use of Christian and ancient Germanic formulas. Village healers cured cattle of worms by spitting three times in appeal to the Trinity.[20] Wise women called on God to bless the crystal in which they saw the face of a thief.[21] They concocted infusions of baptismal water against bed-wetting[22] and chanted gospel verses while curing or inflicting an injury.[23] "There is no limit here to the use of superstitious spells, both among those who say them and those who request them to be said."[24] "Charms and spells are the custom here."[25] "Many women hereabouts say incantations."[26] These are typical comments made by pastors to visitation officials. During an inspection of the county of Nassau-Wiesbaden in 1594, visitors discovered that

> the use of spells [*das Segensprechen*] is so widespread among the people here that no man or woman begins, undertakes, does, or refrains from doing, desires or hopes for anything without using some special charm, spell, incantation, or other such heathenish medium. To wit: when they are in pangs of childbirth, when an infant is picked up or laid down (to guard him against sorcery), when a child is taken to be baptized (at which time they bind amulets or bread crumbs into the baby's swaddling cloths to ward off enchantment), when cattle are driven out or brought home or are lost in the fields, when they shut their windows in the evening, and so on; also against all manner of sickness or misfortune. Whenever something has been mislaid, when a person feels sickly or a cow dries up, they make straightway for the soothsayer . . . to find out who has stolen the object or put a bad spell on the animal, and to procure from him some charm to use against the offender. All people hereabouts engage in these unchristian beliefs. They practice them with familiar and strange words, with names, rhymes, and especially with the names of God, the holy Trinity, some special angels, the Virgin Mary, the twelve apostles and the three kings, also with numerous saints, with the wounds of Christ and his seven last words, . . . with gospel verses and certain prayers. These they mumble secretly or openly, or they write them on scraps of paper and give them to be eaten or worn as amulets. They also make outlandish signs and gestures and do strange things with roots, herbs, mandrakes, and Saint-John's-wort. Every action has its special day, hour, and secret place. In their signs and spells they favor the number three. And they do all this to inflict harm or do good to men, women, animals, and crops, to make things better or worse, to bring good or bad luck on themselves and their fellow creatures.[27]

All over Germany visitation protocols record such phenomena. "Every inhabitant here goes to the wise woman to obtain her help and counsel," reported a visitor from a district in Brandenburg.[28] A Saxon cleric complained of "an old woman here with a crystal, and people run to her whenever something troubles them."[29] "A young fellow appeared here [the city of Meissen, in 1598] last summer, who let it be known that he was the disciple of a famous magician. And people from all over the city went in droves to consult him."[30]

With this underground network of wizards, crystal-gazers, sooth-sayers, and wise women the church competed for the faith and alle-giance of its flock. It was an unequal struggle.[31] LeRoy Ladurie's expla-nation of this "surge of obscurantism" as a result, in part, of pastoral neglect of isolated rural communities will not work for Germany.[32] Few peasant hamlets were beyond the reach of Lutheran state churches, whose officials regarded the survival of occult practices as a spur to intervention. But their most intimidating threats went unheeded. Sometimes offenders were fined or punished, more often they were merely cautioned to turn to their parish priests rather than their cun-ning people. They promised to comply, but soon returned to their old habits. Rarely could authorities discover concrete details about these obscure cults. "We asked the local peasants if they knew of any magi-cians, but they fell silent as soon as we put the question. They never re-veal anything, no matter how hard we press them."[33] Clearly, people believed in the effectiveness of spells and talismans. So did their clerical mentors. The latter knew that occult lore was based on idolatry and superstition, but experience told them that it worked. Its means were unnatural and its effects offended the rational mind;[34] but with the devil acting as instigator (as they saw it), nothing was impossible.[35] This admission contributed to their resigned pessimism. The general devotion to ancient cults, and the perseverance of people in defending what they regarded as traditional rights and customs, locked Protes-tant church authorities in an endless battle for the loyalty and trust of their flocks.[36]

In waging this struggle for people's minds, the Protestant estab-lishment was severely hampered by two processes gradually trans-forming the official religion and its institutions. First, creed and church were falling victim to a process of bureaucratization that dried up the movement's original appeal and channeled it into routinized pro-cedures. Second, Protestant theologians accommodated their teach-ings to the social groups dominating the milieu in which their church functioned. Both developments contributed to the erosion of the popular base.

The takeover of the Reformation by rulers and their agents—Auri-faber's lawyers, courtiers, and politicians—was the inevitable con-comitant of the running down of the movement's early hyperactive and emotionally charged heroic phase. The consolidation resulting from the centralizing drives and the passion for achieving uniformity, shared by all governments, widened the distance separating plain people from the official creed and its ministers. This development has been commented upon by some recent Reformation scholars, who have come to suspect that, after the middle of the century, formal religion as it was perceived by the populace served the interests of rulers rather than of their subjects,[37] while Protestant theology must have seemed to benefit ecclesiastical bureaucrats rather than ordinary members of the Christian community. Compulsory conformity to stripped-down observances and rigid doctrines was replacing the voluntary devotions of early Protestantism[38] and the free-wheeling participatory rites of late medieval Catholicism.[39] Mandates and decrees, surveillance and inspection tried to bring everyone to heel. This uninviting attempt to substitute uniformity, routine, and obedience for autonomy in the exercise of one's religion is sure to have breathed new life into traditional forms of popular piety.

The clergy's struggle against these independent cults was not helped by far-reaching changes affecting the pastorate itself as a result of its incorporation in state churches. Although intended to improve the effectiveness of clerical performance, these changes actually widened the gulf between preachers and their auditors. To the extent that the ecclesiastical establishment turned professional and efficient, it isolated itself from the public. As clergymen came to be better trained, more literate, better-spoken, they tended to talk above the heads of their flock (in "courtly and ornate language [*höfflichen und zierlichen reden*]" as a Rhineland superintendent complained in 1607).[40] Coming to their posts from faraway towns and universities, taking their places in a homogeneous caste and assuming the style of a bureaucracy, they grew ever more distant from their parishioners, who must have perceived in the agents of the Protestant church a modernizing force bent on converting them willy-nilly from their ancient ways and habits to a bookish orthodoxy resting on the virtue of conformity. Resistance was implicit in this conflict of interests, and the visitation reports of Lutheran states show the hardening of the mutual alienation resulting from it. In different circumstances Lutheran lay people showed stalwart partisanship; this fact has been noted earlier. Where evangelical congregations had to persevere in hostile environments, as in Catholic Bavaria, they seemed committed to their faith and informed about its principles.[41] In adversity, knowledge and loyalty mattered.[42] But where people had been drawn into the safe and pallid routine of an officially sanctioned orthodoxy, their interest in formal religion quickly cooled. Visitors rediscovered this fact of ecclesiastical life whenever they confronted a new generation of young adults.

Alienation was further exacerbated by the class-oriented direction of the Lutheran message. In their approach to learners, theologians treated all ranks of the laity equally as *Kinder*—docile children to be taught and shaped. Not so when they defined the substance of what they taught. There was nothing egalitarian about the social ethic of Christian education. In formulating their doctrines, Lutherans allowed their model of the desirable Christian citizen to become the paradigm of their pedagogical program, thereby creating a sharp and lasting division among their auditors. As disseminated in sermons, catechisms, tracts, hymns, Bible comments, and housefather books, the Protestant message was pitched to the solid burgher. From his life and work it derived its values and images. Its religious thrust, and its utility in solving problems, instilling confidence, and mitigating misfortune, was best suited to the stable householder. As for the great multitude of men and women, they could have found little survival value in doctrines whose framers made no attempt to integrate their precepts with the practical needs and aspirations of plain people.

Lutheran theologians seem to have been oblivious to the limitations built into their message by its ties to a single segment of society. They could suggest no steps toward an amelioration of the many hardships that made it difficult for poor people to meet their religious obligations and gave them no grounds for showing devotion to a creed that, while it denounced drinking, fornication, and the casting of spells, condoned destitution and insecurity as an inescapable and appropriate condition of the common man's earthly existence. Preaching their message indiscriminately, as though it related equally to all, Lutheran churchmen were left confounded by the slack response it evoked. The modern observer is less puzzled. Its narrow social appeal severely handicapped Protestantism in its ability to touch the minds and lives of all Christians. Under these circumstances, indoctrination could scarcely have achieved the hoped-for universal transformation of the individual and society. Thus the pedagogical endeavor failed. Its breakdown brought to an end the most ambitious, radical, far-reaching, and fervently pursued hope of the Protestant Reformation.

Of course the pedagogical undertaking may not be the best vantage point for judging the achievements of Protestantism. If it was the objective of the Reformation to complete the breaking up of the medieval church, it succeeded. If its goal was to rationalize ecclesiastical administration and coordinate it with the goals of the early modern state, it definitely succeeded. If it sought to channel the religious energies of an intellectual elite, it was in large part successful. But if it was its central purpose to make people—all people—think, feel, and act as Christians, to imbue them with a Christian mind-set, motivational drive, and way of life, it failed. This assertion may seem to suggest a revisionist thesis, but it is not one with which I started work on this book.[43] I did not know, as I began my studies, whether, and to what extent, the Lutheran Reformation succeeded or failed in its effort to convert people to its beliefs. My study of the sources has convinced me, however, that the burden of proof ought now at last to be placed where it belongs: upon those who claim, or imply, or tacitly assume that the Reformation in Germany aroused a widespread, meaningful, and lasting response to its message. Before 1530 this may well have been the case, although even then the resonance was probably confined to a segment of the urban population. Later in the century one finds mostly apathy. The evidence of the visitation records leaves no escape from this conclusion. But this evidence has not been assimilated by Reformation historians; nor has it until now been linked to the reformers' early reliance on the power of pedagogy to effect a transformation in their followers. Only when this body of information has been taken into account, and its implications fully explored, are we likely to gain a balanced understanding of the Reformation and its reception in society.

LIST OF ABBREVIATIONS

BHM	Bayerisches Hauptstaatsarchiv München
B.S.Landsh.	Bayerisches Staatsarchiv Landshut
B.S.Münch.	Bayerisches Staatsarchiv München
CR	C. E. Bretschneider, ed., *Philippi Melanchthonis opera* . . . (*Corpus Reformatorum*).
E.-L.K.A.Dresd.	Archiv des evangelisch-lutherischen Landeskirchenamt Sachsens (Dresden)
H.S.Hann.	Hauptstaatsarchiv Hannover
Hess.H.S.Wiesb.	Hessisches Hauptstaatsarchiv Wiesbaden
LAS	Landeskirchliches Archiv Stuttgart
L.K.A.Braun.	Landeskirchliches Archiv Braunschweig
L.S.-H.	Landesarchiv Schleswig-Holstein
LW	*Luther's Works*, ed. Jaroslav Pelikan and H. T. Lehmann (Saint Louis, Mo., 1955–)
Mertz	Georg Mertz, *Das Schulwesen der deutschen Reformation* (Heidelberg, 1902).
MGP	*Monumenta Germaniae Paedagogica* (Berlin, 1886–)
N.S.S.Old.	Niedersächsisches Staatsarchiv Oldenburg
OEMF	Ordinariatsarchiv des Erzbistums München und Freising
Pallas	Karl Pallas, ed., *Die Registraturen der Kirchenvisitationen im ehemals sächsischen Kurkreise*, Geschichtsquellen der Provinz Sachsen, vols. 41–41[5] (Halle, 1906–14).
Reu	Johann Michael Reu, *Quellen zur Geschichte des kirchlichen Unterrichts in der evangelischen Kirche Deutschlands zwischen 1530 und 1600. Vol. 1. Quellen zur Geschichte des Katechismus-Unterrichts* (Gütersloh, 1911).
S.Bamb.	Staatsarchiv Bamberg
S.Cob.	Bayerisches Staatsarchiv Coburg
S.Dresd.	Staatsarchiv Dresden
S.Hamb.	Staatsarchiv Hamburg
S.Magd.	Staatsarchiv Magdeburg
S.Neub.D.	Bayerisches Staatsarchiv Neuburg an der Donau

S.Nürn.	Staatsarchiv Nürnberg
S.Weim.	Staatsarchiv Weimar
Sdt.Augsb.	Stadtarchiv Augsburg
Sdt.Cob.	Stadtarchiv Coburg
Sdt.Hann.	Stadtarchiv Hannover
Sdt.Leipz.	Stadtarchiv Leipzig
Sdt.Nürn.	Stadtarchiv Nürnberg
Sdt.Ulm	Stadtarchiv Ulm
Sehling	Emil Sehling, ed., *Die evangelischen Kirchenordnungen des 16. Jahrhunderts*, vols. 1–5 (Leipzig, 1902–13); vols. 6 ff. continued by the *Institut für evangelisches Kirchenrecht der evangelischen Kirche in Deutschland zu Göttingen* (Tübingen, 1955–).
Strassb.A.V.	Strasbourg. Archives de la ville
SVfRg	*Schriften des Vereins für Reformationsgeschichte* (Halle/Gütersloh, 1883 ff.)
Vormbaum	Reinhold Vormbaum, ed., *Die evangelischen Schulordnungen des sechszehnten Jahrhunderts*, vol. 1 (Gütersloh, 1860).
WA	*D. Martin Luthers Werke: Kritische Gesamtausgabe* (Weimar, 1883 ff.; reprinted 1964–8).
WHS	Württembergisches Hauptstaatsarchiv Stuttgart

NOTES

CHAPTER 1

1. To mention only the major synoptic works devoting all or much of their attention to Germany: Karl Hartfelder, "Erziehung und Unterricht im Zeitalter des Humanismus"; Ernst Gundert, "Die Reformation," both in *Geschichte der Erziehung . . .* ed. K. A. Schmidt et al., vol. 2, part 2 (Stuttgart, 1892); Friedrich Paulsen, *Geschichte des gelehrten Unterrichts auf den deutschen Schulen und Universitäten . . .* , 3d ed. (Leipzig, 1919); Georg Mertz, *Das Schulwesen der deutschen Reformation* (Heidelberg, 1902), hereafter cited as Mertz, *Schulwesen;* Karl Schmidt, *Geschichte der Pädagogik dargestellt in weltgeschichtlicher Entwicklung,* 3d ed. Vol. 3. *Die Geschichte der Pädagogik von Luther bis Pestalozzi,* ed. Richard Lange (Köthen, 1883). For Europe generally, cf. Josef Dolch, *Lehrplan des Abendlandes: Zweieinhalb Jahrtausende seiner Geschichte* (Ratingen, 1965). For references to more specific works, see the notes to this and later chapters.

2. There is, of course, a controversy on this point. For opposing arguments see the books by Paulsen and Karl Schmidt cited in the preceding note, continued in Fritz Blättner, *Das Gymnasium: Aufgaben der höheren Schule in Geschichte und Gegenwart* (Heidelberg, 1960), pp. 31 ff.; also Ivar Asheim, *Glaube und Erziehung bei Luther* (Heidelberg, 1961), pp. 74 ff.

3. For the controversy on this see Heinrich Heppe, *Geschichte des deutschen Volksschulwesens,* 5 vols. (Gotha, 1858–60; reprinted Hildesheim and New York, 1971), vol. 1; Gunnar Thiele, "Zur Entstehung der deutschen Volksschule," *Zeitschr. Gesch. Erziehung u. d. Unterrichts* 38, no. 3/4 (1938): 185–205; William J. Wright, "The Impact of the Reformation on Hessian Education," *Church History* 44, no. 2 (June 1975): 182–98.

4. On this point, see my discussion in chap. 9.

5. On Luther's views on education, see chap. 2.

6. For older literature on this question of failure cf. pp. 30–31 of my article "Success and Failure in the German Reformation," *Past and Present* 67 (May 1975): 30–63.

7. On this point cf. Luther's quarrel with Karlstadt over the 1521–22 changes in Wittenberg: James Samuel Preus, *Carlstadt's Ordinaciones and Luther's Liberty: A Study of the Wittenberg Movement, 1521–22* (Cambridge, Mass., 1974).

8. *Ordnung eines gemeinen Kastens der Gemeine zu Leisnig* (1523), *WA,* 12:1–30.

9. Asheim, *Glaube und Erziehung,* pp. 267 f.

10. From a letter to the municipal council of Hamburg, written 1526: *Von dem christlichen Glauben und rechten guten Werken. . . . An die ehrenreiche Stadt Hamburg* (I use Nuremberg, 1527), p. 245.

11. *Auslegung deutsch des Vaterunsers* (1519), *WA,* 6:12.

12. Asheim, *Glaube und Erziehung,* pp. 28 ff. and 43–66, examines meticulously and with copious quotations from the sources Luther's statements on the family and education, particularly the analogy of paterfamilias and political ruler. See also chap. 6, below.

13. *Eine Predigt, das man Kinder zur Schule halten solle* (1530), *WA,* 30², passim.

14. These have been collected by Friedrich Roth, *Der Einfluss des Humanismus und der Reformation auf das gleichzeitige Erziehungs- und Schulwesen bis in die ersten Jahrzehnte nach Melanchthons Tod, SVfRg,* no. 60 (Halle, 1898), p. 25.

15. WA, 12:25.

16. *An den christlichen Adel deutscher Nation* (1520), WA, 6:461.

17. Roth, *Der Einfluss des Humanismus,* pp. 25-34.

18. Paulsen, *Geschichte des gelehrten Unterrichts,* pp. 195 ff. and 629 ff. cites figures to document the shocking drop in the number of matriculations and promotions at universities from 1522 on. Paulsen's tendentious and polemical book must, of course, be used with caution. But the decline of German institutions of learning in the mid-1520s is a matter of general agreement. Cf. Friedrich Falk, "Luthers Schrift an die Ratsherren der deutschen Städte und ihre geschichtliche Wirkung auf die deutsche Schule," *Luther-Jahrbuch* 19 (1937): 55-114.

19. *An die Burgermeyster und Radherren allerley Stedte* . . . (1524), WA, 15:28. This sentiment is echoed by nearly all other contemporary observers.

20. Ibid., pp. 32-34.

21. This principle was, in any case, in conflict with a time-honored conviction that home was in fact the worst place for a child's upbringing. See chaps. 3 and 6 for discussions of this point.

22. Wilhelm Maurer, *Der junge Melanchthon,* 2 vols. (Göttingen, 1967-69), 2:230 ff. and 415 ff. argues convincingly that Melanchthon suffered an intellectual and moral crisis during the Wittenberg disturbances while Luther was away. He despaired of his own ability to supply the needed leadership and came to recognize his true vocation as that of scholar and teacher. Education appeared to him the only antidote to the freewheeling spiritualism of the Wittenberg radicals and the willful misinterpretation, as he saw it, of peasant leaders. Guido Kisch, *Melanchthons Rechts- und Soziallehre* (Berlin, 1967), chap. 4, shows how Melanchthon's reaction to the disturbances also prompted him to embrace Roman law as a source of authority and an expression of the divine will.

23. "Dadurch die leut zu frieden und erbarkeyt erzogen werden"; *Widder die artickel der bawrschafft* (1525) in *Melanchthons Werke in Auswahl,* ed. Robert Stupperich, 1 (Gütersloh, 1951): 214. The appendix to this tract, which contains the quoted phrase, was written after the peasant defeat.

24. *Ratio scholae Norembergae nuper institutae* (1526), in Karl Hartfelder, *Melanchthoniana paedagogica: Eine Ergänzung zu den Werken Melanchthons*... (Leipzig, 1892), pp. 6 ff.

25. *Epitome renovatae ecclesiasticae doctrinae* (1524, written for Philip of Hesse), in *Melanchthons Werke in Auswahl,* 1:184. Cf. Luther's "Das tolle volck" in *An die Ratsherren* (1524), WA, 15:32.

26. Maurer, *Der junge Melanchthon,* 2:462-63.

27. *An die Burgermeyster und Radherren allerley Stedte* . . . (1524), WA, 15:33.

28. Ibid., 15:44.

29. Luther to Elector Johann, 22 June 1526, WA, Br., no. 1052 (4:134).

30. *Eine Predigt, dass man Kinder zur Schule halten solle* (1530), WA, 30²: 586-87.

31. Ibid., p. 532.

32. From Luther's preface to Justus Menius's *An die hochgeborene Fürstin, Fraw Sibilla Hertzogin zu Sachsen, Oeconomia christiana* . . . (Wittenberg, 1529), Aiv r. Also WA, 30²:62.

33. WA, 30²:61

34. Ibid., p. 62.

35. *Eine Predigt, dass man Kinder zur Schule halten solle* (1530), WA, 30²:582-85.

36. Ibid., p. 586.

37. Ambrosius Moibanus, *Catechismus* (Wittenberg, 1535) in Reu, 2 (2):737-38.

38. Christoph Vischer, *Bericht aus Gottes Wort* . . . *wie man junge Fürsten und Herrn auffziehen soll* . . . (n.p., 1573), dii r.

39. This is the argument of Steven Ozment, *The Reformation in the Cities* (New Haven, 1975), pp.61-67.

40. Ludwig Hänselmann, ed., *Bugenhagens Kirchenordnung für die Stadt Braunschweig* (Wolfenbüttel, 1885), pp. 41-43.

41. Ibid., pp. 44-45.

42. See, for instance, the texts of the Braunschweig municipal *Kirchenordnungen* of 1535 and 1596, printed in *MGP*, vol. 1 (Berlin, 1886), nos. 9 and 21; and the Lübeck Schulordnungen of 1555 and 1584 (or 1585), given in Heinrich Heppe, *Geschichte des deutschen Volksschulwesens*, 5:293-98.

43. In the final version of the Braunschweig constitution it comes second, after the section on baptism. But it stands as the first section in Bugenhagen's original draft, as it does in the official texts of the Hamburg and Lübeck constitutions.

44. *Eine Predigt, dass man Kinder zur Schule halten solle* (1530), *WA*, 30²:520.

45. Hänselmann, *Bugenhagens Kirchenordnung für . . . Braunschweig*, p. 45.

46. From Luther's preface to Stephan Klingebeil's *Von Priester Ehe* (1528) *WA*, 24:530. Cf. chap. 8 below.

47. See his letter to Elector Johann of Saxony of 20 May 1530, *WA*, Br. 5, no. 1572.

48. Cf. note 35 above.

49. For a careful, if somewhat hair-splitting, consideration of this entire question, see Werner Reininghaus, *Elternstand, Obrigkeit und Schule bei Luther*, Pädagogische Forschungen, no. 38 (Heidelberg, 1969).

50. Maurer, *Der junge Melanchthon*, 2:463. Asheim, *Glaube und Erziehung*, pp. 67-68 creates a conundrum by asking whether Lutheran schools were "secular" or Christian institutions. Is Luther the "prophet of the state school" (H. Böhmer), or did he limit the power of secular authorities to economic and organizational tasks, leaving internal matters to the spiritual authority? This is, of course, a purely academic distinction. Luther himself blurred the division between secular and ecclesiastical competences, and—in any case—events soon passed him by. What Luther meant in matters of education (the subject of Asheim's excellent book) has little to do with what governments did after ca. 1530.

51. I argue this view for the city of Nuremberg and the circumstances of its adoption of Lutheranism in 1525 in "Protestant Dogma and City Government: The Case of Nuremberg," *Past and Present* 36 (April 1967): 38-58.

52. Quoted in Klaus Leder, *Kirche und Jugend in Nürnberg und seinem Landgebiet 1400 bis 1800*, Einzelarbeiten aus der Kirchengeschichte Bayerns, vol. 52 (Neustadt an der Aisch, 1973), p. 60. This was in 1531.

53. "Die oberkeyt als gemeyner vatter"; from a memorandum by theologians of the university of Rostock to Dukes Albrecht and Ulrich of Mecklenburg, 1556, quoted in H. Schnell, *Das Unterrichtswesen der Grossherzogtümer Mecklenburg-Schwerin und Strelitz*, *MGP*, vol. 38 (Berlin, 1907), p. 255.

54. Urban Rhegius, *Catechesis illustriss. principi Francisco Otthoni . . . Brunswicensium Luneburgensiumque Duci puero . . . et toti scholae ducali dicata* (Braunschweig, 1540). I quote from the German translation (Braunschweig, 1545), 15v.

55. From the *Kirchenordnung* of Gengenbach (1538), ed. Ernst-Wilhelm Kohls, *Evangelische Bewegung und Kirchenordnung: Studien und Quellen zur Reformationsgeschichte der Reichsstadt Gengenbach* (Karlsruhe, 1966), p. 29.

56. Ibid., p. 35.

57. Caspar Huberinus, *Der kleine Catechismus . . .* (Augsburg, 1544), Ci v.–Cii v.

58. Not only in Protestant Germany. See the Bavarian school documents printed in Georg Lurz, ed., *Mittelschulgeschichtliche Dokumente Altbayerns*, vol. 1, *MGP*, vol. 41, (Berlin, 1907).

59. A comprehensive, but far from complete, list of these *Schulordnungen* is given in chronological order by Mertz, *Schulwesen*, pp. 162-65. The texts are found, for the most part, in Reinhold Vormbaum, ed., *Die evangelischen Schulordnungen . . .*, vol. 1 (Gütersloh, 1860).

60. The trend continued into the seventeenth century. For a typical example of such a document, see the *Schulmethodus* (1642) of Duke Ernst the Pious of Gotha, printed in Vormbaum, 2:295-345.

61. This comparison is made by Eduard Spranger, *Zur Geschichte der deutschen Volksschule* (Heidelberg, 1949)), p. 33.

62. The *Schulordnung* was published with the *Kirchenordnung* of 1559 and also separately that same year, with additions. In the following description of the Württemberg *Schulordnung* I cite from the edition in Vormbaum, 1:68-165.

63. For punishment provisions see ibid., p. 95. For further discussion of this subject, see chap. 9 below.

64. Visitation records contain frequent complaints from parents about harsh punishments teachers inflicted on their children. They also make it clear that parents did not stand for this treatment. E.g., visitation in Württemberg, 1585: LAS, Synodusprotokolle 1585, 49r: town of Bolingen: a good schoolmaster, but "mit der züchtigung der kinder gar zu hart, also dass die burger ire kinder aus der schule thon. Pfarrer und geistlicher verwalter haben selbs ire kinder aus der schul genommen."

65. These provisions touched only Latin school teachers. Instructors for German schools were installed without corresponding ceremonies.

66. The *forma obligationis*, to be signed by parent or guardian in the presence of an official, is given in Vormbaum, 1:105-6.

67. For a painstaking school-by-school description of the Latin schools throughout the duchy, see the *Geschichte des humanistischen Schulwesens in Württemberg*, issued by the *Württembergische Kommission für Landesgeschichte* (Stuttgart, 1912-18), vols. 2-3. Unlike most other territorial rulers, Duke Christoph left the properties and revenues of former Catholic monasteries in place but ordered them employed to finance the new schools. Only five of the original thirteen *Klosterschulen* were left by 1599. See Rudolf W. Keck, *Geschichte der mittleren Schule in Württemberg, Veröffentlichungen der Kommission für geschichtliche Landeskunde in Baden-Württemberg, Reihe B: Forschungen*, vol. 47 (Stuttgart, 1968), p. 41.

68. *Instruktion, was die Räte und Abgeordneten . . . zu tun haben* (1536), printed in Eugen Schmid, *Geschichte des Volksschulwesens in Altwürttemberg* (Stuttgart, 1927), p. 8.

69. Girls' schools were favored by most reformers for reasons everyone assumed were obvious, but which were nonetheless set out explicitly. E.g., Justus Menius in the preface to his catechism of 1532 (in Reu, 2 [2]:166): "Denn obwol den weibern in der gemeine zu leren nicht geziemet, so wird dennoch das niemand leugnen können, das ein fromme, verstendige, und gottselige hausmutter iren Kindlin im hause zu christlicher erkenntnis und zucht . . . Überaus wol dienen kann. Und solche hausmutter muss man freilich von jugend auf in schulen ebensowol auferziehen als ander leut und geschickte mannspersonen." Bugenhagen championed the same principle in his *Schulordnungen;* cf. Julius Robert Rost, *Die pädagogische Bedeutung Bugenhagens* (Leipzig-Reudnitz, 1890), pp. 26-27.

70. This assertion is based on my examination of visitation records in WHS, A 281, Büschel 46-49, and in the LAS, Synodusprotokolle (no other signature) for 1581 ff. See also the list of existing German schools compiled for the years 1581 and 1600 in Eugen Schmid, *Geschichte des Volksschulwesens in Altwürttemberg*, pp. 31-32, 35-36. By 1600 more than 400 *Orte* (i.e., villages, large villages, and market villages) had schools, as opposed to only 150 in 1559.

71. See my discussion of this question in chap. 12.

72. Cf. *Articul, dorauff die Land Visitatores fragen sollen*, issued by Duke Christoph in 1562, WHS, A 38, Büschel 8.

73. I have studied documentation for the reigns of Dukes Christoph (1550-68) and Ludwig (1568-93) in the WHS, especially A284: *Kirchenrat und Spezialakten* organized according to localities.

74. For another such example of direct control by a ruler over the appointment of local schoolmasters, see L.K.A. Braun., Voges 132 and 159: correspondence between Duke Julius of Braunschweig-Wolfenbüttel and the magistrates of towns in his realm.

75. To cite one typical case: WHS, A284. Heidenheim Kl.FV.B213.

76. E.g., WHS, A38, B9.

77. E.g., WHS, A63, B21.

78. Martini's memorandum stands as a preamble to the printed *Schulordnung*. I use the edition by Karl Meyer, ed., "Die Schulordnung des Gymnasiums der freien Reichsstadt Nordhausen a. Harz vom Jahre 1583," *Mitteilungen der Gesellschaft für deutsche Erziehungs- und Schulgeschichte* 2 (1892): 66-73.

79. This came into existence very slowly in many territories. In Pfalz-Neuburg, in the Upper Palatinate, for example, Elector Ottheinrich established Lutheranism in 1542 and reorganized the school system in 1558, but not until the beginning of the seventeenth century was the number of particular schools in the territory increased significantly. Cf. Georg Rückert, "Beiträge zur Geschichte der katholischen Volksschulen im K. Bezirksamt Dillingen," *Jahrb. katholischen Vereins Dillingen* 29 (1916): 93-95.

80. In some places the smaller particular schools, limited to one or two forms, were called *Trivialschulen*.

81. For a list of gymnasiums and paedagogiums established by Protestant governments in Germany, see Mertz, pp. 192–204. In some places the gymnasium was attached to the university (e.g., Marburg); in others to particular schools (e.g., Stuttgart). Some gymnasiums were independent (e.g., Gandersheim). The *Gymnasium academicum* or *Gymnasium illustre* (also called *Academia, Athenaeum,* or *Lyceum*) represented a compromise between gymnasium and university, offering not only the regular gymnasium subjects, but also university-level lectures in philosophy, medicine, jurisprudence, and theology. For a history of the gymnasium in Germany see Fritz Blättner, *Das Gymnasium* . . . (Heidelberg, 1960).

82. Examples: the *Klosterschulen* of Württemberg mentioned above, and the *Landesschulen,* or *Fürstenschulen,* founded by Maurice of Saxony in 1543. The abundant documentary material concerning the housing, feeding, clothing, and general treatment of pupils in these schools makes it clear that they constituted a privileged elite. Two examples: *Verzeichnis, Underhaltung der acht schüler* [in St. Georgen *Klosterschule*] (1576) WHS. A284. St. Georgen Kl.V und FV. B187. *Ordnung, wie es mit Kuchin und keller . . . im Kloster Blawbeüren . . . gehalten werden soll* (1576), WHS, A284 Blaubeuren Kl.V und FV. B356. All menus, etc., were read by the duke himself and signed by him to indicate his approval. Cf. Heppe, *Volksschulwesen,* passim, especially 1:11–12, 24–30. The discussion of German schools is confused by historians' use of the word *Volksschule,* which begins to appear only in the eighteenth century.

84. Friedrich Michael Schiele, "Luther und das Luthertum in ihrer Bedeutung für die Geschichte der Schule und der Erziehung," *Preussische Jahrbücher* 132 (1908): 381–95, especially p. 390; Gunnar Thiele, "Zur Entstehung der deutschen Volksschule," *Zeitschr. Gesch. Erziehung Unterrichts* 28, no. 3/4 (1938): 181–205, especially p. 200. For the bibliography of the debate, see Wright, *Impact of the Reformation,* pp. 182–98. Wright himself adds nothing new to the discussion. For the entire medieval background to the German schools of the Reformation period, see Eva Hesselbach, "Die deutsche Schule im Mittelalter," *Zeitschr. Gesch. Erziehung Unterrichts,* N.F. 10 (1920): 1–56.

85. *Reformatio ecclesiarum Hassiae* (1526), chap. 30: *De scholis puerorum,* ad 31: *De scholis puellarum,* ed. Wilhelm Diehl, in *MGP,* 27 (1903): 487–88.

86. Luther to Landgraf Philip of Hesse, 7 January 1527. *WA,* Br. 4, pp. 157–58.

87. Heppe, *Volksschulwesen,* 1:283.

88. Wilhelm Diehl, *Die Schulordnungen des Grossherzogtums Hessen, MGP,* 33 (1905):7–14, 228–46.

89. Heppe, *Volksschulwesen,* 1:283–304.

90. F. M. Rendtorff, ed., *Die Schleswig-Holsteinischen Schulordnungen* (Kiel, 1902), pp. 25–29.

91. The full text of the *Kirchenordnung* is in S.Hamb., IIIA 1 a, 119.

92. Cf. the series of memoranda by various pastors to the city council, *Bedenken der Herrn Pastorn von den Klippschulen,* S.Hamb. Cl.VII, Lit H^e, no. 3, vol. 4, dated between 1540 and 1544.

93. Albert Richter, *Kursächsische Volksschulordnungen* (Leipzig, 1891), p. 21. The entire *Schulordnung* is given in Vormbaum, 1:230–97. See also Julius Richter, *Geschichte der sächsischen Volksschule, MGP* 29 1930: 48–50.

94. The evidence for the existence of town and village schools in Saxony in the 1580s and 1590s is laid out in Pallas, passim, all volumes.

95. S.Cob. B2492, 2r and v. Also ibid., 72r and v; 2493, 15r, and many others. This plea was part of an instruction sent out in 1591, based on information gathered in the territorial visitation of 1589.

96. The evidence for this assertion will be given in chap. 12.

97. *Ordnung der leermeyster zu Strassburg* (1534) printed in Marcel Fournier and Charles Engel, *Les statuts et privilèges des universités françaises . . . ,* vol. 2, 4, fasc. 1: *Gymnase, académie, université de Strasbourg* (Paris, 1894), p. 10.

98. From a visitation in Thuringia, 1570, S.Weim. Reg. 1, no. 43, 29r.

99. From the Württemberg *Schulordnung* (1559) in Vormbaum, 1:69. Reprinted verbatim in the Electoral Saxon *Schulordnung* of 1580, ibid., 1:232.

100. There are amusing descriptions of chaotic conditions existing where no *Ordnung* was observed. E.g., the *Schulordnung* of Breslau, 1570 (Vormbaum, 1:206): Where pupils are not given a fixed timetable, there is always "ein scheutzlich durcheinander lauffen, eine Treppen auff, die ander nider . . . ," resulting in "ein unformlich geschrey."

101. *Lübeckische Kirchenordnung* (1531), Biii r and v.
102. Visitation instructions for County Mansfeld, printed in Reu, 1 (1):263.
103. From the Württemberg *Schulordnung* (1559), in Vormbaum, 1:160.
104. From the Mecklenburg *Kirchenordnung* of 1552, printed in H. Schnell, *Das Unterrichtswesen der Grossherzogtümer Mecklenburg-Schwerin . . . , MGP*, 38 (1907):204.
105. *Unterricht der Visitatoren an die Pfarrherrn im Kurfürstentum zu Sachsen WA*, 26:237.
106. Good examples (among many more): Bremen, Nuremberg, Hannover. In the last of these cities I pursued the conflict between school authorities, on the one hand, and private schools and burghers who supported them, on the other, into the eighteenth century. In Nuremberg the government was forced to organize forty-eight private schools into a licensed guild in 1613 after unsuccessfully fighting them throughout the sixteenth century. For an interesting account of one school proprietor's struggle with governmental bureaucracy, see the autobiography of Thomas Platter, who became a private schoolmaster in Basel in 1544: *Selbstbiographie*, ed. Heinrich Boos (Leipzig, 1878), pp. 99-104 and 130 ff.
107. From a teacher's complaint to the council in Hannover, Sdt.Hann., XIII, W1., no. 1.
108. For example, in the principality of Waldeck (1581), Heppe, *Volksschulwesen*, 2:355.
109. Quoted in Theo Dietrich and Job-Günter Klink, *Zur Geschichte der Volksschule* (Bad Heilbronn, 1964), p. 28.
110. Sdt.Ulm, A (1836), 13v. This was in 1586.
111. Mertz, p. 429.
112. S.Hamb., Ministerial-Archiv, IIIAld, 234.
113. E.G., visitors' instructions during general visitation in Brandenburg, 1527, Berlin, Geheimes Staatsarchiv, Preussischer Kulturbesitz, Pr. Br. Rep. 8, no. 382, no foliation. See also an ordinance against begging issued by the city council of Strassburg, 1564, quoted in Fournier and Engel, *Statuts et privilèges*, vol. 2, 4, fasc. 1, p. 77.
114. Foster Watson, trans., *Tudor School-Boy Life: The Dialogues of Juan Luis Vives* (London, 1908), p. 36. My generalization is based on descriptions of rural schools in visitation protocols.
115. From the large literature on medieval schools and education I single out: Rudolf Limmer, *Bildungszustände und Bildungsideen des 13. Jahrhunderts* (Munich, 1928), especially pp. 139-82; Josef Dolch, *Lehrplan des Abendlandes . . .* , part 3; Joseph Knepper, *Das Schul- und Unterrichtswesen im Elsass von den Anfängen bis gegen das Jahr 1530* (Strassburg, 1905).
116. Antonius Musaeus, *Ein Ratschlag, wie die Schulen in stetten wider anzurichten seyen* (undated ms., ca. 1530, in S.Weim., Reg. O, no. 544, 2r-v.
117. The model for this was the so-called *Bufflerische Stiftung* in Strassburg, where Martin Bucer and Ambrosius Blaurer persuaded the merchants Peter and Jost Buffler of Isny to set up an endowment for paying the study costs of poor theology students. The money going to the candidates was to be matched by the cities they came from. For the text of the endowment document, see Robert Stupperich, ed., *Martin Bucers deutsche Schriften*, 7 (Gütersloh, 1964):539-46.
118. Musaeus, *Ein Ratschlag*, 15v. For Luther's position on the support of education as a good work, cf. *Eine Predigt, das man Kinder zur Schule halten solle* (1530), *WA*, 30² passim, especially p. 587.
119. For references and excerpts, beginning with the *Leisniger Kastenordnung* of 1523, see Mertz, pp. 213-17. See also the visitation recess of Elector Johann Georg of Brandenburg, 1572, on behalf of girls' schools in the electorate: Geheimes Staatsarchiv Berlin, G. St. A. Pr. Br. Rep. 40, no. 184.
120. S.Weim., Reg. O, no. 546.
121. The Saxon visitation records in the Staatsarchiv Dresden are particularly rich in material about these negotiations: hundreds of petitions from communal leaders of hamlets and towns to the elector, and the latter's replies.
122. For example: correspondence between the city of Leipzig and the dukes of Saxony from 1540 to the end of the century, especially in the reign of Duke Moritz. Sdt.Leipz., Tit. VII B2, 133r and v.
123. Ibid., Duke Moritz and Leipzig, Tit. VII B2, 17r-191v. Another example: correspondence between elders of village of Miehlen and Count Philip III of Nassau-Weilburg, 1556: Hess.H.S.Wiesb., Abt. 153, no. 235.

124. The Saxon visitation protocols in the Staatsarchiv Dresden are particularly interesting on these procedures. Similarly, the *Competenz-Bücher* of the duchy of Württemberg kept in LAS with entries for each parish in cities, towns, and villages for every year from 1559 to 1793, giving a complete financial record of salaries and payments in kind, and their sources, of all clerical and school personnel. For still another example: the material for Brandenburg, 1542-1600, given in Victor Herold, ed., "Die Brandenburgischen Kirchenvisitations-Abschiede und Register . . . ," vol. 1 (*Veröffentlichungen der historischen Kommission für die Provinz Brandenburg* . . . , vol. 4, nos. 1-5 (1928-31); vol. 2, ed. Gerhard Zimmermann and Gerd Heinrich (*Veröffentl. Berliner hist. Komm. beim Friedr.-Meinecke-Inst. d. freien Univ. Berlin*, vol. 6 (1963). Brandenburg visitors entered every community and established there by means of inquiries and searches of local records the precise financial arrangement for each school.

125. From a visitation recess in Brandenburg, 1544, quoted in Herold, *Brandenburgische Kirchenvisitations-Abschiede*, 1:664. Wright, *Impact of the Reformation*, pp. 190-93, gives details on the attempts by Philip of Hesse to equalize the salaries of school personnel in his territory.

126. These examples from Saxony-Coburg, 1578 and 1583. S.Cob., B2473, 98r; 299v; B2480, 89r.

127. For some details of the earliest attempts in Electoral Saxony to come to the aid of needy teachers and needy communities with small sums of money and grain, see Julius Richter, *Geschichte der sächsischen Volksschule*, MGP, 29 (1930): 456-85, 629-30. Some instructive figures on clerical income in the Protestant parts of the Rhineland are displayed in tables and charts in Bernard Vogler, *Le clergé protestant rhénan au siècle de la réforme (1555-1619)* (Paris, 1976), chap. 4.

128. Pallas, 41⁴: 123.

129. S.Dresd., Loc. 1988, 43r–46r. The year was 1617.

130. This particular complaint quoted in Richter, *Volksschule*, p. 453, but identical and similar ones are constant in the documents of all regions.

131. For example: WHS, A284, Kirchenrat Spezialakten, a huge series organized by localities. Nearly each petition is accompanied by a table showing the composition of the teacher's or sexton's income.

132. For example: S.Bamb, C2, no. 2031, for the 1590s.

133. The stars among academic teachers were very well off. Johann Sturm got 150 gulden a year as rector of the Strassburg gymnasium (Fournier and Engel, *Statuts et privilèges*, p. 18). Hieronymus Wolff got 300 gulden as rector of the Saint Anna School in Augsburg (Sdt.Augsb., Evangelisches Wesenarchiv, 1004).

134. Bavaria can serve to test the validity of this generalization for the Catholic parts of the Holy Roman Empire. For the complicated maneuvers constituting Bavarian religious policy in the Reformation, see Max Spindler, ed., *Handbuch der bayerischen Geschichte*, 2 (Munich, 1966): 297-409. These moves culminated in the reigns of Albrecht V, Wilhelm V, and Maximilian I, in strong ducal leadership, tending toward exclusiveness, in all areas of religious life (M. Doeberl, *Entwicklungsgeschichte Bayerns*, 1 [Munich, 1908]: 395), as exemplified by the territorial visitations of the 1550s, 1560s, and 1570s, and the *Religionsmandat* of 1569, which contained Bavaria's first comprehensive *Schulordnung* (it is printed in Lurz, *Dokumente*, 2:29-43). As early as 1553, Albrecht V's councillors had declared "we cannot admit that bishops should have any jurisdiction over schools in the duchy of Bavaria. It is our Gracious Prince and Lord who, as territorial ruler, has the sole authority over schools" (quoted in Heinrich Held, *Altbayrische Volkserziehung und Volksschule* [Munich, 1926-28], 1:163). The *Schulordnung* of 1569 employed this authority to mandate schools "in large towns and small villages" for controlled instruction in orthodox religious doctrine and *Zucht*. Uniformity was achieved by ordering all schools to conform their curricula to the *index lectionum* of the Jesuits in Munich, which was attached to an appendix to the ordinance. Attendance at catechism classes was required under Maximilian I (M. von Freyberg, *Pragmatische Geschichte der baierischen Gesetzgebung*, 3 [1836-39]: 166). In 1616 all rural education was put in the hands of German masters. Talented boys were to be sent to Latin school in the nearest town (Held, *Altbayrische Volkserziehung*, 1:190). Visitation questions and procedures make it clear that the goal of these schools was to produce outward conformity in religious matters. See, for example, the summary report drafted by visitors to the administrative district of Burghausen, 1570,

BHM, Staatsverwaltung 2785, 191-98. Another: Relation of visitation of 1597-98 addressed to Wilhelm V: OEMF, no. 571, 773-96. All the same, the policy resulted in a significant increase in the number of small-town and village schools in Bavaria (for evidence, cf. Lurz, *Dokumente*, 2:26-27.

135. The argument that the Reformation was responsible for the reopening of closed schools and the foundation of new ones can be substantiated from the visitation records of many territories. Among the published ones, a good example is the documentation from Electoral Brandenburg, in which the process can be observed from 1540 into the seventeenth century. See Herold, *Kirchenvisitations-Abschiede* (see note 124 for full reference).

CHAPTER 2

1. *Chronica, durch Magistrum Johan Carion vleissig zusamen gezogen* . . . (Wittenberg, 1532), Gii v. For a discussion of Melanchthon's part in this work and of its role in Lutheran historiography, cf. Gerald Strauss, "The Course of German History: The Lutheran Interpretation," in *Renaissance Studies in Honor of Hans Baron*, ed. Anthony Molho and John A. Tedeschi (Florence, 1971), pp. 678-79.

2. For an explicit statement of this theme, which is implicit in the entire work, see Caspar Peucer's preface to his continuation of Carion's chronicle, *Chronica Carionis* . . . (Wittenberg, 1573), bii r-ciii v. Peucer was a professor at the University of Wittenberg and Melanchthon's son-in-law.

3. I take the quotation from O. Albrecht, "Eine handschriftliche Notiz Melanchthons aus dem Jahre 1559," *Theologische Studien und Kritiken* 70 (1897):797-99. Substantially the same passage occurs on Avii r of the 1532 edition of Johann Carion's chronicle (see note 1, above).

4. *Verlegung etlicher unchristlicher Artikel, welche die Widerteuffer fürgeben* (1536), in *Melanchthons Werke in Auswahl, Sudienausgabe*, ed. Robert Stupperich (Gütersloh, 1951), 1:305.

5. *In Danielem prophetam commentarius* (1543) in *Philippi Melanthonis opera* . . . , ed. C. G. Bretschneider, vol. 13 (Halle, 1846), col. 974.

6. Aurifaber's preface is reprinted in *Dr. Martin Luthers sämtliche Schriften*, ed. Johann Georg Walch, 12 (Halle, 1743):40-54. The reference is to p. 52.

7. Andreas Musculus, *Von des Teuffels Tyranney, macht und gewalt, sunderlich in disen letzten Tagen* . . . (Worms, 1561), Cvi v.

8. Ibid., Aii v.

9. Christoph Vischer, *Auslegung der fünf Hauptstück des heiligen Catechismi* . . . (Schmalkalden, 1543; I use Leipzig, 1578), ii r.

10. Zacharias Rivander, *Der ander Theil Promptuarii Exemplorum, darinnen viel herrliche schöne Historien . . . und Exempel . . . verfasset sind* (Frankfurt am Main, 1581), aiii r.

11. This argument is presented by Lucas Osiander, *Bedencken, ob der newe päpstliche Kalender ein Notturft bey der Christenheit sey* . . . (Tübingen, 1583).

12. Werner Jentsch, *Urchristliches Erziehungsdenken: Die Paideia Kyriu im Rahmen der hellenisch-jüdischen Umwelt* (Gütersloh, 1951), pp. 194-95. See also Robert Bultmann, Das Urchristentum (Zurich, 1949), pp. 231-32.

13. Thus, for example, the Protestant magistrates of the imperial city of Gengenbach deplored, in 1538, the wild and disorderly ways of people "as this last age in which we live produces them," but nonetheless organized obligatory catechism classes for the city's youth. Cf. Ernst-Wilhelm Kohls, *Evangelische Bewegung und Kirchenordnung: Studien und Quellen zur Reformationsgeschichte der Reichsstadt Gengenbach* (Karlsruhe, 1966), p. 35.

14. Luther's ideas on education have been analyzed and interpreted by Ivar Asheim in his excellent *Glaube und Erziehung bei Luther* (Heidelberg, 1961). While maintaining that Luther never developed a systematic pedagogy and that it is illegitimate to compound his many stray remarks on the subject into a pedagogical system, Asheim does, in fact, present a coherent (from the point of view of the reformer's immediate followers, perhaps too coherent) outline of Luther's thought on education. See especially pp. 40-87.

15. Ibid., pp. 116–18.

16. "Ideo, lasse dich unsern herr Gott ziehen suo verbo." Sermon on Eph. 6 (1535), *WA*, 41:408. Cf. Asheim, *Glaube und Erziehung*, p. 286.

17. Ibid., pp. 287–89 for citations.

18. See Luther's Lectures on Genesis (1535–45), *WA*, 42:346–47. Cf. Klaus Petzold, *Die Grundlagen der Erziehungslehre im Spätmittelalter und bei Luther* (Heidelberg, 1969), pp. 84–89.

19. *Lectures on Genesis, WA*, 42:347–51.

20. *Praelectio D. M. Lutheri in psalmum CXXVII* (1533), *WA*, 40³:202-32. Cf. Asheim, *Glaube und Erziehung*, pp. 88 ff.

21. For a discussion, with many citations, of the process of divine "education" on the model of God's treatment of Israel, cf. Asheim, *Glaube und Erziehung*, pp. 120–43.

22. Luther's text read, "'Quoniam figmentum cordis humani malum est ab Adolescentia sua," *WA*, 42:346.

23. Ibid.,p. 351. Translation by George V. Schick, *LW*, 2, "Lectures on Genesis," chaps. 6–14 (Saint Louis, Mo., 1960), pp. 126–27.

24. *WA*, 42:352. Cf. *WA*, Tr. 2, no. 1532; 3, no. 3711a.

25. *WA, Tr. 2, no. 1532.*

26. Ibid., 5, no. 6099; 4, no. 4027.

27. Ibid., 1, no. 730: "Die kinder glauben recht."

28. Ibid., 1, no. 660. Many similar statements passim in Tr.

29. Ibid., 4, no. 4027.

30. "Darum sehen die eltern zu, das sie nach Gottes befel den kindern wol fürsten... weil sie sich noch ziehen, biegen und leiten lassen. . . ." Sermon on the fourth to seventh commandments (1525) *WA*, 16:502. Cf. chap. 5 below for a discussion of this and related problems.

31. *Lectures on Genesis, WA*, 42:352.

32. Cf. Asheim, *Glaube und Erziehung*, pp. 28–29; 88 f. Cf. also Edgar Reimers, *Recht und Grenzen einer Berufung auf Luther in den neueren Bemühungen um eine evangelische Erziehung* (Weinheim, 1958), pp. 131 ff. In trying to find coherence and system in Luther's remarks on education, Reimers argues that Luther, seeing education as an aspect of human and worldly justice, as opposed to divine justification, tied all discussion of the subject to the fourth commandment.

33. Asheim, *Glaube und Erziehung*, pp. 88 ff.

34. Luther to Elector Johann, 22 November 1526. *WA*, Br. 4, no. 1052, p. 133.

35. Johann Agricola, *Hundert und dreissig gemeiner Fragstücke für die jungen Kinder* . . . (Wittenberg, 1528), Aii v; Johannes Rürer, preface to Andreas Althamer, *Catechismus* . . . (Nuremberg, 1528; printed in Julius Hartmann, ed., "Älteste katechetische Denkmale der evangelischen Kirche" (Stuttgart, 1844), p. 53.

36. "Necesse est, ut a puerorum institutione exordium fiat." From *Decem praecepta Wittenbergensi praedicata populo* (1518) *WA*, 1:494. Cf. *Deutsche Messe und Ordnung Gottesdiensts* (1526) *WA*, 19:112.

37. *Oeconomia christiana* (Wittenberg, 1529), Diii v.

38. Agricola, *Hundert und dreissig gemeiner Fragstücke*, Aii v. Johann Bader, *Ein Gesprächbüchlein vom Anfangk Lebens, mit dem jungen Volk zu Landaw* (1526), quoted in J. P. Gelbert, *Magister Johann Baders Leben und Schriften* (Neustadt, 1868), p. 123.

39. Christoph Vischer, *Christliche Auslegung und Erklerung der Haustafel* . . . (Leipzig, 1578), Riiii r and v.

40. E.g., Andreas Musculus, *Prophecey und Weissagung . . . von dem zunahenden Zorn, Straf, Jammer und Unglück über Deutschland* (Erfurt, 1557), which ends with a fervent *Kindergebet* in which the praying child is to ask God to overlook his parents' refusal to reform themselves, and "noch einmal mit uns zu versuchen, uns zeit und raum zur Buss und besserung geben" (Fvii v).

41. It is quoted by John Jones, *The Art and Science of Preserving Bodie and Soule in al Health, Wisdome, and Catholicke Religion* . . . (London, 1579), vol. 1, no. 35 (p. 72).

42. *Eine Predigt, dass man Kinder zur Schule halten solle* (1530), *WA*, 30²:520. Cf. *An die Ratsherren aller Städte . . .* (1524), *WA*, 15:30.

43. Cf. Asheim, *Glaube und Erziehung*, pp. 58, 202.

44. *An die Ratsherren aller Städte* . . . (1524), *WA*, 15:45.

45. E.g., *Hauspostille* (1544), *WA*, 52, passim.

46. *Deutsche Messe und Ordnung des Gottesdienstes* (1526), *WA*, 19:78.

47. Sermon on Eph. 6:1 ff. (1535), *WA*, 41:406.

48. "In summa, sic tractat filios, quemadmodum nos videmus tractari a Deo," *WA*, Tr. 5, no. 5819.

49. Cf. Luther, *De servo arbitrio* (1525), *WA*, 18:673. Cf. chap. 7, below.

50. Johann Agricola, *Sybenhundert und fünfftzig Teutscher Sprichwörter* (Hagenau, 1534), no. 508: "Soll ein kind gedeihen, so mag im der vatter leicht etwas lassen." This proverb, and Agricola's commentary on it, are contradicted by several others, e.g., no. 649: "Je lieber kindt, je grösser rute." For a sketch of Agricola's stormy life and the theological controversies that marked it, see Sander L. Gilman, ed., *Johann Agricola von Eisleben: Die Sprichwörter-Sammlungen* (Berlin, 1971), vol. 2, 335–53.

51. Johann Bader, *Ein Gesprächbüchlein* . . . (1526), quoted in J. P. Gelbert, *Magister Johann Baders Leben*, p. 123.

52. Veit Dietrich, *Kinderpostilla* (Nuremberg, 1549), Av v; 46v.

53. Many interesting ones are provided by Klaus Leder, *Kirche und Jugend in Nürnberg und seinem Landgebiet 1400 bis 1800*, Einzelarbeiten aus der Kirchengeschichte Bayerns, 52 (Neustadt an der Aisch, 1973). Leder shows how serious Lutheran theologians and pastors were about religious instruction in town and countryside, how unremitting in their efforts to persuade the city council to issue appropriate laws and give financial support, and how industrious in producing books for religious teaching.

54. It had eleven editions before 1600. Cf. Friedrich Falk, "Luthers Schrift an die Ratsherren der deutschen Städte und ihre geschichtliche Wirkung auf die deutsche Schule," *Luther-Jahrbuch* 19 (1937): 55–114.

55. For example: popular reactions to the draft of the Braunschweig *Kirchenordnung* of 1528 indicate widespread interest and concern with education (Ludwig Hänselmann, ed., *Bugenhagens Kirchenordnung für die Stadt Braunschweig* [Wolfenbüttel, 1885], xxx–xxxi). My generalization is based on examination of visitation records for the second half of the sixteenth century, and the assumption that interest in education shown in these documents existed also in the earlier 1500s. Examples: WHS series A284, containing correspondence between the dukes of Württemberg and the councils of small towns and *Flecken* on the subject of schools. See also the evidence for Pfalz-Neuburg in 1558, Georg Rückert, "Beiträge zur Geschichte der katholischen Volksschulen im K. Bezirksamt Dillingen," *Jb. kath. Ver. Dillingen* 29 (1916): 91 ff., relating to visitations carried out by the Protestant Duke Ottheinrich. Evidence for Jülich-Berg in 1550–82, in Otto R. Redlich, *Jülisch-Bergische Kirchenpolitik am Ausgange des Mittelalters und in der Reformationszeit*, Publ. Ges. f. rheinische Geschichtskunde, 28, 3 vols., (Bonn, 1907–15), e.g., 2:1, 23, 76, 102. For Bavaria: Georg Lurz, *Mittelschulgeschichtliche Dokumente Altbayerns*, *MGP*, 42 (1908): 23–24 on the struggle of territorial estates for the maintenance of schools in rural districts. See chap. 9 below for an extended discussion of the problem of literacy.

56. Luther, *Eine Predigt, das man Kinder zur Schule halten solle* (1530), *WA*, 30²:531. David Chytraeus, *De ratione discendi et ordine studiorum* . . . (Wittenberg, 1564), A4r.

57. From the *Kirchenordnung* of Zweibrücken promulgated in 1557 by Duke Wolfgang. Printed in K. Reissinger, ed., *Dokumente zur Geschichte der humanistischen Schulen im Gebiet der bayerischen Pfalz*, *MGP*, 49 (Berlin, 1911): 1–3. The section on schools is copied from the Wittenberger Reformation, section *de scholis*. Copied again in the *Kirchenordnung* of Mecklenburg, 1552, in H. Schnell, *Das Unterrichtswesen der Grossherzogtümer Mecklenburg-Schwerin und Strelitz*, *MGP*, 38 (Berlin, 1907): 198–201.

58. E.g., "Young people should be instructed from an early age in religion and the arts, so that they can in later life be useful in spiritual and secular government." From visitation recess 1543 for city of Prenzlau, Brandenburg. Berlin: Geheimes Staatsarchiv, Pr.Br.Rep. 8, no. 382, 5v.

59. Martin Bucer, writing in a memorandum to the Council of Ulm, in Robert Stupperich, ed., *Martin Bucers deutsche Schriften*, 7:508.

60. Wenceslaus Linck, *Vom christlichen Adel oder freyheit der Kinder Gottes und glaubigen Menschen* (1524), printed in Wilhelm Reindell, ed., *Wenzel Lincks Werke* (Marburg, 1894), pp. 278–86. The passage referred to occurs on pp. 279–80.

61. *Unterricht der Visitatorn an die Pfarrherrn ym Kurfürstentum Sachssen* (1528), printed in Robert Stupperich, ed., *Melanchthons Werke in Auswahl* . . . , 1:227.

62. Hänselmann, *Bugenhagens Kirchenordnung*, pp. 41-46.

63. Provisions for German schools in both Braunschweig and Lübeck were primitive. For Braunschweig: "wat gudes to leren ut deme worte Godes . . . " (ibid., p. 61). For Lübeck: "nichts sonderes verordnet" (Johann Bugenhagen, *Lübeckische Kirchenordnung* [Lübeck, 1877], p. 46.

64. "Das volck wurdt zu burgerlicher beywonung uss erfarung und übung des buchstabens dester geschlachter, freuntlicher und geneigter . . ." Bucer et al., to Council, February 1525, printed in Robert Stupperich, ed., *Martin Bucers . . . Schriften*, 2:400.

65. "Wenn Herr Omnes auffstehet . . . ," Luther, *Eine treue Vermahnung . . . zu allen Christen, sich zu hüten vor Aufruhr und Empörung* (1522), *WA*, 8:680.

66. Luther, response to Wolf von Salhausen, August 1524, *WA*, 15:228. Cf. Wilhelm Maurer, *Der junge Melanchthon* (Göttingen, 1967-69), 2:452.

67. *Lectures on Galatians, LW*, 26:343-48 (*WA*, 40¹:529-34).

68. *Lectures on Galatians, LW*, 26:308.

69. *Unterricht der Visitatorn* . . . in Stupperich, ed., *Melanchthons Werke*, 1:228-34.

70. Ibid., p. 234.

71. Melanchthon to Johann Memminger, 5 July 1524, in Otto Clemen, ed., *Melanchthons Briefwechsel* (Leipzig, 1926), 1:247. Also *Loci praecipui theologici* (1559), printed in Stupperich, ed., *Melanchthons Werke*, 2, part 1, p. 239. The biblical reference is to Gal. 3:24.

72. *Wider die himmlischen Propheten, von den Bildern und Sakrament* (1525), *WA*, 18:84. Cf. Luther to Nikolaus Hausmann, March 1522, *WA*, Br. 2, no. 459. Cf. also *Eine treue Vermahnung zu allen Christen* . . . (1522), *WA*, 8:680.

73. *Widder die Artikel der Bawrschaft* (1525), in Stupperich, ed., *Melanchthons Werke*, 1:206, 208.

74. Luther, *WA*, Tr. 6, no. 6764.

75. Caspar Huberinus, *Spiegel der Hauszucht* . . . (1552; I use Nuremberg, 1565), M r.

76. Luther to Elector Johann, 22 November 1526, *WA*, Br. 4:133.

77. Quoted in Arno Heerdegen, *Geschichte der allgemeinen Kirchenvisitation in den ernestinischen Landen im Jahre 1554-55*, Zeitschr. Ver. Thüringische Geschichte und Altertumskunde, N.F. 6, Supplementheft (Jena, 1914), pp. 6-7. Menius had participated in the visitations of Thuringia in 1533 and 1539 and in the endowment of 1544-46.

78. From a memorandum by the preachers of Strassburg to the council, February 1525, printed in Marcel Fournier and Charles Engel, *Les statuts et privilèges des universités françaises* . . . , 2, 4 (Paris, 1894), p. 4.

79. See Robert Stupperich's introduction to the Strassburg preachers' supplication of 1524: *Martin Bucers . . . Schriften*, 2:387-94. On Strassburg's educational system, see Charles Engel, *Das Schulwesen in Strassburg vor der Gründung des protestantischen Gymnasiums 1538* (Strassburg, 1886); Walter Sohm, *Die Schule Johann Sturms und die Kirche Strassburgs in ihrem gegenseitigen Verhältnis, 1530-81* (Munich and Berlin, 1912); Ernst-Wilhelm Kohls, *Die Schule bei Martin Bucer in ihrem Verhältnis zu Kirche und Obrigkeit* (Heidelberg, 1963).

80. See the protocols of the meetings of the *Scholarchen*, Strasb.A.V., Archives St. Thomas 372-75. These documents run from 1535 to 1604.

81. Ibid., Archive St. Thomas 84, carton 48, 99-104 (1536).

82. Ibid., 324, 71-72 (1537).

83. Ibid., 324, 142-45 (1540).

84. Ibid., 84, carton 48, 103-4. See also the various memoranda by Bucer and other ministers to the Strassburg council printed in Stupperich, ed., *Martin Bucers . . . Schriften*, vols. 2 and 7.

85. Strasb.A.V., Archives St. Thomas 84, carton 48, 188v-189v; 200r-201v.

86. Ibid., 84, carton 48, 256v.

87. Cf. Melanchthon, *Ratio scholae Norembergae nuper institutae* (1526), printed in Karl Hartfelder, ed., *Melanchthoniana paedagogica: Eine Ergänzung zu den Werken Melanchthons im Corpus Reformatorum* (Leipzig, 1892), p. 6.

88. From the *Schulordnung* of the duchy of Württemberg (1559), in Vormbaum, 1:98.

89. Caspar Aquila, *Des kleinen Catechismi Erklerung mit schönen christlichen exempeln* . . . (1538), in Reu, 2 (2):173.

90. E.g., Justus Gesenius, *Kleine Katechismus-Schule* . . . , first published anonymously, Lüneburg, 1631, then by Johann Schmidt, Strassburg, 1632 (I use the latter edition), preface, unnumbered pages.

91. Caspar Huberinus, *Spiegel der geistlichen Hauszucht* . . . (Frankfurt am Main, 1569), cxix r.

92. Andreas Musculus, *Vom Himmel und der Hellen* . . . (Frankfurt an der Oder, 1559), Aii v.

93. Heinrich Salmuth, *Catechismus* . . . (Budissin, 1581), ciiii r.

94. Simon Musaeus, *Catechismus* . . . (Frankfurt am Main, 1571), 2v.

95. Musculus, *Vom Himmel und der Hellen* (1559), Diii v.

CHAPTER 3

1. See the many references to *Kinder* in the index to Luther's Table Talk, *WA*, Tr. 6, pp. 595-96.

2. For example: *Das Buch Weinsberg*, ed. Johann Jakob Hässlin (Munich, 1961), which contains childhood memories suggesting that parents and children were closely involved with each other. See chap. 5 for a discussion of this subject.

3. A survey of sixteenth-century medical literature shows that from about 1520 physicians devoted increasing attention to the diseases of infants and children. A growing number of special treatises on pediatrics were published beginning ca. 1540. See also chap. 5, below.

4. Cf. Otto Herding's elaborate identification of Wimpheling's sources in his edition of the *Adolescentia: Jacobi Wimpfelingi opera selecta*, 1 (Munich, 1965): 31-151.

5. Otto Brunfels, *Catechesis puerorum in fide, literis et moribus* . . . (Frankfurt am Main, 1529), bks. 1 and 2.

6. Antonio Mancinelli, *De parentum cura in liberos: De filorum erga parentes obedientia, honore et pietate* (Milan, 1504).

7. *Aphorismi institutionis puerorum* (Strassburg, 1519).

8. E.g., *De ratione studii, deque vita iuventutis instituenda, opuscula diversorum autorum* . . . (Basel, 1541), containing treatises by Vergerio, Vives, Erasmus, Sadoleto, Melanchthon, Rudolf Agricola, Hegendorf, Jerome, Basil, Brunfels; also a collection of precepts from Greek and Roman writers; *Institutionis literae sive de discendi atque docendi ratione. Tomus primus* [containing the works of Johann Sturm], *tomus secundus* [containing writings by various rectors and teachers, e.g., Hieronymus Wolf of the Sankt Anna Gymnasium in Augsburg] (Thorn [Prussia], 1586-87).

9. E.g., Sebald Heiden, *Paedonomia scholastica, pietatis, studii literarii, ac morum honestatis praecepta continens* (Nuremberg, 1533); Johann Fungerus, *De puerorum disciplina et recta educatione liber* (Antwerp, 1584).

10. Quintilian *Institutio oratoria* 12. 11. 12. I use the Loeb Classical Library edition with the English translation by H. E. Butler (London, 1921). The *editio princeps* of Quintilian was Rome, 1470. The first edition printed in Germany was Cologne, 1521. On all editions see N. E. Lemaire, *M. F. Quintilianus* (Bibliotheca classica Latina, Paris, 1825), pp. 277-300. On his influence on subsequent periods, cf. F. H. Colson, ed., *M. Fabii Quintiliani Institutionis oratoriae liber I* (Cambridge, 1924), pp. xliii-lxxxix; Paul Lehmann, "Die Institutio oratoria des Quintilianus im Mittelalter," *Erforschung des Mittelalters*, 2 (Stuttgart, 1959): 1-28; Johann Michael Hofer, *Die Stellung des Desiderius Erasmus und des Johann Ludwig Vives zur Pädagogik des Quintilian* (diss., Erlangen, 1910).

11. Quintilian 1.1.1 f.

12. Augustine *Confessions* 1.19. Cf.2., 4 on the famous incident of robbing the pear tree. I use the Loeb Classical Library edition with the English translation of William Watts of 1631 (London, 1912).

13. Joseph Hogger, *Die Kinderpsychologie Augustins* (Munich, 1937).

14. *De peccatorum meritis et remissione, et de Baptismo parvulorum.* Translated in *A Select Library of the Nicene and Post-Nicene Fathers of the Christian Church*. Vol. 5. *St. Augustin's Anti-Pelagian Works* (New York, 1887), bk. 1, chap. 67, p. 42.

15. Ibid., chap. 69, p. 43.
16. *Confessions* 1. 7. 11. Here I use the translation by Peter Brown, who quotes this passage on pp. 28-29 of his *Augustine of Hippo* (Berkeley and Los Angeles, 1967).
17. Hogger, *Kinderpsychologie*, p. 48, remarks shrewdly about Augustine's explanations of his own childhood that "from a hoard of stored-up psychological knowledge he laid bare only such items as would carry a conscious and unconscious conflict into his philosophy of life."
18. Cf. Klaus Petzold, die Grundlagen der Erziehungslehre im Spätmittelalter und bei Luther (Heidelberg, 1969), chap. 2. The first of many editions of Gerson' works was published in Cologne, 1483-84. The Strassburg edition of 1502 was edited in part by Wimpheling.
19. Jean Gerson, *De innocentia puerili*, in *Opera omnia* (Antwerp, 1706) 3:293-96.
20. For an excellent discussion of this, see Petzold, *Grundlagen der Erziehungslehre*, chap. 2.
21. *Tractatus de parvulis trahendis ad Christum*, in *Opera omnia*, 3:277-91, especially p. 283.
22. The first edition of Wimpheling's *Adolescentia* was printed in Strassburg, 1500. Many others followed within a few years. I use the critical edition by Otto Herding cited in note 4 above. For Wimpheling's debt to Gerson, see introduction, pp. 110-32.
23. *Adolescentia*, pp. 206-38.
24. As advanced, for example, by Clement of Alexandria, *Paedagogus*, ed. H.-I. Marrou and Marguerite Harl (Paris, 1960-70), 1:19-21.
25. For these, for an excellent discussion of the whole problem, and for a large bibliography, see Werner Jentsch, *Urchristliches Erziehungsdenken: Die Paideia Kyriu im Rahmen der hellenisch-jüdischen Umwelt* (Gütersloh, 1951), particularly part 2.
26. Quintilian 2. 19. 1f. cf. Giuseppe G. Bianca, *La pedagogia di Quintiliano* (Padua, 1963), pp. 56-59.
27. Quintilian 1. 1, 3.
28. *De pueris instituendis*, critical edition by J.-C. Margolin, *Opera omnia Desiderii Erasmi*, 1, 2 (Amsterdam, 1971): 39-40.
29. Quintilian 1. 12. 8-9.
30. *De pueris instituendis*, p. 33.
31. Ibid., p. 50.
32. Plato *Laws* 7. 808d.
33. *Confessions* 1. 9-10, 12-13.
34. For the immense literature on the subject of the ages of human life see Franz Boll, "Die Lebensalter: Ein Beitrag zur antiken Ethologie und zur Geschichte der Zahlen," *Neue Jahrb. f. d. klass. Altertum, Gesch. u. deutsche Lit.* 16 (1913): 89-154; and Adolf Hofmeister, "Puer, iuvenis, senex . . . ," in *Papsttum und Kaisertum. . . . Paul Kehr zum 65. Geburtstag dargebracht*, ed. Albert Brockmann (Munich, 1926), pp. 287-316. Boll stresses the numerological sources and significance of the division of the life span into three, four, six, or seven stages.
35. For passages, mostly from the *Confessions* and *De peccatorum meritis*, see Hogger, *Kinderpsychologie*, pp. 63-165.
36. Ibid., pp. 88-89.
37. Cf. Hofmeister (as in note 34) for references.
38. The legal literature agreed with the identification of the fourteenth year as the onset of adolescence. E.g., Ulrich Tengler, *Layenspiegel* . . . (Strassburg, 1544), x r; Justin Göbler, *Handbuch . . . kayserlicher und bürgerlicher Rechten* . . . (Frankfurt am Main, 1564), vol. 1, title 12.
39. 2, 2 and 3. 1.
40. Vincent of Beauvais, *De eruditione filiorum nobilium*, ed. Arpad Steiner (Cambridge, Mass., 1938), chap. 35. Vincent's treatise, written ca. 1250, was first printed in Rostock, 1477, and Basel, 1481. Egidio Colonna (Aegidius Romanus), *De regimine principum* (I use the thirteenth-century French version, ed. S. P. Molenaer, New York, 1899), pp. 220-24. The Latin text was first published in Augsburg, 1473, and printed frequently thereafter.
41. Maffeo Vegio, *De educatione liberorum*, written 1444, reprinted frequently from 1491. I use the German translation by K. A. Kopp in *Bibliothek der katholischen Pädagogik*, 2 (Freiburg im Breisgau, 1889): 122.

42. Ibid., p. 121.

43. Herding edition, pp. 198–99, 242.

44. Jean Gerson, *Doctrina pro pueris ecclesiae Parisiensis*, in *Opera omnia*, 3:717–20; *Expostulatio ad potestates publicas adversus corruptionem juventutis per lascivias imagines*, in ibid., 3:291–92; *Tractatus de pollutione diurna*, in ibid., 3:335–45. Cf. Thomas N. Tentler, *Sin and Confession on the Eve of the Reformation* (Princeton, N.J., 1977), pp. 162–232 for Gerson's preoccupation with sex.

45. Gerson may have been on the right track. Hans Heinrich Muchow, in an interesting study, *Jugendgeneration im Wandel der Zeit: Beiträge zur Geschichte der Jugend* (Vienna, 1964), especially p. 26, argues that although the onset of biological sexuality occurs at about the same age in all periods and among all peoples in history, "psychic-sexual maturity," the psychic acceptance of sexuality and the readiness to employ it, comes later. The length of this lag is determined by cultural and social factors. Repression means a longer lag.

46. Vives, *De institutione feminae christianae*, Bk. 1, chap. 7, in *Joannis Ludovici Vivis . . . opera omnia*, 4 (Valencia, 1783): 98.

47. Quintilian 2. 4.

48. Ibid.

49. This Scholastic argument was presented by Aegidius Romanus, *De regimine principum*, passim.

50. *De eruditione principum*, in *Sancti Thomae Aquinatis . . . opera omnia*, vol. 16 (New York, 1950 [reprint of the edition Parma, 1852–73]), opusculum 37, book 5, chap. 48. The book was attributed to Thomas Aquinas throughout the Middle Ages and the early modern period. On the authorship question see Wilhelm Berges, *Die Fürstenspiegel des hohen und späten Mittelalters* (Leipzig, 1938), pp. 309–13.

51. I leave out of consideration here the matter of eugenics, although a number of early modern writers stressed it, notably Vegio, *De educatione liberorum* (cf. note 41, above), p. 37; "The physical and moral condition of the father at the moment of conception is transmitted directly and inexpungeably to the body and mind of the offspring"; and Erasmus, *De pueris instituendis*, p. 43. Most authors did not advise eugenic practices consonant with those in Plato's *Republic* but confined themselves to counseling continence and abstemiousness before intercourse. In any case, such advice did not enter the province of the sixteenth-century pedagogue.

52. *City of God* 22. 24. I use the Loeb Classical Library edition with the English translation of William M. Green 7 (London, 1960): 327.

53. The pedagogical tradition is unanimous on this point. From Quintilian and Augustine to Vegio, Vergerio, Wimpheling, and Erasmus, authors maintained that intellects differ in natural endowments.

54. "Efficax res est natura, sed hanc vincit efficacior institutio," *De pueris instituendis*, p. 29. Cf. Plutarch *De liberis educandis* (for complete reference, see note 59, below), p. 4.

55. For clearest statement see *Laws* 5. 732e–734e; 2. 653a. Cf. R. C. Lodge, *Plato's Theory of Education* (London, 1947), pp. 193 ff.

56. *De pueris instituendis*, p. 53 and passim. Also *De ratione studii*, critical edition by J-C. Margolin, *opera omnia*, 1, 2 (Amsterdam, 1971): 111–51, passim, with reference to Quintilian 1. 1. 20.

57. Aegidius Romanus, *De regimine principum*, pp. 195–96.

58. These quotations are from Jerome, ep. 107 and 128, respectively. F. A. Wright, ed. and trans., *Select Letters of St. Jerome* (London, 1933), pp. 347, 469.

59. Plutarch *De liberis educandis* 12, 16. I use the Loeb Classical Library edition: *Plutarch's Moralia*, ed. and trans. Frank Cole Babbitt (London, 1927), 1:5–69. Plutarch is probably not the author of this treatise, but throughout the early modern period it was attributed to him. On the authorship question see Daniel Wyttenbach in his edition of Plutarch's *Moralia*. Vol. 6. *Animadversiones* (Oxford, 1810), pp. 29–64. Many Latin translations of this work were published in the fifteenth century, including one by Guarino da Verona.

60. On this point, and for Old Testament passages advocating corporal punishment, see Werner Jentsch, *Urchristliches Erziehungsdenken*, pp. 85–139.

61. Quintilian 1. 3. 13–18.

62. Plutarch *De liberis educandis* 12.

63. Quoted by Pierre Riché, *Education et culture dans l'occident barbare, VIe-VIIIe siècles* (Paris, 1962), p. 504.

64. Epistle 95, p. 3, trans. J. G. Cunningham, in *A Select Library of the Nicene and post-Nicene Fathers of the Christian Church*, vol. 1 (Buffalo, 1886).

65. Battista Guarino, *De ordine docendi et studendi*. I use the English translation by William Harrison Woodward in *Vittorino da Feltre and Other Humanist Educators* (first published 1897; reprinted New York, 1963), pp. 162-63.

66. *De educatione liberorum* 52-53.

67. *Isidoneus Germanicus*. I use the German translation by Joseph Freundgen in *Jakob Wimphelings pädagogische Schriften . . .* (Paderborn, 1898), p. 170.

68. *De pueris instituendis*, pp. 61-62.

69. Ep. 107 (see note 58, above), p. 347.

70. *De ordine docendi et studendi* (see note 65, above), p. 162. His treatise, says Battista, "represents the doctrine of my father Guarino Veronese; so much so that you may suppose him to be writing to you by my pen." Ibid., p. 161. Battista's treatise was first printed in Heidelberg, 1489, and several times thereafter.

71. Vegio, *De educatione liberorum*, pp. 78-82.

72. Vergerio, *De ingenuis moribus*, 11r. I use the edition in the Princeton University Library without place and date, but probably 1472. Vergerio's treatise had at least twenty editions before 1500.

73. "Studio laudis excitari incendique amore gloriae." *Adolescentia*, pp. 194-95.

74. *De ingenuis moribus*, 3v-4r.

75. *Adolescentia*, p. 368.

76. Battista Guarino, *De ordine docendi et studendi*, p. 163.

77. Vegio, *De educatione liberorum*, p. 78.

78. Wimpheling, *Adolescentia*, p. 195; Vergerio, *De ingenuis moribus*, 4r and v.

79. Erasmus, *De pueris instituendis*, pp. 62-63. On the use of the sense of shame for education in the confessional, see Tentler, *Sin and Confession*, pp. 128-30.

80. This is the object of education as stated by, among many others, Wimpheling, *Isidoneus*, p. 167.

81. *Republic* 2. 377b: "Do you know that the beginning of every task is the chief thing especially for any creature that is young and tender? For it is then that it is best molded and takes the impression that one wishes to stamp on it."

82. *De liberis educandis* 3A. I use F. C. Babbitt's translation (see note 59 above) but substitute "moral virtue" for "character," as *ēthikas aretas*. Latin translations of the Greek phrase usually read "cum mores ipsi Graeco sermone nihil sint quam assuefactio diuturna" *(Plutarchi . . . moralia . . .*, trans. Guilielmus Xylander [Basel, 1572], p. 4). Plutarch's phrase was a peripatetic commonplace; see the references by Stobaeus in his anthology, *Ioannis Stobaei Anthologii libri duo priores*, ed. Curt Wachsmuth, 2 (Berlin, 1884): 116-17.

83. Plutarch *De liberis educandis* 3A.

84. Vegio, *De educatione liberorum*, p. 69. Cf. Erasmus, *De pueris instituendis*, p. 33 for an identical statement.

85. *De regimine principum*, pp. 206-7.

86. See note 44, above.

87. E.g., *Tractatus de parvulis trahendis ad Christum*, in *Opera omnia*, 3: 277-91. Citations from pp. 283-84.

88. Erasmus, *De pueris instituendis*, p. 33.

89. Ibid., p. 29.

90. Ibid., p. 29 ff.

91. Ibid., passim. The same arguments are made in Erasmus's *Education of a Christian Prince*, trans. Lester K. Born (New York, 1968), p. 140.

92. *De civilitate morum puerilium*, in *Opera omnia* (Leiden, 1703), vol. 1, col. 1044.

93. Wimpheling, *Adolescentia*, p. 192.

94. Quintilian 1.12.10. Cf. also Pseudo-Thomas, *De eruditione principum* (see note 50 above), pp. 221-28 for the same assertion, with references to Quintilian and Scripture.

95. *De officio mariti liber*, in *Opera omnia*, 4 (Valencia, 1783): 322.

96. Christoph Vischer, *Bericht aus Gottes Wort und verstendiger Leute Büchern, wie man junge Fürsten und Herrn . . . auffziehen soll. . . . Auch dem gemeinen Mann zur Kinderzucht zu gebrauchen* (n.p., 1573), biii r and v.

97. On this last point, cf. Quintilian 1.12.8–9.

98. *De pueris instituendis*, p. 48.

99. Quintilian 1.11.2.

100. Ibid., 10.7.1.

101. Ibid., 10.2.1.

102. Cf. note 82 above.

103. In the Latin translation (see note 82 above): "Neque abs re morales virtutes dixeris virtutes consuetudinis eorum lingua."

104. Aristotle *Nicomachean Ethics* 2.1103a.

105. Ibid., 1103 a–b.

106. *Disputatio contra scholasticam theologiam* (1517), WA, 1:224–28; see especially thesis 41: "Tota fere Aristotelis Ethica pessima est gratiae inimica."

107. Plato *Laws* 1.643d: "The most important part of education is right training in the nursery."

108. Aristotle *Nicomachean Ethics* 2.1104b.

109. Thomas Aquinas *Commentary on the Nicomachean Ethics*, trans. C. I. Litzinger, O.P., *Library of Living Catholic Thought*, 1 (Chicago, 1964): 113–16.

110. Aegidius Romanus, *De regimine principum*, pp. 193–94.

111. Aristotle *Politics* 7.12.7.

112. E.g., Aegidius Romanus, *De regimine principum*, p. 195.

113. "Mala enim consuetudo, diu inroborata, est inextinguibilis." This phrase is quoted by Nonius Marcellus, *De compendiosa doctrina ad filium*, ed. L. Quicheret (Paris, 1872), p. 137. It is attributed there to Varro's *De liberis educandis*. Cf. also Aristotle *Politics* 7.13.21–23 for the same point.

114. "Ingenium habet ambiguum ad utrumque usu et consiliis flexile." Juan Luis Vives, *De officio mariti liber*, in *Opera omnia*, 4:364.

115. Ibid., p. 322.

116. Vives, *De disciplina*. I use the German translation of part 2: "The Art of Teaching," in Rudolf Heine, trans., *Johann Ludwig Vives, Ausgewählte pädagogische Schriften* (Leipzig, n.d.), p. 44.

117. Seneca *De clementia* 1.3. The mind can "by practice make mercy its own [*usu suam faciat*]."

118. Vives, *De institutione feminae christianae* (1523), in *Opera omnia*, 4:258.

119. Galen *De sanitate tuenda libri sex* 1.12: "During these years [ages 7–14] you must shape [the child's] mind by means of strict habituation and learning. In this phase of life, morality and obedience are the best means for the care of the body" (*Claudii Galeni opera omnia*, ed. C. G. Kuhn, 6 [Leipzig, 1823]: 60).

120. E.g., Otto Brunfels, *Weiber und Kinder Apothek . . .* (Strassburg, 1535), xliiii r: "Also gewonheit der kind guter sitten ist inen nützlich am Leib und an sel. Darumb übel gesittet sind sol mann ordenlichen und gemechlich gewenen zu gutten sitten, mit gut und straf, damit si in irer Complexion gebessert werden."

121. "Dan die iugent fast die lehre nicht, so sie nicht zu ausdrücklichem nachsprechen gewehnet wird." From the visitation articles for Electoral Saxony, 1574, printed in Pallas, 41 (Allgemeiner Teil): 91.

122. For all relevant citations cf. R. C. Lodge, *Plato's Theory*, chap. 4.

123. Plato *Republic* 7.541a. I use the translation by Charles M. Bakewell in *The Modern Student's Library* (New York, 1928).

124. For Quintilian: 1:2; for the Renaissance: e.g., Vergerio, *De ingenuis moribus*, 7v.

125. For a good discussion of civic education in Renaissance Italy, and for references to authors, see Gregor Müller, *Bildung und Erziehung im Humanismus der italienischen Renaissance* (Wiesbaden, 1969); "Educazione morale-civile," particularly pp. 204–10 on Francesco Filelfo.

126. E.g., Wimpheling, *Adolescentia*, pp. 188 f.; 208; *Isidoneus*, pp. 82 f.; Vives, *De disciplinis*, p. 26.

127. For a discussion of Augustine's theology with reference to education, and for

relevant passages, see Rudolf Strauss, *Der neue Mensch innerhalb der Theologie Augustins* (Zurich, 1967), particularly pp. 52-55.

128. *De vera religione,* trans. J. H. S. Burleigh, *Library of Christian Classics* 6 (Philadelphia, 1953): 48 ff.

129. *De eruditione principum,* pp. 287-93; Vegio, *De eruditione liberorum,* pp. 137-59; Wimpheling, *Adolescentia,* pp. 209 ff.; Erasmus, *Pietas puerilis* (also called *Confabulatio pia*), in *Colloquia familiaria,* in *Opera omnia,* vol. 1, cols. 648-53; Vives, *De disciplinis,* pp. 56-57.

130. Vives, *De disciplinis,* p. 33.

131. Quintilian 2.4, quoting Cicero *De oratore* 2.21.88.

132. *De pueris instituendis,* p. 51.

133. E.g., Quintilian 1.8.8.

134. Vergerio, *De ingenuis moribus,* 11r.

135. For references to the large number of Italian writers who saw this as the object of education, see Müller, *Bildung und Erziehung,* pp. 321-22.

136. Vegio, *De educatione liberorum,* pp. 159-63.

137. This is too evident in all these writings to require proof. Even Erasmus, despite his talk about the plowboy, concerned himself almost exclusively with the well-born, hoping that ordinary mortals would be beneficially influenced if they observed the children of prominent men working hard at their studies ("si conspexerint heroum liberos a primis statim annis dicari studiis"); *De civilitate morum puerilium* (1529), in *Opera omnia,* vol. 1, col. 1033.

138. See the discussion of the Erasmian ideal as put into action by Johann Sturm in Walter Sohm, *Die Schule bei Johann Sturm und die Kirche Strassburgs . . .* (Munich and Berlin, 1912), pp. 31 ff.

139. Aristotle *Politics* 8.1337a. Cf. also Ibid., 5.1310a, and *Nicomachean Ethics* 10.1180a.

140. Quintilian 1.2.

141. Ibid., 1.2.9-10.

142. Vegio, *De educatione liberorum,* p. 69.

143. Wimpheling, *Germania.* I use the German translation by Joseph Freundgen, *Jakob Wimphelings pädagogische Schriften* (Paderborn, 1898), pp. 377-78.

144. *De pueris instituendis,* p. 52.

145. Ibid., pp. 25-26.

146. Vives, *De disciplinis,* p. 44.

147. Quintilian 1.1.6-7. Maffeo Vegio, *De educatione liberorum,* p. 25.

148. E.g., Vegio, *De educatione liberorum,* pp. 23-24.

149. Ibid., pp. 74-76.

150. *De pueris instituendis,* p. 55. As so often, Erasmus can be quoted in self-contradiction. In his *De ratione studii* (see note 56 above), p. 125, he recommends domestic tutoring as superior to public education. But this is so only for the well-to-do. Erasmus insisted on public control over schools for ordinary boys.

151. Aristotle *Nicomachean Ethics* 10.1180a.25; *Politics* 8.1337a.30.

152. Vergerio, *De ingenuis moribus,* 7v.

153. Notably from the old and New Testaments, where little or nothing was said about schools and formal schooling, but a great deal about the father's rights and about education as, essentially, a body of wisdom handed down from parents to children. Cf. Werner Jentsch, *Urchristliches Erziehungsdenken,* pp. 85-139 for the Old Testament; pp. 226-70 for the New Testament. The principles of education in the Italian Renaissance emphasized the role of the family (cf. especially Leon Battista Alberti, *I libri della famiglia,* ed. Cecil Grayson in *Opere volgari* [Bari, 1960]; Alberti's complete manuscript was not published until 1908) but implicitly assumed the essential harmony between family and state interests. Cf. Müller, *Bildung und Erziehung,* passim, especially pp. 210 ff.

154. Vincent of Beauvais, *De eruditione filiorum nobilium* (see note 40 above), chap. 11; Wimpheling, *Isidoneus,* passim, especially p. 171; Vives, *De disciplinis,* passim, especially p. 60.

155. Jerome, ep. 107 and 128 (see note 58 above). Vincent of Beauvais, *De eruditione filiorum nobilium,* chaps. 42-51; Vives, *De institutione feminae christianae,* vol. 1, chap. 4. For Plato's influential views, cf. *Republic* 5.451c ff.

156. Quintilian 1.1.11.

CHAPTER 4

1. The term "psychology" was coined in the late sixteenth century by the German polymath Rudolph Goclenius, in the title of one of his works. None of the authors considered in this chapter used it. Their terminology remained Aristotle's, as given in the Latin translations of his treatise on the soul, De anima.

2. Karl Hartfelder, Melanchthoniana Paedagogica: Eine Ergänzung zu den Werken Melanchthons im Corpus Reformatorum (Leipzig, 1892), p. 242.

3. The book was originally planned to be part of a comprehensive treatment of the realm of physics, but Melanchthon completed no more than this volume. Cf. Karl Hartfelder, Melanchthoniana Paedagogica, p. 241.

4. [Stephen Batman], Batman upon Bartholome, his Booke "De proprietatibus rerum . . ." (London, 1582), vol. 3.

5. The influential commentary on Aristotle's De anima by Giacomo Zabarella, the late-sixteenth-century Paduan philosopher and medical man, was first published, posthumously, in 1605.

6. Robert Burton, The Anatomy of Melancholy (Oxford, 1621), part 1, sec. 1, member 2, subsecs. 5-13: "Of the Soule and his faculties." Burton uses and discusses the entire literature on the soul from Aristotle to Zabarella.

7. De anima 2.412a. "Soul" is thus one aspect of a single substance possessing two aspects: matter and form, body and soul. I use D. W. Hamlyn, trans. and commentator, Aristotle's "De anima," Books II and III (Oxford, 1968). The review of earlier theories of the soul takes up book 1 of Aristotle's treatise.

8. Cf. Juan Luis Vives, De anima et vita, in Joannis Ludovici Vivis Valentini Opera Omnia (Valencia, 1745 ff.) 3:300-520. Bk. 1, chap. 12: "Anima quid sit, nihil interest nostra scire. Qualis autem est quae eius opera, permultum de anima."

9. e.g., Stephen Batman, Batman upon Bartholome, bk. 3, chaps. 1-5.

10. Nominalists and realists hotly debated the question of definition in the Middle Ages. Is "soul" a mere name for a number of functions? Or is it something more than and above these functions? Realists adopted a modified Platonic view of the soul living eternally within an abstract world of ideas. Nominalists, like Aristotle, concentrated on the study of the senses. Cf. George Sidney Brett, A History of Psychology (London, 1912-21), 2:82-85.

11. Cf. Vives, De anima et vita, pp. 341-42: "Thus the human soul is provided with three functions or faculties or powers or duties, or, as others say, potencies and parts ("ex tribus constat praecipuis, sive functionibus, sive viribus, sive numeribus, ac officiis, sive (ut alii apellant) potentiis, ac partibus").

12. Brett, History of Psychology, 1:197-99; Johann Rump, Melanchthons Psychologie . . . in ihrer Abhängigkeit von Aristoteles und Galenos (Kiel, 1897), pp. 11-12.

13. My guides to the subject are Brett, History of Psychology: On Plato, 1:65-99; on Aristotle, 1:100-155; on the eventual replacement of Aristotle, vol. 2, parts 3 and 4. For Aristotle's psychology, see D. W. Hamlyn, Aristotle's "De anima" and Clarence Shute, The Psychology of Aristotle: An Analysis of the Living Being (New York, 1941); also, John I. Beare, Greek Theories of Elementary Cognition (Oxford, 1906).

14. Liber de anima, in C. G. Bretschneider, ed., Philippi Melanthonis opera . . . (Corpus reformatorum), 13 (Halle, 1846), cols. 6-178.

15. Ibid., col. 13. Melanchthon apparently derived the term Endelechia in his definition (col. 12) from Cicero's Tusculan Disputations 1.10.22.

16. He corresponded with medical men for this purpose and was in close touch with his physician son-in-law Caspar Peucer. For later editions of the book he used Vesalius and Leonhard Fuchs. Cf. Rump, Melanchthons Psychologie, p. 8.

17. Cf. also Vives, De anima, p. 340: "[the soul] sees with the eyes and hears with the ears."

18. See the succinct statement in Nicomachean Ethics 1.1102 a-b.

19. Melanchthon here follows Galen rather than Aristotle. The latter had not distinguished between judgment and the common sense. Cf. Rump, Melanchthons Psychologie, p. 171.

20. Vives, De anima, p. 312, gives a somewhat different picture of sense perception, thus showing how the different traditions available to a sixteenth-century scholar could be combined in the manner most satisfying to him. The function of the medium, he says, is to

make the sense object soft and pliable so that in transmitting itself to the sense organ it leaves all its material properties behind. Gerhard Hoppe, *Die Psychologie des Juan Luis Vives* (Berlin, 1901), p. 17, points out that Vives here revives the ancient atomistic corpuscular theory.

21. Melanchthon, *De anima,* cols. 146–47.

22. Günther Jacob, *Der Gewissensbegriff in der Theologie Luthers* (Tübingen, 1929); Gertrud Jung, "Syneidesis, Conscientia, Bewusstsein," *Archiv f. d. gesammte Psychol.* 89 (1934): 525–40.

23. Paul Eber, *Catechismuspredigten* (given in Wittenberg in 1562 and printed Wittenberg, 1578). I use the edition in Reu, 1, 2 (2). The quotation is on p. 88.

24. Erik H. Erikson, *Identity and the Life Cycle: Selected Papers,* Psychological Issues, 1, no. 1 (1959): 80.

25. Melanchthon, *De anima,* col. 142.

26. Ibid., col. 144.

27. Cf. D. W. Hamlyn, *Aristotle's "De anima,"* pp. 138–39. Aristotle, *De anima* 3.429b–430a. The Latin word *tabula* seems to have been first used by Aegidius Romanus.

28. Bartolomäus Metlinger, *Regiment der jungen Kinder, wie man sie halten und erziehen soll* . . . (Augsburg, 1473), 26r.

29. Wenceslaus Linck, *Vom christlichen Adel* (1524), in W. Reindell, ed., *Wenzel Lincks Werke* (Marburg, 1894), p. 279. Linck's word for mind is *Gemüt,* an ancient term, used, however, in the sixteenth century interchangeably with *mens.*

30. E.g., Vives, *De anima et vita,* p. 345, in the discussion of memory. Juan Huarte, *The Examination of Men's Wits* . . . (trans. Richard Carew, 1594), p. 62. The comparison of the mind to a wax tablet occurs in Plato's *Theaetetus* 191c.

31. *De anima* 3.431a.

32. *De Trinitate,* quest. 1, art. 3.

33. "Primi magistri sunt sensus, in quorum domo est conclusa mens"; *De anima et vita,* bk. 2, chap. 8, p. 373.

34. The human infant as a tabula rasa is sometimes conceptualized by anthropologists describing socialization as a process of cultural conditioning. As a concept it conflicts with the view of socialization as impulse control, employed by psychologists since Freud. Sixteenth-century views matched the model of the psychologists rather than that of the anthropologists. Cf. Robert A. LeVine, "Culture, Personality and Socialization: An Evolutionary View," *Handbook of Socialization Theory and Research,* ed. David A. Goslin (Chicago, 1969), p. 506.

35. On the Augustinian origins of this doctrine of the will, see Rudolf Strauss, *Der neue Mensch innerhalb der Theologie Augustins* (Zurich, 1967), pp. 75–90.

36. *De anima* 406b. Translation by Clarence Shute, *Psychology of Aristotle,* p. 97.

37. Robert Burton, *The Anatomy of Melancholy,* part 1, sec. 1, mem. 2, subsec. 8.

38. "Velle ac nolle." Melanchthon, *De anima,* col. 153.

39. Ibid., cols. 155–56; 159–60.

40. Ibid., cols. 166–67.

41. Aristotle *Eudemian Ethics* 1220a.

42. Cf. Aristotle *De memoria et reminiscentia* 451b–452b. Cf. Beare, *Greek Theories,* p. 314.

43. Melanchthon, *De anima,* col. 167.

44. Vives, *De anima et vita,* bk. 2, chap. 15.

45. Vives, *De disciplinis,* in *Opera,* vol. 6, bk. 2, chap. 3, p. 290.

46. Thomas Aquinas, *Commentary on the Nichomachean Ethics,* trans. C. I. Litzinger, O.P., *Library of Living Catholic Thought,* vol. 1 (Chicago, 1964), no. 253.

47. Ibid., no. 247.

48. Ibid., no. 249.

49. Ibid., no. 254.

50. I take the phrase from John Owen, *A Discourse concerning the Holy Spirit* (1674), bk. 3, chap. 6 (republished by the Calvinistic Book Concern, Xenia, Ohio, 1841), p. 184. In the chapter in which this line occurs, Owen gives an outline of the stages of sinfulness in the young person and adult drawn from Augustine's *Confessions.*

51. He takes this arrangement from Augustine *De Trinitate* 10.11. I use *On the Holy Trinity: A Select Library of the Nicene and Post-Nicene Fathers. . . .* vol. 3 (Buffalo, N.Y.,

1887). Augustine, of course, represented the mind as an image of the Trinity: ibid., 10, chap. 12.

52. Vives, *De anima et vita*, bk. 1, chap. 10, p. 327.

53. Ibid., p. 344.

54. Ibid., p. 327.

55. Ibid., pp. 424-25.

56. Ibid., bk. 3. Cf. Carlos G. Noreña, *Juan Luis Vives* (The Hague, 1970), pp. 269-74.

57. *De anima et vita* bk. 2, chap. 2.

58. Ibid., bk. 2, chap. 6.

59. Ibid., bk. 1, chap. 2.

60. Ibid., p. 349.

61. Ibid., p. 347. Vives follows Galen in accepting the inextricable connection between the thinking faculties of the soul and the body's physiology.

62. Ibid., p. 348.

63. Ibid., pp. 351-52.

64. Ibid., pp. 365-67.

65. This one from *Markgräflich Badisch-Durlach'sche Schulordnung* of 1536, printed in Vormbaum, p. 30.

66. *De anima et vita*, p. 398.

67. Augustine, *De magistro*, in R. P. Russell, trans. *Saint Augustine: The Teacher. . . . The Fathers of the Church: A New Translation*, 59, (Washington, D.C., 1968): 45.

68. Ibid.

69. Erasmus, *De pueris instituendis*, ed. J.-C. Margolin, *Opera Omnia Desiderii Erasmi*, 1,2 (Amsterdam, 1971): 45.

70. Ibid., p. 46.

71. Thomas Aquinas, *De magistro*, art. 1, reply (*Quaestio* 11 of *Quaestiones disputatae de veritate*, trans. James V. McGlynn, S.J., *The Disputed Questions on Truth* (Chicago, 1952-54), 2:77-101. In this treatise Thomas seeks to prove that man *can* teach, against the view ascribed by him to Augustine, that only God teaches.

72. Ibid.

73. Hugh of Saint Victor *Didascalicon* 3.11. I use the critical edition by Charles Henry Buttimer, *Hugonis de Sancto Victore, Didascalicon . . .* (Washington, D.C., 1939).

74. Quintilian *Institutio oratoria* 1.3.1. A good memory has two characteristics; it is "quick to take in and faithful to retain." Cf. also Augustine *Confessions* 10.8-19.

75. Sebald Heiden, *Paedonomia scholastica, pietatis, studii literarii, ac morum honestatis praecepta continens* (Nuremberg, 1553), nos. 115 and 116.

76. Quintilian 1.12.8.

77. Augustine *De Trinitate* (see note 51, above) 10.10-11. On this point, see the comments by Charles Trinkaus, *In Our Image and Likeness: Humanity and Divinity in Italian Humanist Thought* (Chicago, 1970), vol. 1, part 2, chap. 4.

78. For manuals on mnemotechnics see Lambertus Thomas Schenkelius, *Compendium der Mnemonik . . .*, trans. Johann Ludwig Klueber (Erlangen, 1804). See Erasmus's ridicule of these manuals in his colloquy *Ars notoria* of 1529: Craig R. Thompson, trans., *The Colloquies of Erasmus* (Chicago, 1965), pp. 458-61.

79. Vives, *De disciplinis*, pp. 347-48. Cf. also David Chytraeus, *De ratione discendi et ordine studiorum . . .* (Wittenberg, 1564), D7 v.

80. Rudolf Agricola, *De formando studio* (I use the edition Freiburg, 1539), pp. 75-90.

81. Timothy Bright, *A Treatise of Melancholy* (Oxford, 1586), pp. 67-68.

82. Juan Huarte, *Examen de ingenios para las ciencias* (1575), critical edition by Rodrigo Sanz (Madrid, 1930). I use the English translation by Richard Carew (London, 1594): *The Examination of Men's Wits*. The reference is to pp. 24-40.

83. Unlike the followers of the Aristotelian school, Huarte regarded "nature"—an individual's "temperature" (i.e., balance of the four qualities) and complexion resulting from his humoral composition—rather than discipline as the basic determinant of learning. He argued that no one can teach a subject to a child who does not have the disposition for it: Ibid., Bii v. For a similar statement, see Thomas Elyot, *The Castel of Helthe . . .* (London, 1539), 3v-4r. Vives also placed considerable emphasis on individual variations among minds (*ingenia*, i.e., aptitudes) and morals (*mores*) resulting from "the different nature of each person, i.e., of the constitution and temperament of their bodies" (*De disciplinis*, bk. 2, chap. 3).

84. Huarte also explains and, to some extent, justifies intellectual and social stratification by demonstrating its origins in the physiologically conditioned natural distinctions among men's minds. His physiological determinism was drawn directly from Galen. Cf. Rudolph E. Siegel, *Galen's System of Physiological Medicine* (Basel and New York, 1968), p. 240.

85. Brett, *History of Psychology*, 1:146.

86. "Jung gewonet, alt getan." This is quoted frequently, e.g., by Caspar Huberinus, *Spiegel der geistlichen Hauszucht* (Frankfurt am Main, 1569), Gvi v.

87. On the earlier Greek sources of Aristotle's assertions about habits and habituation, see Franz Dirlmeier, *Aristoteles Nikomachische Ethik* (5th ed., Berlin, 1969), p. 297, note 29.

88. John Jones, *The Arte and Science of Preserving Bodie and Soule* . . . (London, 1579), p. 57.

89. Plato *Laws* 2. 653.

CHAPTER 5

1. For a survey of this literature see Walter Hornstein and Andreas Flitner, "Kindheit und Jugendalter in geschichtlicher Betrachtung," *Zeitschr. Pädagogik*, no. 4 (1964), pp. 311–39; "Neue Literatur zur Geschichte des Kindes- und Jugendalters," ibid., no. 11 (1965), pp. 66–85.

2. The quotation is from Martinus J. Langeveld, *Studien zur Anthropologie des Kindes* (Tübingen, 1956), pp. 1–2, where he notes and regrets the indifference of earlier centuries to thinking coherently about the child qua child.

3. Johann Jakob Hässlin, ed., *Das Buch Weinsberg* (Munich, 1961), p. 32. Hermann began writing his memoirs in 1555, extending the chronicle back to his birth in January 1518. For the principles governing the writing of this extraordinary chronicle, see Hermann's preface to his heir (1561), ibid., pp. 4–14. For an example of autobiographical recollections of childhood from the fifteenth century, see Richard C. Trexler, "In Search of a Father: The Experience of Abandonment in the Recollections of Giovanni di Pagolo Morelli," *History of Childhood Quarterly* 3 (1975): 225–52.

4. Hässlin, *Das Buch Weinsberg*, p. 53.

5. Ibid., pp. 38–39.

6. Michel Vovelle, *Mourir autrefois* (Paris, 1974), p. 19, estimates for the seventeenth century the number of stillbirths and of deaths during the first few years of life at 45 to 50 percent of the total number of births. For striking pieces of evidence see pp. 20–23, excerpts from a late-seventeenth-century *livre de raison:* of ten children born to one family in fifteen years, only three lived beyond the sixth year; and plate 1: an Austrian *ex voto* of 1775 showing father, mother, and child praying to the Virgin before the bodies of eight other children: "Lieber Gott, acht Kinder sind bei dir / so schenke das neunte mir."

7. Dürer, *Familienchronik*, in Hans Rupprich, ed., *Dürer: Schriftlicher Nachlass* 1 (Berlin, 1956): 30.

8. From the protocols of the *Scholarchen* (1542), Strasb.A.V., Archives St. Thomas 372, unnumbered leaves.

9. I am unimpressed by Philippe Ariès's attempt to argue that death was "tamed" in the medieval and early modern centuries in the sense of being familiar, close by, and therefore calmly accepted. Philippe Ariès, *Western Attitudes toward Death: From the Middle Ages to the Present*, trans. Patricia M. Ranum (Baltimore, 1974), pp. 1–25. I also fail to see how he can reconcile this conclusion with his thesis about the period's—especially the fifteenth century's—"love of life" (derived from A. Tenenti, *Il senso della morte e l'amore della vita nel Rinascimento* [Turin, 1957]; see *Western Attitudes toward Death*, pp. 44–45). A better case for the acceptance of death as normal could possibly be made from the prevalence of prayers in time of death in prayer books suitable for children, such as Konrad Dietrich's *Christliches Zuchtbüchlein* (Ulm, ca. 1616), part 2. For figures and sources on infant mortality in the early modern period, see Lawrence Stone, *The Family, Sex and Marriage in England, 1500–1800* (New York, 1977), pp. 68–70 and note 59.

10. It would be impossible to write for the sixteenth century the kind of analysis given by Hans Heinrich Muchow in his excellent *Jugend und Zeitgeist: Morphologie der Kulturpubertät* (Reinbeck-Hamburg, 1962), which deals with the developing sense of the youth (*Jüngling*) in the 1770s. The book's thesis is that "the intellectual character of a given

period in history shapes the individual living in it, and especially the young person" (p. 40). Muchow's impressive evidence comes from utterances of youths about themselves and the recollections of adults (see also the same author's *Jugendgenerationen im Wandel der Zeit: Beiträge zur Geschichte der Jugend* [Vienna, 1964]). It seems likely that the marked improvement shown by life and death statistics beginning in the early eighteenth century (cf. Vovelle, *Mourir autrefois*, pp. 183-86) had much to do with this new interest in the psychology and culture of youth. For a balanced discussion of childhood experience in an earlier period, see Mary Martin McLaughlin, "Survivors and Surrogates: Children and Parents from the Ninth to the Thirteenth Centuries," in *The History of Childhood*, ed. Lloyd deMause (New York, 1974), pp. 101-81.

11. On these models see chap. 7 below.

12. For concepts of socialization in the modern context see David A. Goslin, ed., *Handbook of Socialization Theory and Research* (Chicago, 1969); William Kessen, ed., *The Child* (New York, 1965); John W. M. Whiting and Irwin L. Child, *Child Training and Personality: A Cross-Cultural Study* (New Haven, 1953).

13. George Frederick Still, *The History of Pediatrics: The Progress of the Study of Diseases of Children up to the End of the Eighteenth Century* (London, 1931), pp. 2-12; 42-54; Albrecht Peiper, *Chronik der Kinderheilkunde*, 4th ed. (Leipzig, 1966), pp. 28-57, 77-79; Karl Sudhoff, ed., *Erstlinge der pädiatrischen Literatur* (Munich, 1925), pp. xliii-li. Cf. also Johann Lachs, *Die Gynekologie des Galen* (Breslau, 1903), pp. 64-67, and Johannes Iberg, "Die Überlieferung der Gynäkologie des Soranos von Ephesos," *Abhandl. kgl.-sächsischen Ges. d. Wiss., philol.-hist. Kl.*, vol. 28 (1910), no. 2.

14. I have examined works of the following academics: Sebastianus Austrius, *De infantium sive puerorum morborum et symptomatum . . .* ([Basel, 1540]; this book is an almost verbatim plagiarized version of Cornelius Roelans's more famous *De aegritudinis infantium*); Paulus Bagellardus, *Libellus de aegritudinibus infantium* (Padua, 1472; reprinted in Sudhoff, *Erstlinge*); Hieronymus Mercurialis, *De puerorum morbis tractatus . . .* (Frankfurt am Main, 1584).

15. Still, *History of Pediatrics*, pp. 179-80.

16. *Problemata Aristotelis; Mancherley zweiffelhaffte Fragen, gründliche Erörterung und Auflösung des . . . Aristotelis und viel anderer . . . Naturerkündiger . . .* (Frankfurt am Main, 1577), unpaginated.

17. Eucharius Rösslin, *Ein Underweisung, wie sich die schwangeren Frauen halten sollen: In Reimen verfasst* (appended to the same author's *Hebammenbüchlein* [Frankfurt am Main, 1562]), p. 101.

18. See Leonhard Acesius's remark in his expanded edition of Walter Reiff's *Schwangerer Frauen Rosengarten . . .* (Frankfurt am Main, 1569), 7r; also Adam Lonicerus's preface to his 1562 edition of Eucharius Rösslin's *Der schwangeren Frawen und hebammen rossgarten* (Frankfurt am Main, 1562).

19. Ludwig Hänselmann, ed., *Bugenhagens Kirchenordnung für die Stadt Braunschweig . . .* (Wolfenbüttel, 1885), p. 31. The *Hebammenordnung* is given on pp. 31-40.

20. Felix Würtz, *Practica der Wund-Artzney* (n.p., 1563). The *Schönes und nützliches Kinder-Büchlein* is appended to this major work. It is also reprinted in Albrecht Peiper, ed., *Quellen zur Geschichte der Kinderheilkunde* (Bern and Stuttgart, 1966), pp. 59-91. My references are to this edition. Passages referred to in the text: pp. 60-62.

21. Rösslin, *Hebammenbüchlein*, 68v.

22. Diane Hughes, "Domestic Ideals and Social Behavior: Evidence from Medieval Genoa," in *The Family in History*, ed. Charles Rosenberg (Philadelphia, 1975), p. 131.

23. The custom was also rejected by Scipio Mercurio, *La comare o raccoglitrice* (Venice, 1595). The only German treatise I have seen that recommends use of wet nurses over the mother is Oswald Gaebelkhover, *Artzneybuch* (Tübingen, 1595), part 2, pp. 119-20. Gaebelkhover was physician to the court of Duke Ludwig of Württemberg. His practice was restricted to people of blood and aristocracy.

24. Tacitus, *Germania*, 20. For an explicit reference to Tacitus's moral intentions in stressing this point, see his *Agricola*, 28. The *Germania* was first printed in Venice (1470), then Nuremberg (1473). Beatus Rhenanus's edition of it came in 1519, and Andreas Althamer's *Commentary on Tacitus* in 1536.

25. Würtz, *Practica*, pp. 63-64.

26. E.g., Otto Brunfels, *Weiber und Kinder Apothek* (Strassburg, 1535), based for the most part on Avicenna but pervaded by a strong sense of obligation toward infants and children.

27. Würtz, *Practica*, pp. 65, 76-78.

28. Ibid., pp. 85-87.

29. E.g., Bartholomäus Metlinger, *Regiment der jungen Kinder* (Augsburg, 1473), 4r-v.

30. All writers advocate this, partly for cleanliness, partly for medicinal reasons. Since Galen it was thought that bathing preserved the natural moisture of infancy (Galen *De sanitate tuenda libri sex* 1. 7.8-17), although some authors disagreed. Laurentius Friess, *Spiegel der Artzney* . . . (Strassburg, 1519), 51v, thought frequent and lengthy bathing harmful. But most writers followed Galen.

31. "Vor allen dingen soll ir leinwand rein und sauber sein"; Brunfels, *Weiber und Kinder Apothek*, xxvi r.

32. *Artzneybuch köstlich für mancherley kranckheyt des gantzen leibs* . . . (a collection of medical writings by various hands [Erfurt, 1546]), p. cliii v.

33. Metlinger, *Regiment*, 9v.

34. Brunfels, *Weiber und Kinder Apothek*, xliiii r.

35. I have referred only to the German literature here. French, English, Spanish, and Italian writers show the same tendencies.

36. This claim is made emphatically, but without much evidence, by Edward Shorter, *The Making of the Modern Family* (New York, 1975), pp. 200-201, 203. See Christopher Lasch's criticism of this point in his review of Shorter's book, *New York Review of Books*, 11 December 1975, p. 51. Stone, *The Family, Sex and Marriage*, pp. 105-14 also claims that high infant mortality made parents cool and remote toward their children throughout the early modern period.

37. Johann Agricola, *Sybenhundert und fünfftzig Teutscher Sprichwörter* (Hagenau, 1534), no. 695.

38. John R. Gillis does not exhaust the range of the ties between parents and children when he asserts that "children were to pre-industrial society what pensions and disability insurance are to our own"; *Youth and History* . . . (New York, 1974), p. 11.

39. Agricola, *Sybenhundert und fünfftzig Teutscher Sprichwörter*, no. 593.

40. Ibid., no. 321.

41. From the preface by Simon Scheidenreisser, called Minervius, to his translation of the Odyssey, *Odyssea, das seind die vier und zwaintzig bücher . . . Homeri . . .* (Augsburg, 1538), iii v. Cf. Zacharias Rivander, *Der ander Theil Promptuarii Exemplorum . . .* (Frankfurt am Main, 1581), Gggiii r: "Es hat Gott der Herr in menschlicher Natur ein Feuwer angesteckt, dadurch die Menschen in Liebe gegen ire kinder . . . gleich entbrandt werden."

42. In the Table Talk: *WA*, Tr. 5, nos. 5490a-5502.

43. Cf. Luther's comments on the earlier death (1528) of his eight-month-old daughter Elizabeth, in a letter to Nikolaus Hausmann, *WA*, Br. 4, no. 1303.

44. *WA*, Tr. 1, no. 250 (1532).

45. Cf. chap. 2 above.

46. *WA*, Br. 5, no. 1595.

47. Especially in the morbid pages of the *History of Childhood Quarterly*. See the editor, Lloyd deMause's programmatic article, "The Evolution of Childhood" in deMause, *History of Childhood*, pp. 1-73.

48. From the dialogue *Mollis educatio liberorum* in Joannes Morisotus, *Colloquia* of 1549 (bk. 3, no. 6), quoted in A. Bömer, "Aus dem Kampfe gegen die Colloquia familiaria des Erasmus: Die Dialogue des Johannes Morisotus," *Archiv Kulturgesch.* 9 (1911): 58.

49. There is evidence that sixteenth-century pedagogues aspired to a healthy mean between spoiling children with excessive parental affection and neglecting them. Cf. the question *Ob eltern sind, welche ire kinder verzärteln oder ärgern* from the visitation questionnaire used in Coburg, S.Cob. B124, vol. V, 416.

50. Cf. the sermons by Geiler von Kaisersberg and others referred to by Hans Boesch, *Kinderleben in der deutschen Vergangenheit* (Leipzig, 1900), p. 25.

51. For example, Konrad Dietrich, *Christliche Kirchengebet, so . . . in denen Ulmischen Kirchen gebraucht werden* (Ulm, 1616), pp. 350-54.

52. E.g., *Nüwe Stattrecht und Statuten der loblichen Statt Freiburg . . .* (Freiburg, 1520),

redacted by the jurist Ulrich Zasius, 74r and 81r. There are many other examples. The Freiburg *Stadtrecht* (along with other codes) has an enormous amount of material on children: their rights of inheritance, duties of father and mother toward them, and so on. It might be argued that municipal regulations aiming at exact record-keeping also betoken a regard for children as individuals. Cf., for example, Veit Dietrich, *Agendbüchlein für die Pfarrherrn auf dem Lande* (Nuremberg, 1543), viiii r.

53. For some excellent examples, see Baltimore, Walters Art Gallery cod. 274, 82, and 148; New York: Pierpont Morgan Library ms. M268, 26r and v: a series of eight illustrations from a magnificent Swabian picture Bible, late fourteenth century. Cf. Hans Wentzel, "Ad infantiam Christi: Zu der Kindheit unseres Herren," in *Das Werk des Künstlers: Studien zur Ikonographie und Formgeschichte, Herbert Schrade . . . dargebracht*, ed. Hans Fegers (Stuttgart, 1960), pp. 134-60.

54. For illustrations of three versions of Cranach's painting, see Gertrud Schiller, *Ikonographie der christlichen Kunst*, 1 (Gütersloh, 1969): 166 and plate 444; Christine O. Kibish, "Lukas Cranach's 'Christ Blessing the Children,'" *Art Bulletin* 37 (1955): 196-203. The panels were clearly intended to strengthen Lutheran arguments for infant baptism. See Luther's evocation of the scene depicted in Matt. 19:13-15 in his *Sermon for the Third Sunday after Epiphany* (1523) in *WA*, 21:74-83. Andreas Osiander published this as an anti-Anabaptist tract in 1529: *Von der Kinder Tauff und frembden Glauben* (Nuremberg, 1529).

55. *Nachlass*, 2:341-51. For Dürer's memories of a devoted father, see *Familienchronik*, in ibid., 1:28-30. He refers to his father throughout as "mein lieber Vatter."

56. A very good example: family portrait of Bartolomäus Bruyn the elder and his children. *Münchener Gemälde Kataloge*. Vol. 24. *Altdeutsche Gemälde: Köln und Nord-Westdeutschland* (Munich, 1972).

57. For some striking illustrations, see the plates in Albrecht Peiper, *Chronik der Kinderheilkunde*, 4th ed. (Leipzig, 1966). Also Max Sauerlandt, *Kinderbildnisse aus fünf Jahrhunderten* . . . (Königstein and Leipzig, 1921), especially plates 14-32. Ilene H. Forsyth, "Children in Early Medieval Art: Ninth through Twelfth Centuries, *Journal of Psychohistory* 4, no. 1 (summer, 1976): 31-70, argues for the existence of a concept of childhood in that period. See also the sensitive remarks on depictions of the massacre of the innocents by Mary McLaughlin in the article cited in note 10, pp. 133-34.

58. *WA*, Tr. 3, no. 3566A. See also 2, no. 1559.

59. Cyriacus Spangenberg, *Ehespiegel: das ist, Alles, was vom heyligen Ehestande nützliches . . . mag gesagt werden* . . . (Strassburg, 1563; 1st ed. 1561), 48r and v.

60. Caspar Huberinus, *Spiegel der Hauszucht* . . . (Nuremberg, 1565, 1st ed., 1552), Dv v; Hv r.

61. Ecclus. (Jesus Sirach) 30:1, 7-9, 12.

62. For a good introduction to the theological problems, see Kurt Aland, *Die Stellung der Kinder in den frühen christlichen Gemeinden und ihre Taufe*, Theologische Existenz heute, N.F., no. 138 (Munich, 1967).

63. Andreas Althamer, *Von der Erbsünd, das sye der Christen kinder gleich als wol verdamb als der heyden* (Nuremberg, 1527).

64. Althamer raises the question: Are children with or without inherited sin? on D r. My paraphrase and passages are taken from the pages immediately following.

65. Ibid., Eiv v.

66. Huldreich Zwingli, *De peccato originali declaratio* . . . (1526), trans. Henry Preble, in William John Hinke, ed., *The Latin Works of Huldreich Zwingli*, 2 (Philadelphia, 1922): 30. Cf. p. 5: "The original contamination of man is a disease, not a sin, because sin implies guilt, and guilt comes from a transgression or trespass on the part of one who designedly perpetrates a deed."

67. *Confessio Augustana*, art. 2. My translation is from the German version, which is stronger than the Latin. For German, Latin, and an English translation based on the Latin, see *Concordia Triglotta: Die symbolischen Bücher der evangelisch-lutherischen Kirche* (Saint Louis, Mo., 1921), pp. 42-43. For a synopsis of New Testament references to children, and a discussion of their significance, see Aland, *Stellung der Kinder*, pp. 5-9.

68. Nicolaus Hunnius, *Anweisung zum rechten Christenthumb für junge und einfältige Leut . . .* (Lübeck, 1637). A conservative orthodox Lutheran, Hunnius was superintendent in Lübeck during most of his active life.

69. Andreas Osiander, *Catechismus oder Kinderpredig* (1533), in *Die evangelischen Kirchenordnungen des XVI. Jahrhunderts*, ed. Emil Sehling, continued by the *Institut für evangelisches Kirchenrecht der evangelischen Kirche in Deutschland zu Göttingen*, 2 (Tübingen, 1961): 234. On Osiander and his Nuremberg catechism, see also chap. 10 below.

70. Agricola, *Sybenhundert und fünfftzig Teutscher Sprichwörter* (1534), no. 134.

71. Ibid., no. 635.

72. Juan Huarte, *Examen de ingenios para las ciencias*, trans. Richard Carew (London, 1594; reprinted 1959), p. 21.

73. Christoph Vischer, *Christliche Auslegung und Erklerung der Haustafel...* (Leipzig, 1578), Rv r and v.

74. Sermon on 1 Peter 5. *WA*, 47:819. The text is 1 Pet. 5:7. The idea of an "altered" nature was, of course, theologically impossible. Elaborate similes and metaphors, such as the "grafting" procedure just mentioned, were intended to gloss over this. As argued in chap. 2, the reader of the popular pedagogical literature had to conclude that beneficial changes could in fact be brought about by education.

75. Huberinus, *Spiegel der Hauszucht*, Fiiii r.

76. Ecclus. 30:1-13.

77. Huberinus, *Spiegel der Hauszucht*, Nn r.

78. *Herrn Augusten zu Sachsen . . . Ordnung* (1580), in Sehling, 1:423.

79. *Visitations-Abschied für die Stadt Döbeln* (1555), in ibid. 1:548.

80. From correspondence concerning the establishment of a new school in Zwickau in 1542, S.Weim. reg. o, no. 552, 18r and v.

81. Christoph Hegendorf, *Christiana studiosae iuventutis institutio* (Hagenau, 1526), Aaii r.

82. For some conspicuous examples, see David Herlihy, "Vieillir à Florence au quattrocento," *Annales: E.S.C.* 24 (1969): 1338-52.

83. Aristotle *Rhetoric* 2.12. 1389a-b. I use the translation by J. H. Freese in the Loeb Classical Library edition (London, 1947).

84. For other statements by Aristotle on youth, and for a general discussion of views by Greek authors on the subject, see Arnold Bork, *Der junge Grieche: Ein Beitrag zur vergleichenden Jugendpsychologie* (Zurich and Stuttgart, 1959).

85. David Chytraeus, *Der fürnembsten heubtstück christlicher lehr nützliche und kurtze erklerung* (Rostock, 1578), 212r.

86. From a visitation protocol for Pfalz-Neuburg, 1584. S.Neub.D., Grassegger-Sammlung 1535³, 108r.

87. In 1546 the city of Strassburg published prayers for children against Catholics, Turks, war, famine, and inflation. A "Gemein Gebet wider den Erbfeind der gantzen Christenheit, den Türken" was added to Johann Brenz's catechism *Fragstück für die Jugend zu Schwäbischen Hall . . .* of 1528, in *Evangelische Katechismen der Reformationszeit vor und neben Martin Luthers Kleinem Katechismus*, ed. Ernst-Wilhelm Kohls, Texte zur Kirchen- und Theologiegeschichte, no. 16 (Gütersloh, 1971), pp. 33-34.

88. For examples—also of the reverse side of this belief in the efficacy of childish innocence, involving the magic use of child's blood—see Eberhard von Künssberg, "Rechtsbrauch und Kinderspiel," *Sitzb. Heidelberger Akad. Wiss. philos.-hist. Kl.* 7 (1920): 30-34.

89. Jörg Wickram, *Rollwagenbüchlein*, no. 74, in *Georg Wickram: Sämtliche Werke*, ed. Hans-Gert Roloff, 7 (Berlin, 1973): 141.

90. *WA*, Tr. 1, no. 660.

91. Ivar Asheim, *Glaube und Erziehung bei Luther* (Heidelberg, 1961), pp. 225-41. For a less sympathetic view, see Klaus Petzold, *Die Grundlagen der Erziehung im Spätmittelalter und bei Luther* (Heidelberg, 1969).

92. I follow Asheim's presentation of the stages of life as seen by Luther. *Glaube und Erziehung*, pp. 230-35. See there for references to Luther's works.

93. *WA*, Tr. 2, no. 1532.

94. For references to the literature on this, see the works of Franz Boll and Adolf Neumeister cited in note 34 to chap. 3.

95. It is difficult to resist the temptation of presenting this developmental scheme in Eriksonian terms: cf. Erik Erikson, *Identity and the Life Cycle; Selected Papers*, Psychological

Issues, vol. 1, no. 1 (New York, 1959): 50–100; idem, *Childhood and Society*, 2d ed. (New York, 1963) pp. 239 ff. For Luther's exposition of the life cycle, see *Lectures on Genesis* (1535–45), *WA*, 43:271. The text is Gen. 23:1-2.

96. Asheim, *Glaube und Erziehung;* Luther, *WA*, 42:351. The text is Gen. 8:21; 46: 500–501 (*Sermon on Galatians* 5:16); 39¹:502 (*Third Disputation against Antinomians*, 1538).

97. Asheim, *Glaube und Erziehung*, p. 34.

98. *WA*, 37:161 ("das muster und exemplar"), Sermon on Matt. 18:3-5; *WA*, Tr. 3, nos. 4027; 2, 1631; 1, 660; 4, 4367, 4364—all with references to Matt. 18:3.

99. *WA*, Tr. 2, nos. 1406, 2550, and several others.

100. *WA*, Tr. 4, no. 4506.

101. Agricola, *Sybenhundert und fünfftzig Teutscher Sprichwörter*, no. 297.

102. Quintilian, a representative classical writer on this point, called boys under fourteen *pueri*, those up to eighteen or nineteen *adulescentes*, and from then on to adulthood *iuvenes: Institutio oratoria* 2.2-3. On the other hand, Isidore of Seville called *infantia* the ages up to seven, *pueritia* to fourteen, *adolescentia* to twenty-eight, *iuventus* to fifty: Etymologiae 11, chap. 2 (Augsburg, 1472), unpaginated. "Youth" in this sense lasts into a man's prime or even to the end of his fertility. Adolf Hofmeister (for reference see note 34 to chap. 3), pp. 287–316 traces this scheme to Varro. There were other schemes, including one in which *pueritia* lasted to age twenty-eight. See also on this point H.-I. Marrou, *A History of Education in Antiquity*, trans. George Lamb (New York, 1964), pp. 42–43. Rigor in age classification was rarely observed in classical and medieval times. For an argument similar to my own, see Joseph F. Kett, "Adolescence and Youth in Nineteenth-Century America," in *The Family in History: Interdisciplinary Essays*, ed. Theodore K. Rabb and Robert I. Rotberg (New York, 1973), pp. 95–99.

103. *Herrn Augusten, Herzogen zu Sachssen . . . Kirchenordnung* (1580), in Sehling, 1:423.

104. Strassb.A.V., Archives St. Thomas 45, carton 21.1, 647v.

105. Stadtarchiv Hannover XIII, V, 4.

106. Unlike the mainstream reformers, Anabaptists tended to discriminate much more clearly among the young person's stages of development from infancy to youth. Their objective was a different one, however, and schooling played a very subordinate role in most Anabaptist communities. Cf. Hillel Schwartz, "Early Anabaptist Ideas about the Nature of Children," *Mennonite Quarterly Review* 47 (April 1973): 102–14.

107. I take this expression from Hans Heinrich Muchow, *Jugendgenerationen im Wandel der Zeit . . .* (Vienna, 1964), p. 26. See above, chap. 3.

108. Philippe Ariès, *Centuries of Childhood: A Social History of Family Life*, trans. Robert Baldick (New York, 1962), p. 329: "The moralists and pedagogues of the seventeenth century, heirs of a tradition going back to Gerson, to the fifteenth-century reformers of the University of Paris, to the founders of colleges in the late middle ages, succeeded in imposing their considered concept of a long childhood thanks to the success of the educational institutions and practices which they guided and supervised. We find the same men, obsessed with educational questions, at the origins of both the modern concept of childhood and the modern concept of schooling." Ariès is wrong in maintaining that it was only in the eighteenth century that the concept of a long childhood was translated into graded schools. But he is right in supposing that the agents of this change, when it came (much earlier than he thinks) were not humanists, but reformers. See also his fourth chapter of part 2: "The Pupil's Age."

109. Cf. Hans Heinrich Muchow, *Jugendgenerationen*, pp. 24–38 for some interesting evidence; also the same author's *Jugend und Zeitgeist . . .* (Reinbeck-Hamburg, 1962), especially pp. 9–13, for an analysis of evidence from Erasmus's *Colloquies*. For some statistics on sexual maturation among European girls in the late medieval and early modern periods, see J. B. Post, "Ages at Menarche and Menopause: Some Mediaeval Authorities," *Population Studies* 25, no. 1 (March 1971): 83–87; also Peter Laslett, "Age at Menarche in Europe since the Eighteenth Century," in *The Family in History . . .*, ed. Theodore K. Rabb and Robert I. Rotberg, (New York, 1973), pp. 28–47.

110. Andreas Flitner, "Kindheit und Jugendalter in geschichtlicher Betrachtung," *Zeitschr. Pädagogik* 10 (1964): 319.

111. Muchow, *Jugendgenerationen*, p. 37.

112. Cf. the many manuals on *Tischzucht* (table manners) and conversation. Correct behavior for children was adult behavior.

113. Fourteen was generally accepted as the age of discretion. See the sixteenth-century comment on the *Sachsenspiegel:* Melchior Kling, *Das gantze Sechsisch Landrecht mit Text und Gloss in eine richtige Ordnung gebracht*... (Leipzig, 1571), 198r and v. Kling maintains that children can tell good from bad at age thirteen or fourteen and can therefore from that age be held responsible.

114. Caspar Huberinus, *Postilla Teutsch über alle sonntägliche Evangelien* . . . (Augsburg, 1545), 2: Sv r.

115. Thomas Elyot, *The Education or Bringinge up of Children, Translated oute of Plutarche* . . . (1533), Fi v.

116. For an interesting discussion of adult attitudes toward the young, see Frank Musgrove, *Youth and the Social Order* (Bloomington, Ind., 1965). Musgrove argues that modern adults dislike and distrust the young and force them into "adolescent" roles by refusing to incorporate them into the social order until they are adults. "The adolescent as a distinct species is the creation of modern social attitudes and institutions. A creature neither child nor adult, he is a comparatively recent socio-psychological invention, scarcely two centuries old" (p. 13). For Erik Erikson's view of adolescence as periods of "institutionalized psycho-social moratoria during which a lasting pattern of inner identity is scheduled for relative completion" see *Identity and the Life Cycle*, p. 111.

117. Ariès, *Centuries of Childhood*, p. 26. Vivian C. Fox, "Is Adolescence a Phenomenon of Modern Times?" *The Journal of Psychohistory* 5:2 (1977), 271-90, also challenges the contention of Ariès, John R. Gillis, John Demos, and others that the concept of adolescence emerged only as late as the nineteenth century.

118. Luther, *Vom ehelichen Leben* (1522), *WA*, 10²:275-304; *Das siebente Kapitel S. Pauli zu den Korinthern* (1523), *WA*, 12:92-142. Several other treatises also deal with the subject. On the whole question, cf. the excellent article by Reinhold Seeberg, "Luthers Anschauung von dem Geschlechtsleben und der Ehe und ihre geschichtliche Stellung," *Luther-Jahrbuch* (1925), pp. 77-122. Seeberg inserts Luther's utterances into a theological frame in which they appear very distinct from medieval, Scholastically based views.

119. *Vom ehelichen Leben, WA*, 10²:276.

120. Ibid. Luther adopted the "naturalist" position of such medieval theologians as Thomas Aquinas and Duns Scotus, against the Augustinian "ascetic" position. On these cf. Tentler, *Sin and Confession*, pp. 167-70, 224-25.

121. *Das siebente Kapitel* . . . *zu den Korinthern, WA*, 12:92-142.

122. Ibid., p. 114.

123. *Wider den falsch genannten geistlichen Stand* . . . (1522), *WA*, 10²:156.

124. *Das siebente Kapitel* . . . *zu den Korinthern, WA*, 12:114-15.

125. Ibid., pp. 117-18.

126. *Vom ehelichen Leben, WA*, 10²:279.

127. *Eine christliche Schrift an H. Wolfgang Reissenbach* . . . *sich in den ehelichen Stand zu begeben* (1525), *WA*, 18:276.

128. "Wiltu nicht, sso wil eyn andere, wil fraw nicht, sso kum die magd"; *Vom ehelichen Leben, WA*, 10²:290.

129. Seeberg, "Luthers Anschauung," pp. 105-6, is embarrassed by these words; he interprets them as a threat. But Luther does say that if a wife fails to respond to two or three such warnings, she may be put aside for another woman: *Vom ehelichen Leben, WA*, 10²:290. See also the comments by Walther I. Brandt to his translation of the treatise in *LW*, 45:33.

130. Aristotle *History of Animals* 7. 581a-582a.

131. Luther, *Vom ehelichen Leben*, referred to what must have been unanimous medical opinion in his time that withholding sperm tends to poison the body: *WA*, 10²:301.

132. ". . . als kind oder gar alte lüt," Laurentius Friess, *Spiegl der Artzny* (Strassburg, 1519), 49r.

133. "Messig der lieb pflegen erquikt den Leib, / Doch anders nit, dann mit seinem Eheweib." *Problemata Aristotelis: Mancherley zweiffelhaffte Fragen* . . . (Frankfurt am Main, 1577), n.p.; chap. "Von dem natürlichen samen."

134. Aristotle *History of Animals* 7.581a.28-32; Laurentius Friess, *Spiegl der Artzny*, 49v. Friess has a touching page on the plight of deprived cloistered nuns as he says (ibid.) he has

observed it. Jacques Duval, *Des hermaphrodits: Accouchemens des femmes* . . . (Rouen, 1612), in his discussion of the female pudenda, says that the common name for the clitoris is *gaude mihi*.

135. Spangenberg, *Ehespiegel,* 131v.

136. Innumerable regulations could be cited for evidence: e.g., in the Württemberg *Kirchenordnung* of 1559. Exceptions were made for young children: for example, in Strassburg a girl under eight might go with an older brother to a boys' school. But from the age of eight on, "yder in die schul, dahin er gehört." See Robert Stupperich, ed., *Martin Bucers deutsche Schriften,* 7 (Gütersloh, 1964):514, for the text of the *Ordnung.* In practice these regulations proved impossible to apply consistently.

137. Strassb.A.V., Archives St. Thomas 372, 20r (1546).

138. Ibid., 324, 2v. Like all principles, this one too broke down in practice. Visitation documents record conditions very much at variance with declared intentions. E.g., WHS A64, B10, where a schoolmaster complains of having one hundred boys and sixty girls sitting in one room. This was in 1571.

139. Otto Brunfels, *Catechesis puerorum* . . . (Frankfurt am Main, 1529), 48v.

140. "Des fleisses [of vigilance] in disem schlüpfflichen alter mage nit zu fil angewendt werden." Martin Bucer to the Strassburg council, 1534. Stupperich, ed., *Martin Bucers deutsche Schriften,* 7:530.

141. S.Weim. Reg. O, no. 552, 19r. For a discussion of the elaborate precautions taken in sixteenth-century Jesuit boarding schools, see Josef Schröteler, *Die Erziehung in den Jesuiteninternaten des 16. Jahrhunderts* (Freiburg im Breisgau, 1940), pp. 329–35.

142. Spangenberg, *Ehespiegel* 132v.

143. Brunfels, *Catechesis puerorum* . . . , 48r.

144. Caspar Huberinus, *Der klaine Catechismus* . . . *für die jugent zugebrauchen* (Augsburg, 1544), Biii r and v. For a similar example, see the catechism by Andreas Musculus given in note 146, Hii v–Jiii v. Jesuit teachers, on the other hand, were instructed not to mention sexual offenses to the boys. Punishment was always for "immodest conduct." See the *Cantelae et observationes ad puritatem inter convictores conservandam* of 1592, given in Schröteler, *Erziehung in den Jesuiteninternaten,* p. 334.

145. Johann Böhm, *Ein christliches Radtbüchlin für die Kinder* (Wittenberg, 1536), Aii v–Aiii r.

146. "Wie mans immer mer erdenken kann." Andreas Musculus, *Catechismus, Kinderpredig, wie die in* . . . *der Stadt Nürnberg Oberkeiten* . . . *gepredigt werden* (Frankfurt an der Oder, 1566), Hviii v.

147. For an extraordinary instance of the openness with which sexual material was presented to children, see the *Colloquia* of Joannes Morisotus (Jean Morisot) of 1549, written for the author's son. It is described in detail by A. Bömer, "Aus dem Kampf gegen die *Colloquia familiaria* des Erasmus . . . ," *Archiv f. Kulturgesch.* 9 (1911): 1–73. For some comments on the free attitude toward sexual matters that prevailed in the early modern period, see Stone, *The Family, Sex and Marriage,* pp. 160–61.

148. Johann Agricola, *Eine christliche Kinderzucht inn Gottes Wort und Lere* . . . (Wittenberg, 1527), xviii v.

149. Heinrich Salmuth, *Catechismus* . . . (Budissin, 1581), Piii r.

150. Andreas Musculus, *Catechismus* . . . (1566), 6 vii r.

151. Memo by a group of Latin teachers to the Strassburg city council, 1540. Strassb.A.V., Archives St. Thomas 324, 142–45. I have contracted the argument slightly.

CHAPTER 6

1. Matt. 10:37. Cf. Luke 12:51–53, 14:26. For statement and discussion of the problem, see Helmut Begemann, *Strukturwandel der Familie,* 2d ed. (Witten, 1966), pp. 82–104, especially the summary on pp. 103–4. The contradiction among scriptural passages on family loyalty bedeviled all commentators in the sixteenth century. See the exegesis by Nicolaus Hunnius, *Anweisung zum rechten Christenthumb für junge und einfältige leut* . . . (Nuremberg, 1639), p. 98.

2. Matt. 15:4; Mark 7:10; Luke 18:20; Eph. 6:2.

3. Eph. 5:21-6:9; Col. 3:18-4:1; 1 Tim. 3:2-5; 1 Pet. 2:18-3:7.

4. E.g., Eph. 5:21-25; 1 Cor. 11:3.

5. For a discussion of the theological foundation of the Christian family, see Begemann, *Strukturwandel der Familie*, chap. 6.

6. Especially Ecclus. 25-33; 37-42. For the many books on household management dressed up as commentaries on these chapters, see below.

7. Col. 1:18. Cf. also Eph. 4:15.

8. For references and citations see Joseph E. Kerns, S.J., *The Theology of Marriage* (New York, 1964), p. 27 and notes 25-27; also Reinhold Seeberg, "Luthers Anschauung von dem Geschlechtsleben und der Ehe . . . ," *Luther-Jahrbuch* (1925), pp. 80-83. *The New Catholic Encyclopedia*, in its article "Marriage (Theology of)," speaks of the "progressive awareness of the Church of the holiness of marriage," (vol. 9, p. 266) but cites no theological opinion before *Rerum novarum* of 1890-91.

9. Luther, *Ein Sermon von dem ehelichen Stand* (1519), *WA*, 2:168-69.

10. The most egregious of these is the alphabet of female vices invented by Giovanni Dominici and taken over by Bishop Antoninus of Florence (*Summa*, part 3, tit. 1, cap. 25: "de diversis vitiis mulierum per alphabetum" [Verona, 1790; reprinted Graz, 1959], vol. 3, col. 117) and by countless authors thereafter. The *Malleus maleficarum* incorporates it in part 1, *quaestio* 6. Misogynism was, of course, as virulent among some Protestants as among some Dominicans.

11. Thomas Aquinas, *Commentum in quatuor libros sententiarum Magistri Petri Lombardi*, bk. 4, dist. 26, *quaestio* 1, art. 3 (*sol.*). *Sancti Thomae Aquinatis . . . Opera Omnia* (Parma, 1852-73; reprinted New York, 1948), 7²:919.

12. For references to these, see Franz Falk, *Die Ehe am Ausgange des Mittelalters*, Erläuterungen und Ergänzungen zu Janssens Geschichte des deutschen Volkes, 6, no. 4, (Freiburg im Breisgau, 1908), 21 ff.

13. Of the writings on wedded life mentioned immediately below, the most anti-monastic is the treatise of 1523, *Das siebente Kapitel S. Pauli zu den Korinthern*. It was occasioned by a pamphlet published in 1522 by one Johann Faber, attacking Luther's rejection of vows and affirming celibacy as a condition more godly and more conducive to the pious life than marriage. Luther replied with a long exegesis, from his newly developed point of view, of the critical text for the discussion of these issues: 1 Cor. 7. Many of Luther's arguments and proofs had already been employed by Erasmus in his *Declamatio matrimonii* of 1518. See Emile V. Telle, *Erasme de Rotterdam et le septième sacrement* (Geneva, 1954), vol. 2, chap. 1 (pp. 153-84). For a general discussion of Luther's comments on family and household see Wilhelm Maurer, "Luthers Lehre von den drei Hierarchien und ihr mittelalterlicher Hintergrund," *Bayer. Akad. d. Wiss., philos.-hist. Kl., Sitzb.* 1970, Heft 4 (Munich, 1970), esp. pp. 3-44.

14. *Ein Sermon von dem ehelichen Stand* (1519), *WA*, 2:166-71. I here use the translation by James Atkinson in *LW*, 44:13.

15. *Das siebente Kapitel* . . . (1523), *WA*, 12:105.

16. *Ein Sermon von dem ehelichen, Stand LW*, 44:9.

17. *Das siebente Kapitel* (1523), *WA*, 12:106-7.

18. Ibid., p. 108.

19. *Vom ehelichen Leben*, *WA*, 10²:275-304. I use the translation by Walther I. Brandt, *LW*, 45:46.

20. Ibid., pp. 43-45.

21. *Predigt* . . . *vom Ehestand* (1545), *WA*, 49:800.

22. *Vom ehelichen Leben*, *LW*, 45:18-19.

23. "Also ist einem Christen die gantze Welt eitel heiltum, reinigkeit, nutz und frummen." *Das siebente Kapitel* (1523), *WA*, 12:122.

24. Ibid., p. 114.

25. Ibid., pp. 103, 116-17.

26. Ibid., pp. 100, 103. 1 Cor. 7:2. For a systematic analysis of Calvin's views on sexuality and marriage—they compare interestingly with Luther's—see André Biéler, *L'homme et la femme dans la morale Calviniste* (Geneva, 1963), especially pp. 35-69.

27. *Vom ehelichen Leben*, *LW*, 45:21.

28. *Das siebente Kapitel* (1523), *WA*, 12:99-100.
29. Ibid., p. 104.
30. Ibid., p. 138. 1 Cor. 7:32-34.
31. Ibid., p. 141.
32. Ibid., p. 93.
33 *Vom ehelichen Leben, WA*, 10²:292-94.
34. Ibid., p. 295.
35. Ibid., p. 296.
36. *Vom ehelichen Leben, LW*, 45:42.
37. *Ein kurtzer Auszug auss der Christlichen Oeconomia Justi Menii*, with [anonymous] *Ein kurtze summa der rechten waren lehre unsers heyligen christlichen glaubens . . .* (Regensburg, 1554), unpaginated. See first plate of this series of woodcuts. On the *Hausväterliteratur* generally, see Otto Brunner, "Das 'Ganze Haus' und die alteuropäische Ökonomik," *Neue Wege der Sozialgeschichte* pp. 33-36; Begemann, *Strukturwandel der Familie*, pp. 104-7. On the support given by Protestant theology to the nuclear family and its head the *paterfamilias*, see Lawrence Stone, *The Family, Sex and Marriage in England, 1500-1800* (New York, 1977), pp. 135-42.
38. Cyriacus Spangenberg, *Ehespiegel: Das ist, Alles, was vom heyligen Ehestande nützliches . . . mag gesagt werden . . .* (Strassburg, 1563; preface dated 1561), 1 v. The terms are *Ehestand, Predigtamt*, and *Regieramt*.
39. Ibid., Aii v.
40. Ibid., 13v.
41. Leonhard Culman, *Jungen Gesellen, Junckfrawen und Witwen, so eelich wöllen werden zu nutz, ein undterichtung . . .* (Nuremberg, 1532), Aviii r.
42. Spangenberg, *Ehespiegel*, 3r.
43. Christoph Vischer, *Christliche Auslegung und Erklerung der Haustafeln wie sich alle drey stende . . . christlich in ihrem Ampte . . . verhalten sollen* (Leipzig, 1578), B v.
44. Culman, *Jungen Gesellen*, Biii v.
45. Veit Dietrich, *Kinder-Postilla* (Nuremberg, 1549), 48v.
46. Vischer, *Christliche Auslegung*, Mii v.
47. Ibid., N v.
48. Hieronymus Rauscher, *Loci communes doctrinae christianae: Die fürnembsten Artickel christlicher Leere* (Nuremberg, 1557), unpaginated.
49. Culman, *Jungen Gesellen*, Aiii r.
50. Vischer, *Christliche Auslegung*, Oiii v.
51. Culman, *Jungen Gesellen*, Cv r.
52. Spangenberg, *Ehespiegel*, 193v.
53. William Tyndale, *The Obedience of a Christian Man* (Marburg, 1528; reprinted 1970), xc r. Tyndale had been to Wittenberg three years before writing this tract.
54. Luther, *Ein Sermon vom ehelichen Stand* (1519), *WA*, 2:169.
55. Preface by Johann Salmuth to his father, Heinrich Salmuth's, *Catechismus . . .* (Budissin, 1581), bii r.
56. Caspar Huberinus, *Postilla Teutsch . . .* (Augsburg, 1545), IIvvi r. For some interesting information on medieval law and practice in domestic education, see Elisabeth Germain, *Langages de la foi à travers l'histoire: Mentalités et catéchèse . . .* (Paris, 1972).
57. Peter Laslett, ed., *Household and Family in Past Time* (Cambridge, 1972), p. 16.
58. On the many interrelated meanings of the word *oeconomia* as used in the early modern period, see the article by Otto Brunner cited in note 37 above, pp. 33-61. Also: article *Hausväterliteratur* in the *Handwörterbuch der Sozialwissenschaften*, vol. 5 (Stuttgart, etc., 1956).
59. Justus Menius, *An die hochgeborne Fürstin, Fraw Sibilla Hertzogin zu Sachsen, Oeconomia Christiana . . .* (Wittenberg, 1529), Biii r-Biv v. Luther's preface is printed in *WA*, 30²:60-63.
60. Urban Rhegius, *Catechesis illustriss. principi Francisco Otthoni, Brunswicensium . . . Duci puero . . . et toti scholae Ducali dicata* (Braunschweig, 1540), p. 15.
61. Johann Agricola, *Eine christliche Kinderzucht inn Gottes Wort und Lere: Aus der Schule zu Eisleben* (Wittenberg, 1527), viii v.
62. Justin Göbler, *Der Rechte Spiegel . . .* (Frankfurt am Main, 1550), xiiiir and v.
63. Laslett, ed., *Household and Family*, p 29.

64. Lawrence Stone, "The Rise of the Nuclear Family in Early Modern England," in *The Family in History*, ed. Charles Rosenberg (Philadelphia, 1975), p. 25.

65. For some clues and references to this debate, see the three review articles by Christopher Lasch, "The Family in History," in *New York Review of Books*, 13, 27 November, 11 December, 1975. On the significance to social history of the shift in the nuclear family, see John Bossy, "Holiness and Society," *Past and Present* 75 (May 1977):119-37. The whole debate is summarized in Stone, *The Family, Sex and Marriage*, pp. 23-26. Cf. also Lutz Berkner, "Recent Research on the History of the Family in Western Europe," *Journal of Marriage and the Family* 35 (1973):395-405.

66. For a rather spotty discussion of the possible roles of youth associations and various kinds of male and female social groups in competing with family loyalties, see Shorter, *Making of the Modern Family*, pp. 206-9, 227-34. Also Natalie Davis, "The Reasons of Misrule," in *Society and Culture in Early Modern France* (Stanford, Calif., 1975), pp. 104-14.

67. Helmut Begemann, *Strukturwandel der Familie* (Hamburg, 1960), pp. 24-28. On the loss of "traditional" economic and political functions of the modern family, see Talcott Parsons and Robert F. Bales, *Family, Socialization and Interaction Process* (New York, 1955), pp. 16-17. I do not associate myself with Parsons's and Bales's analytical scheme, or with their acceptance of the historicity of what they assume to have been traditional. But their formulation of the problem (first paragraph, p. 16) is useful. The usurpation of former family prerogatives by the early modern state is one of the main themes of Philippe Ariès's *Centuries of Childhood*.

68. For the background in Germanic customs and law, see Jacob Grimm, "*Vatergewalt*" in *Deutsche Rechtsaltertümer*, 4th ed. (Leipzig, 1899), 1:627 ff. Cf. also the fascinating article by Jost Trier, "Vater, Versuch einer Etymologie," *Zeitschr. Savigny-Stiftung f. Rechtsgesch: Germanistische Abt.* 65 (1947): 232-60, making the argument that the word father is itself of political, rather than biological or "sentimental" origin: "dass der Vaterbegriff der Indogermanen einen politischen Schwerpunkt, einen Kern von Macht hat, der sein eigentliches Wesen ausmacht" (p. 259). This political core survived the transition from the extended to the nuclear family.

69. Caspar Huberinus, *Spiegel der Hauszucht, Jesus Sirach genannt* (Nuremberg, 1565; preface dated 1552), Oiiii r.

70. Cf. Otto Brunner (as in note 37), p. 44. For a compilation of passages from Luther, see the article "*Hausvater*" in Jacob and Wilhelm Grimm, *Deutsches Wörterbuch*, vol. 4, no. 2, cols. 694-95. The King James and RSV translate the word weakly as "householder."

71. *WA*, Tr. 1, no. 386 (1532).

72. E.g., *WA*, 30¹:58, 132; 27:444. See also Erwin Mülhaupt, "Elternehre und Elternpflicht in reformatorischer Sicht," *Luther: Zeitschrift der Luther-Gesellschaft* 35 no, 2 (1964):49-60. Likening the father's power to a bishop's occurred at least as early as Augustine: "Quodlibet pater familias, quia super intendit domui episcopus dici potest." I take the citation from Levin L. Schücking, *Die puritanische Familie*, 2d ed. (Bonn and Munich, 1964), p. 64.

73. "Ut in tota vita mea ex homine vix audierim verbum, quod potentius in me sonuerit: 'Et non etiam (dicebas) audisti tu parentibus esse obediendum?'" From the preface to *De votis monasticis* (1521), *WA*, 8:574. Luther's emphasis on the joint authority of father and mother as parents was not, of course, intended to dilute the authority of the husband over his wife. Cf. Eph. 5:23, "For the husband is head of the wife as Christ is head of the church, his body."

74. Prov. 3:12. See also Deut. 8:5; Jer. 10:24.

75. Jer. 31:9.

76. Ps. 2:7.

77. Caspar Huberinus, *Der klaine Catechismus . . . für die Jugend zu gebrauchen* (Augsburg, 1544), Cv r.

78. Johann Spangenberg, *Der gros Catechismus und Kinder Lere D. Martin Lutheri für die jungen Christen in Fragstücke verfasset* (Wittenberg, 1551; preface dated 1541), Lvii r and v. The same point is made in *Des kleinen Catechismi und der Haustafel kurtzer Begriff . . .* (Wittenberg, 1549; preface dated 1543), Bvii v.

79. Caspar Huberinus, *Vierzig kurze Predig* (Nuremberg, 1550), Fv r and v.

80. From a manuscript *ABC und Namen Büchlein* written for schoolchildren in Ulm, Sdt. Ulm 1836/1.

81. For examples of such laws, see Franz Beyerle, ed., *Quellen zur neueren*

Privatrechtgeschichte Deutschlands, 1 (Weimar, 1936-38), 1¹:142 (Wormser Reformation, 1498); 1¹:261 (Freiburg Stadtrecht, 1520); 1²:117-18 (Württemberg Landrecht, 1555); 1²:198 (Solmer Landrecht, 1571); etc. Especially informative is the Freiburg code of 1520 drawn up by Ulrich Zasius. This has recently been republished: *Nüwe Stadtrechten und Statuten der loblichen Statt Fryburg* . . . (Aalen, 1968). Cf especially tract. 3, tit. 1. The table of contents alone makes it clear that property was the guiding motive in all laws regarding the relations of parents and children. See also *Der Stadt Nürnberg verneute Reformation 1564* (Nuremberg, 1565), which is particularly explicit on the circumstances of disinheritance. On the last point—limiting children's right to marry without parental consent, see Ulrich Tengler, *Layenspiegel* . . . (Strassburg, 1544), xxx r; *Gräflich—Mansfeldische geistliche Consistorial-ordnung* (1586), in Sehling, 2:205-6; *Kurfürstlicher Pfalz verneuerte Ehe und Ehegerichts-ordnung* (1582), in Franz Beyerle, *Quellen*, 2² (Weimar, 1969: 35).

82. See chap. 11.

83. Luther, *Das Eltern die Kinder zur Ehe nicht zwingen noch hindern sollen* (1524), *WA*, 15:167.

84. See chap. 10.

85. For example, Huberinus, *Spiegel der Hauszucht*. Huberinus condemns tyrannical husbands (Hiii v–Hiv r) but is led into a tirade against *böse weiber* (clxxiii r ff.). For Luther's ideas on the place of women see *WA*, Tr. 1, no. 1046; 2, no. 1979; also 20:149; 25:45–46. Seeberg, *Luthers Anschauung*, p. 113 characterizes Luther's views as "solide deutsche Bürgerlichkeit."

86. Luther, *Deutsche Messe und Ordnung Gottesdients* (1526), *WA*, 19:76.

87. For a reproduction of part of the sole surviving specimen of such a *Tafel*, entitled *Catechismus Lutheri pro pueris et familia*, see *WA*, 30¹:241. Discussion: ibid., pp. 561-72. Cf. also Georg Buchwald, *Die Entstehung der Katechismen Luthers und die Grundlage des grossen Katechismus* (Leipzig, 1894), pp. xi-xii. The better-known Greater and Shorter catechisms of 1529 were intended principally for pastors, not *Hausväter*.

88. Cf. Franz Falk, "Katechismus-Haustafeln als Lehrmittel des ausgehenden Mittelalters," *Literarische Beilage zur Kölner Volkszeitung*, no. 23 (1908).

89. Johann Bugenhagen, *Ein Catechismus* . . . *wo eyn Christen huesswirth syn ghesynde schol upt eyentfoldigheste leeren* . . . (1529).

90. Luther, preface to his *Deudsch Catechismus* (the Greater Catechism), 1529, *WA*, 30¹:128.

91. *Vom ehelichen Leben*, *WA*, 10²:301.

92. Ibid.: "For to God there can be nothing dearer than the salvation of souls."

93. *Ein Sermon von dem ehelichen Stand* (1519), *WA*, 2:170.

94. Huberinus, *Postilla Teutsch* 2:vv–vi r.

95. Quoted in Robert Kolb, "Parents Should Explain the Sermon: Nikolaus von Amsdorf on the Role of the Christian Parent," *Lutheran Quarterly* 25, no. 3 (August 1973): 231-40.

96. Huberinus, *Spiegel der Hauszucht*, Aii v.

97. Huberinus, *Spiegel der geistlichen Hauszucht* . . . (Frankfurt am Main, 1569), Aii v.

98. Georg Lauterbeck, *Jesus Sirach Buch von der Hauszucht, allen Hausvetern, Kindern und Hausgesinde notwending und nützlich zu lesen* (Wittenberg, 1555; preface dated 1549), unpaginated.

99. These points are made by Caspar Huberinus, *Vierzig kurze Predig* (Nuremberg, 1550), iii v.

100. Caspar Huberinus, *Der Catechismus* . . . *Allen frummen Hausvätern sehr nützlich für ire jugent zugebrauchen* (Augsburg, 1543), passim.

101. The evangelical and ethical impulse continues to motivate the *Hausväterliteratur* into its heyday in the seventeenth century, when it addresses itself increasingly to practical matters in familial and social relations and the management of home and farm. For a very good example of this latter type, see Johannes Coler's three-volume *Oeconomia ruralis et domestica* (Wittenberg, 1593-1604).

102. On Huberinus, see Günther Franz, *Huberinus-Rhegius-Holbein: Bibliograph-ische und druckgeschichtliche Untersuchung der verbreitetsten Trost- und Erbauungs-schriften des 16. Jahrhundert* (Nieuwkoop, 1973), pp. 3-5, 147-209, 213-24.

103. Lauterbeck, *Jesus Sirach Buch Von der Hauszucht*.

104. Otto Brunfels, *Pandect Büchlin* (Strassburg, 1529).

105. Huberinus, *Vierzig kurze Predig*, title page.

106. E.g., Sebastian Fröschel, *Catechismus* . . . (Wittenberg, 1559), preface, Avi r. Huberinus, *Catechismus*, title page.

107. Spangenberg, *Der gros Catechismus*, Axi v; Konrad Dietrich, *Biblisches Spruchbüchlin* (1616), p. 11.

108. E.g., Spangenberg, *Der gros Catechismus*.

109. Christoph Vischer, *Auslegung der fünf Heubtstück des heiligen Catechismi* (Schmalkalden, 1573), Cvi v. For a similar one see Spangenberg, *Der gros Catechismus*, Bv v.

110. *Ein Sermon von dem ehelichen Stand* (1519), *WA*, 2:170.

111. *Nüwe Stattrechten und Statuten der* . . . *Statt Fryburg* . . . (1520; reprinted Aalen, 1968), 59v. Cf. also Württemberg Landrecht (1555), in Franz Beyerle, *Privatrechtgeschichte*, 1²:159.

112. E.g., Saxon *Kirchenordnung* (1580), in Reu, 1, 2 (1):142.

113. Dietrich, *Kinder-Postilla*, 45v.

114. Leonhard Culman, *Teutsche Kinder-Tafel* (n.p., ca. 1530), 7r.

115. Leonhard Culman, *Ein schön teutsch geistlich Spiel von der Widtfrau* . . . , in *Schauspiele aus dem 16. Jahrhundert*, ed. Julius Tittmann (Leipzig, 1868), p. 143.

116. Spangenberg, *Ehespiegel*, 56r.

117. See chap. 9.

118. From instructions to superintendents in Albertine Saxony, printed in *Die evangelischen Kirchenordnungen*, 1:313. It is not possible now to determine whether "household" (*Haus*) was defined in the minds of contemporaries in such a way as to exclude the poor in city, town, and countryside. My guess is that it was not.

119. Huberinus, *Spiegel der Hauszucht*, Aiiii r.

120. 1565 visitation in bishopric of Eichstätt. BHM Staatsverwaltung 2783, 203v.

121. Visitation in bishopric of Freising, 1560. OEMF, no. 566, 321.

122. Parish of Au, Bishopric of Freising, 1560. Ibid., p. 213.

123. BHM, Staatsverwaltung 2784, 90r.

124. Natalie Davis, "Printing and the People," in *Society and Culture in Early Modern France*, pp. 212–15 has some interesting things to say on how people in the sixteenth century shared, bought, resold, and passed on books.

125. For a collection of such examples, from a book written for pastors, teachers, and householders, cf. Andreas Hondorff, *Promptuarium exemplorum: Historien und Exempelbuch* (Leipzig, 1580; 1st ed. 1568), 203v–206r.

126. Heinrich Boos, ed., *Das Tagebuch des Felix Platter* (Leipzig, 1878), p. 141.

127. BHM, Hochstift Literalien, Passau 83, xi, 40v.

128. OEMF, no. 566, 64.

129. BHM, Staatsverwaltung 2780, 250r.

130. From the summary and recess of the visitation in superintendency Bischofswerda in Saxony, 1581. S.Dresd., Loc. 1999, 13r. There is no point in giving a few sample citations to visitation protocols, nearly all of which deal with this question and present the evidence passim.

131. Spangenberg, *Der gros Catechismus*, Bv r.

132. Ibid.

133. Dietrich, *Kinder-Postilla*, 43v; idem, *Von der Kinderzucht: Aus dem Evangelio Luce 2, Lehr und Vermanung* (Nuremberg, 1566), aiiii r.

134. A good illustration is the section "Von deutschen Schulen in Dörfern und Flecken," in the *General-Artikel* issued for Saxony in 1580. Such schools are needed, it was said, "because so many subjects are poor and must leave home to find work elsewhere, and therefore have no time to teach and instruct their own children."

135. Looking at the Catholic situation in the Counter Reformation, John Bossy argues that bishops in France and Italy turned against family worship as a dangerous practice likely to encourage religious deviance. Bossy regards this move as a "failure of nerve" that cut official Catholicism off from a powerful source of popular support for reform. "The Counter-Reformation and the People of Catholic Europe," *Past and Present* 47 (May 1970): 68–70.

136. From the *Schulordnung* of the city of Nordhausen (1583), printed in Karl Meyer, ed., "Die Schulordnung des Gymnasiums der freien Reichsstadt Nordhausen . . . ," *Mitt. Ges. f. deutsche Erziehungs- u. Schulgesch.* 2 (1892):116.

137. For some interesting comments on this, see Werner Reininghaus, *Elternstand, Obrigkeit und Schule bei Luther*, Pädagogische Forschungen, no. 38 Heidelberg, 1969). Philippe Ariès is certainly wrong in claiming that "men of that period [the late Middle Ages] were profoundly and rapidly socialized. The family did not intervene to delay the socialization of the child." *Western Attitudes toward Death: From the Middle Ages to the Present*, trans. Patricia M. Ranum (Baltimore, 1974), p. 28.

138. From an instruction to visitors in the Coburg part of Ernestine Saxony, 1583, S.Cob., B2480, 29r.

139. Sdt.Ulm, A(1836), 48r. The date is 1626.

140. Christoph Vischer, *Auslegung der fünf Heubtstück*, Cv v.

CHAPTER 7

1. Luther, *De servo arbitrio*. I use the translation by Philip S. Watson in *Luther and Erasmus: Free Will and Salvation* (Philadelphia, 1969), pp. 184–85. The quotation from Erasmus's *De libero arbitrio* is from the translation by E. Gordon Rupp in ibid., p. 91.

2. In another context Werner Jäger writes, of the importance of models or ideal types, that education in the sense of *Bildung* is not possible "ohne ein dem Geiste vorschwebendes Bild des Menschen, wie er sein soll.... Bildung zeigt sich in der gesamten Form des Menschen, in seinem äusseren Auftreten und Gebaren wie in seiner inneren Haltung. Beides entsteht nicht von ungefähr, sondern nur als Produkt bewusster Züchtigung." *Paideia: Die Formung des griechichen Menschen*, 2d ed. (Berlin and Leipzig, 1936–55) 1:24.

3. In the Apocrypha. This is a part of the didactic wisdom literature of the Old Testament. Along with Ecclesiasticus (also apocryphal), it had been a favorite source of social, particularly matrimonial and general moral, instruction since the fifteenth century. On this point see *The Cambridge History of the Bible*, 2 (Cambridge, 1969): 488.

4. Michael Saxo, *Das erst Teil des christlichen Zeitvertreibers oder Geistlichen Rätzelbuchs . . .* (Dresden, 1599; first printed 1593), 103r and v.

5. From the title page to *Ein schön unnd nützliches Biblischs Spiel von dem Heiligen und Gottforchtigen Tobia . . .* , first performed in Colmar, 1550. Printed in *Georg Wickrams sämtliche Werke*, 11 (Berlin, 1971): 122.

6. Ibid., p. 213.

7. Ibid., p. 302.

8. Ibid., pp. 228–29.

9. Saxo, *Zeitvertreiber*, 102r and v.

10. From preface to Simon Schaidenreisser's translation of the Odyssey, *Odyssea . . .* (Augsburg, 1538), iii v–iiii r. Werner Jäger, *Paideia: The Ideals of Greek Culture . . .* trans. Gilbert Highet, 1 (Oxford, 1939): 55, calls Telemachus the "model of a pliant young man led to action and fame by the eagerly accepted advice of an experienced friend."

11. Zacharias Rivander, *Der ander Teil Promptuarii exemplorum, darinnen viel herrliche schöne Historien . . . und Exempel von Tugend und Untugend . . . verfasset sind. Alles nach den heiligen zehn Geboten Gottes fein ordenlich distribuirt . . .* (Frankfurt am Main, 1581), 205r.

12. Ibid., 205v.

13. Ibid.

14. Ibid., 206r and v.

15. Ibid., 206 r.

16. Ibid., 207v.

17. Ibid., 207r. For a similar book of examples for use in schools, see Georg Fabricius, *Virorum illustrium seu Historiae sacrae libri*, bk. 9 (Leipzig, 1564; expanded edition in ten books, Leipzig, 1578).

18. "Virtus condonans, excusans et dissimulans quaedam errata parentum et superiorum." Valentin Trotzendorf, *Catechesis scholae Goltpergensis* (Wittenberg, 1558), E8r.

19. For a good illustration, see ibid., E7r.

20. The Vulgate has *virilia* for "nakedness." Luther's German translation gives *Schame*

(*WA*, Deutsche Bibel, 8:60). The original Hebrew word also has definite sexual meaning, conveying in addition an association of lewdness, shame, and incest.

21. Luther, *Lectures on Genesis, WA*, 42:383-84. English translation by George V. Schick, *LW*, 2:173.

22. Trotzendorf, *Catechesis Scholae Goltpergensis*, E8r. Medieval illustrations of Gen. 9:21-23, of which there are many, had a different iconological purpose. Except where it makes only a general comment on life, or provides a grotesque decoration (as on choir stalls), the depiction of Noah's nakedness and Ham's ridicule of his father serves to make deliberate comment on two passion scenes with which it nearly always occurs in juxtaposition: the stripping of Jesus and his being mocked. Ample evidence for this may be found in the files of the Index of Christian Art at Princeton University. For Catholic teachings on the fourth commandment before the Reformation cf. Wilhelm Maurer, "Luthers Lehre von den drei Hierarchien und ihr mittelalterlicher Hintergrund," *Bayer. Akad. d. Wiss., philos.-hist. Kl., Sitzb.* 1970, Heft 4 (Munich, 1970), pp. 9-18.

23. Laurentius Drabitius, *Catechismus-Büchlein* . . . (Leipzig, 1595), Cviii r.

24. Caspar Huberinus, *Spiegel der geistlichen Hauszucht Jesus Sirach genandt* . . . (Nuremberg, 1565), Evi r.

25. Christoph Vischer, *Bericht aus Gottes Wort . . . wie man junge Fürsten . . . auffziehen soll* . . . (1573), gii v, gvi r.

26. "Es ist nit mein will." "In uns ist nichts guts." "On dein tun wirst selig." Printed in facsimile in Heinrich Fechtner, ed., *ABC-Bücher des 15., 16., und 17. Jahrhunderts*, no. 1 (Berlin, 1906).

27. Paul Rebhun, *Susanna*, act 2, scene 3, printed in Hermann Palm, ed., *Paul Rebhuns Dramen*, Bibliothek des litterarischen Vereins in Stuttgart, 49 (1859): 26-27.

28. See Bernhard Duhr, S.J., *Geschichte der Jesuiten in den Ländern deutscher Zunge im XVI. Jahrhundert* (Freiburg im Breisgau, 1907), chap. 8.

29. From Linck's preface to Leonhard Culman's play *Ein christlich Teutsch spil, wie ein Sünder zur Bus bekärt wird* (Nuremberg, 1539), quoted in Julius Tittmann, ed., *Schauspiele aus dem sechzehnten Jahrhundert*, Deutsche Dichter des sechzehnten Jahrhunderts, 2 (Leipzig, 1868), p. 110. The expense account for the Latin school in Hannover lists the following dramas: in 1567, the Passion; 1571, Daniel; 1577, Tobias; 1578, Joseph, etc.

30. Elaborate incidents featured in most of these dramas were also mandated by the fact that, written for performance by townspeople, they had to include a very large number of characters.

31. Leonhard Culmann, *Ein schön teutsch spiel von der Widtfraw* . . . , in Julius Tittmann, ed., *Schauspiele aus dem sechzehnten Jahrhundert*, p. 159.

32. E.g., evidence from Bavarian visitations of 1558-60. All Latin and German schoolmasters were to be asked whether they perform "comedies" and, if so, which ones. The evidence shows that most did not, while a few, especially in German schools, staged them regularly. OEMF, no. 565, passim; nos. 567, 547. See also B.S.Landsh., Rep. 82, fasc. 67, no. 43, Saal 17: "Schulacta der Schulen in Landshut," 10v.

33. Zacharias Rivander, *Der ander Teil*, 204v.

34. Erasmus Alberus, *Zehen Dialogi für Kinder, so anfangen zu reden* (Nuremberg, n.d., ca. 1550), Aiii r.

35. Ibid., dialogue 3.

36. *Von des Teuffels Tyranney, Macht und Gewalt* . . . (Worms, 1561), Cvii v.

37. Andreas Musculus, *Betbüchlein* (Leipzig, 1569), Aiiii v.

38. *WA*, Tr. 4, no. 4329.

39. Ibid., 6, no. 6546. Cf. also "Uber das schlehet zu das schendlich laster und haimlich böse geschmeiss [i.e., plague] der sicherheit . . . ," from preface to Larger Catechism, *WA*, 30¹:126.

40. Melanchthon, *Catechismus*, trans. into German by Caspar Brusch (Nuremberg, 1543), Rviii r.

41. Andreas Musculus, *Prophecey und Weissagung . . . von dem zunahenden . . . Zorn, Straff, Jammer und Unglück über Deutschland* (Erfurt, 1557), passim.

42. Johann Tettelbach, *Das güldene Kleinod. D. Martini Lutheri Catechismus in kurtze Frage gefasst* (Breslau, 1568), p. 52.

43. Ibid., p. 51.

44. Caspar Huberinus, *Postilla Teutsch* . . . (Augsburg, 1545), 2:i v viii r.
45. Simon Musaeus, *Catechismus* . . . (Frankfurt am Main, 1571), lxiiii r.
46. Huberinus, *Postilla Teutsch*, 2:s v r.
47. Musculus, *Betbüchlein*, Gii r.
48. Cf. Erasmus's colloquy *Confabulatio pia seu pietas puerilia*, first printed 1522, trans. as *The Whole Duty of Youth* by Craig Thompson, *The Colloquies of Erasmus* (Chicago, 1965), pp. 32-41.
49. Caspar Huberinus, *Der klaine Catechismus* . . . (Augsburg, 1544), Ci r-Cii v.
50. *Ein Vermanung an die jungen Knaben und Töchterlin in der Vorbereitung, wann . . . sie . . . das hochwürdig Sacrament . . . unseres Herrn Jesu Christi entpfahen wöllen . . .* (Strassburg, 1554), unpaginated.
51. Another example from a catechism: the *Kinder Beicht* from Johann Meckhardt's *Catechismus: Ain kurtze christliche Leer und Underweysung für die Jugent* (Augsburg, 1551): "Lieber Herr, ich komm zu euch als zu einem Diener Christi und seiner Kirchen, und bekenn mich vor Gott und euch, das ich laider ein armer sünder bin, und das mein ganzes Leben, und was Gott nit in mir wirkt, nichts ist, dann lauter sünd und übertrettung der Gepot Gottes. In Sonderheit bekenn ich, das ich meinen Eltern, Schul- und Leermaistern ungehorsam gewesen bin, sie oft erzürnet und zu fluchen bewegt hab. Das alles ist mir laid, und beger den Trost der hailsamen Absolution."
52. Huberinus, *Spiegel der Hauszucht*, Eiii r.
53. Otto Brunfels, *Pandect Büchlin* (Strassburg, 1529), "Vom ampt der jünglinge," paraphrasing Ecclus. 32:7-8.
54. Huberinus, *Spiegel der Hauszucht*, Diii v.
55. Ibid., Eii v.
56. Ibid., Evi r.
57. Ibid., K r.
58. Ibid., Riiii v-Rv v.
59. Andreas Musculus, *Catechismus: Kinderpredig* . . . (Frankfurt an der Oder, 1566), Aii r and v.
60. Printed in Palm, ed., *Paul Rebhuns Dramen* (see note 27), pp. 26-27.
61. From the dedication in the first edition of the play, Zwickau, 1536, quoted in Julius Tittmann, ed., *Schauspiele aus dem sechzehnten Jahrhundert*, pp. 22-23.
62. Jörg Wickram, *Von guten und bösen Nachbarn* (1556), printed in *Bibliothek des litterarischen Vereins Stuttgart*, 223 (1901):181.
63. Ibid., p. 183.
64. From the Gräflich-Schwarzburgische *Kirchenordnung* of 1574, printed in Sehling, 2:134.

CHAPTER 8

1. Jörg Wickram, *Der jungen Knaben Spiegel* (1554) in *Georg Wickram: Sämtliche Werke*, ed. Hans-Gert Roloff, 3 (Berlin, 1968):5.
2. From the Württemberg *Schulordnung* of 1559, printed in Vormbaum, pp. 159-65.
3. See chap. 1. The Württemberg *Schulordnung* states: "Damit auch die Jugend in und bei unsern deutschen Schulen mit der Furcht Gottes, rechter Lehre und guter Zucht wol unterrichtet . . . und hierunter Gleichheit sei. . . ." Ibid., p. 159.
4. Johann Michael Dilherr, *Sermon oder Rede von der rechten Kinderzucht und Unterrichtung der Jugend* (Nuremberg, 1642), p. 3.
5. In his correspondence with the Nuremberg council concerning the establishment of a gymnasium there, Sdt.Nürn., Y841.
6. See the memoranda by Strassburg preachers, notably Bucer, 1536 and 1547, in Strass.A.V., Archives St. Thomas 84, carton 48, 99-104, 105-8, 182 ff.
7. References to *gemainer nutz* are constant in the Strassburg documents. See, for example, Marcel Fournier and Charles Engel, *Les status et privilèges des universités françaises* . . . , part 2, vol. 4, fasc. 1 (Paris, 1894), pp. 13, 34, 36, etc. Identical statements are found

everywhere in German territories. E.g., *Waldeckische Kirchenordnung* (1556), in Heinrich Heppe, *Geschichte des deutschen Volksschulwesens* (Gotha, 1858-60; reprinted 1971), 1:10.

8. The concern with this combination continued into the seventeenth century. E.g., Hamburg *Schulordnung* 1634: S.Hamb., Ministerial-Archiv IIIA 1e (1552): "Dieweil auch die Schulen nicht allein der Kirchen, sondern auch des gemeinen Nutzens seminaria sind."

9. See chap. 2.

10. Sermon on Luke 2:17 ff. (December 1533). *WA*, 37:246.

11. See Günther Dohmen, *Bildung und Schule: Die Entstehung des deutschen Bildungsbegriffs und die Entwicklung seines Verhältnisses zur Schule*, 1 (Weinheim, 1964): 65-66, 118 ff. The word *einbilden* is mystic in origin. Eckhardt used it to suggest the *einbilden*, that is to say forming a picture of, God in the *Seelengrund*, the ground of the soul. Luther, of course, rejected all ideas of a mystic union. Not until the seventeenth-century educational reformers, especially Wolfgang Ratke, was the concept fully developed as a pedagogical tool, but sixteenth-century Lutherans knew and used it.

12. Xenophon *Cyropaedia* 1. ii.2-3. The English translation is by Walter Miller, Loeb Classical Library (London, 1914). The first Latin version by Francesco Filelfo was printed in 1476. For Montaigne's praise of Persian education in virtue, see *Essais* 1. 3, 25; 2.22; 3.6, 10.

13. Plutarch *De liberis educandis* 4. For full reference, see note 59 to chap. 3. For the great weight given to habituation in the thought of Galen see Walther Riese, *Galen on the Passions and Errors of the Soul* (Columbus, Ohio, 1963), pp. 123-24.

14. E.g., Caspar Huberinus, *Spiegel der Hauszucht . . .* (Nuremberg, 1565), Gvi v.

15. From a memorandum on the improvement of teaching in the Sankt Anna Gymnasium and other schools, Augsburg, 1593. Sdt.Augsb., Evangelisches Wesensarchiv, no. 1041.

16. Veit Dietrich, *Kinder-Postilla* (Nuremberg, 1549), 44v.

17. Huberinus, *Spiegel der Hauszucht*, Hh r.

18. In Vormbaum, pp. 159-65.

19. Cyriacus Spangenberg, *Ehespiegel . . .* (Strassburg, 1563), 48v-49r.

20. Christoph Vischer, *Bericht aus Gottes Wort . . .* (1573), dvii r.

21. Bugenhagen, in his general outline of a curriculum, written for the city of Hamburg in 1526. The low German text is printed in Eduard Meyer, *Geschichte des hamburgischen Schul- und Unterrichtswesens im Mittelalter* (Hamburg, 1843), p. 178.

22. Caspar Huberinus, *Der Catechismus . . . allen frommen Hausvättern sehr nützlich . . .* (Augsburg, n.d., preface dated 1543), Avi r.

23. Cited in Mertz, p. 246.

24. From a memorandum in the Stadtarchiv Augsburg. Evangelisches Wesensarchiv, no. 1041.

25. See Helga Hajda, *Das mnemotechnische Schrifttum des Mittelalters* (Vienna, 1936), passim. In the later sixteenth century, and the seventeenth, reliance on repetition was codified in school ordinances, which specified the number of times every passage had to be repeated. See, for example, the *Schulordnung* of Duke Ernst of Gotha (1642), in Woldemar Boehne, *Die pädagogischen Bestrebungen Ernst des Frommen von Gotha* (Gotha, 1888), p. 126.

26. E.g., in Saalfeld, under the instructions of Superintendent Caspar Aquila. Cf. Caspar Aquila, *Des kleinen Catechismi Erklerung . . .* (1538), preface, printed in Reu, 1, 2 (2):173.

27. *WA*, Tr. 1, no. 838.

28. Letter to Nikolaus von Amsdorf, March 1534, concerning Erasmus's Catechism. *WA*, Br. 7, no. 2093. Cf. Tr. 1, no. 838.

29. "L'imprégnation est le procédé simple mais fondamental de toute la pédagogie de la Renaissance. . . . Elle est assurée par un certain nombre d'actes coordonnés, qui finissent par créer chez l'élève un véritable conditionnement." Pierre Mesnard, "La pietas litterata de Jean Sturm et le developpement à Strasbourg d'une pédagogie oecumenique (1538-1581)," *Société de l'histoire du protestantisme français. Bulletin* (October-December 1965), p. 291. Also in *XII Congrès international des sciences historiques* (1965), *Rapports* 3: *Commissions*, p. 96.

30. Johannes Clajus, *Grammatica Germanicae Linguae . . . ex bibliis Lutheri Germanicis . . .* (Leipzig, 1578), in Friedrich Weidling, Älteste deutsche Grammatiken in Neudrucken, 2 (Strassburg, 1894): 172.

31. Laurentius Albertus, *Teutsch Grammatick oder Sprachkunst . . .* (Augsburg, 1573), ed. Carl Müller-Fraureuth, *Ältere deutsche Grammatiken in Neudrucken* (Strassburg, 1895).

32. *Anfang des christlichen Glaubens und Teutscher Sprach, wie sie die jungen Kinder in den teutschen Schulen lernen sollen* (Nuremberg, 1534). Facsimile reprint in Heinrich Fechtner, *ABC Bücher des 15, 16, und 17. Jahrhunderts,* vol. 1 (Berlin, 1906).

33. *Elementa literatum et pietatis quae in Augustana schola proponi solent,* quoted in Leonhard Lenk, *Augsburger Bürgertum im Späthumanismus und Frühbarock* (Augsburg, 1968).

34. ABC Book in Sdt.Ulm, 1836/1. Others: 27340, 27340/1, etc.

35. "Dan die jugent fast die lehre nicht, so sie nicht zu ausdrücklichem nachsprechen gewehnet wird." From *Instruktions-Artikel* for the visitation of 1574 in Electoral Saxony, printed in Pallas, 41 (Allgemeiner Teil): 91.

36. Quoted in Klaus Leder, *Kirche und Jugend in Nürnberg und seinem Landgebiet . . .* (Neustadt an der Aisch, 1973).

37. In Luther's preface to Stephan Klingebeil's *Von Priester Ehe* (Wittenberg, 1528), *WA,* 26:530.

38. Ibid.

39. In 1529. See Georg Buchwald, *Die Entstehung der Katechismen Luthers und die Grundlage des grossen Katechismus* (Leipzig, 1894).

40. Luther to Elector Johann, 20 May 1530. *WA,* Br. 5, no. 1572.

41. This is stated by Johann Aurifaber in his preface to Luther's Table Talk (1566), printed in *Dr. Martin Luthers sämtliche Schriften,* ed. Georg Walch, 22 (Halle, 1743): 30.

42. From his lectures on the Song of Solomon, given in 1530-31 and published 1539. *WA,* 31²:613.

43. "Der Catechismus Luther klein / daz höchste Buch auff Erden / das fast die gantze Schrift so fein / in kurtze summ zu lernen. Verse in a catechism published in 1592, cited in Friedrich Hahn, *Die evangelische Unterweisung in den Schulen des 16. Jahrhunderts* (Heidelberg, 1957), p. 66.

44. *Apud adversarios nulla prorsus est catechesis puerorum.* Art. 8 of *Apology of the Augsburg Confession,* in *Concordia Triglotta: The Symbolical Books of the Evangelical Lutheran Church* (Saint Louis, Mo., 1921), p. 324 (Latin), and p. 325 (English).

45. "Uthwendig leren, dagelick wedderholen und ere gantze leven langk beholden." From preface of the *Corpus Doctrinae* for Mecklenburg (1563), quoted in H. Schnell, *Das Unterrichtswesen der Grossherzogtümer Mecklenburg-Schwerin und Strehlitz, MGP* 38 (Berlin, 1907): 120.

46. On this subject see Carl Adolf Gerhard von Zezschwitz, *System der christlich kirchlichen Katechetik* (Leipzig, 1863-74), 2 vols.; Johannes Geffcken, *Der Bilder-catechismus des fünfzehnten Jahrhunderts und die catechetischen Hauptstücke in dieser Zeit bis auf Luther* (Leipzig, 1855); Werner Jentsch, *Urchristliches Erziehungsdenken: die Paideia Kyriu im Rahmen der hellenisch-jüdischen Umwelt* (Gütersloh, 1951); Franz Xaver Eggersdorfer, *Der heilige Augustinus als Pädagoge und seine Bedeutung für die Geschichte der Bildung* (Freiburg im Breisgau, 1907); Ernst-Wilhelm Kohls, *Evangelische Katechismen der Reformationszeit vor und neben Luthers Kleinem Katechismus,* Texte zur Kirchen- und Theologiegeschichte, no. 16 (Gütersloh, 1971); Rudolf Padberg, *Erasmus als Katechet* (Freiburg, 1956). A very good concise survey of pre-Lutheran catechisms in Germany is offered by Steven E. Ozment, *The Reformation in the Cities* (New Haven, 1975), pp. 22-32. See also Elisabeth Germain, *Langages de la foi à travers l'histoire: Mentalités et catéchèse: Approche d'une étude des mentalités* (Paris, 1972).

47. For surveys of earlier catechisms and catechization given by Lutheran writers, see Johann Tettelbach, *Das güldene Kleinod: D. Martini Lutheri Catechismus in kurtze Frage gefasset* (Breslau, 1568), vol. 2, and Heinrich Salmuth, *Catechismus . . .* (Budissin, 1581), aiii r–biii v.

48. New Testament references to *katēchein:* Acts 21:21; Rom. 2:18; 1 Cor. 14:19; Gal. 6:6; etc. On Augustine and catechization see Eggersdorfer, *Der heilige Augustinus,* and Peter Brown, *Augustine of Hippo* (Berkeley, 1967), pp. 124-25.

49. On the evolution of the question and answer form, see the very interesting remarks by von Zezschwitz, *System der Katechetik,* vol. 2, part 2, sect. 2, chaps. 1-2. On memorization: ibid., vol. 2, part 2, sec. 1, chaps. 16-19.

50. "The best guide to the vast medieval literature on these subjects, particularly confession, is Geffcken, *Bildercatechismus.* Geffcken sets out to prove, and does prove, that the

means existed in the late Middle Ages, notably in the fifteenth century, for an informed piety among lay people.

51. In a notable change of emphasis, the Decalogue gradually replaced the catalog of deadly sins as an instrument for guiding confession. Geffcken, *Bildercatechismus*, pp. 20-22, shows that the Decalogue was presented and explained more often and more comprehensively in the fourteenth and fifteenth centuries than any other parts of the Creed. On the Ten Commandments in Augustine's pedagogical activities, see Eggersdorfer, *Der heilige Augustinus*, pp. 164-69.

52. For a discussion of titles and contents of instructional books (such as the many *Beichtbüchlein*, *Spiegel der Leyen*, etc.) circulating in the fifteenth century, see Padberg, *Erasmus als Katechet*, pp. 31-43.

53. For a guide to the literature on popular piety in the late Middle Ages, and a judgment on it, see Steven E. Ozment, *Reformation in the Cities*, pp. 15-22.

54. This exclusive concentration on religion is true also of the *Children's Questions*, the catechism of the Bohemian Brethren written in 1502 and translated into German in 1521, when Luther saw it.

55. For the catechisms of Gerhart, Sam, Althamer, Capito, and Brenz—all published before Luther's catechisms of 1529—see Kohls, *Evangelische Katechismen*, pp. 7-11. For a few other titles see Reu, 1. 1(1): 3-38.

56. From the preface to the Larger Catechism, *WA*, 30¹:129.

57. The evidence is published in part in Pallas, vols. 41-41⁵ (Halle, 1906-14). See also C. A. H. Burkhardt, *Geschichte der sächsischen Kirchen- und Schulvisitationen von 1524 bis 1545* (Leipzig, 1879).

58. Zezschwitz, *System der Katechetik*, 1:567. The letters referred to are in *WA*, Br. 5, nos. 1371, 1397, 1408, 1418, 1420 (all 1529).

59. Luther, arguing in art. 8 of the Schmalkald Articles (written 1537, printed 1538) for the retention of confession and absolution: "sol die Beicht oder Absolutio bey leib nicht lassen abkomen . . . auch umb des jungen rohen volcks willen, damit es verhöret und unterrichtet werde inn der Christlichen lere." *WA*, 50:244.

60. From the preface to the Larger Catechism, *WA*, 30¹:127, 129.

61. Ibid., p. 126.

62. See Luther's statement in his *Deutsche Messe und Ordnung Gottesdiensts* (1526), in which he called for a "grobe schlechte einfeltige Catechismus." *WA*, 19:76.

63. Veit Dietrich, *Kinder-Postilla* (Nuremberg, 1549), Av r.

64. On the genesis and appearance of Luther's two catechisms, see Buchwald, *Entstehung der Katechismen*, and the introductions to the edition of the two catechisms in *WA*, 30¹:426-665. The Larger Catechism is printed in *WA*, 30¹:125-238; the Shorter Catechism, ibid., pp. 243-425.

65. Preface to Larger Catechism, ibid., p. 125.

66. Not all the versions in which the Shorter Catechism was first printed are identical in form. See *WA*, 30¹:239-425 for these versions.

67. From the preface to the Shorter Catechism, ibid., pp. 267-69.

68. Ibid., pp. 276-81.

69. Ibid., pp. 264-67.

70. Ibid., pp. 272-73.

71. *Deutsche Messe und Ordnung Gottesdiensts* (1526) *WA*, 19:77.

72. *WA*, 30¹:270-73.

73. E.g., preface to Larger Catechism, ibid., pp. 125-26.

74. Ibid., p. 128.

75. Ibid., pp. 268-69.

76. Ernst-Wilhelm Kohls, *Evangelische Bewegung und Kirchenordnung: Studien und Quellen zur Reformationsgeschichte der Reichsstadt Gengenbach* (Karlsruhe, 1966), p. 4.

77. From the *Kirchenordnung* of Wintzingerode, in Reu, 1, 2 (1):240.

78. *Von der Freiheit eines Christenmenschen* (1520), *WA*, 7:23-24.

79. Luther had commissioned Johann Agricola, a teacher in Eisleben, to write a catechism in 1528. The result, *Hundert und dreissig gemeyner Fragestücke für die jungen Kinder ynn der deudschen Meydin Schule zu Eyssleben* (Wittenberg, 1528), reprinted in Ferdinand Cohrs, *Die evangelischen Katechismusversuche vor Luthers Enchiridion*, MGP, 20 (Berlin,

1900): 273-311, displeased him not only for its unsystematic character, but especially because it presented the Decalogue as a code of laws, useful, but not binding on Christians: "114. Sol die Christen auch Moses gesetz zwingen? Antwort. Christen thun aus lust und liebe alles, was Gott von yhn foddert. Denn sie sind durch den freywilligen geist Christi versiegelt, darumb sol sie kein gesetz zwingen. . . . 115. Wie sollen wirs denn brauchen? Antwort. Wie die Christen brauchen aller Creaturen . . . wenn, wu, wie offt es sie gelüstet, auch Kriechische und lateinische Bücher . . . , also brauchen sie auch Mosen." Ibid., p. 293. Agricola had quarreled with Melanchthon in 1527 over the latter's emphasis on the Decalogue as a means of awakening a sense of sin in the believer. On Luther's struggle against antinomianism, see Mark U. Edwards, Jr., *Luther and the False Brethren* (Stanford, 1975), chap. 7.

80. *Deutsch Messe und Ordnung Gottesdients* (1526), *WA*, 19:76.

81. Daniel Kauxdorf, *Ein sehr nützliches und tröstliches Handtbüchlein von allen stücken christlicher Lehr, welche im heiligen Kinder Catechismo . . . Doctor Martini Lutheri . . . verfasset sein* (Mühlhausen, 1575), a v r and v.

82. Caspar Huberinus, *Vierzig kurze predig über den ganzen Katechismus* (Nuremberg, 1550), introduction, Biii v-Biv r.

83. Good examples are Johann Brenz, *Fragstück für die Jugend zu Schwäbischen Hall* (1528) and Martin Bucer, *Kinderlehr in deudscher und lateinischer Spraach* (Marburg, 1549), both in Kohls, *Evangelische Katechismen*. Also: Georg Maior, *Catechismus D. Mar. Luth. Düdesch unde Lateinisch: Daruth de Kinder lichtliken yn dem lesende underwyset mögen werden* (Hamburg, n.d.). In 1575, Luther's Shorter Catechism was used as a *libellus elementarii* for the youngest pupils at Saint Sebald's school in Nuremberg; reference in Leder, *Kirche und Jugend in Nürnberg*, p. 89.

84. E.g., Lucas Loss, *Questiunculae methodicae de Christiano catechismo, in formam dialogi . . .*, and *Ein korte summe des Catechismi . . . vor die jungen kinder* (both Wittenberg, 1545).

85. Quoted in Johannes Geffcken, *Die hamburgischen niedersächsischen Gesangbücher des 16. Jahrhunderts* (Hamburg, 1857), pp. 12-13.

86. E.g., Johannes Hoffer, *Icones catecheseos et virtutum ac vitiorum illustratae numeris* (Wittenberg, 1558).

87. Many are listed in Ferdinand Cohrs, "Der religiöse Unterricht der Kleinen in der evangelischen Kirche seit der Reformation," *Pädagogisches Magazin*, no. 1346 (Langensalza, 1931).

88. For Luther's *Haustafel*, see *WA*, 30¹:326-39.

89. E.g., in a sermon on Eph. 6 in 1535: *WA*, 41:404-10.

90. For a good example of a *Haustafel* other than Luther's see the catechism for the city of Gengenbach, printed 1545 but in use even before Luther's, published in Ernst-Wilhelm Kohls, *Der evangelische Katechismus von Gengenbach . . .* (Heidelberg, 1960), pp. 42-45.

91. *Catechismus oder christlicher Kinderbericht, in fragweis . . . zu Ulm in der pfarr gepredigt* (Ulm, 1536), unpaginated.

92. The same catechism in a later edition, *Catechismus oder Kinder Bericht: Für die christliche Jugendt zu Ulm in Stadt und Land* (Ulm, 1561), unpaginated. The reference is to 1 Pet. 5:5.

93. Many of these independent works are listed in Friedrich Hahn, *Die evangelische Unterweisung in den Schulen des 16. Jahrhunderts* (Heidelberg, 1957), p. 65. For Melanchthon's catechisms, which never became popular, see Ferdinand Cohrs, ed., *Philipp Melanchthons Schriften zur praktischen Theologie. Vol. 1. Katechetische Schriften*, Supplementa Melanchthonia, part 5 (Leipzig, 1915).

94. For full reference see List of Abbreviations.

95. C. Mönckeberg, "Die Geschichte des hamburgischen Katechismus," *Zeitschr. Ver. hamburgische Gesch.* 4 (1858): 581.

96. Leder, *Kirche und Jugend in Nürnberg*, pp. 92-94.

97. Cf. preface to the catechism for the city of Gengenbach, printed in Kohls, *Der evangelische Katechismus von Gengenbach*, p. 27.

98. From 1575 to 1585 the heads of the *Klosterschulen* in Württemberg were asked to report to Duke Ludwig the number of copies of Johann Brenz's catechism in each school. For the most part there were none, the masters reported, because students had been told to leave their catechisms at their previous Latin schools. Replies in LAS 699, no. 1.

99. Cf. Vogt. (no first name given), "Luthers Catechismus als Unterrichtsmittel," *Zeitschr. praktische Theologie* 11 (1889):311–38.

100. Quoted in Ernst-Wilhelm Kohls, *Evangelische Bewegung und Kirchenordnung: Studien und Quellen zur Reformationsgeschichte der Reichsstadt Gengenbach* (Karlsruhe, 1966), p. 36.

101. Quoted in Georg Buchwald, ed., *Johann Bugenhagens Katechismuspredigten* (*Quellen und Darstellungen aus der Geschichte des Reformationsjahrhunderts*, 9 (Leipzig, 1909): 1.

102. Tettelbach, *Das güldene Kleinod*, preface.

103. A late example: Nicolaus Hunnius, *Anweisung zum rechten Christenthumb für junge und einfältige Leut* . . . (Nuremberg, 1639), signature vi r.

104. Caspar Huberinus, *Catechismus . . . Allen frommen Hausvätern* . . . (Nuremberg, 1558; preface dated 1543), A4r and v.

105. *Unterricht der Visitatoren an die Pfarrherren* . . ., *WA*, 26:230, 238–39.

106. Cf. the excerpts brought together by Reu, 1, 2 (1): 130–32.

107. From *Instruktions-Artikel* for the 1574 visitations in Electoral Saxony, in Pallas, 41 (Allegemeiner Teil):92.

108. Printed in Sehling, 1:423–25 and Reu, 1, 2 (1):140–45.

109. *Ordenung der christlichen Kinderzucht für die Kirchen im Fürstentum Hessen* (1538), in Wilhelm Diehl, *Zur Geschichte der Konfirmation: Beiträge aus der hessischen Kirchengeschichte* (Giessen, 1897), pp. 124–28. Originating in the urgent need to meet the Anabaptist arguments that people were admitted indiscriminately to communion, the ordinance was frequently republished in augmented form after 1538.

110. In 1539. Cf. Reu, 1, 2 (1):402.

111. Visitation protocols give much evidence for this, as already noted in chap. 1. Two more examples: S.Dresd., Loc. 1997, iii r; and S.Magd., Rep. A12, Generalia 2440. 24 r.

112. E.g., the Saxon *Kirchenordnung* of 1533; the Pomeranian of 1535; Hessen, 1537; Lippe, 1538; etc.

113. As stated explicitly in the *Württembergische Schulordnung* (1559) in Vormbaum, pp. 159–65.

114. Sdt.Augsb., Wesensarchiv 1129, vol. 1.

115. Sdt.Ulm, A (1836), 72v.

116. S.Magd., Rep. A2, no. 92, 47r. The date was 1583. The archbishopric turned Protestant in 1566 under Archbishop Sigismund. From 1566 to 1598 the archbishop was Margrave Johann Friedrich of Brandenburg.

117. From a memorandum on city schools in the duchy of Zweibrücken, 1603, in *Dokumente zur Geschichte der humanistischen Schulen im Gebiet der bayerischen Pfalz*, ed. K. Reissinger, *MGP*, 49 (1911):176. Cf. also instruction for visitation of 1542 in Electoral Saxony, town of Würzen, S.Weim., Reg. Ii, no. 10, 74v.

118. Reu, 1, 2 (1): 43–44. The schoolmaster was Johannes Toltz. His *Inhalt christlicher Lehre* is printed in Reu, 1, 2 (2):494–96; the *Handbüchlein für junge Christen* (1526) is in Ferdinand Cohrs, *Die evangelischen Katechismusversuche . . . MGP*, 20 (Berlin, 1900): 247–60.

119. This is stated explicitly in a report by Electoral Saxon visitors in 1577, printed in Pallas 41¹:139.

120. From the Landesordnung for Hessen, 1537, in Reu, 1, 2 (1):401.

121. This is a summary of visitation records in the S.Hamb., Ministerial-Archiv IIIA i d. Cf. Dieter Klemenz, *Der Religionsunterricht in Hamburg von der Kirchenordnung von 1529 bis zum staatlichen Unterrichtsgesetz von 1870* (Hamburg, 1971).

122. E.g., in Saxony, 1578 visitations, Pallas, 41⁴:130–31.

123. E.g., in Nuremberg in 1560. Gerhard Hirschmann, "Die zweite Nürnberger Kirchenvisitation 1560/61," *Zeitschr. bayerische Kirchengesch.*, 32 (1963):118.

124. Several such lists have survived in Strassburg for 1600. Strass.A.V., Archives St. Thomas 46, carton 21.2.

125. Luther in his Shorter Catechism (1529), *WA*, 30¹:268.

126. From Memorandum to Nuremberg council (1531), quoted in Leder, *Kirche und Jugend*, p. 58.

127. From Württemberg *Schulordnung*, 1559, in Vormbaum, p. 160.

128. From *Kirchenordnung* for Hessen (1566), in Reu, 1, 2 (1):424–25.

129. From visitation instructions for County Mansfeld, 1580, in Thuringia, in Reu, 1, 1 (1):263.

130. For example: Thomas Lindner, *Catechismus vor die evangelischen Kirchen und Schulen zu Ravensburg* (1546), which begins with "Etlich spruech von allerley heilige orden und staend." Printed in Ernst-Wilhelm Kohls, *Evangelische Katechismen der Reformationszeit,* p. 53.

131. From Württemberg *Schulordnung* (1559), in Vormbaum, p. 161.

132. From instruction for visitation in Pfalz-Neuburg, 1566. S.Neub.D., Grassegger-Sammlung, no. 15329, 7v.

133. Abraham Lange, *Christlicher Kinder Lehre* . . . (Jena, 1608), Ar.

134. From visitation in Hessen 1542. Hess.H.S.Wiesb., Abt. 153, no. 457, unpaginated.

135. From Josua Opitz's *Kinderbibel* (1583), quoted in Friedrich Hahn, *Die evangelische Unterweisung* . . . (Heidelberg, 1957) p. 66.

136. Christoph Vischer, *Auslegung der fünf Heuptstück des heiligen Catechismi* . . . (first published 1573; I use Leipzig, 1578), vi r–vii v.

137. Tettelbach, *Das güldene Kleinod,* p. 1.

138. Vischer, *Auslegung der fünf Heuptstück,* Aii v–iii r.

139. A good example: Justus Jonas's preface to Johann Spangenberg's *Des kleinen Catechismi und der Haustaffel kurtzer begriff* . . . (first published Wittenberg, 1541; I use Wittenberg, 1549), Aii v–vi v.

140. Caspar Huberinus, *Catechismus: Mit vielen schönen sprüchen und historien der heyligen schrifft gegründet* . . . (Augsburg, 1543; I use Nuremberg, 1558), unnumbered leaves 3 r–4 r.

141. Mattheus Judex, *Das kleine Corpus doctrinae . . . für die kinder in den Schulen und heusern* (Ursel, 1578), no. xxxiii.

142. Vischer, *Auslegung der fünf Heuptstück,* preface, ii r and v; vi r and v.

143. Cf. Bavarian visitation 1558–60: BHM, Hochstift Literalien, Passau 83, xi, passim. Ibid., Staatsverwaltung 2783, 233. Johannes Bauermann. "Ein Paderborner Visitationsbericht vom Jahre 1575," *Westfalia Sacra* 4 (1973): 14. S.Bamb., B57[vi], no. 6, 1–2; B49, no. 285, 2r.

144. Thirteen early Catholic catechisms are printed in Christoph Moufang, *Katholische Katechismen des 16. Jahrhunderts in deutscher Sprache* (Mainz, 1881). The Tridentine catechism was published in 1566. Peter Canisius's Latin and German catechisms were published 1555–66. On the activities of the Jesuits, see Bernhard Duhr, S.J., *Geschichte der Jesuiten in den Ländern deutscher Zunge im XVI. Jahrhundert* (Freiburg im Breisgau, 1907).

145. For an explicit statement of this position by a Protestant authority, see the promulgation by Count Johann of Oldenburg, 1598, in N.S.S.Old., Best. 20, Titel 19, no. 22.

146. Cf. Elizabeth Eisenstein, "L'avènement de l'imprimerie et la Réforme," *Annales: E.S.C.* 26 (1971): 1355–82. English translation: "The Advent of Printing and the Protestant Revolt: A New Approach to the Disruption of Western Christendom," in *Transition and Revolution,* ed. Robert M. Kingdon (Minneapolis, Minn., 1974).

147. Huberinus, *Vierzig kurze predig,* Aiii v–iiii r.

148. Quoted in Leder, *Kirche und Jugend,* p. 57. The same definition is given by Vischer, *Auslegung der fünf Heuptstück,* Av v.

149. Huberinus, *Vierzig kurze predig,* vii v.

150. Tettelbach, *Das güldene Kleinod,* a 3 r.

151. Paulus Franzius, *Christliche nützliche Fragen und Antwort von den fürnembsten Heuptstücken warer evangelischer Religion* . . . (Wittenberg, 1590), Aix r. Ioannus Thomas Freigius, an all-round pedagogue and follower of Ramus, recommended the question and answer form as the easiest and quickest method for learning any subject. Cf. *Paedagogus, hoc est libellus ostendens qua ratione prima artium initia pueris quam facillime tradi possint* (Basel, 1582). Zezschwitz, *System der Katechetik,* vol. 2, part 2, sec. 2, chaps. 1–2, traces the entire history of the question and answer form from antiquity to the Reformation.

152. There are many examples of regulations requiring or suggesting this method, and many descriptions of its being done. Two are given in Leder, *Kirche und Jugend,* pp. 105, 107. An example from a visitation protocol: S.Dresd., Loc. 1985, 304r.

153. Augustine, *De catechizandi rudibus,* trans. J. P. Christopher (Westminster, Md.,

1946), chap. 13. This entire chapter is a painstaking consideration of the best approaches to be taken in catechization.

154. Heinrich Salmuth, *Catechismus* . . . (Budissin, 1581), Ciiii v.

155. E.g., the recommendations of Andreas Musculus, *Catechismus: Kinderpredig, wie die in . . . Brandenburgk und . . . Nürnberg . . . gepredigt werden* (Frankfurt an der Oder, 1566), preface.

156. From a discussion among Augsburg ecclesiastics in 1602 of the problems of catechism teaching among the city's youth. Documents in Sdt.Augsb., Evangelisches Wesensarchiv 1129, vol. 1.

157. A point often made in visitation recesses. E.g., Brandenburg, 1572: Berlin: Geheimes Staatsarchiv, Preussischer Kulturbesitz: Pr. Br., Rep. 40, no. 184.

158. From a report by a visitor in the duchy of Braunschweig-Grubenhagen, 1579. Printed in Friedrich Spanuth, "Die Grubenhagensche Kirchenvisitation von 1579 durch Superintendent Schellhammer," *Jahrb. Gesellsch. niedersächsische Kirchengesch.* 52 (1954):116.

159. From instructions for a teacher of religion in the gymnasium of Hornbach, duchy of Zweibrücken, 1580, in K. Reissinger, *Dokumente zur Geschichte d. humanistischen Schulen*, p. 139.

160. For Nuremberg, S.Nurnb., Rep. 54a, II, 228 and Gerhard Hirschmann, "Die zweite Nürnberger Kirchenvisitation," p. 118. For Saxony: *General-Artickel und gemeiner Bericht* (1557) in Sehling, 1: 325. For Halberstadt: Gustav Nebe, ed., *Die Kirchenvisitationen des Bisthums Halberstadt in den Jahren 1564 und 1589* (Halle, 1880), p. 63. For Zweibrücken: S.Neub.D., Depot Heimatverein Neuburg, no. 81, 45v.

161. E.g., information given to visitors in Meissen in 1579: S.Dresd., Loc. 1980, 4v.

162. Tettelbach, *Das güldene Kleinod*, Av r.

163. From visitation of duchy of Braunschweig-Grubenhagen in 1579, printed in Friedrich Spanuth, "Die Grubenhagensche Kirchenvisitation," p. 116.

164. B.S.Münch. 1375, no. 9, 530r. This was in 1630.

CHAPTER 9

1. On Ramus generally, see Walter J. Ong, *Ramus, Method, and the Decay of Dialogue* (Cambridge, Mass., 1958); Frank P. Graves, *Peter Ramus and the Educational Reformation of the Sixteenth Century* (New York, 1912). On the concept and practice of "method," see Neal W. Gilbert, *Renaissance Concepts of Method* (New York, 1960).

2. For German editions and translations of Ramus and Ramist works, see Walter J. Ong, *Ramus and Talon Inventory* (Cambridge, Mass., 1958).

3. Michael Neander, *Bedencken an einen guten Herrn und Freund, wie ein Knabe zu leithen und zu unterweisen, das er one gros jagen, treiben und eilen, mit Lust und Liebe, vom sechsten jare seines alters an, bis auff das achtzehende, wol und fertig lernen möge pietatem, linguam latinam, Graecam, Hebraeam, Artes, und endlich universam philosophiam*. 1st ed. (Eisleben, 1580; I use Eisleben, 1583), 16r. Neander taught at Nordhausen from 1547 to 1550, then went to Ilfeld. He died in 1595.

4. Ibid., 15v–16r; 43r.

5. From the preface to a catechism published in Mecklenburg in 1540, cited in H. Schnell, *Das Unterrichtswesen der Grossherzogtümer Mecklenburg-Schwerin und Strehlitz, MGP*, 38 (1907):119.

6. Nathan Chytraeus, rector of a school in Rostock, *Ludi literarii* (1580), cited in ibid., pp. 389–92.

7. "Das man sie auch mit büchern und lection keineswegs überschütte, . . . man sol sie auch nit beschweren mit früw auffsteen, ... man sol die kinder auch nit zu hart halten." From the Electoral Saxon visitation of the city of Würtzen (1542), S.Weim., Reg. 1, no. 10, 74r, 76r, 77r.

8. The policy is also reflected in frequent student protests against long lectures and heavy assignments. E.g. S.Nürn., Rep. 90, no. 83: petition by pupils of the Heilig Geist Spital in Nuremberg in the 1550s.

9. From the *Kirchenordnung* of Gengenbach, cited in Ernst-Wilhelm Kohls, *Evangelische Bewegung und Kirchenordnung* . . . (Karlsruhe, 1966), p. 36.

10. "Jedoch hierinn nit eilen, dann es begiebt sich, das in dem fall die letsten die ersten werden. Darumb allwegen das alter und mores der knaben fleissig seind zu bedenken." Printed in Vormbaum, p. 95. See ibid., pp. 73–74 for instructions on dividing pupils in each grade into groups corresponding to their respective abilities.

11. From the dedication to Philipp Melanchthon of Marcus Croedel's *Institutiones grammaticae Latinogermanicae* . . . (Basel, 1541), reprinted in Karl Hartfelder, *Melanchthoniana Paedagogica* . . . (Leipzig, 1892), pp. 49–54.

12. Caspar Huberinus, *Catechismus* . . . (Nuremberg, 1558), Aix v.

13. E.g., Michael Neander, *Bedencken an einen guten Herrn und Freund.* Johann Sturm preferred the age of seven: *De literarum ludis recte aperiendi liber* (Strassburg, 1538). Matthias Lechner, *Erziehung und Bildung in der griechisch-römischen Antike* (Munich, 1933), p. 81, shows that the custom of beginning elementary schooling at six or seven goes back at least as far as Hellenistic times.

14. Examinations of pupils at the school of the Heilig Geist Spital in Nuremberg in the 1570s show this clearly. In 1574, for example, thirty-five boys were examined; one was twelve years old, four were thirteen, eight were fourteen, three were fifteen, ten were sixteen, three were eighteen, one was nineteen, two were twenty, three were twenty-one. Sdt.Nürn., rep. 90, no. 84.

15. An influential statement of this: Juan Huarte, *Examen de ingenios para las ciencias* (1575), trans. Richard Carew (London, 1594), Bvi r.

16. E.g., Luther, *Eine Predigt, dass man Kinder zur Schule halten solle* (1530), in *WA*, 30²:526. The *Unterricht der Visitatoren* (1528) forbade German teaching in Latin schools: *WA*, 26:236.

17. This was said inter alia by Johann Muschler, a schoolmaster in Oettingen, in a treatise *Von Schulzucht* dedicated to the town council of Leipzig in 1529 (quoted in Friedrich Paulsen, *Geschichte des gelehrten Unterrichts auf den deutschen Schulen und Universitäten* [Leipzig, 1885], 1:282; and by officials conducting a visitation of the city of Coburg in 1577 and recommending the collapsing of the city's three German schools into one: S.Cob., B2468, 17v–18r.

18. S.Cob., B2468, 58v, 85v, 180r.

19. One example: WHS A284: Leonberg G.V., B202, which contains letters from pastors reporting deserving students to the duke, and also petitions from fathers for their sons, together with supporting documents from local officials and pastors. In each case the action taken is indicated.

20. Two examples from Württemberg: ibid., A469, B2 (visitation of a Latin school attached to the *Klosterschule* of Adelsberg, 1560) and LAS: Synodus-Protokolle 1585, 45v.

21. The most impressive follow-through I have seen occurred in the Coburg and Gotha principalities of Saxony. Year after year visitors sent in the names of promising students whose parents were too poor to support their studies. In most cases the duke either appropriated a small sum for the boy's upkeep or arranged for a pastor near a Latin school to take him in as a boarder in exchange for help with catechism instruction. Many of these boys must have made it to the university and a professional career. The documents are in S.Cob., B2461–2539.

22. Ibid., B2480, 92r.

23. "Der gemeine Nutz"—a ubiquitous phrase in educational connections.

24. From a memorandum by Johann Marbach on reorganizing the school system of the duchy of Zweibrücken, 1558, printed in K. Reissinger, ed., *Dokumente zur Geschichte der humanistischen Schulen im Gebiet der bayerischen Pfalz, MGP*, 49 (1911):15. The same procedures operated in Bavaria in 1560: Cf. OEMF, 565–71: visitations of diocese of Freising and Munich, 1560 ff., and Staatsbibliothek München, Cgm. 1737: visitation protocols for diocese of Passau, 1588–60.

25. This particular list, typical of humanist definitions of intellectual ability, was given by Johann Murmellius, an indefatigable German humanist and teacher, in his *opusculum* of 1505. Critical ed. by A. Bömer, *Des Münsterischen Humanisten Johannes Murmellius Opusculum de discipulorum officiis, quod enchiridion scholasticorum inscribitur* (Münster, 1892).

26. This was said by the *Kirchenrat* of Pfalz-Neuburg in 1584 to the father of a boy in the Latin school of Lauingen who was found to be a slow learner. S.Neub.D., Grassegger-Sammlung no. 1535³, 138r.

27. S.Weim., reg. 1, no. 6, 207r for instruction to city of Torgau. Passim for other cities and towns.

28. This principle of organization can be seen at work even where economy mandated large classes. E.g., the records of the Strassburg *Scholarchen:* Strassb.A.V., Archives St. Thomas 324.

29. Ibid., 8v; 10r and v, etc. Classes must not be so small that there are "zu wenig, sy in lust zu behalten und etwas anzureizen." See also the passages from Martin Bucer's Ratslag und bedacht der Schulherrn und ettlicher Gelerten alhie, eyne gemeyne schulen zun Predigern fürzunehmen (1538), quoted in Ernst-Wilhelm Kohls, *Die Schule bei Martin Bucer . . .* (Heidelberg, 1963), p. 85.

30. A phrase used by Loyola, this became a basic educational principle for Jesuits. See Joseph Schröteler, *Die Erziehung in den Jesuiteninternaten . . .* (Freiburg im Breisgau, 1940), pp. 404-6, 460, etc.; and Bernhard Duhr, S.J., *Geschichte der Jesuiten in den Ländern deutscher Zunge . . .* (Freiburg im Breisgau, 1907), pp. 245, 248-49, etc.

31. For a collection of examples of the use of ambition and sense of honor and pride in Protestant education, see Mertz, pp. 379-85.

32. Edward Eggleston, *The Hoosier Schoolmaster* (New York, 1892), p. 53.

33. E.g., John S. Brubacher, *A History of the Problems of Education,* 2d ed. (New York, 1966), p. 142.

34. Giovanni Dominici, *Regola del governo di cura familiare.* I use Augustin Rösler, trans., *Kardinal Johannes Dominicis Erziehungslehre,* in *Bibliothek der katholischen Pädagogik,* 7 (Freiburg im Breisgau, 1894):42-43. Dominici's treatise was not printed in his lifetime.

35. Johann Böhm, *Ein christliches Radtbüchlin für die kinder* (Wittenberg, 1536), unpaginated.

36. Johann Agricola, *Sybenhundert und fünfftzig teutscher Sprichwörter* (Hagenau, 1534), no. 649.

37. "Ach du liebe ruth' / Mach du mich gut,/ Mach du mich fromm,/ Das ich nicht zum Henker komm'." Quoted in Heinrich Heppe, *Geschichte des deutschen Volksschulwesens* (Gotha, 1858; reprinted Hildesheim and New York, 1971), 1:301. Geiler von Kaisersberg, in his *Seelenparadiss* of 1510, gives a different version of this verse: "Liebe rut, trute rut, werest du nicht, ich tet nimmer gut." Quoted in Jakob Grimm and Wilhelm Grimm, *Deutsches Worterbuch,* vol. 8, col. 1561 (see the entire article on *Rute* for a collection of proverbs).

38. Quoted in Caspar Huberinus, *Spiegel der geistlichen Hauszucht* (Frankfurt am Main, 1569), Diiii r.

39. Eberhard von Künssberg, "Rechtsbrauch und Kinderspiel," *Sitzb. Heidelberger Akad. Wiss., philos.-hist. Kl.* 7 (1920): 20-23 argues that the frequency of remarks on the beneficent results of corporal punishment was traceable to the late medieval and early modern custom of giving blows to children as painful reminders of something learned and witnessed. The idea was to fix the occasion and the message in the child's mind by associating it with a painful sensation.

40. Philippe Ariès, *Centuries of Childhood . . . ,* trans. Robert Baldick (New York, 1962), 258, 262. Ariès refers primarily to France but clearly intends his judgments to apply to western European society as a whole.

41. Luther, *WA,* Tr. 3, no. 3566A; 2, no. 1559. Cf. also Hermann von Weinsberg in *Das Buch Weinsberg,* ed. Johann Jakob Hässlin (Munich, 1961) 1:37, 42-43, Also Bartholomäus Sastrow, *Bartholomäi Sastrowen Herkommen, Geburt und Lauff seines gantzen Lebens . . . von ihm selbst beschriben,* ed. G. C. F. Mohnike (Greifswald, 1823-24), 1:77-78. In Sastrow's case the father's severity was mitigated by the mother. Also Johann Butzbach's autobiography, English trans. by R. F. Seybolt and P. Monroe, *The Autobiography of Johannes Butzbach* (Ann Arbor, Mich., 1933), vol. 1, chap. 2.

42. For a good example of such a line of reasoning: Huberinus, *Spiegel der Hauszucht,* Dv v–Ev v.

43. *Leges et statuta, den Schülern so in classibus anfengklichs gegeben* (Strassburg, 1538), in Marcel Fournier and Charles Engel, *Les statuts et privilèges des universités françaises*

..., part 2, vol. 4, fasc. 1 (Paris, 1894), p. 28. The same rule, verbatim, was proposed in Ulm in 1586: Sdt.Ulm, A (1836), 11.

44. From the Electoral Saxon *Kirchenordnung* of 1580 in Vormbaum, pp. 275–76.

45. From visitation instruction to city of Torgau in Electoral Saxony, 1534. S.Weim, reg. 1, no. 6, 269r.

46. *WA*, Tr. 3, no. 3566.

47. *Schulordnung* of Nordhausen (1583), in Vormbaum, p. 380.

48. E.g., Strassburg: Strassb.A.V., Archives St. Thomas, 372. These are the protocols of quarterly examinations of all municipal teachers by the *Scholarchen*. A good case in point: ibid., 3v (1535).

49. "Väterliche Castigation" occurs in one such dossier from Württemberg: WHS A280, B108, relating to the Latin school in Schorndorf (1587).

50. See Walter Hävernik, *Schläge als Strafe: Ein Bestandteil der heutigen Familiensitte in volkskundlicher Sicht* (Hamburg, 1964), pp. 30–35. For a violent polemic against this book and the phenomenon it is said to represent, see Klaus Horn, *Dressur oder Erziehung: Schlagrituale und ihre gesellschaftliche Funktion* (Frankfurt am Main, 1967).

51. Hess.H.S.Wiesb., no. 137 Xa, no. 1., 18r (1594). Other examples: ibid., Abt. 171, K209, 23r; S.Cob., B2480, 92r; B.S.Lansh. Rep. 82, fasc. 67, no. 43, Saal 17, 40r; Jörg Wickram, *Der jungen Knaben Spiegel* (1554) in *Bibl. litt. Ver. Stuttgart* 223 (1901):12–13.

52. S.Cob., B2480, 53v.

53. See chap. 5, note 49.

54. *WA*, Tr. 2, no. 3566 A and B. The remark comes from Plutarch, *De liberis educandis*, in *Plutarch's Moralia*, ed. and trans. F. C. Babbitt (London, 1927) 1:12.

55. Otto Brunfels, *Weiber und Kinder Apothek...* (Strassburg, 1535), xliiii r. The phrase comes verbatim from Bartolomäus Metlinger, *Ein Regiment der jungen Kinder* (Augsburg, 1473), 26r.

56. Bartholomäus Sastrow, *Bartholomäi Sastrowen Herkommen*, 1:77–78.

57. E.g., Hess.H.S.Wiesb., Abt. 133, no. 3, 16v. For Catholic regulations, particularly Jesuit practices, see Schröteler, *Die Erziehung in den Jesuiteninternaten*, pp. 387–90; Duhr, *Geschichte der Jesuiten*, p. 265; and G. M. Pachtler, S.J., *Ratio studiorum et Institutiones Scholasticae Societatis Jesu, MGP*, 5 (1887): 397.

58. "In dieser übertrefflichen geschwinden teuren zeit." Sdt.Cob., B186, 352–53.

59. Cf. the description in Eugen Schmid, *Geschichte des Volksschulwesens in Alt-württemberg* (Stuttgart, 1927), pp. 67–68.

60. For a vivid example, see WHS, A64, B10.

61. For examples see Julius Richter, *Geschichte der sächsischen Volksschule, MGP*, 29 (1930), e.g., p. 457. Also Mertz, pp. 417–27. Also Pallas, passim.

62. These particular ones from Württemberg (1567), WHS A282, B1025.

63. Printed in Pallas, 41³:60.

64. Johann Murmellius, *De magistri et discipulorum officiis epigrammatum liber* (Cologne, 1510), epigram 4.

65. Juan Luis Vives, *De tradendis disciplinis libri quinque* (1531), trans. Foster Watson (Cambridge, 1913; reprinted Totowa, N.J., 1971), p. 57.

66. E.g., Jacob Frey, *Die Gartengesellschaft* (1556), ed. Johannes Bolte, in *Bibl. litt. Ver. Stuttg.* 209 (1896):17.

67. In Strassburg, elementary school teachers could not leave the city without the permission of the school board. Cf. Ernst-Wilhelm Kohls, *Die Schule bei Martin Bucer*, p. 28, note 22.

68. These documents are in the series A284: Kirchenrat Spezialakten in the WHS. They are organized by localities and cover the entire duchy.

69. Ibid., A280, B82.

70. One example: In 1542 Duke Maurice of Saxony sent a printed notice to local authorities in his realm, ordering them to submit exact information on the income of each clergyman and schoolteacher. See Sdt.Leipz., Tit. VII, B2, 159v–160r for this document and a copy of the city council's answer with detailed data.

71. E.g., S.Bamb., C2, nos. 1899 and 1902, and Sdt.Augsb., Evangelisches Wesensarchiv 1129, vol. 1. The latter collection also contains letters from women applicants.

72. Examples from the evidence for this: ibid., 1129, vol. 1; 1042, part 2. Sdt.Ulm,

Ratsprotokolle for entire sixteenth and seventeenth centuries. LAS, *Synodus-Protokolle* from 1581. The 1580 *Kirchenordnung* in Saxony provided a pension for superannuated clerics and schoolmasters and for six months' support for their widows—Cf. Julius Richter, *Geschichte der sächsischen Volksschule*, MGP, 29 (1930); 559, 588–89—but left it up to the individuals concerned to petition for help.

73. E.g., S.Cob., B2468, 58v; LAS, *Synodus-Protokolle*, 1581, 65r, etc.

74. One case as an example: Johann Koch, schoolmaster in Altdorf, Württemberg, was described as "ein blöder mann" in 1583, at age forty-nine; in 1585: "nimmt ab an kräfften," in 1588: "nimmt hefftig an seinen krefften, sinn und verstand ab." In 1590 he was still in office. The series breaks off at this point, to resume in 1621, when a new name shows up in Altdorf. Ibid., 1583, 1585, 1588, 1590, 1621 (unpaginated, but organized by locality). For another case: WHS A284, Herrenberg St.V. Gültstein, Kl.Hirsamer Pfl., B237.

75. I cite a few of the printed materials from which information about teachers' salaries can be obtained: Mertz, passim, especially pp. 211–12, 417–27. Eugen Schmid, *Geschichte des Volksschulwesens in Altwürttemberg* (Stuttgart, 1927), pp. 59 ff., information based on *Kompetenzbücher* of 1559–1600. Victor Herold, ed., "Die Brandenburgischen Kirchenvisitations-Abschiede und Register. . . ." 1. *Veröffentlichungen der historichen Kommission für die Provinz Brandenburg . . .*, vol. 4, nos. 1–5 (1928–31), 2d ed. Gerhard Zimmermann and Gerd Heinrich, *Veröffentlichungen der Berliner historischen Kommission beim Friedrich-Meinecke-Institut der freien Universität Berlin*, vol. 6 (1963). Herold cites exact figures for 1540–45, 1550–58, 1573–81, and 1600. Pallas, passim, all volumes. Julius Richter, *Geschichte der sächsischen Volksschule*, MGP, 29 (1930): 447 ff., 618–20. Gustav Nebe, ed., *Die Kirchenvisitationen des Bisthums Halberstadt . . .* (Halle, 1880). Massive additional information is contained in unpublished visitation protocols. To compare salary figures with cost of living, cf. "Preise und Löhne in der ersten Hälfte des 16. Jahrhunderts," in *Das Visitationsbuch der Hamburger Kirchen 1508-1521*, ed. Erich Keyser and Helga-Maria Kühn, (Hamburg, 1970); and Moritz Elsass, *Umriss einer Geschichte der Preise und Löhne in Deutschland . . .* (Leiden, 1936).

76. S.Cob., B2468, 17v; B2473, 406r and v.

77. E.g., Braunschweig-Kalenberg (1588), the first general church reform of this territory after its acquisition by Duke Julius. Cf. Karl Kayser, "Die General-Visitation von 1588 im Lande Göttingen-Kalenberg," *Zeitschr. Ges. niedersächsische Kirchengesch.* 8 (1904):131.

78. For an illuminating illustration, see the tabulation of payments due to the teaching sexton of the Saxon village of Leundorf, in Julius Richter, *Geschichte der sächsischen Volksschule* (1930), pp. 618–20. Detailed information for the county of Oldenburg is available in a typescript by Heinrich Meyer, *Dokumentation zur frühen Geschichte der oldenburgischen Volksschule*, 1:1575–1670, in the N.S.S.Old.

79. My information about artisan occupations of village schoolmasters comes from visitation documentation in the S.Dresd., in which the names of schoolmasters are listed for each parish throughout the sixteenth century and their occupations nearly always given. Cf. also the five volumes of Heinrich Heppe, *Geschichte des deutschen Volksschulwesens*, e.g., the decree by Duke Johann Casimir of Saxony-Coburg, 1626, 2:209.

80. S.Nürn. Rep. 41a, no. 454, 2–4.

81. Visitors continued to admonish teachers to be *fleissiger* and *gelerter*, that is to say, prepare themselves better. E.g., OEMF, 565, 693.

82. S.Cob., B2461, 154v.

83. Two excerpts from a batch of reference letters and examination results of prospective teachers in the Nuremberg territory, 1550s, S.Nürn., Rep. 19a.

84. E.g., ibid., rep. 40a SI, L. 597.

85. From draft instruction to visitors in Pfalz-Neuburg, 1576. S.Neub.D., Grassegger-Sammlung, no. 15327, 129r.

86. Cf. instruction to visitors in Brandenburg, 1581, in "Die Brandenburgischen Kirchenvisitations-Abschiede," ed. Victor Herold, p. 344.

87. E.g., rules relating to teachers, Strassburg, in Fournier and Engel, *Les statuts et privilèges*, passim, especially p. 48. Also Sdt.Augsb., Evangelisches Wesensarchiv 1004.

88. On this, see the information compiled by Mertz, pp. 405–16.

89. For these and other examples of early Reformation estimates of the shorter time required for learning, cf. Mertz, pp. 361–62. Luther wrote in 1524, in his treatise *An die*

Ratherren aller Städte . . ., "Meyn meynung ist, das man die Knaben des tags eyn stund odder zwo lasse zu solcher schule gehen . . . ," *WA*, 15:47.

90. Vacations were considered to benefit not pupils, but teachers. E.g., Nordhausen *Schulordnung* in Mertz, p. 380. Some other examples: Ulm, two to three weeks in the summer, one week each in autumn and Lent. Braunschweig, one week at Christmas, Easter, and Whitsun. The Jesuit *ratio* of 1599 was one of the earliest regulations to set up a schedule of fixed annual vacations of one to two months' duration for the top classes down to one week only for the lowest grammar-school class. Cf. G. M. Pachtler, *Ratio studiorum . . .*, *MGP*, 5 (1887):265.

91. From the *Schulordnung* of Altdorf (1575), in Vormbaum, p. 627. See the whole section "Von kurtzweilen, spatzirn gehen, und andern dergleichen ergetzfligkeiten," for an illustration of the role of recreation in early modern education. Similarly, *Schulordnung* of Braunschweig (1543) in ibid., p. 51, and that of Brieg (1581), in Mertz, p. 391. Erasmus mentions most of the schoolboy sports of his day in the colloquy "Sport," Craig Thompson, trans., *The Colloquies of Erasmus* (Chicago, 1965), pp. 22–30. For contemporary theoretical discussions of games and recreation, mainly in relation to health, see Hieronymus Mercurialis, *Artis gymnasticae apud antiquos celeberrimae, nostris temporibus ignoratae, libri sex* (Venice, 1569), especially bk. 5, chaps. 11–12 on *deambulatio*, walking for health, which becomes *spazieren gehen* in German. Also Sebald Heiden, the rector of Saint Sebald School, Nuremberg, *Paedonomia scholastica* (Nuremberg, 1553), who thought music the best of all recreational activities (cf. no. 504). Cf. Joseph Dolch, *Lehrplan des Abendlandes . . .* (Ratingen, 1965), pp. 215–16 for more references.

92. Franz Xaver Buchner, *Schulgeschichte des Bistums Eichstätt . . .* (Kallmünz, 1956), passim. Eugen Schmid, *Geschichte des Volksschulwesens in Altwürttemberg*, pp. 70–74.

93. Cf. Philippe Ariès's comments on the traditionality of humanist educators generally: *Centuries of Childhood*, pp. 330–31.

94. Printed in Georg Lurz, *Mittelschulgeschichtliche Dokumente Altbayerns . . .*, *MGP*, 42 (1908):431.

95. Many have been published. A sampling: the earliest of Lutheran school plans was the three-form curriculum of the Latin school of Eisleben, printed in Karl Hartfelder, *Melanchthoniana paedagogica . . .* (Leipzig, 1892), pp. 1–6. The Latin schools of the duchy of Zweibrücken from the 1550s: K. Reissinger, ed., *Dokumente zur Geschichte der humanistischen Schulen im Gebiet der bayerischen Pfalz*, *MGP*, 47, 49 (1910–11). A representative selection is given by Vormbaum, passim.

96. Donatus was still recommended by the Ramist Johann Thomas Freigius in his *Paedagogus* (Basel, 1582), a6r. He does add: "hodie plerique praeferunt Philippum, aut Ramum."

97. The preceding sketch is a composite picture based on my reading of a score, at least, of Latin school curricula issued between 1530 and ca. 1600. Cf. Mertz for detailed information, based almost entirely on sixteenth-century *Schulordnungen*, about subjects, classes, textbooks, etc. On the learned curriculum, generally, and its relations to the medieval trivium and quadrivium, cf. Dolch, *Lehrplan des Abendlandes*, especially pp. 198–216. Mertz, pp. 295–305, gives a comprehensive list of the classical authors read in the sixteenth century, based on his examination of Protestant *Schulordnungen*.

98. Melanchthon's *Enchiridion elementorum puerilium* (or *Elementa puerilia*) of 1523 is printed in Ferdinand Cohrs, *Philipp Melanchthons Schriften zur praktischen Theologie.* 1. *Katechetische Schriften*, Supplementa Melanchthonia, 5 (Leipzig, 1915):20–56. The reference is to p. 20. For Luther's view on the connection between gospel and *Schrift*, see *An die Ratsherren aller Städte . . .* (1524), *WA*, 15:37.

99. It had been originally intended for the private pupils in his *schola domestica*. On Melanchthon's work in religious and catechism instruction, see Robert Stupperich, *Der unbekannte Melanchthon* (Stuttgart, 1961), pp. 41–55: "In der katechetischen Arbeit."

100. Sebald Heyden, *Formulae puerilium* (Nuremberg, 1530), unpaginated.

101. *ABC und Namenbüchlein zum kurtzen und gründlichen Unterricht der Schulkinder im Buchstabiren*, in Sdt.Ulm, 1836/1, 27340.

102. On Cato, see Hans Rupprich, *Die deutsche Literatur vom späten Mittelalter bis zum Barock*, part 1 (Munich, 1970), pp. 293–94; part 2 (Munich, 1973), p. 404. Also Friedrich

Zarncke, *Der deutsche Cato: Geschichte der deutschen Übersetzungen der im Mittelalter unter dem Namen Cato bekannten Distichen* (Leipzig, 1852), introduction. Cato was translated into many languages, including English. For the original Latin poem see Zarncke, *Der deutsche Cato*, pp. 174–83.

103. Leonhard Culman, *Sententiae pueriles* . . . (I use Augsburg, 1544, and Leipzig, 1544). No two editions of this work are identical. The English edition was published in London, 1658, with English translation of the Latin sentences.

104. Walter J. Ong, "Latin Language Study as a Renaissance Puberty Rite," *Studies in Philology* 56 (April 1959):103–24. Reprinted in George D. Springer, ed., *Education and Culture* (New York, 1963), pp. 444–66.

105. The statements quoted come from the *Schulordnungen* of Goldberg (1546) and Lauingen (1565), both in Mertz, p. 270; and from a note by a member of the board of *Scholarchen* in Strassburg on a memorandum on teaching submitted by Martin Bucer, printed in Robert Stupperich, ed., *Martin Bucers deutsche Schriften,* 7 (Gütersloh, 1964): 534.

106. *Unterricht der Visitatoren* . . . (1528) *WA*, 26:238.

107. From the *Kirchenordnung* of Mecklenburg (1552), in Vormbaum, p. 65.

108. For a list of grammatical textbooks in use in Reformation schools see Mertz, pp. 270–71. A curious episode in the history of Latin language and literature in the Reformation is Martin Bucer's rejection of the idea of the continuity of Latin culture and his consequent attempt to rout Latin from the curriculum in Strassburg. See Kohls, *Die Schule bei Martin Bucer*, pp. 69–73. Bucer got nowhere in this struggle. Wittenberg as well as Strassburg remained firmly committed to Latin.

109. This right was stated unequivocally in the Augsburg *Schulordnung* of 1537: "Books shall be authorized and, if necessary, corrected only by [the members of the school board], and no schoolmaster shall have power in this matter to decide anything on his own." Quoted in Martin Niesseler, *Schulvolkskunde der Elementarschulen in der freien Reichsstadt Augsburg* (Augsburg, 1970), p. 8.

110. For the information brought to the Bavarian authorities on this, see Heinrich Held, *Altbayrische Volkserziehung und Volksschule* (Munich, 1926–28), 3:54, and the visitation documents of the diocese of Freising in OEMF, 565–71. For some figures on the wide distribution of Melanchthon's works in pastoral libraries in the Rhineland, see Bernard Vogler, *Le clergé protestant rhénan* . . . , pp. 240–42.

111. From the Bavarian *Schulordnung* of 1569, in Lurz, *Mittelschulgeschichtliche Dokumente*, 42:35–36.

112. Ibid., p. 45. Visitors were instructed to look through every library and printing shop and lock up copies of forbidden books. Also, they were to examine the stocks of itinerant book dealers. BHM, Staatsverwaltung 3019, 267r; Hochstift Literalien Passau, 83, 11, 19v.

113. "Eyn alt gewonheit lest sich nicht / Bald (wie man an Papisten sicht) / Abstelln, wann man da widder fecht / Was tausend jar war ungerecht; / Das wird drum nit für recht erkennt, / On von dem, der da ist verblent." Erasmus Alberus, *Praecepta morum utilissima ex variis autoribus* . . . (Frankfurt, 1536). Catholics could play this game too, of course, as J. Brodrick remarks in his book about Canisius (*Saint Peter Canisius, S.J.* [London, 1939], p. 236). Canisius's short Latin catechism was printed with grammar texts for Catholic schools. For a discussion of Johann Agricola's proverb collection as polemical literature, see Sander L. Gilman, "Johannes Agricola of Eisleben's Proverb Collection (1529): The Polemizing of a Literary Form and the Reaction," *The Sixteenth-Century Journal* 8:1 (April 1977), 77–84.

114. Mattäus Judex, *Der kleine Corpus Doctrinae . . . für die kinder in den schulen und Heusern* . . . (Ursel, 1578), no. 22. Johann Spangenberg, *Der gross Catechismus und Kinder Leere* . . . (Wittenberg, 1541), in Reu, 1, 2 (2), p. 304.

115. Mertz, p. 341.

116. Std. Ulm, A (1836), 21r.

117. These from Joachim Camerarius's *Dialogus de vita decente aetatem puerilem* . . . (Leipzig, 1572), in Latin and German.

118. See the discussions of this aspect of the dialogues of Erasmus and Morisotus in A. Bömer, "Aus dem Kampfe gegen die Colloquia familiaria," pp. 1–73.

119. Elizabeth Eisenstein, "Some Conjectures about the Impact of Printing on Western

Society and Thought: A Preliminary Report," *Journal of Modern History* 40, no. 1 (1968):1–56.

120. The same point is made in a different context by Natalie Z. Davis, *Society and Culture in Early Modern France* (Stanford, Calif., 1975), p. 221.

121. A 1536 instruction to visitors in Württemberg ordered German schools in small towns closed where they interfered with Latin schools. In 1546 Duke Ulrich ordered all vernacular schools closed (Schmid, *Geschichte des Volksschulwesens*, p. 8). For a similar move by the bishops of Passau, Salzburg, and Freising in 1540, see Lurz, *Mittelschulgeschichtliche Dokumente*, 41:215.

122. Lawrence Stone has considered both religion and the political drive for social control as factors determining educational policy, institutions, and procedures: "Literacy and Education in England, 1460–1900," *Past and Present* 42 (1969): 76–86. I do not find that Protestantism—at least in its sixteenth-century German version—gave as great a stimulus to mass education as he suggests (pp. 76–83). There was a wide gap between programmatic announcements by governments and consistories, on the one hand, and the public response to these on the other. The incentive to become literate arose mainly from pragmatic considerations.

123. *Von deutschen Schulen in Dörfern und Flecken*. From the *General-Artikel* of 1580, in Albert Richter, *Kursächsische Volksschulordnungen* (Leipzig, 1891), p. 12.

124. L.S.-H., 218: Lauenburgisches Konsistorium, no. 653, 216v. Cf. the complaint of the government of Braunschweig-Grubenhagen in 1639 that inhabitants of the country's mining towns take their boys out of school "wann sie kaum schreiben und lesen können" and put them to work in the mines. Landeskirchliches Archiv Braunschweig Voges, 1926, 7–8.

125. E.g., visitation instruction for Albertine Saxony (1557), in Sehling, 1:323.

126. Jacob Griessbeutel, *Ein besonder fast nützlich stymmen büchlein mit figuren, welche die stymmen an in selb anzeygen, mit silben und namen, in welchem die Gesellen, Eehalten, und ander alt leut, auch die Kinder, weyb und mann, bald (als in xxiv Stunden auff das minst) leytlich mögen lesen lernen* (Augsburg [1531] and many later editions). Valentin Ickelsamer, *Die rechte Weis auffs kürtzist lesen zu lernen* (1527); *Ein Teutsche Grammatica, darauss einer von im selbs mag lesen lernen . . .* (Augsburg, 1534; both titles reprinted in facsimile in Heinrich Fechtner, *Vier seltene Schriften des sechzehnten Jahrhunderts* [Berlin, 1882]). Peter Jordan, *Leyenschul: Wie man kunstlich und behend schreyben und lesen soll lernen. Darneben auch ein Unterricht, wie die ungelerigen köpf, so eyns groben verstands seyn, on buchstaben, durch figuren und charakteren, so inen selb anmutig, allerley zur noturfft zu schreyben und zu lesen sollen, underweyst werden* (Mainz, 1533; reprinted in Fechtner, *Vier seltene Schriften*). Other authors of reading and writing instructions for adults are Ortholph Fuchssperger, *Leesskonst . . .* (Ingolstadt, 1542; reprinted in Johannes Müller, *Quellenschriften und Geschichte des deutschsprachlichen Unterrichts . . .* (Gotha, 1882), pp. 166–88; Johann Kolross, *Enchiridion, das ist Handbüchlin tütscher Orthographi . . .* (Basel [1530], in Müller, *Quellenschriften*, pp. 64–91); Johann Meichssner, *Handbüchlin gruntlichs berichts, recht und wolschreybens*, in Müller, *Quellenschriften*, pp. 160–66.

127. Jordan, *Leyenschul*, Ai v.

128. On Valentin Ickelsamer, cf. Heinrich Noll, *Der Typus des religiösen Grammatikers im 16. Jahrhundert, dargestellt an Valentin Ickelsamer* (Marburg, 1935).

129. Ickelsamer, *Ein Teutsche Grammatica*, Biiii r–Bvii r. Ickelsamer also gives rules of orthography in his book but thinks it is a hopeless undertaking to teach Germans how to spell their language (ibid., Cvi r.).

130. E.g., County Nassau-Wiesbaden, Oberamt Idstein, visitation 1619: Hess.H.S.Wiesb., Abt. 133, no. 5, 72. Ibid., Abt. 153, no. 235. Negotiations between Dukes Wilhelm V and Maximilian I of Bavaria and deputies of the *Landschaft*, 1578–1616, with frequent references to local desires for schools and schooling: Lurz, *Mittelschulgeschichtliche Dokumente*, 42:12–27.

131. This correspondence, 1564–65, is in WHS, A284. Heidenheim Kl.F.V., B213.

132. Quoted in August Kluckhohn, "Die Jesuiten in Baiern mit besonderer Rücksicht auf ihre Lehrtätigkeit," *Historische Zeitschrift* 31 (1874):406.

133. Letter from pastor in Amt Rosenfeld to Duke Ludwig of Württemberg, 1582. WHS, A284, Rosenfeld G.V., B108.

134. From 1577 visitation of city of Coburg. S.Cob., B2468 17v-18r.

135. *Das Buch Weinsberg*, ed. Johann Jakob Hässlin, p. 67.

136. For a comparable case, cf. the autobiography of Bartolomäus Sastrow of Greifswald mentioned in note 41, above, especially the description of his father's reading skills and his own schooling: 1:20, 61. Cf. also the autobiography of Hans von Schweinichen, who, in his ninth year, in 1561 "habe ich . . . zum Dorfschreiber Jörg Pentzen gehen und allda zwei Jahr schreiben und lesen lernen müssen." *Memorialbuch . . . des schlesischen Ritters Hans von Schweinischen*, ed. Engelbert Hegaur (Munich, n.d.), p. 9.

137. For evidence involving fifteenth- and sixteenth-century artisans, see Dolch, *Lehrplan des Abendlandes*, p. 243.

138. "Du solst anhalten mit lesen, trösten unnd leren. . . ." From the *Schulordnung* of Mecklenburg (1552), Vormbaum, p. 60.

139. Valentin Ickelsamer is the best example of this. For other names, see Noll, *Der Typus des religiösen Grammatikers*.

140. Kolross, *Enchiridion*, in Müller, *Quellenschriften*, pp. 64-65.

141. Ortholph Fuchssperger, *Leesskonst . . .* (Ingolstadt, 1542), in Müller, *Quellenschriften*, pp. 166-67.

142. Valentin Ickelsamer, *Teutsche Grammatica* (ca. 1534) in Fechtner, *Vier seltene Schriften*, Aiiii r and v.

143. Ibid., Aiiii v-Av r.

144. Kohls, *Die Schule bei Martin Bucer*, p. 76.

145. S.Hamb., Cl. 7 Lit. He., no. 3, vol. 4. The year was 1568.

146. OEMF, 565, fol. 442 ff. Much more evidence in Lurz, *Mittelschulgeschichtliche Dokumente, passim*.

147. The range from farm to town is covered in German by the terms *Hof*, a single farmstead with its lands and buildings; *Weiler*, a small settlement of several such farmsteads; *Dorf*, the village, usually with the parish church, but sometimes as *eingepfarrtes Dorf* attached to a nearby parish; *Flecken*, a place somewhere between *Dorf* and town in population, including, along with peasants, tradespeople and artisans; and finally *Stadt*, the town.

148. See above, chap. 1. The documentation is the series A284 in WHS: records of correspondence between the duke and localities on church and school matters.

149. S.Cob., B2468.

150. Ibid., 121v; 215v; 266v; 156r; ibid., B2473 (1578), 282r.

151. The record of the visitation is published in Johann B. Götz, ed., "Die grosse oberpfälzische Landesvisitation unter dem Kurfürsten Ludwig VI," *Verhandl. hist. Ver. Oberpfalz und Regensburg* 85 (1935): 148-244; 86 (1936) 277-362. See summary: 85:166.

152. I have used visitation protocols in S.Dresd. (Loc. 1579-7367), S.Weim., Reg. Ii, nos. 1-69 and Reg. O, nos. 543-52, and Archiv des evangelisch-lutherischen Landeskirchenamts Sachsens (Dresden), Visitationsmatrikel Chemnitz 1575, Visitationen 1580, Matrikel des Consistoriums Dresden, and Visitationen 1582. Much information on town and village schools can also be found in Pallas, *passim*.

153. On village society and leadership, see Georg Ludwig von Maurer, *Geschichte der Dorfverfassung*, vol. 1 (Erlangen, 1865), and Peter Blickle, *Landschaften im alten Reich: Die staatliche Funktion des gemeinen Mannes in Oberdeutschland* (Munich, 1973).

154. S.Dresd., Loc. 1997, 29r-30r.

155. Sachsenburg in Saxony, S.Dresd., Loc. 1989, 389r.

156. A very good example: list of duties and income for office of sexton, schoolmaster, and village scribe, village of Sielmingen, Amt Stuttgart, Württemberg. WHS, A284. Stuttgart St. und G.V. B444. For similar documents for Kalenberg-Göttingen, see Karl Kayser, "Die General-Kirchenvisitation von 1588. . . ." *Zeitschr. Ges. niedersächsische Kirchengesch.* 8 (1904): 93-238; 9 (1904): 22-72.

157. On these methods, see C. Kohr and G. Schlimbach, *Die Methodik des sprachlichen Elementarunterrichts* (Gotha, 1866). Ickelsamer's is not yet the proper analytic method, which does not come into use until Wolfgang Ratke, ca. 1600.

158. Neander, *Bedencken* (see note 3, above), 15r. Bugenhagen, in the *Kirchenordnung* of Braunschweig (1543), said that girls could learn "schryven und lesen, edder tom wenigsten alleine lesen . . . in einem edder twen jaren," Vormbaum, p. 50. According to the Württemberg *Schulordnung* of 1559 and the Saxon one of 1580, it took only one year, working six hours a

day throughout the school year: Vormbaum, pp. 75–77 (Württemberg); pp. 237–38 (Saxony).

159. Valentin Ickelsamer, *Die rechte Weis auffs kürtzest lesen zu lernen* (1527), in Müller, *Quellenschriften*, p. 52.

160. From Hans Fabritius, *Eyn nutzlich Büchlein etlicher gleichstimmender Wörter, aber ungleichs Verstandes* (Erfurt, 1532), in Johann Meier, ed., *Ältere deutsche Grammatiken in Neudrucken*, 1 (Strassburg, 1895): 13–14.

161. Sdt.Augsb., Evangelisches Wesensarchiv, no. 1045.

162. Sdt.Ulm. A (1836): a memorandum concerning schools submitted by eight pastors in 1586.

163. *Schülerordnung Gründlach* (a village in the territory of Nuremberg), Sdt.Nürn., Y779, no. 15

164. *Schulordnung* of Saxony (1580), in Vormbaum, pp. 237–38. Most of this is based on the Württemberg *Schulordnung* of 1559, Vormbaum, pp. 76–77.

165. From the 1559 Württemberg *Schulordnung*, Vormbaum, p. 76.

166. Andrzey Wyczanski, "Alphabétisation et structure sociale en Pologne au 16ᵉ siècle," *Annales, E.S.C.* 29, no. 3 (May–June 1974): 705–13. Wyczanski takes a sample of about a thousand tax self-assessments containing signatures from the years 1564–65 in the Cracow region, enabling him to relate literacy (= ability to take pen in hand and sign) to social standing. For a discussion of the relationship of signatures to literacy, see F. Furet and W. Sachs, "La croissance de l'alphabétisation en France, XVIIIᵉ–XIXᵉ siècle," *Annales, E.S.C.* 29, no. 3 (May–June 1974): 714–37. The authors conclude (after much hedging) that signatures are a valid measure of literacy. See also Pierre Goubert, *L'ancien régime.* Vol. 1. *La société* (Paris, 1969), pp. 244 ff. Goubert utilizes the unpublished work of Louis Maggiolo with signatures and marks on marriage contracts and concludes that four-fifths of all Frenchmen, and an even greater part of Frenchwomen, were totally illiterate in 1685 (78.7% and 86%, respectively, based on 219,047 cases). Literacy was greater in the north of France than in the west, center, and south. It seems to have been tied to the existence of village schools, and Protestantism "ne s'accommode jamais de l'ignorance totale" (p. 244). Goubert's data were used before him by M. Fleury and A. Valmary, "Les progrès de l'instruction élémentaire de Louis XIV à Napoléon III . . . ," *Population* (January–March 1957), pp. 71–92, who conclude, however, that no correlation exists between the prevalence of schools and the ability to sign. Emmanuel LeRoy Ladurie, measuring the frequency of signatures of artisans in Montpellier and Narbonne in 1575, finds only 25% of them illiterate in the former place, 33% in the latter. In the countryside he finds 72% illiteracy among peasants in Montpellier, 90% among rural workers in the Narbonne region: *The Peasants of Languedoc*, trans. John Day (Urbana, Ill., 1974), pp. 150, 161–64. Natalie Davis, "City Women and Religious Change," in her *Society and Culture in Early Modern France* (Stanford, Calif., 1975), pp. 72–73, studies 1,200 contracts from Lyon in the 1560s and 1570s, concluding that 28% of women, all of them from merchant and publisher families, and a much higher proportion of men, including artisans, could sign their names. For some English evidence in the late sixteenth and the seventeenth and eighteenth centuries, see Peter Clark, "The Ownership of Books in England, 1560–1640: The Example of Some Kentish Townfolk," in *Schooling and Society: Studies in the History of Education*, ed. Lawrence Stone (Baltimore, 1976), pp. 102–3, 106, 109. Clark finds a notable extension of literacy to "lower ranks of respectable society," i.e., artisans. Also R. S. Schofield, "The Measurement of Literacy in Pre-Industrial England," in *Literacy in Traditional Societies*, ed. Jack Goody (Cambridge, 1968), pp. 311–25, especially p. 319, for discussion of signatures as indicators of literacy. Also Victor E. Neuburg, *Popular Education in Eighteenth-Century England* (London, 1971); Lawrence Stone, "Literacy and Education in England, 1460–1900," *Past and Present* 42 (1969): 69–139. Cf. also Carlo M. Cipolla, *Literacy and Development in the West* (Baltimore, 1969), and H. J. Martin, *Livre, pouvoirs et société à Paris au 17ᵉ siècle* (Geneva, 1969), and Harvey J. Graff, "Notes on Methods for Studying Literacy from the Manuscript Census [in nineteenth-century Canada]," *Historical Methods Newsletter* 5, no. 1 (December 1971).

167. Cited in Dolch, *Lehrplan des Abendlandes*, p. 243.

168. Cited in Willy Biendkapp, "Zur Geschichte der 'Teutschen Schulen' zu Frankfurt a.M. im 16. Jahrhundert," *Frankfurter Schulzeitung* (1892), nos. 1–3.

169. Rudolf Engelsing, *Analphabetentum und Lektüre: Zur Sozialgeschichte des Lesens zwischen feudaler und industrieller Gesellschaft* (Stuttgart, 1973), especially chaps. 5–7, is a disappointingly general and superficial book that in no way justifies its promising title.

170. Cf. especially *Galmy* (1539), in Hans-Gert Roloff, ed., *Jörg Wickram: Sämtliche Werke*, vol. 1 (Berlin, 1967), chaps. 15–18, 22, 48, 49; *Gabriotto* (1541), in ibid., vol. 2 (1967), chaps. 19–20, 41, etc.; *Der Goldfaden* (1557), in ibid., vol. 5 (1968), chaps. 11, 41, 58; but also chap. 15, with an illiterate shepherd.

171. On the vernacular literature of the time in relation to its society, see Inge Leipold, "Untersuchungen zum Funktionstyp 'Frühe deutschsprachige Druckprosa . . . ,'" *Deutsche Vierteljahrsschr. Literaturwiss. Geistesgesch.* 48, no. 2 (May 1974):264–90. On the entertainment literature generally, see Hans Rupprich, *Die deutsche Literatur vom späten Mittelalter bis zum Barock*, vol. 2, in H. DeBoor and Richard Newald, *Geschichte der deutschen Literatur*, 4² (Munich, 1973):165–84.

172. Jörg Wickram, *Der irr reitende Pilger* (1556), in Roloff, ed., *Jörg Wickram*, 6:84–85:

> Holding the Bible, he drew near
> To the good pilgrim, saying, "hear
> How I find my greatest pleasure
> And spend my evening hours of leisure.
> My labor done in field and stable,
> I place the Bible on my table
> And study it two hours or three.
> On holidays, when I am free
> Of work, I spend the day
> Reading the Scriptures, for my way
> To church is far, two hours to reach
> My parish to hear the pastor preach."

How, the pilgrim wanted to know, could such a simple man be sure that he understood the Bible correctly?

> The peasant answered, "here by my side
> I have some other books, to wit
> Explanations of Holy Writ,
> And these I use to teach myself."
> He showed the pilgrim a tall shelf
> Filled with bound volumes: history,
> Chronicles and theology,
> All German titles, well selected,
> Which this simple peasant had collected.

There are many references to reading peasants in the pamphlet literature of the time. To cite only a few examples found in modern editions: "Neuw Karsthans," in *Satiren und Pasquille aus der Reformationszeit*, ed. Oskar Schade (Hannover, 1863), 2:1–44; "Hans Toll und Klaus Lamp," ibid., 2:128–34; "Wie ein bauer mit aim frauenbruder münich redt," ibid., 2:155–59; "Ein Diagolos . . . zwischen einem Vater und Sohn," in *Flugschriften aus den ersten Jahren der Reformation*, ed. Otto Clemen (Halle, 1907–11), 1:25–47.

173. From the censorship mandate of Albrecht V (1569), in BHM, Staatsverwaltung 2783, 230v. Also ibid., 2784, 90r.

174. Ibid., 2784, 91r.

175. E.g., list of books submitted to Bavarian government from the city of Straubing in 1578: BHM, Staatsverwaltung 2787, 137–46. In the city of Wasserburg, a parish priest is quoted as suspecting that "in allen heusern der stadt seind verbotne verdechtliche puecher." OEMF, 566, 321. Very often the entry reads: "viel paueren haben verfierische puecher," e.g., parish of Au in bishopric of Freising and Munich, 1560, ibid., 566, 213, and parish of Päng in the same diocese, also 1560, in Lurz, *Mittelschulgeschichtliche Dokumente*, 41:260. I assume this to refer to peasant householders and not to agricultural laborers.

176. Visitation instruction to *Pfleger* in *Rentamt* (administrative district) Munich, 1569, Lurz, *Mittelschulgeschichtliche Dokumente*, 42:51.

177. Printed in Sehling, 1:313.

178. Preface by Caspar Creutziger of Wittenberg to Ambrosius Moibanus, *Catechismus* (Wittenberg, 1535); printed in Reu, 1, 2 (2):714.

179. WHS, A284. Adelberg Kl.V, B473.

180. B.S.Münch., 1375 no. 9, 493a r.

181. There is a mass of evidence for the insistence of townspeople on instruction in literacy and their preference, by and large, for more practical private instruction. Some examples: S.Magd., Rep. A 12aI, no. 1974, 207-8: the "fürnembsten bürger [in Halle] verdingen ire söne in privat schulen" (1583). S.Hamb., Cl.VII Lit. He., no. 3, vol. 4: same situation (1560s, 1585, 1646). Pallas, 41⁴:430 reports the same for a village in parish of Arzberg, Saxony, 1578. The city council of Bremen published an edict in 1592 against *Bei- und Klippschulen*, with no success: Hinrich Wulff, *Geschichte der bremischen Volksschule* (Bad Heilbrunn, 1967), pp. 22-23. In Hannover public teachers complained in 1569 "dass [privateers] itzo den merern teil meiner discipuli ... zu sich gezogen." Sdt.Hann., XIII Wl, no. 1. In Nuremberg, where private schools were outlawed, more than eighty of them were counted as late as 1637. Cf. Leder, *Kirche und Jugend in Nürnberg* (Neustadt an der Aisch, 1973), p. 180.

182. Pierre Goubert, *l'ancien régime* (1969), pp. 244-45, ties literacy to the presence of village schools. The most literate regions had two or three times as many schools easily accessible to its population as less literate regions.

CHAPTER 10

1. *Index verborum trilinguis secundum coniugationum seriem* (Augsburg, 1596).

2. Leonhard Culman, *Sententiae pueriles pro primis latinae linguae tyronibus* (Augsburg, 1544), C3r.

3. Sebald Heyden, *Nomenclatura rerum: Formulae colloquiorum puerilium* (Strassburg, n.d.), 1st sec., *De deo, coelo, ac temporibus.*

4. Konrad Mercklin, *Dicta insigniora latino-germanica . . . Etliche fürnemme sprüche aus dem Alten und Newen Testament, beyde in Teutscher und Lateinischer sprach, für die Jungen angehende Schüler zusammen gebracht* (Frankfurt am Main, 1583).

5. Sebastian Fröschel, *Catechismus, wie er in der Kirchen zu Wittenberg nu viel jar . . . gepredigt worden ist* (Wittenberg, 1559). See Aiv v for reference to children: "was wir auch unsere kindlin allhie leren."

6. For what follows I used the edition of Fröschel in Reu, 1, 2 (2):59-82, especially pp. 65-71.

7. Ibid., p. 75.

8. Johann Meckhart, *Catechismus: Ein kurtze christliche Lehr und unterweysung für die Jugend* (Augsburg, 1551: I cite according to Augsburg, 1567), Dvi r and v.

9. *Articuli visitationis in Misnia Anno 1592*, S.Bamb., C7/X, no. 1, 469v.

10. Konrad Dietrich, *Ausführung zum Catechismo . . .* (Frankfurt am Main, 1618), p. 234.

11. *Articuli visitationis in Misnia . . .* , S.Bamb., C7/X, no. 1, 466r.

12. Fröschel, *Catechismus*, in Reu, 1, 2 (2):80.

13. Andreas Musculus, *Gründliche Anzeygung, was die Theologen des Churfürstentums der Mark zu Brandenburg von der christlichen evangelischen Lehre halten . . .* (1552), quoted in C. W. Spieker, *Lebensgeschichte des Andreas Musculus* (Frankfurt an der Oder, 1858), pp. 34-35.

14. On the principles of this controversy see Albrecht Ritschl, *The Christian Doctrine of Justification and Reconciliation*, trans. H. R. Mackintosh and A. B. Macaulay (Edinburgh, 1900), pp. 122-25.

15. As in Canisius's catechism of 1584. Cf. Fridericus Streicher, S.J., ed., *S. Petri Canisii . . . Catechismi Latini et Germanici*, Societatis Iesu Selecti Scriptores, 1 (Rome and Munich, 1933-36): 196-200. See also the shorter versions of this catechism in ibid., pp. 219-20 and 241-42. For an interesting contemporary comparison of Catholic (Tridentine) and Lutheran views on sin, see Martin Chemnitz, *Examen Concilii Tridentini* (1563-73), trans. Fred Kramer, *Examination of the Council of Trent* (Saint Louis, Mo., 1971) topics 3-4.

16. From Michael Coelius, *Ein nützliche Vermanung an die, so beychten und die heilige Absolution empfahen wollen . . .* (1557), in Reu, 1, 2 (2):358-59. Coelius was pastor in Mansfeld from 1525 to 1559.

17. Konrad Dietrich, *Ausführung zum Catechismo: Das ist, wie man den Catechismo des theuren Manns Gottes D. Martini Lutheri . . . recht unter Augen sehen, erwegen und lernen soll . . .* (Frankfurt am Main, 1618), pp. 238-39.

18. Ibid., p. 249.

19. The phrase is borrowed from Melanchthon: "paedagogia in Christum." *Liber de anima,* in *CR,* vol. 13, col. 161. The entire passage quoted here is Fröschel's paraphrase of what Melanchthon writes on free will in that work (cols. 157-63).

20. Fröschel in *Catechismus,* pp. 63-64.

21. Ibid., p. 65.

22. Caspar Aquila, *Des kleinen Catechismi Erklerung . . .* (1538), in Reu, 1, 2 (2): 178-79. The statement concerning boys memorizing and reciting the sermons is from the preface, pp. 173-74.

23. Ibid., p. 182.

24. Ibid., p. 193.

25. Another example: ibid., p. 177, on the fate of those who don't fear, love, and trust God. Also, Leonhard Culman, *Ein unterrichtung von den eltern, kindern, unnd fremden, auch eygenen sünden . . .* (Nuremberg, 1550), with a horrifying picture of the consequences for their children of the sins of parents.

26. On the circumstance of the writing of the *Catechismus oder Kinderpredig* and the question of authorship, cf. Gottfried Seebass, *Das reformatorische Werk des Andreas Osiander* (Nuremberg, 1967), pp. 249-53.

27. See Osiander's statement in the preface. His catechism sermons are printed as *Catechismus oder Kinderpredig,* in Sehling, vol. 11, part 1 (Tübingen, 1961): 206-83. Statement from preface, p. 206.

28. Ibid.

29. Ibid., p. 242.

30. Ibid., pp. 265-66.

31. Ibid., p. 266.

32. The fifty-four editions of the *Kinderpredig* from 1533 to 1567 are given in Gottfried Seebass, *Bibliographia Osiandrica* (Nieuwkoop, 1971), pp. 67-97.

33. The *Kinderpredig* was introduced to the imperial cities of Weissenburg (1533) and Dinkelsbühl (1534).

34. Gottfried Seebass, *Das reformatorische Werk des . . . Osiander,* p. 251.

35. Eck had criticized the Nuremberg-Brandenburg *Kirchenordnung* of 1533, of which Osiander's catechism sermons were a part, in his *Christenliche Unterricht . . . wider die . . . angeber vermainter newer Kirchen-Ordnung* (Ingolstadt, 1533). Osiander responded: *Verantwortung des nürnbergischen Catechismi: Wider den ungelerten zenckischen Sophisten Hansen Mayr zu Ingelstat, der sich lest nennen Johannes Eck* (Nuremberg, 1539; cf. Seebass, *Bibliographia Osiandrica,* p. 121), to which Eck replied (directly to the Nuremberg council): *Schutzred kindlicher Unschuld wider den Catechisten Andre Hosiander* (Eichstätt, 1539). In the 1550s and 1560s Nuremberg theologians abandoned the extreme position on sin as the very substance of man. For the new catechism reflecting the new position, see Andreas Musculus, *Catechismus, Kinderpredig, wie die in Marggrävischer zu Brandenburgk und der Statt Nürnberg Oberkeiten und Gebieten gepredigt werden* (Frankfurt an der Oder, 1566).

36. Ps. 14:3. Osiander, in Sehling, vol. 11, part 1, pp. 233-34.

37. Ibid., p. 234.

38. Ibid.

39. Erasmus, *Liber de sarcienda ecclesiae concordia* (n.p., 1533), p. 84.

40. Thomas Lindner, *Catechismus: Kurze und richtige Auslegung der Hauptstücke christlicher Lehr und Glaubens. Aus dem Nürnbergischen Catechismo in Fragstück gestellt, und vor die evangelischen Kirchen und Schulen in Ravenspurg zusamen gebracht* (1546) printed in Ernst-Wilhelm Kohls, *Die evangelischen Katechismen von Ravensburg . . . und Reichenweier . . .* (Stuttgart, 1963), pp. 31-92. The excerpt is from the attached *Kinder-Litaney für allerley Stände . . . ,* p. 71.

41. *Etliche kurze einfältige Beichten vor die Schul Jugend* (of Ravensburg), printed in ibid., p. 74.

42. From the Catechism for Reichenweier, ibid., p. 125.

43. *Etliche sprüche, darin das gantze christliche Leben gefasst ist* (1527), in *Philipp*

Melanchthons Schriften zur praktischen Theologie, vol. 1, ed. Ferdinand Cohrs, Supplementa Melanchthonia, Abt. 5 (Leipzig, 1915), p. 61.

44. *Hohenlohe-Öhringen'sche Kinderlehre*, a draft in LAS 730, no. 1.

45. Melanchthon in Ferdinand Cohrs, ed., *Philipp Melanchthons Schriften*, 1:64.

46. In Ernst-Wilhelm Kohls, *Evangelische Bewegung und Kirchenordnung: Studien und Quellen zur Reformationsgeschichte der Reichsstadt Gengenbach* (Karlsruhe, 1966), p. 30. The Gengenbach catechism was printed in 1545 but was used before 1529.

47. Konrad Dietrich, preface to *Der kleine Catechismus: D. Martin Luthers . . . für die Ulmische Kirchen und Schulen in Statt und Land* (Ulm, 1616).

48. Caspar Aquila, *Des kleinen Catechismi Erklerung . . .* (1538), in Reu 1, 2 (2):195.

49. E.g., Georg Rhau, *Kinder Glaube* (Wittenberg, 1539), 72r.

50. Michael Saxo, *Das erste Theil des christlichen Zeitvertreibers . . .* (Dresden, 1599), p. 184r.

51. Erasmus Sarcerius, *Catechismus . . .*, trans. into German by Bartolomäus Wagner (Leipzig, 1550), in Reu, 1, 2 (1):100.

52. Caspar Huberinus, *Vierzig kurze Predig über den ganzen Catechismus* (Nuremberg, 1550), Biii v f. Additional examples of implied certainty and immediacy: Urban Rhegius, *Catechesis illustriss. principi Francisco Otthoni . . .* (Braunschweig, 1540), 30r–34v and passim. Justus Menius, *Catechismus*, in Reu, 1, 2 (2):171–72; Johann Brenz, *Der kleine Catechismus in Fragen gestellt . . .* (Hamburg, 1557), unnumbered leaves; Johann Spangenberg, *Des kleinen Catechismi und der Haustafel kurtzer Begriff . . .* (Wittenberg, 1549), Diiii v; David Kauxdorff, *Ein sehr nützliches und tröstliches Handtbüchlein von allen Stücken christlicher Lehr . . .* (Mühlhausen, 1575), in Reu 1, 2 (1):124.

53. For an example of a book trying to refute rival positions within Lutheranism, while offering religious instruction to the simple, see Matthäus Judex, *Das kleine Corpus Doctrinae . . .* (Ursel, 1578).

54. See for example, Konrad Dietrich, *Ausführung zum Catechismo . . .* (1618), p. 245.

55. Ibid., p. 231.

56. From the draft of a *Kinderlehre* for county of Hohenlohe-Öhringen, Württemberg, in LAS, 730, no. 1.

57. Michael Neander, *Menschen-Spiegel, das ist: Von dem Menschen vor dem Fall, nach dem Fall, nach der Widergeburt . . .* (Erfurt, 1618), Axi r.

58. Andreas Musculus, *Von des Teuffels Tyranney, Macht und Gewalt, sonderlich in disen letzten Tagen* (Worms, 1561), Av r and v.

59. Ibid., Avi v; C v–Evii r.

60. *Christliche Fragstücke . . . für die Jugend zu Jauer* [Silesia] (Frankfurt an der Oder, 1591), in Reu, 1, 2 (2):950.

61. An interesting case was the free-will controversy in Coburg in the 1560s. Following the Melanchthon pupil Victorinus Strigel into a synergistic position, the Coburg superintendent Maximilian Mörlin made all clerics in the territory sign a *declaratio* of belief in this position. This was in 1562. Seven years later the antisynergism of Matthias Flacius won out in Coburg. In a new visitation in 1569 the ultra-Lutheran theologian Tileman Hesshusen compelled all pastors to recant their former declarations. These written recantations are in S.Cob., B2461, 31–140. When theologians like Mörlin were confused or misguided on this crucial issue, could the ordinary man be expected to understand?

62. As in Otto Brunfels's *Pandect Büchlin: Beyläuffig aller Sprüch beyder Testament usszugk, in Titel zerlegt . . .* (Strassburg, 1529), 48v–51v, delivering a powerful barrage of scriptural passages to prove that there is no free will in anything. Brunfels translated this book from his own *Pandectarum veteris et novi Testamenti Libri XXII*, 4th ed. (Strassburg, 1529).

63. Lindner, *Catechismus*, p. 72.

64. Charles Trinkaus, *In Our Image and Likeness: Humanity and Divinity in Italian Humanist Thought* (Chicago, 1970), 1:46–47.

65. Nicolaus Hunnius, *Anweisung zum rechten Christenthumb für junge und einfältige Leut im Hause und Schulen . . .* (Nuremberg, 1639), pp. 48–56.

66. Charles G. Finney, *Lectures on Revivals in Religion* (1835), ed. William G. McLaughlin (Cambridge, Mass., 1960), p. 205.

67. Erasmus, *Liber de sarcienda ecclesiae concordia* (n.p., 1533), p. 84.

68. From an instruction to pastors, *Wie mit den leuten in der beicht zu handeln,* for Albertine Saxony (1539), in Sehling, 1:268-69.

69. Andreas Musculus, *Vom Himmel und der Hellen* . . . (Frankfurt an der Oder, 1559), Ji v–Jii r, Jv r.

70. Johann Spangenberg, *Der gros Catechismus und Kinder Lere* . . . (Wittenberg, 1541; I use Wittenberg, 1551), Qvii r. Also in Reu, 1, 2 (2):322.

71. Ibid., Qvii r and v.

72. Ibid., Cv r.

73. Johann Spangenberg, *Auslegung der Episteln und Evangelien* . . . *für die jungen Christen, Knaben und Megdlein* (1543; I use Nuremberg, 1556), vi v.

74. Spangenberg, *Der gros Catechismus,* Qvii v. Reu, 1, 2 (2):322.

75. Musculus, *Vom Himmel und der Hellen,* Jiv v.

76. Musculus, *Catechismus, Kinderpredig,* Cv r.

77. Ibid., Ciii v.

78. Erik H. Erikson, *Identity and the Life Cycle: Selected Papers,* Psychological Issues, 1, no. 1, (1959), p. 71.

79. John M. Whiting and Irvin L. Child, *Child Training and Personality: A Cross-Cultural Study* (New Haven, 1953), pp. 224-26. See the entire chapter "Origins of Guilt" for some highly suggestive comments.

80. Ibid., pp. 240-41.

81. Ibid., p. 261.

82. Ambrosius Moibanus, *Catechismus, auff zehen Artickel Göttlicher schrifft gestellet* . . . (Wittenberg, 1535), in Reu, 2, 2 (2):729.

CHAPTER 11

1. Caspar Huberinus, *Der Catechismus* . . . *allen frommen Hausvättern sehr nützlich* . . . (Augsburg, 1543), Aiii r and v.

2. Good examples of such catechisms are Daniel Kauxdorff, *Ein Gedechtnisbüchlein von den fürnemesten Artickeln christlicher lehre* . . . *welchen frommen Hausvätern und Kindern* . . . *nützlich und dienstlich sein kann* . . . (Leipzig, 1575). See Bi v for explicit statement of polemical purpose; also Caspar Huberinus, *Postilla Teutsch* . . . (Augsburg, 1542), Aii r ff., a prefatory statement by the author calling attention to his objective to defend his position within Lutheran theology.

3. Quoted in Arno Heerdegen, *Geschichte der allgemeinen Kirchenvisitation in den ernestinischen Landen im Jahre 1554-55,* Zeitschr. Ver. Thüringische Gesch. Altertumskunde, N.F. Supplementheft 6 (Jena, 1914), p. 22.

4. On this literature in general, see Hermann Beck, *Die Erbauungsliteratur der evangelischen Kirche Deutschlands.* Part I. *Von Dr. Martin Luther bis Martin Möller* (Erlangen, 1883).

5. Cf. Vincenz Hasak, *Dr. M. Luther und die religiöse Literatur seiner Zeit bis zum Jahre 1520* (Regensburg, 1881: Nieuwkoop, 1967), especially pp. 204-56.

6. *Ein kurze ordenliche Summa der rechten waren lehre unsers heyligen christlichen glaubens, welche ein jeder christlicher hausvater* . . . *seine kinder* . . . *zu leren oder leren zu lassen schuldig ist* (Regensburg, 1554). For another example see Johann Mannich, *Sacra emblemata: Sechs und siebzig geistliche Figürlein* . . . *in welchen eines jeden Evangelii Summa kürtzlichen wird abgebildet* (Nuremberg, 1624).

7. Sebald Heyden, *Paedonomia Scholastica, pietatis, studii literarii, ac morum honestatis praecepta continens* (Nuremberg, 1553), Avi r. The same point of view is expressed by Michael Neander, *Bedencken* . . . *wie ein Knabe zu leithen und unterweisen* . . . (1580; I use Eisleben, 1583), 13r.

8. Sebald Heyden, *Paedonomia Scholastica,* Avi r. On Heyden's work at the *Spital* and Saint Sebald schools in Nuremberg, and his other pedagogical writings, see Klaus Leder, *Kirche und Jugend in Nürnberg* . . . (Neustadt an der Aisch, 1973), pp. 85-86.

9. Josef Dolch, *Lehrplan des Abendlandes* . . . (Ratingen, 1965), pp. 204-6.

10. For a general survey, see Mertz, especially pp. 232-50. Much less useful, though much more recent, is Friedrich Hahn, *Die evangelische Unterweisung in den Schulen des 16. Jahrhunderts* (Heidelberg, 1957).

11. Ludwig Hänselmann, ed., *Bugenhagens Kirchenordnung für die Stadt Braunschweig* . . . (Wolfenbüttel, 1885).

12. From a lesson plan submitted to visitors in 1578. S.Dresd., Loc. 2002, 11r–12r. The psalms taken up in the course of the school year were nos. 1–3, 6, 8, 13–16, 22–23, 67, 79, 85, 90–91, 141.

13. K. Reissinger, ed., *Dokumente zur Geschichte der humanistischen Schulen im Gebiet der bayerischen Pfalz, MGP*, 47 (1910):29–30.

14. S.Magd., Rep. A12 Generalia, no. 2444, 74r.

15. *Disposition: Oder ein christliche ordnung, wie es in der teutschen schulen zu Golzwarden, der vorgeschriben schull instruction nach, zu singen Gebete, fürbitte und Danksagung, mit den Schulknaben Morgens Mittags und Abends gehalten und täglich geübet wird* (ca. 1600) in N.S.S.Old, Bestand 20, Titel 19, no. 53.

16. For another example, an instruction issued by the city of Augsburg for its German teachers, see *Methodus und Lehr-Art* (Augsburg, 1683).

17. These points were made by Martin Bucer, in his preface to the *Strassburger Gesangbuch* of 1541. Printed in Robert Stupperich, ed., *Martin Bucers deutsche Schriften*, 7 (Gütersloh, 1964): 578–89.

18. Quoted in Roland Bainton, *Women of the Reformation in Germany and Italy* (Minneapolis, 1971), p. 72.

19. Luther's introduction to his hymnal of 1524. *WA*, 35:474–75.

20. David Chytraeus, *Der fürnembsten heubtstück christlicher lehr nützliche und kurze erklerung* (Rostock, 1578), in H. Schnell, ed., *Das Unterrichtswesen der Grossherzogtümer Mecklenburg-Schwerin und Strehliz, MGP*, 38 (1907): 329–30.

21. From a school ordinance for the town of Gründlach in the territory of the city of Nuremberg, Sdt.Nürn., Y779.

22. From the title page to *Geistliche Gesang und Psalmen* (Nuremberg, 1545), containing rhymed versions of Luther's catechism.

23. From an instruction to visitors of Coburg by Prince Johann Casimir of Saxony-Coburg, 1613. S.Cob., B2539, 19v.

24. Ibid. Also: a visitation of Electoral Saxony 1578, Pallas, 41 (Allgemeiner Teil):147, 173.

25. From a *Visitationsordnung* in Württemberg, 1557: WHS A63, B27, 39r.

26. E.g., Hess.H.S.Wiesb., Abt. 137, no. 1, 72r.

27. E.g., Pallas, 41 (Allgemeiner Teil):43–44.

28. See the detailed instructions given to the City of Wittenberg in the Saxon visitation of 1528 on the place and performance of hymns, responsive singing, and so on, in the service: Pallas, 41¹:7–10.

29. From the preface to *Der kürzer Catechismus . . . für die Schüler und andere Kinder zu Strassburg* (Strassburg, 1544).

30. E.g., the instruction of the Strassburg *Scholarchen*, 1563, Strass.A.V., Archives Saint Thomas 374, 1v.

31. On the *Kirchenlied* generally, see Philipp Wackernagel, *Das deutsche Kirchenlied von der ältesten Zeit bis zum Anfang des XVII. Jahrhunderts* (Leipzig, 1864–77; reprinted 1964).

32. *Enchiridion, oder ein Handbüchlein . . . zur stetter übung und trachtung geystlicher gesenge. . . . mit dyesen und dergleichen Gesenge sollt man byllich die jungern iugent aufferziehen* (Erfurt, 1524).

33. Wolfgang Figulus, *Deutsche Musica und Gesangbüchlein der Sonntags Evangelien . . . für die Schulkinder, Kneblin und Megdlein, etwa in deutsche Reime verfasst* (Nuremberg, 1560).

34. "O Mensch, bewein dein Sünde gross," in Philipp Wackernagel, *Das deutsche Kirchenlied*, vol. 3, no. 603.

35. *Christliche Psalmen, Lieder und Kirchengesenge in welchen die christliche Lehre zusam gefasset und erklert wird: Trewen Predigern in Stetten und Dörffern . . . nütz und tröstlich* (Leipzig, 1587). Another collection by Selneccer was *Sechs schöner newer geistlicher*

tröstlicher Gesänge über die sechs Hauptstück Christlicher Leere (Lauingen, 1578), containing one hymn on each of the commandments, articles of the Apostles' Creed, etc.

36. An example: text of the catechism set to such tunes by one Magister Holdhausen. Reference in Julius Richter, *Geschichte der sächsischen Volksschule, MGP,* 29 (1930):78. Cf. Luther on the proliferation of hymn settings, in the preface to the *Gesangbuch* edition of 1528: *WA,* 35:475-76.

37. "Deutsche Gesänge" were outlawed in the Bavarian visitations of 1558-60. One schoolmaster, asked whether he taught his pupils German hymns, said no, but he would have more pupils if he did so (OEMF, 567, 446). Many priests stated that "das volk singt bei weilen wider seinen [the priest's] willen den deutschen glauben, Aus tiefer Not. etc." (Ibid., 566, 118).

38. Ibid., 565, passim., e.g., 521.

39. Quoted in Bernhard Duhr, *Geschichte der Jesuiten in den Ländern deutscher Zunge im XVI. Jahrhundert* (Freiburg im Breisgau, 1907), pp. 459-60.

40. Karl Schrems, *Die religiöse Volks- und Jugendunterweisung in der Diözese Regensburg von Ausgang des 15. Jahrhunderts bis gegen Ende des 18. Jahrhunderts* (Munich, 1929), pp. 79-80.

41. This assertion is based on a study of Bavarian visitation protocols in the diocese of Freising. Cf. OEMF, 565, 61, 67 for two examples, and the mandate of the bishop of Freising in 1576, ibid., 1992, unpaginated. Also mandate of Albrecht V in 1570, BHM, Staatsverwaltung 2784, 134r. Also Georg Lurz, *Mittelschulgeschichtliche Dokumente Altbayerns . . . , MGP,* 42 (1908):33.

42. Johannes Geffcken, *Der Bildercatechismus des fünfzehnten Jahrhunderts . . .* (Leipzig, 1855), p. 5, concludes that only a fraction of the huge number of religious hymns printed in the collections of Wackernagel and Hoffmann von Fallersleben were actually sung by Lutheran congregations.

43. From Luther's preface to Babst's *Gesangbuch* of 1545. *WA,* 35:477.

44. *Fraw Musica: Vorrhede auf alle Gute Gesangbücher DML. WA,* 35:483.

45. Ambrosius Moibanus, *Catechismus auff zehen Artikel Göttlicher schrifft gestellet . . .* (Wittenberg, 1535), in Reu, 1, 2 (2):719.

46. Thomas N. Tentler, *Sin and Confession on the Eve of the Reformation* (Princeton, N.J., 1977), pp. 349-63, comes to a different conclusion, but he sustains it by looking only at the works of Luther, Calvin, and Zwingli. These suggest that Christ's sacrifice has made salvation a matter of certainty for all who believe. Salvation no longer depends on completeness of confession or on the power of the sacrament itself. Thus, Tentler argues, the burden has been lifted from the individual. My evidence, on the other hand, suggests that the burden was merely shifted to the problem of belief itself, and that no sense of certainty could be gained from the Lutheran literature of religious instruction.

47. Ambrosius Moibanus, *Catechismus . . . ,* pp. 717-18. The first Latin edition of Moibanus's catechism was published in Wittenberg, 1533. The second Latin edition, 1538, had a preface by Melanchthon. The German edition: Wittenberg, 1535.

48. On the rich strata of meanings and associations in the word "discipline" at the beginning of the modern era, see Walter Dürig, "Disciplina: Eine Studie zum Bedeutungsumfang des Wortes in der Sprache der Liturgie und der Väter," *Sacris Erudiri: Jaarboek voor Godsdienstwetenschappen* 6 (1952):245-79, and Georg Weise, "Der Humanismus und das Prinzip der klassischen Geisteshaltung," *Bibliothèque d'humanisme et Renaissance* 16 (1954):153-71, 284-97. The German word *Zucht* contained meanings and associations ranging from reproduction, nurture, and care, to formal pedagogy, instruction, and—when necessary—punishment, to the result of the educational process in *züchtig* behavior: moderation in all things, a disciplined character and personality.

49. Caspar Huberinus, *Spiegel der Hauszucht . . .* (Nuremberg, 1565), cxvii v.

50. "Dann wo du es [*scil.,* the child] mit der rutten hawest, so darff man es nicht töten." Hieronimus Rauscher, *Loci communes doctrinae christianae: Die fürnembsten Artickel christlicher Leere* (Nuremberg, 1557), n.p., paraphrasing Prov. 23:13: "if you beat him with a rod, he will not die."

51. For a typical statement of this position, see the *Schulordnung* of Nordhausen (1583), in Karl Meyer, ed., "Die Schulordnung des Gymnasiums . . . Nordhausen . . . ," *Mitt. Ges. deutsche Erziehungs- und Schulgeschichte* 2 (1892):72.

52. *Unterricht der Visitatoren an die Pfarrherrn . . .* (1528) *WA,* 26:226.

53. Ibid., p. 96.

54. Peter Brown, *Augustine of Hippo* (Berkeley and Los Angeles, 1967), p. 239.

55. From the Württemberg *Schulordnung* of 1559, in Vormbaum, p. 92.

56. From a series of memoranda on Latin schools in the duchy of Württemberg, 1566, WHS A282, B1025.

57. *WA*, Tr. 4, no. 4082 (1538).

58. Favorite books from which to learn civility were Erasmus's *De civilitate morum puerilium* and Friedrich Dedekind's *Grobianus*; e.g., in all the German schools of Hessen-Darmstadt: Wilhelm Diehl, *Die Schulordnungen des Grossherzogtums Hessen*, MGP, 33 (1905):208.

59. See chap. 7.

60. Melanchthon, *Catechismus, das ist ein kinderlehre Herren Philippi Melanchthonis aus dem Latein ins Deutsche gebracht durch Caspar Bruschen* (Nuremberg, 1543), Gv r.

61. Ibid., vi v.

62. Justus Menius, *Catechismus* (1532), in Reu, 1, 2 (2):172.

63. Andreas Musculus, *Catechismus, Kinderpredig, wie die in Marggrävischer zu Brandenburgk und der Statt Nürnberg Oberkeiten und Gebieten gepredigt werden* (Frankfurt an der Oder, 1566), Fiv v.

64. The most eloquent and sweeping discussion of the application of the fourth commandment to Christian society occurs in the *Catechesis puerilis* of 1543, German version 1544, drawn by Johann Brenz from the writings and lectures of Melanchthon. It is printed in Ferdinand Cohrs, *Philipp Melanchthons Schriften zur praktischen Theologie*. Vol. 1. *Katechetische Schriften*, Supplementa Melanchthonia, Abt. 5 (Leipzig, 1915), pp. 89–336; the section on the fourth commandment, its longest chapter: pp. 151–220. The work had many editions throughout the sixteenth century. Its language is saturated with Melanchthon's brooding concern with rebellion, dissension, the corruption of religion, and the collapse of society. Restoration of obedience is the only solution.

65. Christoph Vischer, *Christliche Auslegung und Erklerung der Haustafel . . .* Leipzig, 1578), Gii v–iii r.

66. For two typical statements to this effect, see Lucas Geierberg, *Wie man den Wiederteuffern auff die yrtumb, so sie in den stücken des Catechismi einfüren, antworten . . . solle* (Marburg, 1562), Bviii v; Caspar Huberinus, *Vierzig kurze Predig . . .* (Nuremberg, 1550), aii r and v (with respect to the clergy).

67. From the council of Lamspringe to Duke Julius of Braunschweig-Wolfenbüttel, 1584. LKA.Braun. Voges 133, n.p.

68. "Nu ist unter allen stücken der Lieb das höhest Gehorsam gegen der Oberkeit. . . ." Melanchthon, *Etliche Sprüche, darinn das ganze christliche Leben gefasst ist* (1527) in Ferdinand Cohrs, *Philipp Melanchthons Schriften*, p. 70.

69. ". . . denn dis ist die rechte ketten, die alle Polliceien zusamen helt und schleusst." Melanchthon, *Catechesis puerilis* (1543), in Ferdinand Cohrs, *Philipp Melanchthons Schriften*, p. 176.

70. Christoph Vischer, *Auslegung der fünf Heubstück des heiligen Catechismi* (Schmalkalden, 1573), Nvii r.

71. Johann Tettelbach, *Das güldene Kleinod: D. Martini Lutheri Catechismus in kurtze Frage gefasset . . .* (Breslau, 1568), pp. 14–15.

72. Konrad Dietrich, *Ausführung zum Catechismo . . .* (Frankfurt am Main, 1618), p. 140.

73. Johann Spangenberg, *Der gros Catechismus und Kinder Lere . . .* (Wittenberg, 1551), Ev v.

74. Simon Musaeus, *Catechismus: Examen mit kurtzen Fragen und Antwort . . .* (Frankfurt am Main, 1571), xxiii v.

75. A typical example: Caspar Huberinus, *Der kleine Catechismus . . . für die jugent zu gebrauchen* (Augsburg, 1544), especially the programmatic statement in the preface: Av r.

76. Dietrich, *Ausführung zum Catechismo*, p. 137.

77. Urban Rhegius, *Catechesis ilustriss. principi Franciso Otthoni . . .* (Braunschweig, 1540), pp. 14–15, applied the principle explicitly to rulers.

78. Huberinus, *Spiegel der Hauszucht*, Aiiii v.

79. *Der kürtzer Catechismus: Das ist christliche Underweisung . . . für die Schüler und andere Kinder zu Strassburg* (Strassburg, 1544), n.p., under section on fourth commandment.

80. Given by, inter alia, Sebastian Fröschel, *Catechismus* . . . (Wittenberg, 1559), in Reu, 1, 2 (2): 71-77.
81. Vischer, *Auslegung der fünf Heubstück des heiligen Catechismi*, Nvi r.
82. Ibid., Niii v.
83. Spangenberg, *Der gros Catechismus*, Fiii r.
84. Melanchthon, *Catechesis, das ist Unterrichtung der Kinder in heiliger christlicher Lehr*, trans. into German by Stephan Agricola (Erfurt, 1551), Fviii r and v.
85. See note 64 above.
86. Huberinus, *Spiegel der Hauszucht*, Rv v.
87. Johann Böhm, *Ein christlykes Radtbökeschen vör de Kinder* . . . (Hamburg, 1600), Biv r. See also note 93 below.
88. Martin Bucer, in Robert Stupperich, ed., *Martin Bucers deutsche Schriften*, 1:58-59.
89. Huberinus, *Spiegel der Hauszucht*, Riiii v.
90. Böhm, *Ein christlykes Radtbökeschen*, Bv r.
91. Andreas Osiander, *Catechismus oder Kinderpredig* (1533), in Sehling, 11:228-29.
92. Gottfried Seebass, *Das reformatorische Werk des Andreas Osiander* (Nuremberg, 1967), pp. 250-51. See also chap. 10 above.
93. Böhm, *Ein christliches Radtbüchlein* (Wittenberg, 1536), Cii r.
94. Lucas Geierberg, *Wie man den Wiederteuffern auff die yrrthumb* . . . *antworten solle* . . . (Marburg, 1562), Cv r.
95. Ibid., Cvi r and v.
96. Luther, Sermons on Matt. 5-7 (1530-32) *WA*, 32:439-40.
97. E.g., Lucas Geierberg, *Wie man den Wiederteuffern*, Cvi r.
98. See note 47, above.
99. Huberinus, *Der Catechismus*, Niii r.
100. Ibid., Mvi r (unpaginated).
101. Ibid., N r and v.
102. Ibid., Nii v.
103. Ibid., Nii v-iii r.
104. Ibid., Niiii v-v r. Huberinus's advice reflects the position assumed by both Luther and Melanchthon (the former reluctantly, the latter with determination) by 1525, that the famous passage Deut. 23:19-20, outlawing the taking of interest among coreligionists, must not be acted upon by individuals. Instead, all reform in economic matters should come from above. For a discussion of this important subject, and for references, see Benjamin Nelson, *The Idea of Usury: From Tribal Brotherhood to Universal Otherhood*, 2d ed. (Chicago, 1969), pp. 29-65.
105. Another interest of propertied readers, catered to in these volumes, is the problem of parental consent to marriage (already referred to in chap. 6). All reformers, catechists, and pedagogues came down heavily on young people who took it upon themselves to enter into wedlock in disregard of parental authority. E.g., Musculus, *Catechismus*, Fv v; Johann Agricola, *750 Teutscher Sprichwörter* (Hagenau, 1534), no. 333. On this point generally, see Lawrence Stone, "The Rise of the Nuclear Family in Early Modern England," in *The Family in History*, ed. Charles Rosenberg (Philadelphia, 1975), pp. 44-45.

CHAPTER 12

1. The overwhelming bulk of visitation materials remains unpublished. Printed visitation records tend to serve the particular and limited interests of the historian of ecclesiastical administration and finance. Most published protocols and relations are also incomplete and therefore not adequate for my purposes (though I have, of course, made grateful use of them). I have consulted unpublished visitation materials in thirty-three state, municipal, and ecclesiastical archives in the Federal Republic of Germany, the German Democratic Republic, and in Strasbourg, in France. A useful, though necessarily incomplete guide to published and unpublished visitation records is contained in Ernst Walter Zeeden and Hansgeorg Molitor, eds., *Die Visitation im Dienst der kirchlichen Reform* (Münster, 1967). The list of archival holdings printed in this volume served me as a point of departure for initial correspondence

with archivists and then visits to archives where promising sources seemed to be available.

2. See the article *Visitieren* in Jacob and Wilhelm Grimm, *Deutsches Wörterbuch*, vol. 12, cols. 382–83. For the explicit meaning of "inspection," see, for example, a memorandum of Bavarian bishops recommending "das die puecher [in churches and schools] mit vleiss visitiert . . . werden." Georg Lurz, *Mittelschulgeschichtliche Dokumente Altbayerns . . . ,* MGP, 41 (1907):240.

3. From the *Vorrhede* to the *Unterricht der Visitatorn an die Pfarherrn ym kurfürstenthum zu Sachssen* (1528), WA, 26:195–96.

4. Nicolaus Hausmann to Elector Johann (1525), in Ludwig Preller, "Nicolaus Hausmann, der Reformator von Zwickau und Anhalt: Zwei Gutachten von ihm über die Reformation in Zwickau . . . ," *Zeitschr. historische Theologie* (1852), pp. 376–77.

5. Ibid., p. 378.

6. Luther to Nicolaus Hausmann, 27 September 1525, WA, Br. no. 926.

7. Luther to Elector Johann, 31 October 1525, WA, Br. no. 937.

8. Luther to Elector Johann, 30 November 1525, WA, Br. no. 950.

9. Ludwig Preller, "Nicolaus Hausmann."

10. *Vorrhede* to *Unterricht der Visitatorn . . . ,* WA, 26:200.

11. For a detailed account of the 1528–29 visitation in Electoral Saxony, see C. A. H. Burkhardt, *Geschichte der sächsischen Kirchen- und Schulvisitationen von 1524 bis 1545* (Leipzig, 1879).

12. I am adopting here the formulation of Karlheinz Blaschke, *Sachsen im Zeitalter der Reformation*, Schriften des Vereins für Reformationsgeschichte, no. 185 (Gütersloh, 1970), p. 113.

13. For a brief sketch of the history of church visitations from the fifth century to the end of the Middle Ages, see August Franzen, ed., *Die Visitationsprotokolle der ersten nachtridentinischen Visitation im Erzstift Köln unter Salentin von Isenburg . . . ,* Reformationsgeschichtliche Studien und Texte, no. 85 (Münster, 1960), pp. 1–3. An older account is by Howard Frere, ed., *Visitation Articles and Injunctions of the Period of the Reformation* (London, 1910), 1:9–169. Another: C. R. Cheney, *Episcopal Visitations in Monasteries in the Thirteenth Century* (Manchester, 1931), chaps. 1 and 3.

14. This "beginning" could come as late as the 1580s where the Reformation was not introduced until then, as in the principality of Kalenberg-Göttingen, for example.

15. Cf. the reference to these types in the visitation reports printed by Johannes Bauermann, "Ein Paderborner Visitationsbericht vom Jahre 1575," *Westfalia Sacra* 4 (1973): 2.

16. *Visitations-Instruktion* 1528 in S.Weim., Reg. Ii, no. 1a, 4–18. The archives of Weimar and Dresden hold the entire documentary record of Saxon visitations in the period of the Reformation, an extraordinarily full, detailed, and unbroken set of documents.

17. Another example of this objective is supplied by the visitations in the Electorate of Brandenburg in the 1540s: Gerhard Zimmermann and Gerd Heinrich, *Die Brandenburgischen Kirchenvisitations-Abschiede und -Register des XVI. und XVII. Jahrhunderts. Vol. 2. Veröffentlichungen der Berliner historischen Kommission beim Friedrich-Meinecke-Institut der Freien Universität Berlin*, vol. 6 (Berlin, 1963), passim. See p. 13 for a particular example: Neuruppin.

18. Cf. chap. 1.

19. Pallas, passim. A Catholic example: Bavarian visitation 1558–60: BHM, Hochstiftliteralien Passau 83, xi, 16r.

20. "Zu anrichtung guter pollicey und äusserlicher zucht, zuvorderst aber pflanzung Göttliches heilmachendes worts. . . ." From title page of the *Visitations-Ordnung* of Württemberg (1557): WHS, A63, B21, 1r. The term *pollicey*, universally used in the sixteenth and seventeenth centuries, referred to administrative rules under the tight reins of government with special attention to the regulation of moral life.

21. BHM, Hochstiftliteralien Regensburg 34, 7r and v.

22. From *Wie man es auff der Visitation in den Kirchen pfleget zu halten*, an instruction in Pfalz-Neuburg, 1566, S.Neub.D., Grassegger-Sammlung no. 15329, 7v–8r.

23. Pallas, 41 (Allgemeiner Teil): 142. Also in Bavaria: BHM, Hochstiftliteralien Passau 83, xi, 16r.

24. E.g., Bavarian visitation 1558 in BHM, Hochstiftliteralien Passau 83, xi, 15v; also Hochstiftliteralien Regensburg 34, 7v.

25. *Artickel darauf die Eingepfarrten zu fragen* (1613) S. Cob., B2539, 25v. The territory included only that part of Coburg that then belonged to Ernestine Saxony.

26. Visitation in Zweibrücken, 1575, in K. Reissinger, ed., *Dokumente zur Geschichte der humanistischen Schulen im Gebiet der bayerischen Pfalz, MGP*, 49 (1911):118.

27. "Solche, die gegen die 10 Gebot ergerlich leben . . . ," S.Dresd., Loc. 2000, 250v.

28. From the Electoral Saxon visitation in 1617, parish of Niba, superintendency Weida. S.Weim., Reg. Ii, no. 51, 85r.

29. Brandenburg visitations, ca. 1578. S.Bamb. C7/X, no. 1, 91 r. The proverb goes "Des Hausvatters augen und Fusstritt machen den Acker satt." The same proverb is quoted in the *Kirchenordnung* of Oldenburg, 1573: N.S.S.Old., Best. 20, Tit. 19.

30. E.g., *Visitations Ordnung* of Mecklenburg (1552), in H. Schnell, *Das Unterrichtswesen der Grossherzogtümer Mecklenburg-Schwerin . . . , MGP* 38 (1907):231.

31. Ibid.

32. For a visitation in the territory of the city of Nuremberg in 1560, the visiting party numbered fourteen or fifteen. Cf. Gerhard Hirschmann, "Die zweite Nürnberger Kirchenvisitation . . . ," *Zschr. bayerische Kirchengesch.* 32 (1963):117. Copious information about the personnel of visiting parties is contained in the final expense accountings of the visitations, handed in at their conclusions.

33. These smaller villages might have *Filialkirchen*, churches without clerical staff assigned to them, or they might have no churches at all, in which case they were called *eingepfarrte Dörfer*, i.e., villages whose people attended service in the *Pfarrdorf*. For an up-to-date discussion of the problems (contemporary as well as for historians) of sixteenth-century Lutheran ecclesiastical organization of the countryside, see Karlheinz Blaschke's introduction to his own, Walther Haupt's, and Heinz Wiessner's *Die Kirchenorganisation in den Bistümern Meissen, Merseburg und Naumburg um 1500* (Weimar, 1969).

34. For an example of such a draft, see the records of the visitations in the county of Sayn-Hachenburg in Hesse, Hess.H.S.Wiesb., Abt. 340, nos. 1605a and 1605b.

35. Count Philipp Ludwig of Pfalz-Neuburg to Friedrich of Zweibrücken, 1592, S.Neub.D., Depot Heimatsverein Neuburg, no. 81, 34v-35r.

36. E.g., for Leipzig: Sdt.Leipz., Tit. VII, B2.

37. For a complete record of this procedure—marginal notes in protocols and relations turned into letters of instruction to secular and clerical personnel at the local level—see the material relating to the visitation of 1582 in Coburg: S.Cob. B2478, B2492-2493 (for the year 1591), and 2494.

38. From *General-Instruktion der visitatorn des Fürstentumbs Neuburg*, 1566; S.Neub.D., Pfalz-Neuburg Akten no. 6269, 15r and v.

39. For typical but particularly graphic examples of this, see S.Dresd., Loc. 7363 and 7367.

40. For an interesting instance of this issue, see the situation created by the attempt of Duke Johann of Jülich-Cleve-Berg and Mark to make his (Catholic) *Kirchenordnung* of 1532 effective by means of a visitation by secular officials. Otto R. Redlich, *Jülisch-Bergische Kirchenpolitik am Ausgange des Mittelalters und in der Reformationszeit* (Bonn, 1907-15), vol. I, no. 239. The engendered quarrels continued under Duke Wilhelm in the 1550s: August Franzen, *Die Visitationsprotokolle der ersten nachtridentinischen Visitation im Erzstift Köln . . .*, Reformationsgeschichtliche Studien und Texte, no. 85 (Münster, 1960), pp. 33–48, 74.

41. For a brief guide to the complex territorial history and dynastic and political organization of the duchies of Brunswick, see the section on Niedersachsen in *Geschichte der deutschen Länder: "Territorien-Ploetz,"* ed. Georg Wilhelm Sante, 1 (Würzburg, 1964: 347-80. For a more detailed account, see Johannes Meyer, *Kirchengeschichte Niedersachsens* (Göttingen, 1939).

42. The instruction and protocols of the 1588 visitation are printed by Karl Kayser, "Die General-Kirchenvisitation von 1588 im Lande Göttingen-Kalenberg," *Zeitschr. Gesellsch. niedersächsische Kirchengesch.* 8 (1904): 93–238; 9 (1904): 22–72. I cite according to this edition. The instruction alone is printed also in Sehling, 6, 2 (1957): 878–89.

43. *Visitatio generalis ducatus Calenbergici, anno 1588* in Kayser, "Die General-Kirchenvisitation," 8 (1904): 97.

44. Ibid., p. 108.

45. Ibid., p. 106.

46. Ibid., p. 107.

47. A good general description of the documentary aspects of Protestant visitations is found in Pallas, 41 (Allgemeiner Teil): 199-232: "Das urkundliche Material."

48. Such a situation is described by Hirschmann, "Die zweite Nürnberger Kirchenvisitation," pp. 119-20.

49. I have made such a synoptic comparison for the visitation of 1579 in the superintendencies under the consistories of Dresden and Meissen: S.Dresd., Loc. 2000, 2002, 2003, 2005, 2009, 2011, 2012, 2050. Also: Archiv des evangelisch-lutherischen Landeskirchenamt Sachsen (Dresden) Matrikel des Consistoriums Dresden.

50. See Hirschmann, "Die zweite Nürnberger Kirchenvisitation," p. 111; Franzen, *Die Visitationsprotokolle*, p. 88.

51. Franzen, *Die Visitationsprotokolle*, p. 88.

52. These points are raised in ibid., pp. 87-88.

53. Peter Blickle, *Landschaften im alten Reich: Die staatliche Funktion des gemeinen Mannes in Oberdeutschland* (Munich, 1973), passim, especially pp. 3-24; 54-156. For an older view, see Georg Ludwig von Maurer, *Geschichte der Dorfverfassung in Deutschland*, vol. 1 (Erlangen, 1865).

54. This point is made emphatically by Maurer, *Geschichte der Dorfverfassung*, p. 155.

55. Johann Adam, *Evangelische Kirchengeschichte der Stadt Strassburg* (Strassburg, 1922), pp. 318-20.

CHAPTER 13

1. *Schreiben der Visitatorn über die mancherlei Unrichtigkeit: Gebrächen und Mängel* (1535), in Pallas, 41 (Allgemeiner Teil): 30.

2. On the condition and qualifications of Lutheran pastors in Ernestine Saxony and Thuringia, see Susan Karant-Boles, *Lutheran Pastors in Ernestine Saxony and Thuringia, 1521-46* (Ph.D. diss., Indiana University 1970). Also Susan Karant-Nunn, "The Economic Position of Lutheran Pastors in Ernestine Thuringia, 1521-1555," *Archiv Reformationsgesch.* 63 (1972): 94-113. Also Bernhard Klaus, "Soziale Herkunft und theologische Bildung lutherischer Pfarrer der reformatorischen Frühzeit," *Zeitschr. Kirchengesch.* 80, no. 1 (1969): 22-49. Klaus's claim that the average clergyman gained significantly in general education and theological cultivation during the sixteenth century (pp. 48-49) is too sweeping. No doubt there was some rise in pastoral competence, but the picture as conveyed in the visitation records is spotty and far from uniform.

3. *Artickel gemeiner Verschaffung*, issued in 1533 for Thuringia, S.Weim., Reg. Ii, no. 4[1], 10r ff.

4. S.Weim., Reg. I, nos. 6-7. The best general map of the territories and jurisdictions of the lands of the Wettin family is Karlheinz Blaschke's "Die Wettinischen Länder," in *Die Reformation in Dokumenten* (Weimar, 1967). For more detailed cartographic information about many (though not all) of the localities given in the Saxon segment of this chapter, see the fifteen maps in Karlheinz Blaschke, et al., *Die Kirchenorganisation in den Bistümern Meissen, Merseburg und Naumburg . . .* (Weimar, 1969). For general information on Saxon history in the age of the Reformation: Karlheinz Blaschke, *Sachsen im Zeitalter der Reformation*, SVfRG, vol. 185 (Gütersloh, 1970), and Rudolf Kötzschke and Herbert Kretzschmar, *Sächsische Geschichte* (Frankfurt am Main, 1965), pp. 162-235.

5. S.Weim., Reg. I, no. 6, 195r.

6. E.-L.K.A.Dresd.,: Matrikel des Consistoriums Dresden (1580), unpaginated, passim. S.Dresd., Loc. 1999 (1581), passim.

7. S.Weim., Reg. Ii, no. 23, 3v-4r.

8. Ibid., 8r and v.

9. Ibid., no. 29, passim.

10. Ibid., no. 29, 3v.

11. Ibid., no. 29, 7v.

12. Ibid., no. 42[i], 6r.

13. Ibid., no. 42[i], 264v.

14. Ibid., no. 42[i], 247v-248r.

15. Ibid., no. 42^i, 237r.
16. Ibid., no. 43, 27r and v.
17. Ibid., no. 45, 71r.
18. Ibid., no. 48, 13r.
19. Ibid., no. 66, passim. This wording is a formula constantly used in the protocols.
20. Ibid., no. 66, 99r.
21. Ibid., no. 66, 106r.
22. Ibid., no. 66, 110r and v.
23. For the prevalence of *Rockenstuben*, see Pallas, all volumes, passim. They were disapproved because they competed with churches as social centers and because the proximity of men and women encouraged sexual encounters. There are frequent references to "lascivious dances" (e.g., S.Dresd., Loc. 2003, 294v) and strange goings-on suggestive of sectarian meetings: "Man sitze die jungen magd zu ihnen [i.e., young men], niemand von den alten dabei, üben seltzame wort und geberd ohne allen schein [i.e., in the dark], sagen, es sei ein alt herkomen." Quoted in Werner Kugler, "Die Kirchenvisitation in der Superintendentur Monheim . . . , *Zeitschr. bayerische Kirchengesch.* 33 (1964): 58. It is also likely that these assemblies (held in the homes of villagers and townspeople according to a system of regular rotation) were suspected of being breeding grounds of deviant religious beliefs and practices. In the sixteenth century, *Rockenstube* was a common symbol for licentious gatherings: e.g., Hans Sachs, *Ein Fassnachtspiel mit Fünf Personen. die Rockenstuben genannt* (Edmund Goetze, ed., *Zwölf Fastnachtspiele aus den Jahren 1518-39* [*Neudrucke deutscher Literaturwerke des XVI. und XVII. Jahrhunderts*, nos. 26-27, Halle, 1880], pp. 124-31.
24. S.Dresd., Loc. 2012, 13r-16r.
25. Ibid., Loc. 1998, 425v.
26. Ibid., Loc. 2002, 122v.
27. A popular ballad reflects the prevailing assumption that such a flagging had occurred. A Saxon traveler in Bavaria confesses his disillusionment to a native of that Catholic country:

> Do not withhold, friend, from my ear
> The tidings I would like to hear:
> How does the gospel stand with you?
> In Saxony, the love that drew
> Us to it years ago is dead,
> Everyone scorns it now instead.
> Vice grows and virtue disappears,
> God's holy word falls on deaf ears.
> I fear that Luther's prophecy
> Will be fulfilled in Saxony:
> Where God's word first came back to light,
> He said, there will it pass from sight.

Pasquillus zwischen einem Bair und Sachssen (ca. 1556, written by an anonymous Bavarian) printed in August Hartmann, ed., *Historische Volkslieder und Zeitgedichte*, vol. 1 (Munich, 1907), no. 8.

28. On the bitter rivalries and struggles among Philippists and orthodox ("Ernestine") Lutherans in the 1570s and 1580s, see Franz Blanckmeister, *Sächsische Kirchengeschichte* (Dresden, 1899), sec. 37, pp. 156-61.

29. The protocols bear out this interpretation: E.g., a visitor's report of a colloquy with villagers accused of *unfleiss* in going to church: "Dises ist den pauren just vorgehalten worden. Sie meinen aber, es sei ihnen an irer narung, deren sie nachgehn müssten, auch viel gelegen. und achtens für ein gerings, die predigten dabey zu verseumen." S.Dresd., Loc. 2003, 266r. For many other examples see Pallas, all volumes, passim. After 1555, demobilized *Landsknechte* roamed the land and quickly learned to make use of Sunday church service to steal chickens and cattle and break into peasant houses (ibid.). In the village of Straach, for instance, the pastor explained that the bark of a dog in the distance was enough to send the congregation racing out of church, "weil der dieb hie viel sich anhero schleichen." (Ibid., 41^1:173.)

30. See the reports printed in Wilhelm Schmidt, ed., "Die Kirchen und Schulvisitation im sächsischen Kurkreise vom Jahre 1555. I. Die kirchlichen und sittlichen Zustände," *SVfRg*, 24^1 (1906): 23-25.

31. Ibid., p. 53.

32. E.g., 1574 visitation in superintendency of Grimma, S.Dresd., Loc. 2002, 50r. For evidence of catechism preaching in 1574, see ibid., Loc. 1991 passim.

33. Ibid., Loc. 2002, 87v (1574).

34. E-L.K.A.Dresd. Visitationsmatrikel Chemnitz 1575, passim.

35. From the Saxon *Kirchenordnung* of 1580 in Sehling, 1:423.

36. Ibid.

37. From visitation of Langenheimersdorf, superintendency Freiberg, 1578. S.Dresd., Loc. 2012, 205v.

38. The vast number of visitation records in Weimar and Dresden make it clear that physical and material conditions remained unsatisfactory in most parishes into the seventeenth century. The overwhelming bulk of information contained in Saxon protocols concerns this state of affairs. As was explained in chap. 12, visitors and their clerks differed among themselves in the thoroughness they brought to their tasks, as did the individuals who redacted the protocols from the raw data. The result is a spotty picture but, given the massiveness of the materials, one rich in concrete information.

39. I failed to record the source of this remark copied from one of the Saxon visitation protocols.

40. From a summary report by the superintendent of Pirna, 1578. S.Dresd., Loc. 2012, 19r.

41. Ibid., 227r.

42. Ibid., Loc. 2002, 33r.

43. Ibid., 74r.

44. Ibid., Loc. 1980, 21r.

45. From visitation in superintendency Leipzig 1579-80. S.Dresd., Loc. 1998, part 1, 28r ff.; part 2, 425r-426v; 430r-435v.

46. Ibid., 426v.

47. Ibid., Loc. 9357[II], 43v.

48. Heinrich Salmuth, *Catechismus. das ist die fürnembsten Hauptstück der heiligen christlichen Lehr der Leipziger Kirchenordnung nach* . . . (Budissin, 1581), Ciiii r.

49. From a visitation in 1581, Pallas, 41[1]:129.

50. From the relation of the visitation in superintendency Dresden (1580), in E-L.K.A. Dresd., Visitation 1580, unpaginated: "Seifersdorf."

51. Ibid., 159v.

52. From 1581 visitation in superintendency Borna. S.Dresd., Loc. 2004, 424v-425r.

53. Ibid., Loc. 1985, 308v.

54. For the 1590s see S.Dresd., Loc. 10601, Loc. 2009, Loc. 2000, Loc. 2005, Loc. 1977, Loc. 1993, all passim.

55. From visitation of superintendency Dresden, 1598-99. S.Dresd., Loc. 2009, 263v.

56. Visitation in superintendency Colditz, 1617. S.Dresd., Loc. 1997, 127v.

57. My evidence for this judgment is taken from a general reading of the visitation reports of the later sixteenth and early seventeenth centuries. See, for instance, the occasionally well-informed answers given by pastors during the investigation of the Flacian "heresy" in the 1570s (some examples from 1573 in S.Cob., B2463) or the frequently impressive catalogs of private libraries submitted by pastors (an example: *Verzeichnis meiner Johann Langepeter, der Zeit zu Capellendorff pfarher, eigene bücher*, submitted in 1570, S.Weim, Reg. 1, no. 53, 21r-24v). Many such lists were copied into the visitation protocols.

58. For the existence of these schools in the duchy of Saxony in the late sixteenth century, see the detailed information printed in Pallas, 41[1-5], passim. The visitation protocols for the 1570s, 1580s, and 1590s are especially explicit on the matter of popular schools, making it clear that village schools were the rule rather than the exception in Saxony. For their organization see Pallas, vol. 41 (Allgemeiner Teil), passim. For examples of school ordinances in Saxony in the sixteenth century, see the many *Schulordnungen* printed in Sehling, vol. 1, passim. A good survey of the Saxon school system before 1580 is given by Georg Müller, "Das kursächsische Schulwesen beim Erlass der Schulordnung von 1580," *Programm des Wettiner Gymansiums zu Dresden*, no. 505 (Dresden, 1888). Müller demonstrates the unsystematic character of popular schools before 1580, a situation the *Schulordnung* of that year, drawn from the earlier Württemberg *Schulordnung*, was intended to correct.

59. Pallas, vol. 41[1-5], passim.
60. Often, when a child went to parish school, his parents removed him before the end of the quarter. One even hears of parents sending two children in alternate weeks: e.g., ibid., 41[5]:120.
61. Ibid., all volumes, passim.
62. Ibid., 41[3]:93.
63. Ibid., 41 (Allgemeiner Teil): 136-37; 141-47.
64. Ibid., pp. 148-49.
65. This summary of abuses is taken from a set of corrective injunctions issued by Duke Johann Casimir of Sachsen-Coburg in 1591. The injunctions were developed from the material put at the duke's disposal in the protocols of the general (i.e., principality-wide) visitation of 1589. For the protocols of this visitation and the duke's ensuing instructions, see S.Cob., B2492 and 2493, passim.
66. For the evidence of this, see ibid., B2468, B2473 (1577-78), and B2476 (1580), passim. The city of Coburg was visited in 1577 (B2468).
67. From *Instruction, welchergestalt in . . . herrn Augusti, herzogen zu Sachsen . . . jährliche Visitation der kirchen und schulen gehalten werden soll* (1577), printed in Sehling, 1:350.
68. Ibid., p. 351.
69. The Protestant margrave Johann Friedrich of Brandenburg was chosen archbishop of Magdeburg in 1566, his predecessor, Sigismund, having already turned Lutheran. On the introduction of the Reformation in the bishopric, see Franz Schrader, ed., *Die Visitationen der katholischen Klöster im Erzbistum Magdeburg durch die evangelischen Landesherren, 1561–1651*, Reformationsgeschichtliche Studien und Texte, 99 (Münster, 1969):1–15. On the distribution and functioning of schools in the bishopric, see the *General-Artikel* of 1585 for Magdeburg: S.Magd., Rep. A12 Generalia, nos. 2434-2670, passim; Rep. A2, no. 511, 93v-94r. Visitors put questions about schools to every town council and group of village elders. Answers are recorded in the above-mentioned protocols.
70. From visitation of archbishopric Magdeburg, 1583. S.Magd., Rep. A2, no. 511, 105v-106r.
71. Ibid., 106r-109v.
72. E.g., ibid., 209r-212v: "Sind etliche so ungelert, das alle hoffnung an inen verloren und schwerlichen im Amt geduldet werden können. Sintemal da kein verstand der seligmachenden warheit ist, auch nicht so viel gedechtnis, das sie etwas aus einem buch auswending lernen und der gemeine verstendlich vortragen könnten, die auch in der Bibel ganz unbelesen sein, auch wol dieselbe nicht einmal recht angesehen haben" (1584).
73. Ibid., 221r and v (1584).
74. Ibid., 226r (1584).
75. Ibid., Rep. A12 Generalia 2445, 2r and v.
76. E.g., the 1583 visitation which concluded "dass in allen orten die leute im catechismo diesmal besser bestanden als vor 20 jaren, da sie in vielen orten nicht die blossen worten . . . gekannt," ibid., Rep. A2, no. 511, 109v.
77. Visitations in the archbishopric Magdeburg in 1561-63 show that identical conditions had prevailed under the preceding Catholic reign (ibid., Rep. A12, Generalia 2434, 2435, 2436, 2440, and Rep. A12 a I, no. 1974). They did not significantly change after the Protestant conversion of the realm. For conditions in the 1640s and 1650s, much affected by the Thirty Years War, see ibid., Rep. A12 a I, no. 1985 and no. 2445.
78. On the complicated and shifting territorial, dynastic, political, and religious divisions of the Brunswick duchies in Niedersachsen, see Johannes Meyer, *Kirchengeschichte Niedersachsens* (Göttingen, 1939).
79. The records of this visitation have been published by Friedrich Spanuth, "Quellen zur Durchführung der Reformation im Braunschweig-Wolfenbüttelschen Lande, 1551 bis 1568," *Zeitschr. Gesellsch. niedersächsische Kirchengesch.* 42 (1937):265-88.
80. Ibid., p. 284.
81. Ibid., p. 275.
82. Cf. the relation of visitations in Braunschweig-Wolfenbüttel (1568-70), in L.K.A. Braun., Voges 448.

83. On the other hand, Duke Julius could not have helped matters by urging his sons Heinrich Julius and Philipp Sigismund to take the tonsure so as to assume the bishoprics of Halberstadt and Verden and Osnabrück, respectively.

84. These are printed in part in Wolters, ed., "Die Kirchenvisitationen der Aufbauzeit (1570–1600) im vormaligen Herzogtum Braunschweig-Wolfenbüttel," *Zeitschr. Gesellsch. niedersächsische Kirchengesch.* 43 (1938): 204–37; 44 (1939): 64–85; 48 (1950): 62–85.

85. Ibid., 43:222–24.

86. Ibid., pp. 233–34.

87. Ibid., p. 234.

88. Ibid., 48:84.

89. Ibid., p. 85.

90. See the documents relating to questions of school financing and appointment of Latin and German schoolmasters, all of them handled by the dukes personally, in L.K.A. Braun., Voges 159 and 132.

91. On the circumstances of these events, see Karl Kayser, *Die reformatorischen Kirchenvisitationen in den welfischen Landen, 1542–1544* (Göttingen, 1897).

92. From the protocol, drawn up in 1580, of the visitation of 1579, printed in Friedrich Spanuth, "Die Grubenhagensche Kirchenvisitation von 1579 durch Superintendent Schellhammer," *Jahrbuch Gesellsch. niedersächsische Kirchengesch.* 52 (1954):106.

93. Ibid., pp. 107, 109, 111, etc.

94. Ibid., p. 116.

95. Ibid., p. 115.

96. Ibid., p. 106.

97. Ibid., p. 117.

98. See the information in Friedrich Spanuth, "Die Herzberger Synoden und Kirchengerichte von 1582 bis 1588, *Jahrbuch Gesellsch. niedersächsische Kirchengesch.* 54 (1956): 18–46; and "Die Generalvisitation in Grubenhagen von 1617," ibid., 53 (1955):49–70. When brought to the synod at Herzberg, pastors were asked about conditions in their respective parishes. The reports they gave are recorded in the minutes of the synod.

99. From visitation in Kalenberg-Göttingen, 1652, in Karl Kayser, ed., "Die Generalvisitation des D. Gesenius im Fürstentum Göttingen 1646 und 1652," *Zeitschr. Gesellsch. niedersächsische Kirchengesch.* 11 (1906):201.

100. E.g., Hess.H.S.Wiesb., Abt. 340, no. 1605a, 174r (visitation of Sayn-Hachenburg in 1585); S.Magd. Rep. A12, Generalia 2445, fol. 165v (visitation of archbishopric Magdeburg, 1650); Strassb.A.V., Archives St. Thomas 45, carton 21.1, 737r and v (1560) and unnumbered pamphlet dated 1586.

101. Visitation of 1583 in H.S.Hann., 83 IV, 77–79. Kalenberg had first been reformed in 1540 by the widow of Duke Erich of Kalenberg, officially recatholicized under Erich II, then rereformed in 1568 after Duke Julius's ascent to the Wolfenbüttel throne.

102. The entire protocol in ibid., no. 101. The visitation took place in 1588. For excerpts: Karl Kayser, "Die Generalvisitation . . . ," *Zeitschr. Gesellsch. niedersächsische Kirchengesch.* 8 (1904): 93–238.

103. Ibid., from examination of Pastor Wilhelm Rauch, pp. 198–99.

104. From summary report on the visitation in the County Hoya, duchy of Kalenberg, 1628. L.K.A.Braun., Voges 1924, unnumbered leaves.

105. Ibid.

106. The condition of the church in Lauenburg, and the competence of its pastors, is shown in the visitation ordered by Franz II in 1581. See W. Dührsen, "Geesthachter Kirchenvisitationen," *Archiv Vereins Gesch. Herzogtums Lauenburg* 2, no. 2 (1888): 22–33.

107. The protocols of the 1581–82 visitation in the duchy of Lauenburg are in the L.S.-H., Abt. 218: Lauenburgisches Konsistorium, no. 653. The reference is to 30r and v. For general religious and moral conditions, see the sections entitled *Abschiede nach gehaltenen Examina mit dem Volcke.*

108. Ibid., 56r–58r.

109. Ibid., 78r.

110. From the visitation of 1590, ibid., Abt. 218: Lauenburgisches Konsistorium Ratzeburg, no. 654, 86r.

111. This had been done in 1581–82. Ibid., no. 653, 37r and v.

112. Ibid., no. 654, 43r and v.
113. Ibid., 63v-64r.
114. For references to "Anabaptists" and "Calvinists," see ibid., 119v, 128r.
115. The visitation of 1568 in Lüneburg is published in Bernhard Lange, ed., "Die General-Kirchenvisitation im Fürstentum Lüneburg 1568," *Jahrbuch Gesellsch. niedersächsische Kirchengesch.* 58 (1960): 41–100.
116. Ibid., pp. 53, 57, 60, 91.
117. E.g., ibid., pp. 76, 91.
118. E.g., visitation in Kalenberg, 1583. H.S.Hann., Hann. 83 IV, nos. 77–79.
119. From a summary relation on visitations of four salt-mining towns in Grubenhagen, 1639: L.K.A.Braun., Voges 1926, 7–8. Also Braunschweig-Lüneburg, 1651–52: ibid., Voges 1927.
120. For examples: ibid., Voges 1926.
121. Ibid., 2.
122. For the school system of Hannover, see Franz Bertram, *Geschichte des Ratsgymnasiums zu Hannover* (Hannover, 1915). For Bugenhagen's school ordinance for Braunschweig, 1528, see Vormbaum, pp. 8–18.
123. As proved by the attention given and the money provided for good Latin schools, and *gute ingenia* to attend them. E.g., L.K.A.Braun., Voges 1929 (1568), 13v–14r: provisions for three advanced schools for *auserlesene ingenia* and six ordinary Latin schools to send their best pupils to them.
124. Ibid., Voges 742.
125. The evidence is in Pallas, vol. 41^{1-5}, with a great number of curricula, book lists, etc. See also K. Pallas, "Der Küster in der evangelischen Kirche . . . ," *Zeitschr. Vereins Kirchengesch. Provinz Sachsen* 19, no. 1 (1922): 3–19. See also the evidence presented by Georg Müller, "Das kursächsische Schulwesen beim Erlass der Schulordnung von 1580," *Programm des Wettiner Gymnasiums . . .* no. 505 (1888).
126. Visitation of 1609: N.S.S.Old., Bestand 73 II, 170v ff. for Geest, 1r–170r for Marsch.
127. E.g., the parish of Stolhamme in Marsch, ibid., 12r–21r.
128. From the report of Superintendent Jacobus Fabricius, in Wilhelm Jensen, "Die Visitationsreise des schleswig-holstein-gottorpischen Generalsuperintendenten Mag. Jacobus Fabricius im Jahre 1639," *Schriften Ver. Schleswig-Holsteinische Kirchengesch.*, ser. 2, 11 (1952): 43–44. Fabricius's report continues in ibid. 12 (1953–54): 1–34. The duchies of Schleswig-Holstein had been Protestant since the late 1520s and under a *Kirchenordnung* (of Christian III, King of Denmark) since 1538, revised in 1542 by Bugenhagen.
129. For some clues to the enormously complicated territorial and political history of Hesse generally, and Hessen-Nassau in particular, see Karl E. Demandt, *Geschichte des Landes Hessen*, 2d ed., (Kassel and Basel, 1972), especially the charts on pp. 374–75.
130. Hess.H.S.Wiesb., Abt. 150. 7, no. 3829, 6v.
131. Ibid., Abt. 153, no. 417, 63v–64v.
132. Ibid., Abt. 150.15, no. 3837, unnumbered.
133. Ibid., Abt. 150.16, no. 3838, unnumbered.
134. Visitation of 1579 in Herrschaft Sayn-Hachenburg (one of the splinter territories of Hessen-Nassau), Ibid., Abt. 340, no. 1605a, 69v.
135. E.g., ibid., Abt. 133, no. 5: Walsdorf (1609 and 1615).
136. *Gebrechen und Beschwerungen der Pfarr zu Mosbach: An den Zuhörern in gemein.* Ibid., Abt. 137.Xa, no. 1, 9r–12r.
137. Visitation of Nassau-Wiesbaden, 1609, ibid., 39r.
138. Ibid., 72v–73r.
139. See LAS, Synodus-Protokolle (from 1581).
140. Even lowly village sextons were examined for fitness by ducal authorities. E.g., WHS, A284: Kirchenrat Spezialakten Calw G–V, B138. On Württemberg's *Volksschulen* generally, see the detailed survey by Eugen Schmid, *Geschichte des Volksschulwesens in Altwürttemberg* (Stuttgart, 1927). The visitation records in Stuttgart, A281, Büschel 46 ff. contain information about the existence of town and village schools but are uninformative on most other counts.
141. This assertion rests on my study of the Synodus-Protokolle and Competenz-Bücher in LAS.

142. For these instances, see Johann B. Götz, ed., "Die grosse oberpfälzische Landesvisitation unter dem Kurfürsten Ludwig VI," *Verhandl. hist. Ver. Oberpfalz Regensburg* 85 (1935): 148–244; 86 (1936): 277–362. See especially 86:290, 329.

143. See also the evidence in Johann B. Götz, *Die religiösen Wirren in der Oberpfalz, 1576-1620*, Reformationsgeschichtliche Texte, 66, (1937):74–75.

144. Quoted in Götz, "Die grosse oberpfälzische Landesvisitation" 85:153.

145. Ibid., 86:354.

146. Robert Dollinger, "Eine oberpfälzische Kirchenvisitation vor dem dreissigjährigen Krieg," *Zeitschr. bayer. Kirchengesch.* 18 (1948): 98–109.

147. Pfalz-Neuburg was reformed by the famous Pfalzgraf Ottheinrich, who issued the *Neuburger Kirchenordnung* in 1543. Catholicism was reintroduced after Charles V's victory in the Schmalkaldic war, but by 1552 the territory was Protestant again and remained so until 1614, when Wolfgang Wilhelm re-Catholicized the land.

148. *Instruction, was sich . . . in visitirung der Kirchen und Schulen in unserm Fürstentumb Neuburg verhalten und ausrichten sollen* (1558). S.Neub.D., Pfalz-Neuburg Akten, no. 6266, 20r ff.

149. Ibid., 31r.

150. Ibid., 34r.

151. Ibid., 155r.

152. Ibid., no. 6269, Br. (1566).

153. Ibid., Grassegger-Sammlung 15326¹, 14v (1575).

154. The document constituting this body is in ibid., 25r ff.

155. The draft of these General Articles is in ibid., no. 15327.

156. Ibid., 55r and v.

157. Ibid., no. 15326² (1577).

158. These are formula phrases, often repeated: e.g., ibid., 14v.

159. Ibid., no. 15326³, passim.

160. S.Neub.D., Grassegger-Sammlung, no. 15335¹ ¹².

161. Ibid., no. 15326⁸, 14r.

162. Werner Kugler, "Die Kirchenvisitation in der Superintendentur Monheim . . . ," *Zeitschr. bayerische Kirchengesch.* 33 (1964): 58.

163. S.Neub.D., Grassegger-Sammlung, no. 15326⁵, 7v. The phrase is a formula.

164. Ibid., Depot Heimatverein Neuburg, no. 83, 32. For visitations of 1586, 1587, 1588, 1591 see ibid., Grassegger-Sammlung, no. 15326⁴ ⁸. The protocols continue annually after 1591.

165. E.g., the consistorial deliberation on the visitation to parish Schmiedmühlen, 1589. Ibid., no. 15335⁴, 17r ff.

166. For a good survey of Bavarian history in the Reformation period, and references to the voluminous literature on the subject, see *Handbuch der bayerischen Geschichte*, vol. 2, ed. Max Spindler (Munich, 1966), pp. 297–409.

167. There is general agreement that the Bavarian dukes used the threat of the Lutheran movement to reduce episcopal power in the duchy. See M. Doeberl, *Entwicklungsgeschichte Bayerns*, 1 (Munich, 1908): 395, and, for a recent view, Helmut Rankl, *Das vorreformatorische landesherrliche Kirchenregiment in Bayern, 1378-1526*, Miscellanea Bavarica Monacensia, no. 34 (Munich, 1971), especially p. 226.

168. This alliance policy was cautiously pursued to the end of advancing Wilhelm IV as a candidate for Roman king to replace Charles V's brother Ferdinand. As long as it lasted, this play required openings to Protestant powers.

169. The oath of 1571 is found in BHM, Staatsverwaltung 1586, 81r–83v. It contains thirty-seven questions based on the Tridentine formulations.

170. For a recent study of the complicated history of the *Geistliche Ratskollegium* in Bavaria, see Richard Bauer, *Der kurfürstliche geistliche Rat und die bayerische Kirchenpolitik, 1768-1802*, Miscellanea Bavarica Monacensia, no. 32 (Munich, 1971).

171. For these, and many other examples, see the huge documentation in BHM, Staatsverwaltung 2780–2789, which contains materials for the years 1558 through the 1580s.

172. See, generally, the documents in Georg Lurz, *Mittelschulgeschichtliche Dokumente Altbayerns*, MGP, vol. 42 (Berlin, 1908).

173. For Bavaria, see the documentation of this struggle between state and church in

ibid., vol. 41 (Berlin, 1907), especially the negotiations of secular and episcopal representatives at meetings in Salzburg, 1549, and Mühldorf, 1553, on such questions as inspection of schools, establishment of curricula, selection of books (ibid. 41:242-243).

174. Ibid., 42:67-75.

175. Quoted in Heinrich Held, *Altbayrische Volkserziehung und Volksschule* (Munich, 1926-28), 1:163. The principle was incorporated in the territorial *Schulordnung* of 1569.

176. The *Schulordnung* of 1569 is printed in Lurz, *Mittelschulgeschichtliche Dokumente*, 42:29-43.

177. On the persistence of Lutheran books and catechisms in the late sixteenth century, see the mandate of 1586 in ibid., 42:86.

178. See Felix Stieve, *Das kirchliche Polizeiregiment in Baiern unter Maximilian I* (Munich, 1876). Maximilian's methods included not only censorship and loyalty oaths, but also domestic visitations (*Haussuchungen*), especially of book dealers' lodgings, monetary rewards for informers, and fines for proved failure to report suspicions, the use of secret spies, and the appointment, in 1629, of a central commission, headed by Maximilian's Jesuit confessor, to conduct an inquisition in Bavaria.

179. From the *Schulordnung* for the city of Pfaffenhausen (1656), in Lurz, *Mittelschulgeschichtliche Dokumente*, 42:148-49.

180. For the mandate introducing Canisius's catechism, a part of the Bavarian *Schulordnung* of 1569, see ibid., 42:31-32. For the catechisms themselves see Friedrich Streicher, S.J., ed., *S. Petri Canisii . . . Catechismi Latini et Germanici* (Rome and Munich, 1933-36). The Greater Catechism was published in Latin in Vienna, 1555, and expanded and adjusted to Tridentine decrees in 1566. The Shorter Catechism for pupils in lower and middle classes came in 1558, in Latin and German. A still shorter one, also in Latin and German, was published in Vienna in 1566, extracted from the revised Larger Catechism of that year.

181. "The idea in binding it up with an elementary Latin grammar was to take on at their own game such Protestants as Melanchthon . . . who made a practice of instilling their doctrines by means of school books." James Brodrick, S.J., *Saint Peter Canisius S.J.* (London, 1939), p. 236.

182. Lurz, *Mittelschulgeschichtliche Dokumente*, 42:40.

183. See the documents in OEMF, 565, relating to the visitation of 1560. E.g., 505. Almost every schoolmaster questioned complained of losing pupils to the Jesuit schools. A reading of the literature and documentation on Jesuit education bears out the accepted idea that the society evinced little interest in instructing or indoctrinating the masses, preferring to concentrate their activities on its leaders.

184. Lurz, *Mittelschulgeschichtliche Dokumente*, 42:40.

185. The Council of Trent enunciated this principle in its twenty-third session (1563): "Concerning Reform," chap. 18 in H. J. Schroeder, trans., *Canons and Decrees of the Council of Trent* (Saint Louis and London, 1941).

186. See the pronouncement in the *Bayrische Landsordnung* of 1553 in Lurz, *Mittelschulgeschichtliche Dokumente*, 42:10-11. On the other hand, Catholic catechisms do not, as do may of the as do many of the Lutheran ones, extend their comments, e.g., on the fourth commandment, to secular civic duties.

187. Ibid., 41:211, 238.

188. Cf. Karl Schrems, "Der 'modus catechizandi' der katholischen Kirchenkatechese in Deutschland im 16. und 17. Jahrhundert," *Verhandl. hist. Ver. Oberpfalz Regensburg*, 106 (1966): 219-41, with a discussion of catechization methods to be used with parishioners in cities, towns, and villages in Catholic Germany. See also Gerhard Bellinger, *Der Catechismus Romanus und die Reformation*, Konfessionskundliche und kontroverstheologische Studien, no. 27 (Paderborn, 1970): p. 71.

189. This judgment is based on my reading of visitation mandates and protocols from the reigns of Albrecht V, beginning with his mandate of 1569, and Wilhelm V. For a good illustration of points of interrogation under these rulers, see BHM, Staatsverwaltung 2785, the relation of a visitation in the administrative district of Burghausen in 1570. For a corresponding instance from another Catholic territory, see the report of a visitation of Styria ordered by Archduke Ferdinand in 1544-45 in Karl Eder, ed., "Die landesfürstliche Visitation von 1544/45 in der Steiermark," *Forschungen zur Verfassungs- und Verwaltungsgeschichte der Steiermark* (Graz, 1955).

190. BHM, Staatsverwaltung 2783, 230.

191. E.g., visitation protocols in Landshut, 1608, B.S.Landsh., Rep. LXXXII, fasc. 67, no. 43, Saal 17: *Schulacta der Schulen*, especially 99r and v. Some of these protocols are printed in Lurz, *Mittelschulgeschichtliche Dokumente*, 42:99–126.

192. B.S.Münch., 1379, no. 9, 492.

193. From a memorandum by the *Geistliche Rat* (1607), in ibid., 493r and v.

194. Archbishop of Salzburg to Duke Maximilian, 1608, ibid., 5a r.

195. Ibid., 10a r–10b v.

196. This conclusion was reached by the *Geistliche Rat* in 1608. Ibid., 13v.

197. Bishop of Salzburg to Maximilian, 1608; ibid., 5b r.

198. For Catholic Europe, this is the argument made by John Bossy, "The Counter-Reformation and the People of Catholic Europe," *Past and Present* 47 (1970): 51–70.

199. The documents are in Hess.H.S.Wiesb., Abt. 171, D221–49, 440, 535–36; K 207–11; 712, 716.

200. Ibid., D222, 22r.

201. Ibid., D243, 46r.

202. Ibid., D227, 26v.

203. See the record of the examination of *seniores* in Nassau-Katzenellenbogen, 1610, ibid., K209, e.g., 34v–35v.

204. Ibid., D243, 46r.

205. For the questionnaire see ibid., D245, 3r–9v. For the procedure as a whole, the protocols of the visitation of 1590 in ibid., passim.

206. Ibid., D535, 10v.

207. Ibid., D535, 65r.

208. Ibid., D535, 66v, 67v.

209. Ibid., D535, 11v.

210. E.g., ibid., K209, 34v–35v.

211. On this point see the article by Carl-Ludwig Furck, "Die Erziehung zu einem bewusst aktiven Leben in der calvinistischen Pädagogik," *Zeitschr. Pädagogik* 10 (1964): 340–60, with many examples from catechisms and similar materials.

212. Hess.H.S.Wiesb., Abt. 171, D535, 76r.

213. Ibid., D245, 53v.

214. See, e.g., the mandate against sundry vices issued in the county of Nassau-Wiesbaden and Idstein in 1588, following unsuccessful appeals in 1576 and 1583: "Und da man sich daran [i.e., earlier mandates] nicht gekheret, und dadurch einem gantzen land für unglück aufgewachsen, wie dann dieser zeit dergleich strafen und heftige plagen vorhanden, . . . so gar nicht geachtet, sondern je lenger je mehr, die greuliche sünden ergerliche schandt und laster, als da seind blutschand, Notzucht, Raub oder Entführung, desgleich Eebruch, unehelich beischlaf, unzucht und huerei eingerissen und im Schwang gehen, also dass die leider bald für kein sünde mehr, welches bei uns Christen erschröcklich zu hören, geachtet werden wölle." Hess.H.S.Wiesb., Abt. 133, no. 1, 4v–5r. The 1588 mandate set the death penalty for adultery; married men convicted of fornication with single girls were exiled after serving time in the stocks; etc. Ibid., 5v–8r.

215. From a summary relation by visitors to the Strassburg council (1660), Strass.A.V., Archives St. Thomas 46, carton 21.2, 415–16.

216. E.g., also L.K.A.Braun., Voges 1926, 73; 1927, 50, 105; Nicolaus Hunnius, *Anweisung zum rechten Christenthumb* . . . (Nuremberg, 1639), signature)(vr.

217. "Der grosse und blinde unverstandt des Catechismi und der gründe christlicher ler. . . ." See note 215, above.

218. S.Neub.D., Grassegger-Sammlung 15326¹⁻¹⁵ for the principality. There is no mention of the city.

219. August Franzen, ed., *Die Visitationsprotokolle der ersten nachtridentinischen Visitation im Erzstift Köln* . . . (Münster, 1960), p. 80.

220. Karl Eder, "Die landesfürstliche Visitation von 1544/45 in der Steiermark," *Forschungen zur Verfassungs- und Verwaltungsgeschichte der Steiermark* (Graz, 1955), p. 37.

221. Nuremberg's first visitation occurred in 1528–29, the second one not until 1560, although tentative plans were made in 1535, 1536, 1540, and 1548.

222. For Dresden: S.Dresd., Loc. 2050, 1r; for Meissen, E.-L.K.A.Dresd., visitation of 1580, 49r; for Leipzig, Sdt.Leipz., Tit. VII B.3, 160v ff.

223. OEMF, 565–71.

224. Cities and towns in the Holy Roman Empire cannot be distinguished by number of inhabitants. A city had the *Stadtrecht*, granted it at one time or another by a ruler or lord, a *Markt* or large village did not. During the sixteenth century the empire had about thirty cities with a population of from 10,000 to 40,000, two hundred to three hundred cities and towns of 2,000 to 10,000, and a great number of places of from 500 to 2,000 inhabitants. Only the privilege of *Stadtrecht* distinguished city (*Stadt*) from town (*Markt*). For an impression of the diminutive size of most *Städte* in the empire, see the visitation records of the bishopric of Halberstadt in 1589 in Gustav Nebe, ed., *Die Kirchenvisitationen des Bisthums Halberstadt...* (Halle, 1880). Many *Städte* in the archbishopric had only from 100 to 200 householders.

225. E.g., Sdt.Leipz., Tit. VII B.3, 111r.

226. E.g., ibid., 161v–162r.

227. E.g., S.Dresd., Loc. 2003, 3r.

228. Sdt.Leipz., Tit. VII B.3, 59 ff.

229. Gesamtkirchliches Archiv Augsburg, Evangelisches Wesensarchiv, vol. 26, no. 6.

230. Johann Meckhardt, *Catechismus, ein kurtze christliche Leer und Underweisung für die jugent* (Augsburg, 1551, 1583, and 1603). On the German schools in Augsburg—private enterprises closely supervised by a group of *Scholarchen*—see the rich documentation in Sdt.Augsb., Evangelisches Wesensarchiv, 1129–30; also Martin Niesseler, *Schulvolkskunde der Elementarschulen in der freien Reichsstadt Augsburg* (Augsburg, 1970). Augsburg had a famous Protestant Latin school, the Sankt Anna Gymnasium, founded in 1531; also a Jesuit college endowed by the Fugger family and opened in 1580.

231. S.Nürn., Reichsstadt Rothenburg Akten 2089.

232. Ibid., 2096.

233. See the printed and manuscript edicts and memoranda in Strassb.A.V., Archives St. Thomas 84, carton 48, beginning in 1535 and going to the end of the century, e.g., 576–77 (for 1573).

234. Christoph Vischer, *Auslegung der fünf Heubtstück des heiligen Catechismi* (Schmalkalden, 1573), Cv r.

235. Simon Musaeus, *Catechismus: Examen mit kurtzen Fragen und Antwort . . .* (Frankfurt am Main, 1571), 2v. Musaeus was superintendent in Gera, Coburg, and Mansfeld.

236. "Also ist der merer teil gesinnet." Ibid., 3r.

237. Veit Dietrich, *Kinder-Postilla* (Nuremberg, 1549), 44r–46v; again, *Von der Kinderzucht* (Nuremberg, 1566), bvii r.

238. S.Nürn., Kirchen und Ortschaften auf dem Lande, 451–54, and Sdt.Nürn., Amb. 658, contain only extracts from the protocols of 1561; the protocols themselves seem to have disappeared, along with those of the visitation of 1560. See also Gerhard Hirschmann, "Die zweite Nürnberger Kirchenvisitation 1560/61," *Zeitschr. bayerische Kirchengesch.* 32 (1963): 111–32, and Klaus Leder, *Kirche und Jugend in Nürnberg und seinem Landgebiet . . .*, pp. 108–25. Leder (pp. 48–50) also cites excerpts from repeated council mandates against blaspheming to show that this vice proved ineradicable.

239. See the documents relating to countryside schools in S.Nürn, 40a: Reichsstadt Nürnberg Gemeinakten, SI, L588, no. 25, and Rep. 90: Erziehung, Unterricht, Bildung, SI, Lade 587, no. 50, also Sdt.Nürn., Y779: curriculum plan for a German school in Gründlach, a countryside parish north of Nuremberg.

240. This was the so-called Second Margrave's War, fought 1552–54 against margrave Albrecht Alcibiades of Brandenburg-Kulmbach.

241. This argument is pressed by Gerhard Hirschmann, "Die zweite Nürnberger Kirchenvisitation."

242. These examples are quoted by Klaus Leder, *Kirche und Jugend in Nürnberg*, pp. 162–63.

243. Ibid., pp. 137–39.

244. On the state of territorial schools in Ulm, see Sdt.Ulm A (1838), no. 1 (1535) and A (1844) (1546), the former a volume of regulations for city and rural teachers, the latter a copy of entries in the *Ratsprotokollbuch* relating to schools and schoolmasters in the country. A

(1838), nos. 5 and 8, give salaries and income figures for both city and territorial teachers in 1635. See also A (9063), part I, 127r–132v: two reports to the council from territorial schoolmasters in 1605, giving their plans of studies for children in two large villages. School matters in Ulm can be investigated systematically from the *Ratsprotokolle*, which are extant for almost the whole sixteenth and seventeenth centuries. The Ulm catechism had been mandatory in the entire territory since at least the early 1550s.

245. Julius Endriss, *Die Ulmer Kirchenvisitationen der Jahre 1557–1615* (Ulm, 1937), p. 35. For earlier visitations in Ulm, see idem, *Die Ulmer Synoden und Visitationen der Jahre 1531–47* (Ulm, 1935).

246. Sdt.Ulm A (9063), part I, 131; A (1836), 43r–49v.

247. Ibid., A (9063), part I, 108r and v.

248. Strassb.A.V., Archives St. Thomas 46, carton 21.1 and 2 contains visitation relations forwarded to the council by its visitors. Each relation, consisting of a pamphlet of twelve to fifteen leaves, written in a tiny script, holds a summary of what visitors found: first a general synopsis of *Mengel und Gebrechen* in the whole territory, then brief notes on each village and parish visited.

249. On Strassburg's school system, see Ernst-Wilhelm Kohls, *Die Schule bei Martin Bucer* . . . (Heidelberg, 1963); Walter Sohm, *Die Schule Johann Sturms und die Kirche Strassburgs* . . . (Munich and Berlin, 1912); Joseph Knepper, *Das Schul- und Unterrichtswesen im Elsass* . . . (Strassburg, 1905) 3:1. The closest insight into school policies in Strassburg is conveyed by the protocols of the meetings of the board of *Scholarchen:* Archives St. Thomas 372.

250. Ibid., Archives St. Thomas 45, carton 21.1, 647v (1556).

251. Ibid., carton 21.1.

252. From the preface, by Johannes Schmidt, president of the *Kirchenkonvent* in Strassburg, to Justus Gesenius's *Kleine Katechismus-Schule* (Strassburg, 1632), unnumbered leaf vii v.

253. From margraviate of Brandenburg visitations: S.Bamb., C2, no. 1821, 49r and v (*Hauptmann und Rät auf dem Gebirg*, i.e., the superintendencies Bayreuth and Hof).

254. Ibid., no. 1823, unpaginated. See also the report on the visitation in Hof, 1589; ibid., no. 1827. Identical conditions prevailed there and in Bayreuth. For similar conditions in the Duchy of Zweibrücken, see Bernard Vogler, *Le clergé protestant rhénan au siècle de la réforme (1555–1619)* (Paris, 1976), pp. 337–38, 351–56.

255. S.Hamb., Cl.VII. Lit. Hd. no. 8, vol. lc, fasc. 1: from Amt Begedorf, 1581.

256. Ibid. The reports continue through the seventeenth century without showing any essential improvement.

257. For an analysis of the appeal of the Lutheran Reformation to the burghers of German cities, see Steven Ozment, *The Reformation in the Cities: The Appeal of Protestantism to Sixteenth-Century Germany and Switzerland* (New Haven, 1975).

CHAPTER 14

1. *WA*, Tr. 6, no. 6795.

2. Johann Aurifaber in the preface to his edition of Luther's *Tischreden* (1566), printed in Johann Georg Walch, ed., *Dr. Martin Luthers sämtliche Schriften*, 22 (Halle, 1743): 49.

3. Andreas Musculus, *Vom Himmel und der Hellen* . . . (Frankfurt an der Oder, 1559), Aii v.

4. For an interesting discussion of the doctrine of malleability as it relates to Soviet and Chinese education, see D. J. Munro, "The Malleability of Man in Chinese Marxism," *China Quarterly* 48 (October-December 1971): 609–40.

5. E.g., Martin King Whyte, *Small Groups and Political Rituals in China* (Berkeley, Calif., 1974), especially pp. 230–35, where Whyte considers the question whether, and to what extent, the *hsiao-tsu* was effective.

6. For a strong plea on behalf of popular piety and its claims to be taken seriously in the study of religion and society, see Natalie Zemon Davis, "Some Tasks and Themes in the Study of Popular Religion," in *The Pursuit of Holiness in Late Medieval and Renaissance Religion*, ed. Charles Trinkaus and Heiko A. Oberman (Leiden, 1974), pp. 307-36.

7. For a discussion of this problem as it touches sixteenth-century Calvinists in the Montpellier region of France, see Emmanuel LeRoy Ladurie, *The Peasants of Languedoc*,

trans. John Day (Urbana, Ill., 1974), pp. 158–61. Also Louis Pérouas, *Le diocèse de La Rochelle de 1648 à 1724: Sociologie et pastorale* (Paris, 1964), pp. 139–44: on the organization of Huguenot communities in La Rochelle.

8. E.g., S.Dresd., Loc. 2003, 266r; Loc. 1998, part II, 339v; S.Magd., Rep. A12, Generalia, no. 2442, 98v; S.Dresd., Loc. 2009, part II, 136r; Loc. 2050, passim; Pallas, 41$^{1-5}$, passim; S.Dresd., Loc. 2000, 215r and v.

9. Cf. John C. Stalnaker's contention that the religious disaffection of the general public was an expression of frustrated "prerevolutionary" hopes coupled with resentment over governmental interventionism: "Residenzstadt and Reformation: Religion, Politics and Social Policy in Hesse, 1509–1546," *Archiv Reformationsgesch.* 46 (1973): 113–46. Marxist historians assume that lack of loyalty to, and interest in, religion was the inevitable reaction of "progressive" groups to the suppression of rural and urban revolts in the early 1520s. For an example of official interventionism in action, see the protocols of the 1552 visitation in the duchy of Mecklenburg printed in H. Schnell, *Das Unterrichtswesen der Grossherzogtümer Mecklenburg-Schwerin und Strelitz, MGP*, vol. 38 (Berlin, 1907), especially pp. 228–29.

10. Or "counter culture," as it is called by Lawrence Stone, "The Disenchantment of the World," *New York Review of Books* 17, no. 9 (2 December 1971):18, 24.

11. For an interesting description of the religious milieu in late medieval Germany, see Immanuel Schairer, *Das religiöse Volksleben am Ausgang des Mittelalters nach Augsburger Quellen* (Leipzig, 1913).

12. Caspar Huberinus, *Spiegel der geistlichen Hauszucht* . . . (Frankfurt am Main, 1569), ccxlv v.

13. E.g., Christoph Vischer, *Auslegung der fünf Heubtstück des heiligen Catechismi* (Schmalkalden, 1573), Cii v.

14. Protestant visitors generally found what they assumed to be a conspiracy of silence among their respondents as to the incidence of magic and magicians. E.g., S.Dresd., Loc. 1997, 174v: "Die gemeine habe einen bund gemacht, das keiner den andern verklagen dorffe" (1617); Loc. 2050, 102v: "Segensprecher hat es wol, aber heimlich" (1585). Johann B. Gotz, "Die grosse oberpfälzische Landesvisitation unter dem Kurfürsten Ludwig VI," *Verhandl. historisch. Vereins Oberpfalz u. Regensburg* 85 (1935): 212.

15. Johann B. Götz, "Die religiösen Wirren in der Oberpfalz 1576–1620," *Reformationsgesch. Studien u. Texte*, no. 66 (Münster, 1937), pp. 79–82.

16. S.Weim., Reg. I, no. 66, 110r and v, 114r. S.Dresd., Loc. 1998, part II, 435v–36r.

17. E.g., Hess.H.S.Wiesb., Abt. 150.15, no. 3837; Abt. 171. D227, 26v.

18. Immanuel Schairer, *Das religiöse Volksleben*, p. 106.

19. Hess.H.S.Wiesb., Abt. 171. D226, 38r.

20. S.Dresd., Loc. 1998, part II, 427r.

21. Ibid., Loc. 1980, 364r.

22. Ibid., Loc. 2009, 34v.

23. S.Bamb., B 26/c, no. 44: *General Instruction von den Druten* (1591), unpaginated.

24. Hess.H.S.Wiesb., Abt. 133, no. 3, 3r.

25. S.Neub.D. Pfalz-Neuburg Akten 6266, 105r.

26. Hess.H.S.Wiesb., Abt. 153, no. 417, 64r.

27. Ibid., Abt. 137, no. 1, 9r.

28. Visitation in superintendency Hof, 1589. S.Bamb., C2, no. 1827, 11r.

29. Visitation in superintendency Bischofswerda, 1579. S.Dresd., Loc. 1980, 366v.

30. Ibid., Loc. 2000, 70r.

31. Nearly all visitation materials give information about the magic subculture of rural and small-town Europe in the early modern period. Particularly revealing sources are: S.Bamb., B26/c, no. 44 (a folder relating entirely to magic and witchcraft); ibid., C2, no. 1821 (1570s, 1580s, 1590s); the protocols in S.Dresd., Loc. 1998, 2000, etc.

32. LeRoy Ladurie, *The Peasants of Languedoc*, pp. 206–7.

33. Quoted in Götz, "Die grosse oberpfälzische Landesvisitation," (as in note 14, above), p. 212.

34. *General Instruction von den Druten*, 1591; *Gemeine General-Instruction, wie sich alle und jede pfleger* . . . *mit Unholden und Hexenwercks verleumbten personen* . . . *zu verhalten haben*. S.Bamb., B 26/c, no. 44.

35. Cf. Luther's own well-known belief in spirits and other occult phenomena as instigated by the devil. E.g., *WA* Tr. 5, no. 5358b.

36. LeRoy Ladurie, *The Peasants of Languedoc*, p. 207, offers another explanation of occult survivals as "a lively reaction of a peasant consciousness disillusioned with the ideologies of urban origin, brutalized after 1560 by war, and haunted by the specters of misery and death—and often by fears of sexual failure." I do not share LeRoy Ladurie's essentially negative view of popular cults (ibid., p. 208), but the elements of this interpretation ring true.

37. Werner Thoma, *Die Kirchenpolitik der Grafen von Fürstenberg im Zeitalter der Glaubenskämpfe 1520-1660*, Reformationsgeschichtliche Studien und Texte, no. 87 (Münster, 1963).

38. Steven E. Ozment, *The Reformation in the Cities* (New Haven, 1975), p. 206, note 235. John Bossy makes the same point for Catholic countries: "The CounterReformation and the People of Catholic Europe," *Past and Present* 47 (May 1970): 51-70, especially p. 68.

39. For a good description of the independent character of late medieval religion, and for a discussion of its impulses and sources of inspiration, see Schairer, *Das religiöse Volksleben*. A more complex and subtly shaded picture is given for late medieval Flanders by Jacques Toussaert, *Le sentiment religieux en Flandre à la fin du moyen âge* (Paris, 1963), especially the *synthèse*, pp. 595-602. See also A. N. Galpern, *The Religions of the People in Sixteenth-Century Champagne*, Harvard Historical Studies, vol. 92 (Cambridge, Mass., 1976), chaps 2-3.

40. Quoted by Bernard Vogler, *Le clergé protestant rhénan au siècle de la réforme (1555-1619)* (Paris, 1976), p. 125.

41. For Bavaria: BHM, Staatsverwaltung 2782, 2783, 2784, 2786, 2787; Staatsbibliothek Munich, Cgm. 1737, and many others.

42. John Bossy has examined the same phenomenon in *The English Catholic Community, 1570-1850* (London, 1975), especially part 2, chap. 6: "Separation: Types of Religious Behaviour."

43. Ernst Walter Zeeden, "Probleme und Aufgaben der Reformationsgeschichtsschreibung," *Geschich. Wiss. Unterricht* 6 (1955): 204-9, invites Reformation scholars to face their own presuppositions and ask themselves the question "Am I 'reading' the Reformation right?" If it is not already clear to the reader of this book, I shall say at this point that I hold no religious convictions of any kind. According to Zeeden, this lack of commitment enables me better than engaged Catholic or Protestant historians to focus on crucial evidence and analyze it objectively. On the other hand, he claims, it tends to shut one off from understanding essential elements of the Reformation that cannot be grasped in an "undogmatic frame of mind" (p. 208). If Zeeden's contention is correct, I hope that my deep and genuine sympathy for the reformers and their cause, though that of an unbeliever, compensates for any blind spots created by my lack of religious engagement.

INDEX

Library of Congress Cataloging in Publication Data

Strauss, Gerald, 1922–
    Luther's house of learning.

    Includes index.
    1. Reformation—Germany.   2. Education—Germany—
History.   3. Lutheran Church—Education—History.
I. Title.
BR307.S76   371.3'0943   77–18705
ISBN 0–8018–2051–0